WITHDRAWN

Stafford Library
Columbia College
1001 Rogers Street
Columbia, Missouri 65216

Statistical Data Mining and Knowledge Discovery

Statistical Data Mining and Knowledge Discovery

Edited by
Hamparsum Bozdogan

Stafford Library
Columbia College
1001 Rogers Street
Columbia, Missouri 65216

CHAPMAN & HALL/CRC

A CRC Press Company
Boca Raton   London   New York   Washington, D.C.

Library of Congress Cataloging-in-Publication Data

Statistical data mining and knowledge discovery / edited by Hamparsum Bozdogan.
    p. cm.
    Includes bibliographical references and index.
    ISBN 1-58488-344-8
      1. Data mining—Statistical methods. 2. Computer algorithms. 3. Knowledge acquisition (Expert systems) I. Bozdogan, H. (Hamparsum), 1945-

QA76.9.D343S685 2003
006.3′07′27—dc21   2003051462

This book contains information obtained from authentic and highly regarded sources. Reprinted material is quoted with permission, and sources are indicated. A wide variety of references are listed. Reasonable efforts have been made to publish reliable data and information, but the author and the publisher cannot assume responsibility for the validity of all materials or for the consequences of their use.

Neither this book nor any part may be reproduced or transmitted in any form or by any means, electronic or mechanical, including photocopying, microfilming, and recording, or by any information storage or retrieval system, without prior permission in writing from the publisher.

All rights reserved. Authorization to photocopy items for internal or personal use, or the personal or internal use of specific clients, may be granted by CRC Press LLC, provided that $1.50 per page photocopied is paid directly to Copyright Clearance Center, 222 Rosewood Drive, Danvers, MA 01923 USA. The fee code for users of the Transactional Reporting Service is ISBN 1-58488-344-8/04/$0.00+$1.50. The fee is subject to change without notice. For organizations that have been granted a photocopy license by the CCC, a separate system of payment has been arranged.

The consent of CRC Press LLC does not extend to copying for general distribution, for promotion, for creating new works, or for resale. Specific permission must be obtained in writing from CRC Press LLC for such copying.

Direct all inquiries to CRC Press LLC, 2000 N.W. Corporate Blvd., Boca Raton, Florida 33431.

Trademark Notice: Product or corporate names may be trademarks or registered trademarks, and are used only for identification and explanation, without intent to infringe.

Visit the CRC Press Web site at www.crcpress.com

© 2004 by CRC Press LLC

No claim to original U.S. Government works
International Standard Book Number 1-58488-344-8
Library of Congress Card Number 2003051462
Printed in the United States of America   2 3 4 5 6 7 8 9 0
Printed on acid-free paper

DEDICATION

Dean of the College of Business Administration
1977 – 2001
The University of Tennessee
Knoxville, TN

DEDICATED TO C. WARREN NEEL FOR HIS OUTSTANDING SERVICE FOR OVER TWO DECADES TO THE COLLEGE OF BUSINESS ADMINISTRATION AND THE UNIVERSITY OF TENNESSEE

FOREWORD

Even before there was a name for it I had been interested in pattern recognition. My first recollection was meeting people who built model aircraft during WW II. The models were used to train observers to recognize differences in the shape of an enemy plane compared to the planes of allies. Mastering the subtleties of different shapes became an important skill of many servicemen.

The second time I was aware of the power of pattern recognition was while working for International Paper. The best executives, so I became aware, were those who could take large diverse data files and form a conclusion about an appropriate strategy for the company. That single capability stood out as a defining trait of the better executives.

While attending graduate schools the thought of differing data processing capabilities of executives again crossed my mind. I broached the subject with several industrial psychologists challenging them to develop an instrument to assess that dimension of executive behavior.

As the years went by I continued to bump in to the executive trait of pattern recognition. It was particularly evident as an organization began a strategic planning process. Some were bound to the process of planning while others could vision an outcome long before data foretold an outcome.

Finally, in the mid-1980s I began to read of chaos theory and focused my thoughts to the math of patterns and concept of fractals. By the 1990s with the emergence of large data files, discussions with faculty interested in neuromechanisms, and the growing awareness of biological models supplanting mechanical models as paradigms, I became more convinced that pattern recognition was to be an extremely important field of study. But, I needed someone to champion the effort at Tennessee.

The idea of hosting an international conference was conceived through e-mail communications during May of 1999 between Professor Ham Bozdogan and myself while he was a Visiting Senior Scientist at Tilburg University in Tilburg, The Netherlands.

When he returned to the University of Tennessee, I encouraged Professor Bozdogan to host a meeting in Data Mining and Knowledge Discovery.

The rest is history.

The book is a wonderful testimony to Professor Bozdogan's creative energy in a new and exciting field. It is indeed an honor to have the work of some of the best minds of the field in this book. And, although undeserved, it is flattering to have this volume dedicated to me.

I know of few events in life that can match the excitement associated with an emerging field of study. Data mining and the growing importance of pattern recognition offers society an invaluable tool to capture the full measure of the information age.

C. Warren Neel
Former Dean
College of Business Administration
The University of Tennessee
Knoxville, TN 37996

EDITOR'S PREFACE

"The value of data is no longer in how much of it you have. In the new regime, the value is in how quickly and how effectively can the data be reduced, explored, manipulated and managed."

Usama Fayyad
President & CEO of digiMine, Inc.

C. Warren Neel International Conference on Statistical Data Mining and Knowledge Discovery took place during June 22-25, 2002 at the Marriott Hotel in Knoxville, Tennessee. It was a privilege to host and chair this prestigious conference.

The idea of hosting a conference of this magnitude was born through e-mail correspondence between me and Dr. Warren Neel, then the Dean of the College of Business Administration (CBA) of the University of Tennessee (UT) during May of 1999. Dean Neel in several e-mail messages asked me to investigate Europe's use of data mining while I was on a research visit as a Senior Scientist at Tilburg University in Tilburg, The Netherlands, during May-June of 1999.

After my inquiries both in The Netherlands and other European countries, I reported to Dean Neel on what Europe was doing in the areas of Data Mining, Knowledge Discovery and E-Business. Then, I proposed to him that we should hold an international conference on this area. In his e-mail dated Tuesday, May 18, 1999, Dean Neel replied:

"Ham,

It sounds very promising to me. Let's talk about the necessary steps when you return. Have a good stay.

Warren"

When I returned to UT, Dean Neel encouraged me to organize a Data Mining conference here at UT, and he told me that he would support such an activity. Shortly after this, he was appointed as the Finance Commissioner by the Governor of the State of Tennessee and left UT for Nashville. Because of his vision and genuine support, it was appropriate for me to name the Conference after Dean Warren Neel.

The primary focus of this important conference was to bring national and international experts and practitioners together in this hot cutting-edge research area to share and disseminate new research and developments covering the wide spectrum of areas such as: market segmentation, customer choice behavior, customer profiling, fraud detection and credit scoring, information complexity and Bayesian modeling, econometric and statistical data mining, prediction, and policy-making, manufacturing, improving information quality in loan approval, web mining between eCustomer care and web controlling, data mining in hyperspectral imaging, direct investments in financial assets, textual data mining, neural networks and airport safety logic, evaluating polygraph data, nuclear power plant load forecasting, implementation of data mining in organizations, mammographic computer-aided detection, genomics, proteomics, and many more areas with emphasis to real-world applications.

About 100 researchers from 15 different countries around the world participated in the conference. There were 70 paper presentations including the following conference keynote lectures:

- The Role of Bayesian and Frequentist Multivariate Modeling In Statistical Data Mining, **S. James Press**, University of California

- Intelligent Statistical Data Mining with Information Complexity and Genetic Algorithms, **Hamparsum Bozdogan**, The University of Tennessee

- Econometric and Statistical Data Mining, Prediction, and Policy-Making, **Arnold Zellner,** University of Chicago

- Visual Data Mining, **Edward J. Wegman**, George Mason University

- Top 10 Data Mining Mistakes, **John Elder**, Elder Research, Inc.,

- Data Mining Evolved: Challenges, Applications, and Future Trends, **Usama Fayyad**, digiMine, Inc.,

- Large Contingency Tables: Strategies for Analysis and Inference, **Stephen Fienberg**, Carnegie-Mellon University

- The Evolution of e-Business Intelligence in the ERP World, **Naeem Hashmi**, Information Frameworks.

Statistical data mining is the process of selecting and exploring large amounts of complex information and data using modern statistical techniques and new generation computer algorithms to discover hidden patterns in the data.

This book contains a collection of selected representative papers of the thematic areas covered during the conference, including some of the keynote lectures. It is with regret that Usama Fayyad and Naeem Hashmi could not make a contribution to this volume as the keynote speakers. I am grateful and extend my sincere thanks to all the contributors to this volume, the Session Organizers and Chairs. All the submitted papers were reviewed and put in the format of Chapman & Hall/CRC book style. As the editor, I am ultimately responsible for any inadvertent errors or omissions.

As the host and the chair of the C. Warren Neel International Conference on Statistical Data Mining and Knowledge Discovery, I am indebted to many sponsors of the conference. They include:

Department of Statistics, College of Business Administration, SAS Institute, UT Science Alliance, Office of Research Administration, Oak Ridge National Laboratory (ORNL), Center of Information Technology & Research (CITR), Statistical Innovations, Inc., and Classification Society of North America (CSNA).

I express my sincere thanks for their generous support, which made this conference a reality.

I would like to acknowledge with my sincere thanks the countless hours of help I received in the beginning from Gina Keeling, and later from Derek Norton, my graduate student, who took the job of coordinating the conference. His computer talents were a tremendous help in maintaining the conference web site, updating, and handling other chores of the organizational matters.

I would like to acknowledge the assistants and the wonderful help of Dr. Halima Bensmail, my Conference Co-Chair, and our Ph.D. students: Yongjae Kwon, Junghun Nam, Kim Cooper, Derek Norton, and Michael Lanning. They drove the conference vans, picked up the participants from the airport, and escorted them to different restaurants during the lunch breaks, and so forth. I am grateful to all of them. I am grateful to Karen Poland, Administrative Services Assistant, and Becky Russell, Principal Secretary of the Department of Statistics, in the handling and for helping me with the administrative details on the financial aspects of the Conference.

Avideo Company provided us with a superb audio-visual capability along with the technical assistants of the Computer Resources Group of the College. I am grateful to Dr. Clifton Woods, III, Vice Provost of the University of Tennessee for loaning us five state-of-the-art laptops used throughout the Conference.

I am grateful to Bob Stern, Senior Editor of Chapman & Hall/CRC, for his understanding, patience, and support throughout the final preparation of the book and who extended the deadline several times before delivery of the final version of this book. Dr. June Kim and my Ph.D. student, Dr. Zhenqiu Liu, have been a tremendous help in fixing and compiling the LaTex format of the manuscripts. I acknowledge their contributions with my sincere thanks. I extend my thanks to my colleagues in the Department of Statistics and anyone whom I left out for creating a congenial atmosphere in which to work.

Finally, it is with great honor and pleasure that I dedicate this book to Dean C. Warren Neel who was behind the initial inception and the delivery of this Conference. Without his vision and encouragement for almost four years ago now, we would not be able to make a mark with the contributions of eminent scholars in this new and emerging field of Statistical Data Mining and Knowledge Discovery.

As we know, the field of Statistics is undergoing a fundamental transformation and it is in an evolutionary stage. Its continued health depends very much on its participation in cross-disciplinary research and scholarly activity in many fields. Today, in the information age we live in, with increasingly sophisticated technology for gathering and storing data, many organizations and businesses collect massive amounts of data at accelerated rates and in ever-increasing detail. Massive data sets pose a great challenge to many cross-disciplinary fields in business, including modern statistics. Such data sets have large number of dimensions and often have huge numbers of observations. They are categorical, discrete, quantitative, and often are mixed data types. This high dimensionality and different data types and structures have now outstripped the capability of traditional statistical methods, data analysis, and graphical and data visualization tools.

It is my hope that the reader will find many interesting ideas and challenges in these invaluable contributed papers covering diverse areas of Statistical Data Mining and Knowledge Discovery and that these contributions will stimulate further research in this new cutting-edge field.

Hamparsum Bozdogan
Toby and Brenda McKenzie Professor in Business,
  Information Complexity, and Model Selection
Department of Statistics
The University of Tennessee
Knoxville, TN 37996

EDITOR'S BIO

Dr. Hamparsum ("Ham") Bozdogan is Toby and Brenda McKenzie Professor in Business, Information Complexity and in Model Selection in the Department of Statistics, College of Business Administration at the University of Tennessee (UT), Knoxville.

Dr. Bozdogan received his B.S. degree in mathematics, 1970 from the University of Wisconsin-Madison, and both his M.S. and Ph.D. degrees in mathematics, 1978 and 1981, respectively, from the University of Illinois at Chicago majoring in probability and statistics (multivariate statistical analysis and model selection) with a full-minor in operations research. He joined the faculty of UT in the Fall of 1990. Prior to coming to UT he was on the faculty of the University of Virginia in the Department of Mathematics, and was a Visiting Associate Professor and Research Fellow at the prestigious "Akaike's Institute," The Institute of Statistical Mathematics in Tokyo, Japan, during 1988.

Ham is a nationally and internationally recognized expert in the area of informational statistical modeling and model selection. In particular, on the celebrated Akaike's (1971) Information Criterion (AIC), he has extended its range of applications broadly, and has identified and repaired its lack of consistency with a new criterion of his own, which is now being used in many statistical software packages including SAS. Dr. Bozdogan is the developer of a new model selection and validation criterion called ICOMP (ICOMP for 'information complexity'). His new criterion for model selection cleverly seeks, through information theoretic ideas, to find a balance among badness of fit, lack of parsimony, and profusion of complexity. This measures the "statistical chaos" in the model for a given complex data structure. From this basic work, he has undertaken the technical and computational implementation of the criterion to many areas of applications. These include: choosing the number of component clusters in mixture-model cluster analysis, determining the number for factors in frequentist and Bayesian factor analysis, dynamic econometric modeling of food consumption and demand in the U.S. and The Netherlands, detecting influential observations in vector autoregressive models, to mention a few. His results elucidate many current inferential problems in statistics in linear and nonlinear multivariate models and ill-posed problems. His informational modeling techniques are currently being used by many doctoral students at UT, in U.S., and around the world.

Dr. Bozdogan is the recipient of many distinguished teaching and research awards at UT such as:

- The Bank of America Faculty Leadership Medal Award of the College of Business Administration (CBA), April 2001.

- The Hoechst Roussel Teaching and Research Award of the College of Business Administration (CBA), April, 1997.

- Won world research competition award in applied econometric modeling among 28 worldwide participating teams to forecast U.S. and Dutch food consumption during September 1996.

- Chancellor's Award for Research and Creative Achievement, the University of Tennessee, Knoxville (UTK), April 7, 1993. This award is given each year to 10 UTK faculty who have recently made significant contributions in their field of study.

His work has been published in many diverse and leading journals. He is the editor of six books:

1. *Multivariate Statistical Modeling and Data Analysis.* Editor with A. K. Gupta, D. Reidel Publishing Company, Dordrecht, Holland, 1987.

2. *Theory & Methodology of Time Series Analysis,* Volume 1, Proceedings of First U.S./Japan Conference on The Frontiers of Statistical Modeling: An Informational Approach. Editor, Kluwer Academic Publishers, Dordrecht, The Netherlands, 1994.

3. *Multivariate Statistical Modeling*, Volume 2, Proceedings of First U.S./Japan Conference on The Frontiers of Statistical Modeling: An Informational Approach. Editor, Kluwer Academic Publishers, Dordrecht, The Netherlands, 1994.

4. *Engineering & Scientific Applications of Informational Modeling*, Volume 3, Proceedings of First U.S./Japan Conference on The Frontiers of Statistical Modeling:

An Informational Approach. Editor, Kluwer Academic Publishers, The Netherlands, 1994.

5. *Measurement and Multivariate Analysis*, Co-editor with S. Nishisato, Y. Baba, and K. Kanefuji, Springer-Verlag, Tokyo, Japan, March 2002.

He is the author of forthcoming modern textbooks:

- *Statistical Modeling and Model Evaluation: A New Informational Approach*,
- *Informational Complexity and Multivariate Modeling*

using an open architecture easy-to-use command driven computational environment MATLAB.

Dr. Bozdogan is a member of many professional societies and serves as the referee to many prestigious statistical journals. His current research innovations are in developing intelligent hybrid models between any complex modeling problem, genetic algorithms (GAs) and his information complexity *ICOMP* criterion as the fitness function. Coupled with this, his current research is focused on a long-standing problem of model selection under misspecification, and combining robustness and misspecification within *ICOMP* criteria. He is developing new techniques which are robust and misspecification resistant. This is important because this new approach provides researchers and practitioners with knowledge of how to guard against the misspecification of the model as we actually fit and evaluate these models, and guard against spurious observations. These new developments and results are very important in many areas of applied and basic research (e.g., in business, engineering, social and behavioral, and medical sciences), which is currently ignored.

LIST OF PRESENTERS

S. James Press
Department of Statistics, University of California, Riverside, CA 92521-0138, USA
jpress@ucrac1.ucr.edu

Hamparsum Bozdogan
Department of Statistics, University of Tennessee, Knoxville, TN 37996-0532, USA
bozdogan@utk.edu

Arnold Zellner
Graduate School of Business, University of Chicago, Chicago, IL 60637, USA
fazellne@gsb.uchicago.edu

Edward J. Wegman
Center for Computational Statistics, George Mason University, Fairfax, VA 22030-4444, USA
ewegman@gmu.edu

Adrian Dobra
ISDS, Duke University, Durham, NC 27708, USA
adobra@stat.duke.edu

Elena A. Erosheva
Department of Statistics, University of Washington, Seattle, WA 98195, USA
elena@stat.washington.edu

Stephen E. Fienberg
Department of Statistics, Carnegie-Mellon University, Pittsburgh, PA 15213, USA
fienberg@stat.cmu.edu

Aleksandra B. Slavkovic
Department of Statistics, Carnegie-Mellon University, Pittsburgh, PA 15213, USA
sesa@stat.cmu.edu

Hyunjoong Kim
Department of Statistics, University of Tennessee, Knoxville, TN 37996-0532, USA
hjkim@utk.edu

Lynette Hunt
Department of Statistics, University of Waikato, Hamilton, New Zealand
lah@stats.waikato.ac.nz

Zhenqiu Liu
Community Health Research Group, University of Tennessee, Knoxville, TN 37996-0532, USA
zliu@utk.edu

Andrei V. Gribok
Department of Electrical and Computer Engineering, University of Tennessee, Knoxville, TN 37996-0532, USA
agribok@utk.edu

Aleksey M. Urmanov
Physical Sciences Center, Sun Microsystems, Inc., San Diego, CA 92121, USA
aleksey.urmanov@sun.com

Christopher M. Hill
Industrial Engineering & Management Systems, University of Central Florida, Orlando, FL 32816-2450, USA
christopher-hill@us.army.mil

Masahiro Mizuta
Center for Information & Multimedia Studies, Hokkaido University, Sapporo, Japan
mizuta@cims.hokudai.ac.jp

Mutasem Hiassat
Automatic Control & Systems Engineering, University of Sheffield, Sheffield, UK
matt@hiassat.freeserve.co.uk

Belle R. Upadhyaya and Baofu Lu
Department of Nuclear Engineering, University of Tennessee, Knoxville, TN 37996-0532, USA
bupadhya@utk.edu and *blu@utk.edu*

Francois Boussu
Ecole Nationale Superieure des Arts et Industries Textiles, Roubaix, 59056, France
francois.boussu@ensait.fr

Jean-Jacques Denimal
Laboratory of Probability and Statistics, University of Sciences and Technologies of Lille, 59655, France
Jean-Jacques.Denimal@univ-lille1.fr

Friedrich Leisch
Institut für Statistik, Vienna University of Technology,
Vienna, A-1040 Austria
Friedrich.Leisch@ci.tuwien.ac.at

Hairong Qi
Department of Electrical and Computer Engineering, University of Tennessee,
Knoxville, TN 37996-0532, USA
hqi@utk.edu

Sami Al-Harbi
School of Information Systems, University of East Anglia, Norwich NR4 7TJ, UK
shh@sys.vea.ac.uk

J. Michael Lanning
Department of Statistics, University of Tennessee, Knoxville, TN 37996-0532, USA
jlanning@utk.edu

Jay Magidson
Statistical Innovations, Belmont, MA 02478, USA
jay@statisticalinnovations.com

M. Ishaq Bhatti
Department of Operations Management & Business Statistics
Sultan Qaboos University, Muscat, Oman
abish@squ.edu.om

Amar Gupta
Productivity From Information Technology (PROFIT) Initiative MIT
Sloan School of Management, MIT, Cambridge, MA 02139, USA
agupta@mit.edu

Dong Xu
Protein Informatics Group, Life Sciences Division,
Oak Ridge National Laboratory, Oak Ridge, TN 37831-6480, USA
xud@ornl.gov

Andreas Geyer-Schulz and Andreas Neumann
Information Services and Electronic Markets,University of Karlsruhe
(TH), 76128 Karlsruhe, Germany
andreas.neumann@em.uni-karlsruhe.de

Michael Berry
Department of Computer Science, University of Tennessee, Knoxville, TN 37996-0532, USA
berry@cs.utk.edu

Julien Blanchard
Ecole Polytechnique de l'université de rue Lu Nantes, 44000 France
julien.blanchard@polytech.univ-nantes.fr

Heping Zhang
Department of Epidemiology and Public Health, Yale University School of Medicine,
New Haven, CT 06520-8034, USA
heping.zhang@yale.edu

Zhicheng Zhang
Laboratoire d'Automatique, de Mécanique et d'Informatique
Industrielles et Humaines, Université de Valenciennes,
Valenciennes, F59313 France
zzhang@univ-valenciennes.fr

Halima Bensmail
Department of Statistics, University of Tennessee, Knoxville, TN 37996-0532, USA
bensmail@utk.edu

R. P. DeGennaro
Department of Finance, University of Tennessee, Knoxville, TN 37996-0532, USA
rdegenna@utk.edu

David L. Banks
Food and Drug Administration, Rockville, MD 20852, USA
banksd@cber.fda.gov

Georgia Panagopoulou
National Statistical Service of Greece, Athens, 10166 Greece
panag@statistics.gr

Contents

1 The Role of Bayesian and Frequentist Multivariate Modeling in Statistical Data Mining   **1**
S. James Press University of California, Riverside, USA
- 1.1 Introduction 1
- 1.2 Is Data Mining Science? 2
- 1.3 Genesis of Data Mining 3
- 1.4 The Data Cube and Databases 3
  - 1.4.1 Some Examples 4
- 1.5 Structured Query Language 5
- 1.6 Statistical Problems with Data Mining 6
- 1.7 Some DM Approaches to Dimension Reduction 7
  - 1.7.1 Graph-Based Multivariate Models 7
  - 1.7.2 Multivariate Bayes Classification and Prediction 8
  - 1.7.3 Markov Independence Models 9
- 1.8 Prior Distributions in Data Mining 9
- 1.9 Some New DM Applications 10

2 Intelligent Statistical Data Mining with Information Complexity and Genetic Algorithms   **15**
Hamparsum Bozdogan University of Tennessee, Knoxville, USA
- 2.1 Introduction 15
- 2.2 What is Information Complexity:ICOMP? 17
  - 2.2.1 The Concept of Complexity and Complexity of a System .. 19
  - 2.2.2 Information Theoretic Measure of Complexity of a Multivariate Distribution 20
  - 2.2.3 Initial Definition of Covariance Complexity 22
  - 2.2.4 Definition of Maximal Covariance Complexity 23
  - 2.2.5 ICOMP as an Approximation to the Sum of Two Kullback-Leibler Distances 27
- 2.3 Information Criteria for Multiple Regression Models 31
  - 2.3.1 ICOMP Based on Complexity Measures 33
  - 2.3.2 ICOMP Under Misspecification 34
  - 2.3.3 AIC and AIC-Type Criteria 36
- 2.4 A GA for the Regression Modeling 36
- 2.5 Numerical Examples 41

      2.5.1   Subset Selection of Best Predictors in Multiple Regression:
A Simulation Example 41
      2.5.2   Subset Selection of Best Predictors in Multiple Regression:
A Real Example 43
  2.6 Conclusion and Discussion 49

3 Econometric and Statistical Data Mining, Prediction and Policy-Making 57

Arnold Zellner University of Chicago, Chicago, USA

  3.1 Introduction 58
  3.2 Brief Comments on Scientific Method and Data Mining 59
  3.3 The Structural Econometric Modeling, Time Series Analysis
(SEMTSA) Approach 61
      3.3.1   The SEMTSA Approach 62
      3.3.2   Statistical Inference Procedures 64
  3.4 Methods Employed in Data Analysis, Modeling and Forecasting . . 67
  3.5 Disaggregation and the Marshallian Macroeconomic Model 71
  3.6 A Complete Marshallian Macroeconomic Model 74

4 Data Mining Strategies for the Detection of Chemical Warfare Agents 79

Jeffrey. L. Solka,[1,2] Edward J. Wegman,[1] and David J. Marchette[2]
[2]Naval Surface Warfare Center (NSWCDD), Dahlgren, VA, [1]George Mason University, Fairfax, VA, USA

  4.1 Introduction 79
  4.2 Results 82
  4.3 Conclusions 90

5 Disclosure Limitation Methods Based on Bounds for Large Contingency Tables With Applications to Disability 93

Adrian Dobra, Elena A. Erosheva and Stephen E. Fienberg Duke University, Durham, University of Washington, Seattle, and Carnegie-Mellon University, Pittsburgh, USA

  5.1 Introduction 94
  5.2 Example: National Long Term Care Survey Data 95
  5.3 Technical Background on Cell Entry Bounds 96
  5.4 Decomposable Frontiers 99
      5.4.1   Calculating Decomposable Frontiers 100
      5.4.2   Analysis of the 2^{16} NLTCS Example 101
  5.5 "Greedy" Frontiers 103
  5.6 Bounds 108
      5.6.1   Bounds in the Decomposable Case 108
      5.6.2   Bounds in the Non-decomposable Case 109
  5.7 Discussion 112
  References 114

6 Partial Membership Models with Application to Disability Survey Data — 117
Elena A. Erosheva University of Washington, USA
- 6.1 Motivation 118
- 6.2 Functional Disability Data 119
  - 6.2.1 Marginal Frequencies and Simple Statistics 120
  - 6.2.2 Frequent Responses 120
  - 6.2.3 Total Number of Disabilities 121
- 6.3 Full Versus Partial Membership 123
  - 6.3.1 Full Membership: Latent Class Model 123
  - 6.3.2 Partial Membership: GoM Model 124
- 6.4 Bayesian Estimation of the GoM Model 125
- 6.5 Analysis and Comparison 127
  - 6.5.1 Latent Class Analysis 127
  - 6.5.2 Grade of Membership Analysis and Comparison 128
- 6.6 Concluding Remarks 132

7 Automated Scoring of Polygraph Data — 135
Aleksandra B. Slavkovic Department of Statistics, Carnegie-Mellon University, Pittsburgh, USA
- 7.1 Introduction 135
- 7.2 Background 136
  - 7.2.1 The Polygraph Examination 136
  - 7.2.2 Instrumentation and Measurements 137
  - 7.2.3 Chart Evaluations 138
- 7.3 Statistical Models for Classification and Prediction 139
- 7.4 The Data 141
- 7.5 Statistical Analysis 144
  - 7.5.1 Signal Processing 144
  - 7.5.2 A Simplified Approach to Feature Extraction 145
  - 7.5.3 Feature Evaluation, Modeling, and Classification 147
  - 7.5.4 Logistic Regression 148
  - 7.5.5 Classification Results 149
- 7.6 Discussion 150
- 7.7 Conclusion 152

8 Missing Value Algorithms in Decision Trees — 155
Hyunjoong Kim and Sumer Yates University of Tennessee, Knoxville, USA
- 8.1 Introduction 155
- 8.2 The Seven Algorithms 156
  - 8.2.1 Probability Split 156
  - 8.2.2 Alternative Split 156
  - 8.2.3 Proxy Split 157
  - 8.2.4 Surrogate Split 158
  - 8.2.5 Root Node Imputation 159

    8.2.6 Nodewise Imputation 159
    8.2.7 Separate Node 159
  8.3 The Simulation Study 159
    8.3.1 Experiment-A 159
    8.3.2 Experiment-B 160
  8.4 Results 162
    8.4.1 Experiment-A 162
    8.4.2 Experiment-B 163
  8.5 Conclusions 166

9 Unsupervised Learning from Incomplete Data Using a Mixture Model Approach 173
Lynette Hunt and Murray Jorgensen University of Waikato, Hamilton, New Zealand
  9.1 Introduction 173
  9.2 Clustering by Mixture Models 175
    9.2.1 Latent Class Models and Local Independence 177
    9.2.2 Generalizing Local Independence: the Multimix Model . . . 177
    9.2.3 Missing Data 178
  9.3 Applications 182
    9.3.1 Example 1: The Iris Data 183
    9.3.2 Example 2: The Cancer Data 186
  9.4 Discussion 188

10 Improving the Performance of Radial Basis Function (RBF) Classification Using Information Criteria 193
Zhenqiu Liu and Hamparsum Bozdogan University of Tennessee, Knoxville, USA
  10.1 Introduction 193
    10.1.1 Binary Classifiers 194
    10.1.2 Logistic Regression and Mixture Model 195
    10.1.3 Multi-Class Classifier 197
  10.2 Regression Trees 197
    10.2.1 Information Criteria 199
    10.2.2 Parameter Estimation 200
  10.3 New Kernel Functions 201
  10.4 The EM Algorithm 204
    10.4.1 Constrained Maximization of a Convex Function 204
    10.4.2 The EM Algorithm 205
    10.4.3 EM-Algorithm for PE Mixture Models 207
  10.5 Hybrid Training 208
  10.6 Computational Results 210
  10.7 Conclusions 212

11 Use of Kernel Based Techniques for Sensor Validation in Nuclear Power Plants   217
Andrei V. Gribok, Aleksey M. Urmanov, J. Wesley Hines, and Robert E. Uhrig University of Tennessee, Knoxville, USA

11.1 Introduction 217
11.2 Collinear, Ill-Posed Problems, Regularization 218
11.3 Kernel Regression and MSET 222
11.4 Support Vector Machines 223
11.5 Data Description and Results 225
11.6 Conclusions 228

12 Data Mining and Traditional Regression   233
Christopher M. Hill, Linda C. Malone, and Linda Trocine University of Central Florida, Orlando, FL, USA

12.1 Introduction 234
12.2 Military Manpower Application 234
12.3 Data Mining and Traditional Regression 236
12.4 General Problems 237
12.5 Attempted Solutions 239
    12.5.1 Algorithmic Improvements 239
    12.5.2 Data Complexity Reduction 240
12.6 Regression Specific Issues 240
    12.6.1 Linear Regression 241
    12.6.2 Logistic Regression 243
12.7 Conclusion 246

13 An Extended Sliced Inverse Regression   251
Masahiro Mizuta Hokkaido University, Sapporo, Japan

13.1 Introduction 251
13.2 Algorithms for SIR Model 252
13.3 Relative Projection Pursuit 254
13.4 SIRrpp 254
13.5 Concluding Remarks 256

14 Using Genetic Programming to Improve the Group Method of Data Handling in Time Series Prediction   257
M. Hiassat, M.F. Abbod, and N. Mort University of Sheffield, Sheffield, UK

14.1 Introduction 257
14.2 The Data 258
14.3 Financial Data 259
14.4 Weather Data 259
14.5 Processing of Data 260
14.6 The Group Method of Data Handling (GMDH) 261
14.7 Genetic Programming (GP) 262
14.8 GP-GMDH 263

14.9	Results and Discussion	264
14.10	Conclusion and Further Work	267

15 Data Mining for Monitoring Plant Devices Using GMDH and Pattern Classification — 269

B.R. Upadhyaya and B. Lu University of Tennessee, Knoxville

15.1	Introduction	269
15.2	Description of the Method	273
	15.2.1 Group Method of Data Handling (GMDH)	273
	15.2.2 Analysis of Residuals for Fault Diagnosis	276
15.3	Analysis and Results	277
15.4	Concluding Remarks	278

16 Statistical Modeling and Data Mining to Identify Consumer Preferences — 281

Francois Boussu[1] and Jean Jacques Denimal[2] [1]Ecole Nationale Superieure des Arts et Industries Textiles, Roubaix, and [2]University of Sciences and Technologies of Lille, France

16.1	Introduction	282
	16.1.1 The Garment Market	282
	16.1.2 Interest of the Proposed Method	282
16.2	Data Mining Method	283
	16.2.1 From Data to Analyses	283
	16.2.2 Proposed Methodology	284
	16.2.3 Data Visualization Tools	288
16.3	Application to a Textile Data Set	288
	16.3.1 Classical and Circular Representations of the Hierarchy	288
	16.3.2 Graphic Plane Representations Associated with Nodes	289
	16.3.3 Shaded Tables Visualizing Associations Between Items and Periods	291
16.4	Conclusion	292

17 Testing for Structural Change Over Time of Brand Attribute Perceptions in Market Segments — 297

Sara Dolničar and Friedrich Leisch University of Wollongong, and Vienna University of Technology, Austria

17.1	Introduction	297
17.2	The Managerial Problem	298
17.3	Results from Traditional Analysis	299
	17.3.1 Brand Image Analysis	299
	17.3.2 Competition Analysis	300
17.4	The PBMS and DynPBMS Approaches	300
	17.4.1 General Principles	300
	17.4.2 Complexity Reduction	301

| | 17.4.3 Tests on Heterogeneity 303
| | 17.4.4 Competition Analysis 305
| 17.5 | Summary 306

18 Kernel PCA for Feature Extraction with Information Complexity 309
Zhenqiu Liu and Hamparsum Bozdogan University of Tennessee, Knoxville, USA

- 18.1 Introduction 310
- 18.2 Kernel Functions 312
- 18.3 Kernel PCA 314
- 18.4 EM for Kernel PCA and On-line PCA 318
- 18.5 Choosing the Number of Components with Information Complexity 319
- 18.6 Computational Results 320
- 18.7 Conclusions 321

19 Global Principal Component Analysis for Dimensionality Reduction in Distributed Data Mining 323
Hairong Qi, Tse-Wei Wang, and J. Douglas Birdwell University of Tennessee, Knoxville, USA

- 19.1 Introduction 324
- 19.2 Principal Component Analysis 326
- 19.3 Global PCA for Distributed Homogeneous Databases 327
- 19.4 Global PCA for Distributed Heterogeneous Databases 330
- 19.5 Experiments and Results 331
  - 19.5.1 Global PCA for Distributed Homogeneous Databases 332
  - 19.5.2 Global PCA for Distributed Heterogeneous Databases . . . 334
- 19.6 Conclusion 336

20 A New Metric for Categorical Data 339
S. H. Al-Harbi, G. P. McKeown and V. J. Rayward-Smith University of East Anglia, Norwich, UK

- 20.1 Introduction 339
- 20.2 Dissimilarity Measure 340
  - 20.2.1 Mahalanobis Distance 341
- 20.3 D_{CV} Metric 343
  - 20.3.1 Weights of Fields 344
- 20.4 Synthetic Examples 345
- 20.5 Exploiting the D_{CV} Metric 348
  - 20.5.1 k-Means Algorithm 348
  - 20.5.2 Case-Based Reasoning 348
  - 20.5.3 Supervised Clustering 349
- 20.6 Conclusions and Future Work 349

21 Ordinal Logistic Modeling Using ICOMP as a Goodness-of-Fit Criterion 353
J. Michael Lanning and Hamparsum Bozdogan University of Tennessee, Knoxville, USA

- 21.1 Introduction 353
- 21.2 Model Selection Criteria 356
  - 21.2.1 Computational Software 358
- 21.3 Ordinal Logistic Regression 359
  - 21.3.1 Cumulative Link Models 360
  - 21.3.2 Cumulative Logit (Proportional Odds) Model 361
  - 21.3.3 Proportional Hazard Model 363
  - 21.3.4 Continuation-Ratio Model 363
  - 21.3.5 Category Boundary Cutoffs (Correlated Data) 363
  - 21.3.6 Model Selection 365
- 21.4 Example Problem: Diabetes Severity 367
  - 21.4.1 Proportional Odds Model 367
  - 21.4.2 Residual (Outlier) Analysis 367
  - 21.4.3 Nested Dichotomous Models 368
  - 21.4.4 Nested Cumulative Link Dichotomous Models 368
  - 21.4.5 Nested Continuation-Ratio Link Dichotomous Models 368
- 21.5 Conclusions 369

22 Comparing Latent Class Factor Analysis with the Traditional Approach in Data Mining 373
Jay Magidson and Jeroen Vermunt Statistical Innovations Inc., USA, and Tilburg University, The Netherlands

- 22.1 Introduction 373
- 22.2 The Basic LC Factor Model 375
- 22.3 Examples 376
  - 22.3.1 Rater Agreement 376
  - 22.3.2 MBTI Personality Items 379
- 22.4 Conclusion 381

23 On Cluster Effects in Mining Complex Econometric Data 385
M. Ishaq Bhatti Sultan Qaboos University, Muscat, OMAN

- 23.1 Introduction 386
- 23.2 The Model 387
- 23.3 An Algorithm for Full Maximum Likelihood Estimation 389
- 23.4 Application of the Model 392
- 23.5 Fixed Coefficient Regression Models 394
- 23.6 Concluding Remarks 395

24 Neural Network-Based Data Mining Techniques for Steel Making 401
Ravindra K. Sarma, Amar Gupta, and Sanjeev Vadhavkar Massachusetts Institute of Technology, Cambridge, USA

24.1 Introduction 402
24.2 Productivity from Information Technology (PROFIT) Initiative . . . 403
24.3 Description of Predictive Model 406
24.4 NNRUN – ANN Training Suite 407
    24.4.1 Data Manipulation 407
    24.4.2 Automated Search For Best Network 408
24.5 Results and Analysis 409
24.6 Conclusions 411

25 Solving Data Clustering Problem as a String Search Problem   415
V. Olman, D. Xu, and Y. Xu Oak Ridge National Laboratory, Oak Ridge, TN, USA
25.1 Introduction 415
25.2 Mathematical Framework 417
    25.2.1 Definition of Cluster 418
    25.2.2 MST-Representation of High-Dimensional Data 418
    25.2.3 Relationship between MSTs and Clusters 418
25.3 Stability of MST Structure Under Noise 421
25.4 Statistical Assessment of Identified Clusters 422
25.5 Applications 423
    25.5.1 Partitioning of Simulated Data 423
    25.5.2 Regulatory Binding Site Identification 424
    25.5.3 Cluster Identification in Gene Expression Profiles 426
25.6 Discussion 428

26 Behavior-Based Recommender Systems as Value-Added Services for Scientific Libraries   433
Andreas Geyer-Schulz 1, Michael Hahsler 2, Andreas Neumann 1, and Anke Thede 1 1Universität Karlsruhe (TH), Germany, 2WU-Wien, Austria
26.1 Introduction 433
26.2 Recommender Services for Legacy Library Systems 435
26.3 Ehrenberg's Repeat-Buying Theory for Libraries 439
26.4 A Recommender System for the Library of the Universität Karlsruhe (TH) 448
26.5 Conclusion 451

27 GTP (General Text Parser) Software for Text Mining   455
Justin T. Giles, Ling Wo, and Michael W. Berry University of Tennessee, Knoxville, USA
27.1 Introduction 455
27.2 Model Facilitated by GTP 456
27.3 GTP Usage and Files Generated 457
27.4 Overview of GTP Options 458
27.5 Query Processing with GTPQUERY 464
27.6 Example 464

27.7 Versions of GTP and GTPQUERY 469
27.8 Code Evolution 470
27.9 Future Work 470

28 Implication Intensity: From the Basic Statistical Definition to the Entropic Version 473

Julien Blanchard, Pascale Kuntz, Fabrice Guillet, and Regis Gras Ecole Polytechnique de l'Universite de Nantes, France

28.1 Introduction 473
28.2 First Definitions 475
28.3 Entropic Version 476
28.4 Experimental Results 478
    28.4.1 Experiments with Synthetic Data 478
    28.4.2 Experiments with Real Data 479
28.5 Conclusion 483

29 Use of a Secondary Splitting Criterion in Classification Forest Construction 487

Chang-Yung Yu and Heping Zhang[1] Yale University, New Haven, USA

29.1 Introduction 487
29.2 A Secondary Node-Splitting Criterion 488
29.3 The Formation of a Deterministic Forest 488
29.4 Comparison Data 489
    29.4.1 Comparison through Cross-Validation 490
    29.4.2 Understanding the Deterministic Forest 490
29.5 Discussion 491

30 A Method Integrating Self-Organizing Maps to Predict the Probability of Barrier Removal 497

Zhicheng Zhang and Frédéric Vanderhaegen University of Valenciennes, Le Mont Houy, France

30.1 Introduction 498
30.2 A Method Integrating Self-Organizing Maps Algorithm 498
    30.2.1 Problematic in BR Data Analysis 498
    30.2.2 A Hierarchical SOM (HSOM) Algorithm-Based Method . . 500
30.3 Experimental Results 503
30.4 Discussions 507
30.5 Conclusions 509

31 Cluster Analysis of Imputed Financial Data Using an Augmentation-Based Algorithm 513

H. Bensmail and R. P. DeGennaro University of Tennessee, Knoxville, TN, USA

31.1 Introduction 513
31.2 Data and Preliminary Tests 514

31.3	Clustering and Bayesian Data Augmentation	518
	31.3.1 Imputation	520
	31.3.2 Posterior Estimation	521
	31.3.3 Algorithm	522
31.4	Bayesian Model Selection for Choosing the Number of Clusters	523
31.5	Analysis of Financial Data	523
31.6	Discussion	525

32 Data Mining in Federal Agencies 529
David L. Banks and Robert T. Olszewski U.S. Food and Drug Administration, Rockville, MD, and University of Pittsburgh, Pittsburgh, PA, USA

32.1	Data Quality	529
	32.1.1 First Steps	530
	32.1.2 Using Poor Quality Data	533
	32.1.3 Estimating the Probability of Bad Data	534
32.2	Indexing Data	534
	32.2.1 A First-Pass Method	535
	32.2.2 Estimating Distance Functions	536
	32.2.3 Computation	536
32.3	Screening for Structure with Locally Low Dimension	537
	32.3.1 Screening Strategy	539
	32.3.2 The Designed Experiment	540
	32.3.3 Regression	544
32.4	Estimating Exposure	545
	32.4.1 Categorical Data	545

33 STING: Evaluation of Scientific & Technological Innovation and Progress 549
S. Sirmakessis[1], K. Markellos[2], P. Markellou[3], G. Mayritsakis[4], K. Perdikouri[5], A. Tsakalidis[6], and Georgia Panagopoulou[7] [1-6]Computer Technology Institute, and [7]National Statistical Services of Greece, IT Division, Greece

33.1	Introduction	549
33.2	Methodology for the Analysis of Patents	550
	33.2.1 Textual Analysis Techniques	552
	33.2.2 Correspondence and Cluster Analysis Techniques	553
	33.2.3 Pre-Processing Steps	558
33.3	System Description	559
	33.3.1 Database Manager Module	560
	33.3.2 Statistical Analysis Module	561
	33.3.3 Results Presentation Module	562
	33.3.4 User Interface	562
33.4	Technology Indicators	563
	33.4.1 Indicators Based on the Technological Sector	564

		33.4.2	Indicators in Level of Continents/Countries/Designated States	565

          33.4.3 Indicators for Inventors/Assignees 566
          33.4.4 Indicators Over Time 567
  33.5 Conclusion 568

34 The Semantic Conference Organizer   571
Kevin Heinrich, Michael W. Berry, Jack J. Dongarra, and Sathish Vadhiyar
University of Tennessee, Knoxville, USA
  34.1 Background 571
  34.2 Latent Semantic Indexing 572
  34.3 Software Issues 573
  34.4 Creating a Conference 575
          34.4.1 A Simple Example 575
          34.4.2 Benchmarks 578
  34.5 Future Extensions 579

Index   **583**

1

The Role of Bayesian and Frequentist Multivariate Modeling in Statistical Data Mining

S. James Press
University of California, Riverside, USA

CONTENTS

1.1	Introduction	1
1.2	Is Data Mining Science?	2
1.3	Genesis of Data Mining	3
1.4	The Data Cube and Databases	3
1.5	Structured Query Language	5
1.6	Statistical Problems with Data Mining	6
1.7	Some DM Approaches to Dimension Reduction	7
1.8	Prior Distributions in Data Mining	9
1.9	Some New DM Applications	10
	References	13

This paper presents an overview of Bayesian and frequentist issues that arise in multivariate statistical modeling involving data mining. We discuss data cubes, structured query language computer commands, and the acquisition of data that violate the usual i.i.d. modeling assumptions. We address problems of multivariate exploratory data analysis, the analysis of non-experimental multivariate data, general statistical problems in data mining, high dimensional issues, graphical models, dimension reduction through conditioning, prediction, Bayesian data mining assuming variable independence, hidden Markov models, and data mining priors. There is also a discussion of some new applications of data mining in the field of Home Security.

1.1 Introduction

This paper presents an overview of statistical and related issues associated with data mining (DM), and some newly recognized applications. We will be particularly concerned with multivariate data. We begin by defining what is meant by DM, and discuss some current and potential applications of the methodology. We also discuss the gaps that exist between the statistical and other tools that have been developed for mining data, and the problems of implementing the results in applications.

What exactly is DM? Data mining involves various computer-intensive methods for searching for relationships among variables. Often, the relationships discovered are unexpected. The methods typically involve analyzing very large (massive) quantities of multidimensional data.

In Section 1.2 we examine the extent to which DM can be considered science, and discuss its relationship with data dredging and data snooping. Section 1.3 notes the multi-disciplinary character of DM, while Section 1.4 presents a discussion of the form in which the data are typically arrayed in a data cube and in databases. Section 1.5 concerns the Structured Query Language that is often used in searching the DM database, while Section 1.6 contains an enumeration of the various types of research problems of a statistical nature that the dictates of DM impose upon the methodologist. Section 1.7 reviews some methods that have been suggested for dimension reduction in DM, Section 1.8 a proposal for using data mining to construct prior distributions, and the paper concludes in Section 1.9 with a discussion of the recently perceived need for applications of DM to homeland security.

1.2 Is Data Mining Science?

To understand the philosophy of the methodological approach used by data miners we need to provide some background and context. Aristotle (b 384BC), and Bacon (1561-1626) advocated an approach to scientific methodology that was used for close to 2000 years. They suggested amassing large quantities of data, searching for patterns, therein, and then hypothesizing about such patterns. Galileo (1564-1642) advocated continuing in this vein but suggested that scientists should also do experiments to check the hypotheses. The Galilean approach to scientific methodology (the Galilean scientific method) was widely accepted within the scientific community for about 300 years; it was still in common use throughout the 19th century.

In the 20th century, however, an important shift in the way the scientific method was practiced took place. Some of the Galilean scientific method was reversed; it was advocated that theory should be postulated first; then experimental data should be collected in an effort to support that theory. This approach to scientific method has been called confirmatory science . From a philosophy-of-science perspective, Data Mining follows the "scientific method" tradition of Galileo. DM reverts to 19th century scientific method in that the data generate the theory; this can be dangerous! When we try to follow the dots , we know the process can be full of pitfalls, but the process can be useful in many situations nevertheless (see Section 1.9). This latter approach to scientific methodology, the DM approach, is sometimes called exploratory science. It is also, disparagingly, sometimes referred to as a fishing expedition. Data snooping or data dredging are other pejorative terms that have been used to describe a process in which we sometimes find patterns where none really exist (see also, Elkan, Oct. 1999, and Jensen, 2000 for discussions of data snooping in economics and finance). DM began with researchers sometimes fitting a wide variety of possible models, and then accepting hypotheses of small (but inconsequential) effects. The scientific field of DM developed and matured to its current position by carefully trying to guard against the pitfalls of that hazardous approach.

1.3 Genesis of Data Mining

Data Mining is a multi-disciplinary field at the confluence of Statistics, Computer Science, Machine Learning, Artificial Intelligence (AI), Database Technology, and Pattern Recognition, listed in no particular order—and perhaps a few other fields. Each field has its own terminology, of course, the result of which has been the development of a jargon that is characteristic of DM, and perhaps not of any of the separate fields from which it has emerged. DM appears to have had its genesis in business, and in particular, in marketing, advertising, finance, and other subfields of business. Now the approach seems to have disseminated throughout the social sciences.

DM methodology draws upon a collection of tools some of which are common in the various subfields from which it has emerged, but it is unusual for these tools to be used jointly, other than in DM. The tools include various types of traditional statistical methods of multivariate analysis, such as those of classification, clustering, contingency table analysis, principal components analysis, correspondence analysis, multi-dimensional scaling, factor analysis, and latent structure analysis, as well as some (usually) computer-based methods developed in other contexts for AI, machine learning, or other fields. For example, in the non-statistics fields workers refer to features and attributes, instead of dependent and independent variables, as they would normally be referred to in statistics. DM also uses tools that appear to have begun their development outside of statistics, such as tree building and tree pruning, support vector machines, link analysis, genetic algorithms, market-basket analysis, and neural network analysis. There is also typically a large amount of use of database technology in all of these fields, as well as in DM.

1.4 The Data Cube and Databases

Sizes of data sets of interest in DM are generally thousands, hundreds of thousands, or even in millions, or more. For example, the marketer who wants to analyze supermarket scanner data is typically dealing with a situation in which there is data for the number of times shopper j bought both products k & m, at store location p, in month q; the number of dimensions, that is, the number of variables per observation vector, might also be in the thousands, or millions, or larger.

Observation vectors are frequently available over many time points, or many space points, or both, so that the discrete, or discretized data sets occupy three- or four- or five- or higher, dimensional hyper-rectangles. Moreover, many of the cells in such hyper-rectangles are often empty, representing missing data.

Such data collections (multi-dimensional contingency tables) are usually referred to in the DM literature as the data cube, which is really a misnomer since such arrayed data generally have different sizes. The data cube may be represented by many flat, or text, files (which is the way statisticians refer to 2-dimensional data) (rows of cases, and columns of attributes), or the data cube may be represented in relational data base format (which is the way computer scientists refer to it). Relational databases are databases related to one another by a single attribute common to all the databases, an attribute such as an identifying number. For example, if the objects being studied are people, their social security numbers, driver's license numbers, or other identifying characteristics could be used to link all of the databases. One of the databases could relate to purchasing behavior of certain consumers, another could represent TV- viewing behavior of the same consumers, another could represent political beliefs of the same consumers, etc. These databases, taken together, represent a relational database, or data cube that is very rich with information about this collection of subjects.

1.4.1 Some Examples

Example (1) Marketing Data: The Co-Occurrence Cube

As an example of a large data set consider the purchasing behavior of consumers at supermarkets. To arrange for the shelf locations of items within the market that are mostly likely to improve sales, it is of interest to the management to know which items are likely to be purchased together. The co-occurrence cube is a special type of DM data cube. It was created to answer such questions that arise naturally in marketing, but it has found uses in many non-marketing applications as well. It summarizes the co-occurrences of certain events so that the frequencies of such co-occurrences can be tracked. In some marketing applications (see Fig. 1), off-diagonal elements are numbers of transactions with those co-occurences (in a 3-dimensional cube there can be 3 items purchased together); in a 4-dimensional cube there can be 4 items purchased together, etc. Diagonal elements are numbers of transactions of just a particular item. In Fig. 1.1 there are 5 items: detergent, soda, milk, window cleaner, and orange juice (OJ). In the figure, OJ, window cleaner, and milk appear together in only one transaction.

Example (2) Jail Inmates

There were 549,630 inmates of the Los Angeles County Jail during the period Dec. 10, 1996-Jan. 23, 2000. Records were kept on all of these inmates requiring a database of many hundreds of attributes—ID number, housing location over time, type of crime, court-related information, time to be served, etc. There were perhaps 200 million cells in a flat file, and there were a variety of such flat files.

Ordinary computers would not handle such massive numbers of records. Computers with very large storage capacities and with ability to carry out computations

Statistical Data Mining and Knowledge Discovery

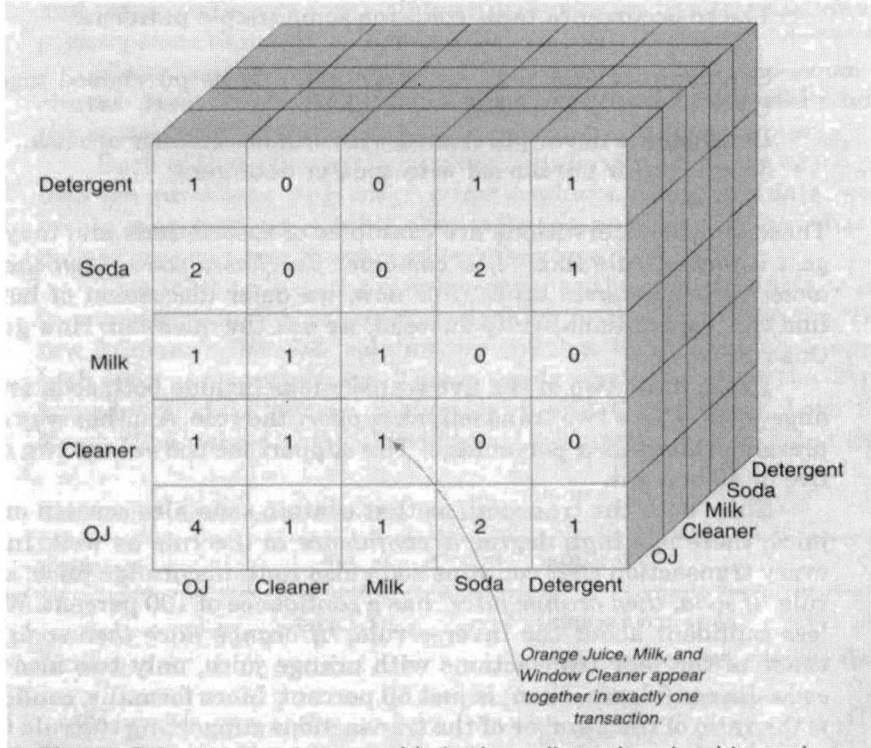

FIGURE 1.1
Co-occurrence cube. From Berry and Linoff (1997, p. 132).

on such a large scale were required to handle the manipulations required for various studies of this data.

1.5 Structured Query Language

To analyze the data in large databases, such as those described above, data miners sometimes use Structured Query Language (SQL) to manipulate the data.

Consider the following example of a typical query in a portfolio analysis context. The machine is asked to select attributes from tables where certain conditions are satisfied, such as: select *"tech stocks"* from the table of possible tech stocks, where the price per share, p, satisfies $\$30 < p < \$75$. When queried, the machine looks for pairings, that is, associations by item (items might be high tech securities in a finance context, or they might be market-basket products in a marketing context, or related threats to the US in an FBI query), temporal associations, and spatial associations.

1.6 Statistical Problems with Data Mining

The data in a data cube are all made to be discrete approximations, if they do not start out as discrete. Those data that began as continuous, or mixed continuous and discrete are discretized. The best way to discretize continuous data is not a simple issue.

The data collected typically violate many of the desired assumptions of traditional statistics, such as attributes being independent, identically distributed, and having low correlation over time and space. Often, the data are highly correlated spatially or temporally, or both. Violation of any of these assumptions can generate major problems when the decision maker is trying to draw substantive conclusions. These data are generally just collections of multidimensional observations, without regard to how they were collected. Traditional experimental design does not typically enter the problem at this point. Sample estimates are used to approximate probabilities, and other approximations might be used as well.

The data cube is searched for relationships by proceeding through the cube systematically along all of its principal axes, and diagonally, in steps. Search of the data cube is open to any and all kinds of multivariate exploratory data analysis such as stochastic modeling, clustering, classification, regression, and visual displays of all kinds.

The procedures described above lead inevitably to many statistical problems:

1) Searching for patterns in data often results in concluding that there seem to be patterns, when in fact the apparent patterns are merely random fluctuations.

2) In statistics, sample size is generally very small, whereas in data mining, sample size is generally very large. As a result, in DM, likelihood ratio methods of hypothesis testing (for large samples), and p-value significance level testing (for large samples) will tend to make the tiniest effects appear to be significant. Bayesian methods are preferable because they are more conservative in rejecting null hypotheses (Berger& Selke, 1987).

3) Data are often unmanageable because data in a relational database may be hierarchical, and distributed (located in different places).

4) Data sizes often exceed machine capacity.

5) In DM, the data are often based on convenience sampling, rather than on probability sampling. Convenience sampling is well known to introduce all kinds of biases into the estimates of the population parameters.

6) As in most statistical inference, results may be strictly associative (and often spurious), but not causal.

7) The high dimensionality of the data cube usually causes modeling problems. One such major problem is sometimes referred to as "the $n << p$ problem." The problem is that when there are many variables, p, often, p greatly exceeds the number of replications, n.

This is opposite to the usual case in statistics where sample size, n, normally greatly exceeds p. We are approaching this problem using "singular value decomposition" (see Jampachaisri and Press (2002)).

8) High dimensional modeling requires study of the behavior of large numbers of jointly dependent variables. This is always difficult.

9) High dimensional probability distributions are difficult to evaluate numerically. For example, it is quite difficult to evaluate the orthant probabilities for an ordinary multivariate normal distribution in, say, as few as 25 dimensions.

10) Correlation matrices in high numbers of dimensions are difficult to understand, even if they can be manipulated in statistical models.

11) To analyze high-dimensional contingency tables using the usual statistical models it is necessary:

a) to collapse many of the dimensions to generate a lower dimensional and more manageable table; or

b) to bring substantive prior information (vague priors are excluded) to bear to permit Bayesian analysis of the data in the very high dimensional contingency table that includes missing data; or

c) both.

1.7 Some DM Approaches to Dimension Reduction

There is a strong need for simplification and dimension reduction in the high dimensional spaces of data mining problems. We now discuss some approaches that have been suggested.

1.7.1 Graph-Based Multivariate Models

Graphical representations are now commonly used for representing multivariate models for visualizing patterns in data mining (and Bayesian neural networks).

DAGS (Directed Acyclic Graphs)(see Figure 1.2) are now central to such modeling. There is a node for every random variable in the model, and nodes in the directed acyclic graph are represented by circles. The arcs (lines) connecting the nodes making up the graph are ordered (the lines end with arrows). The term acyclic refers to graphs that have no loops or cycles, that is, they have no repeated paths.

Dimension Reduction by Conditional Independence

One simple method of reducing dimensionality of multivariate probability distributions is to assume mutual independence of the variables (but it assumes away what may be most interesting). An alternative solution, one which is less than ideal but still retains some of the inherent dependence structure, is to assume conditional independence, a Markov-process type of assumption. In the likelihood function this conditional independence assumption translates to the joint pdf being expressible as a product:

$$f(x) = f_1(x_1) f_2(x_2 \mid x_1) \cdots f_p(x_p \mid x_1, \ldots, x_{p-1}) \tag{1.1}$$

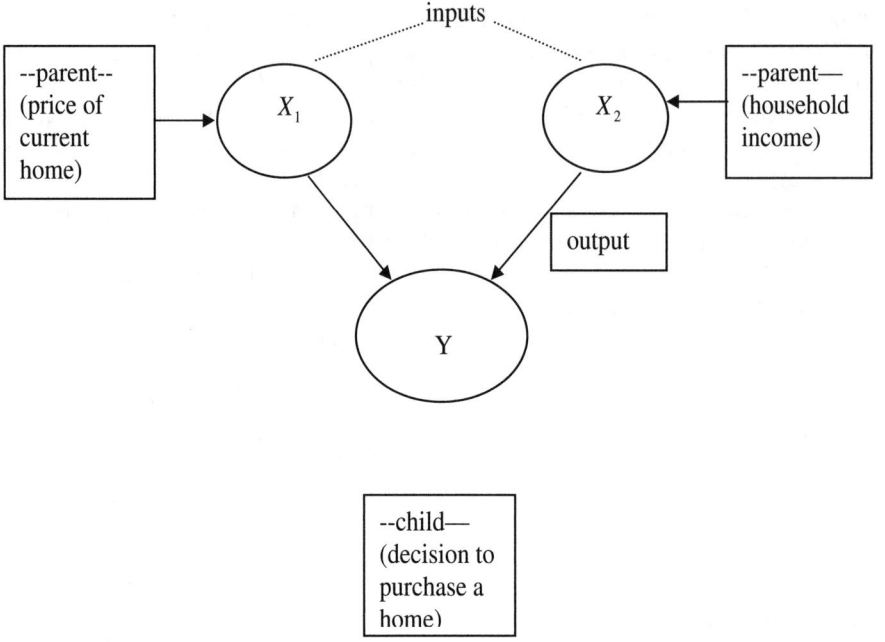

FIGURE 1.2
A simple directed acyclic graph.

1.7.2 Multivariate Bayes Classification and Prediction

The multivariate Bayes approach to classification (briefly summarized below) is used often in data mining.

There are K *multivariate normal* populations, $\pi_1, \ldots, \pi_K$, with unknown mean vectors, and with unknown, and generally unequal, covariance matrices. The observed attribute vector $X = x$ has derived from one of these populations, but we don't know which one. Geisser (1964) has shown that by direct application of Bayes' theorem (for discrete X), the predictive distribution for classifying X into population π_i is given by:

$$P(\pi = \pi_i \mid X = x) \propto P(X = x \mid \pi_i) h(\pi_i) \tag{1.2}$$

for $i = 1, \ldots, K$, where $h(\pi_i)$ denotes the prior probability for classifying X into population π_i, and $P(X = x \mid \pi_i)$ denotes the pdf of a multivariate Student t-distribution. If the populations are non-normal the same approach followed in the normal case can be applied.

Approximate Approach To Bayesian Classification (Naïve Bayes)

Next, we note that if X is just 30 dimensional, and if each component is binary, there are approximately $2^{30} = 10^9 = 1$ billion probabilities to estimate, an enormous undertaking, but not atypical in data mining applications. We use what is sometimes

Statistical Data Mining and Knowledge Discovery

referred to as a naive Bayes approach. First approximate the data likelihood, with a substantial reduction in the number of probabilities to be estimated, by an independence likelihood:

$$P\{X = x \mid \pi_i\} = \prod_{j=1}^{p} P\{X_j = x_j \mid \pi_i\}. \tag{1.3}$$

The approximate multivariate Bayesian predictive distribution is given by

$$P\{\pi = \pi_i \mid X = x\} \propto P\{\pi = \pi_i\} \prod_{j=1}^{p} P\{X = x_j \mid \pi_i\}. \tag{1.4}$$

Therefore, the approximate log posterior odds for classification is given by:

$$\log\left\{\frac{P\{\pi = \pi_i \mid X\}}{P\{\pi = \pi_k \mid X\}}\right\} = \log\left\{\frac{P\{\pi = \pi_i\}}{P\{\pi = \pi_k\}}\right\} + \sum_{j=1}^{p} \log\left\{\frac{P\{X_j = x_j \mid \pi_i\}}{P\{X_j = x_j \mid \pi_k\}}\right\}. \tag{1.5}$$

1.7.3 Markov Independence Models

Now model each of the conditional data distributions. Some of the conditioned variables drop out naturally, reducing the dimension of the problem. We can model the conditional distributions as DAGs. We assume Markov independence of the conditionals. Some of the variables are latent (unobserved); such models are called hidden Markov models. There is always an issue with such modeling as to how many hidden Markov models there should be. The answer depends upon how many it takes to model the actual data conveniently, and sufficiently accurately. It could take just a couple, or (in a neural network) 100 could be required.

A new and promising approach to the dimension reduction problem was proposed by Du Mouchel, 1999b.

1.8 Prior Distributions in Data Mining

Development of subjective prior distributions for unknown quantities in statistical models typically involves considerable introspection. An analyst might search for underlying theory to bring some real information to bear about the underlying process generating the outcome variables, and then must be able to assess prior distributions for the underlying variables of interest. We propose here to use data mining to establish the relationships required for assessing the desired prior distributions. Fortunately, assessment of a prior distribution does not require that methods used to generate it necessarily be rigorous mathematically, or statistically. The only requirement is that the distribution be the analyst's best guess, judgment, or intuition about the underlying process; the relationships suggested by data mining procedures fit such a requirement very well. We suggest below a procedure for developing a prior distribution using DM methods.

Suppose there is a vector of unknown parameters, β, and an analyst would like to assess a prior distribution for it. We have available in the data cube input variables that we believe are comparable to the variables in the output model, and we have available at least one output variable, y, upon which we think these input variables might depend. We have many observations of these variables as well (of course they might not be i.i.d, etc.). We might form a score (objective) function, such as:

$$f(\beta) = \sum_i (y_i - x'\beta)^2, \qquad (1.6)$$

and select β to minimize $f(\beta)$. This value of β could be used as the mean of a family of prior distributions for β. We are now able to generalize because typically in data mining, there are large numbers of observations. Therefore, there are many possible courses of further action.

The data set could, for example, be subdivided into k groups, and the same objective function could be calculated for each group. The values of β obtained by minimizing those objective functions could be used to form a sample *cdf* for β. The sample *cdf* for β could then be used as the prior distribution for β. A kernel density for β could be estimated as well.

1.9 Some New DM Applications

The term data mining has now reached the point where it has almost become a household word. George Will, a news commentator, in commenting on baseball, recently said that "On a Saturday evening last month the Devil Rays scored 4 runs in the bottom of the 9th to beat the Orioles 6-4, thereby snapping a 15 game losing streak."[*] Almost immediately, Tim Kurkjian, a TV sports commentator, said on the ESPN sports program, Baseball Tonight, "This was the first time ever that an American League team had snapped a double digit losing streak by scoring more than 2 runs in the ninth." Mr. Will then begged the question about how such baseball data ever get mined. He then went on to explain about the Elias Sports Bureau. He pointed out that the business of this company is to examine the statistical histories of the major professional sports using custom-written software that will retrieve the answers to these kinds of questions. This is certainly one kind of DM.

On May 29, 2002, Robert Mueller, the Director of the FBI, announced new guidelines for the FBI in terms of how it might carry out future surveillance regarding

---

[*]Will, George F., *Newsweek*, June 24, 2002, p. 96.

possible terrorist attacks against the U.S. The next day, the New York Times ran an editorial which said,

"There is certainly a need to create a central analytical office at the FBI to sort through data from field offices to see if there are connections like those about flight training programs in Arizona and Minnesota that Headquarters failed to spot last summer."

Laura Murphy,[†] representing the American Civil Liberties Union, said,

"Data Mining can be used by the FBI to collect and analyze data to hypothesize about the chances of the United States being attacked by terrorists."

This a particularly interesting and important application of DM.[‡] It can and should be used by the FBI, the CIA, the new-proposed cabinet-level Department of Homeland Security, and other federal agencies.

A recent magazine article[§] was entitled, "Reading the Threat Matrix," and it displayed a checkerboard whose squares showed pictures of Osama Bin Laden, Mohamed Atta (suspected to be the pilot who hit the north tower of the World Trade Center, Sept. 11, 2001), the Statue of Liberty, the Brooklyn Bridge, the Capitol, an airport, a subway station, and other possible targets. Director of the FBI, Robert Mueller,[¶] referred to the use of "commercial data mining establishments" to assist the FBI in connecting the dots to predict terrorist attacks before they happen.

The term connecting the dots has become very popular lately on the Washington, DC scene. It's a term that is appealing to people in that it is easy to understand because it is the basis of some children's games. But it is a game that can be fraught with hazards in that connecting the dots in a DM matrix can be problematic. We don't know which dots to connect, and connecting the wrong ones can lead to all kinds of pitfalls, as explained above. The statistics literature is full of examples of how researchers in earlier years claimed they saw patterns in the data, which on later examination turned out to be random variations. Least squares regression is of course about which dots to connect.

Many of the nation's commercial establishments have long ransacked commercial databases hoping to determine which consumers are likeliest to buy a particular luxury car or life insurance policy. Now, the FBI hopes to sift through the same databases to identify threats before they occur.

Attorney General John Ashcroft recently announced that the Justice Department was loosening its guidelines to allow FBI agents to, among other things, dig into the vast treasure trove of commercial data on the buying behavior of consumers, their preferences and their characteristics. Such databases often correlate an individual, and his various IDs, with his attributes, such as smoking behavior, clothing size, any arrest records, household income, magazine subscriptions, height, and weight, contributions to religious, political or charitable groups, chronic health conditions

---

[†] Jim Lehrer's PBS News Hour, May 30, 2002.
[‡] See also, Jeanene Harris, "Statistics and Homeland Security," *Amstat News*, July, 2002, p.5
[§] *US News*, June 3, 2002, pp.26-30.
[¶] Address to the Judiciary Committee of the US Congress, June 6, 2002.

like diabetes or asthma, the books the person reads, and many other characteristics. People concerned with privacy worry that the FBI's use of such databases could lead to intrusions on the privacy of innocent people. Inaccuracies in the databases could create false alarms.

The FBI hasn't publicly declared how agents would use data obtained from data mining. The bureau will of course use data mining to spot relationships in extremely large data sets. The previous guidelines, which agents viewed as limiting their use of such databases, had grown from efforts to prevent the kind of FBI surveillance abuses that occurred in the 1960s and 1970s. At that time The Bureau kept dossiers on civil rights and anti-war activists. The Bush administration, however, believed those guidelines would hamper the nation's domestic war on terrorism. We're talking about the databases and the data accessible to the business public. The FBI now claims that the same unrestrained access that's available to businesses should be available to them, to thwart further acts of terrorism.

Law-enforcement and intelligence agencies have used other forms of data mining. For instance, some police departments have used DM to sift crime data for trends to predict where future crimes are most likely to occur. Such agencies also have used DM on intelligence information, though not as effectively as they might have. For instance, FBI Director Robert Mueller has said that the Sept. 11 attacks might have been thwarted if intelligence agencies had better integrated and mined data to discern patterns. Meanwhile, the FBI and the Immigration and Naturalization Service have used private look-up services such as ChoicePoint Inc. in Alpharetta, Ga., that collect and sort information about most Americans to find fugitives, illegal immigrants, and other subjects of investigations. But mining commercial databases would take the practice even further, which raises public concerns about individual privacy. Many kinds of information about individuals are collected and tracked, without the individuals being aware of it.

Terrorists are consumers too, because terrorists buy products, rent apartments, and use credit cards. The FBI hopes that DM analysis of the data will reveal patterns that could help prevent future attacks. For instance, the Sept. 11, 2001 hijackers flew together on numerous occasions as they cased airlines in preparation, sometimes buying tickets with credit cards. Some also shared apartments, opened bank accounts, took flying lessons, rented cars, and went to health clubs. All of those could easily have been captured in consumer databases.

Individuals fear that some activities by innocent consumers could inappropriately raise FBI suspicions. The problem is that any number of innocent events can trigger a "suspicion algorithm." Someone who travels on short notice and uses a credit card in two cities on the same day, withdraws a large amount of money from a bank, or who moves frequently might draw suspicion even though he or she had legitimate reasons for doing so.

A critique of the Justice Department's new guidelines by the Center for Democracy and Technology, an advocacy group, said the FBI will now be conducting "fishing expeditions" using the services of the people who decide what catalogs to send you or what spam e-mail you will be interested in. But there is a major difference between the marketers and the FBI; the direct marketers can only annoy you by calling you during dinner time or mailing you another credit card offer based on that information; the FBI can arrest you. Since Sept. 11, 2001, the FBI has in fact arrested and held people based on innocent activity. "Such fears are unwarranted," said Paula DeLucas.[||] She indicated that only when the outcome substantiates further identification of individuals that investigators are likely to discover more details about specific individuals.

DM has been employed by research workers in marketing, advertising, finance, and other areas of business and management for at least a decade. It is only recently, however, that the field has been recognized as one having many challenging technical problems, in many disciplines, and in many non-business related applications. Because of these problems, it has become a new frontier of emerging, cutting-edge technology.

A great deal of time and effort has been devoted by methodologists to developing better DM techniques, and our community will continue to do so. But there has been only a relatively small and inappropriate effort devoted to implementation of the results of DM in the field; that is, in the business and social science communities, and in governmental agencies. These organizations are insufficiently informed about how to take the algorithms developed by methodologists and utilize them efficiently to achieve their objectives. That problem will require much greater attention in the coming years.

References

Berry, Michael, J.A. and Linoff, Gordon (1997). *Data Mining Techniques*, New York, John Wiley and Sons, Inc.

Berger, J.O. and Selke, T. (1987). Testing a point null hypothesis: the irreconcilability of p-values and evidence, *J. Am. Stat. Assoc.*, Vol. 82, 397, pp. 112-122.

DuMouchel, William (Aug. 1999a). Bayesian data mining in large frequency tables, *American Statistician*.

DuMouchel, W., Volinski, C., Johnson, T., Cortes, C., and Pregibon, D. (1999b). Squashing flat files flatter. In *Proc. of the 5th ACM Conference on Knowledge Discovery and Data Mining*, pp. 6-15.

Edelstein, Herbert A. (1999). *Introduction to Data Mining and Knowledge Discovery*, third ed., Potomac, MD: Two Crows Corp.

Elkan, Charles (Oct., 1999). Towards Self-Financing Research, *Computer Science and Engineering*, UCSD, a talk.

[||] Public safety strategist with SAS Institute Inc., North Carolina.

Geisser, Seymour (1964). Posterior odds for multivariate normal classification, *J. R. Stat. Soc.* (B), 26, 69-76.

Hand, David (May, 1998). Data mining, statistics and more?, *American Statistician*.

Hand, David, Mannila, Heikki, and Smyth, Padhraic (2001). *Data Mining, Cambridge*: MIT Press.

Hastie, Trevor, Tibshirani, Robert, and Friedman, Jerome (2001). *The Elements of Statistical Learning*, New York: Springer-Verlag.

Jampachaisri, Katechan and Press, S. James (2002). Bayesian Inference in Applications of Singular Value Decomposition to Biology, presented at the Annual Meetings of the American Statistical Association, Aug. 2002, and to appear in the *Proc. of the Section on Bayesian Statistical Sciences of the American Statistical Association*, 2003.

Jensen, David (2000). Data Snooping, Dredging and Fishing: The Dark Side of Data Mining, *A SIGKDD99 Panel Report*, Vol. 1, Issue 2, p. 53.

Maimon, Oded and Last, Mark (2001). *Knowledge Discovery and Data Mining*, Dordrecht: Kluwer.

Smyth, Padhraic (Sept 2000). Data mining: data analysis on a grand scale. In *Statistical Methods in Medical Research*.

2

Intelligent Statistical Data Mining with Information Complexity and Genetic Algorithms

Hamparsum Bozdogan
University of Tennessee, Knoxville, USA

CONTENTS

2.1	Introduction	15
2.2	What is Information Complexity:ICOMP?	17
2.3	Information Criteria for Multiple Regression Models	31
2.4	A GA for the Regression Modeling	36
2.5	Numerical Examples	41
2.6	Conclusion and Discussion	49
	Acknowledgments	51
	References	51

This paper develops a computationally feasible intelligent data mining and knowledge discovery technique that addresses the potentially daunting statistical and combinatorial problems presented by subset regression models. Our approach integrates novel statistical modelling procedures based on an information-theoretic measure of complexity. We form a three-way hybrid between: information measures of complexity, multiple regression models, and genetic algorithms *(GAs)*. We demonstrate our new approach using a simulated example and on a real data set to illustrate the versatility and the utility of the new approach.

2.1 Introduction

In regression type problems whether it is in multiple regression analysis, in logistic, or in ordinal logistic regression, model building and evaluation and selection of relevant subset of predictor variables on which to base inferences is a central problem in data mining to reduce the "curse of dimensionality," a term coined by Richard Bellman (see, Bellman, 1961) almost 42 years ago. Also, see, e.g., Sakamoto et al., 1986, Miller 1990, Boyce et al., 1974. Often a quantitative, binary, or ordinal level response variable is studied given a set of predictor variables. In such cases it is often desirable to determine which subsets of the predictors are most useful for forecasting the response variable, and to interpret a large number of regression coefficients, since this can become unwieldy even for moderately sized data, and to achieve parsimony of unknown parameters, allowing both better estimation and clearer interpretation of the parameters included in these models.

The problem of selecting the best regression models is a non-trivial exercise, particularly when a large number of predictor variables exist and the researcher lacks precise information about the exact relationships among the variables.

In many cases the total possible number of models reaches over millions (e.g., more than 20 predictor variables) or perhaps into the billions (e.g., 30 predictor variables) and evaluation of all possible combinations of subsets is unrealistic in terms of time and cost.

Therefore, numerical optimization techniques and strategies for model selection are needed to explore the vast solution space. In general the problem of subset selection using numerical techniques requires two components:

**(1) an algorithm for the efficient searching of the solution space, and
(2) a criterion or measure for the comparison of competing models to help guide the search.**

Most statistical packages for statistical analysis provide a *Backward* and *Forward stepwise selection* strategy for choosing the best subset model. However, it is well known that both *Backward* and *Forward stepwise selection* in regression analysis do not always find the best subset of predictor variables from the set of k variables. Major criticisms levelled on *Backward* and *Forward stepwise selection* are that, little or no theoretical justification exists for the order in which variables enter or exit the algorithm (Boyce et al., 1974, p. 19, Wilkinson, 1989, p. 177-178), and the arbitrary choices of the probabilities specified a priori to enter and remove the variables in the analysis. Another criticism is that stepwise searching rarely finds the overall best model or even the best subset of a particular size (Mantel, 1970, Hocking, 1976, 1983, Moses, 1986).

Lastly, and most importantly, because only local searching is employed, stepwise selection provides extremely limited sampling from a small area of the vast solution space. Stepwise selection, at the very best, can only produce an "adequate" model (Sokal and Rohlf, 1981, p. 668).

Based on the above shortcomings of existing problems in regression analysis, the purpose of this paper is to introduce and develop a computationally feasible intelligent data mining and knowledge discovery technique based on the genetic algorithm (*GA*) and information-based model selection criteria for subset selection in *multiple regression* models. Our approach has been also extended to *logistic regression* and *ordinal logistic regression* models as a three-way hybrid. For space considerations, we will report and publish the results of these elsewhere. However, for more on subset selection of best predictors in *ordinal logistic regression* models, we refer the reader to Lanning and Bozdogan (2003) in this volume.

A *GA* is a stochastic search algorithm which is based on concepts of biological evolution and natural selection that can be applied to solving problems where vast numbers of possible solutions exist. *GAs* have been used in a wide variety of fields such as engineering, economics, game theory (Holland, 1992), computational sciences (Forrest, 1993), marketing (Bauer, 1994) and biology (Sumida et al., 1990). Unlike conventional optimization approaches, the *GA* requires no calculation of the gradient of the objective function and is not likely to be restricted to a local optima (Goldberg, 1989). A *GA* treats information as a series of codes on a binary string, where each string represents a different solution to a given problem. These strings are analogous models to the genetic information coded by genes on a chromosome. A string can be evaluated, according to some *"fitness"* value, for its particular ability to solve the problem. On the basis of the fitness values strings are either retained or removed from the analysis after each run so that, after many runs, the best solutions have been identified. One important difficulty with any *GA* is in choosing an appropriate fitness function as the basis for evaluating each solution.

With respect to *multiple regression* analysis, the fitness value is a subset selection criterion for comparing subset models in a search of the best subset. This can be easily determined by using informational model selection criteria.

The format of this paper is as follows. In Section 2.2, we discuss what information complexity is, and present its general form in model selection. In Section 2.3, we give the derived closed form analytical expressions of information complexity *ICOMP* of Bozdogan (1988, 1990, 1994, 2000), and Akaike's (1973, 1974) information criterion *AIC*, and Rissanen's (1978, 1986) *MDL*, Schwarz's (1978) *SBC* or *BIC*, and Bozdogan's (1987) *Consistent AIC with Fisher information CAICF* as decision rules for model selection and evaluation in multiple regression models. In Section 2.4, we develop the *GA* for the general regression modelling and discuss the new statistical software we developed with graphical user interface (GUI) in a flexible Matlab computational environment. Section 2.5 is devoted to simulated and real data examples in multiple regression models to demonstrate the versatility and utility of our new approach.In Section 2.6, we draw our conclusions.

2.2 What is Information Complexity:ICOMP?

In general statistical modeling and model evaluation problems, the concept of model complexity plays an important role. At the philosophical level, complexity involves notions such as connectivity patterns and the interactions of model components. Without a measure of *"overall"* model complexity, prediction of model behavior and assessing model quality is difficult. This requires detailed statistical analysis and computation to choose the best fitting model among a portfolio of competing models for a given finite sample. In this section, we develop and present information-theoretic ideas of a measure of *"overall"* model complexity in statistical modelling to help provide new approaches relevant to statistical inference.

Recently, based on Akaike's (1973) original *AIC*, many model-selection procedures that take the form of a *penalized likelihood* (a negative log likelihood plus a penalty term) have been proposed (Sclove, 1987). For example, for *AIC* this form is given by

$$AIC(k) = -2\log L(\widehat{\theta}_k) + 2m(k) \tag{2.1}$$

where $L(\widehat{\theta}_k)$ is the maximized likelihood function, $\widehat{\theta}_k$ is the maximum likelihood estimate of the parameter vector θ_k under the model M_k, and $m(k)$ is the number of independent parameters when M_k is the model.

In *AIC*, the compromise takes place between the maximized log likelihood, i.e., $-2\log L(\widehat{\theta}_k)$ (the lack of fit component) and $m(k)$, the number of free parameters estimated within the model (the penalty component) which is a measure of complexity that compensates for the bias in the lack of fit when the maximum likelihood estimators are used. In using *AIC*, according to Akaike (1987, p. 319), the accuracy of parameter estimates is measured by a universal criterion, namely

$$Accuracy\ Measure = E\ [loglikelihood\ of\ the\ fitted\ model] \tag{2.2}$$

where E denotes the expectation, since *AIC* is an unbiased estimator of minus twice the expected log likelihood.

We are motivated from considerations similar to those in *AIC*. However, we base the new procedure *ICOMP* on the *structural complexity* of an element or set of random vectors via a generalization of the *information-based covariance complexity index* of van Emden (1971).

For a general multivariate linear or nonlinear model defined by

$$Statistical\ model = Signal + Noise \tag{2.3}$$

ICOMP is designed to estimate a loss function:

$$Loss = Lack\ of\ Fit + Lack\ of\ Parsimony + Profusion\ of\ Complexity \tag{2.4}$$

in several ways using the additivity properties of information theory. We further base our developments on similar considerations to Rissanen (1976) in his *final estimation criterion (FEC)* in estimation and model identification problems, as well as *Akaike's (1973) AIC*, and its analytical extensions in Bozdogan (1987).

The development and construction of *ICOMP* is based on a generalization of the *covariance complexity index* originally introduced by van Emden (1971). Instead of penalizing the number of free parameters directly, *ICOMP* penalizes the covariance complexity of the model. It is defined by

$$ICOMP = -2\log L(\widehat{\theta}) + 2C(\widehat{\Sigma}_{Model}), \tag{2.5}$$

where $L(\widehat{\theta}_k)$ is the maximized likelihood function, $\widehat{\theta}_k$ is the maximum likelihood estimate of the parameter vector θ_k under the model M_k, and C represents a real-valued complexity measure and $\widehat{Cov}(\widehat{\theta}) = \widehat{\Sigma}_{Model}$ represents the estimated covariance matrix of the parameter vector of the model.

Since there are several forms and justifications of *ICOMP*, based on (2.5), in this paper, for brevity, we will present the most general form of *ICOMP* referred to as *ICOMP(IFIM)*. *ICOMP(IFIM)* exploits the well-known asymptotic optimality properties of the *MLE's*, and uses the information-based complexity of the *inverse-Fisher information matrix (IFIM)* of a model. This is known as the celebrated *Cramér-Rao lower bound (CRLB)* matrix. See, e.g., Cramér (1946) and Rao (1945, 1947, 1948).

Before we derive *ICOMP(IFIM)*, we first introduce some background material to understand the concept of complexity and give the definition of the complexity of a system next.

2.2.1 The Concept of Complexity and Complexity of a System

Complexity is a general property of statistical models that is largely independent of the specific content, structure, or probabilistic specification of the models. In the literature, the concept of complexity has been used in many different contexts. In general, there is not a unique definition of complexity in statistics, since the notion is *"elusive"* according to van Emden (1971, p. 8). Complexity has many faces, and it is defined under many different names such as those of *"Kolmogorov Complexity"* (Cover, Gacs, and Gray, 1989), *"Shannon Complexity"* (Rissanen, 1989), and *"Stochastic Complexity"* (Rissanen, 1987, 1989) in information theoretic coding theory, to mention a few. For example, Rissanen (1986, 1987, 1989) similar to Kolmogorov (1983) defines complexity in terms of the shortest code length for the data that can be achieved by the class of models, and calls it *Stochastic Complexity (SC)*. The Monash School (e.g., Wallace and Freeman, 1987, Wallace and Dowe, 1993, Baxter, 1996) define complexity in terms of *Minimum Message Length (MML)* which is based on evaluating models according to their ability to compress a message containing the data.

An understanding of complexity is necessary in general model building theory and inductive inference to study uncertainty in light of the data. Statistical models and methods are not exactly deductive since human beings often reason on the basis of uncertainties. Instead, they generally fall under the category of inductive inference. Inductive inference is the problem of choosing a parameter, or model, from a hypothesis, or model space, which best *'explains'* the data under study (Baxter, 1996, p. 1). As discussed in Akaike (1994, p. 27), reasoning under uncertainty was studied by the philosopher C. S. Pierce (see, e.g., Pierce, 1955), who called it the *logic of abduction*, or in short, *abduction*. Abduction is a way of reasoning that uses general principles and observed facts to obtain new facts, but all with a degree of uncertainty. Abduction takes place using numerical functions and measures such as the information theoretic model selection criteria. Pierce insisted that the most original part of scientific work was related to the abductive phase, or the phase of selection of proper hypotheses. Therefore, developing a systematic procedure for abductive inference with the aid of the notion of complexity is *"a prerequisite to the understanding of learning and evolutionary processes"* (von Neumann, 1966). In this context, statistical modelling and model building is a science of abduction which forms the philosophical foundation of *data mining* and *knowledge discovery*. Hence, the study of complexity is of considerable practical importance for model selection of proper hypotheses or models within the data mining enterprise.

We give the following simple system theoretic definition of complexity to motivate a statistically defined measure.

Definition 2.1. Complexity of a system (of any type) is a measure of the degree of interdependency between the whole system and a simple enumerative composition of its subsystems or parts.

We note that this definition of complexity is different from the way it is frequently now used in the literature to mean the number of estimated parameters in a model. For our purposes, the complexity of a model is most naturally described in terms of interactions of the components of the model, and the information required to construct the model in a way it is actually defined. Therefore, the notion of complexity can be best explained if we consider the statistical model arising within the context of a real world system. For example, the system can be physical, biological, social, behavioral, economic, etc., to the extent that the system responses are considered to be random.

As complexity is defined in *Definition 2.1*, we are interested in the amount by which the whole system, say, S, is different from the composition of its components. If we let C denote any real-valued measure of complexity of a system S, then $C(S)$ will measure the amount of the difference between the whole system and its decomposed components. Using the information theoretic interpretation, we define this amount to be the discrimination information of the joint distribution of the probability model at hand against the product of its marginal distributions. Discrimination information is equal to zero if the distributions are identical and is positive otherwise (van Emden, 1971, p. 25).

Thus, to quantify the concept of complexity in terms of a *scalar index*, we only have to express the interactions in a mathematical definition. We shall accomplish this by appealing to information theory since it possesses several important analytical advantages over the conventional procedures such as those of *additivity* and *constraining properties*, and *allowance to measure dependencies*.

For more details on the system theoretic definition of complexity as background material, we refer the reader to van Emden (1971, p. 7 and 8), and Bozdogan (1990).

2.2.2 Information Theoretic Measure of Complexity of a Multivariate Distribution

For a random vector, we define the complexity as follows.

Definition 2.2. The complexity of a random vector is a measure of the interaction or the dependency between its components.

We consider a continuous p-variate distribution with joint density function $f(x) = f(x_1, x_2, \ldots, x_p)$ and marginal density functions $f_j(x_j), j = 1, 2, \ldots, p$. Following Kullback (1968), Harris (1978), Theil and Fiebig (1984), and others, we define the *informational measure of dependence* between random variables $x_1, x_2, \ldots, x_p$ by

$$I(x) = I(x_1, x_2, \ldots, x_p) = E_f \left[\log \frac{f(x_1, x_2, \ldots, x_p)}{f_1(x_1) f_2(x_2) \cdots f_p(x_p)} \right].$$

Or, it is equivalently defined by

$$I(x) = \int_{-\infty}^{\infty} \cdots \int_{-\infty}^{\infty} f(x_1, x_2, \ldots, x_p) \log \frac{f(x_1, x_2, \ldots, x_p)}{f_1(x_1) f_2(x_2) \cdots f_p(x_p)} dx_1 \cdots dx_p, \qquad (2.6)$$

where I is the *Kullback-Leibler (KL) (1951) information divergence against independence*. $I(x)$ in (2.6) is a *measure of expected dependency* among the component variables, which is also known as the *expected mutual information* or the *information proper*.

- *Property 1.* $I(x) \equiv I(x_1, x_2, \ldots, x_p) \geq 0$, i.e., the expected mutual information is nonnegative.

- *Property 2.* $f(x_1, x_2, \ldots, x_p) = f_1(x_1) f_2(x_2) \cdots f_p(x_p)$ for every p-tuple $(x_1, x_2, \ldots, x_p)$ if and only if the random variables $x_1, x_2, \ldots, x_p$ are mutually statistically independent. In this case the quotient in (2.6) is equal to unity, and its logarithm is then zero. Hence, $I(x) \equiv I(x_1, x_2, \ldots, x_p) = 0$. If it is not zero, this implies a dependency.

We relate the *KL divergence* in (2.6) to *Shannon's (1948) entropy* by the important identity

$$I(x) \equiv I(x_1, x_2, \ldots, x_p) = \sum_{j=1}^{p} H(x_j) - H(x_1, x_2, \ldots, x_p), \qquad (2.7)$$

where $H(x_j)$ is the marginal entropy, and $H(x_1, x_2, \ldots, x_p)$ is the global or joint entropy. Watanabe (1985) calls (2.7) the *strength of structure* and a *measure of interdependence*. We note that (2.7) is the sum of the interactions in a system with $x_1, x_2, \ldots, x_p$ as components, which we define to be the entropy complexity of that system. This is also called the *Shannon Complexity* (see, Rissanen, 1989). The more interdependency in the structure, the larger will be the sum of the marginal entropies to the joint entropy. If we wish to extract fewer and more important variables, it will be desirable that they be statistically independent, because the presence of interdependence means redundancy and mutual duplication of information contained in these variables (Watanabe, 1985).

To define the information-theoretic measure of complexity of a multivariate distribution, we let $f(x)$ be a multivariate normal density function given by

$$f(x) = f(x_1, x_2, ..., x_p) = (2\pi)^{-\frac{p}{2}} |\Sigma|^{-\frac{1}{2}} exp\left\{-\frac{1}{2}(x-\mu)'\Sigma^{-1}(x-\mu)\right\} \quad (2.8)$$

where $\mu = (\mu_1, \mu_2, ..., \mu_p)'$, $-\infty < \mu_j < \infty$, $j = 1, 2, ..., p$ and $\Sigma > 0$ (p.d.). We write $x \sim N_p(\mu, \Sigma)$. Then the joint entropy $H(x) = H(x_1, x_2, ..., x_p)$ from (2.7) for the case in which $\mu = 0$ is given by

$$H(x) = H(x_1, x_2, ..., x_p) = -\int f(x) \log f(x) \, dx$$

$$= \int f(x) \left[\frac{p}{2} \log(2\pi)|\Sigma| + \frac{1}{2}(x-\mu)'\Sigma^{-1}(x-\mu)\right] dx$$

$$= \frac{p}{2} \log(2\pi)|\Sigma| + \frac{1}{2} tr \left[\int f(x) \Sigma^{-1}(x-\mu)(x-\mu)' dx\right]. \quad (2.9)$$

Then, since $E[(x-\mu)(x-\mu)'] = \Sigma$, we have

$$H(x) = H(x_1, x_2, ..., x_p) = \frac{p}{2} \log(2\pi) + \frac{p}{2} + \frac{1}{2} \log|\Sigma|$$

$$= \frac{p}{2}[\log(2\pi) + 1] + \frac{1}{2} \log|\Sigma|. \quad (2.10)$$

See, e.g., Rao (1965, p. 450), and Blahut (1987, p. 250).
From (2.10), the marginal entropy $H(x_j)$ is

$$H(x_j) = -\int_{-\infty}^{\infty} f(x_j) f(x_j) \, dx_j$$

$$= \frac{1}{2} \log(2\pi) + \frac{1}{2} + \frac{1}{2} \log(\sigma_j^2), j = 1, 2, ..., p. \quad (2.11)$$

2.2.3 Initial Definition of Covariance Complexity

Van Emden (1971, p.61) provides a reasonable initial definition of informational complexity of a covariance matrix Σ for the multivariate normal distribution. This measure is given by:

$$I(x_1, x_2, ..., x_p) = \sum_{j=1}^{p} H(x_j) - H(x_1, x_2, ..., x_p)$$

$$= \sum_{j=1}^{p} \left[\frac{1}{2} \log(2\pi) + \frac{1}{2} \log(\sigma_{jj}) + \frac{1}{2}\right] - \frac{p}{2} \log(2\pi) - \frac{1}{2} \log|\Sigma| - \frac{p}{2}. \quad (2.12)$$

This reduces to

$$C_0(\Sigma) = \frac{1}{2}\sum_{j=1}^{p}\log(\sigma_{jj}) - \frac{1}{2}\log|\Sigma|, \qquad (2.13)$$

where $\sigma_{jj} \equiv \sigma_j^2$ is the j-th diagonal element of Σ and p is the dimension of Σ. Note that $C_0(\Sigma) = 0$ when Σ is a diagonal matrix (i.e., if the variates are linearly independent). $C_0(\Sigma)$ is infinite if any one of the variables may be expressed as a linear function of the others ($|\Sigma| = 0$). If $\theta = (\theta_1, \theta_2, \ldots, \theta_k)$ is a normal random vector with covariance matrix equal to $\Sigma(\theta)$, then $C_0(\Sigma(\theta))$ is simply the *KL* distance between the multivariate normal density of θ and the product of the marginal densities of the components of θ. As pointed out by van Emden (1971), the result in (2.13) is not an effective measure of the amount of complexity in the covariance matrix Σ, since:

- $C_0(\Sigma)$ depends on the marginal and common distributions of the random variables $x_1, \ldots, x_p$, and

- The first term of $C_0(\Sigma)$ in (2.13) would change under orthonormal transformations.

2.2.4 Definition of Maximal Covariance Complexity

Since we defined the complexity as a general property of statistical models, we consider that the general definition of complexity of a covariance matrix Σ should be independent of the coordinates of the original random variables $(x_1, x_2, \ldots, x_p)$ associated with the variances σ_j^2, $j = 1, 2, \ldots, p$. As it is $C_0(\Sigma)$ in (2.13) is coordinate dependent. However, to characterize the maximal amount of complexity of Σ, we can relate the general definition of complexity of Σ to the total amount of interaction or $C_0(\Sigma)$ in (2.13). We do this by recognizing the fact that the maximum of (2.13) under orthonormal transformations of the coordinate system may reasonably serve as the measure of complexity of Σ. This corresponds to observing the interaction between the variables under the coordinate system that most clearly represents it in terms of the measure $I(x_1, x_2, \ldots, x_p) \equiv C_0(\Sigma)$. So, to improve on (2.13), we have the following proposition.

Proposition 2.1. A maximal information theoretic measure of complexity of a covariance matrix Σ of a multivariate normal distribution is

$$\begin{aligned}C_1(\Sigma) &= max_T C_0(\Sigma) = max_T \{H(x_1) + \ldots + H(x_p) - H(x_1, x_2, \ldots, x_p)\} \\ &= \frac{p}{2}\log\left[\frac{tr(\Sigma)}{p}\right] - \frac{1}{2}\log|\Sigma|,\end{aligned} \qquad (2.14)$$

where the maximum is taken over the orthonormal transformation T of the overall coordinate systems $x_1, x_2, ..., x_p$.

Proof: Following van Emden (1971, p. 61), Ljung and Rissanen (1978, p. 1421), and filling the gap in Maklad and Nichols (1980, p. 82) to find

$$C_1(\Sigma) = max_T\{H(x_1) + ... + H(x_p) - H(x_1, x_2, ..., x_p)\} \quad (2.15)$$

we must find the orthonormal transformation, say T, of Σ that maximizes

$$\sum_{j=1}^{p} \log(\sigma_{jj}^*) + ... + \log(\sigma_{pp}^*), \quad (2.16)$$

where $\sigma_{jj}^* \equiv \sigma_j^{*2}$'s are the diagonal elements of the covariance of $Tx = T(x_1, x_2, ..., x_p)$, i.e., $Cov(Tx) = \Sigma^*$. Since orthonormal transformations leave $tr(\Sigma) = \sigma_{11} + ... + \sigma_{pp}$ invariant, we

$$maximize \sum_{j=1}^{p} \log(\sigma_{jj}) \quad (2.17)$$

$$subject\ to\ tr(\Sigma) = c, c = constant.$$

To carry out this maximization, we use the geometric and arithmetic mean of $\sigma_{11}, ..., \sigma_{pp}$ given by

$$\left(\prod_{j=1}^{p} \sigma_{jj}\right)^{\frac{1}{p}} \leq \frac{1}{p}\sum_{j=1}^{p} \sigma_{jj} \quad (2.18)$$

with equality if and only if $\sigma_{11} = \sigma_{22} = ... = \sigma_{pp}$.

The equality condition in (2.18) is always achieved by orthonormal transformations T to equalize all variances to within certain error. This is shown by van Emden (1971, p.66). Hence, from van Emden (1971, p.61), and Maklad and Nichols (1980, p.82), (2.17) implies that

$$max \sum_{j=1}^{p} \log(\sigma_{jj}) = max\ \log \prod_{j=1}^{p} \sigma_{jj}$$

$$= p\log\ tr(\Sigma) - p\log\ p = p\log\left[\frac{tr(\Sigma)}{p}\right]. \quad (2.19)$$

Now replacing the first component of $C_0(\Sigma)$ in (2.13), we find

$$C_1(\Sigma) = max_T\{H(x_1)+...+H(x_p)-H(x_1,x_2,...,x_p)\}$$

$$= \frac{p}{2}\log\left[\frac{tr(\Sigma)}{p}\right] - \frac{1}{2}\log |\Sigma| \qquad (2.20)$$

as a maximal information theoretic measure of the complexity of a covariance matrix Σ of a multivariate normal distribution.

$C_1(\Sigma)$ in (2.20) is an upper bound to $C_0(\Sigma)$ in (2.13), and it measures both inequality among the variances and the contribution of the covariances in Σ (van Emden, 1971, p.63). Such a measure is very important in model selection and evaluation problems to determine the *strength of model structures, similarity, dissimilarity, and high-order correlations* within the model. $C_1(\Sigma)$ is independent of the coordinate system associated with the variances $\sigma_j^2 \equiv \sigma_{jj}^2$, $j = 1,2,...,p$. Furthermore, if, for example, one of the σ_j^2's is equal to zero, then $C_0(\Sigma)$ in (2.13) takes the value "$\infty - \infty$" which is *"indeterminate,"* whereas $C_1(\Sigma)$ in (2.20) has the value "∞" *(infinity)* which has a mathematical meaning. Also, $C_1(\Sigma)$ in (2.20) has rather attractive properties. Namely, $C_1(\Sigma)$ is invariant with respect to scalar multiplication and orthonormal transformation. Further, $C_1(\Sigma)$ is a monotonically increasing function of the dimension p of Σ; see Magnus and Neudecker (1999, p. 26). These properties are given and established in Bozdogan (1990).

The contribution of the complexity of the model covariance structure is that it provides a numerical measure to assess *parameter redundancy* and *stability* uniquely all in one measure. When the parameters are stable, this implies that the covariance matrix should be approximately a diagonal matrix. This concept of stable parameter is equivalent to the simplicity of model covariance structure defined in Bozdogan (1990). Indeed, $C_1(\Sigma)$ penalizes the scaling of the ellipsoidal dispersion, and the importance of circular distribution has been taken into account. It is because of these reasons that we use $C_1(\Sigma)$ without using any transformations of Σ, and that we do not discard the use of $C_0(\Sigma)$. If we write (2.20) as

$$C_1(\Sigma) = \frac{1}{2}\log\frac{(\frac{tr(\Sigma)}{p})^p}{|\Sigma|} \qquad (2.21)$$

we interpret the complexity as the *log ratio* between the *geometric mean of the average total variation* and the *generalized variance*, since $tr(\Sigma)/p$ is equal to *average total variation*, and $|\Sigma|$ is the *generalized variance*.

Further, if we let $\lambda_1, \lambda_2, ..., \lambda_p$ be the eigenvalues of Σ, then $tr(\Sigma)/p = \overline{\lambda}_a = 1/p\sum_{j=1}^{p}\lambda_j$ is the arithmetic mean of the eigenvalues of Σ, and $|\Sigma|^{1/p} = \overline{\lambda}_g = \left(\prod_{j=1}^{p}\lambda_j\right)^{1/p}$ is the geometric mean of the eigenvalues of Σ. Then the complexity of Σ can be written as

$$C_1(\Sigma) = \frac{p}{2}\log\left(\overline{\lambda}_a/\overline{\lambda}_g\right). \qquad (2.22)$$

Hence, we interpret the complexity as the *log ratio* between the *arithmetic mean* and the *geometric mean of the eigenvalues* of Σ. It measures how unequal the eigenvalues of Σ are, and it incorporates the two simplest scalar measures of multivariate scatter, namely the *trace* and the *determinant* into one single function. Indeed, Mustonen (1997) in a recent paper studies the fact that the *trace (sum of variances)* and the *determinant* of the covariance matrix Σ *(generalized variance)* alone do not meet certain essential requirements of variability in the multivariate normal distribution.

In general, large values of complexity indicate a high interaction between the variables, and a low degree of complexity represents less interaction between the variables. The minimum of $C_1(\Sigma)$ corresponds to the *"least complex"* structure. In other words, $C_1(\Sigma) \to 0$ as $\Sigma \to I$, the identity matrix. This establishes a plausible relation between information-theoretic complexity and computational effort. Further, what this means is that the identity matrix is the least complex matrix. To put it in statistical terms, orthogonal designs or linear models with no collinearity are the least complex, or most informative, and that the identity matrix is the only matrix for which the complexity vanishes. Otherwise, $C_1(\Sigma) > 0$, necessarily.

Geometrically, $C_1(\Sigma)$ preserves all inner products, angles, and lengths under orthogonal transformations of Σ. An orthogonal transformation T indeed exists which corresponds to a sequence of plane rotation of the coordinate axes to equalize the variances. This can be achieved using *Jacobi's iterative method* or *Gauss-Seidel method* (see, Graham, 1987).

We note that the system correlation matrix can also be used to describe complexity. If we wish to show the *interdependencies* (i.e., *correlations*) among the parameter estimates, then we can transform the covariances to correlation matrices and describe yet another useful measure of complexity. Let R be the correlation matrix obtained from Σ by the relationship

$$R = \Lambda_\sigma \Sigma \Lambda_\sigma, \qquad (2.23)$$

where $\Lambda_\sigma = diag(1/\sigma_1, \ldots, 1/\sigma_p)$ is a diagonal matrix whose diagonal elements equal to $1/\sigma_j, j = 1, 2, \ldots, p$. From (2.20), we have

$$C_1(R) = -1/2 \log |R| \equiv C_0(R). \qquad (2.24)$$

Diagonal operation of a covariance matrix Σ always reduces the complexity of Σ, and that $C_1(R) \equiv C_0(R)$ takes into account the *interdependencies (correlations)* among the variables. For simplicity, the C_0 measure based on the correlation matrix R will be denoted by C_R, and $C_0(R)$ is written as $C_R(\Sigma)$ for notational convenience, since R is obtained from Σ. Obviously, C_R is invariant with respect to scaling and orthonormal transformations and subsequently can be used as a complexity measure to evaluate the interdependencies among parameter estimates. Note that if $|R| = 1$, then $I(x_1, x_2, \ldots, x_p) = 0$ which implies the mutual independence of the variables $x_1, x_2, \ldots, x_p$. If the variables are not mutually independent, then $0 < |R| < 1$ and that $I(x_1, x_2, \ldots, x_p) > 0$. In this sense $I(x)$ in (2.6) or (2.7) can also be viewed as a measure of dimensionality of model manifolds.

Next, we develop the informational complexity *ICOMP(IFIM)* approach to model evaluation based on the maximal covariance complexity $C_1(\bullet)$, and $C_R(\bullet)$.

2.2.5 ICOMP as an Approximation to the Sum of Two Kullback-Leibler Distances

In this section, we introduce a new model-selection criterion called *ICOMP(IFIM)* to measure the fit between multivariate normal linear *and/or* nonlinear structural models and observed data as an example of the application of the covariance complexity measure defined in the previous section. *ICOMP(IFIM)* resembles a penalized likelihood method similar to *AIC* and *AIC-type criteria*, except that the penalty depends on the curvature of the log likelihood function via the scalar $C_1(\bullet)$ complexity value of the *estimated IFIM*.

Proposition 2.2. For a multivariate normal linear or nonlinear structural model we define the general form of ICOMP(IFIM) as

$$ICOMP(IFIM) = -2\log L(\widehat{\theta}) + 2C_1(\widehat{F}^{-1}(\widehat{\theta})), \qquad (2.25)$$

where C_1 denotes the maximal informational complexity of $\widehat{F}^{-1}$, the estimated IFIM. To show this, suppose we consider a general statistical model of the form given by

$$y = m(\theta) + \varepsilon, \qquad (2.26)$$

where:

- $y = (y_1, y_2, \ldots, y_n)$ is an $(n \times 1)$ random vector of response values in $\Re^n$;

- θ is a parameter vector in $\Re^k$;

- $m(\theta)$ is a systematic component of the model in $\Re^n$, which depends on the parameter vector θ, and its deterministic structure depends on the specific model considered, e.g., in the usual linear multiple regression model $m(\theta) = X\theta$, where X is an $(n \times (k+1))$ matrix of nonstochastic or constant design or model matrix with k explanatory variables so that $rank(X) = k + 1 = q$; and ε is an $(n \times 1)$ random error vector with

$$E(\varepsilon) = 0, E(\varepsilon \varepsilon') = \Sigma_\varepsilon. \qquad (2.27)$$

Following Bozdogan and Haughton (1998), we denote θ^* to be a vector of parameters of the operating true model, and θ to be any other value of the vector of parameters. Let $f(y;\theta)$ denote the joint density function of y given θ. Let $I(\theta^*;\theta)$ denote the *KL distance* between the densities $f(y;\theta^*)$ and $f(y;\theta)$. Then, since y_i are independent, $i = 1, 2, \ldots, n$, we have

$$I(\theta^*; \theta) = \int_{\Re^n} f(y; \theta^*) \log \left[\frac{f(y; \theta^*)}{f(y; \theta)} \right] dy$$
$$= \sum_{i=1}^{n} \int f_i(y_i; \theta^*) \log [f_i(y_i; \theta^*)] dy_i - \sum_{i=1}^{n} \int f_i(y_i; \theta^*) \log [f_i(y_i; \theta)] dy_i, \quad (2.28)$$

where f_i, $i = 1, 2, \ldots, n$ are the marginal densities of the y_i.

Note that the first term in (2.28) is the usual negative entropy $H(\theta^*; \theta^*) \equiv H(\theta^*)$ which is constant for a given $f_i(y_i; \theta^*)$. The second term is equal to:

$$-\sum_{i=1}^{n} E[\log f_i(y_i; \theta)], \quad (2.29)$$

which can be unbiasedly estimated by

$$-\sum_{i=1}^{n} \log f_i(y_i; \theta) = -\log L(\theta \mid y_i), \quad (2.30)$$

where $\log L(\theta \mid y_i)$ is the log likelihood function of the observations evaluated at θ. Given a model M where the parameter vector is restricted, a maximum likelihood estimator $\widehat{\theta}_M$ can be obtained for θ, and the quantity

$$-2 \sum_{i=1}^{n} \log f_i(y_i; \widehat{\theta}_M) = -2 \log L(\widehat{\theta}_M) \quad (2.31)$$

evaluated. This will give us the estimation of the first *KL distance*, which is reminiscent to the derivation of *AIC*. On the other hand, a model M gives rise to an asymptotic covariance matrix $Cov(\widehat{\theta}_M) = \Sigma(\widehat{\theta}_M)$ for the *MLE* $\widehat{\theta}_M$. That is,

$$\widehat{\theta}_M \sim N\left(\theta^*, \Sigma(\widehat{\theta}_M) \equiv \widehat{F}^{-1}(\widehat{\theta}_M)\right). \quad (2.32)$$

Now invoking the $C_1(\bullet)$ complexity on $\Sigma(\widehat{\theta}_M)$ from the previous section can be seen as the *KL distance* between the joint density and the product of marginal densities for a normal random vector with covariance matrix $\Sigma(\widehat{\theta}_M)$ via (2.7), maximized over all orthonormal transformations of that normal random vector (see Bozdogan, 1990). Hence, using the estimated covariance matrix, we define *ICOMP* as the sum of two *KL distances* given by:

$$ICOMP(IFIM) = -2 \sum_{i=1}^{n} \log f_i(y_i; \widehat{\theta}_M) + 2C_1\left(\widehat{\Sigma}(\widehat{\theta}_M)\right)$$
$$= -2 \log L(\widehat{\theta}_M) + 2C_1\left(\widehat{F}^{-1}(\widehat{\theta}_M)\right). \quad (2.33)$$

The first component of *ICOMP(IFIM)* in (2.33) measures the lack of fit of the model, and the second component measures the complexity of the estimated *inverse-Fisher information matrix (IFIM)*, which gives a scalar measure of the celebrated

Cramér-Rao lower bound matrix which takes into account the accuracy of the estimated parameters and implicitly adjusts for the number of free parameters included in the model. See, e.g., Cramér (1946) and Rao (1945, 1947, 1948).

This approach has several rather attractive features. If $F_{jj}^{-1}(\theta_K)$ is the j-th diagonal element of the *inverse-Fisher information matrix (IFIM)*, from Chernoff (1956), we know that $F_{jj}^{-1}(\bullet)$ represents the variance of the asymptotic distribution of $\sqrt{n}(\widehat{\theta}_j - \theta_j)$, for $j = 1, ..., K$. Considering a subset of the K parameters of size k, we have that

$$F_{jj}^{-1}(\theta_K) \geq F_{jj}^{-1}(\theta_k). \tag{2.34}$$

Behboodian (1964) explains that the inequality (2.34) means that the variance of the asymptotic distribution of $\sqrt{n}(\widehat{\theta}_j - \theta_j)$ can only increase as the number of unknown parameters is increased. This is an important result that impacts the parameter redundancy. The proof of (2.34) is shown in Chen (1996, p. 6) in his doctoral dissertation: *"Model Selection in Nonlinear Regression Analysis"* under my supervision.

The use of the $C_1(\widehat{F}^{-1}(\widehat{\theta}_M))$ in the information-theoretic model evaluation criteria takes into account the fact that as we increase the number of free parameters in a model, the accuracy of the parameter estimates decreases. As preferred according to the principle of parsimony, *ICOMP(IFIM)* chooses simpler models that provide more accurate and efficient parameter estimates over more complex, overspecified models.

We note that the *trace* of *IFIM* in the complexity measure involves only the diagonal elements analogous to *variances* while the *determinant* involves also the off-diagonal elements analogous to *covariances*. Therefore, *ICOMP(IFIM)* contrasts the *trace* and the *determinant* of *IFIM*, and this amounts to a comparison of the *geometric* and *arithmetic means* of the *eigenvalues* of *IFIM* given by

$$ICOMP(IFIM) = -2\log L(\widehat{\theta}_M) + s\log\left(\frac{\overline{\lambda}_a}{\overline{\lambda}_g}\right), \tag{2.35}$$

where $s = dim(\widehat{F}^{-1}(\widehat{\theta}_M)) = rank(\widehat{F}^{-1}(\widehat{\theta}_M))$.

We note that *ICOMP(IFIM)* now looks in appearance like the *CAIC* of Bozdogan (1987), Rissanen's (1978) *MDL*, and Schwarz's (1978) Bayesian criterion *SBC*, except for using $\log\left(\overline{\lambda}_a/\overline{\lambda}_g\right)$ instead of using $\log(n)$, where $\log(n)$ denotes the natural logarithm of the sample size n. A model with minimum *ICOMP* is chosen to be the best among all possible competing alternative models.

The *greatest simplicity*, that is *zero complexity*, is achieved when *IFIM* is proportional to the identity matrix, implying that the *parameters are orthogonal* and can be estimated with equal precision. In this sense, *parameter orthogonality*, several forms of *parameter redundancy*, and *parameter stability* are all taken into account.

We note that *ICOMP(IFIM)* in (2.33) penalizes the *"bad scaling"* of the parameters. It is important to note that well conditioning of the information matrix needs a simple structure, but the latter does not necessarily imply the former. For example, consider an information matrix that is diagonal with some diagonal elements close to zero. In this case, the corresponding correlation matrix is an identity matrix, which is the simplest. But, the information matrix is poorly conditioned. Therefore, the analysis based on the correlation matrix often ignores an important characteristic, namely, the ratios of the diagonal elements in the information matrix, or the *"scale"* of these components.

Similar to *AIC*, to make *ICOMP(IFIM)* to be scale invariant with respect to scaling and orthonormal transformations in model selection enterprise, we suggest the use of the *correlational form of IFIM* given by

$$F_R^{-1}(\widehat{\theta}) = D_{F^{-1}}^{-1/2} F^{-1} D_{F^{-1}}^{-1/2}. \tag{2.36}$$

Then, $ICOMP(IFIM)_R$ is defined by

$$ICOMP(IFIM)_R = -2\log L(\widehat{\theta}) + 2C_1\left(\widehat{F}_R^{-1}(\widehat{\theta}_M)\right). \tag{2.37}$$

In this way *ICOMP* becomes invariant to one-to-one transformations of the parameter estimates. In the literature, several authors such as McQuarie and Tsai (1998, p. 367), and Burnham and Anderson (1998, p.69), without reviewing the impact and the applications of *ICOMP* to many complex modelling problems, have erroneously interpreted the contribution of this novel approach over *AIC*, and *AIC-type criteria*.

With *ICOMP(IFIM)*, complexity is viewed not as the number of parameters in the model, but as the *degree of interdependence* (i.e., the *correlational structure* among the parameter estimates). By defining complexity in this way, *ICOMP(IFIM)* provides a more judicious penalty term than *AIC*, Rissanen's (1978, 1986) *MDL*, Schwarz's (1978) *SBC (or BIC)*, and Bozdogan's (1987) *Consistent AIC (CAIC)*. The lack of parsimony is automatically adjusted by $C_1(\widehat{F}^{-1}(\widehat{\theta}_M))$ or $C_1(\widehat{F}_R^{-1}(\widehat{\theta}_M))$ across the competing alternative portfolio of models as the parameter spaces of these models are constrained in the model selection process.

Following Morgera (1985, p. 612), we define the *relative reduction of complexity (RRC)* in terms of the *estimated IFIM* as

$$RRC = \frac{C_1(\widehat{F}^{-1}(\widehat{\theta}_M)) - C_1(\widehat{F}_R^{-1}(\widehat{\theta}_M))}{C_1(\widehat{F}^{-1}(\widehat{\theta}_M))}, \tag{2.38}$$

and the *percent relative reduction of complexity* by

$$PRRC = \frac{C_1(\widehat{F}^{-1}(\widehat{\theta}_M)) - C_1(\widehat{F}_R^{-1}(\widehat{\theta}_M))}{C_1(\widehat{F}^{-1}(\widehat{\theta}_M))} \times 100\%. \tag{2.39}$$

The interpretation of *RRC* or *PRRC* is that they both measure heteroscedastic complexity plus a correlational complexity of the model. In general statistical modelling framework, what this means is that, when the parameter estimates are highly correlated, in nonlinear, and in many other statistical modelling, one can remove the correlation by considering parameter transformations of the model. The difference between the complexities $C_1(\widehat{F}^{-1}(\widehat{\theta}_M))$ and $C_1(\widehat{F}_R^{-1}(\widehat{\theta}_M))$ can be used to show how well the parameters are scaled. Parameter transformation can reduce the complexity measure based on the correlation structure, but it can increase the complexity measure based on the maximal complexity. This occurs because the reduction in the correlation does not imply the reduction of scaling effect. Indeed, the reduction in the correlation may even make scaling worse. In this sense, *ICOMP(IFIM)* may be better than *ICOMP(IFIM)$_R$* especially in nonlinear models, since it considers both of these effects in one criterion. For more on these, see, e.g., Chen (1996), Bozdogan (2000), and Chen and Bozdogan (2004).

There are other formulations of *ICOMP*, which are based on the covariance matrix properties of the parameter estimates of a model starting from their finite sampling distributions and Bayesian justification of *ICOMP*. These versions of *ICOMP* are useful in linear and nonlinear models. For more details on this and other approaches, we refer the readers to Bozdogan (2000), and Bozdogan and Haughton (1998) where consistency properties of *ICOMP* have been studied in the case of the usual multiple regression models. The probabilities of underfitting and overfitting for *ICOMP* as the sample size n tends to infinity have been established. Through a large scale Monte Carlo *"misspecification environment,"* when the true model is not in the model set, the performance of *ICOMP* has been studied under different configurations of the experiment with varying sample sizes and the error variances. The results obtained show that *ICOMP class criteria* overwhelmingly agree the most often with the *KL* decision, which goes to the heart of the consistency arguments about information criteria not studied before, since most of the studies are based on the fact that the true model considered is in the model set.

In concluding this section, we note that the difference between *ICOMP* class criteria and *AIC*, *SBC/MDL*, and *CAIC* is that with *ICOMP* we have the advantage of working with both biased as well as the unbiased estimates of the parameters. Further, we have the advantage of using smoothed (or improved) covariance estimators of the models and measure the complexities to study the *robustness properties* of different methods of parameter estimates and improved covariance estimators. *AIC* and *AIC-type criteria* are based on *MLE's*, which often are biased and they do not fully take into account the concept of *parameter redundancy*, *accuracy*, and the *parameter interdependencies* in model fitting and selection process. Also, *ICOMP* class criteria legitimize the role of the *Fisher information matrix (FIM)* (a tribute to Rao, 1945, 1947, 1948) as the natural metric on the parameter manifold of the model, which remained academic in the statistical literature.

2.3 Information Criteria for Multiple Regression Models

We consider the multiple linear regression model in matrix form given by

$$y = X\beta + \varepsilon \qquad (2.40)$$

where y is a vector of $(n \times 1)$ observations on a dependent variable, X is a full rank $(n \times q)$ matrix of nonstochastic predetermined variables in standardized form, and β is a $(q \times 1)$ coefficient vector, and ε is an $(n \times 1)$ vector of unknown disturbance term, such that

$$\varepsilon \sim N(0, \sigma^2 I) \text{ or equivalently } \varepsilon_i \sim N(0, \sigma^2) \text{ for } i = 1, 2, ..., n. \tag{2.41}$$

Given the model in (2.40) under the assumption of normality, we can analytically express the density function of regression model for a particular sample observation as

$$f(y_i | x_i, \beta, \sigma^2) = (2\pi\sigma^2)^{-\frac{1}{2}} \exp\left[-\frac{(y_i - x_i'\beta)^2}{2\sigma^2}\right]. \tag{2.42}$$

That is, the random observation vector y is distributed as a multivariate normal with mean vector $X\beta$ and covariance matrix $\sigma^2 I_n$. The likelihood function of the sample is:

$$L(\beta, \sigma^2 | y, X) = (2\pi\sigma^2)^{-\frac{n}{2}} \exp\left[-\frac{(y - X\beta)'(y - X\beta)}{2\sigma^2}\right], \tag{2.43}$$

and the log likelihood function is:

$$l(\beta, \sigma^2) = -\frac{n}{2}\log(2\pi) - \frac{n}{2}\log\sigma^2 - \frac{(y - X\beta)'(y - X\beta)}{2\sigma^2}. \tag{2.44}$$

Using matrix differential calculus of Magnus and Neudecker (1999), the maximum likelihood estimates (*MLE's*) $(\hat{\beta}, \hat{\sigma}^2)$ of (β, σ^2) are given by:

$$\hat{\beta} = (X'X)^{-1}X'y, \text{ and} \tag{2.45}$$

$$\hat{\sigma}^2 = \frac{(y - X\hat{\beta})'(y - X\hat{\beta})}{n} = \frac{RSS}{n}. \tag{2.46}$$

The *maximum likelihood (ML) covariance matrix of the estimated regression coefficients* is given by

$$\widehat{Cov}(\hat{\beta})_{MLE} = \hat{\sigma}^2 (X'X)^{-1} \tag{2.47}$$

without centering and scaling the model matrix X. Also, the *inverse Fisher information matrix (IFIM)* is given by

$$\widehat{Cov}(\hat{\beta}, \hat{\sigma}^2) = \hat{F}^{-1} = \begin{bmatrix} \hat{\sigma}^2 (X'X)^{-1} & 0 \\ 0 & \frac{2\hat{\sigma}^4}{n} \end{bmatrix}. \tag{2.48}$$

Now, we can define derived forms of *ICOMP* in multiple regression as follows. This can be defined for both $\widehat{Cov}(\hat{\beta})$, $\hat{F}^{-1}$, and the *correlational form of IFIM*, $\hat{F}_R^{-1}$. These are as follows.

2.3.1 ICOMP Based on Complexity Measures

$$ICOMP(Reg)_{C_0} = -2\log L(\widehat{\theta}) + 2C_0(\widehat{Cov}(\widehat{\beta}))$$

$$= n\log(2\pi) + n\log(\widehat{\sigma}^2) + n + 2[\frac{1}{2}\sum_{j=1}^{q}\log(\widehat{\sigma}_{jj}(\widehat{\beta})) - \frac{1}{2}\log\left|\widehat{Cov}(\widehat{\beta})\right|]$$

$$= n\log(2\pi) + n\log(\widehat{\sigma}^2) + n + 2[\frac{1}{2}\sum_{j=1}^{q}\log(\widehat{\sigma}_{jj}(\widehat{\beta})) - \frac{1}{2}\sum_{j=1}^{q}\log(\lambda_j)]. \quad (2.49)$$

based on the original definition of the complexity $C_0(\cdot)$ in (2.13).

$$ICOMP(Reg)_{C_1} = -2\log L(\widehat{\theta}) + 2C_1(\widehat{Cov}(\widehat{\beta}))$$

$$= n\log(2\pi) + n\log(\widehat{\sigma}^2) + n$$
$$+ 2[\frac{q}{2}\log(\frac{tr(\widehat{Cov}(\widehat{\beta}))}{q}) - \frac{1}{2}\log\left|\widehat{Cov}(\widehat{\beta})\right|]$$
$$= n\log(2\pi) + n\log(\widehat{\sigma}^2) + n + 2[\frac{q}{2}\log(\frac{\overline{\lambda}_a}{\overline{\lambda}_g})]. \quad (2.50)$$

based on $C_1(\cdot)$ in (2.14).

If we use the estimated *inverse Fisher information matrix* (*IFIM*) in (2.48), then we define *ICOMP(IFIM)* as

$$ICOMP(IFIM)_{Regression} = -2\log L(\widehat{\theta}_M) + 2C_1\left(\widehat{F}^{-1}(\widehat{\theta}_M)\right)$$
$$= n\log(2\pi) + n\log(\widehat{\sigma}^2) + n + C_1\left(\widehat{F}^{-1}(\widehat{\theta}_M)\right), (2.51)$$

where

$$C_1\left(\widehat{F}^{-1}(\widehat{\theta}_M)\right) = (q+1)\log\left[\frac{tr\widehat{\sigma}^2(X'X)^{-1} + \frac{2\widehat{\sigma}^4}{n}}{q+1}\right]$$
$$-\log\left|\widehat{\sigma}^2(X'X)^{-1}\right| - \log\left(\frac{2\widehat{\sigma}^4}{n}\right). \quad (2.52)$$

In (2.48), as the number of parameters increases (i.e., as the size of X increases), the error variance $\widehat{\sigma}^2$ gets smaller even though the complexity gets larger. Also, as

$\widehat{\sigma}^2$ increases, $(X'X)^{-1}$ decreases. Therefore, $C_1(\widehat{F}^{-1})$ achieves a trade-off between these two extremes and guards against multicollinearity.

To preserve scale invariance, we use the *correlational form of IFIM*, that is, we use $\widehat{F}_R^{-1}$ and define the correlational form of $ICOMP(IFIM)_{Regression}$ given by

$$ICOMP(IFIM)_{Regression} = n\log(2\pi) + n\log(\widehat{\sigma}^2) + n + C_1\left(\widehat{F}_R^{-1}(\widehat{\theta}_M)\right), \quad (2.53)$$

where

$$\widehat{F}_R^{-1}(\widehat{\theta}_M) = D_{F^{-1}}^{-1/2} F^{-1} D_{F^{-1}}^{-1/2} = USV' \quad (2.54)$$

using the *singular value decomposition (svd)* on $\widehat{F}_R^{-1}$. $Svd(\cdot)$ produces a diagonal matrix S, of the same dimension as $\widehat{F}_R^{-1}$ and with nonnegative diagonal elements in decreasing order, which are the singular values of $\widehat{F}_R^{-1}$, and unitary matrices U and V, which satisfy $UU' = VV' = I$, so that $\widehat{F}_R^{-1} = U \cdot S \cdot V'$.

2.3.2 ICOMP Under Misspecification

Although we will not use this form of *ICOMP* in this paper, to be complete and to inform the readers, when the model is misspecified, we define *ICOMP* under misspecification as

$$ICOMP(IFIM)_{Misspec} = n\log(2\pi) + n\log(\widehat{\sigma}^2) + n + 2C_1(\widehat{Cov}(\widehat{\theta})_{Misspec}), \quad (2.55)$$

where

$$\widehat{Cov}(\widehat{\theta})_{Misspec} = \widehat{F}^{-1}\widehat{R}\widehat{F}^{-1} \quad (2.56)$$

is a consistent estimator of the covariance matrix $Cov(\theta_k^*)$. This is often called the *"sandwiched covariance"* or *"robust covariance"* estimator, since it is a correct covariance regardless of whether the assumed model is correct or not. It is called sandwiched covariance, because $\widehat{R}$ is the meat and the two $\widehat{F}^{-1}$s are slices of the bread. When the model is correct we get $\widehat{F} = \widehat{R}$, and the formula reduces to the usual inverse Fisher information matrix $\widehat{F}^{-1}$(White, 1982).

In the regression case, the Fisher information in inner-product form is given as in (2.48) by

$$\widehat{F}^{-1} = \begin{bmatrix} \widehat{\sigma}^2(X'X)^{-1} & 0 \\ 0 & \frac{2\widehat{\sigma}^4}{n} \end{bmatrix} \quad (2.57)$$

and the estimated *outer-product form of the Fisher information matrix* is given by

$$\widehat{R} = \begin{bmatrix} \frac{1}{\widehat{\sigma}^4} X'D^2 X & X'1\frac{Sk}{2\widehat{\sigma}^3} \\ (X'1\frac{Sk}{2\widehat{\sigma}^3})' & \frac{(n-q)(Kt-1)}{4\widehat{\sigma}^4} \end{bmatrix}, \quad (2.58)$$

where $D^2 = diag(\widehat{\varepsilon}_1^2, \ldots, \widehat{\varepsilon}_n^2)$ and X is $(n \times q)$ matrix of regressors or model matrix, Sk is the estimated residual skewness, Kt the kurtosis, and 1 is a $(n \times 1)$ vector of ones. That is,

$$Sk = \text{Coefficient of skewness} = \frac{(\frac{1}{n}\sum_{i=1}^{n}\widehat{\varepsilon}_i^3)}{\widehat{\sigma}^3} \quad (2.59)$$

and

$$Kt = \text{Coefficient of kurtosis} = \frac{(\frac{1}{n}\sum_{i=1}^{n}\widehat{\varepsilon}_i^4)}{\widehat{\sigma}^4}. \quad (2.60)$$

Hence, the *"sandwiched covariance"* or *"robust covariance"* estimator is given by

$$\widehat{Cov}(\widehat{\theta})_{Misspec} =$$

$$\begin{bmatrix} \widehat{\sigma}^2(X'X)^{-1} & 0 \\ 0 & \frac{2\widehat{\sigma}^4}{n} \end{bmatrix} \begin{bmatrix} \frac{1}{\widehat{\sigma}^4}X'D^2X & X'1\frac{Sk}{2\widehat{\sigma}^3} \\ (X'1\frac{Sk}{2\widehat{\sigma}^3})' & \frac{(n-q)(Kt-1)}{4\widehat{\sigma}^4} \end{bmatrix} \begin{bmatrix} \widehat{\sigma}^2(X'X)^{-1} & 0 \\ 0 & \frac{2\widehat{\sigma}^4}{n} \end{bmatrix}. \quad (2.61)$$

Note that this covariance matrix in (2.61) should impose greater complexity than the *inverse Fisher information matrix (IFIM)*. It also takes into account presence of skewness and kurtosis which is not possible with *AIC*, and *MDL/SBC*. For more on model selection under misspecification, see Bozdogan and Magnus (2003).

Another form of *ICOMP* is defined by

$$ICOMP(IFIM)_{Misspec} = n\log(2\pi) + n\log(\widehat{\sigma}^2) + n + 2[tr(\widehat{F}^{-1}\widehat{R}) + C_1(\widehat{F}^{-1})]. \quad (2.62)$$

Similarly, *Generalized Akaike's (1973) information criterion (GAIC)* is defined by

$$GAIC = n\log(2\pi) + n\log(\widehat{\sigma}^2) + n + 2tr(\widehat{F}^{-1}\widehat{R}). \quad (2.63)$$

For this, see, Bozdogan (2000).

Bozdogan and Ueno (2000) modified Bozdogan's (1987) *CAICF* given by

$$CAICF_E = n\log(2\pi) + n\log(\widehat{\sigma}^2) + n + k[\log(n) + 2] + \log\left|\widehat{F}\right| + tr(\widehat{F}^{-1}\widehat{R}), \quad (2.64)$$

which includes *Akaike's* approach and *CAICF* as special cases. For the application and performance of $CAICF_E$, we refer the reader to Irizarry (2001) for model selection in local likelihood estimation.

We note that the term $tr(\widehat{F}^{-1}\widehat{R})$ in (2.62)-(2.64) is important because it provides information on the correctness of the assumed class of potential models as discussed in White (1982). A fundamental assumption underlying classical model selection criteria is that often the true model is considered to lie within a specified class of potential models. In general, this is not always the case, and often the true model may not be within the model set considered. Therefore, our approach guards us against the *misspecification of the probability model* as we actually fit and evaluate the models. In this sense, this result is very important in practice, which is often ignored.

2.3.3 AIC and AIC-Type Criteria

AIC for the regression model to be used as fitness values in the *GA* is given by

$$AIC(Regression) = n\log(2\pi) + n\log(\widehat{\sigma}^2) + n + 2(k+1). \qquad (2.65)$$

Similarly, Rissanen (1978) and Schwarz (1978) (MDL/SBC) criterion is defined by

$$MDL/SBC(Regression) = n\log(2\pi) + n\log(\widehat{\sigma}^2) + n + k\log(n). \qquad (2.66)$$

We note that *ICOMP* and *ICOMP(IFIM)* are much more general than *AIC*. They incorporate the assumption of dependence and independence of the residuals and help the analyst to consider risks of both under- and overparameterized models. *ICOMP* and *ICOMP(IFIM)* relieves the researcher of any need to consider the parameter dimension of a model explicitly (see Bozdogan and Haughton, 1998 for more detailed comparison.)

2.4 A GA for the Regression Modeling

Genetic algorithms *(GAs)* are a part of evolutionary computing. This is a very fast growing area of artificial intelligence (AI). As it is well known, *GAs* are inspired by Darwin's theory about evolution. Simply said, solution to a problem solved by *GAs* is evolved. Genetic Algorithms *(GAs)* were invented by John Holland and developed by him and his students and colleagues. This led to Holland's book *Adaption in Natural and Artificial Systems* published in 1975. In 1992 John Koza used genetic algorithm to evolve programs to perform certain tasks. He called his method *"genetic programming"* (GP). *LISP* programs were used, because programs in this language can be expressed in the form of a *"parse tree,"* which is the object the *GA* works on.

GA is started with a set of solutions (represented by chromosomes) called population. Solutions from one population are taken and used to form a new population. This is motivated by a hope that the new population will be better than the old one. Solutions that are selected to form new solutions (offsprings) are selected according to their fitness value. The more suitable they are the more chances they have to reproduce.

Our implementation of the *GA* for the problem of model selection in multiple linear regression basically follows Goldberg (1989). Recall that the general regression model can be represented as:

$$y = X\beta + \varepsilon. \qquad (2.67)$$

A *GA* for the problem of model selection in subset regression models can be implemented using the following steps. For a comprehensive background of *GAs* and related topics, we refer readers to Goldberg (1989), Michalewicz (1992), and others. Goldberg's *GA* (or called simple genetic algorithm, SGA) contains the following components.

•A genetic coding scheme for the possible regression models

Each regression model is encoded as a string, where each locus in the string is a binary code indicating the presence (1) or absence (0) of a given predictor variable. Every string has the same length, but each contains different binary coding representing different combinations of predictor variables. For example, in a $k=5$ variable regression with a constrant term, the string 1 0 1 0 1 1 represents a model, where *constant term* is included in the model, *variable 1* is excluded from the model, *variable 2* is included in the model, and so on.

•Generating an initial population of models

Population size (i.e., number of models fitted) N is an important parameter of *GA*. Population size says how many chromosomes are in a population (in one generation). If there are too few chromosomes, *GA* has a few possibilities to perform crossover and only a small part of search space is explored. On the other hand, if there are too many chromosomes, *GA* slows down. Research shows that after some limit (which depends mainly on encoding and the problem) it is not useful to increase population size, because it does not make solving the problem faster. We first initialize the first population of N random breeding models. Note that the population size N, representing the number of models to begin the first run, is chosen by the investigator and not by random. Our algorithm is flexible in that it allows one to choose any population size.

•A fitness function to evaluate the performance of any model

In general we can use any one of the model selection criteria described in Section 2.3 as the fitness function used in our *GA* for the regression analysis. However, for the purpose of illustration of the *GA* and for the brevity in this paper, we restrict our attention to the *ICOMP* criterion. Analysts can choose any appropriate model selection criterion based on their needs and preferences.

•A mechanism to select the fitter models

This step involves selecting models based on their *ICOMP(IFIM)* values for composition of the mating pool. After calculating the *ICOMP(IFIM)* for each of the possible subset models in the population, we subtract the criterion value for each model from the highest criterion value in the population. In other words, we calculate

$$\Delta ICOMP_{(i)}(IFIM) = ICOMP(IFIM)_{Max} - ICOMP(IFIM)_{(i)} \qquad (2.68)$$

for $i = 1, ..., N$, where N is the population size.

Next, we average these differences; that is, we compute

$$\overline{\Delta ICOMP(IFIM)} = \frac{1}{N}\sum_{i=1}^{N}\Delta ICOMP_{(i)}(IFIM). \qquad (2.69)$$

Then the ratio of each model's difference value to the mean difference value is calculated; that is, we compute

$$\Delta ICOMP_{(i)}(IFIM)/\overline{\Delta ICOMP(IFIM)}. \qquad (2.70)$$

This ratio is used to determine which models will be included in the mating pool. The chance of a model being mated is proportional to this ratio. In other words, a model with a ratio of two is twice as likely to mate as a model with a ratio of one. The process of selecting mates to produce offspring models continues until the number of offsprings equals the initial population size. This is called the proportional selection or fitting. There is also rank selection or fitting with *ICOMP*. For this see Bearse and Bozdogan (2002).

• **A reproductive operation to perform mating of parent models to produce offspring models**

Mating is performed as a crossover process. A model chosen for crossover is controlled by the crossover probability (p_c) or the crossover rate. The crossover probability (p_c) is often determined by the investigator. A crossover probability of zero simply means that the members of the mating pool are carried over into the next generation and no offsprings are produced. A crossover probability $(p_c) = 1$ indicates that mating (crossover) always occurs between any two parent models chosen from the mating pool; thus the next generation will consist only of offspring models (not of any model from the previous generation).

During the crossover process, we randomly pick a position along each pair of parent models (strings) as the crossover point. For any pair of parents, the strings are broken into two pieces at the crossover point and the portions of the two strings to the right of this point are interchanged between the parents to form two offspring strings as shown in Figure 2.1.

In this case each parent has ten loci. A randomly chosen point along the length of each parent model becomes the crossover point where the models are broken and then reattached to another parent to form two new models. We have a choice of several types of crossover operations. Here, we give just three choices which will suffice for all practical purposes.

Single point crossover - one crossover point is selected, binary string from beginning of chromosome to the crossover point is copied from one parent, the rest is copied from the second parent:

Parent A	Parent B	Offspring
11001011	+ 11011111 =	11001111

Two point crossover - two crossover point are selected, binary string from beginning of chromosome to the first crossover point is copied from one parent, the part from the first to the second crossover point is copied from the second parent and the rest is copied from the first parent:

Parent A	Parent B	Offspring
11001011	+ 11011111 =	11011111

Statistical Data Mining and Knowledge Discovery 39

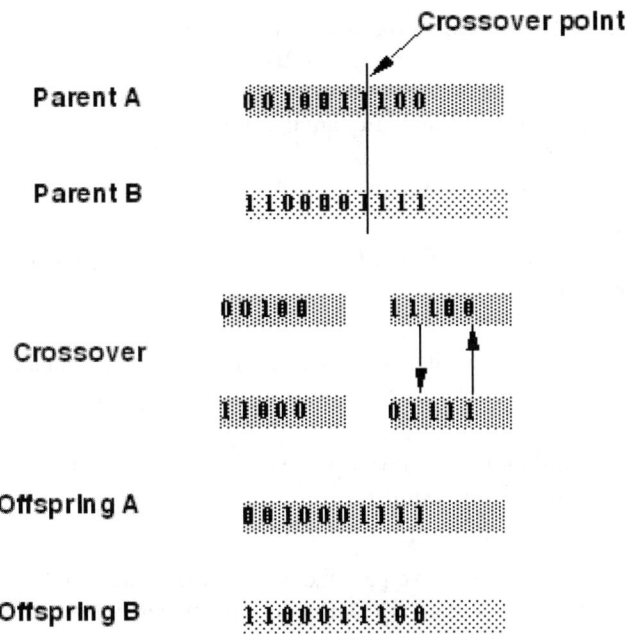

FIGURE 2.1
An example of the mating process, by means of crossing-over, for a given pair of models (strings).

Uniform crossover - bits are randomly copied from the first or from the second parent:

Parent A   Parent B   Offspring
11001011 + 11011101 = 11011111

In our algorithm, the user has the option of choosing any one of the above crossover options. Also, the user has the option of choosing what is called elitism rule. This means that at least one best solution is copied without changes to a new population, so the best solution found can survive to the end of the run.

•**A random effect of mutation to change the composition of new offspring models**

Mutation of models is used in a *GA* as another means of creating new combinations of variables so that the searching process can jump to another area of the fitness landscape instead of searching in a limited area. We permit mutation by specifying a mutation rate or probability at which a randomly selected locus can change from 0 to 1 or 1 to 0. Thus, a randomly selected predictor variable is either added to or removed from the model.

Depending on the particular crossover and mutation rates, the second generation will be composed entirely of offspring models or of a mixture of offspring and parent models. Models in the second generation then go to produce the third generation; the process continues one generation after another for a specified number of generations controlled by the analyst.

In summary, the outline of the steps of *GA* is as follows:

1. [*Start*] Generate random population of N chromosomes (suitable solutions for the problem).

2. [*Fitness*] Evaluate the fitness of each chromosome in the population using one of the model selection criteria.

3. [*New population*] Create a new population by repeating following steps until the new population is complete.

    (a) [*Selection*] Select two parent chromosomes from a population according to their fitness (e.g., ICOMP value)(the better fitness, the bigger chance to be selected).

    (b) [*Crossover*] With a crossover probability cross over the parents to form a new offspring (children). If no crossover was performed, offspring is an exact copy of parents. There are three choices of crossover.

    (c) [*Mutation*] With a mutation probability mutate new offspring at each locus (position in chromosome).

    (d) [*Accepting*] Place new offspring in a new population.

4. [*Replace*] Use new generated population for a further run of algorithm and look for the minimum of the model selection criteria used.

5. [*Test*] If the final condition is satisfied based on the model selection criteria, stop, and return the best solution in current population.

6. [*Loop*] Go to step 2.

In the next section, all our computations are carried out using the newly developed graphical user interface (*GUI*) software in Matlab for the *GA* subset selection of best predictors. *GUI* for solving the subset selection model problem is easy to use and very user friendly. The following is the summary of inputs and outputs and usage of *GUI*.

Statistical Data Mining and Knowledge Discovery 41

List of inputs and usage:

No. of generations:	Key in an integer value
Population size:	Key in an integer value
Fitness Values:	Check an option in the block: *AIC ICOMP ICOMP(IFIM)*
Probability of Crossover:	Key in a real number value from 0 to 1. Single Point Two-point Uniform
Probability of Mutation:	Key in a real number value from 0 to 1.
Elitism Rule	Check/uncheck the option in the checkbox
Input Data files:	Button Y: for the response variable Y Button X: for the set of predictor variables X.
Go:	To solve the problem
Reset:	Reset all keyed-in inputs and outputs
Exit:	Exit the program.

List of outputs and usage:

1. View 2-D/View 3-D buttons:	Shows the 2D/3D plots of criterion values versus generations.
2. Save Figure:	Pop up the current figure showing in the GUI plot window, then the user can save the pop up figure.
3. Output in Matlab	Shows the table of generations of *GA*, Command Window: Shows the fitted chromosomes (Variables) and Binary Strings, and Criterion Score Values.
4. Output File:	Same as the output in Matlab command window.
5. Save Figures:	Simply click on view 2-D/View 3-D after the run.

2.5 Numerical Examples

We consider two examples to illustrate the implementation of the *GA* in subset selection of best predictors.

2.5.1 Subset Selection of Best Predictors in Multiple Regression: A Simulation Example

In this example, we generated the values for y and $x_1, x_2, ..., x_{10}$, using the following simulation protocol.

We simulate the first five predictors using the following:

$$x_1 = 10 + \varepsilon_1,$$
$$x_2 = 10 + 0.3\varepsilon_1 + \alpha\varepsilon_2, \text{ where } \alpha = \sqrt{1 - 0.3^2} = \sqrt{0.91} = 0.9539$$
$$x_3 = 10 + 0.3\varepsilon_1 + 0.5604\alpha\varepsilon_2 + 0.8282\alpha\varepsilon_3,$$
$$x_4 = -8 + x_1 + 0.5x_2 + 0.3x_3 + 0.5\varepsilon_4,$$
$$x_5 = -5 + 0.5x_1 + x_2 + 0.5\varepsilon_5,$$

where ε_i is *independent and identically distributed (i.i.d.)* according to $N(0, \sigma^2 = 1)$, for $i = 1, \ldots, n$ observations, and also $\varepsilon_1, \varepsilon_2, \varepsilon_3, \varepsilon_4, \varepsilon_5 \sim N(0, \sigma^2 = 1)$. The parameter α controls the degree of collinearity in the predictors. Then, we generate the response variable y from:

$$y_i = -8 + x_1 + 0.5x_2 + 0.3x_3 + 0.5\varepsilon_i, \text{ for } i = 1, \ldots, n = 100 \text{ observations}.$$

Further, we generate five redundant variables: $x_6, \ldots, x_{10}$ using the uniform random numbers given by

$$x_6 = 6 \times rand(0,1), \ldots, x_{10} = 10 \times rand(0,1)$$

and fit a multiple regression model of y on $X = [x_0, x_1, x_2, x_3, x_4, x_5, x_6, x_7, x_8, x_9, x_{10}]$ for $n = 100$ observations, where $x_0 = 1$ constant column of $(n \times 1)$ vector of ones.

We expect that the *GA* run should pick the subset $\{x_0, x_1, x_2, x_3\}$ to be the best subset selected using the mininum *ICOMP* value.

The following output from Matlab shows that the *GA* with *ICOMP(IFIM)* as the fitness function can detect the relationship and pick the predictors $\{x_0, x_1, x_2, x_3\}$ to be the best subset chosen as in most of the generations of the *GA*.

Simulation of Collinear Data $n = 100$	
Number of generations	= 15
Population Size	= 30
Fitness Value	=ICOMP(IFIM)
Probability of crossover	= 0.7
	(Two point cross over is used.)
Elitism	= Yes
Probability of mutation	= 0.01

TABLE 2.1
Parameters of the *GA* for the simulated model.

In Table 2.1, we show the results of just one run of the *GA* with the parameters given above.

Statistical Data Mining and Knowledge Discovery   43

Generation	Chromosome (Variables)	Binary String	ICOMP(IFIM)
1	0 1 2 3 9 10	1 1 1 1 0 0 0 0 1 1	160
2	**0 1 2 3**	1 1 1 1 0 0 0 0 0 0	**155**
3	0 1 2 3 8 10	1 1 1 1 0 0 0 0 1 0 1	160.11
4	**0 1 2 3**	1 1 1 1 0 0 0 0 0 0	**155**
5	**0 1 2 3**	1 1 1 1 0 0 0 0 0 0	**155**
6	0 1 2 3 10	1 1 1 1 0 0 0 0 0 1	156.33
7	0 1 2 3 10	1 1 1 1 0 0 0 0 0 1	156.33
8	0 1 2 3 7 10	1 1 1 1 0 0 0 1 0 0 1	157.8
9	0 1 2 3 6 7	1 1 1 1 0 0 1 1 0 0 0	157.77
10	0 1 2 3 7 10	1 1 1 1 0 0 0 1 0 0 1	157.8
11	0 1 2 3 7 10	1 1 1 1 0 0 0 1 0 0 1	157.8
12	0 1 2 3 7 10	1 1 1 1 0 0 0 1 0 0 1	157.8
13	0 1 2 3 7 10	1 1 1 1 0 0 0 1 0 0 1	157.8
14	0 1 2 3 7 10	1 1 1 1 0 0 0 1 0 0 1	157.8
15	0 1 2 3 7 10	1 1 1 1 0 0 0 1 0 0 1	157.8

TABLE 2.2
The results from one run of the *GA* for the simulated model.

Looking at Table 2.2, we note that *GA* picks the best subset $\{x_0, x_1, x_2, x_3\}$ very quickly in the second generation, again in the fourth and in fifth generations. Indeed, we also note that in each of the generations the subset $\{x_0, x_1, x_2, x_3\}$ shows up along with one or two redundant variables.

We can repeat this experiment by simulating new $X - y$ data sets and run the *GA* many times in order to further illustrate the accuracy and efficiency of the *GA*.

2.5.2 Subset Selection of Best Predictors in Multiple Regression: A Real Example

In this example we determine the best subset of predictors of $y =$ Percent body fat from Siri's (1956) equation, using $k = 13$ predictors, $x_1 =$ Age (years), $x_2 =$ Weight (lbs), $x_3 =$ Height (inches), $x_4 =$ Neck circumference (cm), $x_5 =$ Chest circumference (cm), $x_6 =$ Abdomen 2 circumference (cm), $x_7 =$ Hip circumference (cm), $x_8 =$ Thigh circumference (cm), $x_9 =$ Knee circumference (cm), $x_{10} =$ Ankle circumference (cm), $x_{11} =$ Biceps (extended) circumference (cm), $x_{12} =$ Forearm circumference (cm), $x_{13} =$ Wrist circumference (cm) using the *GA* with *ICOMP* as the fitness function.

The data contains the estimates of the percentage of body fat determined by underwater weighing and various body circumference measurements for $n = 252$ men. This is a good example to illustrate the versatility and utility of our approach using multiple regression analysis with *GA*. This data set is maintained by Dr. Roger W. Johnson of the Department of Mathematics & Computer Science at South Dakota School of Mines & Technology (email address: rwjohnso@silver.sdsmt.edu, and web address: http://silver.sdsmt.edu/~rwjohnso).

Accurate measurement of body fat is inconvenient/costly and it is desirable to have easy methods of estimating body fat that are not inconvenient/costly. A variety

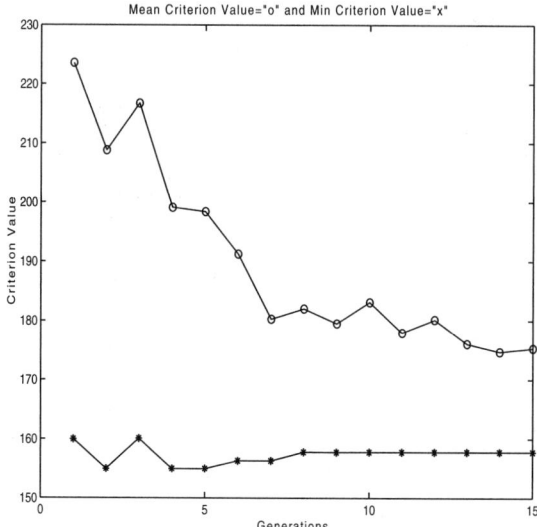

FIGURE 2.2
2D Plot: Summary of a GA Run for the Simulated Data.

of popular health books suggest that the readers assess their health, at least in part, by estimating their percentage of body fat. In Bailey (1994), for instance, the reader can estimate body fat from tables using their age and various skin-fold measurements obtained by using a caliper. Other texts give predictive equations for body fat using body circumference measurements (e.g., abdominal circumference) and/or skin-fold measurements. See, for instance, Behnke and Wilmore (1974, pp. 66-67); Wilmore (1976, p. 247); or Katch and McArdle (1977, pp. 120-132). Percentage of body fat for an individual can be estimated once body density has been determined. One (e.g. Siri (1956))assumes that the body consists of two components: lean body tissue and fat tissue. Letting

D = Body Density (gm/cm^3)
A = proportion of lean body tissue
B = proportion of fat tissue $(A+B=1)$
a = density of lean body tissue (gm/cm^3)
b = density of fat tissue (gm/cm^3)

we have

$$D = 1/[(A/a) + (B/b)].$$

Solving for B we find

Statistical Data Mining and Knowledge Discovery 45

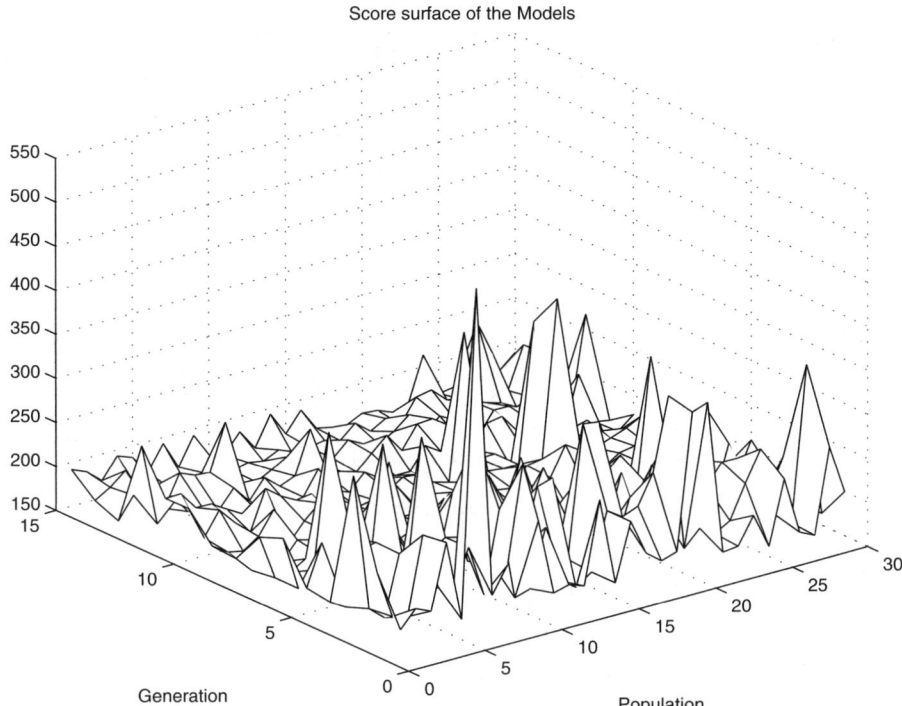

FIGURE 2.3
3D Plot: Model Landscape of all Models Evaluated by ICOMP.

$$B = (1/D) * [ab/(a-b)] - [b/(a-b)].$$

Using the estimates $a = 1.10\ gm/cm^3$ and $b = 0.90\ gm/cm^3$ (see Katch and McArdle (1977), p. 111 or Wilmore (1976), p. 123) we come up with "Siri's equation":

Percentage of Body Fat$(i.e., 100 * B) = 495/D - 450.$

Volume, and hence body density, can be accurately measured a variety of ways. The technique of underwater weighing "computes body volume as the difference between body weight measured in air and weight measured during water submersion. In other words, body volume is equal to the loss of weight in water with the appropriate temperature correction for the water's density" (Katch and McArdle (1977), p. 113). Using this technique,

$$Body\ Density = WA/[(WA - WW)/c.f. - LV]$$

where WA = Weight in air (kg), WW = Weight in water (kg), c.f. = Water correction factor (= 1 at 39.2 deg F as one-gram of water occupies exactly one cm^3 at this temperature, = .997 at 76 – 78 deg F), LV = Residual Lung Volume (liters) (Katch

Rank Number	Variables	ICOMP(IFIM)
1	1 - - 4 - 6 7 8 - - -12 13	1473.9065
2	1 - - 4 - 6 7 8 9 - -12 13	1474.5525
3	1 - 3 4 - 6 7 8 - - -12 13	1474.6751
4	1- - 4 - 6 7 8 - -10 - 12 13	1475.1721
5	1 - - 4 - 6 7 8 - - 11 12 13	1475.2089
6	1 - - 4 - 6 7 8 9 10 - 12 13	1475.5406
7	1 - 3 4 - 6 7 8 9 - - 12 13	1475.6024
8	1 - 3 4 - 6 7 8 - 10 - 12 13	1475.7067
9	1 - - 4 - 6 7 8 9 - 11 12 13	1475.8208
10	- - 3 4 - 6 7 - - - - 12 13	1475.9539
11	1 - 3 4 - 6 7 8 - - 11 12 13	1476.0138
12	1 - - 4 5 6 7 8 - - - 12 13	1476.0362
13	- - - 4 - 6 7 - - - - 12 13	1476.116
14	1 - - 4 - 6 7 8 - 10 11 12 13	1476.3913
15	1 - 3 4 - 6 7 8 9 10 - 12 13	1476.443

TABLE 2.3
The best models chosen by the lowest fifteen *ICOMP(IFIM)* values among all possible models for the body fat data.

Number of runs = 100	
Number of generations	= 30
Population Size	= 20
Fitness Value	=*ICOMP(IFIM)*
Probability of crossover	= 0.5
	(Uniform cross over is used.)
Elitism	= *Yes*
Probability of mutation	= 0.01

TABLE 2.4
Parameters of the *GA* run for the body fat data.

and McArdle (1977, p. 115). Other methods of determining body volume are given in Behnke and Wilmore (1974, p. 22).

For this example, we first evaluated *all possible subset* regression models. Then we picked the top 15 best subset models according to the rankings of the minimum *ICOMP(IFIM)* values. Then, we ran the *GA* for 100 runs with the parameters given in Table 2.4 and picked the top 10 ranking best subset models according to the minimum value of *ICOMP(IFIM)* to determine if the *GA* did indeed find the lowest *ICOMP(IFIM)* model in comparison to the all possible subset selection.

The best top fifteen regression models found by the all possible subset selection procedure are given in Table 2.3.

Statistical Data Mining and Knowledge Discovery 47

GA Ranking	Chromosome (Variables)	Binary String	ICOMP(IFIM)
1	(1) 1 - - 4 - 6 7 8 - - -12 13	0 1 0 0 1 0 1 1 1 0 0 0 1 1	1473.9
2	(2) 1 - - 4 - 6 7 8 9 - -12 13	0 1 0 0 1 0 1 1 1 1 0 0 1 1	1474.6
3	(3) 1 - 3 4 - 6 7 8 - - -12 13	0 1 0 1 1 0 1 1 1 0 0 0 1 1	1474.7
4	(4) 1 - - 4 - 6 7 8 - 10 - 12 13	0 1 0 0 1 0 1 1 1 0 1 0 1 1	1475.2
5	(7) 1 - 3 4 - 6 7 8 9 - -12 13	0 1 0 1 1 0 1 1 1 1 0 0 1 1	1475.6
6	(8) 1 - 3 4 - 6 7 8 - 10 -12 13	0 1 0 1 1 0 1 1 1 0 1 0 1 1	1475.7
7	(9) 1 - - 4 - 6 7 8 9 - 11 12 13	0 1 0 0 1 0 1 1 1 1 0 1 1 1	1475.8
8	(11) 1 - 3 4 - 6 7 8 - - 11 12 13	0 1 0 1 1 0 1 1 1 0 0 1 1 1	1476
9	(13) - - - 4 - 6 7 - - - - 12 13	0 0 0 0 1 0 1 1 0 0 0 0 1 1	1476. 1
10	(15) 1 - 3 4 - 6 7 8 9 10 - 12 13	0 1 0 1 1 0 1 1 1 1 1 0 1 1	1476. 4

TABLE 2.5
Top 10 ranking subsets of the best predictors for the body fat data set from 100 runs of the *GA*.

RSquare	=0.741266
RSquare Adj	=0.733844
Root Mean Square Error	=4.317462
Mean of Response	=19.15079
Observations (or Sum Wgts)	=252

TABLE 2.6
Summary of Fit of best subset model.

Term	Estimated Coeff.	Std Error	t-Ratio	Prob >
Intercept	-0.63164	6.498054	-0.10	0.9226
Age	0.0838616	0.029956	2.80	0.0055
NeckCirc	-0.634546	0.213624	-2.97	0.0033
Abdo2Circ	0.8808665	0.066639	13.22	<.0001
HipCirc	-0.359215	0.118802	-3.02	0.0028
TighCirc	0.2826235	0.129812	2.18	0.0304
ForearmCirc	0.4529919	0.185745	2.44	0.0155
WristCirc	-1.935856	0.481505	-4.02	<.0001

TABLE 2.7
Parameter estimates of the best subset *GA* model.

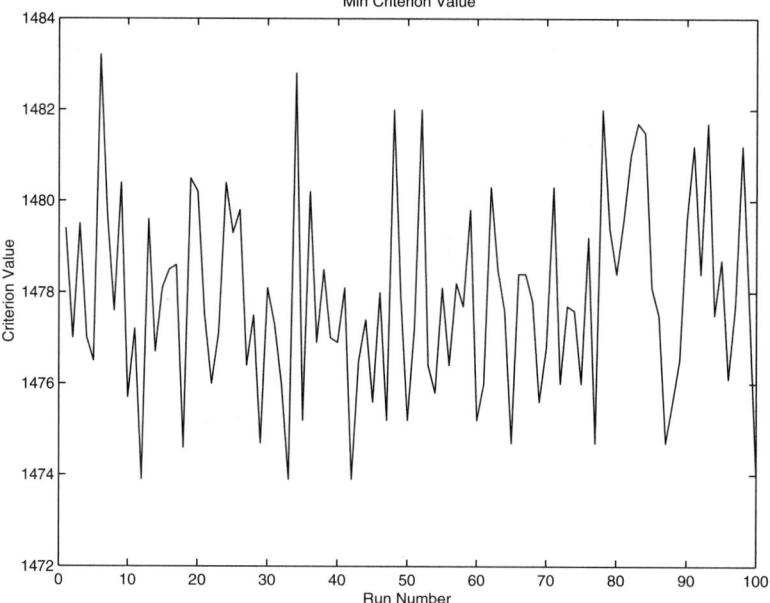

FIGURE 2.4
2D Plot: Summary of 100 Runs of the GA for the Body Fat Data.

If we had to choose one model from this set, the best subset is the first ranking model according to $ICOMP(IFIM) = 1473.9$ with the subset $\{x_1 =$ Age (years), $x_4 =$ Neck circumference (cm), $x_6 =$Abdomen 2 circumference (cm), $x_7 =$Hip circumference (cm), $x_8 =$Thigh circumference (cm), $x_{12} =$ Forearm circumference (cm), $x_{13} =$Wrist circumference (cm)$\}$. Indeed this corresponds to the best subset chosen from all possible subset selection. We further note that GA's selection corresponds to the top seven best subsets from the results of the all possible subsets. This is quite interesting and shows the fact that GA is a highly intelligent statistical model selection device capable of pruning combinatorially large numbers of submodels to obtain optimal or near optimal subset regression models.

Based on our results, the summary of fit and the parameter estimates of the best predictive model are given in Tables 2.6 and 2.7. Figure 2.4 shows the summary of 100 runs of the GA for the body fat data, and Figure 2.5 shows the 3D plot of the model landscape of all models evaluated by the information complexity criterion in 100 runs of the GA for the body fat data.

When we carry out forward stepwise regression analysis on the body fat data set, this approach gives us the full saturated model as the best fitting model, which is not surprising. In other words, stepwise procedure is not able to distinguish the importance of the predictors in the model, since the P-values used in stepwise selection are

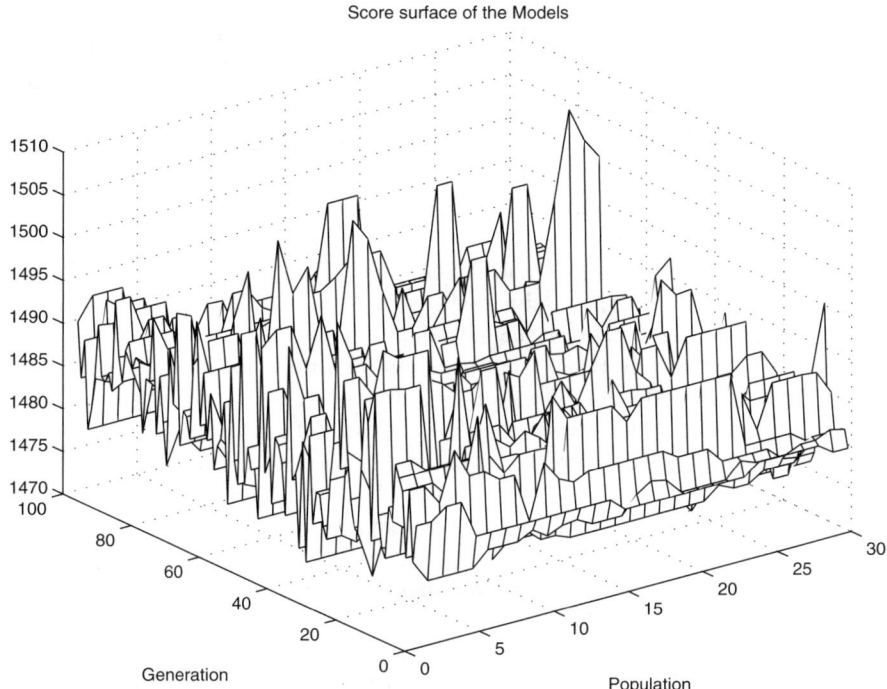

FIGURE 2.5
3D Plot: Model landscape of all models evaluated by ICOMP(IFIM) in 100 runs of the GA for the body fat data.

arbitrary and the F-ratio stopping rule does not have the provision of compensating between the lack of fit and increased model complexity. It does not attempt to find the best model in the model search space.

Therefore, it is time that researchers start critically thinking of abandoning the use of such procedures, which are less than optimal.

2.6 Conclusion and Discussion

In this paper we have demonstrated that the *GA*, an algorithm which mimics Darwinian evolution, is a useful optimization tool for statistical modelling. We view each regression model as a chromosome or a genotype within a population of such entities. The value of an information-based model selection criterion is calculated for each model as a measure of the model's fitness. The collection of all possible fitness values forms a fitness landscape of this "artificial life." Using the biological concepts of natural selection, crossover, and mutation, the *GA* searches over this landscape to find the "best" model.

Our *GA* application to the problem of optimal statistical model selection on the simulated and the body fat indicates that the *GA* can indeed find the best model without having to evaluate all possible regression models. Compare to all possible subset selection, we evaluated only a small proportion of the total model space in each run.

Question can be asked as to: "Will the *GA* always be guaranteed to find the best model for all data sets?" In some situations the *GA* will find "good" models, but may miss finding the overall best one. This is not a failure specific to the *GA*, but rather a limitation faced by any type of optimization algorithm not using an exhaustive search. Researchers often analyze a large number of variables wherein a very large number of possible models exist. In many data sets, we should bear in mind that a single best model may not exist, but rather a number of equally optimal models are present. A *GA* is capable, in such a case, of finding at least some of these best models. For example, in the body fat data example, the *GA* found the best top seven models in the all possible subsets. This is a remarkable achievement.

Another question is: "What are the optimal numbers of both population size and number of generations for use with the GA?" In the literature of *GA*, there are no clear cut answers to this question. The answer will probably depend on the number of predictor variables and the structure of the data set at hand. Understanding the relationships among these factors requires further investigation (Mahfoud 1994). We are currently investigating these problems by trying different combinations of population sizes and generations, and examining their results carefully to see if they have consistent patterns and results.

The *GA* approach in combination with information-based criteria is much more likely to uncover the "best" model as well as "better" models than stepwise selection for several reasons. First, our *GA* approach utilizes an information-based criterion as fitness values to evaluate models instead of treating regression model selection as a problem involving statistical hypothesis-testing, such as P-values used for stepwise selection. Second, the *GA* approach is not limited to simply adding or removing a single variable at a time. Rather, the *GA* evaluates models with new combinations of entire sets of variables obtained by evolutionary mechanisms (such as natural selection and crossover) at each generation. Third, the *GA* is a very flexible optimization algorithm. Several evolutionary mechanisms can be modified by the investigators at different stages of *GA*. For example, different proportional selection schemes can also be used to determine the combination of genotypes in the population in the next generation (Srinivas and Patnaik, 1994). Finally, and most importantly, a *GA* is not a "hill-climbing" searching algorithm like forward, backward, and stepwise procedures. A given *GA* can simultaneously search over multiple areas in the fitness landscape of the solution space.

It is obvious that more research is needed on the application of *GAs* to statistical model selection, in general, not just for linear regression modelling. We are working on other applications of the *GA* in other statistical modelling problems such as in logistic and ordinal logistic regression, in vector autoregressive models (Bearse and Bozdogan, 1998), and in multivariate regression (Bearse and Bozdogan, 2002). We encourage researchers to develop *GAs* for other statistical modelling problems.

Acknowledgments

I was introduced to the genetic algorithms *(GAs)* by Dr. Hang-Kwang (Hans) Luh in 1996 when he was a post doc in Mathematical Ecology here at the University of Tennessee and worked with me for two years taking my advanced statistical modelling and multivariate courses. I am grateful to Hans for pounding into me the importance of this area in which I was doing statistical modelling with information complexity ICOMP, and marrying it with the *GA*.

I acknowledge two of my graduate students and thank Vuttichai Chatpattananan and Xinli Bao for creating graphical user interface (GUI) based on my existing Matlab programs of the *GA* and modifying them. This made the computations much easier.

Finally, I dedicate this paper to Dean Warren Neel for his unending support of my work and area of research since I came to the University of Tennessee in 1990, and for creating a conducive atmosphere to carry out high level research.

References

Akaike, H. (1973). Information theory and an extension of the maximum likelihood principle. In B.N. Petrov and F. Csáki (Eds.), *Second international symposium on information theory*, Académiai Kiadó, Budapest, 267-281.

Akaike, H. (1974). A new look at the statistical model identification. *IEEE Transactions on Automatic Control*, AC-19, 716-723.

Akaike, H. (1987). Factor analysis and AIC. *Psychometrika*, **52**, 317-332.

Akaike, H. (1994). Implications of informational point of view on the development of statistical science. In H. Bozdogan (Ed.), *Engineering & scientific applications of informational modeling*, Volume **3**, pp. 27-38. Proceedings of the first US/Japan conference on the frontiers of statistical modeling: An informational approach. Kluwer Academic Publishers, the Netherlands, Dordrecht.

Bailey, Covert (1994). *Smart Exercise: Burning Fat, Getting Fit*, Houghton-Mifflin Co., Boston, pp. 179-186.

Bauer, R. J. Jr. (1994). *Genetic Algorithm and Investment Strategies.* John Wiley & Sons, New York.

Baxter, R. A. (1996). *Minimum Message Length Inference: Theory and Applications.* Unpublished Ph.D. Thesis, Department of Computer Science, Monash University, Clayton, Victoria, Australia.

Bearse, P. M. and Bozdogan, H. (1998). Subset selection in vector autoregressive (VAR) models using the genetic algorithm with informational complexity as the fitness function. *Systems Analysis, Modeling, Simulation (SAMS)*, 31, 61-91.

Bearse, P.M. and Bozdogan, H. (2002). Multivariate regressions, Genetic Algorithms, and Information Complexity: A Three Way Hybrid. In *Measurement and Multivariate Analysis*, S. Nishisato, Y. Baba, H. Bozdogan, and K. Kanefuji (Eds.), Springer, Tokyo, 2002, 269-278.

Behboodian, J. (1964). *Information for Estimating the Parameters in Mixtures of Exponential and Normal Distributions.* Ph.D.Thesis, Department of Mathematics, University of Michigan, Ann Arbor, MI.

Behnke, A.R. and Wilmore, J.H. (1974). *Evaluation and Regulation of Body Build and Composition*, Prentice-Hall, Englewood Cliffs, NJ.

Bellman, R. (1961). *Adaptive Control Processes: A Guided Tour.* Princeton University Press, Princeton, NJ.

Blahut, R. E. (1987). *Principles and Practice of Information Theory.* Addison-Wesley Publishing Company, Reading, MA.

Bock, H. H. (1994). Information and entropy in cluster analysis. In In *Multivariate Statistical Modeling*, H. Bozdogan (Ed.),Vol. 2, Proceedings of the First US/Japan Conference on the Frontiers of Statistical Modeling: An Informational Approach, Kluwer Academic Publishers, the Netherlands, Dordrecht; 115-147.

Bozdogan, H. (1987). Model selection and Akaike's Information Criterion (AIC): The general theory and its analytical extensions. *Psychometrika,* 52(3), 345-370.

Bozdogan, H. (1988). ICOMP: a new model-selection criterion. In *Classification and Related Methods of Data Analysis*, H. H. Bock (Ed.), Elsevier Science Publishers, Amsterdam; 599-608.

Bozdogan, H. (1990). On the information-based measure of covariance complexity and its application to the evaluation of multivariate linear models. *Communications in Statistics, Theory and Methods*, 19, 221-278.

Bozdogan, H. (1994). Mixture-model cluster analysis using a new informational complexity and model selection criteria. In *Multivariate Statistical Modeling*, H. Bozdogan (Ed.), Vol. 2, Proceedings of the First US/Japan Conference on the Frontiers of Statistical Modeling: An Informational Approach, Kluwer Academic Publishers, the Netherlands, Dordrecht, 69-113.

Bozdogan, H. (2000). Akaike's information criterion and recent developments in information complexity. *Journal of Mathematical Psychology*, 44, 62-91.

Bozdogan, H. (2004). *Statistical Modeling and Model Evaluation: A New Informational Approach.* To appear.

Bozdogan, H. and Haughton, D.M.A. (1998). Informational complexity criteria for regression models. *Computational Statistics and Data Analysis*, 28, 51-76.

Bozdogan, H. and Ueno, M. (2000). A unified approach to information-theoretic and Bayesian model selection criteria. Invited paper presented in the Technical Session Track C on: Information Theoretic Methods and Bayesian Modeling at the 6th World Meeting of the International Society for Bayesian Analysis (ISBA), May 28-June 1, 2000, Hersonissos-Heraklion, Crete.

Bozdogan, H. and Magnus, J. R. (2003). Misspecification resistant model selection using information complexity. Working paper.

Burnham, K. P. and Anderson D. R. (1998). *Model Selection and Inference: A Practical Information-Theoretic Approach.* Springer, New York.

Boyce, D. E., Farhi, A., and Weischedel, R. (1974). *Optimal Subset Selection: Multiple Regression, Interdependence, and Optimal Network Algorithms.* Springer-Verlag, New York.

Chen, X. (1996). *Model Selection in Nonlinear Regression Analysis.* Unpublished Ph.D. Thesis, The University of Tennessee, Knoxville, TN.

Chen, X. and Bozdogan, H. (2004). *Model Selection in Nonlinear Regression Analysis: A New Information Complexity Approach.* Working research monograph.

Chernoff, H. (1956). Large sample theory: parametric case, *Annals of Mathematical Statistics*, 27, 1-22.

Cover, T. M., Gacs, P., and Gray, R. M. (1989). Kolmogorov's contibutions to information theory and algorithmic complexity. *Ann. Prob.*, 17, 840-865.

Cramér, H. (1946). *Mathematical Methods of Statistics.* Princeton University Press, Princeton, NJ.

Forrest, S. (1993). Genetic algorithms: principles of natural selection applied to computation, *Science*, 261(2.4), 872-878.

Graham, A. (1987). *Nonnegative Matrices and Applicable Topics in Linear Algebra.* Halsted Press, a Division of John Wiley and Sons, New York.

Goldberg, D. E. (1989). *Genetic Algorithms in Search, Optimization, and Machine Learning*, Addison-Wesley, New York.

Gosh, J. K. (1988) (Ed.). *Statistical Information and Likelihood: A Collection of Critical Essays by Dr. D. Basu.* Springer-Verlag, New York.

Harris, C. J. (1978). An information theoretic approach to estimation. In M. J. Gregson (Ed.), *Recent Theoretical Developments in Control*, Academic Press, London,

563-590.

Hocking, R. R. (1976). The analysis and selection variables in linear regression, *Biometrics*, 32, 1044.

Hocking, R. R. (1983). Developments in linear regression methodology: 1959-1982, *Technometrics*, 25, 219-230.

Holland, J. (1992). Genetic algorithms. *Scientific American*, 66-72.

Irizarry, R. A. (2001). Information and posterior probability criteria for model selection in local likelihood estimation. *Journal of the American Statistical Association*, March 2001, Vol. 96, No. 453, 303-315.

Katch, F. and McArdle, W. (1977). *Nutrition, Weight Control, and Exercise*, Houghton Mifflin Co., Boston.

Kauffman, S. A. (1993). *The Origins of Order: Self-organization and Selection in Evolution*, Oxford University Press, Oxford.

Kolmogorov, A. N. (1983). Combinatorial foundations of information theory and the calculus of probabilities. *Russian Math Surveys*, 38, 29-40.

Kullback, S. (1968). *Information Theory and Statistics*. Dover, New York.

Kullback, S. and Leibler, R. (1951). On information and sufficiency. *Ann. Math. Statist.*, 22, 79-86.

Lanning, M. J. and Bozdogan, H. (2003). Ordinal Logistic Modeling Using ICOMP as a Goodness-of-Fit Criteria. In *Statistical Data Mining and Knowledge Discovery*, H. Bozdogan (Ed.), Chapman & Hall/CRC, Boca Raton, FL.

Ljung, L. and Rissanen, J. (1978). On canonical forms, parameter identifiability and the concept of complexity. In *Identification and System Parameter Estimation*, N. S. Rajbman (Ed.), North-Holland, Amsterdam, 1415-1426.

Magnus, J. R. and Neudecker, H. (1999). *Matrix Differential Calculus*, 2nd Edition, John Wiley & Sons, New York.

Mahfoud, S. W. (1994). *Population Sizing for Sharing Methods*, Illinois Genetic Algorithms Laboratory Report No. 94005. University of Illinois, Champaign-Urbana, IL.

Maklad, M. S. and Nichols, T. (1980). A new approach to model structure discrimination. *IEEE Trans. on Syst., Man, and Cybernetics*, SMC 10, 78-84.

Mantel, N. (1970). Why stepdown procedures in variables selection, *Technometrics*, 12, 591-612.

Peirce, C. S. (1955). Abduction and Induction. In *Philosophical Writings of Peirce*, J. Buchler (Ed.),Dover, New York, 150-156.

McQuarie, A. D. R. and Tsai, C-L. (1998). *Regression and Time Series Model Selection*. World Scientific Publishing Company, Singapore.

Michalewicz, Z. (1992). *Genetic Algorithms + Data Structures = Evolution Programs*, Springer-Verlag, New York.

Miller, A. J. (1990). *Subset selection in regression*, Chapman and Hall, London.

Morgera, S. D. (1985). Information theoretic covariance complexity and its relation to pattern recognition. *IEEE Trans. on Syst., Man, and Cybernetics*, SMC 15, 608-619.

Mustonen, S. (1997). A measure of total variability in multivariate normal distribution. *Comp. Statist. and Data Ana.*, 23, 321-334.

Moses, L. E. (1986). *Think and Explain with Statistics*, Addison-Wesley, Reading, MA.

Rao, C. R. (1945). Information and accuracy attainable in the estimation of statistical parameters. *Bull. Calcutta Math Soc.*, 37, 81.

Rao, C. R. (1947). Minimum variance and the estimation of several parameters. *Proc. Cam. Phil. Soc.*, 43, 280.

Rao, C. R. (1948). Sufficient statistics and minimum variance estimates. *Proc. Cam. Phil. Soc.*, 45, 213.

Rao, C. R. (1965). *Linear Statistical Inference and Its Applications*. John Wiley & Sons, New York.

Rissanen, J. (1976). Minmax entropy estimation of models for vector processes. In *System Identification*, : R. K. Mehra and D. G. Lainiotis (Eds.), Academic Press, New York, 97-119.

Rissanen, J. (1978). Modeling by shortest data description. *Automatica*, 14, 465-471.

Rissanen, J. (1986). Stochastic complexity and modeling. *Ann. Statist.*, 14, 1080-1100.

Rissanen, J. (1987). Stochastic complexity. (With discussion), *J. of the Royal Statist. Soc.*, Series B, 49, 223-239.

Rissanen, J. (1989). *Stochastic Complexity in Statistical Inquiry*. World Scientific Publishing Company, Teaneck, NJ.

Roughgarden, J. (1979). *Theory of Population Genetics and Evolutionary Ecology: An Introduction*, MacMillian Publishing, New York.

Sakamoto, Y., Ishiguro, M., and Kitagawa, G. (1986). *Akaike Information Criterion Statistics*, KTK Scientific Publishers, Tokyo.

Schwarz, G. (1978). Estimating the dimension of a model. *Ann. Statist.*, 6, 461-464.

Sclove, S. L. (1987). Application of model-selection criteria to some problems in multivariate analysis. *Psychometrika*, 52, 333-343.

Shannon, C. E. (1948). A mathematical theory of communication. *Bell Systems*

Technology Journal, 27, 379-423.

Siri, W.E. (1956). Gross composition of the body. In *Advances in Biological and Medical Physics*, Vol. IV, J.H. Lawrence and C.A. Tobias (Eds.), Academic Press, New York.

Sokal, R. R. and Rohlf, F. J. (1981). *Biometry, 2nd ed.*, W. H. Freeman and Company, New York.

Srinivas, M. and Patnaik, L. M. (1994). Genetic algorithms: a survey, *IEEE Transactions of Signal Processing*, 42 (4), 927-935.

Sumida, B. H., Houston, A. I., McNamara, J. M. and Hamilton, W. D. (1990). Genetic algorithms and evolution. *J. Theoretical Biology*,147, 59-84.

Theil, H. and Fiebig, D. G. (1984). *Exploiting Continuity: Maximum Entropy Estimation of Continuous Distributions*. Ballinger Publishing Company, Cambridge, MA.

van Emden, M. H. (1971). *An Analysis of Complexity*. Mathematical Centre Tracts, Amsterdam, 35.

von Neumann, J. (1966). *Theory of Self-Reproducing Automata*. In A. W. Burks (Ed.), University of Illinois Press, Urbana.

Wallace, C. S. and Freeman, P. R. (1987). Estimation and inference by compact coding. (With discussion). *J. Royal Statist. Soc.*, Series B, 49, 240-265.

Wallace, C. S. and Dowe, D. L. (1993). MML estimation of the von Mises concentration parameter. Technical Report 93/193, Department of Computer Science, Monash University, Clayton 3168, Australia.

Watanabe, S. (1985). *Pattern Recognition: Human and Mechanical*. John Wiley and Sons, New York.

White, H. 1982. Maximum likelihood estimation of misspecified models, *Econometrica*, 50, 1-26.

Wilkinson, L. (1989). *SYSTAT: The System for Statistics*, SYSTAT, Evanston, IL.

Wilmore, Jack (1976). *Athletic Training and Physical Fitness: Physiological Principles of the Conditioning Process*, Allyn and Bacon, Inc., Boston.

3

Econometric and Statistical Data Mining, Prediction and Policy-Making

Arnold Zellner
University of Chicago, Chicago, USA

CONTENTS

3.1 Introduction 58
3.2 Brief Comments on Scientific Method and Data Mining 59
3.3 The Structural Econometric Modeling, Time Series Analysis (SEMTSA) Approach 61
3.4 Methods Employed in Data Analysis, Modeling and Forecasting 67
3.5 Disaggregation and the Marshallian Macroeconomic Model 71
3.6 A Complete Marshallian Macroeconomic Model 74
Acknowledgments 75
References 75

How to formulate models that work well in explanation, prediction and policy-making is a central problem in all fields of science. In this presentation, I shall explain the strategy, our Structural Econometric Modeling, Times Series Analysis (SEMTSA) approach that my colleagues and I have employed in our efforts to produce a macroeconomic model that works well in point and turning point forecasting, explanation and policy-making. Data relating to 18 industrialized countries over the years, taken from the IMF-IFS data base, have been employed in estimation and forecasting tests of our models using fixed and time varying parameter models, Bayesian posterior odds, model combining or averaging, shrinkage, and Bayesian method of moments procedures. Building on this past work, in recent research economic theory and data for 11 sectors of the U.S. economy have been employed to produce models for each sector. The use of sector data and models to forecast individual sectors' output growth rates and from them growth rates of total U.S. output will be compared to use of aggregate data and models to forecast growth rates of total U.S. output. As will be seen, IT PAYS TO DISAGGREGATE in this instance. Last, a description of some steps underway to improve and complete our Marshallian Macroeconomic Model of an economy will be described.

3.1 Introduction

When Professor Ham Bozdogan invited me to present a lecture at the University of Tennessee, C. Warren Neel Conference on Statistical Data Mining and Knowledge Discovery, he mentioned that he had attended my presentation of our modeling and forecasting work at the June 2000 International Society for Bayesian Analysis (ISBA, website: www. Bayesian.org) and Eurostat meeting in Crete and that he thought it was a good example of data mining. This was news to me since I did not have a good definition of data mining and was unsure about how it represented what we were doing in our work with a large data set relating to 18 industrialized countries over a period of about 50 years. After attending this U. of Tennessee Conference, I believe that I have a better understanding of data mining and believe that it is useful to relate it to general views of scientific methodology and some past work in statistics and economics, which I shall do in Section 3.2. I provide a brief overview of scientific methodology and its objectives and indicate where, in my opinion, data mining fits into the overall process and what some of its unique features are.

Then in Section 3.3, I shall describe what Ham called our past data mining efforts with special emphasis on methodological tools that may be useful in other data mining efforts. These include the Structural Econometric Modeling, Time Series Analysis (SEMTSA) approach put forward by F. C. Palm and by myself, Zellner and Palm (1974,1975) and pursued further by many over the years; see papers by leading workers in Zellner and Palm (2003). In this approach, the value of keeping it sophisticatedly simple (*KISS*) is emphasized for "obvious" reasons.... See, e.g., Zellner, Kuezenkamp and McAleer (2001) for further consideration of simplicity and complexity issues. In addition to the overall SEMTSA approach, there is a brief discussion of new results in information processing, including a new derivation of the Bayesian learning model, Bayes' Theorem and generalizations of it; see, Soofi (2000) and Zellner (1997, 2002). One special learning approach is the Bayesian method of moments (BMOM) that permits researchers to derive post data moments and post data densities for parameters and future observations without use of sampling assumptions for the given data, likelihood functions and prior densities. Since, as I learned at this Conference, there is often great uncertainty regarding the forms of likelihood functions and prior densities in data mining, an approach, such as the BMOM approach, which permits individuals to perform inverse inference without specifying the form of the likelihood and using a prior density, will probably be useful. Examples will be provided to illustrate general principles. For more on the BMOM and applications of it see, e.g., Green and Strawderman (1996), Mittelhammer et al. (2000), van der Merwe et al. (2001), Zellner (1994,1997a, b, 2002) and Zellner and Tobias (2001).

In Section 3.4, some details regarding the models and methods employed in analyzing, modeling and forecasting data for 18 industrialized countries will be described. Also, considerations regarding aggregation/disaggregation issues will be briefly discussed along with an example involving alternative methods for forecasting the median growth rate of 18 countries' real output growth rates, which illustrates that, in this instance, it pays to disaggregate; see Zellner and Tobias (2000). Further, disaggregation by industrial sectors using Marshallian models for each sector will be described and some results, taken from Zellner and Chen (2001), of the use of sector models in forecasting aggregate outcomes will be provided and compared to those derived from models implemented with aggregate data. Last, in Section 3.6 considerations regarding the form of a complete *Marshallian Macroeconomic Model* will be presented along with some thoughts regarding future research.

3.2 Brief Comments on Scientific Method and Data Mining

As discussed in Jeffreys (1937,1998) and Zellner (1984,1996,1997), it is the case that scientific work in all areas involves induction, deduction and reduction. Induction involves (a) measurement and description and (b) use of given models or subject matter generalizations to explain features of past data, predict as yet unobserved data and to help solve private and public decision problems. As regards reduction, in Zellner (1996, p. 5) it is pointed out that the famous physicist C.S. Pierce commented that reduction suggests that something may be; that is, it involves studying facts and devising theories to explain them. For Pierce and others the link of reduction with the unusual fact is emphasized. And of course, deduction, that is logical or mathematical proof or disproof, plays a role in induction and reduction but is inadequate alone to serve the needs of scientists. As emphasized by Jeffreys (1937,1998), scientists need to be able to make statements less extreme than "proof," "disproof" and "I don't know." They generally make statements such as "A probably causes B" or "Theory I is probably better than Theory II" or "The parameter's value probably lies between 0.40 and 0.50." Fortunately, Bayesian methods are available to quantify such statements, to update such probabilities as more data become available and to provide predictions that can be checked with additional data; for a survey of Bayesian analysis with many references, some to downloadable, free software for performing Bayesian calculations, see Berger (2000). That Bayesian methods permit updating of probabilities representing degrees of confidence in models is a very important capability. In this connection, note that causality has been defined as predictability according to a law or set of laws, that is, a dependable, subject matter model or set of models that have performed well in past work and thus have high probabilities associated with them. See, e.g., Feigl (1953), Aigner and Zellner (1988), and Zellner (1984), for further discussion of the concept of causality, empirical tests of causality and its relation to applied data analysis and modeling.

There is no doubt but that data miners are involved in inductive, deductive and reductive scientific work involving measurement, description, modeling, explanation, prediction and decision-making. What appears to be rather unique about the current data mining area are the large samples of data utilized and the powerful computers and algorithms that are available for analyzing them. However, as has been recognized by many, there are the old issues of data quality, appropriate measurement procedures and good statistical descriptive measures that are obviously very important. Further, given a tentative model for a very large data set, say a multivariate regression or time series model, the use of appropriate estimation, testing, model evaluation and other inference procedures is critical. For example, use of inappropriate testing and model evaluation methods, e.g., the 5% level of significance in Neyman-Pearson test procedures, can lead to costly errors when sample sizes are very large; see, e.g., Zellner (1996, p 302, ff.) and references cited therein for further discussion of this important problem. Further, the accept-reject framework often used is many times not as good as the use of techniques that permit a set of models to be identified and to use them in model averaging to obtain estimates and predictions. Further, in making decisions or producing forecasts, it has been emphasized that model uncertainty as well as other types of uncertainty should be taken into account, as for example in formal model combining and averaging procedures (see Zellner (1997, Part V), for procedures for model-combining and applications to forecasting problems that appear readily applicable to modeling and forecasting in some data mining problems).

As regards reduction, that is studying data and devising models to explain them, there is the issue of simplicity versus complexity. Some advise researchers to start with a sophisticatedly simple model and complicate it if necessary.

Note that a sophisticatedly simple modeling approach involves taking account of what is already known about a problem in order to avoid making stupid errors. In industry, there is the saying, *"Keep it simple stupid" (KISS)*. Since some simple models are stupid, I changed the interpretation of *KISS* to *"Keep it sophisticatedly simple,"* which is in line with Einstein's advice to make models as simple as possible, but no simpler. On the other hand there are those who advocate starting with a large, complicated, "encompassing" model and testing downward to discover a useful model. Of course, it is impossible to prove deductively whether it is better to *KISS* or to use an "encompassing" approach. However, it is relevant to note that there are many, many complicated encompassing models and if one chooses the wrong one, all that follows will be unsatisfactory. While there are many successful sophisticatedly simple models in the sciences, e.g., $s = 1/2gt^2$, $F = ma$, $PV = RT$, $E = mc^2$, etc., it is difficult to find one successful large, complicated model in any area of science. For additional consideration of these simplicity/complexity issues and some measures of the complexity of models, see Zellner, Kuezenkamp and McAleer (2001).

Since, as mentioned above, recognition of unusual facts is many times very important in leading to new insights and models, it occurred to me that there must be ways of producing unusual or surprising facts. After some thought, I developed a list of eight such procedures, (see Zellner, 1984, pp. 9-10), many of them quite obvious, namely, study unusual groups, e.g., the very poor or the very rich, unusual historical periods, e.g., hyperinflations, or great depressions, produce extreme data that are inconsistent with current models' predictions, etc. Also, with large data sets, there is a tendency to throw away "outlying" observations rather than try to explain why they are "outlying." As is well known, "outlying" points may be evidence that assumed functional forms for relations, e.g., linear forms, and/or assumed distributions for error terms are incorrect. Thus "outlying" or "unusual" data points deserve much attention and explanation, if possible. For brevity, I shall not review analyses that have been adversely affected by deleting rather than explaining outlying data points.

When the available data, say time series data, include many, many variables, as in data relating to the world's numerous economies, and include many unusual features, e.g., similar, but not exactly the same upward and downward movements in growth rates of output and other variables, etc., there is the problem of how to formulate explanatory models that explain past variation and are helpful in predicting new data and in policy-making. Many researchers and governmental units worldwide have approached this problem by building complicated, multi-equation, linear and non-linear, stochastic models, so-called structural econometric models. Unfortunately, not many of these models, if any, have performed satisfactorily in explanation and prediction. Others have resorted to large statistical models, usually vector autoregressive (VAR) models in attempts to get good forecasting models. These attempts, too, have not been successful in the sense that their point and turning point forecasts have not been very good. Faced with these problems and approaches, years ago, Franz Palm and I put forward a combined structural econometric modeling, time series analysis (SEMTSA) approach that attempted to integrate the best features of earlier approaches. See Zellner and Palm (1974,1975,2003) and Zellner (1984, 1997) for descriptions of the approach and applications of it to a variety of problems. The approach involves starting simply with models for individual variables, determining forms for them that reflect past subject matter information, fit the data reasonably well and forecast satisfactorily. Then these tested components are combined to form a multivariate model, and its performance in explaining variation in past data and in forecasting future data is studied and continually improved. Throughout the process, subject matter theory is used in attempts to "rationalize" or "explain" why the empirical models work in practice and in an effort to produce a "structural" or "causal" model rather than just an empirical, statistical forecasting model that does not explain outcomes or possible causal relations very well. See below for further discussion of the SEMTSA approach's properties and some experiences in applying it in our efforts to produce a structural macroeconomic model that works well in explaining past data, predicting new data and in policy-making.

3.3 The Structural Econometric Modeling, Time Series Analysis (SEMTSA) Approach

In the mid-twentieth century, impressive theoretical and empirical developments occurred in the statistical time series analysis area in the work of Quenouille (1957), Box and Jenkins (1970), and others. The univariate and multivariate autoregressive, moving average (ARMA) models employed in this statistical time series analysis approach seemed very different from the causal, dynamic, structural econometric models formulated and estimated by the Nobel Prize winners, Tinbergen, Klein, and Modigliani and many others and used by many governmental units world-wide. Since many were confused about the relationship of these two classes of models, in Zellner and Palm (1974), we clarified the relationship and pointed to some unusual features of multivariate statistical time series and structural econometric models. This led to a strategy of model-building that we called the SEMTSA approach and first applied in a paper, Zellner and Palm (1975), to evaluate a monetary model of the U.S. economy and utilized in other works included in Zellner and Palm (2003).

3.3.1 The SEMTSA Approach

The initial problems considered in the SEMTSA approach were (1) the implications of the basic multiple time series or multivariate ARMA model put forward by Quenouille (1957) and others for properties of processes for individual variables and (2) its relationship to dynamic structural econometric models. In this connection, Quenouille's and others' multiple time series model, that includes a vector autoregression as a special case, for an $m x 1$ vector of variables at time t, $z(t)$ is:

$$H(L)z(t) = F(L)e(t) \text{ for } t = 1, 2, \ldots, T \quad (3.1)$$

where $H(L) = I + H_1 L + \ldots + H_p L^p$ and $F(L) = F_o + F_1 L + \ldots + F_q L^q$ are matrix lag operators with L the lag operator such that $L^r z(t) = z(t-r)$, the H's and F's given matrices and $e(t)$ is a zero mean white noise error vector with covariance matrix I.

Is the model in (3.1) a good one for modeling and forecasting? As Palm and I suggested, a relevant issue is what are the implied processes for individual variables in the vector $z(t)$. If $H(L)$ is invertible, it is straightforward to derive the marginal processes for individual elements of $z(t)$. In general these turn out to be very high order autoregressive-moving average processes, not at all like the models for individual variables identified by many time series workers. Thus the general model in (3.1) has implications that are not in agreement with empirical findings indicating a need for modifications of it, say imposing restrictions, or introducing nonlinearities, etc.

As mentioned above, the relation of (3.1) to dynamic linear structural econometric models (SEMs), discussed in most past and current econometrics textbooks, was unclear to many. Here we pointed out that if the vector of variables, z(t), is partitioned into a sub vector of "endogenous" variables, $y(t)$, and a sub vector of "exogenous" variables, $x(t)$, that is $z(t)' = [y(t)', x(t)']$, the relation would be clear. Note that endogenous variables are variables whose variation is to be explained by the model whereas exogenous variables, e.g., weather variables, etc. are input variables to the model. The assumption that the sub vector $x(t)$ is a vector of exogenous variables leads to a sub matrix of $H(L)$ being identically zero and $F(L)$ being block diagonal, very important restrictions on the general model in (3.1). When these restrictions are imposed, the system becomes:

$$H_{11}(L)y(t) + H_{12}(L)x(t) = F_{11}(L)e_1(t) \quad (3.2)$$

$$H_{22}(L)x(t) = F_{22}(L)e_2(t) \qquad (3.3)$$

where $H_{11}(L), H_{12}(L)$ and $H_{22}(L)$ are sub matrices of $H(L)$ and the assumption that $x(t)$ is exogenous implies that the sub-matrix $H_{21}(L) \equiv 0$. Also, $F_{11}(L)$ and $F_{22}(L)$ are sub matrices of $F(L)$ with the assumption that $x(t)$ is exogenous implying that the off diagonal matrices $F_{12}(L) \equiv 0$ and $F_{21}(L) \equiv 0$.

Equation system (3.2) is in the form of a linear dynamic SEM while (3.3) is the system assumed to generate the exogenous or input variables. Thus there is compatibility between the multiple time series model in (3.1) and the linear dynamic SEM. Further, as emphasized in our SEMTSA approach, it is important to check the implications of (3.2) for the forms of the processes for individual variables in $y(t)$. Given that the matrix lag operator $H_{11}(L)$ is invertible, that is $H_{11}^{-1} = H_{11}^{a}/|H_{11}|$ where the dependence on L has been suppressed, H_{11}^{a} is the adjoint matrix and $|H_{11}|$ is the determinant of H_{11}, a polynomial in L, it is direct to solve for the transfer function system associated with (3.2), namely:

$$|H_{11}|y(t) = -H_{11}^{a}H_{12}x(t) + H_{11}^{a}F_{11}e_1(t). \qquad (3.4)$$

Note that since the same lag operator $|H_{11}|$ hits all the elements of $y(t)$ and if there is no canceling of common roots, this implies that the autoregressive part of the transfer functions for the elements of $y(t)$ should be IDENTICAL, a restriction that can be and has been tested in applied work. Further, restrictions on the coefficients in (3.2) imply testable restrictions on the parameters of the transfer functions in (3.4) that can be and have been tested. Last, empirical procedures for obtaining or identifying forms of transfer functions from information in data are available in the literature and have been applied to determine whether the forms of the transfer function equations derived analytically in (3.4) are the same as those determined or identified empirically. See Zellner and Palm (1975, 2003) for examples in which these procedures are applied to a variety of problems and revealed that the information in the data was in conflict with the implications of models in many cases.

In our initial empirical work to formulate good models to explain and predict macroeconomic variables, in Garcia-Ferrer et al. (1987), we decided to start with analysis of models for a key macroeconomic variable, the rate of growth of real output, as measured by real GDP, of an economy. After determining that simple time series models, e.g., autoregressive models, did not work well in forecasting and with the form of (3.4) in mind, we formulated the following model for the output growth rate of economy i in year t, denoted by the scalar $y_i(t)$,

$$y_i(t) = \beta_{oi} + \beta_{1i}y_i(t-1) + \beta_{2i}y_i(t-2) + \beta_{3i}y_i(t-3) + \qquad (3.5)$$
$$+ \beta_{4i}M_i(t-1) + \beta_{5i}SR_i(t-1) + \beta_{6i}SR_i(t-2) + \beta_{7i}WSR(t-1) + e_i(t)$$

or

$$y_i(t) = x_i(t)'\beta_i + e_i(t) \; t = 1, 2, \ldots, T \text{ and } i = 1, 2, \ldots, N \qquad (3.6)$$

where M = growth rate of real money, SR = growth rate of real stock prices and WSR = the median of the countries' growth rates of real stock prices. The form of (3.5) was rationalized as follows: (a) The AR(3) assumption allowed for the possibility of having complex roots leading to oscillatory movements (see Hong (1989) for supporting empirical evidence). (b) Burns and Mitchell (1946) had established that money and stock prices lead in the business cycle using pre World War II data going back to the 19th century for France, Germany, U.K., and U.S. (c) The variable WSR was included to model common shocks hitting all economies. The model in (3.5) was named an autoregressive, leading indicator (ARLI) model and implemented with data for 9 and then 18 industrialized countries in point and turning point forecasting experiments with encouraging results.

Later (3.5) was modified to include a current measure of world output, $w(t)$, the median of 18 countries' growth rates in year t, and an ARLI model for $w(t)$ was introduced, namely,

$$y_i(t) = \gamma_i w(t) + x_i(t)'\beta_i + e_i(t) \tag{3.7}$$

and

$$w(t) = \alpha_o + \alpha_1 w(t-1) + \alpha_2 w(t-2) + \alpha_3 w(t-3) \tag{3.8}$$
$$+ \alpha_4 MM(t-1) + \alpha_5 MSR(t-1) + \alpha_6 MSR(t-2) + u(t)$$

where MM and MSR are the median growth rates of real money and real stock prices, respectively, and u is an error term. We called this two equation model the ARLI/WI model and showed in Zellner and Hong (1989) that it performed somewhat better in forecasting experiments with data for 18 countries than the one equation ARLI model, shown above in (3.5), using various Stein-like shrinkage estimation and forecasting techniques. Also, the RMSE's of forecast compared favorably with those associated with large, structural OECD forecasting models. In addition, variants of the ARLI and ARLI/WI models performed well in forecasting turning points in countries' growth rates with 70% or more of 211 turning points correctly forecasted for 18 countries with the "downturn" and "no downturn" forecasts being somewhat better than the "upturn" and "no upturn" forecasts; see Zellner and Min (1999) for these and additional results with references to earlier analyses. And very important, the ARLI/WI model was shown to be compatible with various macroeconomic theoretical models, e.g., a Hicksian IS/LM model in Hong (1989), a generalized real business cycle models in Min (1992) and an aggregate supply and demand model in Zellner (1999). This is a fundamental aspect of the SEMTSA approach, namely a fruitful interaction between data analysis and subject matter theoretical models. Some additional variants of these models will be discussed in Sect. 3.4.

3.3.2 Statistical Inference Procedures

With respect to inference procedures for the ARLI and ARLI/WI models, mentioned above, various procedures were employed including least squares (LS), maximum likelihood (ML), traditional Bayesian(TB) and the recently developed Bayesian method of moments (BMOM). For these time series models, while LS and ML procedures readily yielded point estimates, they did not provide, among other things, finite sample standard errors, confidence and predictive intervals, probabilities relating to various models' forms and probability statements regarding possible downturns or upturns in countries' growth rates. In contrast, TB procedures readily provided finite sample results including intervals for parameters and future observations, shrinkage estimates and forecasts, probabilities associated with alternative model forms, etc. given the traditional inputs to TB analyses, namely, a prior density, a likelihood function and Bayes' theorem. As is well known, Bayes' theorem yields the important general result that a posterior density for the parameters is proportional to the prior density for the parameters times the likelihood function, with the factor of proportionality being a normalizing constant that can be evaluated analytically or numerically.

Thus given the inputs, a prior density and a likelihood function, it is direct to obtain a posterior density for the parameters and also a predictive density for future observations. In an effort to relax the need for such inputs, the Bayesian method of moments (BMOM) was introduced in Zellner (1994); see also Zellner (1997) and the references cited in Section 3.1 for further results and applications. The BMOM approach permits investigators to obtain post data moments and densities for the parameters and future observations without using prior densities, likelihood functions and Bayes' theorem and may be useful to data miners in performing statistical inference.

To illustrate the BMOM approach, consider time to failure given observations that are assumed to satisfy, $y(i) = \theta + u(i)$, $i = 1, 2, \ldots, n$ where θ is a parameter of interest with an unknown value. On summing both sides of this relation and dividing by n, we have the given mean of the observations $\bar{y} = \theta + \bar{u}$ and on taking a subjective expectation of both sides, $\bar{y} = E\theta + E\bar{u}$, where it is to be recognized that $\bar{y}$ has a given observed value, e.g., 3.2, whereas θ and $\bar{u}$ have unobserved values that are considered subjectively random. Now if we assume that there are no outliers or left out variables and the form of the above relationship is appropriate, we can assume that the subjective mean of $\bar{u}$ is zero, that is, $E\bar{u} = 0$ that implies $E\theta = \bar{y}$. Thus we have a post data mean for θ without introducing a prior density and a likelihood function. Also, as is well known, the mean is an optimal estimate relative to a quadratic loss function. Further, the maximum entropy or most spread out proper density for θ with given mean $= \bar{y}$ is easily derived and well known to be the exponential density, that is, $g(\theta \mid D) = (1/\bar{y})\exp(-\theta/\bar{y})$ with $0 < \theta < \infty$ and where D denotes the given observations and background information. This post data density can be employed to make inverse probability statements regarding possible values of θ, e.g., $\Pr\{1.2 < \theta < 2.3 \mid D\}$, the objective of Bayes' (1763) original paper and thus the name Bayesian method of moments. This is one example of the BMOM.

To apply the BMOM to equation (3.5) above, express the equation in standard regression form, $y = X\beta + e$ where y is a vector of given observations, X a matrix of observations on the input variables, β a coefficient vector and e a vector of realized error terms. The elements of β and of e are treated as parameters with unknown values, as previously done in the TB literature in Chaloner and Brant (1988) and Zellner (1975). Assuming that X is of full column rank, we can write: $b \equiv (X'X)^{-1}X'y = E\beta + (X'X)^{-1}X'Ee$, where E represents the subjective expectation operator. Assuming that the functional form of the relation is satisfactory, i.e., no left out variables, and no outliers, no errors in the variables, etc., we can make Assumption I: $X'Ee = 0$ which implies from the relation above that $E\beta = b = (X'X)^{-1}X'y$, that is the post data mean for β, b is the least squares estimate. Further, we have $y = XE\beta + Ee$ and thus Assumption I implies that y is the sum of two orthogonal vectors, $XE\beta$ and Ee. In addition, $Ee = y - XE\beta = \hat{e}$, the least squares residual vector. On making a further assumption regarding the post data covariance matrix of the realized error vector, see, e.g., Zellner (1997, p. 291ff) and Zellner and Tobias (2001), the second moment matrix of β is shown to be:

$$E(\beta - E\beta)(\beta - E\beta) = (X'X)^{-1}s^2 \text{ with } s^2 = \hat{e}'\hat{e}/v$$

where $v = T - k$ is the "degrees of freedom" parameter, T is the number of observations, and k is the number of elements of β. Note that all these post data moments have been derived without using a likelihood function and a prior density. However, more prior information can be introduced via use of a conceptual sample and in other ways, as shown in Zellner et al. (1999), and other papers cited above.

With the moments of β as given in the previous paragraph, the least informative, maxent density for β is a multivariate normal density with mean b, the least squares estimate of β, and covariance matrix $(X'X)^{-1}s^2$. This density can be employed to make probability statements regarding possible values of the elements of β and functions of them quite readily. Also, for future, as yet unobserved values of y, assumed to satisfy, $y_f = X_f\beta + e_f$, given X_f, if we make assumptions regarding the moments of e_f, the moments of y_f can be easily derived. For example, if it is assumed that $Ee_f = 0$, then $Ey_f = X_f E\beta = X_f b$, the least squares forecast vector. With a further assumption regarding the second moment of e_f the second moments of the elements of y_f are available and these moments can be used as side conditions in deriving a proper maxent predictive density for y_f. For some computed examples involving these and other assumptions with applications to forecasting turning points, see Zellner et al. (1999).

In addition to providing BMOM post data and predictive moments and densities, information theory has been utilized in Zellner (1988, 1997, 2002) to produce learning models, including Bayes' Theorem, in a very direct approach. Namely information measures associated with inputs and outputs to an information processing problem are considered. In the TB approach there are two inputs, a prior and a likelihood function, and two outputs, a posterior density for the parameters, and a marginal density for the observations. On forming the criterion functional, information out minus information in and minimizing it with respect to the form of the output density for the parameters, subject to its being a proper density, the solution is to take the posterior density for the parameters equal the prior density times the likelihood function divided by the marginal density of the observations, that is the result of Bayes' theorem and when this is done, the information in = the information

Statistical Data Mining and Knowledge Discovery

out and thus this information processing rule is 100% efficient. See comments on these results in Soofi (2000) and by Jaynes, Hill, Kullback and Bernardo in Zellner (1997).

As pointed out in Zellner (1997,2002), one can input just a likelihood function, and no prior, as R. A. Fisher wanted to do in his fiducial approach, and solve for an optimal form for the output density for the parameters that is proportional to the likelihood function. Or one can assign given weights to the input prior and sample information and solve for an optimal form of the output density for the parameters. Also, when the input information is just in the form of given moments for parameters, the optimal form for the output density is the BMOM solution. Dynamic problems in which the output of one period is the input to the next period, along with additional sample information, have been formulated and solved using dynamic programming techniques. Again when the traditional inputs are employed, a prior and a likelihood function, it is optimal to update densities using Bayes' theorem. Having various information processing or learning models "on the shelf" to be used when appropriate is important just as is the case with various static, dynamic and other models in engineering, physics, economics, business and other fields

Having presented some discussion of general methods, attention in the next section will be focused on these and other methods used in our empirical, data mining work.

3.4 Methods Employed in Data Analysis, Modeling and Forecasting

In our work since the mid 1980's, we have used data from the International Monetary Fund's International Financial Statistics database at the U. of Chicago, a very large database with data on many variables for over 100 countries' economies. Since measures of output may contain systematic biases, etc., we thought it wise to log variables and take their first differences to help get rid of proportional measurement biases. Further, these growth rate measures are of great interest. However, we were not too sanguine about inducing covariance stationarity by first differencing given the many different kinds of shocks hitting economies, e.g., wars, strikes, financial crises, droughts, policy blunders, etc.

Very important in our work and in presentations was and is the graphical presentation of our data using boxplot techniques to display general properties of the economic fluctuations for the 18 countries in our sample and for 11 sectors of the U.S. economy in later work. See Fig. 1 for a plot of the growth rates of output, real money and real stock prices for 18 countries. As can be seen, there are somewhat regular fluctuations present in the three variables with the money and stock price variables showing a tendency to lead, as recognized earlier by Burns and Mitchell (1946) in their monumental "data mining" study, *Measuring Business Cycles*, in which they used data for France, England, Germany and the U.S. going back to the 19th century to characterize properties of economic fluctuations in many variables.

From our plots of the data, we noted that there appear to be some outlying points. As yet, we have not formally tested for outliers nor utilized procedures for allowing for outliers in estimation and forecasting. Rather than face possible charges of "rigging the data" or "massaging the data" by eliminating outliers, etc., we decided to use all the data that relate to periods in which unusual events occurred in many countries, e.g., the Korean, Vietnamese and Gulf wars, energy crises of the 1970s, institution of wage and price controls, some abrupt changes in monetary and fiscal policies, etc. No dummy variables or other devices were used to deal with these unusual historical events. It was assumed and hoped that our lagged stock market and monetary variables would reflect the impacts of such events on economies.

With the data described, it was thought important to carry along some "benchmark" models in forecasting. In earlier studies, random walk models and simple time series models, e.g., third order autoregressive models, AR(3) models, or Box-Jenkins ARIMA models had been found to forecast better than some large scale models; see, e.g., the discussion of such studies by Christ, Cooper, Nelson, Plosser and others in Zellner (1984, 1997a). However, we generally found that such benchmark models, as well as other models, tended to make large errors in the vicinity of turning points in economic activity. Thus we thought it very important not just to study point forecasts but also to develop methods for making good turning point forecasts.

With respect to point forecasting, in Zellner and Hong (1989), we estimated the fixed parameter ARLI and ARLI/WI models, discussed above in connection with (3.5)-(3.7), using data, 1954-1973, for first 9 and then 18 industrialized countries and made one-year ahead point forecasts with parameter estimates updated year by year for the period 1974-1984. In this work, our ARLI and ARLI/WI models' performance was much better than that of various benchmark models and competitive in terms of root mean squared errors (RMSEs) to that of some large-scale OECD models. Also, the ARLI/WI model performed better than the ARLI model. Similar results were found to hold in later studies involving extended forecast periods, e.g., 1974-1997. See, e.g., papers in Sect. IV of Zellner (1997) and Zellner and Palm (2003) for some of these results.

The methodological tools utilized in this forecasting work included the following:

(1) Finite sample posterior densities for parameters of relations were employed in estimation of parameters, analyses of the realized error terms and study of the properties of dynamic relations, such as (3.5)-(3.7) above. For example, in Hong (1989) using data for each of 18 countries, draws were made from the trivariate Student t marginal posterior density of the autoregressive parameters of the ARLI model in (3.5) and, for each draw, the three roots of the process were computed. It was found that in a large fraction of the draws, about .85, that there were two complex roots and one real root associated with the model. Also, the computed posterior densities for the periods of the cycle associated with the complex roots were found to be centered at about 3 to 5 years and those for the amplitudes were centered at values less than one for both the real and complex roots. Note that in this

work, there was no need to rely on asymptotic approximate results, usually employed in non-Bayesian work with time series models.

(2) Means of predictive densities for future observations were employed as point forecasts that are optimal relative to a quadratic predictive loss function. With use of diffuse priors and usual likelihood functions or by use of BMOM predictive means, these forecasts were identical to least squares forecasts when fixed parameter models were employed but not in cases involving use of random parameter models and shrinkage assumptions. Recall that a usual predictive density for a future vector of observations, y_f is given by $h(y_f \mid D) = \int q(y_f|\theta)g(\theta|D)d\theta$, where D denotes the given data and $g(\theta D)$ is the posterior density for the vector of parameters θ.

(3) Predictive densities were employed to compute optimal turning point forecasts. For example, given a definition of a turning point, e.g., given two previous growth rates below the third, that is $y(T-2), y(T-1) < y(T)$, where T denotes the current period, if $y(T+1) < y(T)$, this is defined to be a downturn (DT), while if $y(T+1)$ is not below $y(T)$, this outcome is defined to be no downturn (NDT). Given such a sequence of outcomes up to period T and a predictive density for $y(T+1)$, it is direct to compute the probability that $y(T+1)$ is less than $y(T)$, that is the probability of a downturn, P, and that of no downturn, $1-P$. Then on considering a two by two loss structure associated the acts, forecast DT and forecast NDT and the possible outcomes, namely DT or NDT, it is direct to derive the forecast that minimizes expected loss. For example, if the 2×2 loss structure is symmetric, it is optimal for forecast DT when $P > 1/2$ and NDT when $P < 1/2$. Similar analysis applies to forecasting upturns and no upturns. Using such simple turning point forecasting procedures with a number of alternative models, about 70 per cent or more of 211 turning points for 18 countries were forecasted correctly. Also, such turning point forecasts were better than those provided by a number of benchmark procedures, e.g., coin tossing, or systematic optimistic or systematic pessimistic forecasts, etc. Such fine performance in turning point forecasting was a pleasant surprise! See Zellner and Min (1999) for results using many variants of the models in (3.5) and (3.7).

(4) Posterior odds were employed in variable selection, model comparison and model combining. As regards model selection, several researchers using our data and their model identification procedures determined forms for our ARLI model, given in (3.5) above, that differed from ours in terms of lag structures, etc. One group reported models that forecasted much, much better than our models, so much better that I suspected something must wrong. Indeed it turned out that they had used all the data to fit their model and then used a portion of the sample for forecasting experiments. When this error was corrected, the improved performance of their model disappeared. On the other hand several others using their model identification procedures did produce models that are competitive with ours. This prompted our use of posterior odds to compare various variants of our model. We employed 8 input variables, the 7 shown in connection with (3.5) and an eighth, the money variable lagged two periods for a total of 8 possible input variables and thus $2^8 = 256$ possible linear models that included our model and those of our two "competitors." Fortunately, our model compared favorably with the 255 alternative models, including those of our competitors that also performed reasonably well. For methods and

specific results, see Zellner and Min (1993) and Zellner (1997). These methods are applicable to many other model selection problems and involve a correction for the possibility that on considering so many different models, one may have fit the data well just by chance, a "model selection" effect that has been discussed by Jeffreys (1998, p. 253 and p. 278) and in our paper.

Also, posterior odds have been very useful in comparing fixed parameter and time varying parameter models, showing a slight preference for time varying parameters. As regards time varying parameters, they have been widely employed in engineering state space modeling. In our context, there are many reasons why parameters, e.g., those in (3.5) above, might be time varying, including aggregation effects, changes in technology and/or tastes and preferences, effects of changes in economic policies, i.e., Lucas effects, etc. Our earliest work involved use of the assumption that the coefficient vector in (3.5) followed a vector random walk, $\beta_i(t) = \beta_i(t-1) + v_i(t)$ with $v_i(t)$ a white noise error vector and of Bayesian recursive methods to update parameter and predictive densities. Later, other variants were employed, namely

$$(i)\ \beta_i(t) = \theta + u_i(t),$$
$$(ii)\ \beta_i(t) = \theta(t) + u_i(t) \text{ and } \theta(t) = \theta(t-1) + \eta(t),\ etc.$$

Here we are introducing dynamic Stein-like assumptions that the individual country coefficient vectors are distributed about a mean vector that may be a constant, as in (i) or may be generated by a random vector random walk process, as in (ii). These and other models both for our ARLI and ARLI/WI models were implemented with data and found to perform better than models that did not incorporate Stein-like shrinkage effects, both for fixed and time varying parameter versions. Posterior odds for such time varying parameter models versus fixed parameter models were derived and computed. They indicated some support for the use of time varying parameters and much support for the use of shrinkage assumptions. For example, using shrinkage, the median RMSE of forecast for the 18 countries' annual forecasts, 1974 – 87, was 1.74 percentage points while without shrinkage it was 2.37 percentage points. For more on these empirical results, derivations of posterior odds and use of them in combining models, see Min and Zellner (1993) and Zellner (1997). In this work involving combining models and their forecasts, comparisons were made with results of non-Bayesian combining methods of Bates, Granger and others. In these calculations, the Bayesian combining techniques performed slightly better than non-Bayesian combining techniques but did not result in much improvement relative to uncombined forecasts.

(5) As mentioned earlier, our empirical forecasting models were shown to be compatible with certain theoretical macroeconomic models. While this compatibility with economic theoretical models was satisfying, there was still the need to improve the explanatory and forecasting performance of our models and to include additional variables to be forecast. How this was to be done and what was done is the subject of the next section.

3.5 Disaggregation and the Marshallian Macroeconomic Model

In connection with the need to improve and extend our models, it was thought advisable to disaggregate the output variable since with disaggregated data there would be more observations and information that might improve forecasts and provide better explanations of the variation in total output. Further, in Zellner and Tobias (2000) the results of an experiment were published to indicate that disaggregation can be effective in improving forecasting precision. In particular, (a) equation (5a) was employed to forecast future values of w(t), median growth rate of 18 countries. These results were compared to those provided by two other procedures, namely, (b) use of (5a) and (5b) to forecast individual countries' growth rates and use of the median of the 18 forecasts as a forecast and (c) use of just equation (3.5) to forecast individual countries' growth rates and use of the median of these forecasts as a forecast of the median growth rate. These calculations indicated that method (b) that involves disaggregation was much better than methods (a) and (c) indicating that some forms of disaggregation can lead to improved forecasts. These empirical results suggested that improved forecasts of future, aggregate output of a country might be obtained by summing forecasts of its components, as shown theoretically in papers by de Alba and Zellner (1991), Lütkepohl (1986) and others. The main issue was how to disaggregate total output in a meaningful, fruitful and effective manner.

One morning while shaving, it occurred to me that it might be worthwhile to disaggregate by industrial sector, e.g., agriculture, mining, construction, retail trade, etc. using traditional Marshallian demand, supply and firm entry/exit relations for each sector. While demand and supply relations had appeared in many earlier macroeconomic models, few, if any, included entry and exit relations. For example, in real business cycle models, there is the representative firm and one wonders what would happen should this firm shut down.

Fortunately, in earlier work, Veloce and Zellner (1985), we had derived and implemented a model of the Canadian furniture industry to show the importance of taking account of entry and exit of firms and the number of firms in operation in explaining variations in furniture supply. When the variable, number of firms in operation was omitted from the supply equation, as in many previous studies, very unsatisfactory results were obtained whereas with the inclusion of this variable, more sensible estimation results were obtained. In Zellner (2001), a slightly revised version of the original Marshallian sector model was derived that involved competitive conditions with N profit maximizing firms, each with a Cobb-Douglas production function including neutral and factor augmenting technical change. Assuming that firms maximize profits, the firm's supply function was derived and multiplied by $N(t)$, the number of firms in operation at time t and the real price of output, $p(t)$, to obtain a supply relation for industry real sales, $S(t) = p(t)N(t)q(t)$ which, when differentiated with respect to time, led to the following dynamic supply relation:

$$(1/S)dS/dt = (1/N)dN/dt + \eta\,(1/p)\,dp/dt + a \quad SUPPLY \qquad (3.9)$$

where η is a parameter and a denotes a linear function of exogenous variables shifting supply, e.g., rates of growth of the real wage rate, the real price of capital, etc.

Further, with a "log-log" demand function for the sector's output, Q, multiplied by the real price of output, real sales demanded is $S = pQ$ and $\log S$ is a linear function of the logs of real price, real income, real money balances and other variables. On differentiating $\log S$ with respect to t, the following relation is obtained:

$$(1/S)dS/dt = v(1/p)dp/dt + b \quad DEMAND \tag{3.10}$$

where v is a parameter and $b =$ a linear function of the rates of change of variables shifting the demand function, e.g., real income, real money, etc.

As regards entry and exit of firms, we assume:

$$(1/N)dN/dt = c(S - F) \quad ENTRY - EXIT \tag{3.11}$$

where c and F are positive parameters, the latter associated with a cost of entry. Also, in this model, S is proportional to real industry profits.

Thus we have three equations for the three variables, $p(t)$ price, $S(t)$ real sales and $N(t)$ number of firms in operation. On substituting from (3.11) in (3.9) and then eliminating the variable $(1/p)dp/dt$ from the remaining two equations, the final, implied equation for $S(t)$ is:

$$(1/S)dS/dt = r - S/F + g \tag{3.12}$$

where r is a parameter and g is a linear function of the rates of change of the input variables shifting the supply and demand relations, e.g., the real wage rate, the real price of capital services, real income, real money balances, etc. Note too that for $g = constant$ or $g = 0$, (3.12) is in the form of the logistic differential equation with solution the logistic function that has been often used to model many industries' output. Showing that such empirical logistic functions are compatible with a traditional Marshallian model of a competitive industry is indeed satisfying. See Zellner (2001) for more information regarding the derivation of this model.

With the above results available, in Zellner and Chen (2001), discrete versions of (3.12) were formulated and fitted using data for 11 sectors of the U.S. economy. Before turning to particular models, note that it is well known that a discrete version of the homogenous part of (3.12) is in the form of a chaotic model that can have quite unusual outputs; see, e.g., Kahn (1990, Ch. 16) and Koop, Pesaran and Potter (1996) for plots of the outputs of such chaotic models. This raises the question as to whether the world is better modeled using (1) a model using continuous time, (2) a model based on discrete time or (3) a mixed continuous-discrete time model, as for example used in modeling certain biological populations as mentioned in Zellner (2002) with reference to Cunningham (1958). While it would be interesting in future work to entertain a mixed model and to compute posterior odds on it versus a discrete time model, in recent work, Zellner and Chen (2001), we started with discrete time models, one of which is

$$(1-L)\log S_t = \alpha_o + \alpha_1 S_{t-1} + \alpha_2 S_{t-2} + \alpha_3 S_{t-3} + \beta_1(1-L)\log Y_t$$
$$+\beta_2(1-L)\log M_{t-1} + \beta_3(1-L)\log w_t + \beta_4(1-L)\log SR_{t-1} + u_t \quad (3.13)$$

where S denotes real sector sales, Y real income, M real money, w real wage rate, SR real stock price index and u an error term.

It is seen that the rate of change and levels of S enter the equation, a so-called "cointegration effect" that follows from the economic theoretical model presented above. The lags in the S variable were introduced to represent possible lags in the entry equation and in the demand equations. With parameters allowed to vary over sectors, the relation in (3.13) was fitted to 11 sectors' data for the U.S. economy, agriculture, mining, construction, etc. using data, from the early 1950s to 1979 to fit the models and then the relations were employed to forecast one year ahead with estimates updated year by year, 1980 to 1997. With 11 sector forecasts available each year, they were used to produce forecasts of the rate of change of aggregate real output (GDP) year by year. Such forecasts were compared to forecasts obtained from aggregate annual data using (i) an AR(3) model, (ii) an ARLI model and (iii) an aggregate one sector Marshallian model in the form of (3.13) The benchmark AR(3) model missed all the turning points and yielded a *mean absolute error (MAE)* of *forecast=1.71* percentage points and *root mean squared error (RMSE)* = 2.32 percentage points. The aggregate Marshallian model's *MAE = 1.48* and *RMSE = 1.72* percentage points are much lower than those associated with the AR(3) and ARLI models implemented with aggregate data.

When a time series AR(3) model was implemented using least squares methods for each sector and forecasts were aggregated to form forecasts of the rates of growth of aggregate real *GDP*, there was not much improvement, namely a *MAE = 1.65* and *RMSE = 2.26* percentage points. In contrast, the ARLI model and the Marshallian equation in (3.13), implemented with the disaggregated sector data and using least squares estimation and forecasting methods, produced much better annual forecasts of rates of growth of aggregate *GDP* with forecast *MAE = 1.25* and *RMSE = 1.47* percentage points for the Marshallian model in (3.13) and *MAE =1.32* and *RMSE = 1.62* percentage points for the ARLI model. Thus this set of experiments indicates that IT PAYS TO DISAGGREGATE for two of the three models considered above.

In other experiments we employed various estimation and forecasting methods that yielded some improved forecasts relative to those provided by least squares. For example, using a seemingly unrelated regression approach for joint estimation of the 11 sector relations in the form of (3.13), taking account of differing error term variances and their correlations across equations, and one year ahead forecasting with the 11 sectors' data, the aggregate growth rate forecasts had *MAE = 1.17* and *RMSE = 1.40* percentage points. Also, many other estimation and forecasting techniques employed yielded *MAEs* ranging from *1.2* to *1.4* and *RMSEs* ranging from *1.4* to *1.6* percentage points, thus indicating that it was probably the added information provided by disaggregation that produced improved forecasting performance. See Zellner and Chen (2001) for detailed presentation of the data and forecasting results. Also, it should be noted that forecasts for the highly variable agricultural, mining, construction and durable goods industrial sectors were not very accurate and need to be improved, e.g., by introduction of weather variables for the agricultural sector, etc. With such improvements, there will be improvements not only in sector forecasts but also probably in aggregate *GDP* forecasts. Also, perhaps fitting all three relations, shown in (3.9)-(3.11) above, for each sector may lead to improved sector and aggregate forecasts.

Note that a *MAE* of about *1.2* percentage points for forecasting annual real *GDP* for the U.S., as obtained in the above forecasting experiments, compares favorably with *MAEs* reported in Zarnowitz (1986, Table 1, p. 23). As he reports, for the periods, 1969 – 1976 and 1977 – 84, the *MAE = 1.2* percentage points for the one year ahead forecasts of the rates of growth of real GNP made by the U.S. Council of Economic Advisors. Of course, "on line" forecasters have to cope with preliminary data problems not present in our forecasting experiments. However such on line forecasters typically use a lot of judgmental, outside information to adjust their models' forecasts and sometimes combine models' and others' forecasts in efforts to get improved forecasts that we did not do.

In summary, the above results based on our Marshallian sector models are encouraging and further work will be done to get improvements. Along these lines, it will be useful to add relations to get a closed model of the economy, our Marshallian Macroeconomic Model. The first steps in this direction are described in the next section.

3.6 A Complete Marshallian Macroeconomic Model

Above, supply, demand and entry relations were formulated for each sector. Attention was focused on the final product market in which each sectors' producers are assumed to sell. To close the model, there is a need to add factor markets, that is labor, capital and money markets as well as an international sector. The roles of intermediate goods and inventories need attention. And the operations of federal, state and local governments have to be incorporated in the model. Consideration of the births of new sectors and the deaths of old sectors is needed as well as allowance for regulated and imperfectly competitive sectors. Improvements in entry and investment equations are possible. Fortunately, there is much valuable research on many of these topics in the literature, which can be incorporated in our model and, hopefully, improve it. However, what is initially needed is a "bare bones" complete model, that is a "Model T" that works reasonably well.

In our approach to this last problem, we have started analyzing a one sector closed economy *MMM* model by adding labor, capital and money markets to the product market discussed above. From initial analyses, currently underway with G. Israilevich, when such additions are made, the model is mathematically tractable and leads to final equations for the variables of the system that are in forms similar to that presented in (3.12) above. However, when we go to a two sector model, there are interesting interactions between sectors produced by dependencies in demand and supply relations that affect properties of solutions. Elements of stability and instability are encountered for certain values of strategic parameters. Every effort is being made to keep the model in a form so that mathematical analyses of its properties are tractable. If not, computer simulation techniques will be employed to help determine the properties of the overall model including its responses to changes in policy variables, e.g., money, tax rates, etc. as has been done in much past work, including Zellner and Peck (1973). And of course, additional forecasting experiments will be carried forward using as much new data as possible.

It was a pleasure having an opportunity to discuss our work and results with many at this Conference. I hope that the above account of our modeling experiences using large data sets will be of interest and value to many data miners and that our future work will benefit from research that you have done and are currently carrying forward. Hopefully, we shall all strike gold.

Acknowledgments

Research financed by Alexander Endowment Fund, CDC Management Fund and the National Science Foundation.

References

Aigner, D. and Zellner, A. (eds.) (1988). Causality, *Annals Issue J. of Econometrics*, 39, 234.

Berger, J.O.(2000). Bayesian Analysis: a look at today and thoughts of tomorrow, *J. Am. Stat. Assoc.*, 95, Dec., 1269-1276.

Box, G. and Jenkins, G. (1970). *Time Series Analysis: Forecasting and Control*, San Francisco: Holden-Day.

Burns, A. and Mitchell, W. (1946). *Measuring Business Cycles*, New York: Columbia University Press and National Bureau of Economic Research.

Cunningham, R. (1958). *Introduction to Non-Linear Analysis*, New York: McGraw-Hill.

De Alba, E. and Zellner, A.. (1991). Aggregation, disaggregation, predictive precision and modeling, ms., 7 pp.

Feigl, H. (1953). Notes on causality. In *Readings in the Philosophy of Science*, Feigl, H. and Brodeck, M. (eds.), New York: Appleton-Century-Crofts, 408-418.

Garcia-Ferrer, A., Highfield, R., Palm, F. and Zellner, A.(1987). Macro-economic forecasting using pooled international data, *J. of Bus. and Econ. Statistics*, 5, 53-67.

Green, E. and Strawderman, W. (1996). A Bayesian growth and yield model for slash pine plantations, *J. Appl. Statistics*, 23, 285-299.

Hong, C. (1989). Forecasting Real Output Growth Rates and Cyclical Properties of Models. Ph.D. Thesis, Dept. of Economics, University of Chicago.

Jeffreys, H. (1973). *Scientific Inference*. Cambridge: Cambridge University Press, 3rd ed.

Jeffreys, H. (1998). *Theory of Probability*. Oxford Classic Series, Oxford: Oxford University Press, reprint of 3rd revised edition.

Koop, G., Pesaran, M. and Potter, S. (1996). Impulse response analysis in nonlinear multivariate models, *J. Econometrics*, 74, 119-147.

Lütkepohl, H. (1986). Comparisons of predictors for temporally and contemporaneously aggregated time series, *Int. J. Forecasting*, 2, 461-475.

Kahn, P. (1990). *Mathematical Models for Scientists and Engineers*. New York: Wiley.

Min, C. (1992). Economic Analysis and Forecasting of International Growth Rates. Ph.D. Thesis, Dept. of Economics, University of Chicago.

Min, C. and Zellner, A. (1993). Bayesian and Non-Bayesian methods for combining models and forecasts with applications to forecasting international growth rates, *J. Econometrics*, 56, 89-118, reprinted in Zellner (1997a).

Mittelhammer, R., Judge, G., and Miller, D. (2001). *Econometric Foundations*. Cambridge: Cambridge University Press.

Quenouille, M. (1957). *The Analysis of Multiple Time Series*. New York: Hafner Publishing Co.

Soofi, E. (1996). Information theory and Bayesian statistics. In *Bayesian Analysis in Statistics and Econometrics*, Berry, D., Chaloner, K. and Geweke, J. (eds.), New York: Wiley, 179-189.

Soofi, E. (2000). Information theory and statistics, *J. Am. Stat. Assoc.*, 95, Dec., 1349-1353.

Van der Merwe, A., Pretorius, A., Hugo, J. and Zellner, A. (2001). Traditional Bayes and the Bayesian method of moments analysis for the mixed linear model with an application to animal breeding, *S. Afr. Stat. Journal*, 35, 19-68.

Veloce, W. and Zellner, A. (1985). Entry and empirical demand and supply analysis for competitive industries, *J. Econometrics*, 30, 459-471.

Zarnowitz, V. (1986). The record and improvability of economic forecasting, *Economic Forecasts*, 3, 22-31.

Zellner, A. (1984). *Basic Issues in Econometrics*. Chicago: University of Chicago Press.

Zellner, A. (1994a). Time Series Analysis, Forecasting and Econometric Modeling: The Structural Econometric Modeling, Time Series Analysis Approach, invited paper with discussion in *J. of Forecasting*, 13, 215-233.

Zellner, A. (1994b). Bayesian method of moments/instrumental variable analysis of mean and regression models. In *Modelling and Prediction*, Lee, J., Johnson, W. and Zellner, A. (eds.), New York: Springer, 61-76, reprinted in Zellner (1997a).

Zellner, A. (1996). *An Introduction to Bayesian Inference in Econometrics*. Wiley Classics Library, New York: Wiley.

Zellner, A. (1997a). Bayesian Analysis in Econometrics and Statistics: The Zellner View and Papers, invited contribution to M. Perlman and M. Blaugh (eds.), *Economists of the Twentieth Century Series*, Cheltenham, UK: Edward Elgar Publ. Ltd.

Zellner, A. (1997b). The Bayesian method of moments: theory and applications. In *Advances in Econometrics*, Fomby, T. and Hill, R. (eds.), 12, 85-105, Greenwich, CT: JAI Press.

Zellner, A. (1999). Bayesian and Non-Bayesian Approaches to Scientific Modeling and Inference in Economics and Econometrics, invited paper for Ajou University Research Conf. Honoring Prof. Tong Hun Lee, *Korea J. of Money and Finance*, 5, 11-56.

Zellner, A. (2001a). Remarks on a 'Critique' of the Bayesian method of moments (BMOM), *J. Appl. Statistics*, 28, No. 6, 775-778.

Zellner, A. (2001b). The Marshallian Macroeconomic Model. In *Economic Theory, Dynamics and Markets*, T. Negishi et al. (eds.), Boston/Dordrecht: Kluwer Acad. Publishers, 19-29.

Zellner, A. (2002). Information processing and Bayesian analysis, *J. Econometrics*, 107, 41-50.

Zellner, A. and Chen, B. (2001). Bayesian modeling of economies and data requirements, *Macroeconomic Dynamics*, 5, 673-700.

Zellner, A. and Hong, C. (1989). Forecasting international growth rates using Bayesian shrinkage and other procedures, *J. Econometrics*, 40, 183-202.

Zellner, A., Kuezenkamp, H. and McAleer, M. (2001). *Simplicity, Inference and Modelling*. Cambridge: Cambridge University Press.

Zellner, A. and Min, C. (1999). Forecasting turning points in countries' output growth rates: a response to Milton Friedman, *J. Econometrics*, 88, 203-206.

Zellner, A. and Palm, F. (1974). Time series analysis and simultaneous equation econometric models, *J. Econometrics*, 2, 17-54, reprinted in Zellner and Palm (2003).

Zellner, A. and Palm, F. (1975). Time series analysis of structural monetary models of the U.S. economy, *Sankya*, Series C, 37, 12-56, reprinted in Zellner and Palm (2003).

Zellner, A. and Palm, F. (eds.), (2003). *The Structural Econometric Modeling, Time Series Analysis Approach*, to be published by Cambridge University Press.

Zellner, A. and Peck, S. (1973). Simulation experiments with a quarterly model of the U.S. economy. In *Econometric Studies of Macro and Monetary Relations*, Powell, A. and Williams, R. (eds.), Amsterdam: North-Holland, 149-168, reprinted in Zellner (1984).

Zellner, A., Tobias, J. and Ryu, H. (1999a). Bayesian method of moments analysis of time series models with an application to forecasting turning points in output growth rates, *Estadistica*, 49-51, pp. 3-63, with invited discussion.

Zellner, A., Tobias, J. and Ryu, H. (1999b). Bayesian method of moments (BMOM) analysis of parametric and semiparametric regression models, *S. Afr. Stat. Journal*, 31, 41-69.

Zellner, A. and Tobias, J. (2001). Further results on Bayesian method of moments analysis of the multiple regression model, *Int. Econ. Rev.*, 42, No. 1, 121-140.

4

Data Mining Strategies for the Detection of Chemical Warfare Agents

Jeffrey. L. Solka,[1,2] Edward J. Wegman,[1] and David J. Marchette[2]
[2]Naval Surface Warfare Center (NSWCDD), Dahlgren, VA, [1]George Mason University, Fairfax, VA, USA

CONTENTS

4.1 Introduction 79
4.2 Results 82
4.3 Conclusions 90
     Acknowledgments 91
     References 91

This paper discusses a classification system for the detection of various chemical warfare agents. The data were collected as part of the Shipboard Automatic Liquid (Chemical) Agent Detection (SALAD) system. This system is designed to detect chemical agents onboard naval vessels. We explore the intricacies associated with the construction of various classification systems. Along the way we take time to explore some applications of recently developed statistical procedures in visualization and density estimation to this discriminant analysis problem. We focus our discussion on all phases of the discriminant analysis problem. In the exploratory data analysis phase we provide results that detail the use of histograms, scatter plots and parallel coordinate plots for the selection of feature subsets that are fortuitous to the discriminant analysis problem and the discernment of high dimensional data structure. In the discriminant analysis phase we discuss several semiparametric density estimation procedures along with classical kernel, classification and regression trees, and k-nearest-neighbors based approaches. These discussions include some illustrations of the use of a new parallel coordinates framework for the visualization of high dimensional mixture models. We close our discussions with a comparison of the performance of the various techniques through a study of the associated confusion matrices.

4.1 Introduction

The Shipboard Automatic Liquid (Chemical) Agent Detector (SALAD) is a system designed to detect chemical agents onboard naval vessels. The device takes the form of an instrument that is fed with tractor feed reagent paper. This paper reacts with chemical droplets to produce a characteristic color change. The device is designed to sit exposed on the ship waiting for chemical agents to rain down on the reactive paper as it travels through the system. At certain periodic intervals a camera captures images of the paper using 13 spectral filters. Intensity measurements at each of these wavelengths are collected and passed to the classification section of the system for additional processing. In this phase of the process the agents are to be classified according to particular chemical type. It is the classification portion of the system that our work has focused on.

Initially data were collected at the Dahlgren Division of the Naval Surface Warfare Center on simulant chemicals, which are designed to produce paper signatures similar to the actual chemical warfare agents. Although these data were provided to us and we did perform some preliminary analysis on the data, this is not the focus of this paper. In addition, data was collected at the GEOMET Center on several of the live agents at various drop sizes. Creation of a classification system for the signatures of the 1 ml drops was the goal of our analysis. Thirteen band signatures were collected on the chemicals GA, GB, GD, GF, VX, HD, L, GDT, HDT, and the paper without any chemical stimulant.

The collection data was presented to us initially as a set of images. Using the Advanced Distributed Region of Interest Tool (ADROIT) [3] the images were diagnosed. The diagnosis procedure consisted of labeling those pixels from each of the various chemical classes along with a subset of the pixels from the background. In this manner a training set and a test set were created. The training set was used to build the classifier and the test set was used to test it. More sophisticated testing procedures, such as the jackknife, were considered but were deemed unnecessary. The training data consisted of 14,236 observations and the test data consisted of 1,868,070 observations.

For the purposes of our analysis we grouped GA, GB, GD, GF, and GDT into the class G; VX into the class V; and HD, L, and HDT into the class H. Each class was then assigned a numerical class label according to the following scheme. G was labeled as class 0, V was labeled as class 1, H was labeled as class 2, and the background was labeled as class 3. The training set consisted of 2,106 observations from the G class, 569 from the V class, 1,088 from the H class, and 10,473 background observations. The test set was comprised of 13,889 observations from the G class, 2,318 from the V class, 6,662 from the H class, and 1,845,201 from the background class.

The design of the classification system was broken into the usual constituent steps of exploratory data analysis, probability density estimation, classifier design, and classifier testing. The purpose of the exploratory analysis phase is to ascertain any underlying structures that exist in the training data. This is in part done in order to choose particularly fortuitous features sets and also to discover any additional structure that would be important in the density estimation portion of the procedure. Standard statistical visualization procedures such as boxplots and histograms are typically applied to univariate projections of the features. In addition one sometimes examines pairs plots, which represent scatterplots of the various features chosen 2 at a time.

Ultimately one would like to be able to examine the distribution of the features in the full higher-dimensional space. The parallel coordinates method (cf. Wegman [11]) is one technique to do this. In this technique one places the coordinate axes parallel to one another in order to plot the points in the higher-dimensional space. This is necessary since one, in dimension higher than 3, ultimately does not have the ability to place the coordinate axes orthogonal to one another. It turns out that there is a natural correspondence between this coordinate system and projective geometry space. In this manner, we can understand how certain geometric structures in Euclidean space are mapped into the parallel coordinates framework.

Once one has performed a preliminary analysis based on these techniques one performs model-based exploratory analysis on the feature set. There are several different techniques for performing model-based density estimation. These range from the fully nonparametric procedures such as kernel density estimation [8], to semiparamteric density estimation procedures such as the adaptive mixtures density estimator (AMDE) [6] [5], and finally fully parametric models such as finite mixture models [4].

In the kernel estimation approach, one models the underlying distribution as a mixture of component densities. Each component density resides at one of the points of the data set and often takes the simple form of a Gaussian. In equation 1 we present the form of the univariate kernel estimator

$$\hat{f}(x) = \frac{1}{nh} \sum_{i=1}^{n} g\left(\frac{x - x_i}{h}\right). \tag{4.1}$$

In the case of multivariate data it is simplest to use the well-known product kernel.

Mixture models are an alternative to the fully nonparametric kernel estimator. In the simplest case one can model each of the class densities as a single term mixture that has a mean based on each class mean and a common covariance structure. In this case the common covariance matrix is given by

$$\Sigma_c = \sum_{allc} \frac{n_c}{n} \left(\frac{W_c}{n_c - 1}\right) \tag{4.2}$$

where

$$W_c = \sum_{i=1}^{n_c} (x_i^c - \mu^c)^2. \tag{4.3}$$

This classifier is denoted as a linear classifier. One obtains a quadratic classifier by allowing each of the classes to have a different covariance structure.

In the adaptive mixtures density estimation (AMDE) [5] [6] approach one loosens several of the requirements of the above procedures. Namely one allows the number of terms in the model to be driven by the complexity of the data, the location of the terms to be anywhere, the covariances to be nonuniform, and the mixing coefficients to not all be equal. In this case the form of the estimator is

$$\hat{f}(x) = \sum_{i=1}^{m} \pi_i N(x, \hat{\theta}). \tag{4.4}$$

In this equation it is the number of terms that is determined by the complexity of the data, the π's are the mixing coefficients, and N is the normal density determined by parameter set. In this case, the estimator is built in a recursive manner. As each data point is presented, the estimator either updates the existing parameters in the model using a recursive form of the expectation-maximization (EM) algorithm or else adds an additional term to the model as dictated by the complexity of the data.

The last mixture-based approach to be discussed is known as the Shifted Hats Iterated Procedure (SHIP). This method is a hybrid method that employs both kernel estimation techniques and mixture models. The technique switches attention between a mixture model of the data set and a kernel estimate (or more sophisticated semiparametric estimator). The name shifted hats came about since an estimator is typically denoted by the hat symbol and we are shifting our view on which function the estimator represents. A full description of this technique is provided in [7].

The next approach that was used to classify the data is based on the k-nearest-neighbors procedure. In this procedure one assigns a class label for each of the observations in the test set based on the k closest elements of the training set under an appropriate distance metric such as the standard Euclidean metric. In our case the large cardinality of the training set makes a straightforward application of the procedure problematic. We have chosen to use a reduced k-nearest-neighbors method as described by Hand 1997 [1]. This approach selects a subset of the full exemplar set for use in a nearest neighbor classifier. The reader is referred to Hand 1997 [1] for a full treatment of the methodology.

The final approach that was used to classify the data was classification and regression trees (CART). In this approach the algorithm attempts to form a sequence of decision planes perpendicular to the coordinate axes that partition the data into class homogeneous regions. The classifier then takes the form of a sequence of simple if tests. The reader is referred to Venables and Ripley 1994 [10] for a full treatment of this approach.

4.2 Results

Initially we chose to evaluate the classification utility of the features individually. In Figure 4.1 we present histogram plots for each of the 13 bands and each of the classes. We notice a fair degree of separability exhibited in features 7 and 11. This separability led us to utilize these features as one possible choice in subsequent analysis.

Next we turn our attention to an examination of the full thirteen-dimensional features. We have chosen to visualize the full higher dimensional feature set through the use of parallel coordinates, which provides us with a convenient venue for the display of higher dimensional data. In Figure 4.2 we present a parallel coordinate plot of the training data. The plot was produced using the ExplorN package that

Statistical Data Mining and Knowledge Discovery

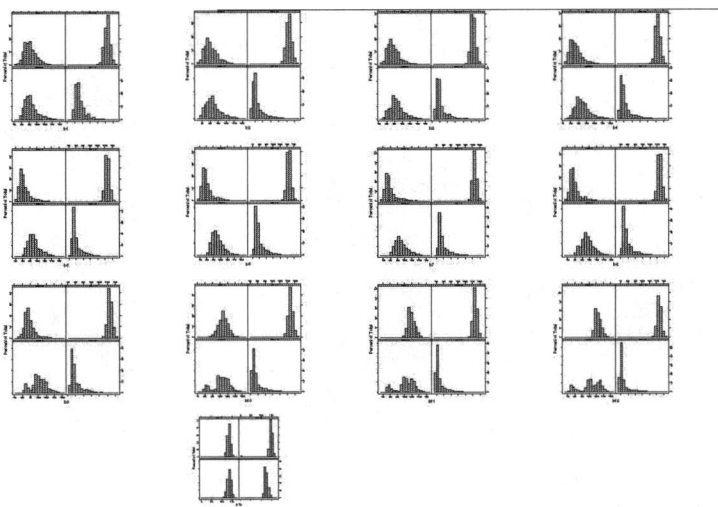

FIGURE 4.1
Histogram plots for each of the 13 bands for each of the 4 classes. The plots are arranged by band from top to bottom. In each case class 0 appears in the lower left corner, class 1 appears in the lower right corner, class 2 appears in the upper left corner, and class 3 appears in the upper right corner.

utilizes saturation brushing, a technique to deal with the overplotting problem associated with large data sets [12] [2]. In the plot the color saturation is computed as a function of the number of lines that traverse a given area. In addition when colored lines overlap one another the package mixes the colors together in the usual additive manner. Class 0 is displayed as red, class 1 as green, class 2 as blue, and class 3 (background) as white. The lowest axis in the figure designates the class label.

There are a few things worthy of note in the plot. First we notice the characteristic scalloped appearance of the class 3 data. This visual feature is associated with a multivariate elliptical density as might be found in a normal data set. It is not surprising to find that the background intensities were normally distributed. We also notice that a small subset of the class 3 observations are outliers as indicated by their far left appearance in band 13. This apparent anomaly is the subject of continued investigation. We also note the amount of class separation in bands 7 and 11. This observation is in keeping with our univariate analysis. Once again we notice that the class 3 observations are well separated from the other classes in most of the bands. We finally note the trimodality of class 0 particularly in band 11. This multimodal type behavior is not surprising since we originally collapsed multiple chemical classes into each of the subsequent classes.

The collectors of the SALAD data also proposed an alternate trivariate feature set. This feature set was chosen to mimic a three-band red, blue, green combination. Adding bands 1 and 2 together formed the first feature, the second feature by adding

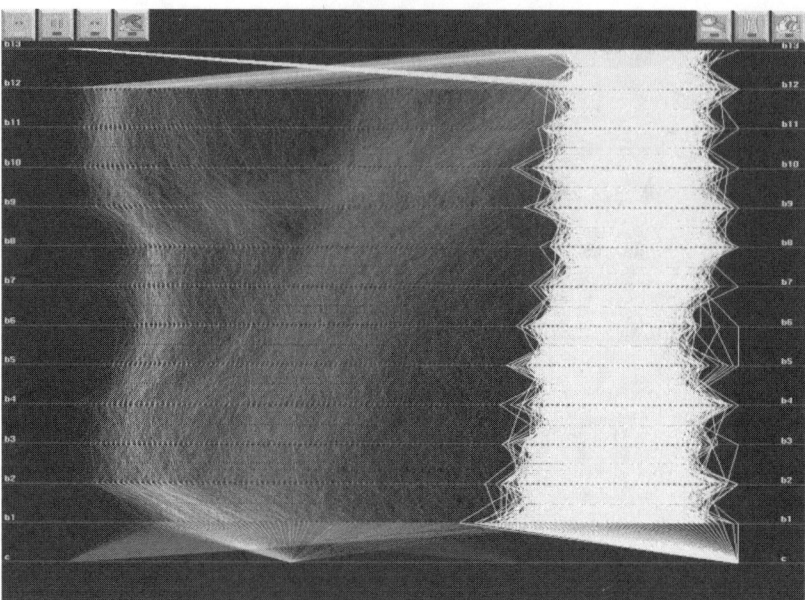

FIGURE 4.2
Parallel coordinates plot of all the training data. Class 0 is rendered in red, class 1 in green, class 2 in blue, and class 3 in white.

bands 6 and 7 and the third feature by adding bands 11 and 12. Besides reducing the dimensionality of the problem to three-space this step also reduced the requirements on the system so that instead of collecting 13 spectral bands they only need to collect 6 bands, or, with a modification of the filter set, 3 bands. In Figure 4.3 we present a scatterplot of these features for the 4 classes. The color scheme is identical to the previous plots with the exception that the background observations have been rendered in black. This plot provides additional evidence for the normality of the class three observations. In addition we see clear separation between the background observations and the other classes. Finally we notice that classes 0 through 2 are also moderately well separated in this feature space.

We now turn our attention to some model-based exploratory data analysis. This provides an alternate means to evaluate the utility of the various features. In Figure 4.4 we present plots of SHIP-based probability density estimates for the various classes based on bands 7 and 11. These models help us evaluate the overlap between the various classes. We point out the trimodality of class 0 in both of the features. We note the separation between class 1 and class 2 in the band 11 feature and the separation of class 0 from both class 1 and 2 in the band 7 feature. Finally we note that the background is fairly well separated from the other classes in both bands.

Alternatively one may build bivariate densities for bands 7 and 11 together. In Figure 4.5 we present bivariate kernel density estimates of the training data using a spherical product kernel. In the right-most figure we color each pixel in the band 7

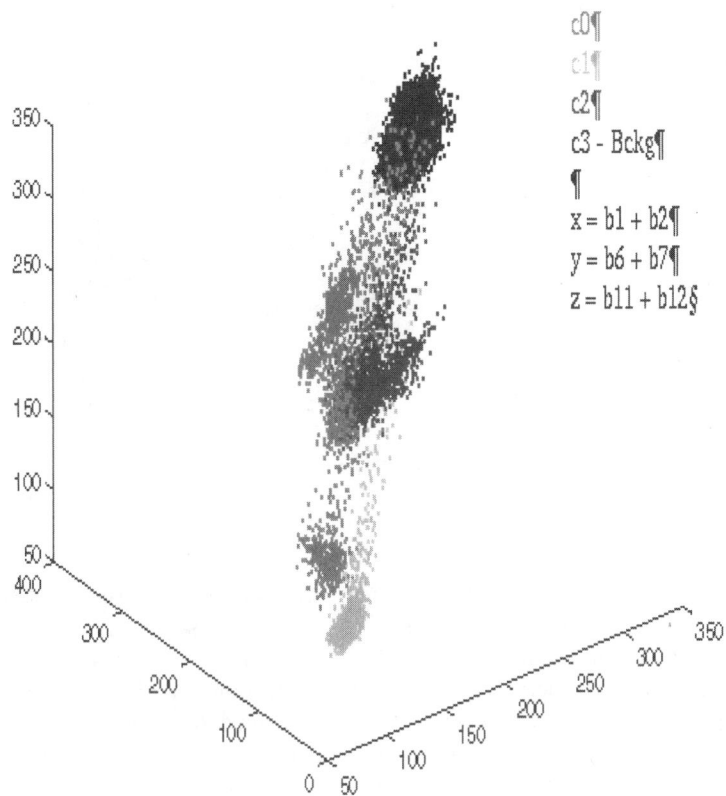

FIGURE 4.3
Scatterplot of the pseudo-RGB features. Class 0 is red, class 1 is green, class 2 is blue, and class 3 is black. Feature 1 (x-axis) is band 1 plus band 2, Feature 2 (y-axis) is band 6 plus band 7, and Feature 3 (z-axis) is band 11 plus band 12.

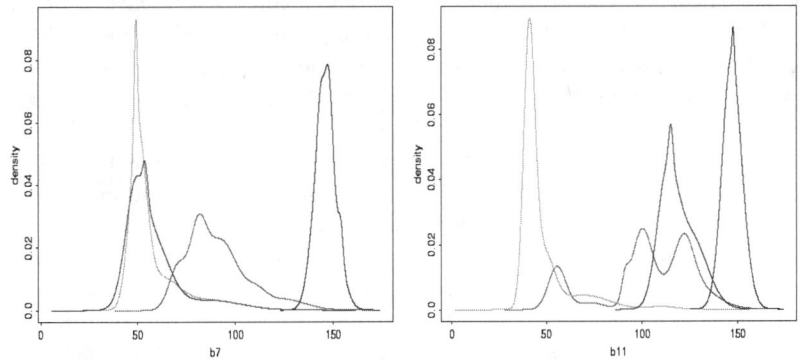

FIGURE 4.4
Univariate SHIP probability density functions for bands 7 and 11.

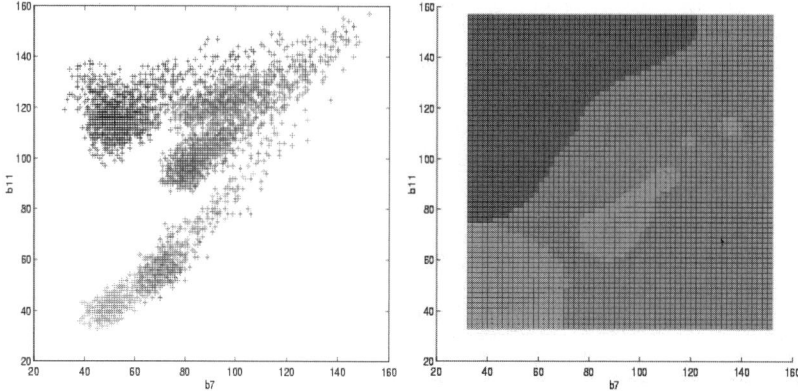

FIGURE 4.5
Multi-class discriminant regions based on a bivariate product kernel. Discriminant regions are plotted on the right and a scatterplot is rendered on the left.

cross band 11 space according to which of the class conditional bivariate probability density functions is higher. In the upper plot we present a scatterplot of the data. As before class 0 is colored in red, class 1 in green, and class 2 in blue. The background class has been omitted in this particular illustration. Pixels where the class conditional probabilities fell below a threshold have been colored white.

In the next set of images we consider the visualization of AMDE models based on the thirteen-dimensional training data. Each model consists of a mixture of thirteen-dimensional Gaussian terms. It is difficult in general to ascertain the match between the training data and the model given the high-dimensional nature of the data. In Figure 4.6 we plot the AMDE model for class 0. The data are rendered in yellow in the plot. In addition we have plotted the means of the terms that constitute the mixture model in red. The first axis has been used to plot a value equal to the scaled mixing coefficients in the case of the mixture terms and a dummy variable in the case of the data. The rendered grayscale images at the bottom of the plot represent the covariance structure of the terms in the mixture with the mixing coefficients explicitly spelled out below the images. White represents a large value in the covariance matrix.

There are a few relationships between the data and the model that are made clear by this plot. We notice that the term with the largest mixing coefficient tracks right through the center of the data set. The covariance image tracks the variability of the data fairly well. The next term, descending by mixing proportion, has a much tighter covariance structure as is indicated by the darkness of the rendering. This term tracks the left-most mode of the data set. The last two terms have very small proportions.

Next we turn our attention to some general discussions on the CART models that were built on the training data. In Figure 4.7 we present the plot of a classification tree based on the training data. The reader will notice that the CART procedure did not utilize all of the 13 bands but merely a subset of them. Specifically bands 1, 5, 7,

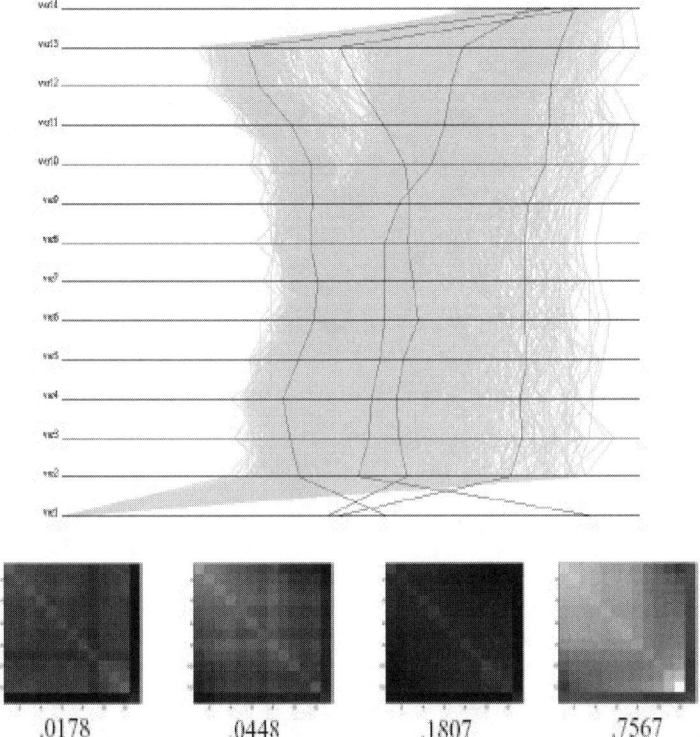

FIGURE 4.6
Parallel coordinates plot of the data, rendered in yellow, and the means of the mixture terms, rendered in red for class 0. The first axis represents a value proportional to the mixing coefficient in the case of the mixture terms. The gray-scale images represent the covariance structure of the given term. The numerical values of the mixing coefficients appear below the images.

8, 10, 12, and 13 were used in the model. These exceed the number of bands "hand picked" by the data collectors by 1, but interestingly enough the model has been built using an appreciably different set of bands.

It is easier to understand the inner workings of the CART procedure if we examine a pedagogical example. Suppose that the spectral signature of an observation is given by (70, 35, 110, 131, 111, 27, 105, 75, 215, 107, 115, 62, 117). The CART processes this observation as follows:

$$b7 = 105 < 129.5, \text{ which implies go left,}$$
$$b8 = 75 > 63.5, \text{ which implies go right,}$$
$$b12 = 62 < 111.5, \text{ which implies go left,}$$
$$b12 = 62 < 88.5, \text{ which implies go left, and}$$
$$b1 = 70$$

which implies go left which designates the observation as class 0.

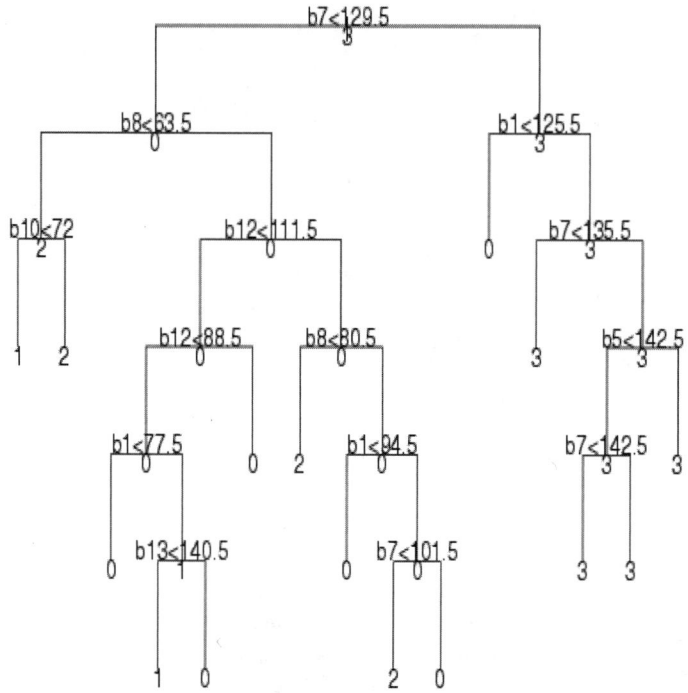

FIGURE 4.7
CART based on all 13 bands.

Next we turn our attention to classification results obtained using the models discussed earlier. In each case we analyze the results via a confusion matrix. The first entry of the confusion matrix represents the probability of calling an observation as class 0 given that the observation came from class 0, denoted $p(c_0|c_0)$. The entry in the first row and second column is the probability of calling an observation class 0 given that it was drawn from class 1 denoted $p(c_0|c_1)$. Similarly the entry in the second row and the first column represents $p(c_1|c_0)$. So the diagonal entries represent the $p(c_i|c_i)$ for $i = 0, 1, 2$, and 3. We have computed confusion matrix results for the adaptive mixtures model based on the full 13 features, adaptive mixtures model based on bands 7 and 11, adaptive mixtures models based on the pseudo RGB features, the linear classifier based on all 13 features, the linear classifier based on bands 7 and 11, the linear classifier based on the RGB features, the quadratic classifier based on all 13 features, the quadratic classifier based on bands 7 and 11, the quadratic classifier based on the RGB features, the spatial CART classifier based on all 13 features, the spatial CART classifier based on RGB features, the knn classifier based on all 13 features, the reduced knn classifier based on 200 exemplars, and the current classification system. We are however not free to provide the details of the current classification system at this time. The reader is referred to [9] for a full listing of the confusion tables.

Statistical Data Mining and Knowledge Discovery

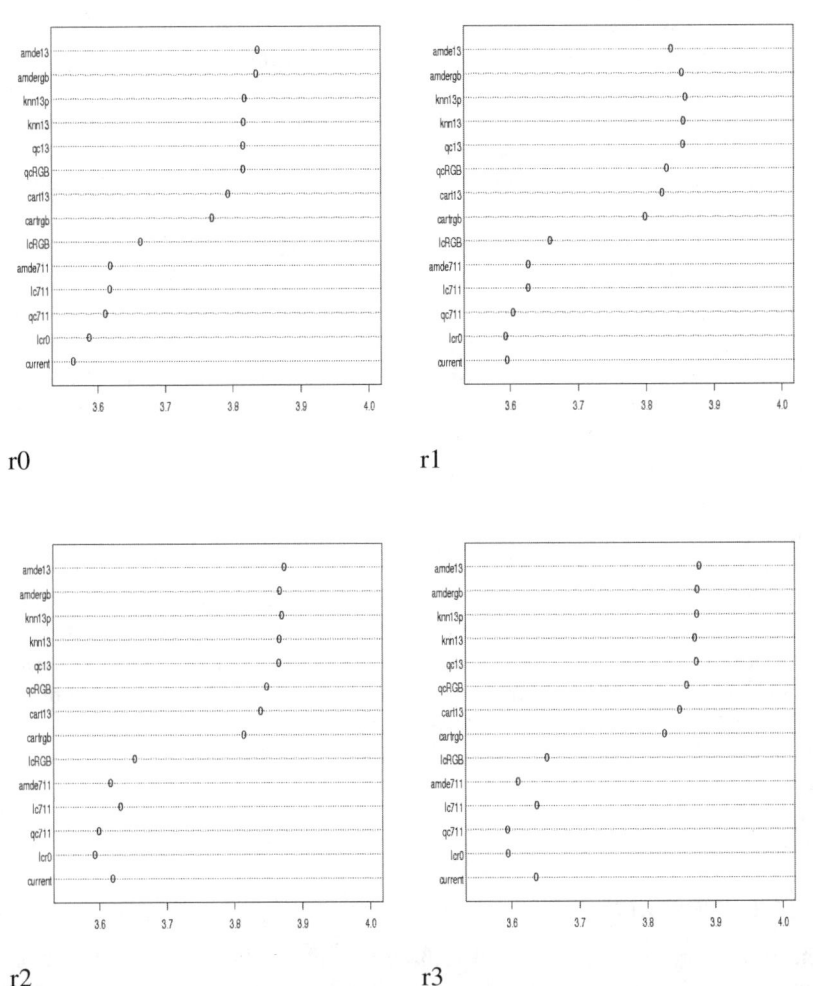

FIGURE 4.8
Sorted score for the various classification systems where the pixel radius varies between 0 and 3.

The $r = 0$ entry in each Table treats the pixels as independent, ignoring the spatial information inherent in the original image. Since processing time is at a premium in this application, we considered the simplest method for utilizing the spatial relationship of the pixels. Initially each pixel is assigned a class as above. Then to determine the final class label for the pixel a vote is taken from all the pixels within a $(2r+1)\text{x}(2r+1)$ box centered at the pixel, with the final class label for the pixel being the one, which wins the vote (ties are broken arbitrarily). We refer to r as the radius. The radii used were 0-3, where a radius of 0 corresponds to the standard classifier with no spatial information.

In Figure 4.8 we present a dot chart of the results. The diagonal of the confusion matrix is summed and plotted on the x-axis. The classifiers were sorted by their performance under this metric in the case where the radius was 0 (single pixel, no spatial information), and this ordering is retained for the rest of the charts. There are several trends that are revealed in the dot chart. We first notice that those classifiers that use the full dimensionality of the data either as all 13 features or as the RGB feature set outperform the other classifiers that use the hand-selected two-dimensional projection. This occurs without fail except in the case of the simple linear classifier on all 13 features. Another thing to notice is that the semiparametric and the nonparametric classifiers outperform the parametric classifiers in general. By this we mean that the adaptive mixtures and knn-based classifiers in general perform better than the linear and quadratic classifiers. We also point out that the CART-based classifiers seem to be outperformed by the quadratic classifiers, but are better than the linear classifiers. We finally note that there is an improvement in performance as we proceed from a radius of 0 to 1 and finally 2. There is, however, a leveling off of the improvement as we reach $r = 3$.

There are a few things that remain to be noted about the current approach. The current approach is bested by virtually all of the approaches at the $r = 0$ level. By the time one proceeds to the $r = 3$ level the performance of the fielded approach has improved sufficiently to allow it to outperform roughly three other classifiers. Even given this improvement the performance of the fielded system can be described as mediocre at best. This performance however may be sufficient depending on the situation at hand. This lackluster performance is a trade-off for a need to rapidly field the system in order to be prepared for a very real threat.

4.3 Conclusions

We have attempted to evaluate the discriminant utility of these features. Our work has consisted of a data-mining phase, a model-building phase, and a model-evaluation phase. We have utilized standard statistical procedures such as histograms to provide univariate views of the data. In addition we have employed the parallel coordinates visualization framework in order to ascertain the structure of the feature set in the full thirteen-dimensional space.

We have employed high-performance probability density estimation procedures to model the distribution of the features sets in both the full space and other fortuitously reduced spaces. The density estimation/classification techniques used have included standard classification and regression trees along with adaptive mixtures, kernel estimators, k-nearest-neighbors, and the recently developed shifted hats iterated procedure.

We have employed a simple scheme to incorporate spatial information into our classifier systems. We have measured the performance of the various classifiers using the standard confusion matrix measure. In order to compare the performance of the classifiers we must turn to the confusion matrix results. As presented in the dotchart of Figure 4.8 we were able to show that the adaptive mixtures model obtained using all 13 features and a spatial radius of 3 proves to be the superior choice.

Assuming that one is very much limited with regard to both time and computational capabilities, then one needs to examine alternate solutions. Under these circumstances we recommend that one employ the CART model based on the full feature set with a spatial radius of 3. This system provides probability of detection that exceeds .85 while obtaining a false alarm rate less than .12. This system provides this level of performance while at the same time offering considerable speed improvements. In fact we would anticipate considerable time savings given the fact that the classifier takes the form of a simple sequence of if tests.

Acknowledgments

The authors would like to thank Greg Johnson of the Naval Surface Warfare Center for providing us with an opportunity to work on a very interesting problem. In addition we would like to thank Dr. Webster West of South Carolina University for provision of a JAVA-based parallel coordinates framework, and Dr. George Rogers of the Naval Surface Warfare Center for provision of the SHIP source code. This paper is an expansion of a part of the Keynote Lecture presented by EJW at the C. Warren Neel Conference on the New Frontiers of Statistical Data Mining, Knowledge Discovery, and E-Business. Other portions of that Keynote presentation may be found in [2].

The first author, JLS, would like to acknowledge the sponsorship of Dr. Wendy Martinez at the Office of Naval Research. The work of the second author, EJW, was completed under the sponsorship of the Air Force Office of Scientific Research under the contract F49620-01-1-0274 and the Defense Advanced Research Projects Agency through cooperative agreement 8105-48267 with Johns Hopkins University. The third author, DJM, would like to acknowledge the sponsorship of the Defense Advanced Research Projects Agency.

References

[1] D. J. Hand. *Construction and Assessment of Classification Rules*. John Wiley and Sons, New York, 1997.

[2] E. J.Wegman. Visual data mining. In *Statistics and Medicine*. 2002.

[3] D. J. Marchette, J. L. Solka, R. J. Guidry, and J. E. Green. The advanced distributed region of interest tool. *to appear Pattern Recognition*, 1998.

[4] G. J. McLachlan and K. E. Basford. *Mixture Models*. Marcel Dekker, New York, 1988.

[5] C. E. Priebe. Adaptive mixtures. *J. Amer. Stat. Assoc.*, 89:796–806, 1994.

[6] C. E Priebe and D. J. Marchette. Adaptive mixture density estimation. *Pattern Recognition*, 26(5):771–785, 1993.

[7] G. W. Rogers, D. J. Marchette, and C. E. Priebe. A procedure for model complexity selection in semiparametric mixture model density estimation. *appearing in the Proceedings of and Presented at the 10th International. Conference on Mathematical and Computer Modelling and Scientific Computing*.

[8] B. W. Silverman. *Density Estimation for Statistics and Data Analysis*. Chapman and Hall, London, 1986.

[9] J. L. Solka, E. J. Wegman, and D. J. Marchette. Data mining strategies for the detection of chemical warfare agents. Technical Report 182, George Mason University, Fairfax, VA, 2002.

[10] W. N. Venables and B. D. Ripley. *Modern Applied Statistics with S-Plus*. Springer-Verlag, Heidelberg, 1994.

[11] E. J. Wegman. Hyperdimensional data analysis using parallel coordinates. *J. Amer. Stat. Assoc.*, 85:664–675, 1990.

[12] E. J. Wegman and Q. Q. Luo. High dimensional clustering using parallel coordinates and the grand tour, 1997. Republished in *Classification and Knowledge Organization*, R. Kaluer and O. Opitz, (eds), Springer-Verlag, Heidelberg.

5

Disclosure Limitation Methods Based on Bounds for Large Contingency Tables With Applications to Disability

Adrian Dobra, Elena A. Erosheva and Stephen E. Fienberg
Duke University, Durham, University of Washington, Seattle, and Carnegie-Mellon University, Pittsburgh, USA

CONTENTS

5.1	Introduction	94
5.2	Example: National Long Term Care Survey Data	95
5.3	Technical Background on Cell Entry Bounds	96
5.4	Decomposable Frontiers	99
5.5	"Greedy" Frontiers	103
5.6	Bounds	108
5.7	Discussion	112
	Acknowledgments	113
	References	114

Much attention has been focused recently on the problem of maintaining the confidentiality of statistical data bases through the application of statistical tools to limit the identification of information on individuals (and enterprises). Here we describe and implement some simple procedures for disclosure limitation based on bounds for the cell entries in contingency tables that result from knowledge about released marginal totals or subtables. Our work draws on the ideas associated with the theory of log-linear models for contingency tables where the minimal sufficient statistics are in fact marginal totals corresponding to the highest-order terms in the model. We draw on recent results associated with decomposable log-linear models and their use in the disclosure limitation context.

Our primary illustration of the methodology is in the context of a 2^{16} contingency table extracted from disability data collected as part of the National Long Term Care Survey. We treat these data as if they involved an entire population and we illustrate the calculation of optimal releases of marginals in such a circumstance. We describe briefly some of the analyses we have carried out on these data using the Grade of Membership model, whose minimal sufficient statistics are not simply marginal totals, and we relate this to the optimal set of releasable margins. We conclude with a discussion of some of the possible implications of our analyses for disclosure limitation in similar data sets.

5.1 Introduction

If government agencies are to collect and publish high quality data, it is essential that they maintain the confidentiality of the information provided by others. Typically agencies promise respondents that their data will be kept confidential and used for statistical purposes only. Disclosure limitation is the process of protecting the confidentiality of statistical data. A disclosure occurs when someone can use published statistical information to identify an individual data provider. Since virtually any form of data release contains some information about the individuals whose data are included in it, disclosure is not an all-or-none concept but rather a probabilistic one. For general introductions to some of the statistical aspects of confidentiality and disclosure limitation see Doyle et al. [13], Duncan et al. [15], Fienberg [20], and Willenborg and De Waal [37, 38].

Disclosure limitation procedures alter or limit the data to be released, e.g., by modifying or removing those characteristics that put confidential information at risk for disclosure. In the case of sample categorical data in the form of a contingency table, a count of "1" can generate confidentiality concerns if that individual is also unique in the population. Much confidentiality research has focused on measures of risk that attempt to infer the probability that an individual is unique in the population given uniqueness in the sample (e.g., see Chen and Keller-McNulty [4], Fienberg and Makov [22, 23], Skinner and Holmes [36], and Samuels [35]). Here we will consider only the case of population data, for which a count of "1" is unique. Moreover, a count of "2" is also problematic for population data since it allows each of the two people in the cell to identify one other! More generally, small counts raise issues of disclosure risk.

In this paper we provide an overview of some recent work to develop bounds for entries in contingency and other non-negative tables (see Dobra and Fienberg [9, 10, 11], and Dobra et al. [12]). We work within a statistical framework for the release of cross-classified categorical data coming originally in the form of a contingency table where requests from users come in the form of (marginal) sub-tables involving a subset of the variables. Clearly, the more such sub-tables that are available, the more information we have about the full joint distribution of the cross-classifying variables. Through a detailed example we illustrate both the utility of data releases in the form of marginals and simple methods for assessing the risk of disclosure using bounds on the individual cell entries. Our interest in this problem grows out of work to develop a Web-based table query system, coordinated by the National Institute of Statistical Sciences [12]. The system is being designed to work with a database consisting of a k-way contingency table and it allows only those queries that come in the form of requests for marginal tables. What is intuitively clear from statistical theory is that, as margins are released and cumulated by users, there is increasing information available about the table entries. Such an approach to disclosure limitation always tell the truth by releasing marginals from the full table, albeit not the whole truth, which would entail releasing the full table (c.f., Dobra et al. [12]).

The approach we outline in this paper draws heavily on the ideas associated with the theory of log-linear models for contingency tables (see Bishop, Fienberg, and Holland [1], and Lauritzen [31]), where the minimal sufficient statistics (MSSs) are in fact marginal totals corresponding to the highest-order terms in the model. This simple statistical fact has profound implications for reporting purposes as well as for disclosure limitation methods based on reporting only subtables. If an agency knows that a particular log-linear model fits a multi-dimensional contingency table well, then, at least in principle, users of the data could get by with only the MSSs. If the agency is able to release a set of marginals which include the MSSs of well fitting log-linear models, then users can also independently assess the fit relevant log-linear models from the released data and consider alternative models as well. It is in this sense that an approach based on releasing marginals leads to conclusions that may be more uncertain, but will not be erroneous.

In the next section, we introduce an example of a 2^{16} contingency table based on disability data from the National Long Term Care Survey, which we use to illustrate our methods. In Section 5.3 we give a brief summary of the key technical background on bounds for cell entries in a table when the marginals correspond to those associated with decomposable and reducible graphical models. Then, in Sections 5.4 and 5.5, we outline a general approach to the determination of optimal releases of marginals based on a search procedure that involves only decomposable cases and apply it to our example. In Section 5.6 we assess our results to the 2^{16} table, and we conclude with a discussion of some of the possible implications for disclosure and statistical analyses.

5.2 Example: National Long Term Care Survey Data

In this paper our primary example is a 2^{16} contingency table **n** extracted from the "analytic" data file for National Long Term Care Survey. Each dimension corresponds to a measure of disability defined by an activity of daily living, and the table contains information cross-classifying individuals aged 65 and above. This extract involves data pooled across four waves of a longitudinal survey, and it involves sample as opposed to population data. We henceforth act *as if* these were population data. For a detailed description of this extract see [17].

The 16 dimensions of the contingency table correspond to responses to 6 activities of daily living (ADLs) and 10 instrumental activities of daily living (IADLs). Specifically, the ADLs are (1) *eating*, (2) *getting in/out of bed*, (3) *getting around inside*, (4) *dressing*, (5) *bathing*, (6) *getting to the bathroom or using a toilet*. The IADLs are (7) *doing heavy house work*, (8) *doing light house work*, (9) *doing laundry*, (10) *cooking*, (11) *grocery shopping*, (12) *getting about outside*, (13) *traveling*, (14) *managing money*, (15) *taking medicine*, (16) *telephoning*. For each ADL/IADL measure, subjects were classified as being either disabled (level 1) or healthy (level 0) on that measure.

Of the $2^{16} = 65,536$ cells in the table, 62,384 (95.19%) contain zero entries, 1,729 (2.64%) contain counts of "1," 499 (0.76%) contain counts of "2." The largest cell count is 3,853, in the $(0,0,\ldots,0)$ cell corresponding to being healthy on all 16 measures. In fact, no relatively simple hierarchical log-linear model provides a reasonable fit to these data in part because they all substantially underestimate the value of this cell count in particular.

In the absence of simple parsimonious log-linear models to describe such disability data, considerable attention has been given to analyses using what is known as the Grade of Membership (GoM) model (see Manton, Woodbury, and Tolley [33] and [19]). The GoM model is a partial or mixed membership model that resembles a more traditional latent class model. For a random sample of subjects, we observe K dichotomous responses, $x_1, \ldots, x_K$. We assume there are J basis subpopulations, which are determined by the conditional (positive) response probabilities, λ_{jk}, $k = 1, \ldots, K$. The subjects are characterized by their degrees of membership in each of the subpopulations, $g = (g_1, \ldots, g_J)$, which are nonnegative and add to 1. Conditional on the subject's membership scores, g, the subject's response probability for item k is given by a convex combination $\Pr(x_k = 1|g) = \sum_j g_j \lambda_{jk}$. We assume that the responses $x_1, \ldots, x_K$ are conditionally independent, given the membership scores. For many purposes we may also want to add the assumption that the membership scores, g, have a Dirichlet distribution with parameters $\alpha = (\alpha_1, \ldots, \alpha_J)$. For the disability data in our example, $K = 16$ and a "reasonable" value of $J = 5$ (e.g., see Erosheva [17, 18]).

The GoM likelihood function is not of the exponential family type, and thus no sufficient statistics exist for the membership scores [17]. This does not allow for conditional likelihood estimation and also means that if the GoM model is an appropriate one to describe the disability data in the 2^{16} table, then we need more than the simple marginal totals associated with any unsaturated log-linear model to estimate the GoM parameters. We return to this point after we explore the disclosure limitation properties of bounds based on the release of marginal tables for these data.

5.3 Technical Background on Cell Entry Bounds

Bounds for entries in two-way contingency tables go back to seminal papers by Bonferonni [2], Fréchet [26], and Hoeffding [27]. For an $I \times J$ table with entries $\{n_{ij}\}$ and row margins $\{n_{i+}\}$ and column margins $\{n_{+j}\}$, these bounds take the form

$$\min\{n_{i+}, n_{+j}\} \geq n_{ij} \geq \max\{0, n_{i+} + n_{+j} - n_{++}\}. \tag{5.1}$$

For simplicity, we refer to these as *Fréchet bounds*. Until recently, the only multidimensional generalizations of this result that have been utilized involved non-overlapping fixed marginals (c.f. the related work described in Joe [28]).

Statistical Data Mining and Knowledge Discovery

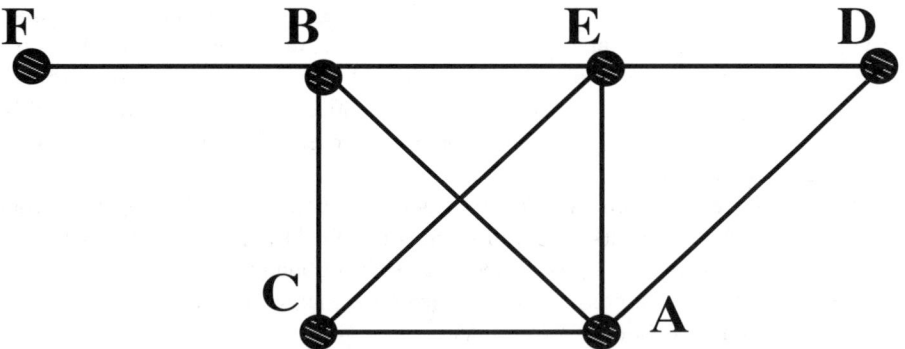

FIGURE 5.1
Independence graph for a 6-dimensional table and a log-linear model induced by the marginals [BF], [ABCE], and [ADE].

Any contingency table with non-negative integer entries and fixed marginal totals is a lattice point in the convex polytope **Q** defined by the linear system of equations induced by the released marginals. The constraints given by the values in the released marginals induce upper and lower bounds on the interior cells of the initial table. These bounds or *feasibility intervals* can be obtained by solving the corresponding linear programming problems. The importance of systematically investigating these linear systems of equations should be readily apparent. If the number of lattice points in **Q** is below a certain threshold, we have significant evidence that a potential disclosure of the entire dataset might have occurred. Moreover, if the induced upper and lower bounds are too tight or too close to the actual sensitive value in a cell entry, the information associated with the individuals classified in that cell may become public knowledge.

The problem of determining sharp upper and lower bounds for the cell entries subject to some linear constraints expressed in this form is known to be NP-hard (see Roehrig et al. [34]). Several approaches have been proposed for computing bounds; however, almost all of them have drawbacks that show the need for alternate solutions.

We visualize the dependency patterns induced by the released marginals by constructing an independence graph for the variables in the underlying cross-classification. Each variable cross-classified in the table is associated with a vertex in this graph. If two variables are not connected, they are conditionally independent given the remaining variables. Models described solely in terms of such conditional independencies are said to be *graphical* (e.g., see Lauritzen [31]). For example, Figure 5.1 shows the independence graph for a 6-variable cross-classification with the variables $\{A,B,C,D,E,F\}$ corresponding to the 6 nodes. Of the 15 possible edges, 6 are absent and correspond to conditional independencies.

Decomposable models are a subclass of graphical models that correspond to triangulated graphs and have closed form structure and special properties. In particular, the expected cell values can be expressed as a function of the fixed marginals. To be more explicit, the maximum likelihood estimates are the product of the marginals divided by the product of the separators. For example, the graph in Figure 5.1 is triangulated and, for the corresponding decomposable log-linear model, the marginals [BF], [ABCE], and [ADE], corresponding to the cliques in the graph, are the MSSs. The cliques are "separated" from one another by subsets of connected nodes, which we refer to as separators.

By induction on the number of MSSs, Dobra and Fienberg [9] developed generalized Fréchet bounds for sets of margins that correspond to the MSSs of any decomposable log-linear model. These generalized Fréchet bounds are sharp in the sense that they are the tightest possible bounds given the marginals and there are feasible tables for which these bounds are attained.

THEOREM 5.1
(Fréchet Bounds for Decomposable Models) *Assume that the released set of marginals for a K-way contingency table correspond to the MSSs of a decomposable log-linear model. Then the upper bounds for the cell entries in the initial table are the minimum of relevant margins, while the lower bounds are the maximum of zero, or sum of the relevant margins minus the separators.*

When the log-linear model associated with the released set of marginals is not decomposable, it is natural to ask ourselves whether we could reduce the computational effort needed to determine the tightest bounds by employing the same strategy used for decomposable graphs, i.e., decompositions of graphs by means of complete separators. An independence graph that is not necessarily decomposable, but still admits a *proper* decomposition (i.e., looks like a decomposable graph but whose components are not fully connected) is called *reducible* (Leimer [32]). Once again, we point out the link with maximum likelihood estimation in log-linear models. We define a *reducible log-linear model* in [9] as one for which the corresponding MSSs are marginals that characterize the components of a reducible independence graph. If we can calculate the maximum likelihood estimates for the log-linear models corresponding to every component of a reducible graph $\mathcal{G}$, then we can easily derive explicit formulae for the maximum likelihood estimates in the reducible log-linear model with independence graph $\mathcal{G}$ [9].

THEOREM 5.2
(Fréchet Bounds for Reducible Models) *Assume that the released set of marginals is the set of MSSs of a reducible log-linear model. Then the upper bounds for the cell entries in the initial table are the minimum of upper bounds of relevant components, while the lower bounds are the maximum of zero, or sum of the lower bounds of relevant components minus the separators.*

Finally, we note that when the released margins correspond to a log-linear model that is neither decomposable nor reducible, a more elaborate form of bounds calculation is required. Dobra [7, 11] has developed an iterative algorithm for this situation, generalizing the original "shuttle" procedure proposed by Buzzigoli and Giusti [3], which can be used to compute sharp bounds. Unfortunately, as the dimensionality of the table grows, this algorithm is computationally elaborate and is not especially useful as the main component of a search for an optimal form of marginal release. Instead we adopt simplified search strategies and then use the algorithm only after we have focused in on a small subset of sets of marginal releases. In the following sections, we turn to such simplified search strategies that exploit the bounds calculation in the decomposable case. When we apply these to the 2^{16} table from Section 5.2, we also describe the results of applying the generalized shuttle algorithm.

5.4 Decomposable Frontiers

Here we briefly describe the method of Dobra et al. [12] to identify a releasable set of marginals based on a search using decomposable bounds and we apply the approach to our 2^{16} example.

The set **S** of all 2^k marginals of a k-way table **n** is partially ordered by set inclusion of variable. If the variables associated with a marginal $\mathbf{n}_1$ are contained in the set of variables associated with another marginal $\mathbf{n}_2$, we say that $\mathbf{n}_1$ is a *child* of $\mathbf{n}_2$ and $\mathbf{n}_2$ is a *parent* of $\mathbf{n}_1$. The *released frontier* $\mathscr{RF}$ of a set $\mathscr{R}$ of released marginals consists of the maximal elements of $\mathscr{R}$–those with no released parents. Clearly, any set of released marginals is completely identified by its frontier. The elements of $\mathscr{RF}$ consist of sets of marginals and they represent the trade-offs that occur when the release of some marginals make others unreleasable. Our goal here is to identify useful elements of $\mathscr{RF}$.

For simplicity, we consider a set $\mathscr{R}$ to be releasable if and only if the minimum difference between the upper and lower bounds for the small count cells of "1" or "2" in table **n** is greater or equal to some threshold β.

In the context of the Web-based query system, the set **S** is partitioned at any time t as follows:

$$\mathbf{S} = \mathscr{R}(t) \cup \mathscr{M}(t) \cup \mathscr{U}(t), \tag{5.2}$$

where $\mathscr{R}(t)$ are the released marginals at time t, $\mathscr{M}(t)$ are the possible future releases at time t, and $\mathscr{U}(t)$ are the marginals that became un-releasable by releasing $\mathscr{R}(t)$. As we release additional marginals, we select elements from $\mathscr{M}(t)$ for inclusion in $\mathscr{R}(t)$ and at the same time move other elements into $\mathscr{U}(t)$.

We may not want to allow all elements in $\mathscr{U}(t)$ to be a potential release at time t because the release of some would essentially foreclose on the possibility of releasing others at a later time. Therefore, the system might also maintain a list of candidate releases $\mathscr{CM}(t) \subset \mathscr{M}(t)$.

Now assume a user requests a marginal $\mathbf{n}_0$. In order to accept or deny this request, the system would have to dynamically evaluate whether the set $\mathscr{R}(t) \cup \{\mathbf{n}_0\}$ is releasable provided that $\mathbf{n}_0$ belongs to $\mathscr{CM}(t)$. If $\mathbf{n}_0$ is released, the system needs to update the sets $\mathscr{U}(t+1)$ and $\mathscr{CM}(t+1)$ very quickly to be ready to process a new request. In addition, evaluating the disclosure risk is a lot more difficult if the system takes into account the fact that it gives away information about **n** when denying a request.

In actual applications, the underlying categorical database **n** might have 40 or more dimensions and/or millions and millions of cells. Consequently, dynamically evaluating whether a marginal is releasable as well as updating the sets $\mathcal{U}$ and $\mathcal{CM}$ involve huge computations that cannot be done on today's computers. Besides scalability issues, there are other concerns relating to user equity: if we release a marginal, some other marginals become unreleasable and hence those users requesting these marginals might suffer if a policy of "first come, first served" would be applied.

A possible solution would be to replace sequential releases with one-time releases. In this case, the complete set of marginal **S** contains the released marginals $\mathcal{R}$ and the un-released marginals $\mathcal{U}$. The only difficulty of this approach is identifying the "best" $\mathcal{R}$ according to some data utility criteria. The tedious dynamic risk computations are now replaced by a one-time computation that can be done offline. Users can be polled on the choice of $\mathcal{R}$. This simplified static version of the table server is not prone to be attacked by intruders as the dynamic server was.

5.4.1 Calculating Decomposable Frontiers

We say that a release $\mathcal{R}$ is *decomposable* if its corresponding frontier defines the MSSs of a decomposable graphical model. A decomposable frontier is the frontier of a decomposable release. In this case, the upper and lower bounds induced by $\mathcal{R}$ can be computed using formulas [9], which reduces to almost zero the computational effort required to establish whether $\mathcal{R}$ is releasable or not.

We quantify the data utility $\mathbf{DU}(\mathcal{R})$ of a release $\mathcal{R}$ by the total number of marginals contained in $\mathcal{R}$. To maximize $\mathbf{DU}(\mathcal{R})$ over the space of decomposable releasable sets $\mathcal{R}$ we use a simulated annealing approach that involves generating random draws from the distribution

$$\pi(\mathcal{R}) \propto \exp(\mathbf{DU}(\mathcal{R})/T), \tag{5.3}$$

where T is a scale parameter called *temperature* The temperature T is slowly decreased toward 0 as the algorithm progresses. Given a current state $\mathcal{R}_0$, a new decomposable set of sub-tables $\mathcal{R}_1$ is selected from a uniform distribution on a neighborhood $N(\mathcal{R}_0)$ of $\mathcal{R}_0$. If $\mathbf{DU}(\mathcal{R}_1) \geq \mathbf{DU}(\mathcal{R}_0)$, $\mathcal{R}_1$ is "accepted" with probability 1, that is $\mathcal{R}_1$ becomes the current state. Otherwise, if $\mathbf{DU}(\mathcal{R}_1) < \mathbf{DU}(\mathcal{R}_0)$, $\mathcal{R}_1$ could be accepted with probability

$$\min\{\exp((\mathbf{DU}(\mathcal{R}_1) - \mathbf{DU}(\mathcal{R}_0))/T), 1\}. \tag{5.4}$$

We repeat this simulation process and the resulting sequence. The Markov chain $\{\mathcal{R}_j\}$ forms a Markov chain that will concentrate in a smaller and smaller region around a local maxima of $\mathbf{DU}(\mathcal{R})$ as T approaches 0. Therefore, at higher temperatures, the simulated annealing algorithm can "escape" local optima of the criterion function and eventually converge to a global optimum.

5.4.2 Analysis of the 2^{16} NLTCS Example

It is standard survey practice to release the one-way marginals for all variables, and thus we begin by assuming that these have already been released. We ran the simulated annealing algorithm for searching a decomposable frontier for three different threshold values, $\beta = 3, 4, 5$. The resulting decomposable frontiers are:

$$\mathcal{RF}(\beta = 3) = \Big\{ [5,10,12,13,14,15,16], [5,10,11,14,15,16], [9,10,12,13,14,15],$$
$$[6,10,12,13,15,16], [4,10,12,13,14,15], [4,8,10,12,13,14],$$
$$[3,4,12,13,14,15], [3,4,7,12,13,15], [2,12,13,14,15,16],$$
$$[1,9,12,13,14,15] \Big\}, \tag{5.5}$$

$$\mathcal{RF}(\beta = 4) = \Big\{ [6,9,12,13,15,16], [6,8,12,13,15,16], [2,6,8,12,13,15],$$
$$[2,6,11,12,13,15], [2,4,6,11,12,13], [2,4,11,12,13,14],$$
$$[2,4,6,10,12,13], [2,4,5,10,12,13], [2,3,6,8,12,13],$$
$$[1,8,12,13,15,16], [2,4,6,7,11] \Big\}, \tag{5.6}$$

$$\mathcal{RF}(\beta = 5) = \Big\{ [6,8,10,14,15,16], [4,6,8,10,14,15], [15,14,8,6,4,3],$$
$$[3,4,6,8,13,15], [3,4,6,12,14,15], [3,4,6,9,13,15],$$
$$[2,4,6,8,13,15,13], [2,4,8,11,13,15], [3,4,6,7,14],$$
$$[4,5,6,12,14,12], [1,4,6,14,15] \Big\}. \tag{5.7}$$

Two of these frontiers contain 6-dimensional marginals, while the third, $\mathcal{RF}(\beta = 3)$, contains a 7-dimensional marginal. Summaries of the released sets of marginals determined by these frontiers are presented in Tables 5.1, 5.2 and 5.3.

The releasable frontier consists of *multiple* sets of releases, and for each the released marginals are maximal in the sense that any additional marginal is unreleasable. The simulated annealing algorithm happened to find the sets of releases on the releasable frontiers given above, but there are likely several other frontier elements.

Dimension	Released Marginals	Total Number of Marginals	Percent
1	16	16	100%
2	66	120	55%
3	125	560	22.32%
4	125	1,820	6.87%
5	66	4,368	1.51%
6	16	8,008	0.20%
7	1	11,440	0.00%

TABLE 5.1
Breakdown of the released set of sub-tables $\mathscr{RF}(\beta = 3)$. The columns show the dimension of sub-tables, how many sub-tables of that dimension are in $\mathscr{RF}(\beta = 3)$, the total number of sub-tables and the percentage of released sub-tables. The total number of released sub-tables is 415.

Dimension	Released Marginals	Total Number of Marginals	Percent
1	16	16	100%
2	64	120	53.33%
3	116	560	20.71%
4	109	1,820	5.99%
5	52	4,368	1.19%
6	10	8,008	0.12%

TABLE 5.2
Breakdown of the released set of sub-tables $\mathscr{RF}(\beta = 4)$. The total number of released sub-tables is 367.

Dimension	Released Marginals	Total Number of Marginals	Percent
1	16	16	100%
2	62	120	51.67%
3	108	560	19.29%
4	97	1,820	5.33%
5	44	4,368	1.00%
6	8	8,008	0.10%

TABLE 5.3
Breakdown of the released set of sub-tables $\mathscr{RF}(\beta = 5)$. The total number of released sub-tables is 335.

As the threshold β decreases, the number of released sub-tables increases for each dimension. Examining the decomposable frontiers for $\beta = 3, 4, 5$, we first notice that they are not nested. For example, the released sets of sub-tables defined by frontiers $\mathscr{RF}(\beta = 4)$ and $\mathscr{RF}(\beta = 5)$ are not subsets of the set of sub-tables defined by $\mathscr{RF}(\beta = 3)$. Note that all marginals of the "most generous" decomposable frontier $\mathscr{RF}(\beta = 3)$ contain 0-2 ADL and 4-6 IADL variables, but most marginals of the frontier $\mathscr{RF}(\beta = 5)$ contain 3 ADL and 3 IADL variables. Thus, it seems that releasing fewer ADL variables in the marginals allows us to maximize the total number of marginals released for a lower value of threshold β. This might be related to an existing theory which says that ADL variables are approximately hierarchical, e.g., see Katz et al. [29]. If the small counts of 1 and 2 are indicative of "imbalance" in the marginals, and if responses on ADL items are more structured than responses on IADL items, releasing more IADL items is "safer" than releasing more ADL items.

5.5 "Greedy" Frontiers

Searching for decomposable releases, although appealing from a computational point of view, can be considered to be too restrictive from a practical perspective. In this section, we present a heuristic procedure for identifying an arbitrary release that is based on a consistent methodology for assessing the disclosure risk associated with releasing a particular marginal. We illustrate the components of this algorithm using the 2^{16} table example.

We begin by introducing the notion of the *most parsimonious* model corresponding to a sub-table. Let $K = \{1, 2, \ldots, k\}$ denote the indices of the variables cross-classified in a k-dimensional table $\mathbf{n} = \mathbf{n}_K$.

DEFINITION 5.1 *The most parsimonious model associated with the C-marginal of $\mathbf{n}$ is the model with minimal sufficient statistics*

$$\{C\} \cup \left[\bigcup_{j \in K \backslash C} \{\{j\}\} \right]. \tag{5.8}$$

Definition 5.1 says that the most parsimonious model in which a given marginal appears is defined by that marginal and by the one-dimensional marginals corresponding to the variables in the table which do not appear in that marginal. For example, the most parsimonious model corresponding to the $[1,2]$-marginal of a six-way table has minimal sufficient statistics $\{[1,2,3], [4], [5], [6]\}$.

We would like to find a way to quantify how "problematic" the release of a certain marginal might be. In this context, "problematic" means "potentially problematic" because a marginal is released after some other marginals have already been released. The level of how "problematic" a marginal might be is therefore relative to the rest of the marginals and is not an absolute measure that would have a meaning if it would be considered alone. To define such a measure, we propose looking at all the models in which a given marginal is involved, i.e., we consider all possible sets of releases containing that marginal. The most parsimonious model is embedded in all these sets of releases, and, because it has the loosest bounds, it suffices for us to study only this model. If the release of this model is problematic, the release of all other models is problematic as well. On the other hand, if the release of the most parsimonious model is not problematic, one cannot say anything about all the other models that include the marginal.

There is an immediate intuitive interpretation of evaluating the disclosure risk of a marginal based on its most parsimonious model: in order to see how much "damage" this marginal could do, we release this marginal alone along with some minimal information about the variables not contained in this marginal. Another attractive feature of these most parsimonious models is that they are decomposable, hence calculating the upper and lower bounds associated with them is straightforward and can be done by means of explicit formulas.

By employing the notion of parsimonious models, we completely drop the (very) strong decomposability constraint we imposed when we searched for a decomposable frontier. Moreover, we take into account sets of releases that are only required to be hierarchical! This represents the highest level of generality we could hope to achieve. In addition, the size of the space of releases we take into consideration is huge. A search strategy similar to simulated annealing is hopeless if employed on a space of this size!

DEFINITION 5.2 *The critical width of a marginal $\mathbf{n}_C$ is the minimum of the difference between the upper and lower bounds for the cells containing small counts of "1" or "2". These bounds are induced by the most parsimonious model associated with $\mathbf{n}_C$.*

The critical width is the minimum of the difference between the relevant bounds for cells with counts of "1" and "2" because all the cells containing small counts in the table have to be protected in order to consider a release to be safe at a given level. If one such small count cell is not adequately protected according to the risk criteria we employ, we consider the entire release to be problematic.

DEFINITION 5.3 *The marginal $\mathbf{n}_{C_1}$ is said to be more problematic than the marginal $\mathbf{n}_{C_2}$ if the critical width of $\mathbf{n}_{C_1}$ is smaller than the critical width of $\mathbf{n}_{C_2}$.*

We calculated the critical widths for all the marginals of the 16-dimensional table. The critical widths corresponding to the one-dimensional marginals of a table are equal by definition since they are all calculated based on the same model–complete independence of the variables in that table. Typically agencies attempt to release at least the one-dimensional marginal corresponding to each variable.

In our case, the critical width associated with the one-dimensional marginals is large, i.e., $2,285$. On the other hand, all the 8-dimensional marginals have a critical width of 1. Hence, by releasing only one eight-way sub-table after releasing all the one-way sub-tables, at least one small count cell will be made public. The critical widths for the marginals of dimension $2, 3, \ldots, 7$ are given in Figure 5.2. As the dimension of released sub-tables increases, the critical widths decrease, tend to be less scattered and gradually cluster around 1.

The most problematic two-way table is, by far, $[7, 8]$ with a critical width of 8. One obvious reason why this marginal is so problematic is the count of 8 in cell $(1, 0)$ which is very small compared with the other three counts in this marginal. This count corresponds to respondents who could not do IADL *light house work*,

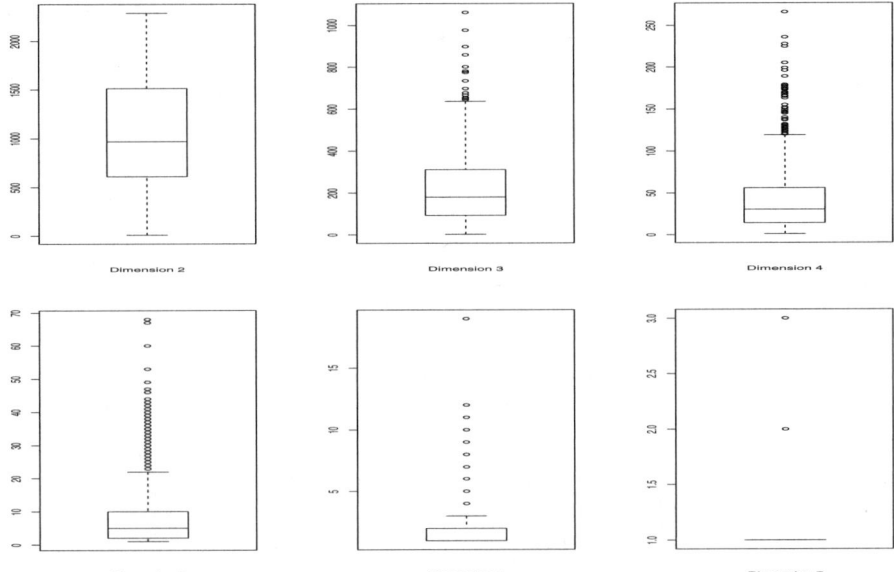

FIGURE 5.2
Boxplots with critical widths associated with marginals of dimension $2, 3, \ldots, 7$.

but were able to do IADL *heavy house work*. The next most problematic two-way marginal is $[1, 7]$ with a critical width of 64, while the third most problematic two-way sub-table is $[5, 1]$ with a critical width of 82. The most problematic three-way marginals are $[7, 8, 12]$, $[7, 8, 10]$ and $[1, 7, 8]$, all with a critical width of 3. We note that $[7, 8]$ is a child of these three marginals. We also note that the decomposable frontiers of Section 1.4.2 do not contain these most problematic three-way marginals. The most problematic four-way marginals have a critical width of 1. Variables 8, 7 and 1 appear in most of the 36 four-way marginals having this critical width. Other variables, such as 16, 12 and 11, also have a significant presence in these marginals.

To choose a release, we construct a list, $\mathscr{L}$, which contains the marginals in decreasing order with respect to their critical widths. Therefore the least problematic marginals will appear at the top of this list, while the most problematic marginals will be placed at the end. According to our definition, two marginals are "equally problematic" if they have the same critical width. However, to maximize the amount of released information, we might prefer to release, if possible, a higher dimensional marginal instead of a lower dimensional marginal if both marginals have the same critical widths. Consequently, we re-order the marginals in $\mathscr{L}$ having a certain fixed critical width in decreasing order with respect to their dimension.

More explicitly, let $\mathbf{n}_{C_1}$ and $\mathbf{n}_{C_2}$ be two marginals with dimensions k_1, k_2 and with critical widths w_1 and w_2. Denote by l_1 and l_2 the ranks of $\mathbf{n}_{C_1}$ and $\mathbf{n}_{C_2}$ in the list $\mathscr{L}$. If $w_1 > w_2$, then $l_1 < l_2$. However, if $w_1 = w_2$ and $k_1 > k_2$, then we also require that $l_1 < l_2$.

Dimension	Released Marginals	Total Number of Marginals	Percent
1	0	16	0%
2	0	120	0%
3	0	560	0%
4	263	1,820	14.45%
5	1,311	4,368	30.01%
6	103	8,008	3.78%

TABLE 5.4
Non-decomposable frontier obtained from the greedy procedure for $\beta = 3$. The total number of sub-tables in this frontier is $1,677$.

Dimension	Released Marginals	Total Number of Marginals	Percent
1	16	16	100%
2	120	120	100%
3	547	560	97.68%
4	1,566	1,820	86.04%
5	1,659	4,368	37.98%
6	103	8,008	3.78%

TABLE 5.5
Breakdown of the released set of sub-tables corresponding to the frontier in Table 5.4. Compare with the released set corresponding with the decomposable frontier $\mathscr{RF}(\beta = 3)$; see Table 5.1. The total number of released sub-tables is $4,011$.

Let $\mathbf{n}_1, \mathbf{n}_2, \ldots, \mathbf{n}_L$ be the marginals of $\mathbf{n}$ in the order in which they appear in $\mathscr{L}$. We want to identify the unique rank $l_0 \in \{1, 2, \ldots, L\}$ such that the set of marginals $\{\mathbf{n}_1, \ldots, \mathbf{n}_{l_0}\}$ is releasable according to our risk criteria, but $\{\mathbf{n}_1, \ldots, \mathbf{n}_{l_0}, \mathbf{n}_{l_0+1}\}$ is not. Instead of sequentially adding new marginals starting from the top of list $\mathscr{L}$, we determine l_0 by employing a much more efficient bisection search strategy.

We used this greedy algorithm to determine a releasable set of marginals for the 16-dimensional table for thresholds 3, 4 and 5. These releases are summarized below. We note that the releases obtained from the greedy algorithm contain 10 times more marginals than the decomposable releases resulting from the simulated annealing search described in Section 5.4. Therefore, when the decomposability constraint is dropped, the resulting set of possible releases is much richer. The fact that a non-decomposable frontier is 10 times larger than a decomposable frontier that satisfies the same constraints tells us that decomposability is a very restrictive constraint.

The released marginals for these three thresholds have dimension six or smaller. For thresholds 4 and 5, only one two-way marginal, $[7, 8]$, is not released. This marginal is contained in the greedy frontier for threshold 3. From the summaries presented in tables below we learn that, if we were considering the data in this table to be the entire population rather than a sample, almost all the three-way marginals would be releasable.

We can modify the greedy algorithm so that the hierarchical frontier identified includes the MSSs of well fitting log-linear models, provided that these MSSs are

Dimension	Released Marginals	Total Number of Marginals	Percent
1	0	16	0%
2	0	120	0%
3	0	560	0%
4	338	1,820	18.57%
5	1,176	4,368	26.92%
6	55	8,008	0.69%

TABLE 5.6
Frontier obtained from the greedy procedure for $\beta = 4$. The total number of sub-tables in this frontier is $1,569$.

Dimension	Released Marginals	Total Number of Marginals	Percent
1	16	16	100%
2	119	120	99.17%
3	546	560	97.5%
4	1,531	1,820	84.12%
5	1,396	4,368	31.96%
6	55	8,008	0.69%

TABLE 5.7
Breakdown of the released set of sub-tables corresponding to the frontier in Table 5.6. Compare with the released set corresponding with the decomposable frontier $\mathscr{RF}(\beta = 4)$; see Table 5.2. The total number of released sub-tables is $3,663$.

Dimension	Released Marginals	Total Number of Marginals	Percent
1	0	16	0%
2	0	120	0%
3	5	560	0.89%
4	405	1,820	22.25%
5	1,110	4,368	25.41%
6	17	8,008	0.21%

TABLE 5.8
Frontier obtained from the greedy procedure for $\beta = 5$. The total number of sub-tables in this frontier is $1,537$.

Dimension	Released Marginals	Total Number of Marginals	Percent
1	16	16	100%
2	119	120	99.17%
3	545	560	97.32%
4	1,480	1,820	81.32%
5	1,189	4,368	27.22%
6	17	8,008	0.21%

TABLE 5.9
Breakdown of the released set of sub-tables corresponding to the frontier in Table 5.8. Compare with the released set corresponding with the decomposable frontier $\mathscr{RF}(\beta = 5)$; see Table 5.3. The total number of released sub-tables is $3,366$.

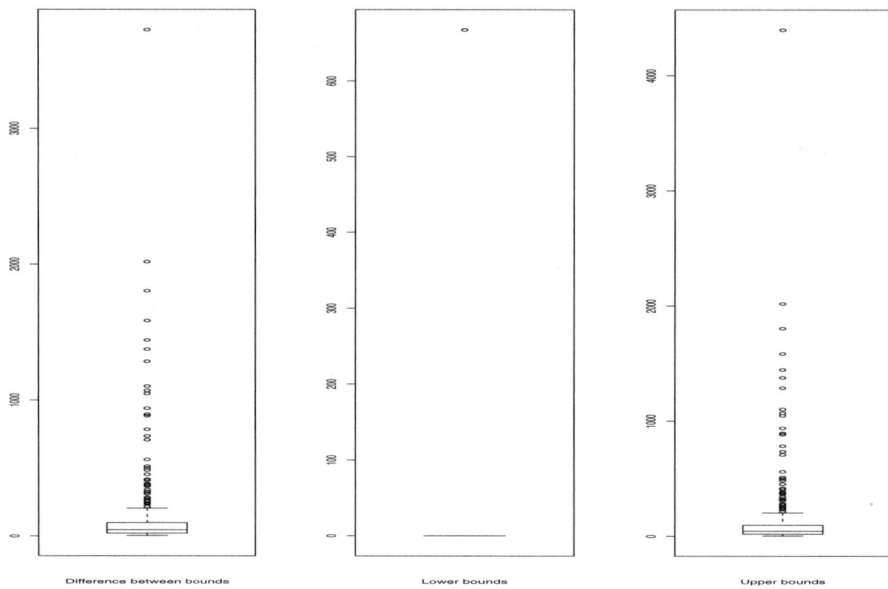

FIGURE 5.3
Boxplots with the bounds for the non-zero cells determined by the frontier $\mathscr{RF}(\beta = 3)$.

simultaneously releasable according to the risk criteria employed. It is sufficient to put the MSSs at the top of the list $\mathscr{L}$, followed by the rest of the marginals in decreasing order of their critical widths. This straightforward approach maximizes the utility of a release from the point of users trying to model the data in the full cross-classification.

5.6 Bounds

In this section, we provide details on the bounds determined by the decomposable and greedy frontiers associated with a threshold equal to "3."

5.6.1 Bounds in the Decomposable Case

We calculated the bounds corresponding to the frontier $\mathscr{RF}(\beta = 3)$ by employing the formulas described in Dobra and Fienberg (2002); see Figure 5.3.

The upper bounds are strictly bigger than the lower bounds for all the cells in the table. The sum of the differences between the upper and lower bounds for the non-zero cells is 345,534. All the cells but one have lower bounds equal to 0. The only cell with a non-zero lower bound is the $(0,0,\ldots,0)$ cell in the table, and this lower bound is equal to 667. This cell contains the largest count in the table and consequently has the largest upper bound and the largest difference between the bounds.

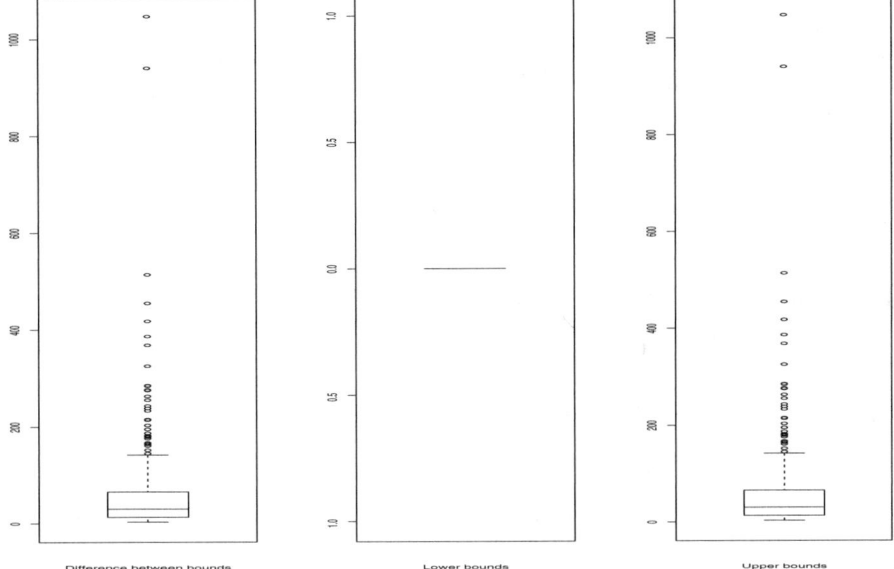

FIGURE 5.4
Boxplots with the bounds for the cells having a count of 1 determined by the frontier $\mathcal{RF}(\beta = 3)$.

The minimum value for the upper bounds is 3 and is attained for 11 cells. There are 36 cells with an upper bound of 4, 27 cells with an upper bound of 5 and 55 cells with an upper bound of 6. All the corresponding lower bounds are 0.

In Figure 5.4 and Figure 5.5 we give the bounds associated with the small count cells of 1 and 2, respectively. All the lower bounds for these cells are zero.

5.6.2 Bounds in the Non-decomposable Case

By employing the generalized shuttle algorithm, we calculated the bounds associated with the greedy frontier from Table 5.4; see Figure 5.6.

A number of the 24,148 cells containing non-zero counts have the upper bounds equal to the lower bounds. However, for the cells having a count of 1, the minimum difference between the bounds is 3 (there are 14 cells for which this minimum is attained), while the minimum difference between the bounds for the cells having a count of 2 is 4 (only two cells have this property).

The sum of the differences between the upper and lower bounds for the non-zero cells is 249,759, hence the bounds are tighter than the bounds for the decomposable frontier $\mathcal{RF}(\beta = 3)$. Moreover, 22 non-zero cells have lower bounds greater or equal to 1. Again, the first cell in the table has the largest lower bound, the largest upper bound and the largest difference between the bounds.

The lower bounds for the small count cells of 1 or 2 are all zero; see Figure 5.7 and Figure 5.8.

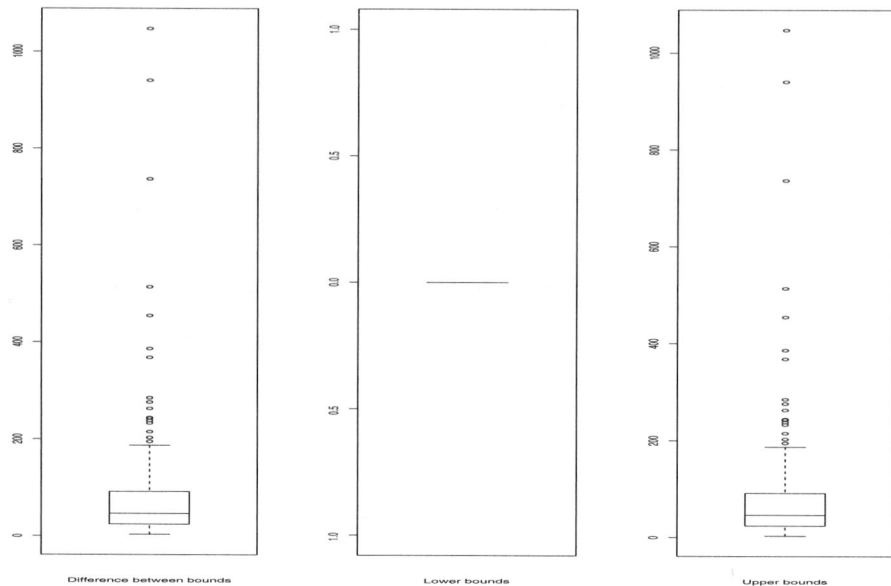

FIGURE 5.5
Boxplots with the bounds for the cells having a count of 2 determined by the frontier $\mathscr{RF}(\beta = 3)$.

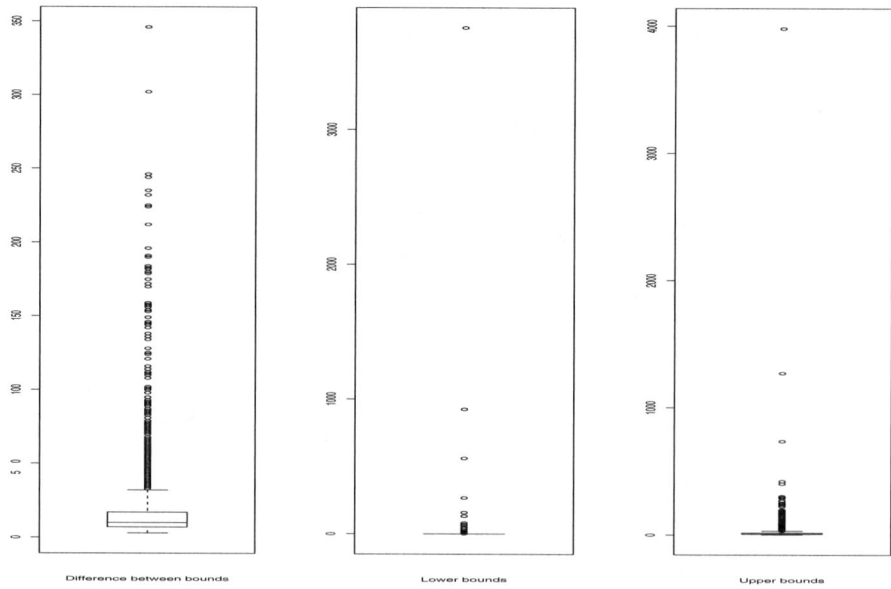

FIGURE 5.6
Boxplots with the bounds for the non-zero cells determined by the frontier from Table 5.4.

Statistical Data Mining and Knowledge Discovery 111

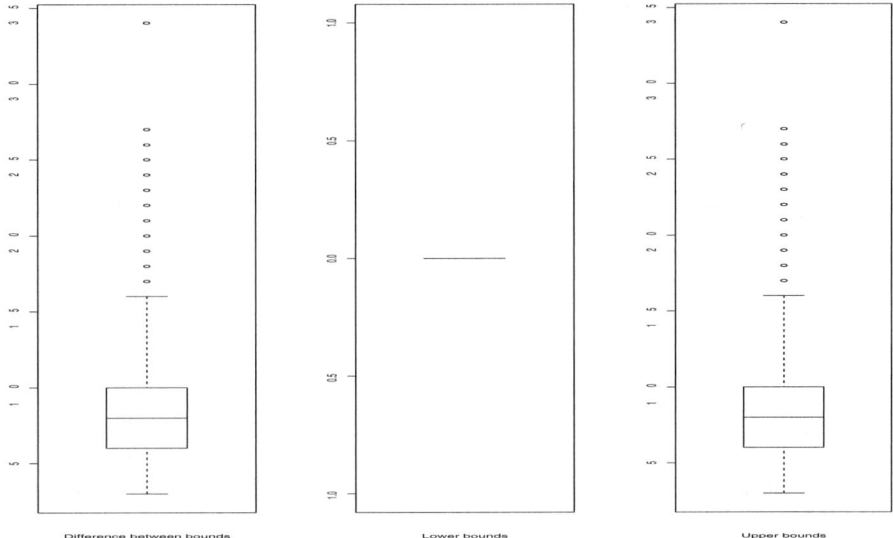

FIGURE 5.7
Boxplots with the bounds for the cells having a count of 1 determined by the frontier from Table 5.4.

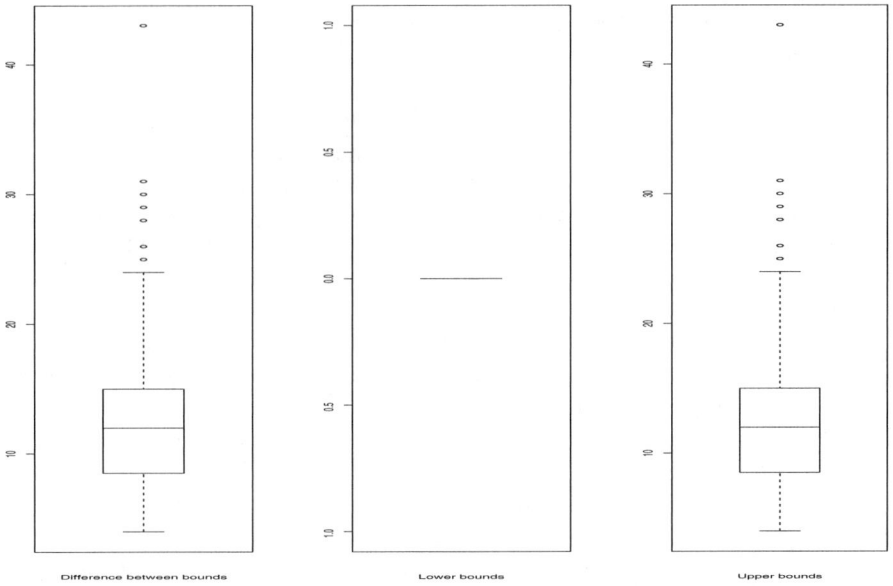

FIGURE 5.8
Boxplots with the bounds for the cells having a count of 2 determined by the frontier from Table 5.4.

Group 1	Variable	1	7					
	Disclosure Score	1.82	1.88					
Group 2	Variable	16	8	11	4	10	9	5	2
	Disclosure Score	2.84	2.91	3.01	3.15	3.17	3.23	3.24	3.26
Group 3	Variable	6	3	12	14	15	13	
	Disclosure Score	3.37	3.39	3.52	3.66	3.74	3.85	

TABLE 5.10
Assessing how problematic every variable in the NLTCS dataset is using disclosure scores.

5.7 Discussion

In this paper we presented two methods for determining a releasable frontier. The first method that computes a decomposable frontier is fast and will work for arbitrarily large tables with any number of dimensions and with millions of cells. The scalability of this approach relates to the fact that it is based on computing bounds based on *formulas* whose usage involve little or no computational effort. The only drawback of using this method is that the decomposability can be a serious constraint in many situations: in our example, the size of the frontiers generated by the two methods differed by an order of magnitude.

The second method relaxes this assumption and computes a hierarchical frontier that could have any structure. The first step in applying this method is calculating the critical widths associated with each marginal and this calculation also scales to arbitrary multi-way tables since it is based on the same formulas for computing the bounds. The critical widths have another immediate use: it provides us with a consistent way of ranking variables with respect to how problematic they are for disclosure. As we mentioned before, as the critical width of a marginal gets larger, that marginal tends to tighten the bounds less. Therefore, one would expect that the "less problematic" variables will be contained in marginals with larger critical widths.

We define the *disclosure score* associated with each variable cross-classified in the target table to be the *mean* of the critical widths for all the marginals in which that variable belongs; see Table 5.10. In our running example, each variable belongs to 32,767 marginals. We ordered the variables in increasing order with respect to their scores. An increase in the score corresponding with a sequence of variables indicates that the variables in that sequence make the bounds less and less tight; therefore those variables become less and less "problematic." In Table 5.10 we grouped the 16 variables in three groups defined by the disclosure scores: Group 1– very problematic variables; Group 2–problematic variables; Group 3–slightly problematic variables. Group 1 contains two variables, 1 (ADL *eating*) and 7 (IADL *doing heavy house work*), which appear to be significantly more "problematic" than the other variables. It seems important to emphasize that this is not in contradiction with our previous findings which identified [8, 7] to be the most problematic combination of two variables for disclosure limitation purposes: combinations of several variables have properties different than the properties of each variable taken by itself. Group 2 contains a combination of ADL and IADL variables. The least problematic variables are four IADL variables and ADLs 3 (*getting around inside*) and 6 (*getting to the bathroom or using a toilet*). Based on disclosure scores, other ADL variables appear to be quite "problematic," with the most problematic ADL *eating*. The IADL variables appear to be divided into two groups: with more "problematic" variables number 7 (*doing heavy house work*), 16 (*telephoning*), 8 (*doing light house work*), and 11 (*grocery shopping*), and less problematic variables number 12 (*getting about outside*), 14 (*managing money*), 15 (*taking medicine*), and 13 (*traveling*).

While there is a natural gap in disclosure scores between groups 1 and 2, groups 2 and 3 are less separate. In fact, the difference in scores between variables 2 and 6 is smaller than that between variables 3 and 12. If we were to place variables 3 and 6 into group 2, then it would contain all of the ADL variables except for variable 1 along with some IADL variables. The methods we have applied are most directly appropriate when the table of counts presents population data. It is worth remembering that the data in this example come from a sample survey where the sampling fraction is relatively small, and thus the release of the entire table might well be deemed safe by most disclosure limitation standards.

Finally, address the potential utility of marginal tables released using methodology illustrated in this paper. Users would like to be able to perform statistical analyses on and draw the same inferences from the released marginals as they would were they in the possession of the complete dataset. In principle, it is straightforward to assure the consistency of inferences by making sure that the relevant marginals involved in log-linear models that fit the data well were released. But in the present example, there is no unsaturated log-linear model that fits the data well, and alternative models such as the grade of membership model discussed by Erosheva [17, 18] seem much more appropriate. These alternative models do a far better job of fitting the very large cells in the table, e.g., the cell corresponding to those with no disabilities, and thus these cells may need to be part of any release, along with a set of marginals. This is an issue we hope to pursue in future research.

Acknowledgments

The preparation of this paper was supported in part by Grant No. 1R03 AG18986-01, from the National Institute on Aging to Carnegie-Mellon University and by National Science Foundation Grant No. EIA-9876619 to the National Institute of Statistical Sciences.

References

[1] Bishop, Y. M. M., Fienberg, S. E., and Holland, P. W. *Discrete Multivariate Analysis: Theory and Practice.* M.I.T. Press, Cambridge, MA, 1975.

[2] Bonferroni, C. E. *Teoria statistica delle classi e calcolo delle probabilitá.* Publicazioni del R. Instituto Superiore di Scienze Economiche e Commerciali di Firenze, **8**, 1936.

[3] Buzzigoli, L. and Giusti, A. An Algorithm to Calculate the Lower and Upper Bounds of the Elements of an Array Given its Marginals. In *Statistical Data Protection (SDP'98) Proceedings*, pages 131–147, Eurostat, Luxembourg, 1999.

[4] Chen, G. and Keller-McNulty, S. Estimation of Identification Disclosure Risk in Microdata, *Journal of Official Statistics* **14**: 79–95, 1998.

[5] Cox, L. H. Some Remarks on Research Directions in Statistical Data Protection. In *Statistical Data Protection (SDP'98) Proceedings*, pages 163–176, Eurostat, Luxembourg, 1999.

[6] Deshpande, A., Garofalakis, M. and Jordan, M. Efficient Stepwise Selection in Decomposable Models. In J. Breese and D. Koller (Ed)., *Uncertainty in Artificial Intelligence, Proceedings of the Seventeenth Conference*, 2001.

[7] Dobra, A. Computing Sharp Integer Bounds for Entries in Contingency Tables Given a Set of Fixed Marginals. Tech. Rep., Department of Statistics, Carnegie Mellon University, 2000.

[8] Dobra, A. Measuring the Disclosure Risk for Multi-way Tables with Fixed Marginals Corresponding to Decomposable Log-linear Models. Tech. Rep., Department of Statistics, Carnegie Mellon University, 2000.

[9] Dobra, A. and Fienberg, S. E. Bounds for Cell Entries in Contingency Tables Given Marginal Totals and Decomposable Graphs. *Proceedings of the National Academy of Sciences*, **97**: 11885–11892, 2000.

[10] Dobra, A. and Fienberg, S. E. Bounds for Cell Entries in Contingency Tables Induced by Fixed Marginal Totals with Applications to Disclosure Limitation. *Statistical Journal of the United Nations ECE*, **18**: 363–371, 2001.

[11] Dobra, A. and Fienberg, S.E. (2002). Bounding Entries in Multi-way Contingency Tables Given a Set of Marginal Totals. *Proceedings of Conference on Foundation of Statistical Inference and Its Applications Jerusalem, Israel*, R. Lerch, (ed.), Springer-Verlag, Heidelberg, to appear, 2002.

[12] Dobra, A., Karr, A. F., Sanil, A. P., and Fienberg, S. E. Software Systems for Tabular Data Releases. *International Journal on Uncertainty, Fuzziness and Knowledge-Based Systems*, in press (2002).

[13] Doyle, P., Lane, J., Theeuwes, J., and Zayatz, L. (eds.) *Confidentiality, Disclosure and Data Access: Theory and Practical Applications for Statistical Agencies*. Elsevier, Amsterdam, 2001.

[14] Duncan, G. T. and Fienberg, S. E. Obtaining Information While Preserving Privacy: a Markov Perturbation Method for Tabular Data. In *Statistical Data Protection (SDP'98) Proceedings*, pages 351–362, Eurostat, Luxembourg, 1999.

[15] Duncan, G. T., Jabine, T. B., and Wolf, V. A. de (Eds.). *Private Lives and Public Policies: Confidentiality and Accessibility of Government Statistics*. National Academy Press, Washington, DC, 1993.

[16] Edwards, D. E. and Havranek, T. A Fast Procedure for Model Search in Multidimensional Contingency Tables. *Biometrika*, **72**: 339–351, 1985

[17] Erosheva, E. Grade of Membership and Latent Structure Models with Application to Disability Survey Data. Department of Statistics, Carnegie Mellon University, Ph.D. Dissertation, 2002.

[18] Erosheva, E. Partial Membership Models with Application to Disability Survey Data. In *Statistical Data Mining and Knowledge Discovery*, Bozdogan, H. (ed.), Chapman and Hall/CRC Press, Boca Raton, FL, Chapter 6, 2004.

[19] Erosheva, E. A., Fienberg, S. E. and Junker, B. W. Alternative Statistical Models and Representations for Large Sparse Multi-dimensional Contingency Tables. *Annales de la Faculté des Sciences de l'Université de Toulouse Mathématiques*, **11**, in press, 2002.

[20] Fienberg, S. E. Conflicts Between the Needs for Access to Statistical Information and Demands for Confidentiality. *Journal of Official Statistics*, **10**, pages 115–132, 1994.

[21] Fienberg, S. E. Fréchet and Bonferroni Bounds for Multi-way Tables of Counts with Applications to Disclosure Limitation. In *Statistical Data Protection (SDP'98) Proceedings*, pages 115–129, Eurostat, Luxembourg, 1999.

[22] Fienberg, S. E. and Makov, U. E. Confidentiality, Uniqueness and Disclosure Limitation for Categorical Data. *Journal of Official Statistics*, **14**: 485–502, 1998.

[23] Fienberg, S. E. and Makov, U. E. Uniqueness and Disclosure Risk: Urn Models and Simulation. *Research in Official Statistics* **4**: 23–40, 2001.

[24] Fienberg, S. E., Makov, U. E., Meyer, M. M., and Steele, R. J. Computing the Exact Distribution for a Multi-way Contingency Table Conditional on its Marginals Totals. In *Data Analysis from Statistical Foundations: Papers in Honor of D. A. S. Fraser*, A. K. Md. E. Saleh (ed.), Nova Science Publishing, Huntington, NY, pages 145–177, 2001.

[25] Fienberg, S. E., Makov, U. E., and Steele, R. J. Disclosure Limitation Using Perturbation and Related Methods for Categorical Data. *Journal of Official Statistics*, **14**, pages 485–502, 1998.

[26] Fréchet, M. *Les Probabilitiés, Associées a un Système d'Evénments Compatibles et Dépendants. Premiere Partie.* Hermann & Cie, Paris, 1940.

[27] Hoeffding, W. Scale-invariant Correlation Theory. Schriften des Mathematischen Instituts und des Instituts für Angewandte Mathematik der Universität Berlin, **5**(3), pages 181–233, 1940.

[28] Joe, H. *Multivariate Models and Dependence Concepts.* Chapman & Hall, New York, 1997.

[29] Katz, A., Ford, A. B., Moskowitz, R. W., Jackson, B. A., and Jaffe, M. W. Studies of Illness in the Aged. The Index of ADL: A Standardized Measure of Biological and Psychosocial Function. *Journal of the American Medical Association*, **185**, 914–919, 1963.

[30] Keller-McNulty, S. and Unger, E. A. A Database System Prototype for Remote Access to Information Based on Confidential Data. *Journal of Official Statistics*, **14**: 347–360, 1998.

[31] Lauritzen, S. L. *Graphical Models.* Clarendon Press, Oxford, 1996.

[32] Leimer, H. G. Optimal Decomposition by Clique Separators. *Discrete Mathematics*, **113**: 99–123, 1993.

[33] Manton, K. G., Woodbury, M. A. and Tolley, H. D. *Statistical Applications Using Fuzzy Sets.* Wiley, New York, 1994.

[34] Roehrig, S. F., Padman, R., Duncan, G. T., and Krishnan, R. Disclosure Detection in Multiple Linked Categorical Datafiles: A Unified Network Approach. In *Statistical Data Protection (SDP'98) Proceedings*, pages 149–162, Eurostat, Luxembourg, 1999.

[35] Samuels, S. M. A Bayesian, Species-sampling-inspired Approach to the Uniques Problem in Microdata Disclosure Risk Assessment. *Journal of Official Statistics*, **14**: 373–383, 1998.

[36] Skinner, C. J. and Holmes, D. J. Estimating the Re-identification Risk Per Record in Microdata. *Journal of Official Statistics*, **14**: 373–383, 1998.

[37] Willenborg, L. and de Waal, T. *Statistical Disclosure Control in Practice.* Lecture Notes in Statistics, Vol. **111**, Springer-Verlag, New York, 1996.

[38] Willenborg, L. and de Waal, T. *Elements of Statistical Disclosure Control.* Lecture Notes in Statistics, Vol. **155**, Springer-Verlag, New York, 2000.

6

Partial Membership Models with Application to Disability Survey Data

Elena A. Erosheva
University of Washington, USA

CONTENTS

6.1	Motivation	118
6.2	Functional Disability Data	119
6.3	Full Versus Partial Membership	123
6.4	Bayesian Estimation of the GoM Model	125
6.5	Analysis and Comparison	127
6.6	Concluding Remarks	131
	References	133

This paper draws on the ideas of full versus partial membership in statistical modelling. We focus on the particular form of the latter, the Grade of Membership (GoM) model, which was developed in the 1970s in the context of medical diagnosis. Other examples of partial membership models include Probabilistic Latent Semantic Analysis and the Latent Dirichlet Allocation model, developed in machine learning; and a genetics clustering model for multilocus genotype data. All these models represent individuals as having partial membership in several subpopulations.

Latent class models provide an example of full membership structure. The GoM model is related to traditional latent class models, but it employs the concept of partial rather than full membership. We illustrate a special case of 2-profile GoM model on a subset of disability data from the National Long Term Care Survey. We use a Bayesian framework for estimation of the GoM model parameters, and compare the results to those of the 2-class latent class model. In the final section, we discuss the broader class of partial membership models.

This work was completed as a part of the author's dissertation research in the Department of Statistics, Carnegie Mellon University. It was supported in part by Grant No. 1R03 AG18986-01 from the National Institute on Aging to Carnegie Mellon University and by National Science Foundation Grant No. EIA-9876619 to the National Institute of Statistical Sciences. The author would like to thank her advisor, Stephen Fienberg, for his encouragement and helpful comments on earlier drafts of this paper.

6.1 Motivation

Consider a setting where several characteristics are observed for a number of objects. The objects represent a random sample from a population of interest. For example, we may consider a sample of news broadcast segments. Words in the script are then the observed characteristics of each segment. Whether the goal is to make inference regarding the set of main topics of news broadcasts or to determine how a particular news segment relates to the main topics, traditional hard classification approaches may not be fully descriptive for the following reason. Given a reasonably small number of topics, a news segment may not belong as a whole to any of the topics, because it may combine different topics to some extent: for example, one-third of a news segment might be covering politics, and two-thirds might be covering education.

For an example of partial membership structure in genetics, consider a random sample of individuals from a population of interest. Suppose we record genotypes of the sampled individuals at a selected number of loci. Depending whether an individual has ancestors from one or from several of the basis subpopulations, we regard the individual as a full or a partial member in the subpopulations, respectively. Thus, an individual may have a mixed or partial membership if his ancestry is shared among several subpopulations.

An analogous partial membership structure may exhibit itself at the social level. For example, consider a survey with questions about *Internet addiction*. Choices of the answers may reveal at least two basic categories of individuals: those who consider themselves Internet addicted and those who do not. However, it is clear that there is a great number of people who do not fall neatly under these two categories but may be described as being somewhere in-between.

The Grade of Membership (GoM) model [14] is an attempt to account for soft classification structure. The GoM model was developed by Max Woodbury in the 1970s as a multivariate statistical technique for medical classification [20, 4]. It is also known as a "fuzzy sets" model because every individual is assumed to be a partial member of several extreme classes simultaneously [14]. GoM applications now cover a wide spectrum of studies, including research on disability in the elderly [1, 15, 13].

Recently, new statistical models have been published in genetics and in machine learning that build on the soft classification structure and are remarkably similar to the GoM model. For example, Pritchard, Stephens, and Donnelly [17] developed a clustering model with admixture for applications to multilocus genotype data. In machine learning, Hofmann's Probabilistic Latent Semantic Analysis [12] and Blei, Ng, and Jordan's Latent Dirichlet Allocation models [3], similar to different variations of the GoM model, are used to study the composition of text documents.

Current estimation methods for different versions of the GoM model are maximum-likelihood based [14, 16]. In this paper, we estimate the GoM model parameters within a Bayesian framework. We illustrate the special case of 2-profile GoM model with an analysis of disability survey data. Because traditional latent class models are based on the concept of full membership, where each individual is considered to be a complete member of one of the latent classes, it is of interest to compare the GoM and latent class models with the same number of basis subpopulations.

In Section 2, we motivate our interest in partial membership structure with an exploration of a 16-way contingency table that contains data on disability in elderly people from the National Long Term Care Survey [5]. In Section 3, we formalize ideas of full and partial membership on the example of latent class and GoM models. We provide a latent class representation of the GoM model, which is the basis of our Bayesian approach, in Section 4. In Section 5 we describe results of the GoM and latent class analyses, and compare the performance of the two models. We discuss general class of partial membership models in Section 6.

6.2 Functional Disability Data

The National Long Term Care Survey (NLTCS), conducted in 1982, 1984, 1989, 1994, and 1999, was designed to assess chronic disability in the U.S. elderly Medicare-enrolled population [5]. The survey aims to provide data on the extent and patterns of functional limitations (as measured by activities of daily living (ADL) and instrumental activities of daily living (IADL)), availability and details of informal caregiving, use of institutional care facilities, and death. We focus on the subset of 16 functional disability variables, extracted from the *analytic* file. The analytic file of the survey data includes various correction factors and consistency checking conducted by the Center for Demographic Studies, Duke University.

The subset consists of dichotomous responses to 6 ADL and 10 IADL measures. Specifically, the ADLs are (1) *eating*, (2) *getting in/out of bed*, (3) *getting around inside*, (4) *dressing*, (5) *bathing*, (6) *getting to the bathroom or using toilet*. The IADLs are (7) *doing heavy house work*, (8) *doing light house work*, (9) *doing laundry*, (10) *cooking*, (11) *grocery shopping*, (12) *getting about outside*, (13) *traveling*, (14) *managing money*, (15) *taking medicine*, (16) *telephoning*. For every ADL/IADL measure, individuals were classified as being either disabled or healthy on that measure.

We use pooled data on 16 ADL/IADL measures from the 1982, 1984, 1989, and 1994 NLTCS waves. Given that the difference in times between any two consecutive waves is at least two years, and that we expect substantial within-individual variability, analysis of the pooled data provides informative findings about the overall structure of disability among the elderly.

Our interest in examining the disability data focuses on conceptual differences between partial and full membership modeling. We use Bayesian framework for parameter estimation of the GoM and latent class models. We compare the fit of the models by examining expected values for frequent response patterns. We also discuss how the full and partial membership models account for heterogeneity in individual responses. For a more in depth discussion of the Bayesian estimation approach for the GoM model, see Erosheva [9].

	ADL/IADL measure	frequency
1	eating	0.106
2	getting in/out of bed	0.276
3	getting around inside	0.403
4	dressing	0.208
5	bathing	0.439
6	getting to the bathroom or using toilet	0.248
7	doing heavy house work	0.676
8	doing light house work	0.217
9	doing laundry	0.355
10	cooking	0.259
11	grocery shopping	0.486
12	getting about outside	0.555
13	traveling	0.493
14	managing money	0.229
15	taking medicine	0.211
16	telephoning	0.146

TABLE 6.1
Marginal frequencies of 16 measures from NLTCS.

6.2.1 Marginal Frequencies and Simple Statistics

Table 6.1 contains marginal frequencies for 16 ADL/IADL measures, pooled across four survey waves, which range from 0.106 for *eating* to 0.676 for *doing heavy house work*.

To give a rough idea about the distribution of counts in the 2^{16} contingency table, consider the following characteristics. The total sample size is 21,574. Out of all possible $2^{16} = 65,536$ combinations of response patterns, 3,152 occurred in the NLTCS sample. Thus, the average number of observed responses per combination is $21574/3152 = 6.84$. Roughly 82% of the counts are less than 5, 9% of the counts are 5 to 9, 5% are from 10 to 19, and 4% are 20 and above. Out of all observed combinations, 55% occurred only once. Observed counts of 1 in contingency tables may lead to confidentiality concerns, if the individual with a unique response in the sample is also unique in the population. Dobra, Erosheva, and Fienberg [7] discuss the problem on maintaining confidentiality and apply disclosure limitation methods to the 16-way disability data.

6.2.2 Frequent Responses

There are 24 response patterns in the data with observed counts greater than 100, and they account for 42% of observations.

As can be seen from Table 6.2, these patterns are of two general types. The first type includes the first 18 rows in the table. These are relatively healthy people with at most four disabilities among the mobility IADLs (*traveling, getting about outside,*

Statistical Data Mining and Knowledge Discovery

	response pattern	count
1	0 0 0 0 0 0 0 0 0 0 0 0 0 0 0 0	3853
2	0 0 0 0 1 0 0 0 0 0 0 0 0 0 0 0	216
3	0 0 0 0 0 0 1 0 0 0 0 0 0 0 0 0	1107
4	0 0 0 0 1 0 1 0 0 0 0 0 0 0 0 0	188
5	0 0 0 0 0 0 1 0 0 0 1 0 0 0 0 0	122
6	0 0 0 0 0 0 0 0 0 0 0 1 0 0 0 0	351
7	0 0 1 0 0 0 0 0 0 0 0 1 0 0 0 0	206
8	0 0 0 0 0 0 1 0 0 0 0 1 0 0 0 0	303
9	0 0 1 0 0 0 1 0 0 0 0 1 0 0 0 0	182
10	0 0 0 0 1 0 1 0 0 0 0 1 0 0 0 0	108
11	0 0 1 0 1 0 1 0 0 0 0 1 0 0 0 0	106
12	0 0 0 0 0 0 0 0 0 0 0 0 1 0 0 0	195
13	0 0 0 0 0 0 1 0 0 0 0 0 1 0 0 0	198
14	0 0 0 0 0 0 1 0 0 0 1 0 1 0 0 0	196
15	0 0 0 0 0 0 1 0 0 0 0 1 1 0 0 0	123
16	0 0 0 0 0 0 1 0 0 0 1 1 1 0 0 0	176
17	0 0 1 0 0 0 1 0 0 0 1 1 1 0 0 0	120
18	0 0 0 0 1 0 1 0 0 0 1 1 1 0 0 0	101
19	0 1 1 1 1 1 1 1 1 1 1 1 1 0 0 0	102
20	1 1 1 1 1 1 1 1 1 1 1 1 1 0 1 0	107
21	0 1 1 1 1 1 1 1 1 1 1 1 1 1 1 0	104
22	1 1 1 1 1 1 1 1 1 1 1 1 1 1 1 0	164
23	0 1 1 1 1 1 1 1 1 1 1 1 1 1 1 1	153
24	1 1 1 1 1 1 1 1 1 1 1 1 1 1 1 1	660

TABLE 6.2
Cell counts for the most frequent observed responses.

grocery shopping) and at most one disability among ADLs (either *bathing* or *getting around inside*). The observed cell counts from the first 18 patterns add up to 7,851, which is 36% of all observed responses. The cell that corresponds to no disabilities on the 16 ADL/IADL measures had the largest observed count of 3,853.

The last six rows in Table 6.2 correspond to the second general type. These are relatively disabled people who are able to perform independently only up to three cognitive IADLs (*managing money, telephoning, taking medicine*) and possibly ADL *eating*. For this type, the largest observed count is 660 for the all-one (disabled on all 16 measures) pattern. The last six patterns account for 1,290 observed responses, which is approximately 6% of the total.

6.2.3 Total Number of Disabilities

It is instructive to examine the distribution of the total number of disabilities per person, even though it gives a simplified, one-dimensional view on the complex distribution of counts in the 16-way table. The distribution of the total number of

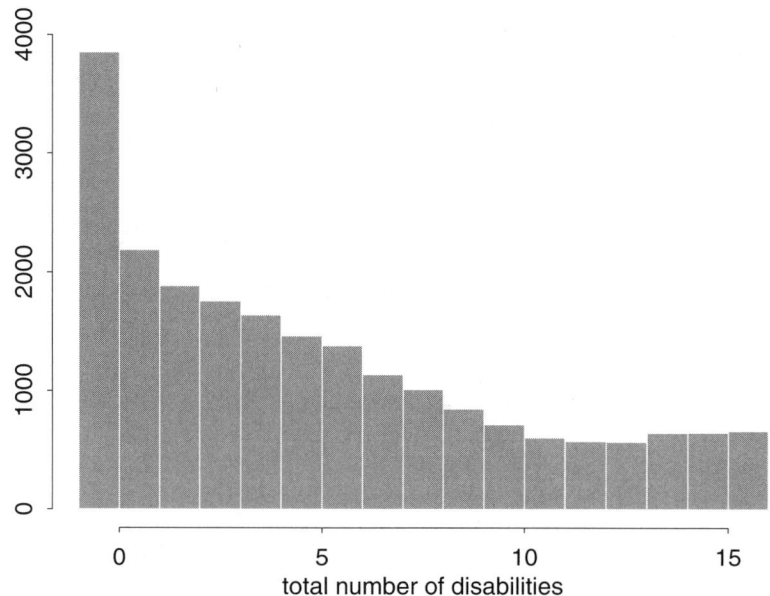

FIGURE 6.1
The number of observed response patterns by total number of disabilities.

disabilities per person, given in Figure 6.1, is consistent with earlier observations on the most frequent response patterns.

There are two modes. The first distinct peak happens at the observed count of zero with 3,853 responses. These are the healthy people with no disabilities. The next bar with the total of one observed disability is almost half the height of the bar for the healthy people. Note that only one cell, all-zero responses, contributes to the first bar, and 16 cells possibly contribute to the second bar. Despite the fact that the number of potential contributing cells rapidly increases up to the category of eight total disabilities, the empirical density steadily decreases up to the category with 13 total disabilities. The second, much less pronounced peak is observed at the all-one response pattern, with all 16 disabilities. From Figure 6.1, however, it cannot be concluded if there are other high probability density points in the multi-way table.

The exploratory data analysis presented in this section shows that there are two substantial 'clusters' in the data that can be labelled 'healthy' and 'disabled.' Representative response patterns from these 'clusters' are shown in Table 6.2 which contains the most frequent responses. The patterns in Table 6.2 account for as much as 50% of the observations.

Next, we describe latent class and the GoM models, which are based on the ideas of full membership in latent classes and partial membership in extreme profiles, respectively. We estimate parameters of these models by using a Bayesian framework.

We then focus on a 2-class and a 2-profile model for the ADL/IADL data extract from the National Long Term Care Survey, and compare the fitted values for the frequent response patterns. Often when latent class models are fitted, observed patterns are then classified on the basis of their posterior probabilities for each latent class. We examine the distribution of posterior probabilities for the latent class model in our example and compare it to the distribution of the partial membership parameters for the GoM model.

6.3 Full Versus Partial Membership

In this section we describe two examples on full membership and partial membership models, namely, latent class and GoM models. The general set-up assumes that discrete responses are recorded on J dichotomous items for N individuals. Here, we only consider dichotomous items, but both latent class and GoM models can deal with polytomous items as well. Let $x_i = (x_{i1}, x_{i2} \ldots, x_{iJ})$ denote a response pattern, where x_{ij} is a binary random variable indicating a response of the ith individual to the jth manifest (observable) variable, $i = 1, 2, \ldots, N$, $j = 1, 2, \ldots, J$.

6.3.1 Full Membership: Latent Class Model

To define a K-class latent class model, let $y_i = (y_{i1}, y_{i2}, \ldots, y_{iK})$ be a latent vector with components representing full membership of subject i in class k. That is, only one component of y_i equals one and the others are zero. The latent class probabilities are $\pi_k = Pr(y_{ik} = 1)$, where $\sum_{k=1}^{K} \pi_k = 1$; these parameters describe the proportions of the population that are members in each of the latent classes. Given the full membership in the kth latent class, $y_{ik} = 1$, denote the conditional probability of positive response on manifest variable j by

$$\mu_{kj} = \Pr(x_{ij} = 1 | y_{ik} = 1), \quad k = 1, 2, \ldots, K; \; j = 1, 2, \ldots, J. \quad (6.1)$$

The conditional probability of negative response on manifest variable j is then

$$\Pr(x_{ij} = 0 | y_{ik} = 1) = 1 - \mu_{kj}, \quad k = 1, 2, \ldots, K; \; j = 1, 2, \ldots, J. \quad (6.2)$$

To deal with multivariate observations, latent class model employs the local independence assumption: given the latent vector y, the manifest variables are assumed to be independent. The observed joint distribution of the manifest variables under the latent class model has the form of a mixture model:

$$f^{LCM}(l_1, l_2, \ldots, l_J) = \sum_{k=1}^{K} \pi_k \cdot \prod_{j=1}^{J} \mu_{kj}^{l_j} (1 - \mu_{kj})^{1-l_j}. \quad (6.3)$$

The marginal probability of observing response pattern $l = (l_1, l_2, \ldots, l_J)$ in equation (6.3) is the sum of the probabilities of observing l from each of the latent classes weighted by their relative sizes, π_k. The latent class model assumes that each person is a member of one and only one latent class out of K.

6.3.2 Partial Membership: GoM Model

Manton et al. provide a standard formulation of the K-profile GoM model [14]. Assume K extreme profiles exist in the population of interest. Each subject can then be characterized by a latent vector of membership (GoM) scores $g_i = (g_{i1}, g_{i2}, \ldots, g_{iK})$, one score for each extreme profile. The membership scores define "proportion" of individual's membership for each of the extreme profiles; they are non-negative and sum to unity over the extreme profiles for each subject:

$$\sum_k g_{ik} = 1, \ i = 1, 2, \ldots, N. \tag{6.4}$$

The extreme profiles are defined by their conditional probabilities of (positive) response for each observed categorical variable:

$$\lambda_{kj} = Pr(x_{ij} = 1 | g_{ik} = 1), \ k = 1, 2, \ldots, K, \ j = 1, \ldots, J. \tag{6.5}$$

The conditional response probability λ_{kj} is the probability of positive response to the question j for a complete member of extreme profile k. Similarly to latent class conditional probabilities of response, response probabilities of the extreme profiles are unknown. Additional assumptions needed to complete formulation of the GoM model [14] are the following: (1) conditional probability of response x_{ij} of individual i to question j, given the GoM scores, is

$$Pr(x_{ij}|g_i) = \sum_{k=1}^{K} g_{ik} \cdot \lambda_{kj}^{x_{ij}} (1 - \lambda_{kj})^{1-x_{ij}}; \tag{6.6}$$

(2) conditional on the values of GoM scores, responses x_{ij} are independent for different values of j; (3) responses x_{ij} are independent for different values of i; (4) the GoM scores g_{ik} are realizations of the components of a random vector with some distribution $D(\alpha)$, parameterized by vector α.

Assumption (1) postulates that individual response probabilities are convex combinations of response probabilities from K extreme profiles weighted by subject-specific membership scores. Assumption (2) is known as the local independence assumption in psychometrics. Assumption (3) corresponds to individuals being randomly sampled from a population. These first three assumptions are essential for the GoM model. Assumption (4), however, has an ambiguous status in the GoM model literature and it is not used in the GoM estimation procedure described by Manton et al. [14] nor is it implemented in the software package for the GoM model [6].

In this paper, we explicitly employ assumption (4) in Bayesian estimation framework for the GoM model. We assume the GoM scores follow a Dirichlet distribution with parameter vector $\alpha = (\alpha_1, \alpha_2, \ldots, \alpha_K)$. Under assumptions (1)-(4), integrating out the latent variables, we obtain the joint distribution of the manifest variables:

$$f^{GoM}(l_1, l_2, \ldots, l_J) = \int \prod_{j=1}^{J} \sum_{k=1}^{K} g_k \cdot \lambda_{kj}^{l_j} (1 - \lambda_{kj})^{1-l_j} dD(g|\alpha). \tag{6.7}$$

The hierarchical structure that follows from the standard formulation of the GoM model (omitting the subject index, for $j = 1, \ldots, J$),

$$x_j | g \sim \text{Bern}\left(\sum_{k=1}^{K} g_k \cdot \lambda_{kj}\right)$$

$$g \sim D(\alpha), \tag{6.8}$$

is inconvenient for Bayesian modeling because it does not produce tractable full conditional distributions. Existing estimation methods that rely on structure (6.8) are maximum-likelihood based [16]. However, the full conditional distributions become tractable under the latent class representation of the GoM model, which we describe next.

6.4 Bayesian Estimation of the GoM Model

The latent class representation of the GoM model is based on a set of constraints, proposed by Haberman [11], such that the marginal distribution of the manifest variables under the resulting latent class model with constraints is exactly the same as under the GoM model.

To define latent classes, we consider the vector of J multinomial latent variables $z = (z_1, z_2, \ldots, z_J)$, each taking on values from the set $\{1, 2, \ldots, K\}$. Here, the integer K is the same as the number of the GoM extreme profiles. Denote by $Z = \{1, 2, \ldots, K\}^J$ the set of all possible vectors z.

Each vector of latent classification variables, $z \in Z$, defines a latent class. Let $g = (g_1, g_2, \ldots, g_K) \in (0,1)^K$ be a random vector with cumulative distribution function $D(\alpha)$, such that $\sum_k g_k = 1$. It can be shown that the functional form

$$\pi_z = \Pr(z) = E_D\left(\prod_{j=1}^{J} g_{z_j}\right) \tag{6.9}$$

places a proper distribution on the latent classes labelled by the z's [8]. From the functional form in equation (6.9), it follows that the latent classification variables $z_1, z_2, \ldots, z_J$ are exchangeable.

To specify the conditional distribution for the manifest variables given the latent variables, we make two additional assumptions. First, we assume that x_j is independent of z_a, $a \neq j$, given z_j:

$$Pr(x_j = l_j | z) = Pr(x_j = l_j | z_1, z_2, \ldots, z_J)$$
$$= Pr(x_j = l_j | z_j), \tag{6.10}$$

where $z_j \in \{1,2,\ldots,K\}$ is the value of the latent classification variable, and $l_j \in \{0,1\}$ is the observed value of the manifest variable x_j. Thus, x_j is directly influenced only by the jth component of the latent classification vector z. Second, we assume that these conditional probabilities are given by

$$Pr(x_j = l_j | z_j = k) = \lambda_{kj}^{l_j}(1 - \lambda_{kj})^{1-l_j}, \quad j = 1,\ldots,J. \tag{6.11}$$

In this fashion, the set of λs is the same as the set of the extreme profile probabilities for the GoM model.

The constrained latent class model is fully defined by J exchangeable latent variables $z_1, z_2, \ldots, z_J$, the conditional probability structure, and the local independence assumption. The probability of observing response pattern $l = (l_1, l_2, \ldots, l_J)$ for the constrained latent class model is

$$f^{HLCM}(l) = \sum_{z \in Z} \left[E_D \left(\prod_{j=1}^{J} g_{z_j} \right) \cdot \left(\prod_{j=1}^{J} \lambda_{z_j j}^{l_j}(1 - \lambda_{z_j j})^{1-l_j} \right) \right], \tag{6.12}$$

where the latent classes are determined by latent realizations of the z's, the latent classification vectors. The probability of observing response pattern l in equation (6.12) is the sum of the conditional probabilities of observing l from each of the latent classes, weighted by the latent class probabilities. The probability of latent class z is the expected value of a J-fold product of the membership scores, $g = (g_1, g_2, \ldots, g_K) \sim D(\alpha)$, which are nonnegative random variables that sum to 1. Notice that the probability of observing response pattern l, given the latent class z, depends on the number of components in z equal $k = 1, 2, \ldots, K$, and does not depend on the order of components.

It can be shown that the probability distribution the GoM model places on the manifest variables coincides with the probability distribution the latent class model with constraints places on the manifest variables [8]. Hence, on the basis of observed data, the GoM model and the constrained latent class model are indistinguishable. Therefore, we refer to the latent class model with constraints as the latent class representation of the GoM model.

The latent class representation of the GoM model adds another level to the model hierarchy. Suppressing the subject index, for $j = 1, 2, \ldots, J$, we have:

$$x_j | z_j \sim Bern \left(\prod_{k=1}^{K} \lambda_{kj}^{z_{jk}} \right),$$
$$z_j | g \sim Mult(1, g_1, \ldots, g_K), \tag{6.13}$$
$$g \sim Dir(\alpha_0, \xi)$$

where the latent realization z_j determines the response probability for the observable x_j. Here, (α_0, ξ) is a reparameterization of the hyperparameters $\alpha = (\alpha_1, \alpha_2, \ldots, \alpha_K)$, such that $\alpha_0 = \sum_{k=1}^{K} \alpha_k$, and $\xi = (\xi_1, \xi_2, \ldots, \xi_K)$, where $\xi_k = \alpha_k / \alpha_0$, $k = 1, 2, \ldots, K$.

We place prior distributions on the structural parameters, λ_{kj}, and hyperparameters, α_0 and ξ, that have the following general forms:

$$\lambda_{kj} \sim Beta(\eta_{1kj}, \eta_{2kj}),$$
$$\alpha_0 \sim Gamma(\tau_1, \tau_2), \tag{6.14}$$
$$\xi \sim Dir(\zeta).$$

The latent class representation of the GoM model leads naturally to a data augmentation approach [19] for computing the posterior distribution of the GoM model parameters. We augment the observed data $\mathbf{x} = \{x_i = (x_{i1}, \ldots, x_{iJ}) : i = 1, \ldots, N\}$ with realizations of the latent classification variables $\mathbf{z} = \{z_i = (z_{i1}, \ldots, z_{iJ}) : i = 1, \ldots, N\}$. Let $z_{ijk} = 1$, if $z_{ij} = k$, and $z_{ijk} = 0$, otherwise. The joint distribution $p(\mathbf{x}, \mathbf{z}, \mathbf{g}, \lambda, \alpha)$ obtained from the latent class representation of the GoM model is

$$p(\lambda)p(\alpha) \left(\prod_{i=1}^{N} Dir(g_i|\alpha) \right) \prod_{i=1}^{N} \prod_{j=1}^{J} \prod_{k=1}^{K} \left(g_{ik} \lambda_{kj}^{x_{ij}} (1-\lambda_{kj})^{1-x_{ij}} \right)^{z_{ijk}},$$

where

$$Dir(g_i|\alpha) = \frac{\Gamma(\sum_k \alpha_k)}{\Gamma(\alpha_1)\ldots\Gamma(\alpha_K)} g_{i1}^{\alpha_1-1} \ldots g_{iK}^{\alpha_K-1},$$

and the parameters are $\mathbf{g} = \{g_i = (g_{i1}, g_{i2}, \ldots, g_{iK}) : i = 1, 2, \ldots, N\}$, $\lambda = \{\lambda_k = (\lambda_{k1}, \lambda_{k2}, \ldots, \lambda_{kJ}) : k = 1, 2, \ldots, K\}$, and $\alpha = (\alpha_1, \alpha_2, \ldots, \alpha_K)$. Complete conditional distributions of $\mathbf{z}$, λ and $\mathbf{g}$, available from equation (??), allow us to construct Markov chain Monte Carlo algorithms for obtaining the posterior distribution. We use Gibbs sampler to draw from posterior distributions of λ and $\mathbf{g}$, and a Metropolis-Hastings step to obtain draws of the hyperparameters. See Erosheva [9] for further details on the Bayesian estimation approach.

6.5 Analysis and Comparison

6.5.1 Latent Class Analysis

We employ a Bayesian framework to obtain posterior mean estimates for the parameters of 2-class latent class model. Placing a uniform prior distribution on the latent class and conditional response probabilities, we obtain posterior distributions of the model parameters by using BUGS [18], and assess convergence by using the CODA package of supplementary Splus functions [2]. In particular, we examine Geweke and Heidelberger and Welch diagnostics, trace plots and summary statistics. For our data, convergence diagnostics for a chain of 4,500 samples, with the first 1,000 of samples discarded as a burn-in, indicated that the chain converged.

Posterior means of conditional response probabilities for the 2-class latent class model are given in Table 6.3. Notice that the conditional response probabilities for the first class are consistently greater than the corresponding probabilities for the second class. This observation is in agreement with previous findings: the classes can be interpreted as 'disabled' and 'healthy,' respectively. Estimated posterior means (standard deviations) of the latent class weights, π_1 and π_2, are $0.345(1e-04)$ and $0.655(1e-04)$, respectively, which means that about one-third of the population is from the 'disabled' class, and two-thirds of the population are from the 'healthy' class.

By using the latent class weights and conditional response probabilities, expected probability for any cell in the 16-way table can be calculated as a weighted sum of the cell probabilities under each class. Expected values for the most frequent response patterns under the latent class model are provided in Table 6.3. It is clear that although on the basis of estimated conditional response probabilities the two classes can be interpreted as 'healthy' and 'disabled,' the fit for the frequent response patterns from these two categories is not very good. The fit is especially poor for the all-zero and all-one responses, for which the expected counts are severely underestimated, as are the expected counts for the 'disabled' most frequent response patterns at the bottom of Table 6.3. There is no clear pattern in the fitted values for the 'healthy' frequent responses in the upper portion of the table; only pattern number 2, where *bathing* is the only disability, and possibly pattern number 3, where the only disability is *doing heavy house work*, are fitted reasonably well.

We should keep in mind that we only examined patterns in Table 6.3, a small portion of all possible response patterns in the 16-way contingency table. Since the table is very sparse, assessing the overall goodness-of-fit with traditional χ^2 statistic is not appropriate in this case because of the questionable adequacy of χ^2 approximations [10].

To obtain a better fitting model, one way would be to increase the number of classes. Another possibility is to try to account for observed heterogeneity by assuming partial membership structure and introducing subject-specific membership parameters for two classes. This is the approach that is taken by the GoM model.

6.5.2 Grade of Membership Analysis and Comparison

Recall, in formulating our Bayesian approach, we use a reparameterization of the hyperparameters, where $\alpha_0 = \sum_k \alpha_k$ is the sum, and ξ is the vector of relative proportions of the Dirichlet components. For most individuals in the sample, we expect their vectors of membership scores to be dominated by one component (i.e., most individuals are close to one of the extreme profiles). Therefore, we set the prior for α_0 to be $Gamma(2, 10)$. We choose the prior for the relative proportions ξ to be uniform on the simplex. We put uniform prior distributions on the conditional response probabilities, λ, as well.

Several MCMC runs with different lengths produced very similar posterior mean estimates. Chains of about 40,000 samples were generally enough to achieve convergence of the structural parameters. A chain of 90,000 samples with thinning

j	μ_{1j}	μ_{2j}	λ_{1j}	λ_{2j}
1	0.298 (2e-04)	0.005 (2e-05)	0.319 (7e-03)	0.000 (9e-05)
2	0.656 (2e-04)	0.075 (7e-05)	0.817 (1e-02)	0.000 (5e-04)
3	0.801 (2e-04)	0.193 (1e-04)	0.962 (6e-03)	0.088 (5e-03)
4	0.542 (2e-04)	0.031 (5e-05)	0.641 (1e-02)	0.000 (3e-04)
5	0.847 (1e-04)	0.223 (1e-04)	0.993 (4e-03)	0.128 (5e-03)
6	0.589 (2e-04)	0.068 (7e-05)	0.722 (9e-03)	0.004 (2e-03)
7	0.983 (5e-05)	0.513 (1e-04)	1.000 (2e-04)	0.475 (6e-03)
8	0.594 (2e-04)	0.018 (4e-05)	0.687 (1e-02)	0.000 (1e-04)
9	0.832 (2e-04)	0.103 (9e-05)	0.982 (6e-03)	0.015 (3e-03)
10	0.692 (2e-04)	0.030 (5e-05)	0.812 (1e-02)	0.000 (1e-04)
11	0.925 (1e-04)	0.253 (1e-04)	1.000 (3e-04)	0.161 (6e-03)
12	0.885 (1e-04)	0.380 (1e-04)	0.988 (3e-03)	0.297 (6e-03)
13	0.848 (1e-04)	0.306 (1e-04)	0.949 (4e-03)	0.222 (6e-03)
14	0.522 (2e-04)	0.075 (8e-05)	0.625 (8e-03)	0.018 (3e-03)
15	0.504 (2e-04)	0.056 (6e-05)	0.598 (9e-03)	0.012 (2e-03)
16	0.349 (2e-04)	0.039 (5e-05)	0.404 (7e-03)	0.011 (2e-03)

TABLE 6.3
Posterior mean(standard deviation) estimates for 2-class LCM and for 2-profile GoM model.
The ADL items are: (1) eating, (2) getting in/out of bed, (3) getting around inside, (4) dressing, (5) bathing, (6) using toilet. The IADL items are: (7) doing heavy house work, (8) doing light house work, (9) doing laundry, (10) cooking, (11) grocery shopping, (12) getting about outside, (13) traveling, (14) managing money, (15) taking medicine, (16) telephoning.

parameter $q = 10$ gave perfect univariate convergence diagnostics for all model parameters, after the first 10,000 samples were discarded as a burn-in. The (joint) log-likelihood convergence diagnostics indicated overall convergence of the multivariate posterior distribution. We examined the plots of successive iterations, and found that the label-switching problem is not encountered in this analysis because the two profiles are very well separated on each item.

Table 6.3 provides posterior mean and standard deviation estimates for the structural parameters of the 2-profile GoM model. For all items, the conditional response probabilities of the first extreme profile, $\lambda_{1j}, j = 1, 2, \ldots 16$, are much higher than those of the second extreme profile. Therefore, similarly to the 2-class latent class model, two profiles in the GoM model can be labelled as 'disabled' and 'healthy,' respectively.

Comparing the estimates of conditional response probabilities with those from the 2-class latent class model, we see that the GoM conditional response probabilities are more extreme, i.e., they are larger for the 'disabled' category and smaller for the 'healthy' category. Since the GoM model accounts for heterogeneity between the extreme profiles by putting some weight on the response probabilities that are in-

n	response pattern	observed	2-class LCM	2-profile GoM
1	0 0 0 0 0 0 0 0 0 0 0 0 0 0 0 0	3853	828	1249
2	0 0 0 0 1 0 0 0 0 0 0 0 0 0 0 0	216	238	212
3	0 0 0 0 0 0 1 0 0 0 0 0 0 0 0 0	1107	872	1176
4	0 0 0 0 1 0 1 0 0 0 0 0 0 0 0 0	188	250	205
5	0 0 0 0 0 0 1 0 0 0 1 0 0 0 0 0	122	295	259
6	0 0 0 0 0 0 0 0 0 0 0 0 1 0 0 0	351	507	562
7	0 0 1 0 0 0 0 0 0 0 0 0 1 0 0 0	206	121	69
8	0 0 0 0 0 0 1 0 0 0 0 0 1 0 0 0	303	534	535
9	0 0 1 0 0 0 1 0 0 0 0 0 1 0 0 0	182	128	70
10	0 0 0 0 1 0 1 0 0 0 0 0 1 0 0 0	108	153	99
11	0 0 1 0 1 0 1 0 0 0 0 0 1 0 0 0	106	37	16
12	0 0 0 0 0 0 0 0 0 0 0 0 0 1 0 0	195	365	386
13	0 0 0 0 0 0 1 0 0 0 0 0 0 1 0 0	198	384	369
14	0 0 0 0 0 0 1 0 0 0 1 0 1 0 0 0	196	130	86
15	0 0 0 0 0 0 1 0 0 0 0 1 1 0 0 0	123	236	174
16	0 0 0 0 0 0 1 0 0 0 1 1 1 0 0 0	176	80	44
17	0 0 1 0 0 0 1 0 0 0 1 1 1 0 0 0	120	19	9
18	0 0 0 0 1 0 1 0 0 0 1 1 1 0 0 0	101	23	12
19	0 1 1 1 1 1 1 1 1 1 1 1 1 0 0 0	102	27	57
20	1 1 1 1 1 1 1 1 1 1 1 1 1 0 1 0	107	12	35
21	0 1 1 1 1 1 1 1 1 1 1 1 1 1 1 0	104	30	122
22	1 1 1 1 1 1 1 1 1 1 1 1 1 1 1 0	164	13	55
23	0 1 1 1 1 1 1 1 1 1 1 1 1 1 1 1	153	16	80
24	1 1 1 1 1 1 1 1 1 1 1 1 1 1 1 1	660	7	36
sum		9141	5305	5917

TABLE 6.4
Observed and expected cell counts for frequent response patterns under 2-class latent class model and 2-profile Grade of Membership model.

between the response probabilities of the extreme profiles, this observation is consistent with our expectations. The posterior means (standard deviations) of the hyperparameters ξ_1, ξ_2 and α_0 are $0.433(4e-02), 0.567(4e-02)$, and $0.521(2e-02)$, respectively. Comparing the estimated latent class probabilities and the estimated relative proportions of Dirichlet distribution, we note that the Dirichlet proportions are closer to 0.5: the latent class model estimates that 34% of the elderly are 'disabled' and 66% are 'healthy,' whereas the corresponding GoM Dirichlet proportions are 0.43 and 0.57. The Dirichlet proportions are the cumulative percentages of responses to individual questions that elderly make as 'healthy' or 'disabled.' The estimate of α_0 equals 0.521, which corresponds to a bath-tub shaped Dirichlet (Beta) distribution of the membership scores.

The frequent response patterns, their observed and expected values under the 2-profile GoM model, are given in Table 6.4. Comparing these results with the expected counts obtained under the 2-class latent class model, we first note that although the expected values for the all-zero and all-one response patterns are still much lower than observed, the GoM model fits the all-zero and all-one response patterns better than the latent class model. Similarly, the fitted values look much better in the lower part of the table with 'disabled' frequent response patterns. Even though the latent class model provides a better fit to a few response patterns from Table 6.4, the GoM model does a better job overall. The sum of squared differences between the expected and the observed counts for the frequent response patterns is 7,472,788 for the 2-profile GoM model compared to 9,931,869 for the 2 class latent class model.

The latent class model is built on the assumption that each observation is originating from a particular latent class. After the model is estimated, the observations are often classified into the latent classes on the basis of posterior probabilities:

$$Pr(class\ k|l) = \frac{Pr(l|class\ k) \cdot \pi_k}{\sum_{a=1}^{K} Pr(l|class\ a) \cdot \pi_a}, \quad k = 1, 2, \ldots, K.$$

Although the latent space is discrete, it seems that posterior probabilities can be thought of as being analogous to membership scores. However, since the posterior probabilities are not parameters, they do not account for additional heterogeneity. Given the latent class model, the posterior probabilities can only provide an assessment of uncertainty that goes in assigning observations to latent classes. The GoM model, on the other hand, accounts explicitly for additional heterogeneity by introducing subject-level partial membership parameters. One should avoid making direct comparisons of posterior probabilities and membership scores primarily because the posterior probabilities are not parameters of the model. Having said that, it can be instructive to know what is the distribution of uncertainty in the class assignments of the latent class model, and how it compares to the distribution of the membership scores in the GoM model.

Figure 6.2 shows the distribution of the posterior probabilities of an observation coming from the first ('disabled') latent class with the Beta distribution of the membership score in the first ('disabled') extreme profile under the GoM model. Two lower curves on Figure 6.2 are the nonparametric and Beta density estimates of the distribution of the posterior probabilities. The density estimates are obtained from a set of posterior probabilities calculated for each observation in the data. The nonparametric density roughly follows the shape of a Beta distribution, telling us that most observations can be classified as 'healthy' or 'disabled' with only a small degree of uncertainty. However, multiple distinct bumps farther away from 0 and 1 on the abscissa indicate presence of groups of observations that might be better described as partial members in the 'healthy' and 'disabled' latent classes.

The upper smooth curve in Figure 6.2 is the estimated density function of Beta distribution of the partial membership score in the first ('disabled') extreme profile from the GoM model. This density appears to place more mass in between the extreme points than do both parametric and nonparametric estimates of the density of posterior probabilities. That is not particularly surprising because individual response probabilities determined by the GoM model are bounded with the extreme profile response probabilities, respectively, which are more extreme than the latent class conditional response probabilities.

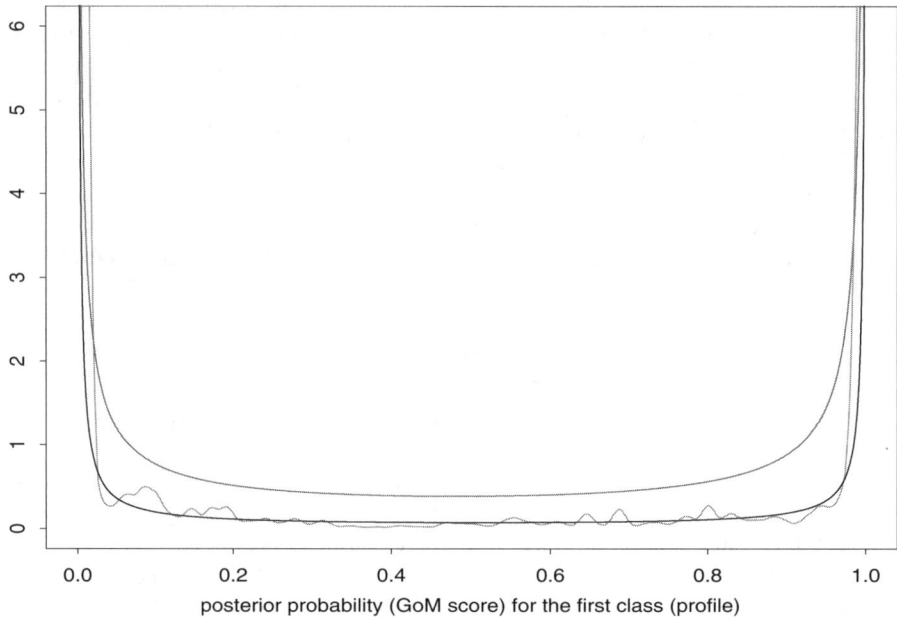

FIGURE 6.2
Latent class model: Nonparametric and Beta density estimates of the distribution of posterior probability of being a member of the 'disabled' class (lower curves). GoM model: Beta distribution of the membership score in the 'disabled' extreme profile (upper curve).

6.6 Concluding Remarks

In this paper, we have not considered the question whether the low-dimensional special cases of the models are sufficient to describe the data well, but we rather focused our attention on distinct capabilities that the full and partial membership models provide with respect to modeling heterogeneity in observed discrete responses. On the example of ADL/IADL disability data from the National Long Term Care Survey, we have seen that introducing the partial membership structure into the model may improve the fit as well as provide us with a more realistic approach to model heterogeneity in individual responses.

The latent class representation of the GoM model makes it possible not only to use a Bayesian approach, but also to make a connection with partial membership models that recently appeared in the genetics and machine learning literatures. In contrast with the Grade of Membership model, partial membership models in other literatures have been originally based on the idea of latent classification variables.

In the clustering model with admixture [17], the latent classification variables represent unknown subpopulations of origin of particular alleles. The genetics application provides clear intuitive interpretations for the model parameters. Drawing a parallel with the GoM model for multinomial discrete data, the set of subpopulations in the clustering model plays the role of extreme profiles, the loci play the role of items, and the number of possible alleles at a locus is equivalent to the number of possible responses for an item. The only substantive difference between the two models lies in the data generating process: whereas there are two allele copies corresponding to two independent realizations of the subpopulation of origin at each locus for the multilocus genotype data, there is only one realization of the observed response for each item in the survey type data for which the GoM model was developed.

In the information retrieval area, the process of generating words in a document for the Latent Dirichlet Allocation model [3] includes three steps: (1) drawing membership scores for each of the K topics, (2) drawing a topic, conditional on the values of membership scores, and (3) drawing a word, conditional on the topic. Following the traditional 'bag-of-words' assumptions, all words in the document are considered as independent draws. Under this assumption, one characteristic in a document (a word) is observed with the number of replications that equals the length of the document. Thus, the sampling scheme is again different from that of the GoM model which assumes that single replications of J distinct characteristics are observed.

Despite different sampling schemes, the models from different literatures described above share a common idea of partial membership. Understanding connections among these models will allow us to borrow approaches and results across different literatures.

References

[1] L. Berkman, B. Singer, and K. G. Manton. Black/white differences in health status and mortality among the elderly. *Demography*, 26(4):661–678, 1989.

[2] N. Best, M.K. Cowles, and K. Vines. CODA: Convergence diagnosis and output analysis software for Gibbs sampling output (version 0.30). Technical report, MRC Cambridge, UK, 1996.

[3] D. M. Blei, A. Y. Ng, and M. I. Jordan. Latent Dirichlet Allocation. *Advances in Neural Information Processing Systems*, 14, 2001.

[4] J. Clive, M. A. Woodbury, and I. C. Siegler. Fuzzy and crisp set-theoretic-based classification of health and disease. A qualitative and quantitative comparison. *Journal of Medical Systems*, 7(4):317–331, 1983.

[5] L. S. Corder and K. G. Manton. National surveys and the health and functioning of the elderly: The effects of design and content. *Journal of the American Statistical Association*, 86:513–525, 1991.

[6] Decision Systems, Inc. *User Documentation for DSIGoM. Version 1.0.*, 1999.

[7] A. Dobra, E. A. Erosheva, and S. E. Fienberg. Disclosure limitation methods based on bounds for large contingency tables with applications to disability. In *C. Warren Neel Conference on the New Frontiers of Statistical Data Mining, Knowledge Discovery, and E-Business*, 2002.

[8] E. A. Erosheva. *Grade of Membership and Latent Structure Models with Application to Disability Survey Data*. PhD thesis, Carnegie Mellon, 2002.

[9] E. A. Erosheva. Bayesian estimation of the grade of membership model. In *Bayesian Statistics 7. Proceedings of the Seventh Valencia International Meeting (to appear)*, 2003.

[10] S.E. Fienberg. *The Analysis of Cross-Classified Categorical Data*. The Massachusetts Institute of Technology, 1994.

[11] Shelby J. Haberman. Book review of *Statistical Applications Using Fuzzy Sets*, by Manton, K. G., Woodbury, M. A., and Tolley, H. D. *Journal of the American Statistical Association*, pages 1131–1133, 1995.

[12] T. Hofmann. Unsupervised learning by probabilistic latent semantic analysis. *Machine Learning*, 42:177–196, 2001.

[13] K. G. Manton, E. Stallard, and M. A. Woodbury. A multivariate event history model based upon fuzzy states: Estimation from longitudinal surveys with informative nonresponse. *Journal of Official Statistics*, 7:261–293, 1991.

[14] K. G. Manton, M. A. Woodbury, and H. D. Tolley. *Statistical Applications Using Fuzzy Sets*. Wiley-Interscience, 1994.

[15] K.G. Manton and M. A. Woodbury. Grade of Membership generalizations and aging research. *Experimental Aging Research*, 17(4):217–226, 1991.

[16] R. G. Potthoff, K. G. Manton, M. A. Woodbury, and H. D. Tolley. Dirichlet generalizations of latent-class models. *Journal of Classification*, 17:315–353, 2000.

[17] J. K. Pritchard, M. Stephens, and P. Donnelly. Inference of population structure using multilocus genotype data. *Genetics*, 155:945–959, 2000.

[18] D. Spiegelhalter, A. Thomas, N. Best, and W. Gilks. BUGS 0.5: Bayesian Inference Using Gibbs Sampling Manual (version ii). Technical report, MRC Cambridge, UK, 1996.

[19] M. A. Tanner. *Tools for Statistical Inference. Methods for the Exploration of Posterior Distributions and Likelihood Functions (Third Edition)*. Springer-Verlag, 1996.

[20] M. A. Woodbury, J. Clive, and A. Garson. Mathematical typology: A grade of membership technique for obtaining disease definition. *Computers and Biomedical Research*, 11:277–298, 1978.

7

Automated Scoring of Polygraph Data

Aleksandra B. Slavkovic
Department of Statistics, Carnegie-Mellon University, Pittsburgh, USA

CONTENTS

7.1 Introduction 135
7.2 Background 136
7.3 Statistical Models for Classification and Prediction 139
7.4 The Data 141
7.5 Statistical Analysis 144
7.6 Discussion 150
7.7 Conclusion 152
      Acknowledgments 153
      References 153

The objective of automated scoring algorithms for polygraph data is to create reliable and statistically valid classification schemes minimizing both false positive and false negative rates. With increasing computing power and well developed statistical methods for classification we often launch analyses without much consideration for the quality of the datasets and the underlying assumptions of the data collection. In this paper we try to assess the validity of logistic regression when faced with a highly variable but small dataset of 149 real-life specific incident polygraph cases. The data exhibit enormous variability in the subject of investigation, format, structure, and administration, making them hard to standardize within an individual and across individuals. This makes it difficult to develop generalizable statistical procedures. We outline steps and detailed decisions required for the conversion of continuous polygraph readings into a set of features. With a relatively simple approach we obtain accuracy rates comparable to those reported by other more complex algorithms and manual scoring. Complexity underlying assessment and classification of examinee's deceptiveness is evident in a number of models that account for different predictors giving similar results, typically "overfitting" with the increasing number of features. While computerized systems have the potential to reduce examiner variability and bias, the evidence that they have achieved this potential is meager at best.

7.1 Introduction

Polygraphs are used by law enforcement agencies and the legal community for criminal investigations, in the private sector for pre-employment screening, and for testing for espionage and sabotage. Polygraph proponents claim high accuracy rates of 98% for guilty subjects and 82% for innocent [23, 2]. These rates are typically calculated by leaving out inconclusive cases and ignoring the issue of sampling bias, e.g., when the accuracies and inter-raters reliability are calculated using only subjects for which there is an independent validation of their guilt or innocence (i.e., ground truth).

The polygraph as an instrument has been recording changes in people's relative blood pressure, respiration and the electrodermal response (palmar sweating) in some form since 1926. These psychophysiological responses, believed to be controlled by the autonomic nervous system, are still the main source of information from which the polygraph examiners deduce an examinee's deceptive or nondeceptive status. The underlying premise is that an examinee will involuntarily exhibit fight-or-flight reactions in response to the asked questions. The autonomic nervous system will, in most cases, increase the person's blood pressure and sweating, and affect the breathing rate. These physiological data are evaluated by the polygraph examiner using a specified numerical scoring system and/or statistically automated scoring algorithms. The latter are the main focus of this report. Current methods of psychophysiological detection of deception (PDD) are based on years of empirical work, and are often criticized for a lack of thorough scientific inquiry and methodology.

The objective of automated scoring algorithms for polygraph data is to create reliable and statistically valid classification schemes minimizing both false positive and false negative rates. The statistical methods used in classification models are well developed, but to the author's knowledge, their validity in the polygraph context has not been established. We briefly describe the polygraph examination framework and two automated scoring algorithms relying on different statistical procedures in Section 7.2. Section 7.3 provides some background on statistical models one might naturally use in settings such as automated polygraph scoring. In Section 7.4 we evaluate collection of real-life polygraph data of known deceptive and nondeceptive subjects. In Section 7.5 we outline steps and detailed decisions required for the conversion of continuous polygraph readings into a set of numeric predictor variables and present results of a logistic regression classifier. Our approach is simpler than other proposed methods, but appears to yield similar results. Various data issues that are not addressed or captured by the current algorithms indicate a deficiency in the validity of methods applied in the polygraph setting.

7.2 Background

7.2.1 The Polygraph Examination

The polygraph examination has three parts [24, 20, 6]. The *pre-test* phase is used to formulate of a series of 8 to 12 "Yes and No" questions which are custom-made for the examinee based on the exam topic (see Table 7.1). During the *in-test* phase, these questions are asked and data are collected. Typically, the same questions are asked

Statistical Data Mining and Knowledge Discovery

TABLE 7.1
Example questions for the Zone Comparison Test (ZCT) format.

X	This test is about to begin.
1	Is today Tuesday?
2	Regarding that stolen property, do you intend to answer truthfully each question... ?
3	Are you convinced that I will not ask you a surprise question on this test?
4C	Before 1995, did you ever steal anything from an employer?
5R	Did you steal any of that missing property?
6C	Before 1995, did you ever steal anything?
7R	Did you steal any of that missing property from building —— ?
1A	Is this the month of January?
8C	Before 1995, did you ever steal something and not get caught?
9R	Do you know for sure who stole any of that missing property?
10C	Before 1995, did you ever tell a serious lie to ...?
11	Is there something else you are afraid I will ask you a question about...?
XX	Test is over...

at least 3 times, with or without varying the order of the questions. One repetition represents a polygraph chart limited to approximately 5 minutes (Figure 7.1).

There are three main types of questions. *Irrelevant* ("Is today Tuesday?") questions are meant to stabilize the person's responses with respect to external stimuli such as the examiner's voice. *Relevant* (R) questions address the main focus of the exam. *Comparison* (C) or *control* questions address issues similar in nature but unrelated to the main focus of the exam. There might be "wild-type" questions too [6].

In the *post-test* part the examiner evaluates the charts by comparing the responses on the relevant and comparison questions, and tries to obtain a confession from the examinee. It is expected that a deceptive person will show stronger reactions to the relevant questions, while an innocent person will be more concerned with comparison questions. Depending on the test format, the agency conducting the exam and examiner's training, the number, type and order of questions may differ.

Specific issue exams address known events that have occurred, e.g., a theft. We are concerned with two Comparison Question Test formats: the Zone Comparison Test (ZCT), and the Multiple General Question Test (MGQT). According to the Department of Defense Polygraph Institute (DoDPI), these have pre-defined formats, although in practice they are highly variable (cf. § 7.4).

7.2.2 Instrumentation and Measurements

A polygraph instrument records and filters the original analog signal. The output is a digital signal, a discretized time series with possibly varying sampling rates across instruments and channels. The polygraph typically records thoracic and abdominal respirations, electrodermal and cardiovascular signals (Figure 7.1).

Pneumographs positioned around the chest and the abdomen measure the rate and depth of respiration. Subjects can control their breathing and influence the recorded measurements. Changes in respiration can also affect heart rate and electrodermal activity. For example coughing is manifested in electrodermal activity.

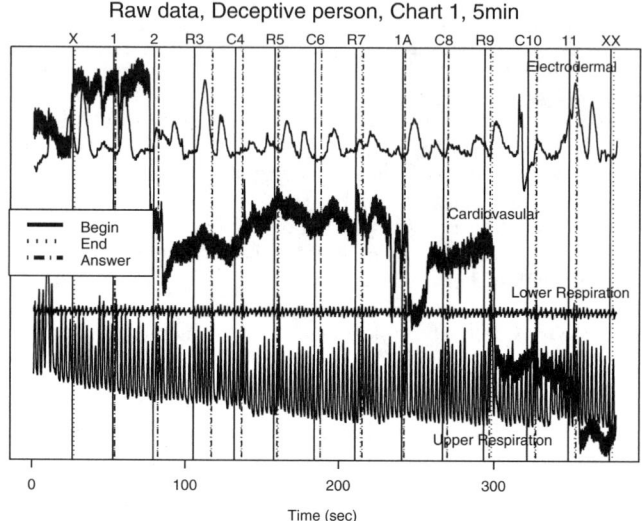

FIGURE 7.1
The lower recordings are thoracic and abdominal respirations, the middle series is cardiovascular signal and the upper is electrodermal signal. The scale is arbitrary. The labels on the upper axis correspond to the Table 7.1 question sequence.

Electrodermal activity (EDR) or sweating is measured via electrodes (metal plates) placed on two fingers, and it is considered the most valuable measure in lie detection. Either skin conductance (SC) or its reciprocal, skin resistance (SR), is recorded. Some have argued [8] that the size of the response on a question depends on which of SC or SR, is recorded. This is a controversial issue discussed in more detail in the psychophysiological literature and in [6].

Cardiovascular activity is measured by a blood pressure cuff placed above the biceps. As a hybrid signal of relative blood pressure and heart rate, it is the most complex of the four measurements. The cardiovascular response is coactivated or coinhibited by other physiological responses, making its evaluation more difficult, e.g., [0.12Hz-0.4Hz] frequency band in the heart rate is due to respiration. This coupling may differ within a person and across different environmental settings [3].

It is unclear whether these physiological responses reflect a single psychological process (such as arousal) or the extent to which they are consistent across individuals. The psychophysiological literature includes contradictory claims on how internal emotional states are mapped to physiological states, and the extent to which emotional states represent deception [6, 11, 17, 14].

7.2.3 Chart Evaluations

A critical part of polygraph examination is the analysis and interpretation of the physiological data recorded on polygraph charts. Polygraph examiners rely on their subjective global evaluation of the charts, numerical methods and/or computerized algorithms for chart scoring.

Numerical Scoring. The scoring procedure may differ by the PDD exam type, the agency and the examiner's training and experience. In the 7-Position Numerical Analysis Scale the examiner assigns values from -3 to 3 to the differential responses on pairs of relevant and comparison questions. The negative values, for example, indicate higher reaction on the relevant questions. The values are summed across pairs, channels and charts. A total score of +6 or greater indicates nondeception, -6 or less deception, and in-between are inconclusive cases [20, 25].

Computerized Scoring Algorithms. We focus on two computerized polygraph systems currently used with U.S. distributed polygraph equipment. Other systems have been developed more recently [24, 9]. The Stoelting polygraph instrument uses the Computerized Polygraph System (CPS) developed by Scientific Assessment Technologies based on research conducted at the University of Utah [18, 19, 5]. The Axciton and Lafayette instruments use the PolyScore algorithms developed at the Johns Hopkins University Applied Physics Laboratory [12, 13, 22]. Performance of these algorithms on an independent set of 97 selected confirmed criminal cases was compared by [9]. CPS performed equally well on detection of innocent and guilty subjects while the other algorithms were better at detecting deceptives (cf. § 7.6). More details on the polygraph instruments and history of the development of computerized algorithms can be found in [20, 19, 1].

The methods used to develop the two existing computer-based scoring algorithms both fit within the general statistical framework described below. They take the digitized polygraph signals and output estimated probabilities of deception. While PolyScore uses logistic regression or neural networks to estimate these probabilities, CPS uses standard discriminant analysis and a naive Bayesian probability calculation (a proper Bayesian calculation would be more elaborate and might produce markedly different results). They both assume equal a priori probabilities of being truthful and deceptive. The biggest differences that we can discern between them are the data they use as input, their approaches to feature development and selection, and the efforts that they have made at model validation and assessment. Appendix G of [6] and [24] give a more detailed review of these algorithms. Computerized systems have the potential to reduce bias in the reading of charts and inter-rater variability. Whether they can actually improve accuracy also depends on how one views the appropriateness of using other knowledge available to examiners, such as demographic information, historical background of the subject, and behavioral observations.

7.3 Statistical Models for Classification and Prediction

This section provides some background on the statistical models that one might naturally use in settings such as automated polygraph scoring. The statistical methods for classification and prediction most often involve structure:

$$\text{response variable} = g(\text{predictor variables, parameters, random noise}), \quad (7.1)$$

where g is some function. For classification problems it is customary to represent the response as an indicator variable, y, such that $y = 1$ if a subject is deceptive, and $y = 0$ if the subject is not. Typically we estimate y conditional on the predictor variables, X, and the functional form, g. For linear logistic regression models, with k predictor variables $x = (x_1, x_2, ..., x_k)$, we estimate the function g in equation (7.1) using a linear combination of the k predictors:

$$\text{score}(x) = \beta_0 + \beta_1 x_1 + \beta_2 x_2 + ... + \beta_k x_k, \quad (7.2)$$

and we take the response of interest to be:

$$\Pr(\text{deception}|x) = \Pr(y|x) = \frac{e^{\text{score}(x)}}{1 + e^{\text{score}(x)}}. \quad (7.3)$$

This is technically similar to choosing $g = \text{score}(x)$, except that the random noise in equation (7.1) is now associated with the probability distribution for y in equation (7.3), which is usually taken to be Bernoulli. We are using an estimate of the score equation (7.2) as a hyperplane to separate the observations into two groups, deceptives and nondeceptives. The basic idea of separating the observations is the same for nonlinear approaches. Model estimates do well if there is real separation between the two groups.

Model development and estimation for such prediction/classification models involve a number of steps:

1. Specifying the possible predictor variables (features of the data) to be used.
2. Choosing the functional form g in model (7.1) and the link function.
3. Selecting the features to be used for classification.
4. Fitting the model to data to estimate empirically the prediction equation to be used in practice.
5. Validating the fitted model through some form of cross-validation.

Different methods of fitting and specification emphasize different features of the data. Logistic regression models make no assumptions about the distribution of the predictors. The maximum likelihood methods typically used for their estimation put heavy emphasis on observations close to the boundary between the two sets of observations. Common experience with empirical logistic regression and other prediction models is that with a large number of predictor variables we can fit a model to the data (using steps 1 through 4) that completely separates the two groups of observations. However, once we implement step 5 we often learn that the achieved separation is illusory. Thus many empirical approaches build cross-validation directly into the fitting process, and set aside a separate part of the data for final testing. A thorough discussion on classifcation/prediction models, cross-validation, and related methodologies such as black box approaches can be found in [15].

7.4 The Data

The Department of Defense Polygraph Institute (DoDPI) provided data from 170 specific incident cases that vary by the collection agency, type of crime, formats and questions. We analyzed 149 cases,* a mix of ZCT and MGQT tests (see Table 7.2). We had to discard 21 cases due to missing information on one or more charts. The type of data missing could be any combination of type of questions, onset of the question, time of the answer, and others. All data were collected with Axciton polygraph instruments.

Each examination (subject/case) had three to five text data files corresponding to the exam charts, each approximately five minutes long. The data were converted to text from their native proprietary format by the "Reformat" program developed by the JHUAPL program, and the identifiers were removed. Each data file contained demographic information (when available), the sequence of questions asked during the exam, and the following fields:

1. Sample: index of observations; sampling rate is 60 Hz for all measurements.
2. Time: the time, relative to the test beginning, when the sample was taken.
3. Pn1: recording of the thorax respiration sensor.
4. Pn2: recording of the abdomen sensor.
5. EDR: data from an electrodermal sensor.
6. Cardio: data from the blood pressure cuff (60 and 70 mmHg inflated).
7. Event: time for the begining and end of the question and time of the answers.

Figure 7.1 shows raw data for one subject. Each time series is one of the four biological signals plus unknown error. In our analysis we use an addional series (pulse frequency that we extracted from the cardio signal)(see § 7.5.1). Demographic data such as gender, age, and education are typically available to the examiner. We had limited demographic data and did not utilize it in the current analysis.

Respiratory tracing consists of inhalation and exhalation strokes. In manual scoring the examiner looks for visual changes in the tracings for breathing rate, baseline, and amplitude, where for example 0.75 inches is the desired amplitude of respiratory activity. Upper and lower respiration recordings are highly correlated as are the features we extract on these recordings.

TABLE 7.2
Number of cases by test type and ground truth.

	Deceptive	Nondeceptive	Total
ZCT	27	24	51 (51)
MGQT	90	29	119 (98)
Total	117 (98)	53 (51)	170 (149)

---

*These data overlap with those used in the development of PolyScore.

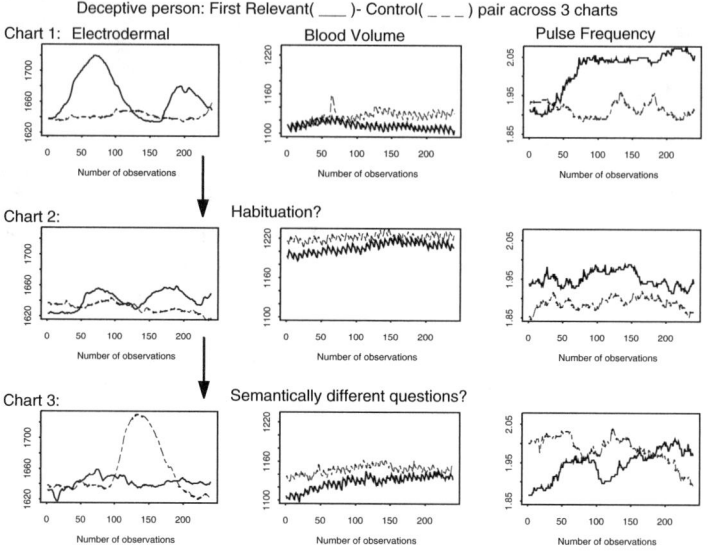

FIGURE 7.2
Overlaid response windows for electrodermal, blood volume, and pulse frequency series on charts 1, 2, and 3 of a deceptive person for the first relevant-comparison question pair. Sampling rate here is 12 Hz.

Electrodermal (EDR) tracing is the most prominent signal. Based on the limited information about the Axciton instrument, our EDR signal is a hybrid of the skin conductance and skin resistance [9] and little of known psychophysiological research can be applied. In manual scoring an evaluator may look for changes in amplitude and duration of response. When there is no reactivity the tracing is almost a horizontal line. Psychophysiology literature reports a 1-3 second delay in response to a stimulus. We observe EDR latency of 1-6 seconds from the question onset.

Research has shown that stronger stimulation elicits larger EDR response, but repetitive stimulation leads to habituation [8]. In Figure 7.2 notice the decrease in the response on the first relevant question across three charts. This could be a sign of habituation where a response to a stimulus is reduced with repeated exposure to the same question. However, in a number of cases the sequence of the questions may not be the same across the charts; so, we might be observing different responsiveness to semantically different questions and not habituation. For example, the first relevant question on chart 1 may appear in the third postion on chart 3. In addition, different people have different responsiveness to the same stimulus (Figure 7.3).

Cardiovascular tracing records systolic stroke (pen up), diastolic stroke (pen down), and the dichotic notch. The evaluator looks for changes in baseline, amplitude, rate and changes in dichotic notch (position, disappearance). For cardiovascular activity the blood pressure usually ranges from 80 mmHg to 120 mmHg, but we cannot utilize this knowledge since the scale is arbitrary with respect to known physiolog-

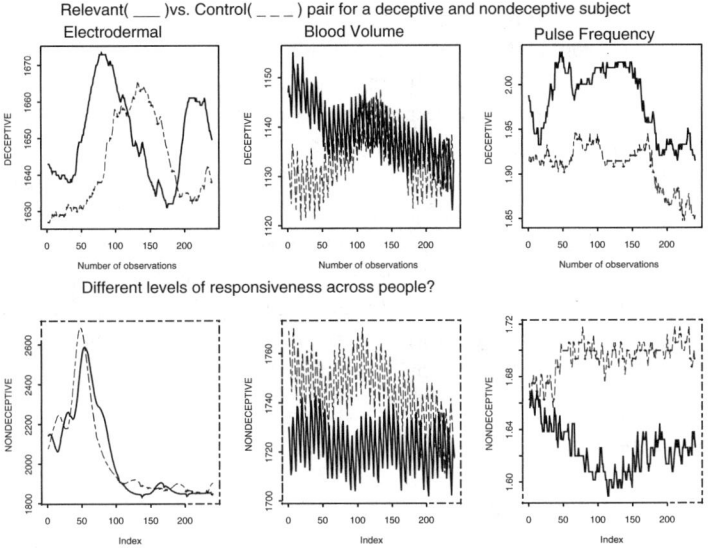

FIGURE 7.3
Overlaid response windows for electrodermal, blood volume, and pulse frequency series on chart 1 of a deceptive and a nondeceptive person for a relevant-comparison question pair.

ical units. In fight-or-flight situations, heart rate and blood pressure typically both increase.

Besides habituation there are other issues manifested in these data that may influence feature extraction, evaluation, and modeling. There are latency differences present across different question pairs. In Figure 7.5, notice how the latency changes for the EDR as we move from the first relevant-comparison pair to the third. We can also observe different responsiveness (e.g., magnitude) across different questions. This phenomenon, however, may actually be due to a body's tendency to return to homeostasis and not due to a different reaction to different stimuli.

Our analysis revealed diverse test structures even within the same test format. The ZCT usually has the same number of comparison (C) and relevant (R) questions. A typical sequence is CRCRCR. The MGQT proposed sequence is RRCRRC. These sequences may be interspersed with other question types, and in our data we found at least 15 different sequences. The questions varied greatly across tests and were semantically different among subjects within the same crime. The order of questions varied across charts for the same person. Two problems we faced were the variable number of charts and variable number of relevant questions. Missing relevant questions should be treated as missing data; however, in this project we did not have sufficient evidence to properly impute these values. Thus we chose to drop the fourth relevant-comparison pair when it existed. For eight subjects who were missing the third relevant-comparison pair, we replaced their value by zero, i.e., we assumed that there was no difference in the response on that particular relevant-comparison pair. Elimination of both the fourth chart and the fourth relevant-comparison pair when missing, and replacement of missing values with zeros did not significantly change the model coefficients nor the final result of classification. These types of differences across cases pose major problems for both within- and between-subject analyses, unless all the responses are averaged.

The crucial information for the development of a statistical classifier of polygraph data is ground truth (i.e., knowledge of whether a subject was truly deceptive or nondeceptive). Ideally, determination of ground truth should be independent of the observed polygraph data, although it is not clear how the ground truth was established for some of our cases. This introduces uncertainty in class labels, in particular for innocent cases since their ground truth is typically set based on someone else's confession. We proceed as though the ground truth in our data is correct.

7.5 Statistical Analysis

We follow the general framework described in § 7.3 for development and estimation of the logistic regression classification model. The analysis can be broken into Signal Processing, Feature Extraction, Feature Evaluation, Modeling and Classification, and Cross-Validation.

7.5.1 Signal Processing

With modern digital polygraphs and computerized systems, the analog signals are digitized and the raw digitized signals are used in the algorithm development. The primary objective of signal processing is to reduce the noise-to-information ratio. This traditionally involves editing the data (e.g., to detect artifacts and outliers), some signal transformation, and standardization. Our goal is to do a minimal amount of data editing and preserve the raw signal since we lack information on actual instrumentation and any type of filtering performed by either the machine or the examiner.

We first subsampled the 60 Hz data by taking every fifth observation for each channel. Next we transformed the cardiovascular recording. We separated the relative blood volume from the pulse, constructing a new series for the relative blood pressure and another one for the pulse frequency. This was done by first calculating the average signal by applying a moving average with a window of size five. This gives a crude measurement of relative blood pressure. The averaged signal was subtracted from the original signal to produce the pulse. The pulse frequency time series is obtained by first removing ultra-high frequency by applying a low pass filter.[†] The filtered signal is made stationary by subtracting its mean. For each window of size 199 observations, we computed the spectral density of a fitted sixth order auto-regressive model.[‡] Via linear interpolation we calculated the most prominent

---
[†] We used the MATLAB built-in *Butterworth* filter of the 9th order at frequency 0.8.
[‡] We explored different AR models as well, but AR(6) models seem to capture the changes sufficiently.

Statistical Data Mining and Knowledge Discovery 145

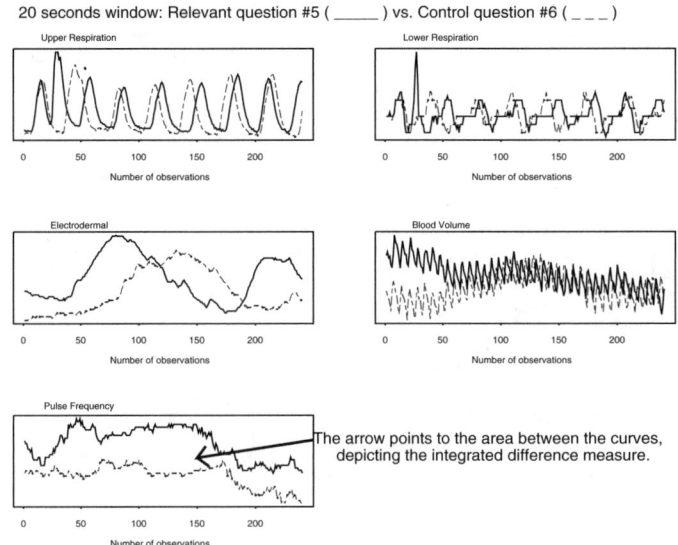

FIGURE 7.4
Overlaid response windows of a relevant and a comparison question for respirations, electrodermal, blood volume, and pulse frequency series on chart 1 of a deceptive person.

frequency. The procedure was repeated for the length of the time series to obtain a new series representing the frequency of a person's pulse during the exam.

7.5.2 A Simplified Approach to Feature Extraction

The discussion of general statistical methodology for prediction and classification in § 7.3 emphasized the importance of feature development and selection. A feature can be anything we measure or compute that represents the emotional signal. Our goal was to reduce the time-series to a small set of features with some relevance to modeling and classifying the internal psychological states such as deception.

Our initial analysis tried to capture low and high frequency changes of the given measurements. To capture slow changes we extracted *integrated differences* and *latency differences* features within a 20-second window from the question onset. Within the same response interval, we extracted *spectral properties differences* to capture high frequency changes. These three features are crude measures of differential activity on relevant and comparison questions. We used the same features for all signals except for the respiration where we did not use the latency.

Integrated Differences. The integrated difference is the area between two curves.

$$d_{ijkl} = \sum_{l=1}^{n}(R_{ijkl} - C_{ijkl}) \tag{7.4}$$

is the integrated difference of the ith relevant (R) question versus the ith comparison

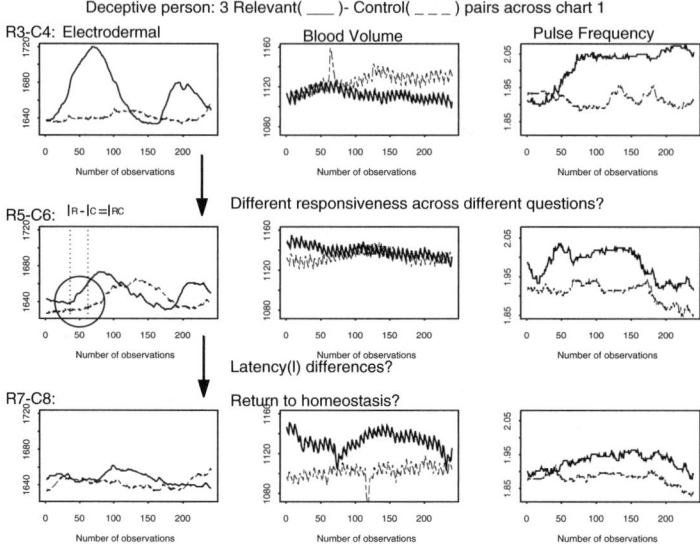

FIGURE 7.5
The overlaid response windows for 3 pairs of relevant and comparison questions on electrodermal, blood volume, and pulse frequency series on chart 1 of a deceptive person.

(C) question of the jth channel on the kth chart, where $n = 240$ is the number of observations in the response window (see Figure 7.4).

Latency Differences. We calculated latency for each 20-second window for comparison and relevant questions on all channels except respiration as follows:

1. Take the absolute value of the differenced time series, $Y_t = |\triangle X_t|$.
2. Calculate the cumulative sum, $Y_j = \sum_{k=0}^{j} X_k$, and normalize it, i.e., $Z_j = \frac{Y_j}{Y_n}$.
3. Define latency as the minimum Z_j such that $Z_j > 0.02$, i.e., $\ell = \min\{Z_j : Z_j \geq 0.02\}$.
4. Define the latency difference feature as the difference in the latency for the relevant and the comparison questions: $\ell_{rc} = \ell_r - \ell_c$.

Spectral Properties Differences. High frequency measure is the difference between spectral properties that we defined in the following way:

1. Apply a high pass filter[§] on a 20-second window for each comparison and relevant question.
2. Generate periodograms as an estimator measure of spectrum.
3. Assess the spectral properties difference:
   (a) Calculate a mean frequency component, $f_c = \int_0^\pi \lambda S_c(\lambda) d\lambda$, where λ is the spectral density of the process, and S_c is the estimated measure of the spectrum.

[§]We used built-in *Butterworth* filter from MATLAB.

(b) Calculate the variance of the frequency component, $v_c = \int_0^\pi \lambda^2 S_c(\lambda)\,d\lambda - f_c^2$.

(c) Combine (a) and (b) to get $h_{rc} = |f_r - f_c| + |\sqrt{v_r} - \sqrt{v_c}|$.

These extracted features are measures of responsiveness to the stimuli. For integrated and latency differences measures we expect positive values if the response is higher on the relevant question, negative if it's higher on the comparison questions, and zero if there is no difference. Spectral properties differences only give the magnitude of the differential activity.

7.5.3 Feature Evaluation, Modeling, and Classification

This section reviews aspects of feature selection and of statistical modeling involving the development of scoring rules into classification rules. The extracted features were considered in three types of comparisons between relevant and comparison questions:

1. each relevant compared to its nearest comparison,
2. each relevant compared to the average comparison,
3. averaged relevant compared to the average comparison.

In the first two settings the maximum number of continuous variables per subject was 240 (4 relevant-comparison pairs × 5 channels × 4 charts × 3 features), while the third setting had 60. Since the potential variable space is large relative to the sample size and the variables are highly correlated, particularly in the first two settings, we evaluated features graphically, via clustering, principal-component analysis (PCA) and with univariate logistic regression trying to reduce dimensionality. The remainder of this report will focus on setting 3. The other two settings are briefly discussed in [24].

Figure 7.6 shows separation of the two classes given the integrated difference feature for the electrodermal (dEdr) channel or the electrodermal latency difference (lEdr) versus the integrated difference for blood volume (dBv). These are values averaged across charts. Most deceptive subjects (the 1s in the figure) have values greater than zero on dEdr and their distribution is slightly skewed left on pulse frequency (Fqp). Nondeceptive subjects (represented with 0s) mostly have values less than zero on dEdr. They are less variable on Fqp and are centered around zero. Most deceptive subjects have a positive latency difference measure; their latency is longer on relevant than on comparison questions (when averaged within and across charts). Nondeceptives show a tendency of having less variable values that are less than zero (i.e., longer latency on EDR on comparison questions, but not as much between variability as for deceptive subjects). A bivariate plot of the integrated difference for blood volume and pulse frequency shows less clear separation of the two groups. Deceptive subjects show a tendency to have higher blood volume responses on relevant than on comparison questions while the opposite holds for nondeceptive examinees.

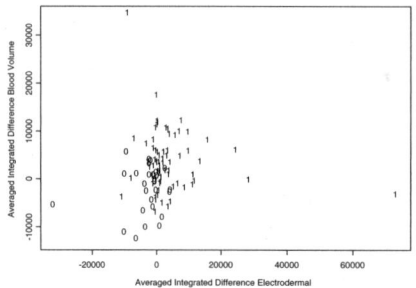 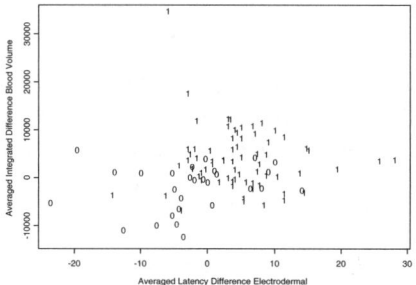

FIGURE 7.6
Bivariate plots of averaged integrated difference feature for electrodermal (dEdr) versus averaged integrated difference feature for blood volume (dBv), averaged latency difference for electrodermal(lEdr) versus dBv.

7.5.4 Logistic Regression

We used data from 97 randomly chosen subjects (69 deceptive, 28 nondeceptive) for evaluation and selection of the best subset of features for the classification model, and saved the remaining 52 cases (29 deceptive, 23 nondeceptive) for testing. Since the questions across subjects are semantically different and there is no consistent ordering we developed a model based on comparison of the averaged relevant questions versus the averaged comparison questions. Logistic regression models developed on variables from the first two settings even when principal components are used as predictors yield multiple models with at least 9 predictors. These predictors vary across different models and perform poorly on the test set, although they may achieve perfect separation on the training dataset [24].

Average Relevant vs. Average Comparison. For each chart, each channel and each feature we calculated the average relevant and average comparison response over the 20-second window. Typically, if we have a noisy signal, one simple solution is to average across trials (i.e., across charts) even though we lose some information on measurement variability between different charts.

$\bar{R}_{ij.} = \frac{\sum_{k=1}^{nr_i} R_{ijk}}{nr_i}$ is the averaged relevant response and $\bar{C}_{ij.} = \frac{\sum_{k=1}^{nc_i} C_{ijk}}{nc_i}$ is the averaged comparison response on the ith chart, j^{th} channel, where nr_i is the number of relevant questions and nc_i is the number of comparison questions on the ith chart. We calculate the averaged relevant ($\bar{R}_{.j.}$) and comparison ($\bar{C}_{.j.}$) responses across m charts producing a total of 13 predictors: 5 for integrated differences, 5 for spectral proportion differences, and 3 for latency differences.

The logistic regression was performed for each feature independently on each chart, across the charts, and in combination to evaluate the statistical significance of the features. A stepwise procedure in Splus software was used to find the optimal set of features. Neither clustering nor PCA improved the results. The following models are representative of performed analyses on each feature and when combined: In-

TABLE 7.3
Features with the estimated logistic regression coefficients and standard errors for models M1, M2, and M4.

Model	M1	M2	M4
Features	$\hat{\beta}$ (SE)	$\hat{\beta}$ (SE)	$\hat{\beta}$ (SE)
Intercept$\times 10$	+4.90 (3.03)	+6.80 (2.50)	−3.07 (2.96)
Integrated Diff. Electrodermal$\times 10^4$	+3.15 (1.02)		+1.59 (0.62)
Integrated Diff. Blood Volume$\times 10^4$	+2.14 (0.75)		+1.07 (0.44)
Integrated Diff. Pulse Frequency$\times 10$	−3.72 (1.44)		−2.49 (0.87)
Latency Diff. Electrodermal$\times 10$		+1.43 (0.404)	+0.35 (0.38)
Spectral Diff. Blood Volume$\times 10$			+0.36 (0.23)

TABLE 7.4
Percents of correctly classified subjects in hold-out-set cross-validation.

Model	Training		Test	
	Deceptive(%)	Nondeceptive(%)	Deceptive(%)	Nondeceptive(%)
M1	94	64	97	52
M2	96	29	90	9
M3	99	7	100	9
M4	93	61	97	48

tegrated Difference (M1), Latency Difference (M2), Spectral Properties Difference (M3): Score $= \hat{\beta}_0 + \hat{\beta}_1 \text{hPn1} + \hat{\beta}_2 \text{hEdr} + \hat{\beta}_3 \text{hBv} + \hat{\beta}_4 \text{hFqp}$, and all 3 features (M4).

We considered models on individual charts and observed almost identical models across charts. Chart 3 did worse on cross-validation than the other two, and relied more on high frequency measures of respiration and sweating. Chart 2 added significantly to the detection of innocent subjects in comparison to chart 1. For chart 2 the latency difference on blood volume was a slightly better predictor than the high frequency measure which is more significant on chart 1 [24].

The linear combination of integrated differences was the strongest discriminator. Latency had the most power on the electrodermal response. Our high frequency feature on any of the measurements was a poor individual predictor, particularly on nondeceptive people; however, it seems to have some effect when combined with the other two features. All features show better discrimination on electrodermal response, blood volume, and pulse frequency than on the respiration measurements.

7.5.5 Classification Results

We tested the previously described models for their predictive power on an independent test set of 52 subjects. Table 7.4 summarizes the classification results based on a 0.5 probability cutoff. A probability of 0.5 or above indicates deception, and a probability less than 0.5 indicates truthfulness.

We ran the same subsets of training and test data through the Polyscore. Figure 7.7 shows receiver operating characteristic curves (ROCs) of model M4 performance

TABLE 7.5
5-fold cross-validation results at 0.5 probability cutoff value.

	Training (N=119)				Test(N=30)			
	Deceptive%		Nondeceptive%		Deceptive%		Nondeceptive%	
	M1	M4	M1	M4	M1	M4	M1	M4
Mean	91	90	60	57	92	92	70	66
St.Error	4.1	2.1	2.3	2.1	5.4	5.6	21.6	21.5

and of a PolyScore 5.1 on 52 test cases. This is not an independent evaluation of PolyScore algorithm since some of these test cases were used in its development. ROC and the area under the curve give a quantitative assessment of a classifier's degree of accuracy. [7] showed that ROC overestimates the performance of the logistic regression classifier when the same data are used to fit the score and to calculate the ROC.

Since k-fold cross-validation works better for small data sets [15] we performed 5-fold cross-validation on models M1 and M4. The results are presented in Table 7.5. The number of innocent subjects in training runs vary from 39 to 47 out of 51, and deceptive from 72 to 80 out of 98. In the first run with only four nondeceptive test cases our models achieve 100% correct classification which is highly inconsistent with the other runs. The average area under the ROC for M4 is $0.899(\pm 0.05)$. When we apply shrinkage correction proposed by [7] the average area under the curve is approximately 0.851.

7.6 Discussion

The objective of the automated scoring algorithms for polygraph data is to create reliable and statistically valid classification schemes minimizing both false positive and false negative rates. Beginning in the 1970s, various papers in the polygraph literature have offered evidence claiming to show that automated classification methods for analyzing polygraph charts could do so. According to [9], the accuracies of five different computer algorithms range from 73% to 89% on deceptive subjects when inconclusives are included and 91% to 98% when they are excluded. For innocent subjects these numbers vary from 53% to 68%, and 72% to 90%.

Our analyses based on a set of 149 criminal cases provided by DoDPI suggest that it is easy to develop such algorithms with comparable recognition rates. Our results are based on a 0.5 probability cutoff for two groups: deceptive (probability greater than 0.5) and nondeceptive (probability less than 0.5). Other cutoff values would allow us to balance the errors differently. Neither clustering nor PCA significantly improve our results, which is consistent with the recent work of [5].

One possible explanation for the relatively poor classification performance is the small sample size and, in particular, the small number of nondeceptive cases. However, PolyScore algorithms, for example, had a much larger database [22, 12], but their accuracy rates are not significantly better than ours.

Statistical Data Mining and Knowledge Discovery 151

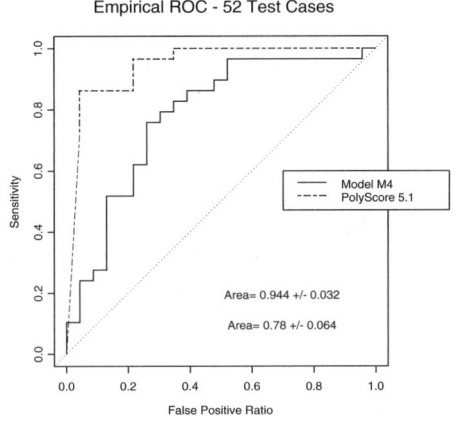

	M4	PolyScore 5.1	Others*
≥ 0.5 cutoff			
Deceptive	90%	86%	73-100%
Nondeceptive	48%	78%	53-90%

FIGURE 7.7
ROCs for classification results of PolyScore 5.1 and M4 on 52 test cases. The table shows percent correct when 0.5 is a cutoff value. In practice PolyScore 5.1 uses 0.95 and 0.05 as the cutoff values for classifiying deceptive and nondeceptive subjects. (*)These values are based on different cutoffs and range over the results when inconclusives are included and excluded giving higher percent correct when inconclusive cases are excluded.

Another possible explanation could be high variability and presence of measurment errors that come with real-life polygraph data, where there is a lack of standards in data collection and recording. Our exploratory data analysis points to problems with question inconsistency, response variability within an individual and across individuals (due to nature, gender, etc.), and possible learning effects. It is not always clear where differences in responses comes from; are we dealing with habituation or comparing semantically different questions across the charts and hence having different responsivness to different questions? Since in our data the questions are semantically different, and no consistent ordering within and across charts could be established, we averaged the relevant and comparison responses and then look at their difference. PolyScore and CPS algorithms take the same approach. This methodology ignores the question semantics which could be a flaw in our approach. These phenomena could be better studied in the screening type tests or with more standardized laboratory cases¶ where there is consistency in the order and the type of questions asked within and across both charts and individuals. Athough CPS algorithms have been developed on laboratory data, they have not achieved significantly better results.

¶See discussion on possible downfalls of lab data in [6].

These points and numerous aspects of each of the steps of the analysis are discussed further in [24]. Perhaps it is not reasonable to expect that a single algorithm will successfully be able to detect deceptive and truthful examinees. A solution may lay in the data collection and on detailed research on underlying theory for polygraphs, before proper statistical modeling can be effectively utilized.

Finally, we note that in the cases we examined there is little or no information available on the assessment of ground truth, differences among examiners, examiner-examinee interactions, and delays in the timing of questions. Most of these are not addressed by current scoring algorithms. More discussion on these issues and their implications for inflated accuracies can be found in Appendix G of [6].

7.7 Conclusion

This paper presents an initial evaluation and analysis of polygraph data for a set of real-life specific incident cases. With a very simple approach, in a short period of time, we have managed to obtain accuracy rates to a certain degree comparable to what's currently being reported by other algorithms and manual scoring. The fact that we are able to produce a number of different models that account for different predictors yet give similar results points to the complexity that underlines assessment and/or classification of examinee's deceptiveness.

This work can be redefined and extended in a number of ways. More features could be extracted and explored. Thus far these efforts have not resulted in significantly smaller errors; hence, it raises a question how far could this approach go? One could imagine improvements to current methods by running a proper Bayesian analysis and incorporating prior knowledge on prevalence. Our inclination would be to do a more complex time series analysis of these data. The waveform of each channel can be considered and the analysis would gear towards describing a physiological signature for deceptive and nondeceptive classes. Clearly the ordering of the questions should be accounted for. A mixed-effects model with repeated measures would be another approach, where repetitions would be measurements across different charts. In other areas with similar data researchers have explored the use of Hidden Markov Models [10].

There has yet to be a proper independent evaluation of computer scoring algorithms on a suitably selected set of cases, for either specific incidents or security screening, which would allow one to accurately assess the validity and accuracy of these algorithms. One could argue that computerized algorithms should be able to analyze the data better because they execute tasks which are difficult even for a trained examiner to perform, including filtering, transformation, calculating signal derivatives, manipulating signals, and looking at the bigger pictures, not merely adjacent comparisons. Moreover, computer systems never get careless or tired. However, success of both numerical and computerized systems still depends heavily on the pre-test phase of the examination. How well examiners formulate the questions inevitably affects the quality of information recorded. We believe that substantial improvements to current numerical scoring may be possible, but the ultimate potential of computerized scoring systems depends on the quality of the data available for system development and application, and the uniformity of the examination formats with which the systems are designed to deal. Computerized systems have the potential to reduce the variability that comes from bias and inexperience of the examiners and chart interpreters, but the evidence that they have achieved this potential is meager at best.

Acknowledgments

The author would like to thank Stephen E. Fienberg and Anthony Brockwell, for their advice and support on this project. The author is also grateful to the members of the NAS/NRC Committee to review the scientific evidence on polygraphs for the opportunity to work with them, and to Andy Ryan and Andrew Dollins of the Department of Defense Polygraph Institute for providing the data.

References

[1] Alder, K. 1998. To Tell the Truth: The Polygraph Exam and the Marketing of American Expertise. *Historical Reflections*. 24(3), pp.487-525.

[2] American Polygraph Association. *www.polygraph.org*

[3] Brownley, K.A., Hurwitz, B.E., Schneiderman, N. 2000. Cardiovascular psychophysiology. Ch. 9, pp. 224-264, in [4].

[4] Cacioppo, J.T., Tassinary, J.T., Bernston, G.G., Eds. 2000. *Handbook of Psychophysiology*. Second Edition. New York: Cambridge University Press.

[5] Campbell, J.L. 2001. *Individual Differences in Patterns of Physiological Activation and Their Effects on Computer Diagnoses of Truth and Deception*. Doctoral Dissertation. The University of Utah.

[6] Committee to Review the Scientific Evidence on the Polygraph. 2002. *The Polygraph and Lie Detection*. Washington, DC: National Academy Press.

[7] Copas, J.B., Corbett, P. 2002. Overestimation of the receiver operating characteristic curve for logistic regression. *Biometrika*, 89(2), pp. 315-331.

[8] Dawson, M., Schell, A.M., Filion, D.L. 2000. The electrodermal system. Ch. 8, pp. 200-223, in [4].

[9] Dollins, A.B., Kraphol, D.J., Dutton, D.W. 2000. Computer Algorithm Comparison. *Polygraph*, 29(3), pp.237-257.

[10] Fernandez, R. 1997. *Stochastic Modeling of Physiological Signals with Hidden Markov Models: A Step Toward Frustration Detection in Human-Computer Interfaces*. Master's Thesis. Massachusetts Institute of Technology.

[11] Gratton, G. 2000. Biosignal Processing. Ch. 33, pp. 900-923, in [4].

[12] Harris, J.C., Olsen, D.E. 1994. Polygraph Automated Scoring System. U.S. Patent #5,327,899.

[13] Harris, J. 1996. Real Crime Validation of the PolyScore 3.0 Zone Comparison Scoring Algorithm. Johns Hopkins University Applied Physics Laboratory.

[14] Harver, A., Lorig, T.S. 2000. Respiration. Ch. 10, pp. 265-293, in [4].

[15] Hastie, T., Tibshirani, R., Friedman, J. 2001. *The Elements of Statistical Learning: Data Mining, Inference and Prediction*. New York: Springer-Verlag.

[16] Hosmer, D.W., Lemeshow, Jr., S. 1989. *Applied Logistic Regression*. New York: John Wiley & Sons.

[17] Jennings, R.J., Stine, L.A. 2000. Salient method, design, and analysis concerns. Ch. 32, pp. 870-899, in [4].

[18] Kircher, J.C., Raskin, D.C. 1988. Human versus computerized evaluations of polygraph data in a laboratory setting. *Journal of Applied Psychology* 73:291-302.

[19] Kircher, J.C., Raskin, D.C. 2002. Computer methods for the psychophysiological detection of deception. Chapter 11, pp. 287-326, in *Handbook of Polygraph Testing*, M. Kleiner, ed. London: Academic Press.

[20] Matte, J.A. 1996. *Forensic Psychophysiology Using Polygraph-Scientific Truth Verification Lie Detection*. Williamsville, NY: J.A.M. Publications.

[21] McLachlan, G.J. 1992. *Discriminant Analysis and Statistical Pattern Recognition*. New York: John Wiley & Sons.

[22] Olsen, D.E, Harris, J.C., Capps, M.H., Ansley, N. 1997. Computerized Polygraph Scoring System. *Journal Forensic Science* 42(1):61-71.

[23] Raskin, D.C., Hont, C.R., Kircher, J.C. 1997. The scientific status of research on polygraph techniques: The case for polygraph tests. In D.L. Faigman, D.Kaye, M.J. Saks, J. Senders (Eds.) *Modern Scientific Evidence: The Law and Science of Expert Evidence*. St.Paul, MN:West.

[24] Slavkovic, A. 2002. *Evaluating Polygraph Data*. Technical report 766. Department of Statistics. Carnegie Mellon University.

[25] Swinford, J. 1999. Manually Scoring Polygraph Charts Utilizing the Seven-Position Numerical Analysis Scale at the Department Of Defense Polygraph Institute. *Polygraph*, 28(1), pp.10-27.

8

Missing Value Algorithms in Decision Trees

Hyunjoong Kim and Sumer Yates
University of Tennessee, Knoxville, USA

CONTENTS

8.1 Introduction 155
8.2 The Seven Algorithms 156
8.3 The Simulation Study 159
8.4 Results 162
8.5 Conclusions 166
    References 168

Seven decision tree algorithms for missing values were compared based on split point selection, split variable selection, and the predictive accuracy. The simulation experiments were carried out under two scenarios. We found that the performance of missing value algorithms depends on the characteristic of data set under the analysis and none can outperform others in all cases.

8.1 Introduction

In the real world, missing values are common and can occur in both training and test data for classification. Missing values can dramatically affect classification algorithms and their performances. Among classification algorithms, decision trees are known to be less sensitive to missing values mainly because it uses only one variable at each node of the tree. Many decision tree algorithms were developed to deal with missing values in different ways. This study is to evaluate the performance of these algorithms. In particular, we will study the missing value effect on the tree structure and classification accuracy. For more general information on classification trees, see Breiman et al. (1984).

Seven missing value algorithms were considered for this study: probability split, alternative split, proxy split, surrogate split, root-node imputation, mean imputation, and taking a designated node for the missing values. All graphs and tables concerning the algorithms will be labeled with either the numbers or algorithm name given below:

1. Probability Split
2. Alternative Split
3. Proxy Split
4. Surrogate Split
5. Root Node Imputation
6. Nodewise Imputation
7. Separate Node

A simulation study was designed and conducted to assess the seven algorithms. Decision tree programs used for the evaluation were C4.5 (Quinlan 1993), CRUISE (Kim and Loh 2001), QUEST (Loh and Shih 1997), RPART (Therneau and Atkinson 2001), and S-PLUS (Clark and Pregibon 1993).

8.2 The Seven Algorithms

Each of the seven algorithms will be briefly discussed in the following subsections.

8.2.1 Probability Split

The probability split algorithm was evaluated using C4.5 (Quinlan 1993). In C4.5, split variables and split points are selected based on a greedy search algorithm using non-missing observations in the training data. At each stage of tree growing, observations with missing values in the split variable will take down all the branches in the node with different probabilities. The probabilities are determined proportional to the number of non-missing data that takes each branch. On the other hand, observations with no missing values will take down one branch with probability one. This procedure is repeated for each sub-partition until a stopping rule is satisfied. Pruning is used to simplify the tree structure and to prevent over-fitting. When a future data point arrives at a node, the data point is compared to the split rule. The split rule is usually a simple rule based on one variable such as $X_1 < 2$. If the value for the split variable is missing in the future data, C4.5 uses the probability assigned to that node. The future data will travel all possible paths in the tree; a probability is assigned after it travels each particular split in the tree. The probability of reaching each terminal node is assessed and the path with the greatest probability is selected.

8.2.2 Alternative Split

The alternative split algorithm was evaluated using one of the missing value options available in CRUISE (Kim and Loh 2001). This algorithm uses the p-values from the chi-square test of independence to rank the split variables; the test examines the relationship between the variable and the class membership. If there are missing values in the variables, only non-missing cases are included for the test; thus different number of cases may be counted for each test. When a variable is continuous, it is

Statistical Data Mining and Knowledge Discovery

Y	X1: Number of Observations			
	Quartile1	Quartile2	Quartile3	Quartile4
1	25	25	0	0
0	0	0	25	25
	p-value $<$ 0.0001			

Y	X2: Number of Observations			
	Quartile1	Quartile2	Quartile3	Quartile4
1	15	18	10	8
0	10	7	15	17
	p-value = 0.0182			

Y	X3: Number of Observations			
	Quartile1	Quartile2	Quartile3	Quartile4
1	12	10	14	15
0	13	15	11	10
	p-value = 0.5009			

TABLE 8.1
Alternative split example. The rows represent the classes of Y and the columns represent the four quartiles of the continuous predictor variables.

converted to a discrete variable categorized on sample quartiles. Suppose that there are 25 observations per quartile for a data set and there are three variables X_1, X_2, and X_3 to classify the response Y as 0 or 1. Table 8.1 shows the frequency between the quartile dispersion and the classes. The largest association, as shown by the smallest p-value, is between Y and X_1; therefore, X_1 will be the selected split variable. For categorical variables, quartiles are replaced by observed categories of the variable.

The alternate split is determined as follows. The remaining two variables will be ranked according to their p-values and used when the value for X_1 is missing. Therefore, if an observation has a missing value for X_1 and it arrives at the node that splits on X_1, X_2 will be used instead; if X_2 is also missing, X_3 will be used to determine the path.

8.2.3 Proxy Split

The proxy split algorithm was evaluated using one of the missing value options in CRUISE (Kim and Loh 2001). The split variable is determined by the method de-

		X_1	
		Left	Right
X_2	Left	5	0
	Right	0	5
	p-value = 0.0016		

		X_1	
		Left	Right
X_2	Left	7	1
	Right	2	5
	p-value = 0.0201		

TABLE 8.2
Proxy Split Example. The row and columns represent the path of a node in the tree.

scribed in Section 8.2.2. To determine the proxy split, this algorithm considers the number of cases the split variable and the other variables send the same way. Chi-square tests of independence are then performed for each combination. The variable having the greatest association with the original split variable, as shown by the smallest p-value, is selected as the proxy split. The variables are ranked according to their p-values, and used in that order in case of missing values for more than one variable. In Table 8.2, there are twenty total observations in the data set. For the purpose of illustration, consider that X_1 has five missing values and is determined to be the original split variable. Further assume that X_2 also has five missing values among 15 non-missing cases, while X_3 has no missing values. From the tables, the proxy split chosen would be X_2 because it has the greatest association with X_1. Therefore, at a node that splits on X_1, and if an observation has missing value for X_1, X_2 will be used instead; if X_2 is also missing, X_3 will be used to determine the path.

8.2.4 Surrogate Split

The surrogate split algorithm was developed by Breiman et al. (1984). This algorithm ranks the variables according to the number of cases that variables send the same way as the split variable. A greedy search algorithm is initially used to determine the split, and then the total number of observations that both variables send to the same subnode is counted. Consider Table 8.2 from Section 8.2.3; the surrogate split in this case would now be X_3 because it sends more observations to the same node than X_2 does. The surrogate split algorithm was evaluated using RPART (Therneau and Atkinson 2001).

8.2.5 Root Node Imputation

The root node imputation algorithm considered in this simulation was one of the missing value treatment options available in the CRUISE (Kim and Loh 2001) software. The tree construction is done by the same method as the one described in 8.2.2. The difference lies on the way to deal with the missing values in a test data. Before the test data are evaluated by the decision tree, the missing values are imputed by an imputation algorithm. We used a non-parametric regression method assuming missing at random. It explores both linear and non-linear relationships among variables. Variable to be imputed is treated as response and others as predictors. The predicted value replaces the missing value. The test dataset is considered to be non-missing after imputation and takes down the tree for classification.

8.2.6 Nodewise Imputation

In the nodewise imputation algorithm used by QUEST (Loh and Shih 1997), the split variable is selected using non-missing data by the one-way Analysis of Variance for continuous variables and chi-square test of independence for categorical variables. Missing values in training data are replaced by the mean or mode of all other non-missing data points available at the current node. For a test data classification, missing values are also imputed by the sample mean or mode values at each node.

8.2.7 Separate Node

For any predictor with missing values, the separate node algorithm will assign a node for missing values. Therefore, if an observation has a missing value for the split variable (continuous or categorical), it takes the path to the node designated for missing values. We used S-PLUS (Clark and Pregibon 1993) for this algorithm.

8.3 The Simulation Study

The goal of the simulation study was to compare the missing value algorithms on three aspects: variable selection in the presence of missing values, split point selection in the presence of missing values, and the classification accuracy of test data containing missing values.

8.3.1 Experiment-A

Three variables, X_1, X_2, and X_3, were generated and used in the decision tree construction in an attempt to classify the binomial response variable, Y. The response determinant is X_1 and X_2 can be the determinant also when the correlation with X_1 is high. X_1 was distributed as $X_1 \sim N(0,1)$ when Y=0 for approximately 42% of the

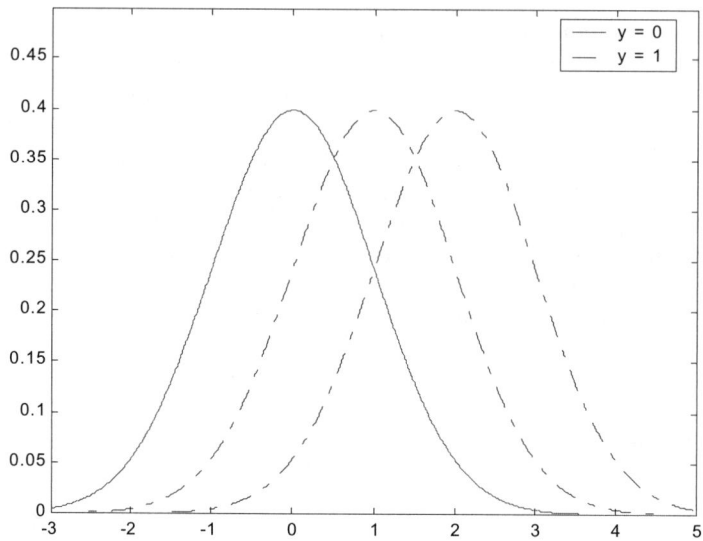

FIGURE 8.1
Distribution of X_1 for varying Y.

observations; Y=1 and $X_1 \sim N(2,1)$ for approximately 25% of the observations; Y=1 and $X_1 \sim N(1,1)$ for approximately 33% of the observations.

Figure 8.1 illustrates the distributional curves of X_1. As the response determinant, X_1 is expected to be the split variable for the first node in the tree if it does not have any missing values. For the purposes of this study X_1 contained three percentages of missing values: 10%, 30%, and 50%. The remaining variables X_2 and X_3 had no missing values; where X_2 follows Exponential(1)+δX_1 and X_3 has Uniform(0,1). The X_2 variable is correlated with X_1 at four levels, δ=0, 0.5, 1, 5. The correlations between X_1 and X_2 are 0, .45, .71, and .98. Scatter plot representations of the varying relationship between X_1 and X_2 are given in Figure 8.2. Note that X_2 is also expected to be the split variable if the correlation with X_1 is high. X_3 is a noise variable for classification of Y. The sample size for both the training and test data set was 1000 observations. There were 1000 iterations of each correlation and missing values combination, for a total of 12,000 iterations.

8.3.2 Experiment-B

Three variables, X_1, X_2, and X_3, were generated again to classify the binomial response variable, Y. The response determinants are variables X_1 and X_2 which are distributed as Normal. X_3 becomes the determinant if the correlation with X_1 is

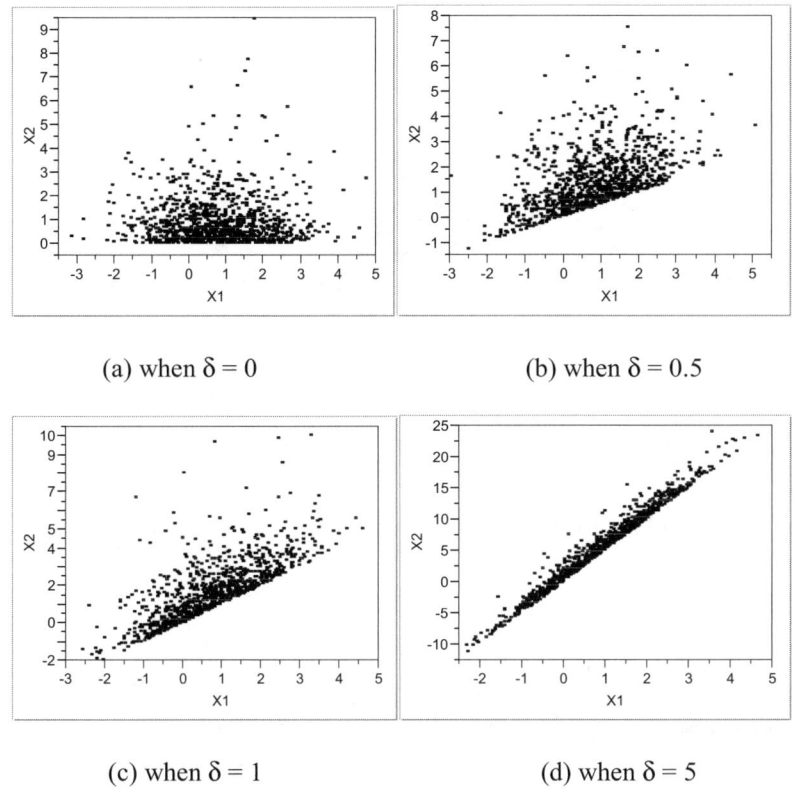

FIGURE 8.2
Scatter plots of X_1 versus X_2 for varying degrees of correlation.

high. When Y=1, $X_1 \sim N(2,1)$ and $X_2 \sim N(0,1.69)$ for approximately 50% of the observations; when Y=0, $X_1 \sim N(2,1)$ and $X_2 \sim N(2,1)$ for approximately 17% of the observations and $X_1 \sim N(0,1)$ and $X_2 \sim N(0,4)$ for approximately 33% of the observations. Figure 8.3 presents the scatter plot of X_1 and X_2 with class labels for each observation. For the purposes of this study X_1 contained three percentages of missing values: 10%, 30%, and 50% and X_2 has one missing percentage value: 30%. The remaining variable X_3 had no missing values; where X_3 has Exponential(1) + δX_1. The X_3 variable was correlated with X_1 at four levels, $\delta=0, 0.5, 1, 5$. As the response determinants, either X_1 or X_2 are expected to be the split variable for the first node in the tree, especially for low missing percentages. Note that X_3 is also expected to be the split variable when the correlation with X_1 is high. The sample size for both the training and test data set was 500. There were 200 iterations of each correlation and missing values combination, for a total of 2,400 iterations.

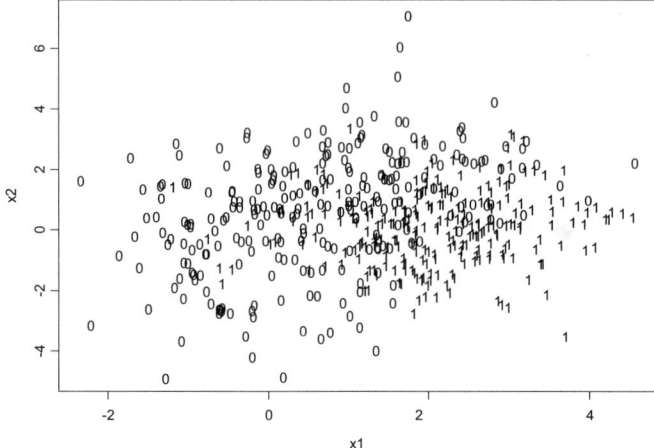

FIGURE 8.3
Scatter plots of X_1 and X_2 with class labels superimposed. The plot is based on 500 observations.

8.4 Results

8.4.1 Experiment-A

As mentioned in the previous section, X_1 and X_2 are the response determinant, therefore, the correct choice for the initial split variable. In general, as the correlation between X_1 and X_2 increased, the algorithms selected X_2 more often. This result is reasonable because X_1 loses classification power due to missing values while X_2 maintained the same level of classification power. Among the algorithms, the separate node algorithm performed differently because it selected X_1 most of the time. This result is displayed in Figure 8.4.

From the distributions of X_1, the split point selection was expected to be somewhere between 0.5 and 1, depending on the percentage of missing values. From the box plots given in Figure 8.5, the median split point for all seven algorithms is within the expected range for the first two levels of correlation. The alternative split, the proxy split, and the separate node algorithms have the least amount of variation; but the separate node algorithm selects slightly lower split point when X_1 has 30% and 50% missing, and slightly higher split point when X_1 has 10% missing. For the high correlation (r = .98) case, the split point values are larger because of the tendency for the algorithms to pick X_2 instead of X_1. In all cases the least variation occurred in the alternative split, the proxy split, and the root-node imputation algorithms.

Figures 8.6 to 8.9 show the test error for the three levels of missing values by correlation between X_1 and X_2. For low correlation case ($r = 0$ or .45), as X_1 has more missing values, the median test error rate also increased for all algorithms. The impact of missing values decreased as the correlation increased except for the separate node algorithm. For high correlation case ($r = .98$), the error rates are very similar. The differences of error rates among algorithms are larger for the low correlation, but it decreases as the correlation between X_1 and X_2 increases. These two relationships can be attributed to the fact that X_2 has no missing values and as the correlation increases, the algorithms select X_2 more often. The probability split, alternate split, and proxy split algorithms gave uniformly low median test error rates. The separate node algorithm has the highest median test error rate in all twelve scenarios, and is significantly different from the others.

8.4.2 Experiment-B

Note that all the variables are the response determinants. At 10% missing for X_1 and 30% missing for X_2 and for low correlations between X_1 and X_3 ($r = 0$ or .45), X_1 was selected most often across all algorithms. However, as X_1 takes more missing values, X_2 is selected more often. This result is reasonable because X_1 loses classification power due to missing values while X_2 maintained the same level of classification power. X_3 was not selected often due to the low correlation with X_1. For high correlation cases ($r = .98$), X_3 picks up the classification power of X_1, thus selected most often. This behavior generally holds for all the methods considered. This suggests that all seven methods are doing a reasonable job in selecting variables. The results are in Figure 8.10.

For the split point selection as displayed in Figure 8.11, we can observe that the split points are more widely distributed compared to Section 8.3.1. This is due to the fact that all of the variables can be determinants and their split points make the box plot spread out. At 10% missing percentage and low correlations ($r = 0$ or .45), all the methods have small variations as X_1 is selected most of the time. As missing percentages increase for low correlation, some algorithms like alternate split, proxy split, root node imputation, and separate node algorithms have large variation because X_2 or X_3 are selected alternatively as the split variable. For 30% or 50% of missing percentage with high correlations ($r = .98$), the variation reduced again due to the fact that X_3 was selected most of the time. The probability split, the surrogate split, and the nodewise imputation algorithms had small variations on split points consistently.

Figures 8.12 to 8.15 show the test error for the three levels of missing values by correlation between X_1 and X_3. As in Experiment-A, the impact of missing values decreased as the correlation increased except for the separate node algorithm. The differences of error rates among algorithms are smaller in general compared to Experiment-A. Among algorithms, the nodewise imputation algorithm gives lower test error rates consistently. Unlike experiment-A, the separate node algorithm performed well in low correlation ($r = 0$), but poor in high correlation case ($r = .98$).

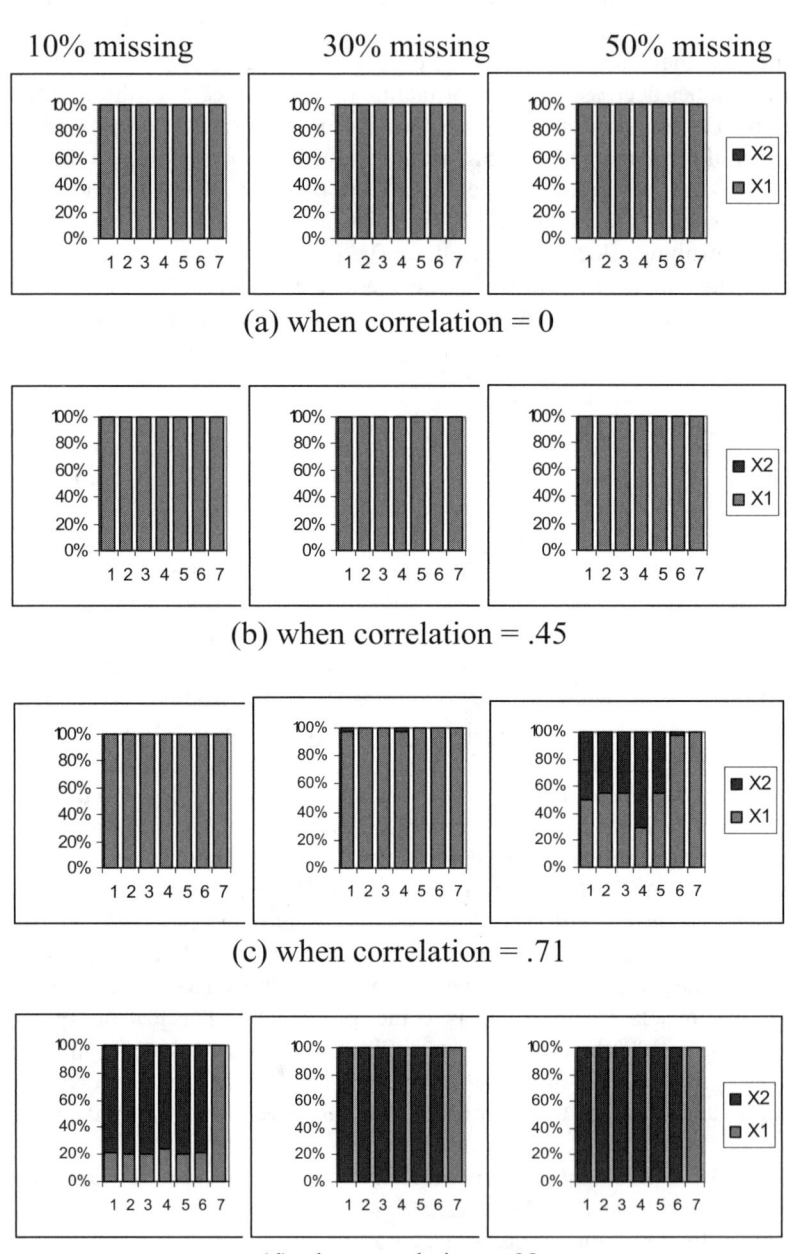

FIGURE 8.4
Initial Split variable selection for all twelve cases – Experiment-A.

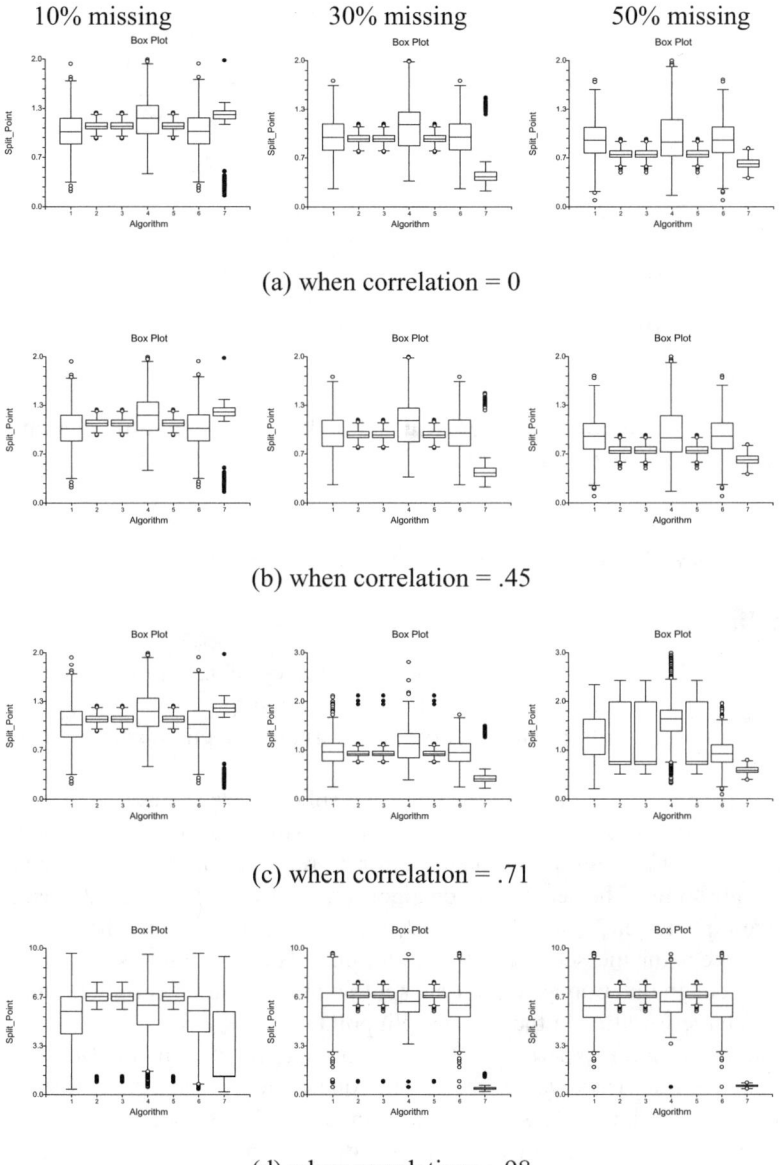

FIGURE 8.5
Box plots of selected split points – Experiment-A.

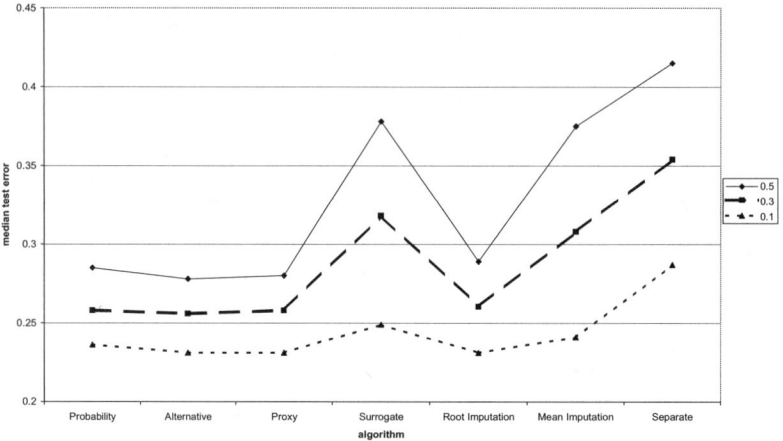

FIGURE 8.6
Median test error rate of all seven algorithms, for three missing value percentages and no correlation between X_1 and X_2 ($\delta = 0$).

8.5 Conclusions

This study is to evaluate the performance and the accuracy of seven missing value algorithms in decision trees. There were three criteria used to evaluate the performance of the algorithms: split point selection, split variable selection, and test error rate.

For the experiment-A, the alternative and proxy split appear to have the lowest test error rate for all correlations and missing values. However, as the correlation increases, the effect of missing values on test error decreases as does the differences between the algorithms. The separate node algorithm performs poorly in all cases. As the correlation between X_1 and X_2 increased, X_2 was selected more often as the split variable except for the separate node algorithm. The alternative split, proxy split, and root-node imputation gave accurate split points with small variation; other algorithms had large variation in the chosen split point.

On the other hand for the experiment-B, the nodewise imputation method showed the lowest test error rate. However, as the correlation between X_1 and X_3 increases, the effect of missing values on test error rate decreased. The separate node algorithm performs reasonably well in most cases. Both X_1 and X_2 are selected as the split variables for low correlation case. As the correlation between X_1 and X_3 increased, X_3 was selected more often as the split variable. The probability split, the surrogate split, and the nodewise imputation algorithms gave accurate split points with small variation; other algorithms had large variation in the chosen split point.

Statistical Data Mining and Knowledge Discovery

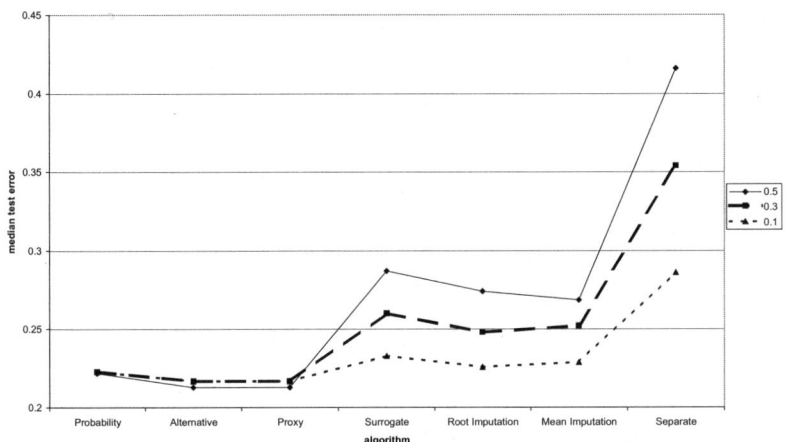

FIGURE 8.7
Median test error rate of all seven algorithms, for three missing value percentages. Correlation between X_1 and X_2 is .45 ($\delta = 0.5$).

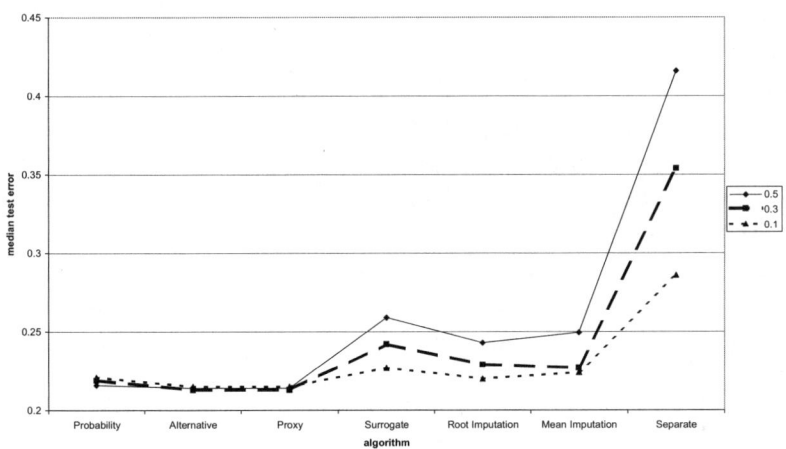

FIGURE 8.8
Median test error rate of all seven algorithms, for three missing value percentages. Correlation between X_1 and X_2 is .71 ($\delta = 1$).

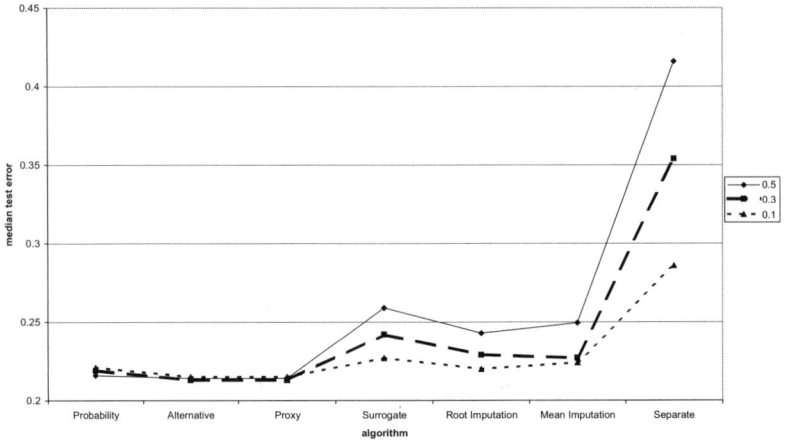

FIGURE 8.9
Median test error rate of all seven algorithms, for three missing value percentages. Correlation between X_1 and X_2 is .98 ($\delta = 5$).

As a conclusion, there was no clear winner that outperformed other algorithms in all three criteria. The performance of missing value algorithms depends on the characteristic of data set under the analysis.

References

[1] Breiman, L., Friedman, J., Olshen, R., and Stone, C. *Classification and Regression Trees*. Chapman & Hall, London, 1984.

[2] Clark, L.A. and Pregibon, D. Tree-based models. In *Statistical Models in S*, J.M. Chambers and T.J. Hastie (eds), pages 377-419, 1993.

[3] Kim, H., and Loh, W.-Y. Classification Trees With Unbiased Multiway Splits. *Journal of the American Statistical Association 96*, pages 598-604, 2001.

[4] Loh, W.-Y. and Shih, Y.-S. Split Selection methods for classification trees. *Statistica Sinica 7*, pages 815-840, 1997.

[5] Quinlan, J. R. *C4.5: programs for Machine Learning*. San Mateo, CA: Morgan Kaufmann, 1993.

[6] Therneau, T., and Atkinson, B. Recursive partitioning and regression trees. http://www.mayo.edu/hsr/Sfunc.html, 2001.

Statistical Data Mining and Knowledge Discovery

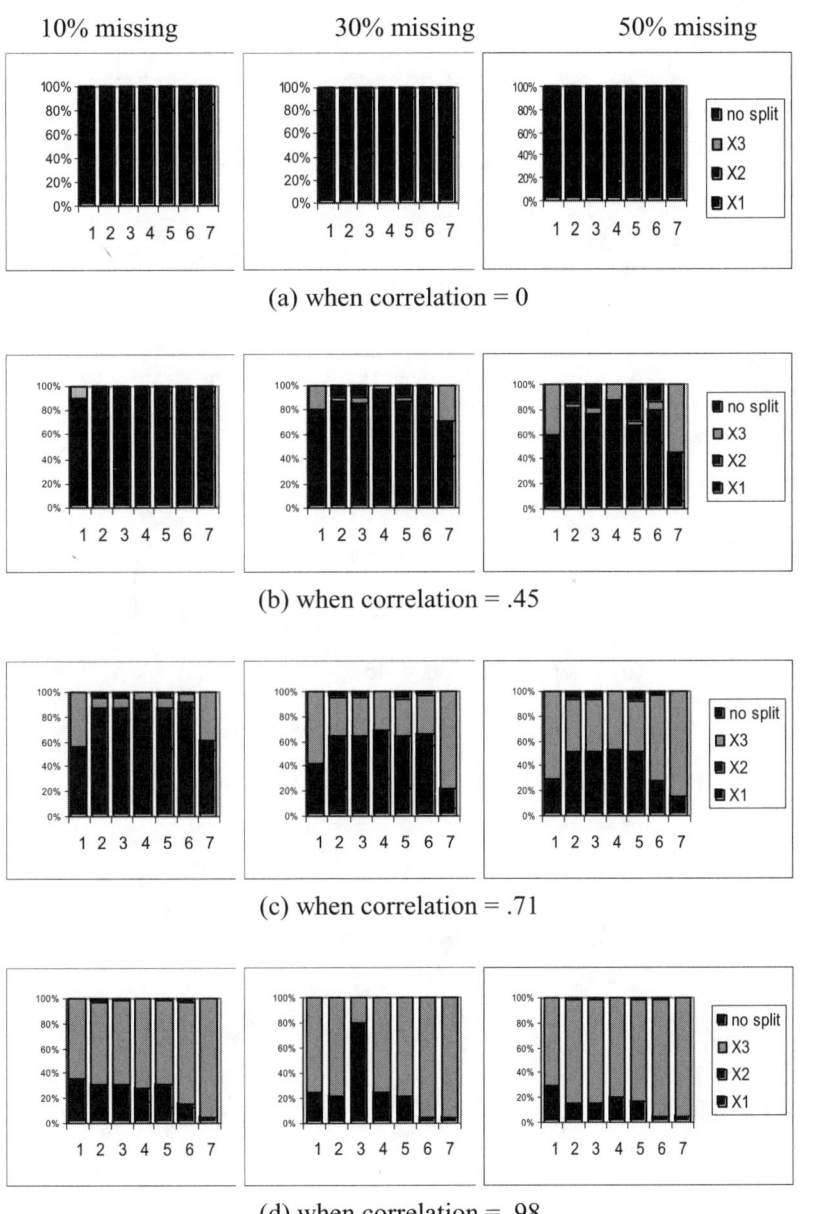

FIGURE 8.10
Initial split variable selection for all twelve cases. No split represents the case when the first node is a terminal node – Experiment-B.

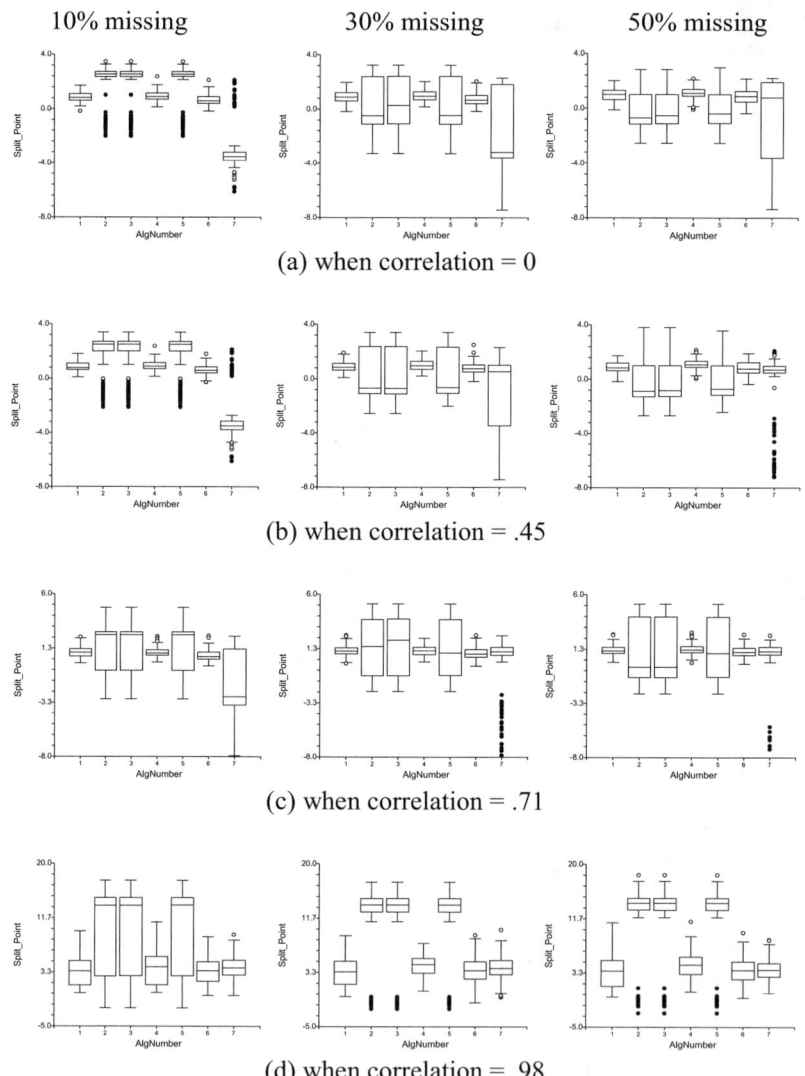

FIGURE 8.11
Box plots of selected split points – Experiment-B.

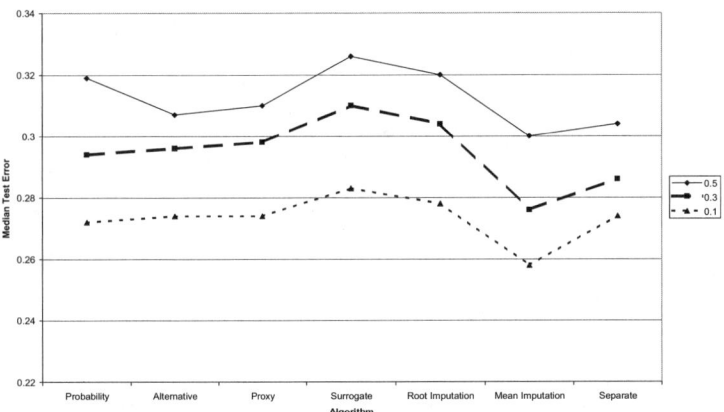

FIGURE 8.12
Median test error rate of all seven algorithms, for three missing value percentages and no correlation between X_1 and X_2 ($\delta = 0$).

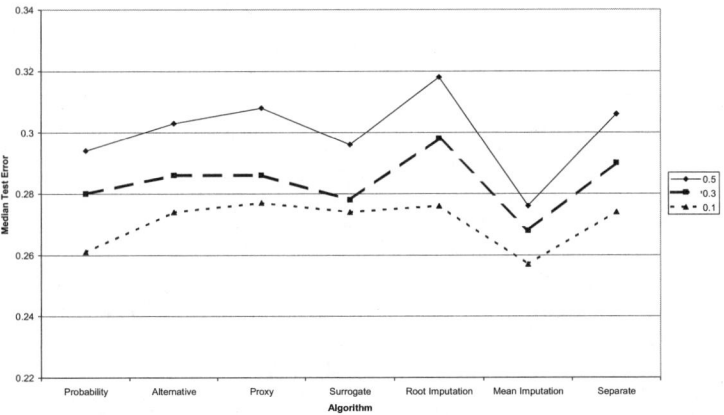

FIGURE 8.13
Median test error rate of all seven algorithms, for three missing value percentages. Correlation between X_1 and X_2 is .45 ($\delta = 0.5$).

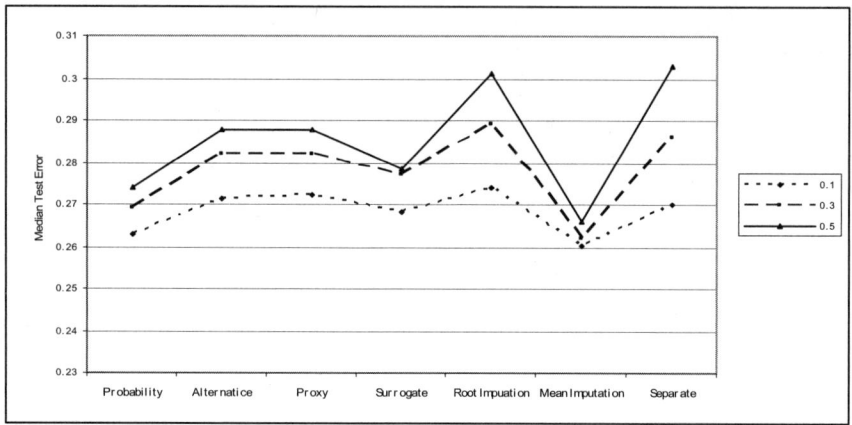

FIGURE 8.14
Median test error rate of all seven algorithms, for three missing value percentages. Correlation between X_1 and X_2 is .71 ($\delta = 1$).

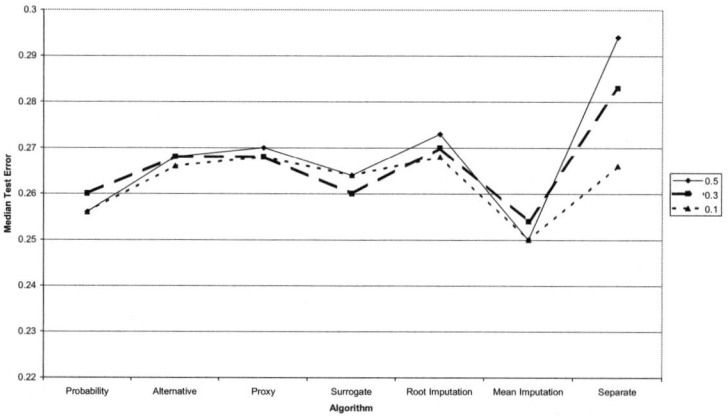

FIGURE 8.15
Median test error rate of all seven algorithms, for three missing value percentages. Correlation between X_1 and X_2 is .98 ($\delta = 5$).

9

Unsupervised Learning from Incomplete Data Using a Mixture Model Approach

Lynette Hunt and Murray Jorgensen
University of Waikato, Hamilton, New Zealand

CONTENTS

9.1 Introduction 173
9.2 Clustering by Mixture Models 175
9.3 Applications 182
9.4 Discussion 188
   References 189

Many unsupervised learning tasks involve high dimensional data sets where some of the attributes are continuous and some are categorical. One possible approach to clustering such data is to assume that the data to be clustered arise from a finite mixture of populations. The mixture likelihood approach has been well developed and much used, especially for mixtures where the component distributions are multivariate normal. Hunt and Jorgensen [17] presented methodology that enabled the clustering of mixed categorical and continuous data using a mixture model approach.

However many multivariate data sets encountered also contain unobserved or missing values. In this paper we demonstrate that the mixture approach to clustering can handle mixed categorical and continuous data where data are missing at random in the sense of Little and Rubin [20]. The methodology is illustrated by clustering two data sets.

9.1 Introduction

The computer discovery of structure in large multivariate data sets is variously known as "unsupervised learning," "clustering" and "cluster analysis." We will use the three terms synonymously. Although there is now a large literature on the mixture model approach to unsupervised learning, it is unlikely to have much impact in applications unless it is of use for clustering the kind of multivariate data sets which occur in practice. Two particular complications that are relatively common in practice are that the variables may be of mixed data types, some categorical and some continuous, and that values of some variables may be missing for some observations.

As described by Hunt and Jorgensen [17], the Multimix program accommodates both categorical and continuous variables. In this note we will describe the ideas behind the approach taken to missing data in Multimix, and demonstrate by clustering some example data sets with missing values.

Mainstream statistical packages employ a range of approaches to the missing data problem in cluster analysis. If the number of observations with missing values is small it is usual to discard those observations. With larger numbers of observations with missing values the practice of analyzing only complete observations both wastes information and can lead to misleading results if the complete cases are not representative of the full data set.

For this reason clustering packages usually implement some method of using the information in the incomplete cases. For example the GenStat directive FSIMILARITY forms similarity matrices by implementing Gower's [14] general (dis)similarity coefficient. This coefficient takes the form of a weighted average over variables in which the weight is taken as zero when calculating the similarity between two observations whenever the variable being considered has either value missing. Effectively this assumes that the contribution that would have been provided by the incompletely recorded variable to the proximity between the two items is equal to the weighted mean of the contributions provided by the variables for which complete information is available. Gower gives an example to show that the resultant similarity matrix need not be positive definite when data are missing. It is clear that when the assumption is not met the resultant similarity matrix may be misleading even when it is positive definite.

Another example of the handling of missing values in unsupervised learning comes from the SAS procedure FASTCLUS [30]. This is an iterative clustering algorithm of the "k-means" type, which maintains a set of k "cluster seeds," allocates observations to the cluster whose seed is closest in a distance measure, and updates the cluster seeds according to the observations so allocated. The cluster seeds are chosen to have all component variables nonmissing, and when allocating an observation to a cluster the missing variables are effectively disregarded.

Both FSIMILARITY and FASTCLUS are purely algorithmic procedures that are not based on any statistical model. One advantage of adopting a model-based framework for clustering is that we can take advantage of the considerable literature on missing data when fitting statistical models. Review papers in this literature include [1], [15], [28], and [10]. Also [20] and [31] are monographs on partially missing data. The approaches appropriate for handling such data in classification studies have traditionally been restricted due to the reluctance of the investigator to make assumptions about the data noted by Gordon [13] and the lack of a formal model for cluster analysis. It should, however, be noted that although an algorithm that is not model-based may not formally make any assumptions about the joint distributions of the variables, it may well be that the behavior of the algorithm is likely to be unsatisfactory unless some such conditions are satisfied.

Data are described as 'missing at random' when the probability that a variable is missing for a particular individual may depend on the values of the observed variables for that individual, but not on the value of the missing variable. That is, the distribution of the missing data mechanism does not depend on the missing values. For example, censored data are certainly *not* missing at random. Although SAS FASTCLUS does not assume any statistical model, it could yield misleading results given data with values missing, but not at random. For example it might be that variables close in value to that of a particular cluster seed become missing. This could cause observations that should be allocated to this cluster to be allocated elsewhere by FASTCLUS.

Rubin [29] showed that the process that causes the missing data can be ignored when making likelihood based inferences about the parameter of the data if the data are 'missing at random' and the parameter of the missing data process is 'distinct' from the parameter of the data. When the data are missing in this manner, the appropriate likelihood is simply the density of the observed data, regarded as a function of the parameters. 'Missing at random' is a central concept in the work of Little [20].

The EM algorithm of [10] is a general iterative procedure for maximum likelihood estimation in incomplete data problems. Their general model includes both the conceptual missing data formulation used in finite mixture models (that is, the assignments to classes are missing) and the accidental missing data discussed earlier. Many authors, for example McLachlan and Krishnan [24], have discussed the EM algorithm and its properties.

Little and Schluchter [22] present maximum likelihood procedures using the EM algorithm for the general location model with missing data. They note that their model reduces to that of Day [8] for K-variate mixtures when there is one K-level categorical variable that is completely missing. Little and Rubin [20] and Schafer [31] point out that the parametric mixture models lend themselves well to implementing incomplete data methods. We implement their approach to produce explicit methodology that enables the clustering of mixed (categorical/continuous) data using a mixture likelihood approach when data are missing at random. It is shown that the proposed methodology can detect meaningful structure in mixed data even when there is a fairly extreme amount of missing information.

9.2 Clustering by Mixture Models

Finite mixture models with multivariate component distributions have been used by several researchers as the basis for an approach to unsupervised learning with explicit statistical models. An extensive listing of mixture model software may be found on the web page maintained by David Dowe* although not all of these programs are suitable unsupervised learning in the sense discussed here. Some examples of mixture model clustering programs for multivariate data sets incorporating both continuous and categorical variables are

---

*http://www.csse.monash.edu.au/~dld/mixture.modelling.page.html

Snob developed by Chris Wallace, David Dowe and colleagues at the Department of Computer Science at Monash University, Melbourne;

AutoClass developed by Peter Cheeseman and colleagues at NASA;

Multimix developed by Lyn Hunt and Murray Jorgensen at the Department of Statistics, University of Waikato, New Zealand;

Mplus developed by Bengt Muthen and colleagues at the Graduate School of Education and Information Studies at UCLA;

Latent Gold developed by Jay Magidson and Jerome Vermunt of Statistical Innovations, Inc.

These models are usually fitted to large data sets and can involve large numbers of parameters. Other mixture model software is described by McLachlan and Peel [25] in their Appendix A2, but not all of this may be considered as cluster analysis software as some packages are oriented toward the univariate case.

We adopt the following notation for finite mixture models for multivariate data. Suppose that p attributes are measured on n individuals. Let $\mathbf{x}_1, \ldots, \mathbf{x}_n$ be the observed values of a random sample from a mixture of K underlying populations in unknown proportions $\pi_1, \ldots, \pi_K$. Let the density of $\mathbf{x}_i$ in the kth group be $f_k(\mathbf{x}_i; \theta_k)$, where θ_k is the parameter vector for group k, and let $\phi = (\theta', \pi')'$, where $\pi = (\pi_1, \ldots, \pi_K)'$, and $\theta = (\theta_1, \ldots, \theta_K)'$. The density of $\mathbf{x}_i$ can be written as

$$f(\mathbf{x}_i; \phi) = \sum_{k=1}^{K} \pi_k f_k(\mathbf{x}_i; \theta_k)$$

where $\sum_{k=1}^{K} \pi_k = 1$ and $\pi_k \geq 0$, for $k = 1, \ldots, K$.

Let $\hat{\phi}$ denote the maximum likelihood estimate of ϕ. Then each observation, $\mathbf{x}_i$, can be allocated to group k on the basis of the estimated posterior probabilities. (The estimation is not necessarily Bayesian, but the allocation of observations to clusters involves a Bayes Theorem step.) The estimated probability that observation $\mathbf{x}_i$ belongs to group k is given by

$$\hat{z}_{ik} = \frac{\hat{\pi}_k f_k(\mathbf{x}_i; \hat{\theta}_k)}{\sum_{k=1}^{K} \hat{\pi}_k f_k(\mathbf{x}_i; \hat{\theta}_k)} \quad (k = 1, \ldots, K);$$

and $\mathbf{x}_i$ is assigned to group k with the greatest $\hat{z}_{ik}$.

If the purpose of clustering is to recover the underlying structure of the components, rather than to assign individuals to their most probable class, another assignment procedure is sometimes used whereby $\mathbf{x}_i$ is assigned to group k with probability $\hat{z}_{ik}$. This assignment method is particularly useful in the case where clusters may overlap. Of course if the clusters identified do not overlap the two assignment mechanisms will usually agree.

Finite mixture models are frequently fitted where the component densities $f_k(\mathbf{x}; \theta_k)$ are taken to be multivariate normal; i.e., $\mathbf{x}_i \sim N_p(\mu_k, \Sigma_k)$, if observation i belongs to group k. This model has been studied in [32], and [23]. Computational details on the maximum likelihood estimates of the components of ϕ are given in [25] (p. 82).

9.2.1 Latent Class Models and Local Independence

The latent class model described, for example, in [11] is a finite mixture model for data where each of the p attributes is discrete. Suppose that the jth attribute can take on levels $1, \ldots, M_j$ and let λ_{kjm} be the probability that for individuals from group k, the jth attribute has level m. Then, conditional on individual i belonging to group k, the probability function is $f_k(\mathbf{x}_i; \theta_k) = \prod_{j=1}^{p} \lambda_{kjx_{ij}}$. In other words, within each group the distributions of the p attributes are independent. This property has been termed *local independence*.

Local independence is often viewed as a very strong assumption to make in an exploratory analysis of multivariate data. However when clusters are well separated it is not necessary to model the shape of a cluster accurately to get good assignments of observations to clusters. Furthermore, a cluster showing lack of local independence may itself often be decomposed into a finite mixture of approximately locally independent sub-clusters, restoring the validity of the latent class model. Local independence is not often assumed for multivariate normal attributed but there is no reason why this could not be done, for example reducing the number of parameters when a large number of components are being fitted. In this case each component multivariate normal would have a diagonal covariance matrix.

Local independence may be weakened by partitioning the variables into cells or blocks, such that variables in different cells would be independent within each component. In the multivariate normal case this leads to block-diagonal dispersion matrices for each component. This partitioning also provides a way around the problem of the shortage of tractable models for multivariate distributions where some variables are discrete and some are continuous. One need merely ensure that the cells of the partition contain either discrete or continuous variables but not both. In the next section we discuss a program that takes advantage of this.

9.2.2 Generalizing Local Independence: the Multimix Model

Jorgensen and Hunt ([18], [17]) proposed a general class of mixture models to include data having both continuous and categorical attributes. This model, which they dubbed the 'Multimix' model, was conceived of initially as a joint generalization of both latent class models and mixtures of multivariate normal distributions. We suggested an approach based on a form of local independence by partitioning the observational vector $\mathbf{x}_i$ such that

$$\mathbf{x}_i = (\breve{\mathbf{x}}_{i1} | \ldots | \breve{\mathbf{x}}_{il} | \ldots | \breve{\mathbf{x}}_{iL})'$$

where the attributes within partition cell $\breve{\mathbf{x}}_{il}$ are independent of the attributes in partition cell $\breve{\mathbf{x}}_{il'}$, for $l \neq l'$ within each of the K sub-populations. Thus the density of individual i with respect to group k can be written

$$f_k(\mathbf{x}_i) = \prod_{l=1}^{L} f_{kl}(\breve{\mathbf{x}}_{il}).$$

In this paper, we restrict ourselves to the following distributions suggested for the partition cells:

Discrete distribution where $\breve{\mathbf{x}}_{il}$ is a one dimensional discrete attribute taking values $1, \ldots, M_l$ with probabilities λ_{klM_l}.

Multivariate Normal distribution where $\breve{\mathbf{x}}_{il}$ is a p_l dimensional vector with a $N_{p_l}(\mu_{kl}, \Sigma_{kl})$ distribution if individual i is in group k.

It may be noted that the EM framework makes it easy, in principle, to extend the repertoire of available distributions for blocks of variables to other members of the exponential family. The original version of Multimix includes a distribution where conditional on a discrete variable D taking the value d, q continuous variables have the distribution $N_q(\mu_d, \Sigma)$, providing one way of modelling within-cluster associations between discrete and continuous variables. This distribution is due to Olkin and Tate [27] and is referred to as the *location model*.

Hunt and Jorgensen [17] discuss maximum likelihood estimation in Multimix. Multimix models include the latent class model and mixtures of multivariate normal distributions as special cases. *Multimix* models with only continuous variables are mixtures of multivariate normals in which the covariance matrices are each block-diagonal with the same block pattern. Banfield and Raftery [3] consider other kinds of restrictions to covariance matrices in mixtures of multivariate normals, with possible limitations on volume, orientation and shape of the component distributions.

9.2.3 Missing Data

In this paper we put forward a method for mixture model clustering based on the assumption that the data are missing at random and hence the missing data mechanism is ignorable. It is reasonable to ask whether we can do without the 'missing at random' assumption and work with non-ignorable missing data mechanisms. However the effective use of non-ignorable models requires knowledge of the missing data mechanism that will quite often be lacking in an exploratory clustering situation. The use of non-ignorable models is discussed by Molenberghs, Goetghebeur, Lipsitz and Kenward [26] in the context of longitudinal categorical data. They note that such models cannot be tested by the data and advocate using a range of models in a sensitivity analysis, while employing as much context-derived information as possible. Because our interest in this paper is directed towards the general clustering problem we confine ourselves to methods that are technically valid when the missing data mechanism is ignorable.

We now present a form of Multimix suitable for multivariate data sets with missing data. This model reduces to that given in [17] when all the data are observed.

Suppose the observation vector $\mathbf{x}_i$ is written in the form $(\mathbf{x}_{obs,i}, \mathbf{x}_{miss,i})$, where $\mathbf{x}_{obs,i}$ and $\mathbf{x}_{miss,i}$ respectively denote the observed and missing attributes for observation i. Note that this is a formal notation only and does not imply that the data need to be rearranged to achieve this pattern. In fitting the mixture model, there are now two types of missing data that have to be considered; one is the conceptual 'missing' data, the unobserved indicator of group membership, and the other is the unintended or accidental missing data values. However these unintended missing values can also be of two different types. They may be continuous and belong to a multivariate normal partition cell, or they may be a categorical variable involved in a partition cell with a discrete distribution.

The E step of the EM algorithm requires the calculation of $Q(\phi, \phi^{(t)}) = E\{L_C(\phi) \mid \mathbf{x}_{obs}; \phi^{(t)}\}$, the expectation of the complete data log-likelihood conditional on the observed data and the current value of the parameters. We calculate $Q(\phi, \phi^{(t)})$ by replacing z_{ik} with

$$\hat{z}_{ik} = \hat{z}_{ik}^{(t)} = E(z_{ik} \mid \mathbf{x}_{obs,i}; \phi^{(t)})$$
$$= \frac{\pi_k f_k(\mathbf{x}_{obs,i}; \theta_k^{(t)})}{\sum_{k=1}^{K} \pi_k f_k(\mathbf{x}_{obs,i}; \theta_k^{(t)})}.$$

That is, z_{ik} is replaced by $\hat{z}_{ik}$, the estimate of the posterior probability that individual i belongs to group K.

The remaining calculations in the E step require the calculation of the expected value of the complete data sufficient statistics for each partition cell l, conditional on the observed data and the current values of the parameters for that partition cell.

For each discrete partition cell l and each value m_l of $\breve{\mathbf{x}}_{il}$, the E step calculates

$$E(z_{ik}\delta_{ilm} \mid \mathbf{x}_{obs,i}; \theta_k^{(t)}) = \begin{cases} \hat{z}_{ik}\delta_{ilm} & x_{il} \text{ observed,} \\ \hat{z}_{ik}E(\delta_{ilm} \mid \mathbf{x}_{obs,i}; \theta_k^{(t)}) & x_{il} \text{ missing.} \end{cases}$$

$$= \begin{cases} \hat{z}_{ik}\delta_{ilm} & x_{il} \text{ observed,} \\ \hat{z}_{ik}\hat{\lambda}_{ilm}^{(t)} & x_{il} \text{ missing,} \end{cases}$$

where δ_{ilm} is an indicator variable given by

$$\delta_{ilm} = \begin{cases} 1 & \text{if } x_{il} = m, \\ 0 & \text{otherwise.} \end{cases}$$

Suppose we let

$$\hat{\delta}_{ilm} = \begin{cases} \delta_{ilm} & x_{il} \text{ observed,} \\ \lambda_{ilm} & x_{il} \text{ missing.} \end{cases}$$

Then we can write this expectation in the form

$$E(z_{ik}\delta_{ilm} \mid \mathbf{x}_{obs,i}; \theta k^{(t)}) = \hat{z}_{ik}\hat{\delta}_{ilm}$$

for $k = 1, \ldots, K$; each categorical $\breve{\mathbf{x}}_{il}$ and each value m_l of $\breve{\mathbf{x}}_{il}$.

For multivariate normal partition cells, depending on the attributes observed for individual i in the cell, these expectations may require the use of the sweep operator described originally in [5]. We use the version of sweep defined by Dempster [9]; also described in [20] (pp. 112-119). The usefulness of sweep for maximum likelihood estimation in multivariate missing-data problems is shown in [20], [31]. This approach was implemented by Hunt [16] with mixtures of multivariate normal distributions. The approach is adapted in the following manner:

Suppose we use the current estimates of the parameters for group k in cell l to form an augmented covariance matrix A_l given by

$$A_l = \begin{pmatrix} -1 & \mu_{k1} & \mu_{k2} & \cdots & \mu_{kp_l} \\ \mu_{k1} & \sigma_{k11} & \sigma_{k12} & \cdots & \sigma_{k1p_l} \\ \mu_{k2} & \sigma_{k21} & \cdots & \cdots & \sigma_{k2p_l} \\ \vdots & \vdots & \vdots & \vdots & \vdots \\ \mu_{kp_l} & \sigma_{kp1} & \cdots & \cdots & \sigma_{kp_lp_l} \end{pmatrix}$$

for $k = 1, \ldots, K$.

Suppose we index the rows and columns of A_l from 0 to p_l. Then sweeping on row and column j of A_l corresponds to sweeping on x_{ij}. The sweep operator has a close relationship with regression. Sweeping A_l on the rows and columns corresponding to the observed x_{ij} in cell l yields the conditional distribution (regression) of the missing $x_{ij'}$ on the observed x_{ij} in the cell. Sweeping on a variable converts that variable from an output variable into a predictor variable. Hence we can find the predicted value of the missing variables for observation i in partition l from the regression of $\mathbf{x}_{miss,i}$ in cell l on the variables in $\mathbf{x}_{obs,i}$ in cell l, evaluated at the current estimates of the parameters.

The remaining calculations in the E step for multivariate normal partition cells are as follows:

$$E(z_{ik}x_{ij} \mid \mathbf{x}_{obs,i}; \theta_k^{(t)}) = \begin{cases} \hat{z}_{ik}x_{ij} & x_{ij} \text{ observed,} \\ \hat{z}_{ik}E(x_{ij} \mid \mathbf{x}_{obs,i}; \theta_k^{(t)}) & x_{ij} \text{ missing.} \end{cases}$$

$$\begin{aligned} & E(z_{ik}x_{ij}^2 \mid \mathbf{x}_{obs,i}, \theta_k^{(t)}) \\ &= E\left(z_{ik} \mid \mathbf{x}_{obs,i}; \theta_k^{(t)}\right) E\left(x_{ij}^2 \mid \mathbf{x}_{obs,i}; \theta_k^{(t)}\right) \\ &= \begin{cases} \hat{z}_{ik}x_{ij}^2 & x_{ij} \text{ observed,} \\ \hat{z}_{ik}\left[\left(E\left(x_{ij} \mid \mathbf{x}_{obs,i}; \theta_k^{(t)}\right)\right)^2 + \text{Var}\left(x_{ij} \mid \mathbf{x}_{obs,i}; \theta_k^{(t)}\right)\right] & x_{ij} \text{ missing.} \end{cases} \end{aligned}$$

For $j \neq j'$,

$$E(z_{ik}x_{ij}x_{ij'}|\mathbf{x}_{obs,i};\theta_k^{(t)})$$
$$= \begin{cases} \hat{z}_{ik}x_{ij}x_{ij'} & x_{ij} \text{ and } x_{ij'} \text{ observed,} \\ \hat{z}_{ik}x_{ij}E(x_{ij'}|\mathbf{x}_{obs,i};\theta_k^{(t)}) & x_{ij} \text{ observed}, x_{ij'} \text{ missing,} \\ \hat{z}_{ik}E(x_{ij}|\mathbf{x}_{obs,i};\theta_k^{(t)})x_{ij'} & x_{ij} \text{ missing}, x_{ij'} \text{ observed,} \\ \hat{z}_{ik}\left[E(x_{ij}|\mathbf{x}_{obs,i};\theta_k^{(t)})E(x_{ij'}|\mathbf{x}_{obs,i};\theta_k^{(t)})\right. \\ \left. + \text{Cov}(x_{ij},x_{ij'}|\mathbf{x}_{obs,i};\theta_k^{(t)})\right] & x_{ij} \text{ and} x_{ij'} \text{ missing,} \end{cases}$$

for $i = 1,\ldots,n;\ k = 1,\ldots,K;\ x_{ij} \in \breve{\mathbf{x}}_{il}$ where $\breve{\mathbf{x}}_{il}$ is a multivariate normal partition cell.

It can be seen from the above expectations, that when there is only one factor x_{ij} missing, the missing x_{ij} are replaced by the conditional mean of x_{ij}, given the set of values $\mathbf{x}_{obs,i}$ observed for that individual in that cell and the current estimates of the parameters for the cell. However, for the conditional expectations $E(z_{ik}x_{ij}^2 | \mathbf{x}_{obs,i};\theta_k^{(t)})$ and $E(z_{ik}x_{ij}x_{ij'} | \mathbf{x}_{obs,i};\theta_k^{(t)})$, that are to be used in the calculation of the covariance matrix, then respectively if x_{ij} is missing, or if x_{ij} and $x_{ij'}$ are missing in that cell, the conditional mean of x_{ij} is adjusted by the conditional covariances as shown above. These conditional means and the nonzero conditional covariances are found by using the sweep operator on the augmented covariance matrix which has been created using the current estimates of the parameters for that particular multivariate normal partition cell. The augmented covariance matrix is swept on the observed attributes $\mathbf{x}_{obs,i}$ in cell l such that these attributes are the predictors in the regression equation and the remaining attributes are the outcome variables for that cell.

In the M step of the algorithm, the new parameter estimates $\theta^{(t+1)}$ of the parameters are estimated from the complete data sufficient statistics.

Mixing proportions:

$$\hat{\pi}_k^{(t+1)} = \frac{1}{n}\sum_{i=1}^n \hat{z}_{ik}^{(t)} \qquad \text{for } k = 1,\ldots,K.$$

Discrete distribution parameters:

$$\hat{\lambda}_{klm} = \frac{1}{n\hat{\pi}_k}\sum_{i=1}^n \hat{z}_{ik}\hat{\delta}_{ilm} \qquad \text{for } k = 1,\ldots,K\ ;\ m = 1,\ldots,M_l;$$

and where l indexes a discrete partition cell $\breve{\mathbf{x}}_l$.

Multivariate Normal parameters:

$$\hat{\mu}_{kj}^{(t+1)} = \frac{1}{n\hat{\pi}_k} E\left(\sum_{i=1}^{n} \hat{z}_{ik}^{(t)} x_{ij} \mid \mathbf{x}_{obs,i}, \theta_k^{(t)}\right)$$

$$\hat{\Sigma}_{kjj'}^{(t+1)} = \frac{1}{n\hat{\pi}_k} E\left(\sum_{i=1}^{n} \hat{z}_{ik}^{(t)} x_{ij} x_{ij'} \mid \mathbf{x}_{obs,i}, \theta_k^{(t)}\right) - \hat{\mu}_{kj}^{(t+1)} \hat{\mu}_{kj'}^{(t+1)}$$

for $k = 1, \ldots, K$. Here j and j' index the continuous attributes belonging to a Multivariate Normal cell $\breve{\mathbf{x}}_l$.

Because of the adjustment needed for the conditional means when both x_{ij} and $x_{ij'}$ in partition $\breve{\mathbf{x}}_l$ are missing, it is convenient to use similar notation to that given in [20], p. 144. Let the conditional covariance between attributes j and j' for individual i, given that individual i belongs in group k at iteration t, be defined as

$$C_{kir,jj'}^{(t)} = \begin{cases} 0 & \text{if } x_{ij} \text{ or } x_{ij'} \text{ is observed,} \\ \text{Cov}(x_{ij}, x_{ij'} \mid \mathbf{x}_{obs,i}, \theta_k^{(t)}) & \text{if } x_{ij} \text{ and } x_{ij'} \text{ are missing,} \end{cases}$$

and the imputed value for attribute j of individual i, given the current value of the parameters and that the individual belongs in group k, be defined as

$$\hat{x}_{ij,k}^{(t)} = \begin{cases} x_{ij} & \text{if } x_{ij} \text{ is observed,} \\ E(x_{ij} \mid \mathbf{x}_{obs,i}, \theta_k^{(t)}) & \text{if } x_{ij} \text{ is missing.} \end{cases}$$

Then we can write the parameter estimates for the mean and the variance or covariance terms in the form

$$\hat{\mu}_{kj}^{(t+1)} = \frac{1}{n\hat{\pi}_k} \sum_{i=1}^{n} \hat{z}_{ik}^{(t)} \hat{x}_{ij,k}^{(t)}$$

$$\hat{\Sigma}_{kjj'}^{(t+1)} = \frac{1}{n\hat{\pi}_k} \sum_{i=1}^{n} \hat{z}_{ik}^{(t)} \left[(\hat{x}_{ij,k}^{(t)} - \hat{\mu}_{kj}^{(t+1)})(\hat{x}_{ij',k}^{(t)} - \hat{\mu}_{kj'}^{(t+1)}) + C_{ki,jj'}^{(t)}\right]$$

for $k = 1, \ldots, K$. Here again j and j' index the continuous attributes belonging to a Multivariate Normal cell $\breve{\mathbf{x}}_l$.

9.3 Applications

In this section we illustrate the above approach to clustering by considering two examples. The well-known iris data set considered by Fisher [12] was chosen to demonstrate this approach to clustering mixtures where the component distributions are multivariate normal and where data are missing at random. The prostate cancer clinical trial data of Byar [6], also reproduced in [2], was chosen to demonstrate this unsupervised learning procedure where we have mixed categorical and continuous attributes and data are missing at random.

As we are primarily interested in clustering data where data are missing at random, we have artificially created missing observations, where the probability of an observation on an attribute being missing was taken independently of all other data values. The missing values generated in this manner are missing completely at random, and the missing data mechanism is ignorable for likelihood inferences [20], [31]. Both of these chosen examples have a known classification of the observations into groups, enabling us to permit some judgement on the usefulness of this method of clustering.

Missing values were created in the following way. Each attribute of each individual was assigned a random digit generated from the discrete [0,1] distribution, where the probability of a zero was taken respectively as 0.10, 0.15, 0.20, 0.25 and 0.30. Attributes for an individual were recorded as missing when the assigned random digit was zero. This process was repeated ten times for each of the probabilities chosen. For both examples, we report the results from one pattern of missing data where the probability of an observation on an attribute being missing was 0.30. This illustrates the Multimix approach to clustering incomplete data on a fairly extreme case of the type of data that would be analyzed using these methods.

There has been much work on determining the number of groups in a finite mixture and there does not appear to be a single superior method of determining the group number (see, for example, [7] and the references therein). The problem of determining the group number is a peripheral question to the theory being illustrated here. The number of clusters to be fitted in the mixture in the following two examples will be the same as the specified number of classifications in that data.

9.3.1 Example 1: The Iris Data

The complete data set consists of the measurements of the length and width of both sepals and petals from each of 50 plants of three species of Iris, *I. Setosa*, *I. Versicolor*, and *I. Virginica*. Many clustering techniques have been applied to this data set, and it is well known that the species *I. Versicolor* and *I. Virginica* are more similar to each other than either is to the *I. Setosa*. (See for example [21] for further details and references.)

The data set to be reported in this paper contained 49 *Setosa* and all the *Versicolor* and *Virginica* plants. (The missing data process had created one observation with all four attributes recorded as missing and this was deleted from further analysis.) Nine plants have three attributes recorded as missing, 40 plants have two attributes recorded as missing, 55 plants have one attribute recorded as missing, and 42 plants have all four attributes recorded.

We regard the data as a random sample from the distribution

$$f(\mathbf{x}_i; \phi) = \sum_{k=1}^{3} \pi_k f_k(\mathbf{x}_i; \theta_k)$$

	Classification Model		
Species	Group 1	Group 2	Group 3
I. Setosa	47	2	0
I. Versicolor	1	41	8
I. Virginica	0	1	49

TABLE 9.1
Agreements and differences between the species and the model classifications for Example 1 with 30% missing data.

where each component $f_k(\mathbf{x}_i; \theta_k)$ is $N_4(\mu_k, \Sigma_k)$ density. We will refer to this model as Model 1.

Model 1 was fitted iteratively using the EM algorithm with various initial groupings, including the species classification. Several local maxima were found, and the solution of the likelihood was taken to be the one corresponding to the largest of these. It corresponded to a log-likelihood of -183.1 (calculated to base e).

Note that the first M step is performed on the basis of the specified initial groupings. For a multivariate normal cell, the estimates of the means are calculated using the available data for that cell and in that group. The estimates for the variance covariances are calculated in this first M step by replacing the missing values in the cell by the group mean for that cell and then calculating the estimates using the 'filled in' data set. The convergence criterion used was to cease iterating when the difference in log-likelihoods at iteration t and iteration $t-10$ was 10^{-10}.

Each plant was then assigned to the group to which it has highest estimated posterior probability of belonging. It can be seen from Table 9.1 that there are 12 plants where the species and the model classifications differ. Suppose we define a plant as *decisively assigned* to a group when $\max_k \hat{z}_{i,k} \geq 0.95$ for $k=1,\ldots,3$. Examination of the posterior probabilities showed that 125 of the 149 plants are decisively assigned to a group. For the 12 misclassified observations, five are decisively assigned to a different group from the one corresponding to the species.

The two *I. Setosa* and the *I. Versicolor* plants that are misclassified by the model are of particular interest. One misclassified *I. Setosa* plant has a posterior probability of assignment to Group 1 and 2 respectively of 0.11 and 0.61. This plant has only the sepal length recorded, and this value (5.7) is similar to that for a *I. Versicolor* plant (see Table 9.2). The other *I. Setosa* plant has two attributes recorded as missing. Comparison of these attributes with the parameter estimates in Table 9.2 indicates this plant has a sepal width that is more similar to that for *I. Versicolor* species. The *I. Versicolor* plant that is classified into the group corresponding to the *Setosa* species has only the sepal width recorded and this value (3.4) is like that for the *I. Setosa* plants.

Another comparison between the species classification and the Model 1 fit can be obtained by comparing the estimated parameters for Model 1 with their counterparts

	Model 1 Estimates	**Species Estimates**

Mean Vectors

$$\hat{\mu}_1 = (4.999\ 3.419\ 1.462\ 0.251) \quad (5.006\ 3.428\ 1.462\ 0.246)$$
$$\hat{\mu}_2 = (5.835\ 2.761\ 4.153\ 1.284) \quad (5.936\ 2.770\ 4.260\ 1.326)$$
$$\hat{\mu}_3 = (6.575\ 2.953\ 5.498\ 1.975) \quad (6.588\ 2.974\ 5.552\ 2.026)$$

Variance Covariance Matrices:[†]

$$\hat{\Sigma}_1 = \begin{pmatrix} 0.107 & & & \\ 0.080 & 0.104 & & \\ 0.007 & 0.001 & 0.030 & \\ 0.007 & 0.010 & 0.008 & 0.013 \end{pmatrix} \quad \begin{pmatrix} 0.122 & & & \\ 0.097 & 0.141 & & \\ 0.016 & 0.011 & 0.030 & \\ 0.010 & 0.009 & 0.006 & 0.011 \end{pmatrix}$$

$$\hat{\Sigma}_2 = \begin{pmatrix} 0.307 & & & \\ 0.096 & 0.087 & & \\ 0.194 & 0.092 & 0.207 & \\ 0.055 & 0.043 & 0.054 & 0.028 \end{pmatrix} \quad \begin{pmatrix} 0.261 & & & \\ 0.083 & 0.096 & & \\ 0.179 & 0.081 & 0.216 & \\ 0.055 & 0.040 & 0.072 & 0.038 \end{pmatrix}$$

$$\hat{\Sigma}_3 = \begin{pmatrix} 0.412 & & & \\ 0.097 & 0.115 & & \\ 0.335 & 0.091 & 0.367 & \\ 0.103 & 0.076 & 0.076 & 0.105 \end{pmatrix} \quad \begin{pmatrix} 0.396 & & & \\ 0.092 & 0.102 & & \\ 0.297 & 0.070 & 0.298 & \\ 0.048 & 0.047 & 0.048 & 0.074 \end{pmatrix}$$

TABLE 9.2
Parameter estimates for Example 1 under Model 1 and Fisher's iris data using the species classifications. The attributes are Sepal length, Sepal width, Petal length, and Petal width, Group 1 corresponds to *I. Setosa*, Group 2 to *I. Versicolor*, and Group 3 to *I. Virginica*.

using the species classification. It can be seen from a comparison of the parameter estimates in Table 9.2 that the agreement is fairly close.

The estimates of the mixing proportions in Groups 1 to 3 respectively for the model are 0.3188, 0.2997 and 0.3815, leading to expected numbers in the three groups respectively of 47.50, 44.66 and 56.85. This is very close to the 49/50/50 division in the species.

The estimates of the variance covariance matrices for the model appear to be reasonable, and as is expected, they are always positive definite. In the current version of the program written to analyze this type of data, equal covariance matrices cannot be imposed for the component distributions. It may be an advantage to impose this condition on this data set, as this would reduce the numbers of parameters to be estimated from the small data set, even though Hawkins's test indicated normality with heteroscedascity (see [4]).

We have demonstrated that with 28% of the attributes recorded as missing, the approach of multivariate finite mixture models with data missing at random has been able to detect the structure present in the data exceedingly well. Note that in the analogous model fitted to the iris data set with no missing data values, there were 5 observations misclassified in the *Versicolor* and the *Virginica* species.

9.3.2 Example 2: The Cancer Data

We will now consider the clustering of cases using the pre-trial variables of the prostate cancer clinical trial data of Byar [6]. The data were obtained from a randomized clinical trial comparing four treatments for 506 patients with prostatic cancer where clinical criteria had been used to classify these patients into two groups, Stage 3 and Stage 4 of the disease. Stage 3 represents local extension of the disease with no clinical evidence of distant metastasis, whilst Stage 4 represents distant metastasis as evidenced by acid phosphatase levels, X-rays, or both [6].

There are twelve pre-trial covariates measured on each patient, seven may be taken to be continuous, four to be discrete, and one variable (SG) is an index nearly all of whose values lie between 7 and 15, and which could be considered either discrete or continuous. We treat SG as a continuous variable. Two of the discrete covariates have two levels, one has four levels and the fourth discrete covariate has seven levels. A preliminary inspection of the data showed that two variables, SZ and AP, were both skewed variables. As detailed in [17], these two variables have been transformed to make their distributions more symmetric.

Thirty one individuals have at least one of the pretrial covariates missing, giving a total of 62 missing values. We refer to this data as Cancer1. As there are only approximately 1% of the data missing, we have also artificially created more missing observations using the procedure described above. We refer to this latter data set as Cancer30.

Cancer30 had 1870 values recorded as missing. These missing values were such that only five individuals had all attributes observed and varying to the other extreme where two individuals had only 1 attribute observed.

Hunt and Jorgensen [17] report a complete case clustering of the twelve pretrial covariates where individuals that had missing values in any of these covariates were omitted from further analysis, leaving 475 out of the original 506 individuals available. In [16] and [17] they discuss a fitting strategy for incorporating local associations within the model. We report the results for model using the partitioning preferred by Hunt [16] where the three attributes WT, SBP and DBP are in one partition cell. We compare the classifications under the model for Cancer1 and Cancer30.

The data are regarded as a random sample from the distribution

$$f(\mathbf{x}; \phi) = \sum_{k=1}^{2} \pi_k \prod_{l=1}^{10} f_{kl}(\mathbf{x}; \theta_{kl})$$

		Classification for Cancer30	
		Group 1	Group 2
Classification for Cancer1	**Group 1**	277	14
	Group 2	29	185

TABLE 9.3
Agreements and differences between the Model Classifications for Cancer1 and Cancer30.

where the component distributions $f_{kl}(\breve{\mathbf{x}}_{il}; \theta_{kl})$ are $N_3(\mu_{kl}, \Sigma_{kl})$ for the partition cell containing WT, SBP and DBP, $N(\mu_{kl}, \sigma_{kl}^2)$ for the remaining continuous attributes, and $D(\lambda_{kl1}, \ldots, \lambda_{klm_l})$ for each of the four categorical attributes.

This model was fitted iteratively using the EM algorithm with various initial groupings, including the one based on the clinical classification. As described in the previous section, these initial groupings are used to implement the first M step. For discrete partition cells the initial estimates of the probabilities λ_{klm}, $m = 1, \ldots, M_l$ are calculated using the available data. For multivariate normal cells, the estimates of the means and the variance covariances are calculated as described previously. The convergence criterion was again to cease iterating when the difference in log-likelihoods at iteration t and iteration $t - 10$ was 10^{-10}. Several local maxima were found, and the solution of the likelihood was taken to be the one corresponding to the largest of these. For Cancer1 the solution corresponded to a log-likelihood of -8378.5 (calculated to base e), while for Cancer30 the solution had a log-likelihood of -11895.8. Each individual was assigned to the group to which it had highest estimated posterior probability of belonging.

Table 9.3 indicates that the model classifications for Cancer1 and Cancer30 differ for 43 individuals. The posterior probabilities of these individuals were examined for both data sets. Using the posterior probabilities for Cancer1, it was found that six of the fourteen individuals assigned to Group 1 for Cancer1 and Group 2 for Cancer30 had appreciable membership[‡] in both Group 1 and Group 2. Using the posterior probabilities for Cancer30, it was found that a different six of the fourteen individuals also had appreciable membership in both groups. Examination of the posterior probabilities for both Cancer1 and Cancer30 showed that four of the 29 individuals also had appreciable membership in both groups. Note that these were not the same four individuals.

The differences between the model and the clinical classifications were investigated for both Cancer1 and Cancer30.

It can be seen from Table 9.4 that for Cancer1 the clinical classification and the 'statistical diagnosis' are different for 43 individuals. Five of these individuals have appreciable membership in both groups. For Cancer30, it was found that the clinical

---
[‡]Greater posterior probabilities were between 0.5 and 0.6.

	Model Classification			
Clinical	Cancer1		Cancer30	
Classification	Group 1	Group 2	Group 1	Group 2
Stage 3	270	22	265	26
Stage 4	21	193	40	174

TABLE 9.4
Agreements and differences between the Clinical and Model classifications.

classification and the 'statistical diagnosis' differed for 66 individuals, with ten of these individuals having appreciable membership in both groups.

Hunt [16] found in the complete case analysis that 40 of the 475 individuals were assigned to a different group than the one corresponding to the clinical classification. A comparison of the assignments for the 475 individuals from the complete case analysis with those individuals in Cancer1 showed that three individuals were classified differently. These three observations had appreciable membership in both groups. Hunt [16] also investigated the differences between the 'statistical diagnosis' and the clinical classifications and found that Survival Status gave insight into the model classifications. The model classification gave a better indication of prognosis with patients in Group 1 having a higher probability of being alive or dying from other causes, whereas patients in Group 2 had more chance of dying from prostatic cancer.

Another comparison between the clinical classification and the model fit can be obtained by comparing the estimated parameters for the model with their counterparts using the clinical classification. Agreement was fairly close for both Cancer1 and Cancer30.

9.4 Discussion

The mixture approach to clustering data is well defined and has been much used, particularly for mixtures where the component distributions are multivariate normal. However when clustering real multivariate data sets, it is unusual to find data sets where the attributes are all continuous or all categorical. We usually find that the attributes are mixed categorical and continuous variables, and we often have missing observations to deal with.

There has been considerable interest recently in the analysis of incomplete data [20], [31]. The finite mixture model lends itself well to implementing incomplete data methods. We have a well specified, flexible model whose parameters can be estimated by maximum likelihood. The *Multimix* approach to clustering mixed data is able to be extended to cope with incomplete data.

We have demonstrated from our investigations that the approach works well for data sets that have a large amount of missing data and where the data are missing at random. The model has been able to detect the structure known to exist in the data and simultaneously cope with an extreme amount of missing data. However as with all problems involving missing data, the mechanism that led to certain values being missing needs careful investigation.

References

[1] Afifi, A. A. and Elashoff, R. M.(1966). Missing Observations in Multivariate Statistics I: Review of the Literature. *Journal of the American Statistical Association*, 61, 595–604.

[2] Andrews, D. A. and Herzberg, A. M.(1985). *Data: a Collection of Problems from Many Fields for the Student and Research Worker*. Springer-Verlag, New York.

[3] Banfield, J.D. and Raftery, A.E.(1993). Model-based Gaussian and Non-Gaussian Clustering. *Biometrics*, 49, 803–821.

[4] Basford, K. E. and McLachlan, G. J. (1985). Estimation of Allocation Rates in a Cluster Analysis Context. *Journal of the American Statistical Association*, 80, 286–293.

[5] Beaton, A. E. (1964). The Use of Special Matrix Operators in Statistical Calculus. *Educational Testing Service Research Bulletin*, RB, 64–51.

[6] Byar, B. P. and Green, S. B. (1980). The Choice of Treatment for Cancer Patients Based on Covariate Information: Application to Prostate Cancer. *Bull. Cancer*, 67, 477–490.

[7] Celeux, G. and Soromenho, G.(1996). An Entropy Criterion for Assessing the Number of Clusters in a Mixture Model. *Journal of Classification*,13, 195–212.

[8] Day, N. E.(1969). Estimating the Components of a Mixture of Normal Components. *Biometrika*, 56, 464–474.

[9] Dempster, A. P.(1969). *Elements of Continuous Multivariate Analysis*. Addison-Wesley, Reading, MA.

[10] Dempster, A. P., Laird, N. M., and Rubin, D. B.(1977). Maximum Likelihood from Incomplete Data via the EM Algorithm (with Discussion). *Journal of the Royal Statistical Society B*, 39, 1–38.

[11] Everitt, B.S.(1984). A Note on Parameter Estimation for Lazarsfeld's Latent Class Model using the EM Algorithm. *Multivariate Behavioral Research*, 19, 79–89.

[12] Fisher, R. A.(1936). Multiple Measurements in Taxonomic Problems. *Annals of Eugenics*, 7, 179–188.

[13] Gordon, A. D.(1999). *Classification*. Chapman & Hall/CRC, London.

[14] Gower, J. C. (1971). A General Coefficient of Similarity and Some of its Properties. *Biometrics*, 27, 857–874.

[15] Hartley, H. O. and Hocking, R. R.(1971). The Analysis of Incomplete Data. *Biometrics*, 14, 174–194.

[16] Hunt, L.A. (1996). *Clustering Using Finite Mixture Models*. PhD thesis, Dept. of Statistics, University of Waikato, New Zealand.

[17] Hunt, L. A. and Jorgensen, M. A. (1999). Mixture Model Clustering Using the Multimix Program. *Australian & New Zealand Journal of Statistics*, 41, 153–171.

[18] Jorgensen, M. A. and Hunt, L. A.(1996). Mixture Model Clustering of Data Sets with Categorical and Continuous Variables. In *Proceedings of the Conference on Information, Statistics and Induction in Science*, Melbourne, 375–384.

[19] Lauritzen, S. L. and Wermuth, N.(1989). Graphical Models for Associations Between Variables, Some of Which are Qualitative and Some Quantitative. *Annals of Statistics*, 17, 31–57.

[20] Little, R. J. A. and Rubin, D. B. (1987). *Statistical Analysis with Missing data*. Wiley, New York.

[21] Mardia, K. V., Kent, J. T., and Bibby, J. M. (1979). *Multivariate Analysis*. Academic Press, New York.

[22] Little, R. J. A. and Schluchter, M. D. (1985). Maximum Likelihood Estimation for Mixed Continuous and Categorical Data with Missing Values. *Biometrika*, 72, 497–512.

[23] McLachlan, G. J. and Basford, K. E.(1988). *Mixture Models: Inference and Applications to Clustering*. Marcel Dekker, NewYork.

[24] McLachlan, G. J. and Krishnan, T. (1997). *The EM Algorithm and Extensions*. Wiley, New York.

[25] McLachlan, G. J. and Peel, D. (2000). *Finite Mixture Models*. Wiley, New York.

[26] Molenberghs, G., Goetghebeur, E. J. T., Lipsitz, S. R., and Kenward, M. G.(1999). Nonrandom Missingness in Categorical Data: Strengths and Limitations. *American Statistician*, 53, 110–118.

[27] Olkin, I. and Tate, R. F.(1961). Multivariate Correlation Models with Mixed Discrete and Continuous Variables, *Annals of Mathematical Statistics*, 32, 448–465.

[28] Orchard, T. and Woodbury, M. A. (1972). A Missing Information Principle: Theory and Applications. *Proceedings of the 6th Berkeley Symposium* I, 697–715.

[29] Rubin, D. B. (1976). Inference and Missing Data. *Biometrika*, 63, 581–593.

[30] SAS Institute Inc. *SAS/STAT® User's Guide, Version 8*. SAS Institute, Cary, NC, 1999.

[31] Schafer, J. L. (1997). *Analysis of Incomplete Data*. Chapman &Hall, London.

[32] Titterington, D. M., Smith, A. F. M., and Makov, U. E. (1985). *Statistical Analysis of Finite Mixture Distributions*. Wiley, NewYork.

10

Improving the Performance of Radial Basis Function (RBF) Classification Using Information Criteria

Zhenqiu Liu and Hamparsum Bozdogan
University of Tennessee, Knoxville, USA

CONTENTS

10.1 Introduction 193
10.2 Regression Trees 197
10.3 New Kernel Functions 201
10.4 The EM Algorithm 204
10.5 Hybrid Training 208
10.6 Computational Results 210
10.7 Conclusions 212
      Acknowledgments 212
      References 212

Successful implementation of *radial basis function* (*RBF*) networks for classification tasks must deal with architectural issues, the burden of irrelevant attributes, scaling, and some other problems. In this paper, we introduce a new class of kernel functions and try to build a three-way hybrid between the *EM algorithm*, *regression trees*, and the *new kernel functions*. Instead of using linear output and least squares error function, we introduce nonlinear sigmoid function and cross entropy error function into *radial basis function* (*RBF*) network. The new resulting network is easy to use, and has favorable classification accuracy. Numerical experiments show that our new model has better performance than logistic regression in binary classification and has equivalent performance in multiple classification as compared with MLP and other nonparametric classification procedures.

10.1 Introduction

We assume that we are given data set D which consists of real or discrete inputs $\{\mathbf{x}\}_{n=1}^{N}$ in some space. Let t_n denote the corresponding target categorical variables which can take a finite and known number of, say, integer values. We wish to model such a data set and hence find the predictive distribution over the classes for a new observation point $\mathbf{x}_{N+1}$. In what follows, we shall first discuss the case of binary (two class) classification. Then, we shall introduce the case of multiple-class classification.

10.1.1 Binary Classifiers

The standard approach is to model the data using Bayesian conditional classifier which predicts t conditional on $\mathbf{x}$. To do this we assume the existence of a function $a(\mathbf{x})$ which models the 'logit' $log\frac{P(t=1|\mathbf{x})}{P(t=0|\mathbf{x})}$ as a function of $\mathbf{x}$. Thus

$$y = P(t=1|\mathbf{x},\mathbf{a}(\mathbf{x})) = \frac{1}{1+exp(-a(\mathbf{x}))}. \tag{10.1}$$

To develop the model, we place a prior distribution over the unknown function $a(\mathbf{x})$. There are two approaches to this. One is to model the $a(\mathbf{x})$ directly using the Gaussian process. This involves modelling the joint distribution of $\{a(\mathbf{x_n})\}$ with a Gaussian process. Williams and Barber (1998) have implemented classifiers based on Gaussian process prior using the Laplace approximation, and Neal (1997) has used Monto Carlo approach to implement a Gaussian process classifier.

Alternatively, we can use a neural network approach. Output $a(\mathbf{x})$ is a function of $a(\mathbf{x};w)$, where the parameters $\mathbf{w}$ might be, say, the weights of the neural network or the coefficients of the linear expansion

$$a(\mathbf{x};\mathbf{w}) = \sum_j w_j K_j(x). \tag{10.2}$$

Different kernel functions $K_j(\mathbf{x})$ would produce different models. When $K_j(\mathbf{x}) = x_j$, the model is called the logistic regression.

$$a(\mathbf{x};\mathbf{w}) = \sum_j w_j x_j.$$

On the other hand, if we take

$$K_j(\mathbf{x}) = exp\{-\frac{||x-c_j||^2}{2r_j^2}\}, \tag{10.3}$$

where $K_j(\mathbf{x})$ is now the Gaussian kernel function, we get the *RBF* network with sigmoid output.

The popular RBF networks for classification use linear instead sigmoid function in their output layer (Kubat, 1998). The structure of the *RBF* network is shown in Figure 10.1.

It is easy to compute the *RBF* network using linear output layer after all the kernel parameters are predetermined. However, these kinds of models do not perform well. Sometimes they have no comparable structures with logistic regression and other statistical tools.

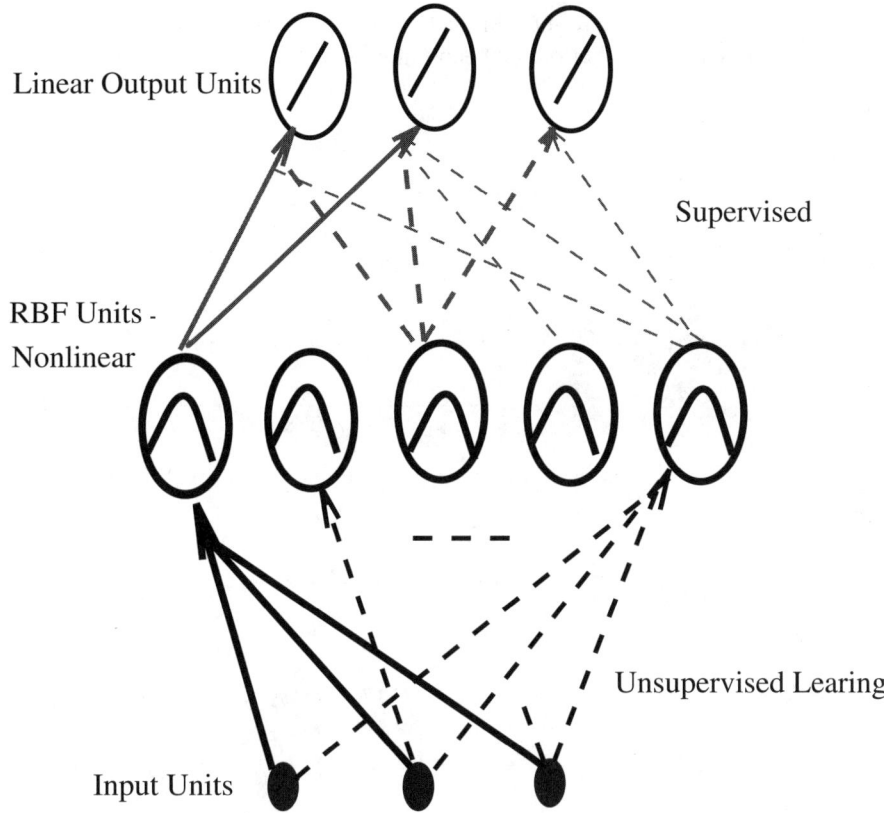

FIGURE 10.1
A radial basis function (RBF) network structure.

10.1.2 Logistic Regression and Mixture Model

Logistic regression has been extensively studied in the last decade. Since it is a special case of *RBF* neural network, we explore an interesting relationship between the Gaussian mixture model and the logistic regression.

Claim: When the covariance matrices between the mixture clusters are indeed equal, the posterior class probability $P(t|\mathbf{x}, c_0, c_1, \Sigma)$ computed from a Gaussian mixture model, i.e.,

$$P(t=1|\mathbf{x}, c_1, c_0, \Sigma) = \frac{P(\mathbf{x}|c_1, \Sigma)P(t=1)}{P(\mathbf{x}|c_1, \Sigma)P(t=1) + P(\mathbf{x}|c_0, \Sigma)P(t=0)}, \quad (10.4)$$

conforms to a logistic regression model:

$$P(t=1|\mathbf{x}, \mathbf{w}) = g(w_0 + \sum_{i=1}^{m} w_i x_i). \quad (10.5)$$

Proof: We establish the proof of this as follows.

Let's divide both the numerator and denominator by

$$P(\mathbf{x}|c_1, \Sigma)P(t=1)$$

giving us

$$P(t=1|\mathbf{x}, c_0, c_1, \Sigma) = \frac{1}{1 + \frac{P(\mathbf{x}|c_0, \Sigma)P(t=0)}{P(\mathbf{x}|c_1, \Sigma)P(t=1)}}. \tag{10.6}$$

Rewriting this we get:

$$\frac{1}{1 + \frac{P(\mathbf{x}|c_0, \Sigma)P(t=0)}{P(\mathbf{x}|c_1, \Sigma)P(t=1)}} = \frac{1}{1 + exp\{log\frac{P(\mathbf{x}|c_0, \Sigma)P(t=0)}{P(\mathbf{x}|c_1, \Sigma)P(t=1)}\}} \tag{10.7}$$

$$= \frac{1}{1 + exp - \{log\frac{P(\mathbf{x}|c_1, \Sigma)P(t=0)}{P(\mathbf{x}|c_0, \Sigma)P(t=1)}\}}. \tag{10.8}$$

We note that this is already in the logistic form $(1 + exp(-z))^{-1}$ provided that the argument

$$\mathbf{a} = log\frac{P(\mathbf{x}|c_1, \Sigma)P(t=0)}{P(\mathbf{x}|c_0, \Sigma)P(t=1)} = logP(\mathbf{x}|c_1, \Sigma) - logP(\mathbf{x}|c_0, \Sigma) + log\frac{P(t=1)}{P(t=0)} \tag{10.9}$$

has the desired linear form. To this end,

$$\mathbf{a} = [-\frac{1}{2}(\mathbf{x} - c_1)^T \Sigma^{-1}(\mathbf{x} - c_1) - log((2\pi)^{\frac{n}{2}}|\Sigma|^{\frac{1}{2}})]$$

$$- [\frac{1}{2}(\mathbf{x} - c_0)\Sigma^{-1}(\mathbf{x} - c_0)] + -log((2\pi)^{\frac{n}{2}}|\Sigma|^{\frac{1}{2}})] + log\frac{P(t=1)}{P(t=0)}$$

$$= -\frac{1}{2}(\mathbf{x} - c_0)\Sigma^{-1}(\mathbf{x} - c_0) - \frac{1}{2}(\mathbf{x} - c_1)\Sigma^{-1}(\mathbf{x} - c_1) + log\frac{P(t=1)}{P(t=0)}$$

$$= (c_1 - c_0)^T \Sigma^{-1} \mathbf{x} - \frac{1}{2}c_1^T \Sigma^{-1} c_0 + log\frac{P(t=1)}{P(t=0)}. \tag{10.10}$$

We can now write a closed form expression of the weights as a function of the means and the covariance:

$$w_0 = \frac{1}{2}c_1 T \Sigma^{-1} c_1 + \frac{1}{2}c_0^T \Sigma^{-1} c_0 + log\frac{P(t=1)}{P(t=0)} \tag{10.11}$$

$$w_i = \sum_j (c_{0j} - c_{1j})\Sigma_{ji}^{-1}, \quad i > 0 \tag{10.12}$$

$\Rightarrow$

$$\mathbf{a}(\mathbf{x}; \mathbf{w}) = w_0 + \sum_{j=1}^{m} w_j x_j$$

which is the logistic regression.

One can now ask the question: "Which method will perform better, the logistic regression or the mixture model?" Based on our results, usually, logistic regression has a better performance, as it estimates the weights (coefficients) through optimizing the error function. We will illustrate this point by giving a simple example later.

10.1.3 Multi-Class Classifier

Having considered the binary classifier, let us now investigate the problem of multi-class classification. In the binary case, we used the sigmoid function j to define $P(t = 1|a(\mathbf{x}))$ where $a(\mathbf{x})$ was a real function of $\mathbf{x}$. In the multi-class case, for a problem with I classes, we define the probability of the point $\mathbf{x}$ being in class j in terms of *softmax function* (Bridle 1989):

$$P(t = j|a^{(1)}(\mathbf{x}), a^{(2)}(\mathbf{x}), \ldots, a^{(I)}(\mathbf{x})) = \frac{exp(a^{(j)}(\mathbf{x}))}{\sum_{i=1}^{I} exp(a^{(i)}(\mathbf{x}))}, \quad (10.13)$$

where we have introduced I functions $a^{(1)}, a^{(2)}, \ldots, a^{(I)}$ to model the probability of being in any one class across the input space. Note that throughout this section, superscripts will refer to different classes whereas subscripts will refer to different data points. We shall also denote the vector $(a_1^{(i)}, a_2^{(i)}, \ldots, a_N^{(i)})$ as $\mathbf{a}^i$ and the vector $(a_n^{(1)}, a_n^{(2)}, \ldots, a_n^{(I)})$ as $\mathbf{a_n}$ where $a_n^{(i)} = a^{(i)}(\mathbf{x}_n)$.

Softmax model is a generalization of the binary classification to multi-way classification problem. Let $K_j(\mathbf{x})$ be the kernel functions, $j = 1, 2, \ldots, m$, i.e., $\mathbf{K}(\mathbf{x}) = [K_1(\mathbf{x}), K_2(\mathbf{x}), \ldots, K_m(\mathbf{x})]$ then the $a^{(i)}$ is defined as follows:

$$a^{(1)}(\mathbf{x}; \mathbf{w}) = w_{10} + w_{11}K_1(\mathbf{x}) + \ldots + w_{1m}K_m(\mathbf{x}) \quad (10.14)$$

$$a^{(2)}(\mathbf{x}; \mathbf{w}) = w_{20} + w_{21}K_1(\mathbf{x}) + \ldots + w_{2m}(\mathbf{x})K_m(\mathbf{x}) \quad (10.15)$$

$$\ldots\ldots$$

$$a^{(I)}(\mathbf{x}; \mathbf{w}) = w_{I0} + w_{I1}K_1(\mathbf{x}) + \ldots + w_{Im}K_m(\mathbf{x}). \quad (10.16)$$

It is easy to show that when $I = 2$ and $K_i(\mathbf{x}) = x_i$, softmax reduces to a logistic model. In the logistic when regression $k = 2$, we write $a^{(i)}$'s in a more compact form given by

$$a^{(1)} = w_{10} + \mathbf{w}_1^T \mathbf{x}, \quad a^{(2)} = w_{20} + \mathbf{w}_2^T \mathbf{x}. \quad (10.17)$$

As a result, we get

$$P(t = 1|\mathbf{x}; \mathbf{w}) = \frac{exp(a^{(1)})}{exp(a^{(1)}) + exp(a^{(2)})} = \frac{1}{1 + exp[-(a^{(1)} - a^{(2)})]}, \quad (10.18)$$

where

$$(a^{(1)} - a^{(2)}) = (w_{10} - w_{20}) + (\mathbf{w}_1 - \mathbf{w}_2)^T \mathbf{x} \quad (10.19)$$

is a linear predictor as we wanted. Note the fact that the labels are $\{1, 2\}$ as opposed to $\{0, 1\}$ makes no difference since we can always rename them.

10.2 Regression Trees

The basic idea of regression trees is to partition the input space recursively in two, and approximate the function in each half by the average output value of the samples it contains. See Breiman et al. (1984). Each bifurcation is parallel to one of the axes and can be expressed as an inequality involving of the input components e.g., $x_k > a$. The input space is divided into hyperrectangles organized into a binary tree where each branch is determined by the dimension (k) and boundary (a) which together minimize the residual error between model and the data (Orr et al. (1999)).

Further, from Orr et al. (1999), we note that the root node of the regression tree is the smallest hyperrectangle that will include all of the training data $\{x_i\}_{i=1}^{N}$. Its size (half-width) s_k and center c_k in each dimension k are

$$s_k = \frac{1}{2}(max_{i \in s} x_{ik} - min_{i \in s} x_{ik}) \tag{10.20}$$

$$c_k = \frac{1}{2}(max_{i \in s} x_{ik} + min_{i \in s} x_{ik}), \tag{10.21}$$

where $k \in K$, with

$$K = \{1, 2, \ldots, P\}$$

denoting the set of predictor indices, and

$$S = \{1, 2, \ldots, N\}$$

denoting the set of training indices. A bifurcation of the root node divides the training samples into left and right subsets, S_L and S_R, on either side of a boundary b in one of the dimensions k such that

$$S_L = \{i : x_{ik} \leq b\},$$

$$S_R = \{i : x_{ik} > b\}.$$

The mean output value on either side of the bifurcation is

$$\bar{\mathbf{y}}_L = \frac{1}{N_L} \sum_{i \in S_L} \mathbf{y}_i, \tag{10.22}$$

$$\bar{\mathbf{y}}_R = \frac{1}{N_R} \sum_{i \in S_R} \mathbf{y}_i, \tag{10.23}$$

where N_L and N_R are the number of samples in each subset. The mean square error is then

$$E(k,b) = \frac{1}{N}\{\sum_{i \in S_L} \|\mathbf{y}_i - \bar{\mathbf{y}}_L\|^2 + \sum_{i \in S_R} \|\mathbf{y}_i - \bar{\mathbf{y}}_R\|^2\}. \tag{10.24}$$

As discussed in Orr et al. (1999) in detail, the bifurcation that minimizes $E(k,b)$ over all possible choices of k and b is used to create the "children" of the root node and is found by simple discrete search over m dimensions and n observations. The children of the root node are split recursively in the same manner and the process terminates when every remaining bifurcation creates children containing fewer than n_{min} samples, where n_{min} is a parameter. The children are shifted with respect to their parent nodes and their sizes reduced in dimension k. One should note that in our approach our generalization is based on multivariate regression as opposed to the usual multiple regression with one response variable as in Orr et al. (1999).

Regression trees can both estimate a model and indicate which components of the input vector are most relevant to the modelled relationship. Dimensions that carry the most information about the output tend to split earliest and most often. Cases where the relevant dimensions are **x**-dependent are indicated by local clustering of the bifurcation boundaries. This form of *automatic relevance determination* is a natural feature of regression trees.

10.2.1 Information Criteria

The complexity of a nonparametric regression model increases with the number of independent and adjustable parameters, also termed *degrees of freedom*, in the model. According to the qualitative principle of *Occam's razor* (Orr et al. 1999), we need to find the simplest hypothesis that fits the observed data. The principle states that to be effective, the model complexity must be controlled. This also means we need to provide a trade off between how well the model fits the data and the model complexity.

On the other hand, the complexity of the model grows dramatically as the dimensionality of input space m increases. To provide best trade off between model complexity and dimensionality of the input, we exploit the following common properties of real data. Input variables tend to be correlated in some way, i.e., data points tend to be located in some specific regions of the space and/or in some sub-spaces featuring a so-called true or intrinsic dimensionality which is usually much lower than m (Orr et al. 1999). Thus horizontal subset selections are used to find the best subspace.

The information criteria used to evaluate and compare different horizontal and vertical subset selections can be regarded as another most important parameter. There are several distinct criteria. Here, we use Akaike's information criterion *AIC* (Akaike 1973):

$$\mathbf{AIC}(p) = n\log_e(2\pi) + n\log_e(\frac{(y-\mathbf{H}\alpha)^T(y-\mathbf{H}\alpha)}{n}) + n + 2(p+1),$$

Schwarz's Bayesian information criterion *SBC* (Schwarz 1978):

$$\mathbf{SBC}(p) = \frac{n+(\log_e n - 1)p}{n(n-p)}(y-\mathbf{H}\alpha)^T(y-\mathbf{H}\alpha),$$

Consistent Akaike's information criterion *CAIC* (Bozdogan 1987):

$$CAIC(p) = n\log_e(2\pi) + n\log_e(\frac{(y-\mathbf{H}\alpha)^T(y-\mathbf{H}\alpha)}{n}) + n + (\log_e n + 1)p,$$

and Bozdogan's *ICOMP*, a new information measure of complexity for model selection (Bozdogan 1988, 1990, 1994, 2000):

$$\mathbf{ICOMP}(p) = nlog_e(2\pi) + nlog_e\hat{\sigma}^2 + n + (p+1)log_e(\frac{tr(\mathbf{H}^T\mathbf{H})^{-1} + \frac{2\hat{\sigma}^2}{p}}{p+1})$$

$$- log_e|(\mathbf{H}^T\mathbf{H})^{-1}| - log_e(\frac{2\hat{\sigma}^2}{n}).$$

where

$$\hat{\sigma}^2 = \frac{(y - \mathbf{H}X)^T(y - \mathbf{H}X)}{n - p}.$$

For each horizontal subset, during the vertical subset selection process the current model and its potential successors differ only by the addition, subtraction, or replacement of one or two basis kernel functions. The matrix inverse involved in calculating the model selection information criterion is therefore not expensive as it can be calculated incrementally using matrix partition.

CAIC and ICOMP are more conservative than AIC and SBC in the sense that the former impose more penalty for model complexity and therefore lead to a less complex model. Our experimental results show that CAIC and ICOMP out-perform AIC and SBC in preventing overfitting for the unstable real data.

10.2.2 Parameter Estimation

In order to estimate the mean vector and the covariance matrices, we need marry the regression tree, kernel function, and information criteria together and to transfer the tree node to kernel functions. As we know, the regression tree contains a root node, some nonterminal nodes (having children) and some terminal nodes (having no children). Each node is associated with a hyperrectangle of input space having a center $\mathbf{c}$ and size $\mathbf{s}$ as described in Section 10.2. The node corresponding to the largest hyperrectangle is the root node and that is divided up into smaller and smaller pieces progressing down the tree. To transform the hyperrectangle in the node into a Gaussian kernel function (see, e.g., equation (10.3)), we use its center $\mathbf{c}$ as the kernel function center and its size $\mathbf{s}$, scaled by a parameter β, as the kernel function parameters $\mathbf{r}$,

$$\mathbf{r} = \beta\mathbf{s}. \tag{10.25}$$

The control parameter β is the same for all nodes.

After the tree nodes are transformed into kernel functions, we select a vertical subset to be included in the model. The standard methods for vertical subset selection include forward selection (the basis kernel functions are added until overfitting occurs), backward elimination (the basis kernel functions are pruned until overfitting is prevented), a combination of the two (e.g., two forward selection steps followed by one backward elimination step) or all vertical subset selection (full combinatorial search). The last is generally too computationally expensive. In any of the standard methods for vertical subset selection, we control the model complexity using information criteria and the basis kernel functions generated from the regression tree. No distinctions are made between the basis kernel functions corresponding to different nodes in the tree. Intuitively, kernel functions with large s_j should be included first, to synthesize coarse features of the data, and functions with small s_j last, to modify the fine details. This, in turn, suggests searching the basis kernel function candidates by traversing the tree from the largest hyperrectangle (and kernel functions) at the root to the smallest hyperrectangle (kernel functions) at the terminal nodes. Thus the first decision should be whether to include the root node in the model, the second is whether to include any of the children of the root node, and so on, until the terminal nodes are reached (Kubat, 1998).

After we find the best subset and the kernel function centers, we need to estimate the initial value of the mean vector and the covariance matrices of the kernel functions. Let us assume that node p includes N_p input values in a subset $\{\mathbf{X_j}\}$. We estimate the function center μ_j by the sample average $\hat{\mu}_j$:

$$\mu_j \approx \hat{\mu}_j = \frac{1}{N_j} \sum_{x \in X_j} \mathbf{x} \qquad (10.26)$$

and the covariance matrices by

$$\Sigma_j \approx \hat{\Sigma}_j = \frac{1}{N_j} \sum_{x \in X_j} (\mathbf{x} - \mu_\mathbf{j})(\mathbf{x} - \mu_\mathbf{j})^T. \qquad (10.27)$$

10.3 New Kernel Functions

In this section we introduce a new class of kernel functions, called *power exponential* (*PE*) distribution function (Bozdogan, 2002). Let $X \sim PE(\mu, \sigma, \beta)$ with density function

$$f(x; \mu, \sigma, \beta) = \frac{1}{\sigma \Gamma(1 + \frac{1}{2\beta}) 2^{1+\frac{1}{2\beta}}} exp(-\frac{1}{2} |\frac{x - \mu}{\sigma}|^{2\beta}), \qquad (10.28)$$

where the parameters μ, $-\infty < \mu < \infty$ and $\sigma > 0$ are, respectively, location and scale parameters and $\beta \in (0, \infty)$ is related to the kurtosis parameter. In this way, it indicates the nonnormality of the distribution. When $\beta = 1$ the density in (10.28) is normal. The Figures (10.2-10.4) are the *PE* with different β values.

In the multivariate case, the *PE* has the distribution given by

$$f(\mathbf{x}) = \frac{p\Gamma(\frac{p}{2})}{\pi^{\frac{p}{2}} \Gamma(1 + \frac{p}{2\beta}) 2^{1+\frac{p}{2\beta}}} \Sigma^{-1/2} exp\{-\frac{1}{2}[(\mathbf{x} - \mu)^T |\Sigma|^{-1}(\mathbf{x} - \mu)]^\beta\}, \qquad (10.29)$$

where p is the dimension of variable $\mathbf{x}$; Σ is the variance-covariance matrix of $\mathbf{x}$; β is related to the kurtosis parameter. When $\beta = 1$, we have the multivariate normal

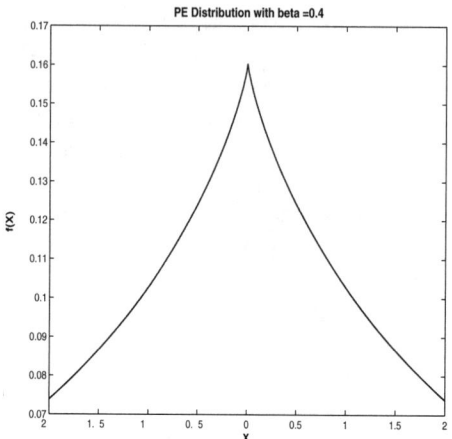

FIGURE 10.2
PE distribution with $\beta = 0.4$.

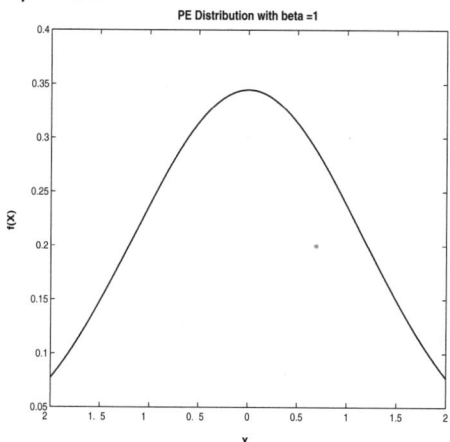

FIGURE 10.3
PE distribution with $\beta = 1$ which is Gaussian.

distribution:

$$f(\mathbf{x}) = (\frac{1}{2\pi})^{\frac{p}{2}} |\Sigma|^{-1/2} exp\{-\frac{1}{2}[(\mathbf{x}-\mu)^T \Sigma^{-1}(\mathbf{x}-\mu)]\}. \quad (10.30)$$

An advantage of *PE* class is that it is adaptive to both *peakedness* and *flatness* in the data set through varying the value of β.

Taking the exponential part of the *PE* distribution and ignoring the constant terms in equation (10.29), we get the new *PE* kernel function:

$$K(\mathbf{x}) = exp\{-[(\mathbf{x}-\mu)^T \Sigma^{-1}(\mathbf{x}-\mu)]^\beta\}. \quad (10.31)$$

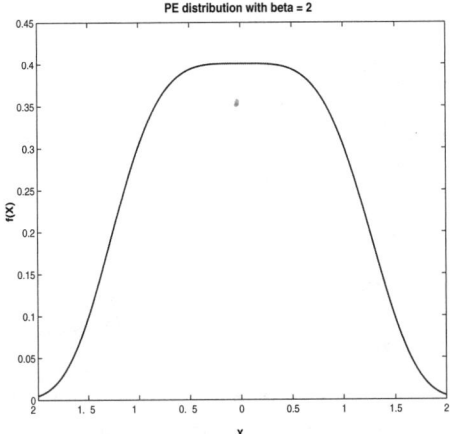

FIGURE 10.4
PE distribution with $\beta = 2$.

Hence, when $\beta = 1$, *PE* kernel becomes a simple Gaussian kernel:

$$K(\mathbf{x}) = exp[-(\mathbf{x}-\mu)^T \Sigma^{-1}(\mathbf{x}-\mu)]. \quad (10.32)$$

When Σ is a diagonal covariance matrix with diagonal elements r_i, the *PE* kernel becomes

$$k(\mathbf{x}) = exp\{-[\sum_i \frac{(x_i - \mu_i)^2}{r_i^2}]^\beta\}. \quad (10.33)$$

If all of the diagonal elements are equal to r, then the *PE* kernel becomes

$$K(\mathbf{x}) = exp\{-[\frac{\|\mathbf{x}-\mu\|^2}{r^2}]^\beta\}. \quad (10.34)$$

Bozdogan (2002) gives several ways to estimate the parameter β of the *PE* distribution. We just give two of them here. Let N be the number of observations, and m be the number of variables; we have:

$$d_i = (\mathbf{x}_i - \mu)^T \Sigma^{-1}(\mathbf{x}_i - \mu),$$

$$\bar{d} = \frac{1}{N}\sum_{i=1}^{N} d_i,$$

$$\mathbf{d} = [d1, \ldots, d_N]^T.$$

1. Method of moments for Gamma parameters:

$$\hat{\beta} = \frac{\bar{d}}{\sigma_d^2}.$$

2. Loglikelihood of Mahalanobis squared distance:

$$\hat{\beta} = \frac{m}{4\bar{d}}.$$

In this paper, however, we don't intend to estimate the parameter β. We treat it as a free parameter to add some flexibility to the classification model.

10.4 The EM Algorithm

The EM algorithm is a standard tool in statistics for dealing with missing values in maximum likelihood parameter/structure estimation. See the classic paper by Dempster et al. (1977) and the refinements provided by Neal and Hinton (1998). In this section, we present a more general view of this algorithm. We start by describing a simple algorithm for maximizing convex functions within nonconvex sets. Carrying this algorithm over to a probabilistic setting gives the standard EM-algorithm as a special case.

10.4.1 Constrained Maximization of a Convex Function

Suppose we have a convex continuously differentiable function $f(\mathbf{x})$ $\mathbf{x} \in \chi$, and we would like to find the maximum of this function within some compact set $\mathbf{x} \in \chi_c \subseteq \chi$. Neither χ_c nor χ need to be a convex set. More precisely, we want

$$\mathbf{x}_c = \arg\max_{\mathbf{x} \in \chi_c} f(\mathbf{x}). \qquad (10.35)$$

The set χ_c may be fragmented and thus finding the maximum may require a rather exhaustive search. To deal with this difficulty, we develop instead a simple iterative algorithm that is no longer guaranteed to find the global maximum but will nevertheless always find a local maximum that depends on an initial guess x_0 provided by the user. Whenever the set χ_c is convex, however, the iterative algorithm will find the global maximum.

Our assumption guarantees that we can find a tangent plane for the function f at any point $\mathbf{x}_0$:

$$L(\mathbf{x}; \mathbf{x}_0) = \nabla f(\mathbf{x}_0)^T (\mathbf{x} - \mathbf{x}_0) + f(\mathbf{x}_0). \qquad (10.36)$$

Since f is convex we must have

1. $L(\mathbf{x}; \mathbf{x}_0) \leq f(\mathbf{x})$ for all $\mathbf{x} \in \chi$
2. $L(\mathbf{x}_0; \mathbf{x}_0) = f(\mathbf{x}_0)$

Suppose now that we were able to find $x_1 \in \chi_c$ such that $L(\mathbf{x}_1; \mathbf{x}_0) > L(\mathbf{x}_0; \mathbf{x}_0)$. Then the above properties imply that

$$0 < L(\mathbf{x}_1; \mathbf{x}_0) - L(\mathbf{x}_0; \mathbf{x}_0) = L(\mathbf{x}_1; \mathbf{x}_0) - f(\mathbf{x}_0) \leq f(\mathbf{x}_1) - f(\mathbf{x}_0) \qquad (10.37)$$

or, equivalently, $f(\mathbf{x}_1) > f(\mathbf{x}_0)$, which is what we want. By applying this argument iteratively, we get the following Frank Wolfe algorithm for maximizing f (Bertsekas, 1995):

Algorithm 1

1. Choose $\mathbf{x}_0 \in \chi_c$.

2. Compute $L(\mathbf{x}; \mathbf{x}_{t-1})$.

3. Find $\mathbf{x}_t \in \chi_c$ such that $L(\mathbf{x}_t; \mathbf{x}_{t-1}) > L(\mathbf{x}_{t-1}; \mathbf{x}_{t-1})$.

4. Iterate until $L(\mathbf{x}_t; \mathbf{x}_{t-1}) - L(\mathbf{x}_{t-1}; \mathbf{x}_{t-1}) < \varepsilon$.

This algorithm generates a sequence $\mathbf{x}_0, \mathbf{x}_1, \ldots, \mathbf{x}_t$ with the property that

$$f(\mathbf{x}_0) < f(\mathbf{x}_1) <, \ldots, f(\mathbf{x}_t) \qquad (10.38)$$

and stops whenever

$$\arg\max_{\mathbf{x} \in \chi_c} L(\mathbf{x}_t; \mathbf{x}_{t-1}) = L(\mathbf{x}_{t-1}; \mathbf{x}_{t-1}) = f(\mathbf{x}_{t-1}). \qquad (10.39)$$

At this point we reach a local maximum. Note that we may still be able to find $\mathbf{x}_t \neq \mathbf{x}_{t-1}$ such that $L(\mathbf{x}_t; \mathbf{x}_{t-1}) = f(\mathbf{x}_{t-1})$; the local maximum function is unique in terms of the value of the function, not in terms of $\mathbf{x}$ that achieves the value.

Finally note that to find $\mathbf{x}_t$ from $\mathbf{x}_{t-1}$ as required by the algorithm we do not need to evaluate $L(\mathbf{x}; \mathbf{x}_{t-1})$ but only the part that depends on x.

$$\mathbf{x}_t = \arg\max_{\mathbf{x} \in \chi_c} \{L(\mathbf{x}; \mathbf{x}_{t-1})\} = \arg\max_{\mathbf{x} \in \chi_c} \{\nabla f(\mathbf{x}_{t-1})^T \mathbf{x}\}. \qquad (10.40)$$

The stopping criterion also relies on computing only $\nabla f(\mathbf{x}_{t-1})^T \mathbf{x}$:

$$L(\mathbf{x}_t; \mathbf{x}_{t-1}) - L(\mathbf{x}_{t-1}; \mathbf{x}_{t-1}) = \nabla f(\mathbf{x}_{t-1})^T \mathbf{x}_t - \nabla f(\mathbf{x}_{t-1})^T \mathbf{x}_{t-1}. \qquad (10.41)$$

10.4.2 The EM Algorithm

Suppose we have a parametric model

$$P(\mathbf{x}|\theta) = P(x_1, \ldots, x_n|\theta) \qquad (10.42)$$

over $\mathbf{x} \in A$, where $\theta \in \Theta$ denotes the parameters. Let $\mathbf{x}_v$ be the set of observed variables. We would like to maximize

$$\log P(\mathbf{x}_v|\theta) = \log \sum_{\mathbf{x} \setminus \mathbf{x}_v} P(\mathbf{x} \setminus \mathbf{x}_v, \mathbf{x}_v|\theta) \qquad (10.43)$$

with respect to the parameters $\theta \in \Theta$. Typically there are multiple observations and possibly over different sets of variables. Our simple case here is readily extended to the more general setting.

The EM algorithm proceeds to maximize the log-likelihood by starting with an initial guess Θ_0, and successively refining the parameters by finding the maximum of

$$Q(\theta|\theta_0) = E_{\theta_0}\{\log P(\mathbf{x} \setminus \mathbf{x}_v, \mathbf{x}_v|\theta_0)|\theta_0\} = \sum_{\mathbf{x}\setminus\mathbf{x}_v} P(\mathbf{x} \setminus \mathbf{x}_v|\mathbf{x}_v, \theta_0) \log P(\mathbf{x}|\theta) \quad (10.44)$$

with respect to $\theta \in \Theta$. The advantage of this formulation is that due to the factorization of the joint distribution, $\log P(\mathbf{x}|\theta)$ often reduces to a simple sum that considerably simplifies the maximization step. The computation of the Q-function, i.e., carrying out the expectation over the missing values, is called the *E-step* and the maximization with respect to θ is known as the *M-step*. We can write the algorithm as follows:

Algorithm 2

1. Choose $\theta_0 \in \Theta$.

2. E-step: Compute $Q(\theta|ta_{t-1})$.

3. M-step: find $\theta_t \in \Theta$ such that $Q(\theta_t|\theta_{t-1}) > Q(\theta_{t-1}|\theta_{t-1})$.

4. Iterate until $Q(\theta_t|\theta_{t-1}) - Q(\theta_{t-1}|\theta_{t-1}) < \varepsilon$.

This is similar to our previous algorithm. We can establish the connection formally as follows. Let Φ be the space of all real functions $\Phi(x)$ whose components are indexed by the configuration $x \in A$. Also let Φ_c be the set of all functions $\Phi(x) = \log P(\mathbf{x}|\theta)$ for all $\theta \in \Theta$. Thus maximizing the log-likelihood is equivalent to maximizing

$$\log \sum_{\mathbf{x}\setminus\mathbf{x}_v} P(\mathbf{x}|\theta) = \log \sum_{\mathbf{x}\setminus\mathbf{x}_v} e^{\log P(\mathbf{x}|\theta)} = \log \sum_{\mathbf{x}\setminus\mathbf{x}_v} e^{\Phi(x)} = f(\Phi) \quad (10.45)$$

with respect to $\Phi \in \Phi_c$. It can be shown that $f(\Phi)$ is a convex function of Φ. This is a well known property in the physics literature and can be shown easily by computing the Hessian and showing that it must be positive (semi-) definite. The gradient of f with respect to a particular component of Φ, say $\Phi(\tilde{x})$, is given by

$$\frac{\partial f(\Phi)}{\partial \Phi(\tilde{x})} = \frac{1}{\sum_{\mathbf{x}\setminus\mathbf{x}_v} e^{\Phi(x)}} \sum_{\mathbf{x}\setminus\mathbf{x}_v} \delta(\mathbf{x}_v = \tilde{\mathbf{x}}_v) = \frac{1}{\sum_{\mathbf{x}\setminus\mathbf{x}_v} e^{\Phi(x)}} e^{\Phi(\tilde{x})} \delta(\mathbf{x}_v = \tilde{\mathbf{x}}_v)$$

$$= \frac{1}{P(\mathbf{x}_v|\theta)} P(\tilde{\mathbf{x}}|\theta) \delta(\mathbf{x}_v = \tilde{\mathbf{x}}_v) \quad (10.46)$$

so long as $\Phi \in \Phi_c$, thus

$$\nabla f(\Phi_0)^T \Phi = \sum_{\tilde{x}} \left[\frac{1}{P(\tilde{\mathbf{x}}_v|\theta_0)} P(\tilde{\mathbf{x}}|\theta_0) \delta(\mathbf{x}_v = \tilde{\mathbf{x}}_v)\right] \log P(\tilde{\mathbf{x}}|\theta) \quad (10.47)$$

$$= \sum_{\mathbf{x}\setminus\mathbf{x}_v} \frac{P(\mathbf{x}|\theta_0)}{P(\mathbf{x}_v|\theta_0)} \log P(\mathbf{x}|\theta) \quad (10.48)$$

$$= \sum_{\mathbf{x}\setminus\mathbf{x}_v} P(\mathbf{x} \setminus \mathbf{x}_v|\mathbf{x}_v, \theta_0) \log P(\mathbf{x}|\theta) = Q(\theta|\theta_0), \quad (10.49)$$

Statistical Data Mining and Knowledge Discovery

which completes the connection. The analysis of the EM-algorithm follows the analysis of the previous algorithm. Therefore EM-algorithm is a specific case of the Algorithm 1.

10.4.3 EM-Algorithm for PE Mixture Models

In the previous section, we introduced the EM-algorithm for mixture model using Gaussian kernels. Here we derive the EM for the PE mixture directly from log-likelihood function.

We have a mixture m PE where we use t and j to denote specific mixture components and i indexes training examples. θ contains all the adjustable parameters in the mixture PE model.

The log-likelihood of the observed data is given by

$$Q(\theta) = \sum_{i=1}^{n} \log P(\mathbf{x}_i|\theta) = \sum_{i=1}^{n} \log \left[\sum_{j=1}^{m} P(\mathbf{x}_i, t=j|\theta) \right] \quad (10.50)$$

$$= \sum_{i=1}^{n} \log \left[\sum_{j=1}^{m} P(t=j|\theta) P(\mathbf{x}_i|t=j,\theta) \right] \quad (10.51)$$

$$= \sum_{i=1}^{n} \left[\sum_{j=1}^{m} p_j P(\mathbf{x}_i|\mu_j, \Sigma_j) \right], \quad (10.52)$$

where $\theta = \{p_1, \ldots, p_m, \mu_1, \ldots, \mu_m, \Sigma_1, \ldots, \Sigma_m\}$ and $p_j = P(j|\theta)$ is the prior probability of selecting component j. Note the PE kurtosis parameter β is a predetermined constant. That is, it is given *a priori*. So, we can simply test the effect of the kurtosis β by specifying different values.

Algorithm 3:

1. Choose $\theta_0 \in \Theta$.

2. E-step: compute

$$Q(\theta|\theta_0) = \sum_{i=1}^{n} E_{\theta_0}\{\log P(\mathbf{x},t|\theta)|\mathbf{x}_i\} \quad (10.53)$$

$$= \sum_{i=1}^{n} \left[\sum_{j=1}^{m} P(t=j|\mathbf{x}_i,\theta_0) \log P(\mathbf{x}_i, t=j|\theta) \right]. \quad (10.54)$$

3. M-step: find $\theta_t \in \Theta$ such that $Q(\theta_t|\theta_{t-1}) > Q(\theta_{t-1}|\theta_{t-1})$.

4. Iterate until $Q(\theta_t|\theta_{t-1}) - Q(\theta_{t-1}|\theta_{t-1}) < \varepsilon$.

In the M-step the parameters μ_j and Σ_j can be estimated using the general maximum log-likelihood method. The prior probability $\hat{p}_j$, however, can be found through maximizing $Q(\theta|\theta_0)$ directly.

In order to optimize $\hat{p}_j$, we need to add the constraint $\sum_{j=1}^{m} \hat{p}_j = 1$. This creates a new optimization that we wish to maximize:

$$\hat{Q}(\theta|\theta_0) = \sum_{i=1}^{n}\sum_{j=1}^{m} P(t=j|\mathbf{x}_i,\theta_0)\log P(\mathbf{x}_i,t=j|\theta) - \lambda\left(\sum_{j=1}^{m}\hat{p}_j - 1\right). \quad (10.55)$$

Excluding boundary conditions, taking the derivative related to $\hat{p}_j$, and simplifying the formulas, we can get

$$\hat{p}_j = \frac{1}{n}\sum_{i=1}^{n} P(t=k|\mathbf{x}_i,\theta_0). \quad (10.56)$$

10.5 Hybrid Training

Hybrid training is composed of two separate stages. In the first stage, the kernel's parameters (the PE centers and covariance) are determined using the unsupervised training approach. Then the second layer multiplicative weights are trained using the regular supervised technique.

The first stage can be performed with the regression tree and EM-algorithm, which was introduced above. In each iteration of the EM algorithm, the new prior class probabilities are calculated from the current posterior probabilities. Then, the PE's centers and covariances are calculated using the new priors. Finally, new posteriors are extracted from these new parameters, and are used in the next iteration, and so on. The kurtosis parameter β is preassigned, so that we can test the effect of different β by simply giving different values of β.

The second stage is equivalent to solving a system of linear equations, in which the second-layer weights (coefficients) are the unknowns, and the target output values are the free variables. There are two kinds of methods for solving this second stage problem. The first is the pseudo-inverse technique for batch learning. The second method is the gradient descent learning rule. We will employ the second method in this paper.

In the binary case, output $y = P(t|\mathbf{x},\mathbf{w}) = \frac{1}{1+exp(a(\mathbf{x}))}$ and $a(\mathbf{x}) = w_0 + \sum_{j=1}^{m} w_j K_j$. To compute the gradient

$$\frac{\partial}{\partial w_j} y = \frac{\partial}{\partial w_j} \log P(t|K(\mathbf{x}),\mathbf{w}) \quad (10.57)$$

first, we know $y(-a) = 1 - y(a)$ and

$$\frac{\partial}{\partial a} y(a) = y(a)y(-a), \quad \frac{\partial}{\partial a} y(-a) = -y(a)y(-a) \quad (10.58)$$

since

$$\log P(t|K(\mathbf{x}),\mathbf{w}) = t\log y(a) + (1-t)\log(1-y(a)) \quad (10.59)$$

Statistical Data Mining and Knowledge Discovery

$$\frac{\partial}{\partial a} \log P(t|K(\mathbf{x}), w) = t \frac{\partial}{\partial a} \log y(a) + (1-t) \frac{\partial}{\partial a} \log y(-a). \tag{10.60}$$

This is just a difference between the binary output label and our prediction of the probability that the label is 1. The difference becomes zero only if we predict the correct label with probability one. Now,

$$\frac{\partial}{\partial w_0} \log P(t|K, \mathbf{w}) = \frac{\partial a}{\partial w_0} \cdot \frac{\partial}{\partial a} \log P(t|K, \mathbf{w}) = 1.(t - y(a)) \tag{10.61}$$

$$\frac{\partial}{\partial w_j} \log P(t|K, \mathbf{w}) = \frac{\partial a}{\partial w_j} \cdot \frac{\partial}{\partial a} \log P(t|K, \mathbf{w}) = K_j.(t - y(a)). \tag{10.62}$$

Updating rules depend merely on the prediction difference $(t - y(a))$ in addition to the middle layer output. These are are often called **delta rules**. Then the weights (coefficients) are updated as follows:

$$w_j \leftarrow w_j + \varepsilon \sum_{i=1}^{n} \frac{\partial}{\partial w_j} \log P(t_i | K_i(\mathbf{x}), \mathbf{w}), \tag{10.63}$$

where $\varepsilon = 1/\sqrt{nm}$, n is the number of training examples, and m is the number of centers in the middle layer. Set of weights w_j can be initialized to 0 or to very small random numbers.

Similarly for the multi-class classification with *softmax* output, the gradient descent learning rule for *softmax* is

$$w_{ij} \leftarrow w_{ij} + \varepsilon \frac{\partial}{\partial w_{ij}} \log P(t|K, \mathbf{w}). \tag{10.64}$$

By the chain rule (recall the definition of $a^{(i)}$ in multi-class classification)

$$\frac{\partial}{\partial w_{ij}} \log P(t|K, \mathbf{w}) = \frac{\partial a^{(i)}}{\partial w_{ij}} \cdot \frac{\partial}{\partial a^{(i)}} \log P(t|K, \mathbf{w}) \tag{10.65}$$

$$= K_j \cdot \frac{\partial}{\partial a^{(i)}} \left(a^{(t)} - \log \sum_{j=1}^{m} e^{a^{(j)}} \right) \tag{10.66}$$

$$= K_j \cdot \left(\delta_{t,i} - \frac{1}{\sum_{j=1}^{m} e^{a^{(j)}}} \frac{\partial}{\partial a^{(i)}} \left(\sum_{j=1}^{m} e^{a^{(j)}} \right) \right) \tag{10.67}$$

$$= K_j \cdot \left(\delta_{t,i} - \frac{1}{\sum_{j=1}^{m} e^{a^{(i)}}} \right) \tag{10.68}$$

$$= K_j \cdot (\delta_{t,i} - P(t = i|K, \mathbf{w})), \tag{10.69}$$

where $\delta_{t,i} = 1$ if $t = i$ and zero otherwise. We have assumed here that $j > 0$. The derivative with respect to w_{i0} is obtained analogously but K_j would be replaced with 1. This has the form of a delta rule since it is a difference between that target $\delta_{t,i}$ (assigning 1 to the correct label and zero for others) and our predictions $P(t = i|K, \mathbf{w})$.

The hybrid training approach has several advantages. It is much faster than the supervised method, and is easier to interpret. It is especially useful when labelled data are in short supply, since the first stage can be performed on all the data without using the label.

The hidden units in a *RBF* network are actually the component densities of a *PE* mixture model.

The second layer weights are their mixture coefficients. The first stage of unsupervised training determines the *PE* distributions, thus partitions the data into multi-dimensional radialclusters. The second stage of the training sets the mixing coefficients, in order to map the *PE* (actually the distance of the input vector from each *PE*) to validate output values.

10.6 Computational Results

In order to illustrate various features of our new method, we first generate a two dimensional toy example to show the effect for classification with different β values. Figures (10.5 - 10.8) show that different β values give different classification boundary contours. Therefore, we have quite different classification decisions. It is shown that parameter β is critical in *RBF* classification.

The second data set is created by sampling from a distribution model that we constructed. There are 3 classes: 100 examples of each class, and each example has 2 feature values. The data set is contained in three matrices. The feature values for each example are collected in the input matrix. Each example is stored as a row. The correct class of the i'th example is stored in the i'th row of the target matrix. There is one column in the target matrix for each class. The column that contains the value 1 is the correct class; the other column will contain 0. A third matrix called test contains a collection of test examples. The classification results for test data are visualized in Figures (10.9-10.11).

Classification using *RBF* network with *PE* kernel and $\beta = 0.95$ has the lowest test error.

Our third example is a binary data file. The training and test data sets are "3"s and "5"s. We have assigned $y = 1$ for all "3"s and $y = 0$ for all "5"s. The results are given in Table 10.1.

Our last example is a credit screening problem. The credit database was obtained via FTP from the machine learning database repository maintained by UC-Irvine. The task is to predict whether or not an application will default. For each of 690 applicant case histories, the database contains 15 features describing the applicant plus the class label indicates whether or not a default ultimately occurred. The descriptions of the features are left out for propriety reasons. Only 6 features were used in the analysis reported here. After omitting the cases having missing features, we use 666 observations in the experiments.

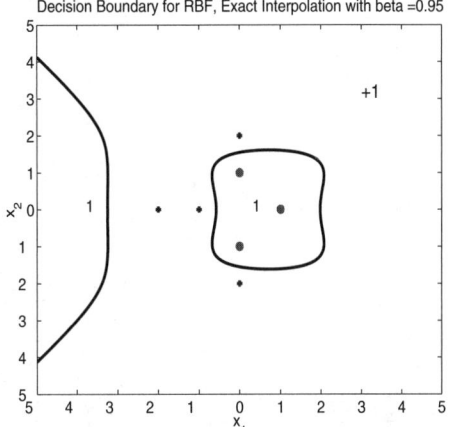

FIGURE 10.5
RBF classification using PE kernel with $\beta = 0.95$.

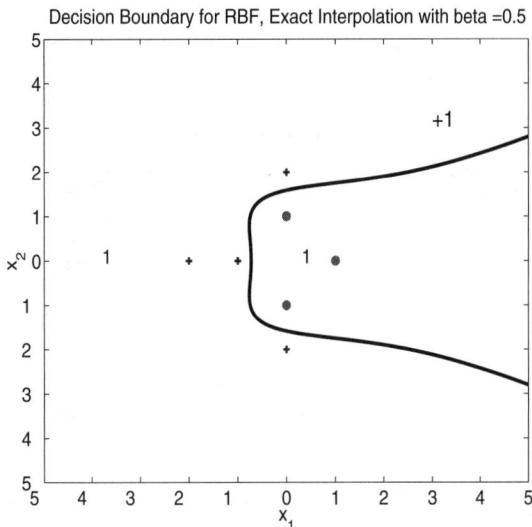

FIGURE 10.6
RBF classification using PE kernel with $\beta = 0.5$.

In all the analyses, the data were randomly partitioned in 100 different ways into 400 training data and 266 test data. The results shown in Table 10.2 are averaged over 100 different partitions. RBF using PE kernel gives the best test error. Such a modest but statistically significant improvement in test error could translate into a substantial increase in profit for the bank.

Models	Test Error(# of Misclassifications)
Mixture of Gaussian Classifier	96
Logistic Regression	48
RBF with PE kernel $\beta = 0.98$	40

TABLE 10.1
Model performance comparison for the binary data.

Models	Training Error	Test Error
Multilayer Perceptron	$18.6\% \pm 0.2$	$22.3\% \pm 0.3$
RBF using Gaussian kernel	$19.1\% \pm 0.3$	$21.8\% \pm 0.1$
RBF with PE kernel $\beta = 0.87$	$18.7\% \pm 0.1$	$20.6\% \pm 0.3$

TABLE 10.2
Model performance comparison for the credit data base.

10.7 Conclusions

In this paper, we proposed *RBF* using *PE* kernels which generalize the Gaussian kernels. These kinds of kernel functions together with a hybrid training scheme result in a higher classification accuracy. The results are encouraging. In the future, we may estimate the conditional probability for the mixture Power Exponential distribution using the same scheme and use different β for different *PE* components. In order to improve the performance, we may pick up the best β through using genetic algorithm (*GA*).

Acknowledgments

This work is based on the results of the Ph.D. thesis of the first author under the supervision of Professor Bozdogan. The first author would like to express his sincere gratitude to Professor Bozdogan. The results of this paper would not have been possible without his guidance, knowledge, encouragement, and patience.

References

Akaike, H. (1973). Information theory and an extension of the maximum likelihood principle. In B.N. Petrov and F. Csáki (Eds.), *Second International Symposium on Information Theory*, Budapest: Académiai Kiadó, 267-281.

Statistical Data Mining and Knowledge Discovery 213

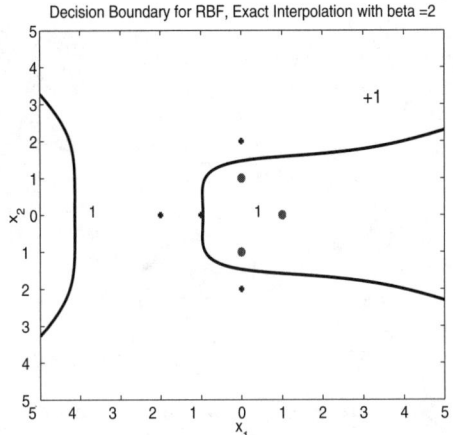

FIGURE 10.7
RBF classification using PE kernel with $\beta = 2$.

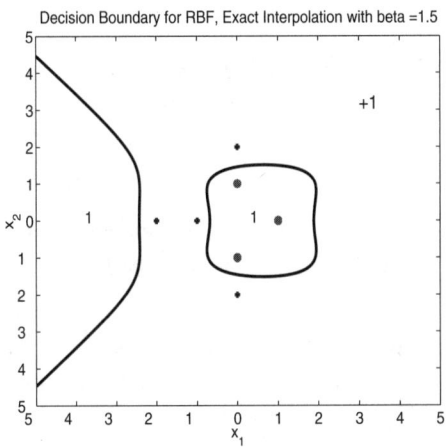

FIGURE 10.8
RBF classification using PE kernel with $\beta = 15$.

Bertsekas, D. (1995). *Nonlinear Programming*, Athena Scientific, Belmont, MA.

Breiman, L., Friedman, J., Olsen, J., and Stone, C. (1984). *Classification and Regression Trees*. Wadsworth, Belmont, CA.

Bridle, J. S. (1989). Probabilistic interpretation of feedforward classification network ooutputs, with relationships to statistical pattern recognition. In *Neuro-computing: Algorithms, Architectures and Applications*, Spring-Verlag, Heidelberg, 227-236.

Bozdogan, H. (1987). Model selection and Akaike's Information Criterion (AIC):

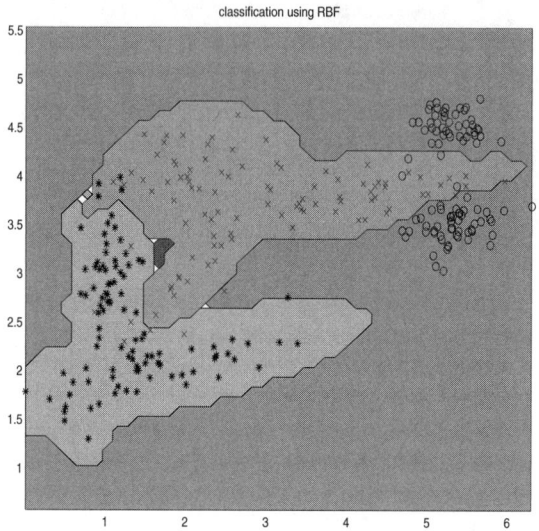

FIGURE 10.9
RBF classification using $\beta = 0.95$; test error 14.

The general theory and its analytical extensions. *Psychometrika*, 52(3), 345-370.

Bozdogan, H. (1988). ICOMP: a new model-selection criterion. In *Classification and Related Methods of Data Analysis*, H. H. Bock (Ed.), Elsevier Science Publishers, Amsterdam, 599-608.

Bozdogan, H. (1990). On the information-based measure of covariance complexity and its application to the evaluation of multivariate linear models. *Communications in Statistics, Theory and Methods*, 19, 221-278.

Bozdogan, H. (1994). Mixture-model cluster analysis using a new informational complexity and model selection criteria. In *Multivariate Statistical Modeling*, H. Bozdogan (Ed.), Vol. 2, Proceedings of the First US/Japan Conference on the Frontiers of Statistical Modeling: An Informational Approach, Kluwer Academic Publishers, Dordrecht, the Netherlands, 69-113.

Bozdogan, H. (2000). Akaike's information criterion and recent developments in information complexity. *Journal of Mathematical Psychology*, 44, 62-91.

Bozdogan, H. (2002). A new generation multivariate mixture-model cluster analysis of normal and non-normal data using information measure of complexity. Invited Paper Presented at The 8th Meeting of IFCS-2002, July 16-19, Cracow, Poland, 2002.

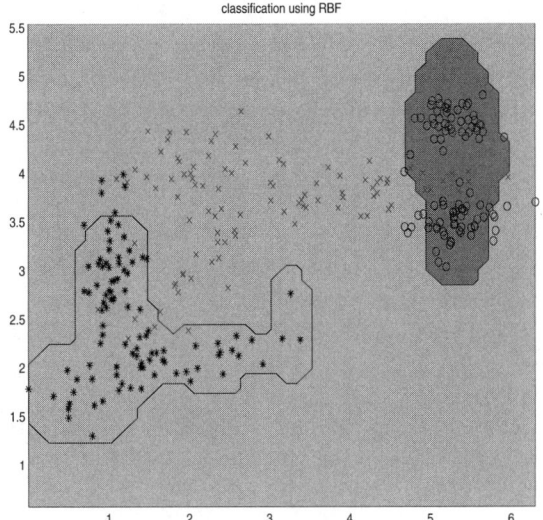

FIGURE 10.10
RBF classification using $\beta = 1$; test error 22.

Dempster, A. P., Laird, N. M., and Rubin, D. B. (1977). Maximum Likelihood from incomplete data via the EM algorithm. *J. Roy. Statist. Soc. B*, 39, 1–38.

Kubat, M. (1998). Decision trees can initialize radial basis function networks. *IEEE Transactions on Neural Networks*, 9(5): 813-821.

Neal, R. M. (1997). Monte Carlo implementation of Gaussian process models for Bayesian regression and classification. Technical Report No. 9702, Department of Statistics, University of Toronto.

Neal R. M. and Hinton, G. E. (1998). A view of the EM algorithm that justifies incremental, sparse and other variants. In *Learning in Graphical Models*. Ser. Adaptive Computation and Machine Learning, M. I. Jordan, (Ed.), MIT, Cambridge, MA.

Orr, M., Hallam, J., Takezawa, K., Murray, A., Ninomiya, S. , Oide, M., and Leonard, T. (1999). Combining regression tree and radial basis function networks. *http://www.cns.ed.ac.uk/people/mark.html*.

Schwarz, G. (1978). Estimating the dimension of a model. *Ann. Statist.*, 6, 461-464.

Williams, C.K.I. and Barber, D. (1998). Bayesian classification with Gaussian processes. *IEEE Transactions on Pattern Analysis and Machine Intelligence*, 20(12), 1342-1351.

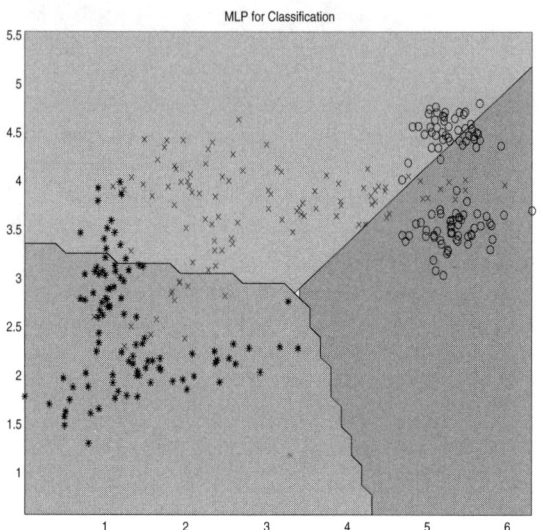

FIGURE 10.11
Linear classification test error 49.

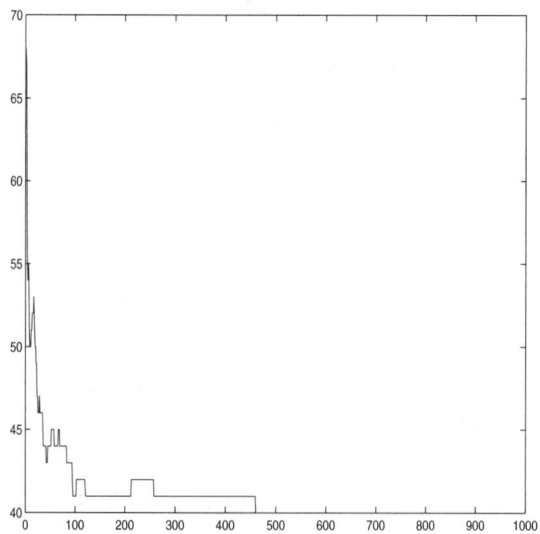

FIGURE 10.12
Training errors for the RBF.

11

Use of Kernel Based Techniques for Sensor Validation in Nuclear Power Plants

Andrei V. Gribok, Aleksey M. Urmanov, J. Wesley Hines, and Robert E. Uhrig
University of Tennessee, Knoxville, USA

CONTENTS

11.1 Introduction	217
11.2 Collinear, Ill-Posed Problems, Regularization	218
11.3 Kernel Regression and MSET	222
11.4 Support Vector Machines	223
11.5 Data Description and Results	225
11.6 Conclusions	228
Acknowledgments	229
References	230

Several techniques have been proposed recently for sensor validation in nuclear as well as fossil power plants. They are all based on the same idea of using redundant information contained in collinear data sets to provide an estimation of monitored sensor value. Being data driven statistical techniques they are all prone to the instabilities and inconsistencies caused by collinear finite data sets. This paper examines these techniques from a unifying regularization point of view and presents some experimental comparison of their performance on real plant data. The results show that without proper regularization all the statistical techniques are sensitive to minor variations in the data. Regularization may effectively stabilize the inference making results repeatable and consistent.

11.1 Introduction

The safe and economical operation of Nuclear Power Plants (NPP) requires knowledge of the state of the plant, which is obtained by measuring critical plant parameters with sensors, and their instrument chains. Traditional approaches used to validate the sensors are operating correctly involve the use of redundant sensors coupled with periodic instrument calibration. Since few of the sensors are actually out of calibration, the end result is that many instruments are unnecessary maintained. An alternative condition based technique is desirable.

When implementing condition based calibration methods, the instruments are calibrated only when they are determined to be out of calibration. On-line, real-time sensor calibration monitoring identifies faulty sensors, which permits reduced maintenance efforts and increases component reliability.

Inferential sensing is the prediction of a sensor value through the use of correlated plant variables. Most calibration monitoring systems produce an inferred value and compare it to the sensor value to determine the sensor status. There are a number of techniques, which were proposed for on-line inferential sensing during recent years. Most notable are neural nets (NN) (Hines, 1997,1998) and multivariate state estimation techniques (MSET) (Gross, 1997, Zavaljevski, 1999). Both of these methods use related sensors as inputs to estimate a model (sets of weights) that is subsequently used to infer the sensor's value based on the input values. A peculiar feature of any on-line sensor validation system is that this system should not only accurately infer the sensor's value but it should also be robust to moderate changes in input values. This means that the sensor validation system should resolve a subtle compromise between accuracy and robustness. Recently, the role of regularization in this process was realized (Hines, 1999, Gribok, 1999, Zavaljevski, 1999, Hines, 2000).

11.2 Collinear, Ill-Posed Problems, Regularization

The problems, which arise in inferential sensing, are twofold. First, the use of correlated sensors as inputs to an inferential system leads to a significantly non-uniform eigenvalue spectrum of the data matrix. This causes some weights to be unreasonably large and hence decreases the system's robustness to minor perturbations. The second problem is that these techniques, being statistically based, can significantly overfit the training data set, again providing poor performance on the test data. Regularization techniques can remedy both of these problems and provide a stable and accurate system. Currently, neural nets, as well as MSET, use regularization and include regularization parameters either in an explicit form (weight decay parameter for NN) or in both explicit and implicit forms (regularization parameter and kernel width for MSET). Both techniques can be considered as a subset of the recently developed method of support vectors or support vector machines (SVM) (Vapnik, 1995)

To illustrate the problems with the ordinary least squares (OLS) solution for sensor validation, let us consider a simple linear multiple regression fit to a set of plant data. Eighty two variables, recorded at a TVA plant, arranged in a data matrix X (1000×82), are used as predictor variables to infer the value of response variable Y which is the sensor under surveillance. The ordinary least squares (OLS) solution is produced by solving the normal equations and can be written in terms of data matrix X and response variable Y as:

$$w = (X^t X)^{-1} X^t Y \qquad (11.1)$$

Statistical Data Mining and Knowledge Discovery

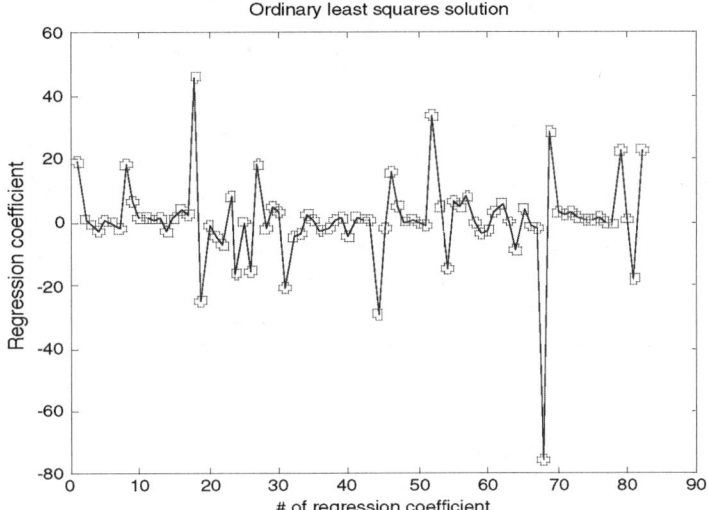

FIGURE 11.1
Regression coefficients produced by OLS solution.

which is the minimizer of the ordinary least squares functional:

$$E(w) = (Y - Xw)^t (Y - Xw) \qquad (11.2)$$

The number of samples used to estimate the OLS solution is 1000 and condition number of standardized matrix X is 740. The OLS solution is shown in Figure 11.1.

We can see that it has a number of large weights and inference would rely heavily on these weights to make predictions on future unseen data. As we pointed out, the condition number of matrix X is 740 indicating severe collinearity (Belsley, 1980). As a result of collinear data the confidence intervals on regression coefficients w are very wide indicating that OLS solution essentially consists of random numbers poorly determined by the data. For example, confidence intervals on some of the 82 regression coefficients are shown in Table 11.1.

As we can see from Table 11.1, all confidence intervals are wide and all but one change sign, indicating that the regression coefficients do not significantly differ from zero. Obviously, such a solution would produce dubious results when used in prediction. The inference of a sensor value Y based on new unseen data using OLS solution is shown in Figure 11.2.

We can see that the prediction becomes horrible. The reason for this is that one sensor, #53, changed its behavior drastically, thus changing the prediction. The readings from this sensor are shown in Figure 11.3.

This example shows that the OLS solution, although fitting training data quite well, may not be appropriate for future use because of the lack of robustness and stability. Dropping the signal #53 from the list of predictor variables does not help because other sensors having non-stationary behavior will affect the predictions. As

Regression coeff. #	Parameter value	Lower confidence	Upper confidence
50	-0.6319	-9.57	8.493
51	-1.336	-11.38	8.713
52	33.89	-55.05	122.8
53	4.555	-9.446	18.56
54	-14.6	-37.41	8.214
55	6.114	-5.614	17.84
56	4.549	-1.514	10.61
57	7.902	-5.156	20.96
58	-0.2155	-44.75	44.32
59	-3.919	-7.632	-0.2059

TABLE 11.1
Regression coefficients and their confidence intervals.

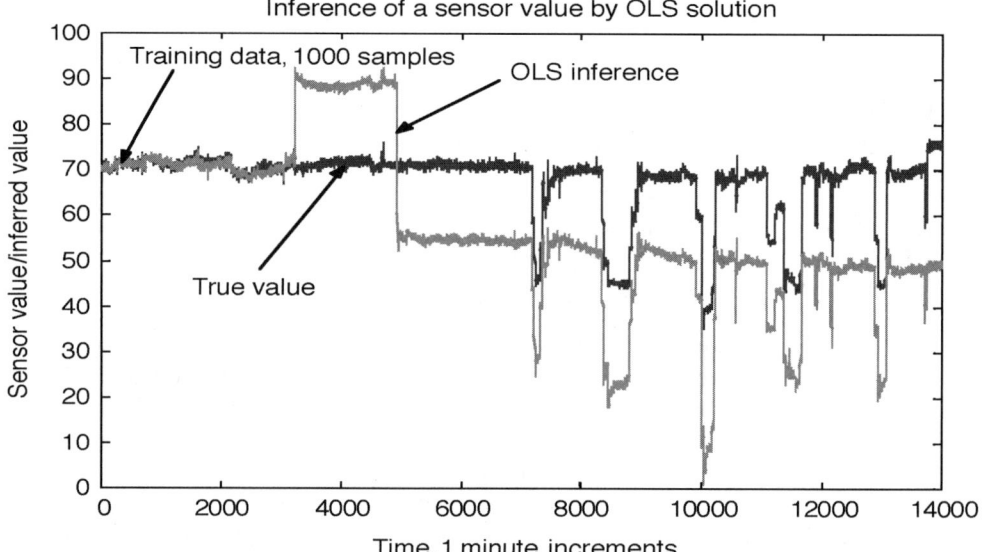

FIGURE 11.2
Inconsistency of inference by OLS solution.

has been pointed out, the main reason for unstable, non-robust prediction is statistical inconsistency of the regression coefficients obtained from collinear data sets. A simplest form of regularization known as ridge regression (RR) can be used to stabilize the solution. The ridge solution can be calculated as (Hoerl, 1970)

$$w = (X^t X + \lambda I)^{-1} X^t Y \qquad (11.3)$$

which is the minimizer of the following regularized functional:

$$E(w) = (Y - Xw)^t (Y - Xw) + \lambda w^t w \qquad (11.4)$$

Ridge regression is a shrinkage estimator: it shrinks large regression coefficients towards zero, simultaneously reducing their variance, thus making them statistically

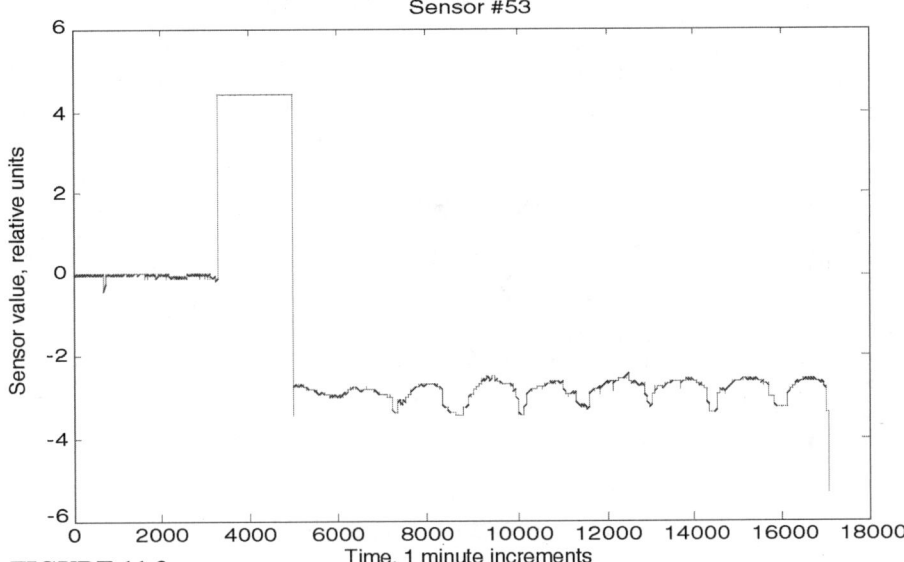

FIGURE 11.3
Inconsistency of inference by OLS solution.

significant. Parameter λ is called the ridge or regularization parameter and has to be estimated from the data if not known *a priori* (very rare situation in practice). The prediction on the same set of data using ridge regression is shown in Figure 11.4.

As we can see the prediction is very stable and was not affected by changes in sensor #53 (compare to Figure 11.2). This simple but instructive example shows the benefits that regularization provides for sensor validation systems. However, ridge regression is a linear technique and can be used effectively only when the system under consideration is essentially a linear one. Although the degree of nonlinearity of the data sets generated by a real plant is still a subject of research interest, it is clear that sensor validation systems would benefit from using nonlinear information provided a stable solution can be found. A natural candidate model to be used in nonlinear sensor validation system would be the artificial neural network (ANN). However, practical applications of ANNs were always shadowed by the inherent ill-posedeness of ANN training. The ANN error surface has many local minima, and training guarantees convergence to one of them. However the quality of this solution (its predictive value) can not be guaranteed because this solution depends on many factors: in particular on the weight initialization, training technique used, number of hidden neurons, stopping rule, the hidden neuron activation function and, finally, on the training data itself as well as the order in which the samples are presented. All this makes ANNs ill-controlled learning machines, although in many practical applications neural networks produced good or excellent results. Much effort has been dedicated to the problem of ANN regularization. Presently, the most promising and consistent approach is Bayesian regularization (BR) (MacKay, 1992), which allows

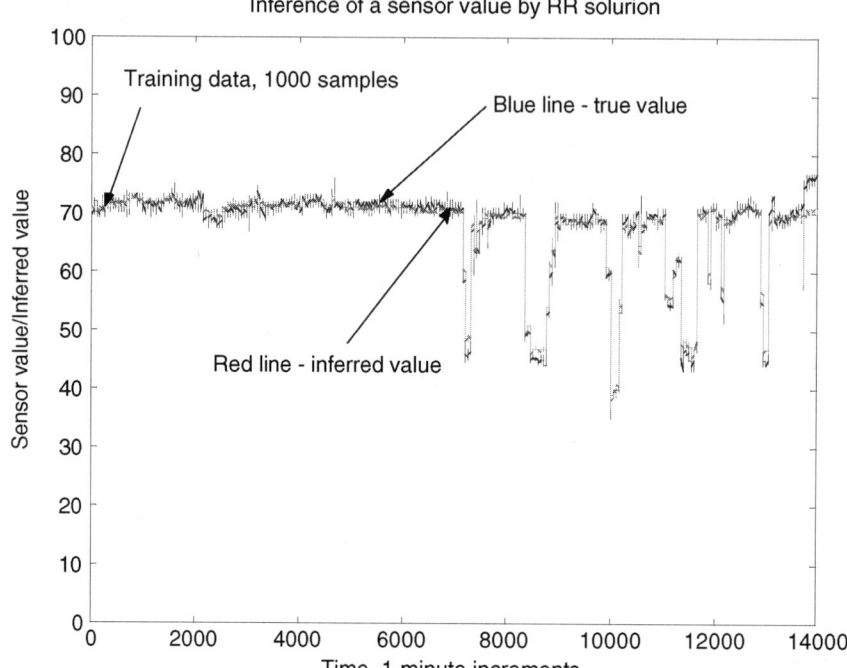

FIGURE 11.4
Inference by regularized solution.

the selection of the ANN architecture as well as the value of regularization parameter to be "automatic" based on evidence approximation. However, BR is computationally time consuming so in this study we adopted the weight decay regularization technique with the regularization parameter selected empirically.

11.3 Kernel Regression and MSET

An alternative approach to incorporating nonlinear information into a sensor validation system is to use other nonparametric regression methods such as kernel regression (Cherkassky, 1998) or MSET, which proves to be a kernel regression in disguise (Zavaljevski, 1999). The kernel regression estimator can be written in the form:

$$\hat{Y} = \frac{\sum\limits_{i=1}^{N} K(\frac{x-x_i}{h}) Y_i}{\sum\limits_{i=1}^{N} K(\frac{x-x_i}{h})} = \sum\limits_{i=1}^{N} w_i Y_i \qquad (11.5)$$

where N is the number of training samples and K is a properly chosen kernel function, such as the Gaussian function $K(u) = (2\pi\sigma)^{1/2}\exp(-u^2/2\sigma^2)$. We can see that the weights "w" map Y into its estimate "$\hat{Y}$" which is a smoother version of Y. The parameter h is called the smoothing parameter or bandwidth and controls the degree of smoothing. This parameter should be optimized to resolve a trade-off between data fit and smoothness of the regression function. It should be emphasized that kernel regression requires the proper choice of kernel type and bandwidth to make sensible estimations. The choice of kernel type is equivalent to the choice of NN architecture (number of hidden neurons) and the choice of bandwidth is equivalent to the choice of weight decay parameter when training ANN with weight decay. Kernel regression is based on the kernel density estimation technique (Cherkassky, 1998) and its own drawback: for high dimensional data, estimation may become inconsistent due to the curse of dimensionality and be very sensitive to the kernel selection. Kernel regression can be made consistent by using regularization techniques similar to those used in ridge regression.

11.4 Support Vector Machines

Recently Vapnik (1995) introduced a regularized kernel based technique called Support Vector Machines (SVM).

The technique corresponds to minimization of the following functional:

$$E(f) = \frac{C}{N}\sum_{i=1}^{N} |Y_i - f(x_i)|_\varepsilon + \frac{1}{2}\|f\|^2 \quad (11.6)$$

where

$$|Y_i - f(x_i)|_\varepsilon = \begin{cases} 0 \text{ if } |Y_i - f(x_i)| < \varepsilon \\ |Y_i - f(x_i)| \text{ otherwise} \end{cases} \quad (11.7)$$

is Vapnik's ε-*Insensitive Loss Function* (*ILF*). An important point is that this function assigns zero loss to errors less than ε, thus safeguarding against overfitting. In other words, this function does not fit a crisp value but instead fits a tube with radius ε to the data. This is similar to a fuzzy description of the function. The other important aspect of this loss function is that it minimizes a least modulus but not least squares. It is known that least squares are optimal, strictly speaking, for Gaussian noise models. However if the noise is not Gaussian then as Huber (1964) showed under the assumptions of symmetry and convexity of the noise probability density function, the best approximation is provided by a least modulus but not least squares. Thus, if one has only general information about noise density (which is usually the case) then it is better to minimize the least modulus. The parameter ε also plays an important role by providing a sparse representation of the data, as we shall see later. Note that (11.6) is very similar to ridge functional (11.4) with $\lambda = 1/2C$.

In (Vapnik, 1998) it is shown that the minimizer of (11.6) under very general conditions can be written as:

$$f(x) = \sum_{i=1}^{N} c_i K(x_i, x) \qquad (11.8)$$

where c_i are the solutions of a quadratic programming (QP) problem. $K(x_i,x)$ is the so-called kernel function that defines the generalized inner product and is a commonly used tool to perform nonlinear mapping. Several choices for the kernel K are available, such as *Gaussian, sigmoid, polinomial, splines*. The interesting fact is that for different kernels, SVM corresponds to different approximation techniques. Gaussian kernel corresponds to RBF networks, the sigmoid to the multilayer perceptron (MLP) with one hidden layer and the polynomial to polynomial approximation. Thus SVM comprises several different learning techniques "under one roof." The kernel K should be chosen prior to application of the SVM. The only item defined by the data are the coefficients "c_i," which are obtained by maximizing the following quadratic form:

$$\min(E(c)) = \frac{1}{2} \sum_{i,j=1}^{N} c_i c_j K(x_i, x_j) - \sum_{i=1}^{N} c_i Y_i + \varepsilon \sum_{i=1}^{N} |c_i| \qquad (11.9)$$

subject to the constraints

$$\sum_{i=1}^{N} c_i = 0, \quad -\frac{C}{N} \leq c_i \leq \frac{C}{N}, \quad i = 1...N \qquad (11.10)$$

The fundamental notion about (11.9) is that it is a QP problem and hence it possesses *a unique* solution. Thus in contrast to neural network training, which performs a complex nonlinear optimization with *many local minima*, SVM performs quadratic optimization with a *single global minimum* meanwhile providing capabilities to learn any nonlinear relations and emulate neural networks. Due to the nature of this quadratic programming problem only a number of coefficients "c_i" will be different from zero and the data points associated with them are called support vectors, hence the name SVM. Parameters C and ε are regularization parameters that control the flexibility or complexity of the SVM. These parameters should be selected by the user using resampling or other standard techniques. However, it should be emphasized that, in contrast to the classical regularization techniques (Tikhonov, 1963, MacKay, 1992), a clear theoretical understanding of C and ε is still missing and is a subject of theoretical as well as experimental efforts. Three different kernel types were investigated in this study:

Polynomial(*POLY*) $= K(x_i, x_j) = (x_i * x_j + 1)^d, d = 1, 2, \ldots$ – degree of polynomial

Gaussian Radial Basis Function(*GRBF*) $= K(x_i, x_j) = \exp(\frac{(x_i - x_j)^2}{2\sigma^2})$

$$Exponential\ Radial\ Basis\ Function(ERBF) = K(x_i, x_j) = \exp(\frac{|x_i - x_j|}{2\sigma^2})$$

11.5 Data Description and Results

We experimented with MSET, ANN and SVM using data provided by Florida Power Corporation for the venturi meter fouling problem (Kavaklioglu, 1994, Gribok, 1999). The venturi fouling problem is described and analyzed in detail in papers by Kavaklioglu (1994), and Gribok (1999, and 2000). In this paper we provide a brief description of the problem.

In the United States, a nuclear power plant's operating limit is directly related to its thermal power production. The simplified energy balance equation can be written as (Chan and Ahluwalia et al., 1992):

$$Q_c = m_{fw}(h_s - h_{fw}) + Losses, \tag{11.11}$$

where Q_c is core thermal power, h_s and h_{fw} are enthalpies of steam and feedwater, respectively, and m_{fw} is feedwater flow rate.

Since the enthalpies of steam and feedwater can be determined accurately, uncertainties in thermal power estimation often come from feedwater flow rate measurements (Chan and Ahluwalia et al., 1992). The majority of PWRs and some BWRs utilize venturi meters to measure feedwater flow rate because of their ruggedness and precision. However, these meters are susceptible to measurement drift due to corrosion products in the feedwater building up on the meter's orifice. This increases the measured pressure drop across the meters, which results in an over-estimation of the flow rate. Consequently, the reactors' thermal power is also overestimated (Chan and Ahluwalia et al. 1992).

To overcome this problem, an inferential sensing system is being developed at the University of Tennessee to infer the "true" feedwater flow rate. This system infers feedwater flow rate by integrating information from correlated sensors. A least squares model (linear or nonlinear) can be "trained" to map appropriate input variables to feedwater flow. This estimation can then be used in the calculation of reactor thermal power to avoid unnecessary derating. Twenty four variables have been selected as predictor variables to infer feedwater flow rate. The difference between the inferred and measured values is referred to as drift in this study and is the subject of primary interest. An example inference is shown in Figure 11.5.

A check point is selected about 6 months into the fuel cycle to evaluate the difference between measured and estimated feed flow rates. The stability of this inference is of primary concern. Several models including MSET, its regularized version

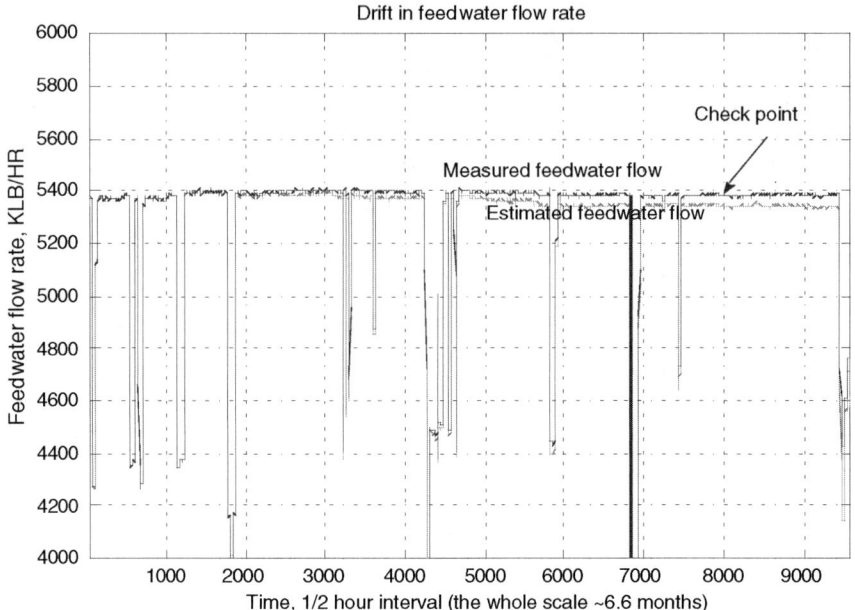

FIGURE 11.5
An example of inference using linear regression technique.

RMSET (Zavaljevski, 1999) as well as a neural network in form of multi-layer perceptron with one hidden layer were used to estimate the drift in the check point. The consistency of these estimates with respect to different number of training points was evaluated. The results are summarized in Table 11.2.

For comparison, the results provided by two linear techniques are presented in the first two columns. As we can see from Table 11.2. the regular MSET and OLS proved to be the most unstable techniques with respect to different numbers of training points. OLS was unstable due to collinearity in the data matrix and MSET proved to be very prone to overfitting. Clearly, both techniques are probably not suitable candidates for inferential sensing. RMSET proved to be more stable than regularized neural network and they were both outperformed by ridge regression which provided most consistent results in this study. The reason for this is that this data set is essentially linear and nonlinear techniques tend to overfit, trying to discover "nonlinearities." The results provided by RMSET were very close to those of ridge regression because the degree of the polynomial kernel used was chosen to be 2, assuring near linear performance. Note that the neural network was also regularized using weight decay with the regularization parameter $\lambda = 0.9$. Regularization parameter for RMSET was selected based on L-curve (Hansen, 1992).

The results presented comparing the SVM, MSET, and RMSET results all used a polynomial kernel. This is not a usual kernel for local regression techniques such

Statistical Data Mining and Knowledge Discovery

Number of data points	OLS solution klb/hr	Ridge regression, klb/hr	Neural network, 32 hidden neurons $\lambda = 0.9$ klb/hr	MSET, polynomial kernel of degree 2 klb/hr	RMSET polynomial kernel of degree 2, $\lambda=1.42$ klb/hr
200	25.08	39.73	23.30	6.03	43.39
300	16.25	39.65	31.08	61.70	40.59
400	9.82	39.41	38.77	92.60	39.64
500	11.98	39.13	33.25	5.67	37.93
600	39.46	39.68	37.84	40.37	39.28
700	42.86	39.68	33.94	61.07	40.00
800	42.02	39.23	37.14	67.05	39.35
900	39.00	39.06	37.21	65.68	39.01

TABLE 11.2
Drift dependence on the number of training points for different inference methods.

MSET, klb/hr			RMSET, klb/hr			SVM, klb/hr		
POLY	RBF	ERBF	POLY	RBF	ERBF	POLY	RBF	ERBF
6.03	43.92	50.99	43.39	47.44	54.41	38.63	43.85	57.25

TABLE 11.3
Dependence of inference on kernel type.

as MSET but was used to be consistent with the SVM code. However, neither of the three above methods produced results as consistent as the regularized linear techniques. The number of training vectors, selection of training vectors, scaling method and kernel function shaping parameters all caused variability in the drift prediction.

As was mentioned above, kernel based techniques require the selection of a kernel which can be done either a priori or a posteriori using resampling techniques. We investigated the dependence of the inference provided by three kernel based techniques using different types of kernels to implement the inner product. The results are summarized in Table 11.3. The number of training points was 200 for all cases and the polynomial kernel had degree 2 and RBF kernels had $\sigma^2 = 1$.

As we can see the drift inference indeed depends on the type of the kernel used. However, for larger data sets this dependence might be much less because in kernel density estimation with large data sets the kernel type matters less than bandwidth. The kernel parameters such as d and σ^2 are regularization parameters and have to be selected properly. We also want to emphasize that the application of SVM was straightforward without any fine tuning of regularization parameters. No engineering judgement was used; however, it is known that in engineering applications tailoring of the system to the data can significantly improve performance. The SVM gives rich opportunities for such adjustments.

# of training points	MSET, klb/hr	RMSET,klb/hr	SVM,klb/hr
200	6.03	43.39	38.65
300	61.70	40.59	38.50
400	92.60	39.64	38.62

TABLE 11.4
Comparison of different kernel based techniques.

Finally, the stability of SVM with respect to different numbers of training points was checked. The results are summarized in Table 11.4. Due to hardware and software constraints only a limited number of cases were investigated. The kernel type was polynomial with d=2, regularization parameter C was 10^4 and parameter ε was set to be 17 which reflects noise level estimated by linear techniques.

As we can see, SVM outperformed the two other techniques with stability matching that of regularized linear methods.

11.6 Conclusions

The stability of inference provided by different statistical techniques was investigated. It was determined that kernel methods without proper regularization tend to overfit training data providing highly inconsistent inference. With regularization they can match the stability of regularized linear systems meanwhile being able to process nonlinear information. The SVM seems to be a very promising technique taking into account its universality, inherent regularization properties and hence stability. It also has very solid theoretical foundations. A very important advantage of the SVM is the interpretability of support vestors (SV). Figure 11.6 shows one of the predictor signals along with support vectors.

We can see that support vectors represent important or most informative data points, which are essential for function representation and thus provide a clear and instructive interpretation for SVM. This interpretability is in sharp contrast to neural networks where the weights usually lack any meaningful interpretation. The interpretability of SVM solutions has tremendous appeal for engineering applications. It should be pointed that the number of support vectors reflects how effectively the training data are encoded or compressed by a model. This fact reveals a tight connection between SVM and the Minimum Description Length (MDL) principle (Rissanen, 1989), a powerful inductive principle that enjoyed few practical applications in nonlinear learning systems due to technical difficulties. In our case, the number of support vectors is 19, which corresponds to 9.5% of all 200 training samples. It means that the solution can be recovered just using 9.5% of the data points. If training data need to be stored we only need to keep the 19 samples instead of all

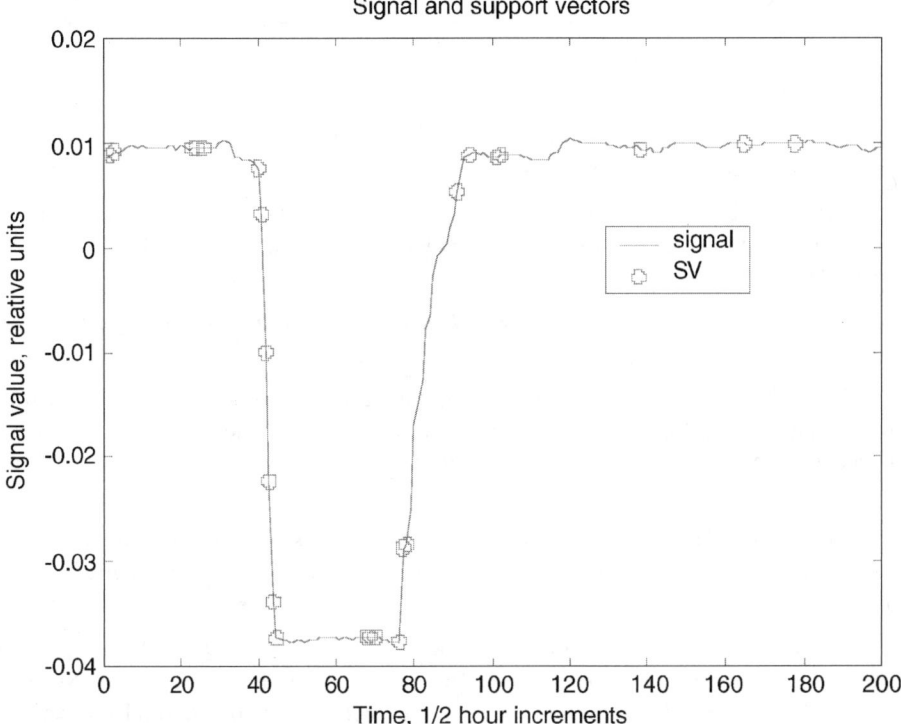

FIGURE 11.6
Support vectors interpretation.

200. With this small data set we will still be able to completely recover the solution. The degree of compressibility is controlled by parameter ε. The obtained results show that SVM has great potential for engineering applications as a robust nonlinear inferential technique.

Acknowledgments

We would like to acknowledge Florida Power Corporation and TVA for providing the data, and Idaho National Engineering and Environmental Laboratory for funding this research. We also would like to acknowledge the use of the MATLAB freeware SVM Toolbox by Steve Gunn, http://svm.first.gmd.de/

References

Belsley, D.A., Kuh, E., Welsch, R.E. (1980). *Regression Diagnostics: Identifying Influential Data and Sources of Collinearity*. John Wiley and Sons, New York.

Chan, A.M.C. and Ahluwalia, A.K. (Nov. 1992). Feedwater flow measurement in U.S. nuclear power generation stations, EPRI TR-101388, Electric Power Research Institute.

Cherkassky, V. and Miller, F. (1998). *Learning from data*. John Wiley and Sons, New York.

Hines, J.W., Uhrig, R.E., Black, C., and Xu, X. (1997). An Evaluation of Instrument Calibration Monitoring Using Artificial Neural Networks. In the *Proceedings of the 1997 American Nuclear Society Winter Meeting*, Albuquerque, NM, November, 16-20.

Hines., J. W., Uhrig, R. E., and Wrest, D.J. (1998). Use of Autoassociative Neural Networks for Signal Validation, *Journal of Intelligent and Robotic Systems*, 21,143-154.

Gribok, A.V., Attieh, I., Hines, J.W., and Uhrig, R E. (1999). Regularization of Feedwater Flow Rate Evaluation for Venturi Meter Fouling Problems in Nuclear Power Plants, Ninth International Meeting on Nuclear Reactor Thermal Hydraulics (NURETH-9), San Francisco, CA, Oct 3-8, 1999. Accepted for publication in *Nuclear Technology*.

Gribok, A.V., Attieh, I., Hines, J.W., and Uhrig, R E., 2000. Stochastic Regularization of Feedwater Flow Rate Evaluation for Venturi Meter Fouling Problems in Nuclear Power Plants, submitted for publication in *Inverse Problems in Engineering*.

Gross, K. C., Singer, R. M., Wegerich, S. W., Herzog, J. P., Van Alstine, R., and Bockhorst, F. K. (1997). Application of a Model-based Fault Detection System to Nuclear Plant Signals, *Proc. of the Intl. Conf. on Intelligent System Application to Power Systems*, Seoul, Korea. pp.60-65.

Hansen, P.C. (1992). Analysis of discrete ill-posed problems by means of the L-curve, *SIAM Review* vol. 34, No.4, pp. 561-580.

Hines, J.W., Gribok, A., Attieh, I., and Uhrig, R.E. (1999). The Use of Regularization in Inferential Measurements, Presented at the Enlarged Halden Programme Group (EHPG) Meeting, Loen, Norway, May 24-29, 1999.

Hines, J. W., Gribok, A., Attieh, I., and Uhrig, R. E. (2000) Regularization Methods for Inferential Sensing in Nuclear Power Plants, in *Fuzzy Systems and Soft Computing in Nuclear Engineering*, Da Ruan (Ed.), Springer Verlag, Heidelberg, January 2000, pp.285-310.

Hoerl, A.E. and Kennard, R.W. (1970). Ridge regression: biased estimation for nonorthogonal problems. *Technometrics*, 12, pp.55-67.

Huber, P. (1964). Robust estimation of location parameter. *Annals of Mathematical Statistics, 35,(1)*

Kavaklioglu, K. and Upadhyaya, B. R. (1994). Monitoring feedwater flow rate and component thermal performance of pressurized water reactors by means of artificial neural networks. *Nuclear Technology*, Vol. 107, July, pp.112-123.

MacKay, D.J.C. (1992). A practical Bayesian framework for backprop networks, *Neural Computation*, 4, pp. 448-472.

Rissanen, J. (1989). *Stochastic Complexity in Statistical Inquiry,* World Scientific Publishing Co., Singapore.

Tikhonov, A.N. (1963). Solution of incorrectly formulated problems and the regularization method, *Doklady Akad. Nauk USSR* 151, pp. 501-504.

Vapnik, V. N. (1995). *The Nature of Statistical Learning Theory*, Springer-Verlag, New York.

Vapnik, V. N. (1998). *Statistical Learning Theory.* John Wiley and Sons, New York.

Zavaljevski, N., Gross, K.C., and Wegerich, S.W. (1999). Regularization Methods for the Multivariate State Estimation Technique (MSET), *Proc. of the Int. Conf. on Mathematics and Computations, Reactor Physics and Environmental Analysis in Nuclear Applications*, September 27-30, 1999, Madrid, Spain, pp.720-729.

12

Data Mining and Traditional Regression

Christopher M. Hill, Linda C. Malone, and Linda Trocine
University of Central Florida, Orlando, FL, USA

CONTENTS

12.1 Introduction	233
12.2 Military Manpower Application	234
12.3 Data Mining and Traditional Regression	236
12.4 General Problems	237
12.5 Attempted Solutions	239
12.6 Regression Specific Issues	240
12.7 Conclusion	246
References	247

Data mining has emerged in response to a need from industry for effective and efficient analysis of large data sets. It is used with great success in the business world in areas such as marketing. Traditional regression techniques have not generally been used in data mining but may be more attractive in some applications. An example of such an application is military manpower analysis. We introduce how we will approach this problem using logistic and linear regression.

This paper provides a general overview of data mining and discusses how regression analysis may be used in the large data set scenarios. It also presents general analytical problems with analysis of large data sets and discusses attempted solutions. We discuss issues of using traditional regression techniques, such as linear and logistic regression, on large data sets. The paper provides a sampling of relevant papers and research in these areas.

Our research is focused on improving the performance of traditional regression methods with respect to analyzing large data sets, specifically with respect to variable selection, estimation, and prediction. This paper explores the issues both through a description of the large sample effects on statistics used in model building and through a demonstration on a large set of simulated data with known coefficients and correlation. This analysis provides an explanation of the issues of using traditional methods and identifies ways to make traditional regression methods more useable in analysis of large data sets.

12.1 Introduction

The proliferation of information technology over the last decade has caused almost all organizations to automate their business practices, and as a result has provided them with large quantities of data available for analysis. The existence of these massive amounts of data has permeated many industries and applications. Applications of large data sets include marketing, quality management, finance, supermarkets, banking, astronomy, chemistry, medicine, and military applications. The field that has emerged in response to analysis of these large data sets is data mining, and there is a wide range of techniques available to the analyst depending on the objective of the analysis at hand. Each of these techniques face a group of common challenges resulting from the large data sets. In addition, each technique faces unique issues as well. This paper will identify a class of large data problems that are well suited to analysis by traditional linear and logistic regression analysis. It will discuss the traditional regression in terms of its relationship to data mining in general and to the general analysis issues from large data. It will also explore the issues specific to traditional regression and illustrate them with simulation examples. Some problems seem to be particularly well suited to traditional linear and logistic regression analysis. The example that will be used to motivate a class of large data problems is military manpower analysis.

12.2 Military Manpower Application

Manpower acquisition methods have historically had a significant impact on the ability of the United States Army to effectively conduct its wartime mission. Maintaining an all volunteer force (AVF), especially during prosperous economic times for our nation, is expensive, difficult to manage, and requires significant attention from the strategic leaders of the nation. The Army has gone through cycles of manning the Army with volunteers, and rounding out the force with compulsory service methods in times of National emergencies. In 1973 while near the conclusion of the Viet Nam conflict, the modern AVF was born, and the Army has sustained its force structure exclusively through volunteers since. Since the military has faced varying degrees of difficulty maintaining the volunteer force, its leadership uses instruments like pay increases, enlistment bonuses, educational incentives, and advertising to recruit the numbers needed for the AVF (Hill, 2000). Because the acquisition of quality military manpower is such a significant strategic imperative for the success of the Army, analysis of the personnel system is one of the most important and meaningful functions performed by military researchers. The problems associated with analysis of large data sets directly affect this research.

While the entire military personnel management system is an excellent application of the problem of analysis of large data, this paper will focus on a specific subset—attrition in the Army Recruiting Command's Delayed Entry Program (DEP). The general recruiting process begins with a contact between a recruiter and a prospect. The recruiter conducts a basic qualification assessment of education level, mental ability, and moral standards for the potential recruit. If the recruiter feels the prospect is qualified and available, he will begin a detailed sales pitch with specific individual features oriented to the prospect. If the prospect remains interested, the recruiter completes an application and makes an appointment for the applicant to visit a Military Entrance Processing Station (MEPS) where detailed qualification and contracting are completed. At the MEPS, the potential recruit faces detailed physical, medical, moral, and mental qualification. If the applicant successfully negotiates these phases, he or she meets with a guidance counselor to begin negotiation for specific aspects of the contract, such as job, incentives, locations, and term of service. This part of the process is very difficult because the Army is trying to match its needs with the applicant's desires. Many times these two do not match, so the Army will try to negotiate through the offering of incentives to move the applicant towards the needs of the Army. If the youth has made it through qualification and finds an appealing enlistment package, the applicant will complete an enlistment contract, sign it, and enter the Army's DEP. While in the DEP the applicant must wait on results of drug testing, other medical tests, security checks, and potential waiver submissions to clear before becoming completely qualified and available to begin training. The wait period may also be tied to specific training start dates. The period of waiting in the DEP can be as short as a few weeks but can extend up to a year. It is common within the Army to portray the DEP as an inventory of finished goods awaiting shipping. The recruiter interacts with the applicant at various points during the waiting period to bolster the morale and validate the qualification of the youth (AR 601-210, 1995).

The real-world process has attrition behavior present at all phases in the process. Applicants can become unqualified or uninterested anywhere in the process from the beginning meeting with the recruiter all the way through the time waiting in the DEP. Reasons that contribute to this attrition are generally grouped as disqualification, such as emergence of a medical problem, and apathy, the applicant changes his or her mind. Some natural attrition in the DEP is healthy; the Army does not need soldiers who are neither qualified nor motivated. However, the amount of resources, including both monetary and non-monetary, invested in an applicant up to the point of signing a contract is very high. Naturally, the Army wants to reduce this attrition, and they spend a great deal of time analyzing it. This analysis generally takes two forms—describing relationships and predicting the response. The Army seeks to understand the influence of a group of independent variables, like unemployment rates, incentive levels, advertising levels, etc., on the dependent attrition variable. This allows them to react tactically and plan strategically to mitigate attrition. They are also interested in predicting the attrition of a group of applicants in the DEP so they can better align production and inventory levels to Army manpower requirements. In the last five years, the average number of contracts signed by DEP members has been about 87,000 per year, so any analysis of the DEP that spans several years will face large data sets. The Army Recruiting command needs a tool to help decision makers divide and assign resource priorities and emphasis. The DEP attrition problem seems to be very well suited for a traditional regression application.

12.3 Data Mining and Traditional Regression

The recruiting attrition problem introduces a class of problems that seem to be particularly well suited for analysis by traditional linear and logistic regression analysis. These problems may range in size from a several thousand to millions of observations. The decision-makers need a prediction capability, but they also need to be able to accurately measure relative impact and contribution of individual variables on a response, since decision-makers will want to understand the basic relationships of the variables as well as a prediction output. This characteristic will cause issues for many of the so-called black box methods. Although there are other data mining techniques that fit these criteria, linear and logistic regression seem to meet these objectives exceptionally well. However, it is important to understand how regression fits in the data mining world.

There are many available data mining tools, and traditional regression may not typically come to the forefront in a data miner's choice set. Data mining activities are a good point to start understanding the relationship between regression and data mining. Berry and Linoff (2000) provide a good description of the activities involved in data mining. They state the major activities include classification, estimation, prediction, affinity grouping or association rules, clustering, and description and visualization. The activities common to most data mining methods and traditional regression are prediction and estimation. One difference between the methods is in the definition of estimation. In data mining, estimation may mean estimating the value of a variable based on values and relationships with other variables. In regression, it applies more to the estimation of coefficients, which estimate the impact of the variable on the response.

Another significant characteristic of data mining approaches in comparison to traditional statistical studies is that many data mining studies are exploratory in nature. Businesses will filter through large amounts of raw data for information that provides the organization a competitive edge. The intent is to find subtle but significant patterns previously unseen to researchers (Patterson, 2000). These massive data sets are typically full of passive data with large amounts of low-grade information. The data are typically observed and are not collected specifically for the data mining study (Gunter, 1996). The general nature of this data by itself provides several analytical challenges.

This exploratory approach with the intent of finding previously undiscovered patterns does not apply to all situations. There are many examples in industry, manufacturing, engineering, and the military where the purpose of the research is of a directed nature. These types of problems are more commonly associated with traditional regression applications. Examples include using extremely large sets of data to predict future production given current conditions, or exploring the relationship be-

Statistical Data Mining and Knowledge Discovery 237

tween a set of independent variables and a response in a manufacturing application. These examples illustrate that the penalty of error, either Type I or Type II, may vary greatly in different applications. As a result, the technique used for analysis must be able to address the analytical challenges accompanying large sets of data, but the nature of some problems may warrant different concerns than in a typical data mining application where the risk of error may not be as great. A more detailed example of one of these scenarios is a manufacturing process that sprays a thermal protection coating on a part, while collecting data on multiple independent variables numerous times per second during the process. Another example in the military environment is the attempted identification of whether an inbound airborne object is friendly or hostile based on numerous sensors feeding real time information; these sensors update multiple times per second. Contrast the risk in these scenarios with a typical data mining example where analysts attempt to look through a massive database in an exploratory type of search attempting to find a sub market or niche market to target with a direct mail campaign. Clearly, the penalties for mechanical failure of an assembled component or the identification of a hostile airborne object are much greater than for sending a piece of direct mail to the wrong segment or potential customer.

Data mining does not necessarily entail modeling of the data. Its emphasis has been on identification of associations between variables with less attention on statistical modeling of the data, especially in the predictive model activities. This is partially because statisticians did not design their modeling methods for modeling large-scale problems (Cortes, Pregibon, and Volinsky, 1998). In addition, data mining has evolved independently of statistics, as statisticians have been traditionally interested in making use of relatively sparse data (Rocke, 1998). As a result, the approach of a data mining activity may be of a completely different nature than that of a traditional statistical approach. The statistician may begin with a detailed hypothesis, whereas the data miner may be looking for some previously undiscovered pattern. However, both approaches are susceptible to problems associated with analysis of large data sets.

Given the diversity of the kind of information desired from a large data set, it is important to note that there is no specific technique that can address all the relevant questions or that for a given question consistently outperforms the others. However, traditional regression seems to be the right tool when you need prediction, estimation of coefficients, and the ability to explain the methodology and results to a decision maker. In addition to the challenge of finding the right tool for the right problem, all of the techniques are susceptible to many general problems associated with analysis of large data sets.

12.4 General Problems

There are many potential problems associated with the analysis of large sets of data in general, and they classify as finding insignificant patterns as significant, size related problems, and data quality issues. Perhaps the most significant of these is detection of patterns or results in the data that are not actually significant. The detection of these patterns can occur for a variety of reasons. Hand (1998 and 2000) discusses the detection of spurious relationships and goes on to say that most unexpected patterns found in data mining will prove to be due to problems in the data rather than representing any real structure. Hand (2000) also mentions the impact of Ramsey's theory, which states that patterns are certain to arrive somewhere in large enough data sets as a consequence of combinatorial relationships and not simply of chance. Elder and Pregibon (1995) mention the possibility of Simpson's paradox, where automated search procedures can often be fooled by anomalous association patterns.

Another set of challenges associated with the analysis of large data sets is generally described as size related problems. These include main memory limitations of computers (Hand, 1998) and limitations of manipulating gigabyte or larger data files (Downing, Fedorov, Lawkins, Morris, and Ostrouchov, 2000). Leung, Ma, and Zhang (2001) also point out that classical regression techniques typically analyze data sets as a whole, and this is not practical in large data sets. This may be due to problems associated with restriction on functional form, or because subtle relationships may be difficult to find in large, complex data sets. Sampling based approaches may also have difficulty in capturing these subtle relationships.

The last group of general problems with analysis of large data sets is data quality related. Hand (1998 and 2000) points out the high likelihood of problems within individual records such as missing data or incorrect data entry. Hand (1998 and 2000), Leung et al. (2001), and Downing et al. (2000) all mention the high probability of data in large sets violating the classic assumptions of traditional regression approaches. Hand (1998 and 2000) and Elder and Pregibon (1995) discuss issues of selection bias within the data. All together, these problems mount serious challenges for any analytical approach.

There are other issues relating more directly to some of the data mining specific applications. According to Chatfield (1995), the issue of model uncertainty is very serious in applications where model formulation, fitting, and checking occur on the same data in an iterative, interactive way. This general approach is common to many of the data mining algorithms. The results may be biased estimates of model parameters and residual variance. The analyst will likely believe the model is better than it is, and the prediction intervals will be too narrow. Salzberg (1997) also points out a problem with iterative techniques called repeated tuning. This occurs when researchers continually strive for algorithm modifications that achieve better performance on a given data set. They end up modeling nuances of the specific data set as opposed to finding global conclusions about algorithmic improvement.

The effects of all these challenges narrow into a small group of impacts on the models—effectiveness and efficiency. The unguided, blind search approach of data mining techniques may lead to discovery of purely random patterns, which are actually spurious patterns, Simpson's paradox, or Ramsey theory issues. Another way to think about this is discovery of statistical significance in the absence of practical significance. This issue affects the accuracy and as a result effectiveness of the method and/or model. Problems with data leading to contravention of assumptions, bias, or other data quality issues will directly affect the model's accuracy or the effectiveness of the model as well. Another common problem is the issue of interpretability.

Some algorithms provide results that are often not interpretable, and the modelers often pass judgment of their significance to domain experts for translation. The interpretability issue can affect both effectiveness, in the case of an incorrect interpretation, and efficiency, in the case of multiple looks to obtain a solution. Problems with the sheer size of the data set can lead to complex and slow algorithms, which may affect efficiency. In general, when researchers modify algorithms to improve efficiency, they generally find a trade-off with accuracy or effectiveness. The same trade-off is true between improvements in effectiveness and reduced efficiency. This trade-off is relevant regardless of the modeler's approach—data mining or regression based. There is a need to find ways to improve modeling approaches for large data analysis within each activity that allows for both efficiency and effectiveness.

12.5 Attempted Solutions

The data mining, statistical, and machine learning or artificial intelligence communities have addressed these problems in a variety of ways. There exists a myriad of papers on methods to improve specific data mining, statistical, and artificial intelligence algorithms. There are many other papers oriented more specifically to computer science based or data engineering approaches. It is not the intent of this portion of the paper to be a complete literature review of all of these issues. The intent is to focus on the techniques specific to regression applications, like prediction and parameter estimation, and to provide a sampling of work attempting to overcome many of the issues pointed out in the previous section.

In the face of the challenges associated with large data sets researchers from the data mining, statistical, and artificial intelligence communities have embarked on finding methods that were not adversely affected by quality problems of the data, or that avoided the issues altogether. Their applications generally center on one of two approaches: finding ways to improve the algorithms to handle the larger data, or employing techniques designed to reduce the complexity of the data.

12.5.1 Algorithmic Improvements

The first group of selected regression and prediction approaches to analysis of large data sets centers around finding ways to improve the algorithms. Several papers serve as examples for this approach. Kooperberg, Bose, and Stone (1997) combine nonparametric regression techniques with Polychotomous regression to obtain their classification methodology. Denison, Mallick, and Smith (1998) provide a list of methods for conducting regression: additive models, CART, projection pursuit, alternating conditional expectations, and MARS. Gao (1999) combines a smoothing spline ANOVA model and a log-linear model to build a partly flexible model for multivariate Bernoulli data. Torgo (2000) tries to address the issue of functional form in regression domains with nonparametric approaches such as local regression modeling. Hong and Weiss (2001) review the key theoretical developments in the probably approximately correct (PAC) and statistical learning theory that have led to the development of support vector machines and to the use of multiple models for increased predictive accuracy.

12.5.2 Data Complexity Reduction

In addition to the algorithmic improvement methods, there are numerous examples of attempts to reduce the complexity of data. Chen in 1978 considers sampling strategies to reduce the size and complexity of the data set. John and Langley (1996) also reduce complexity and speed up the data mining process by using the probably close enough (PCE) criterion to describe the desired properties of a sample. Cheng (1998) considers data generalization or discretization, which generalizes the raw data into higher levels of abstraction (i.e., collection of data in ranges rather than precise values) to reduce complexity. Cortes, Pregibon, and Volinsky (1998) discuss both data reduction and algorithmic improvement by using approaches that build profiles for customers based on calling patterns, and then they look at new calls to determine if they generally match the patterns. They do not use all of the millions of data points once they establish a profile; they only look at the new records. Downing, Fedorov, Lawkins, Morris, and Ostrouchov (2000) believe it is necessary to segment data and conduct local analysis on each segment, then analyze the results globally. Naik, Hagerty, and Tsai (2000) introduce a method, Sliced Inverse Regression (SIR), to enable managers to gain better insights and improve decision-making in data-intensive marketing environments. SIR reduces dimensionality and attains high predictive accuracy. Leung, Ma, and Zhang (2001) used a type of switching regression to identify regression classes, via a random sampling methodology. They call the approach Regression-Class Mixture Decomposition (RCMD). Finally, Hershberger and Kargupta (2001) present a method for distributed multivariate regression using wavelet-based collective data and show that generation of accurate parametric multivariate regression models is possible from distributed, heterogeneous, data sets with minimal data communication overhead compared to that required to aggregate a distributed data set.

Many of the techniques briefly described above do a satisfactory job of avoiding some of the statistical problems associated with large data sets as they strive to gain an effective and efficient method. However, most of these approaches trade off efficiency or speed with effectiveness. Ones that are effective are not simple and efficient while the ones that are more efficient are not as statistically powerful and effective. It may be useful to explore some of the problems specific to application of traditional regression methods in analysis of large data sets.

12.6 Regression Specific Issues

Discussion of specific issues with traditional regression is difficult to find in the literature. There are papers that compare tools, but it is difficult to find specific issues relating to traditional regression analysis. A good comparison paper is Harris-Jones and Haines (1998). They discuss the impact of information gains from varying sample size on traditional regression and other data mining techniques. Statisticians will generally believe that the larger the sample the more accurate the results up to some limit (which is not known). Data miners do not believe in the limit—more is better. The authors compared linear regression, logistic regression, C4.5 rule induction, C5 rule induction, and multi-layer perceptron neural networks. Regression models converge on a stable solution more rapidly, as quickly as with 1000 records, and have little improvement after 3200 records. Rule induction and neural nets continue to improve throughout the full range of the data sets. Regression models are very stable once the data set exceeds 100 observations, but the other methods are much less stable, show considerable variation among data sets for the same sample size, and also are much less predictable. Execution times were generally small with most under a minute, but at the larger sample size execution times often approached an hour for most algorithms, with neural nets extending into days. The authors' conclude where collection costs are high regression approaches can produce stable results with relatively little data. When costs are less important, or costs of misclassification are extremely high, then rule induction and neural nets may be more appropriate. The impact of the paper is that there is tremendous potential with traditional techniques in analysis of large data sets, to get results that are more accurate more quickly, and seem to be at worst comparable to the other techniques.

Regardless of the cause of absence of research concerning traditional regression models in large data set applications, there is a relevant need for such study. The traditional linear and logistic regressions show promise and many applications are well suited for traditional regression. This is partially due to the nature of the problem, like desire for prediction or study of a set of independent variables, but it may also be due to the difference in risk environment and impact of errors as discussed in the manufacturing and military examples. Given that the techniques are comparable at worst, the fact that traditional regression is so widely accepted, easily implemented, and generally understood makes it even more attractive. Each traditional regression technique will be explored both from a conceptual nature and with a simulation example for illustration. The simulations allow introduction of problems with known relationships and comparison of tests at varying data sizes to determine the impact of the number of observations. The two specific issues of concern with traditional regression methods are how the statistics are affected by the number of observations and how effectively the models perform in selecting the correct variables. Large data sets affect many of the statistics used in traditional regression analysis. This is especially true during the model building stage.

12.6.1 Linear Regression

Some of the statistics used in model building for the linear model, such as the F-statistic, Mean Squared Error (MSE), Adjusted R^2, and t-statistic, become ineffective variable selection tools with analysis of large samples. The F-statistic helps determine whether or not there is a relationship between a set of independent variables and a response. Using this statistic is a good first step in model building to get an idea of the effectiveness of the group of independent variables. The computation of the F-Statistic is:

$$Fo = \frac{SSR/k}{SSE/(n-k-1)}.$$

In the formula, SS_R is the regression sum of squares, SS_E is the error sum of squares, k is the number of terms, and n is the number of observations. As the sample size, n, becomes extremely large, the F-statistic will also grow while the critical value will decrease as the degrees of freedom increases. As a result, the null hypothesis, which states all of the estimated coefficients are equal to zero, will be easily rejected. This effect causes the F-statistic to lose its value to a modeler.

Sample size also affects the adjusted R^2 statistic. This statistic determines whether the impact of increasing explained variability in the response by adding an additional independent variable in the model is worth the cost in degrees of freedom. Computation for adjusted R^2 is:

$$R^2_{adj} = 1 - \left(\frac{n-1}{n-p}\right)(1-R^2),$$

where n is the number of observations, p is the number of terms including the intercept, and R^2 is the coefficient of determination. As the sample size, n, becomes larger, the value of the adjusted R^2 will approach the value of R^2. This result is intuitive since in very large samples the penalty degrees of freedom will not be an issue. The result is that in large data sets, adjusted R^2 loses meaningful value.

The Mean Square Error (MSE) statistic is helpful when faced with the omission of a relevant independent variable; this situation is common and sometimes unavoidable in an observed data setting. The statistic helps determine whether the decreased variance of the estimated coefficients is valuable enough to offset the bias associated with the variable omission. Decreasing the MSE will generally improve predictive ability of a model. MSE is calculated with:

$$MSE = \frac{SSE}{n-p},$$

where SS_E is the error sum of squares, n is the number of observations, and p is the number of terms including the intercept. Sample size, n, will grow much faster than p, which remains constant. As a result, the denominator will grow very large. The numerator will also grow but not as fast as the denominator. As a result, the MSE in extremely large samples will approach σ^2 and will not be sensitive to addition or deletion of a single variable.

The t-statistic determines the impact of an individual independent variable on a response. The t-statistic is computed with:

$$t_o = \frac{bj}{se(bj)},$$

where b_j is the estimated coefficient and *se* is its standard error. As the sample size becomes larger, the coefficient estimates will be increasingly precise, so the standard error will shrink. The standard error shrinks as a function of an increasing sample size—the larger the sample size, the lower the standard error. This statistic loses it effectiveness as the statistic becomes extremely sensitive to the denominator in some variable selection applications. This means detecting meaningful, subtle, and truly significant influences of independent variables will be more difficult to observe.

As the description above indicates, statistical tools commonly used by regression modelers may not be as effective in the presence of large data sets. The greatest impact of these problems is in the modeling stage where the analyst must decide which variables to include in the models. A simple example may best illustrate these adverse effects. This example will use a set of simulated data with a known relationship between the variables and the response. Five hundred thousand observations of 18 different independent variables were generated with Minitab Version 13 using a Uniform (-1,1) distribution. Two additional variables were generated as a function of some of the original 18 variables. This resulted in 20 independent variables. Additionally, each independent variable was multiplied by a randomly chosen constant to introduce scale differences among the X's.

The error term was generated using a normal (N(0,1)) distribution with the same random number generator. Summing the X1, X5, X15, and Error terms formed the response. Subsets of the data were used to build regression models and compare the effects of increasing sample size. Table 12.1 shows some of the results of this experiment. As the table shows, the F-statistic becomes extremely large and unusable. The adjusted R^2 converges to the R^2 and becomes of little value. The MSE converges to σ^2, which in this case is 1, and is of no help. The results also show how erratic the p-values of the individual t-statistics can be as the sample size increases. In this experiment, all of the correct variables were chosen, but other insignificant variables were picked at varying sample sizes from $n = 50$ to $500,000$. In addition, the inclusion of insignificant terms seems random and may be due to spurious patterns. Other more ill-behaved experiments also show errors in omitting significant terms.

12.6.2 Logistic Regression

Employing logistic regression for analysis of a dichotomous response in a large data set brings a different set of statistics and challenges. First, the method of estimation of parameters is the method of maximum likelihood, not ordinary least squares as in the linear models. Next, the error term is neither normally distributed, nor constant. This makes the representation of the error term more challenging in the logistic regression simulation experiments. The statistics are different as well. The statistics of interest are the deviance, pseudo R^2, and Wald statistic. The log likelihood is used as the basis for computing many of the statistics. It is computed by

$$L(\beta) = \ln[l(\beta)] = \sum_{i=1}^{n} \{yi \ln[\pi(xi)] + (1 - yi) \ln[1 - \pi(xi)]\},$$

	n=500		n=25,000		n=100,000		n=500,000	
	P-value	In Model?	P-value	In Model?	P-value	In Model?	P-value	In Model?
Constant	0.497		0.369		0.903		0.142	
X1	0	Y	0	Y	0	Y	0	Y
X2	0.181		0.098		0.456		0.117	
X3	0.861		0.796		0.365		0.657	
X4	0.879		0.306		0.266		0.51	
X5	0	Y	0	Y	0	Y	0	Y
X6	0.158		0.89		0.873		0.786	
X7	0.579		0.855		0.04	Y	0.91	
X8	0.784		0.353		0.963		0.494	
X9	0.499		0.974		0.573		0.607	
X10	0.174		0.393		0.396		0.581	
X11	0.953		0.232		0.806		0.537	
X12	0.294		0.089		0.076		0.294	
X13	0.886		0.528		0.584		0.044	Y
X14	0.084		0.38		0.931		0.149	
X15	0	Y	0	Y	0	Y	0	Y
X16	0.471		0.688		0.528		0.559	
X17	0.281		0.021	Y	0.004	Y	0.669	
X18	0.946		0.337		0.57		0.137	
X19	0.699		0.788		0.677		0.657	
X20	0.293		0.523		0.881		0.071	
F-stat	1444.16		75374		301326		1509000	
R^2	98.4		98.4		98.4		98.4	
ADJ R^2	98.3		98.4		98.4		98.4	
MSE	0.9		1		1		1	

TABLE 12.1 Results of linear regression models of simulated data. (True model variables are shaded.)

where $\pi(x)$ is the conditional mean of Y given x. This value should continue to get smaller and smaller as the sample size increases. These decreasing values will affect some of the logistic regression diagnostics.

Hypothesis testing is based on likelihood ratio tests using a statistic called deviance. The deviance, which compares the log-likelihood of a saturated model with the log-likelihood of the fitted model, is used to assess the fit of the model and plays a similar role to residual sum of squares in the linear model. The deviance statistic is computed as follows:

$$G = -2\ln\left[\frac{\text{(likelihood of fitted model)}}{\text{(likelihood of saturated model)}}\right].$$

In large samples, this statistic approaches a χ^2 distribution with degrees of freedom equal to the number of terms in the model. In very large samples, we expect these statistics to become larger while the critical values remain constant; so, rejection of the null hypothesis becomes easier, and differentiation of adding or removing terms will be more difficult.

The pseudo-R^2 statistic is analogous to R^2 in a linear regression model. This value shows improvement in log likelihood relative to the baseline model that is due to the set of independent variables under consideration. Because the likelihood values continue to grow, the pseudo-R^2 may become less sensitive to subtle changes at large sample sizes. The statistic is computed as

$$R^2L = 1 - \frac{Lp}{Lo}.$$

Tests on individual coefficients are based on a t-like statistic referred to as the Wald inference (Montgomery, Peck, & Vining, 2001). The statistic is

$$zo = \frac{\hat{\beta}j}{se(\hat{\beta}j)},$$

which is essentially the same as the t-statistic in the linear model. In fact, we would expect the behavior of this statistic to be the same in the two models.

In order to simulate the logistic regression scenario, an experiment with 20 independent variables was generated with 300,000 observations, again using the Minitab software. The X's were randomly generated with a uniform U(0,1) distribution. This data set has 12 significant terms, four of which were correlated, and eight insignificant terms, four of which were correlated. One of the significant terms, X20, was used in the calculation of the response, but it was omitted from the candidate group of independent variables during regression. The following X's were used to generate the response: X2, X3, X4, X6, X8, X10, X14, X15, X16, X17, X19, and X20. The response was formed by calculating g(x) and $\pi(x)$, and comparing $\pi(x)$ to a random error term generated by U(0,1) to introduce error in the simulation. If the value of $\pi(x)$ exceeded the error value, then the response was coded as 1; otherwise, the response was 0. This approach yielded about 28.8 percent of the response as positive. Excerpts of the results are shown in Table 12.2.

As expected, the log likelihood values increase as sample size increases. These increases directly affect some of the other statistics used during the model building process. The deviance continues to increase as sample size grows, while the model degrees of freedom remain constant. This will make it easier to find a significant difference when comparing a set of independent variables and the response. In fact, as these values continue to get larger and larger, they become less sensitive to subtle changes and relationships. The pseudo-R^2 value converges and becomes less sensitive to subtle changes, even when comparing the full model to models with terms omitted.

The tests on individual coefficients are erratic as well. There is evidence of both Type I and Type II errors in the simulation models. The erratic results also vary by sample size.

The implications of this experiment are that the logistic regression technique will experience many of the same issues as the linear model, even though the method of estimation and statistics are different. The most significant implications are the same as in the linear models—some of the statistics used in model building are directly affected by sample size and will complicate the variable selection process.

	n=5K		n=25K		n=100K		n=300K	
	P-Value	In Model	P-Value	In Model	P-Value	In Model	P-Value	In Model
Constant	0.236		0.668		0.005	Y	0.000	Y
X1	0.307		0.499		0.122		0.053	Y
X2	0.000	Y	0.000	Y	0.000	Y	0.000	Y
X3	0.856		0.005	Y	0.000	Y	0.000	Y
X4	0.489		0.071		0.000	Y	0.000	Y
X5	0.659		0.775		0.582		0.341	
X6	0.000	Y	0.000	Y	0.000	Y	0.000	Y
X7	0.682		0.543		0.054		0.662	
X8	0.035	Y	0.000	Y	0.000	Y	0.000	Y
X9	0.929		0.372		0.103		0.227	
X10	0.716		0.788		0.861		0.904	
X11	0.434		0.324		0.231		0.548	
X12	0.872		0.232		0.376		0.648	
X13	0.479		0.377		0.244		0.054	Y
X14	0.000	Y	0.000	Y	0.000	Y	0.000	Y
X15	0.000	Y	0.000	Y	0.000	Y	0.000	Y
X16	0.005	Y	0.000	Y	0.000	Y	0.000	Y
X17	0.000	Y	0.000	Y	0.000	Y	0.000	Y
X18	0.728		0.783		0.013	Y	0.022	Y
X19	0.803		0.006	Y	0.000	Y	0.000	Y
Loglikelihood	-2418.147		-11674.966		-46854.617		-140597.722	
Deviance	1243.266		6614.966		26175.852		79150.945	
Pseudo-R Square	0.2045		0.2208		0.2183		0.2197	

TABLE 12.2 Results of logistic regression models of simulated data. (True model variables are shaded.)

12.7 Conclusion

The examination of traditional regression techniques through simulated data allows investigation of performance of the models at varying sample sizes and data conditions. Both linear and logistic models seem to have similar problems: some of the routine statistics used in model building become less useful in large data sets and they seem to have difficulty selecting correct variables. However, the techniques are promising even with these issues. They do routinely achieve between a 75 and 100 percent correct selection of variables in a variety of simulated conditions. In addition, these techniques are at worst comparable to other data mining techniques in these applications. There certainly exists a class of problems, large data sets with a need for estimation of parameter coefficients and prediction of the response, where regression seems particularly well suited. More research is necessary to better bound the specific issues for linear and logistic regression.

The next steps for our research will focus on two fronts—messy data and adjustments. The first area is consideration of even messier data sets and larger sample sizes. There is a need to more clearly articulate the level and conditions when traditional regression methods become more susceptible to spurious patterns and see at what point the methods routinely have trouble with other data problems such as multicollinearity, assumption violations, and outliers. Other adjustments and rules of thumb that may be useful in helping with variable selection, like a Bonferroni adjustment, will be explored for their usefulness. Even with adjustment, the need to be able to ascertain a difference in statistical and practical significance will likely remain. In addition to these areas there is also potential for considering other methods that use less than the entire data set, such as sampling based methods. Additional problem description coupled with investigation of methods for improving variable selection may help improve the performance of and solidify the traditional regression techniques as a viable alternative in large data analysis applications.

References

Berry, M. J. A., and Linoff, G. (2000). *Mastering Data Mining, The Art and Science of Customer Relationship Management*. John Wiley and Sons, New York.

Chatfield, C. (1995).Model Uncertainty, Data Mining and Statistical Inference, *Journal of the Royal Statistical Society*, Series A, 158, Part 3, 419-466.

Chen, C. (1978). An examination of the Use of Subsampling a Large Data File in Conjunction with Maximum Likelihood Estimation of the Coefficients of the Logistic regression Model. Master's Thesis, University of Massachusetts.

Cheng, S. (1998). Statistical Approaches to Predictive Modeling in Large Databases. Master's Thesis, Simon Frasier University, British Columbia, Canada.

Cortes, C., Pregibon, D., and Volinsky, C. (1998). Prediction Models for Massive Data Sets: Applications in Telecommunications. *Proceedings of the Second International Conference on the Practical Application of Knowledge Discovery and Data Mining*, London, U.K., pp.1-9.

Denison, D. G. T., Mallick, B.K., and Smith, A.F.M. (1998). Bayesian MARS, *Statistics and Computing*, 8, 337-346.

Department of the Army (1995). Army Regulation 601-210, Personnel Procurement, regular Army and Army Reserve Enlistment Program. Headquarters, Department of The Army, Washington, D. C.

Downing, D.J., Fedorov, V.V., Lawkins, W.F., Morris, M.D., and Ostrouchov, G. (2000). Large Data Series: Modeling the Usual to Identify the Unusual, *Computational Statistics and Data Analysis*, 32, pp. 245-258.

Elder, J. F., and Pregibon, D. (1995). A statistical perspective on KDD. In *Proceedings, The First International Conference on Knowledge Discovery and Data Mining (KDD-95)*, Fayyad, U. M. and Uthurusamy, R. (Eds.), AAAI Press, Menlo Park, CA, pp. 87-93.

Gao, F. (1999). Penalized Multivariate Logistic Regression with a Large Data Set. Doctoral Dissertation, University of Wisconsin, Madison, WI.

Gunter, B. (1996). Data Mining: Mother Lode of Fool's Gold? *Quality Progress*, April, 113-117.

Hand, D. J. (1998). Data Mining: Statistics and More? *The American Statistician*, 52, 2, 112-118.

Hand D. J. (2000). Data Mining, New Challenges for Statisticians, *Social Science Computer Review*, 18, 4, 442-449.

Harris-Jones, C. and Haines, T. L. (1998). Sample Size and Misclassification: Is More Always Better? In *Proceedings of the Second International Conference On the Practical Application of Knowledge Discovery and Data Mining*, London, U.K., 301-312.

Hershberger, D. E. and Kargupta, H. (2001). Distributed Multivariate Regression Using Wavelet-based Collective Data Mining. *Journal of Parallel and Distributed Computing*, 61, 372-400.

Hill, C. M. (2000). The All-Volunteer Army: Historical Challenges. *Military Review*, LXXX, 3, 76-78.

Hong, S. J. and Weiss, S. M. (2001). Advances in Predictive Models for Data Mining, *Pattern Recognition Letters*, 22, 55-61.

Hosmer, D. W. and Lemeshow, S. (2000). *Applied Logistic Regression*, (2nd ed.). John Wiley and Sons, New York.

John, G. H., and Langley, P. (1996). Static Versus Dynamic Sampling For Data Mining. In *Proceedings, Second International Conference on Knowledge Discovery and Data Mining (KDD-96)*, Simoudis, E., Han, J., and Fayyad, U. (Eds.), AAAI Press,. Menlo Park, CA, pp. 367-370.

Kooperberg, C., Bose, S., and Stone, C. J. (1997). Polychotomous Regression, *Journal of The American Statistical Association*, 92, 437, 117-127.

Leung, Y., Ma, J. H., and Zhang, W. X. (2001). Regression Classes in Large Data Sets, *IEEE Transactions on Pattern Analysis and Machine Intelligence*, 23, 5-21.

Myers R. H. and Montgomery, D. C. (1995). *Response Surface Methodology, Process and Product Optimization Using Designed Experiments*. John Wiley and Sons, New York.

Naik, P.A., Hagerty, M. R., and Tsai. C. (2000). A New Dimension Reduction Approach for Data-Rich Marketing Environments: Sliced Inverse Regression, *Journal of Marketing Research*, XXXVII, 88-101.

Pampel, F. C. (2000). *Logistic Regression, A Primer*. Sage Publications, Thousand Oaks, CA.

Patterson, T. D. (2000). Data Mining for Golden Opportunities, Scope Out Valuable Resources Form Mountains of Information. [On-line]. *Computing: 50 Hot Technologies, 8, 1*. http://www.smartcomputing.com/editorial/article.asp.

Rocke, D. M. (1998). A Perspective on Statistical Tools for Data Mining Applications Center for Image Processing and Integrated Computing. *Proceedings of the Second International Conference on the Practical Application of Knowledge Discovery and Data Mining*, London, U.K., 25-27, March 1998, 313-318.

Salzberg, S. L. (1997). Methodological Note, On Comparing Classifiers: Pitfalls to Avoid and a Recommended Approach, *Data Mining and Knowledge Discovery*, 1, 317-328.

Torgo, L. (2000). Efficient And Comprehensible Local Regression. In the *Proceedings of Knowledge Discovery and Data Mining Current Issues And New Applications, 4th Pacific-Asian Conference PAKDD 2000)*, Terano, T., Liu, H., and Chen, A. L. P. (Eds.), Kyoto, Japan, April 18-20, 2000, Springer-Verlag, Berlin, pp. 376-379.

13

An Extended Sliced Inverse Regression

Masahiro Mizuta
Hokkaido University, Sapporo, Japan

CONTENTS

13.1 Introduction 251
13.2 Algorithms for SIR Model 252
13.3 Relative Projection Pursuit 254
13.4 SIRrpp 254
13.5 Concluding Remarks 256
    References 256

In this paper, we propose a new algorithm for Sliced Inverse Regression (SIR). SIR is a model for dimension-reduction of explanatory variables. There are several algorithms for the SIR model: SIR I, SIR II, etc. We have proposed an algorithm named SIRpp (SIR with Projection Pursuit). They find out a set of linear combinations of explanatory variables. In most of SIR algorithms, there is a serious restriction; the distribution of explanatory variables is elliptically symmetric distribution or normal distribution. The restriction should be removed for actual data analysis.

We develop a concept of relative projection pursuit: an extension of Projection Pursuit. The main concept of ordinary Projection Pursuit is to find out non-normal structures in the dataset. The non-normality is evaluated by a degree of difference between the distribution of the projected dataset and the normal distribution. The relative projection pursuit searches a singular structure in a target dataset based on a degree of difference between the distribution of the projected target dataset and that of the reference dataset designated by the user. We can construct the new SIR algorithm free from the restriction of the distribution of explanatory variables using the relative projection pursuit.

13.1 Introduction

Multiple regression analysis is a fundamental and powerful method for data analysis. There are many approaches to study regression analysis. One of them is non-linear regression. The number of explanatory variables is an important factor for non-linear regression analysis, because if the number is large, it is very difficult to get useful results within reasonable computational time.

There are many studies on reduction of the dimension of the space of explanatory variables: explanatory variable selection, Projection Pursuit Regression (PPReg), Alternating Conditional Expectation (ACE), etc. Li [5] proposed an excellent concept named Sliced Inverse Regression (SIR). The aim of SIR is also to find out a set of linear combinations of explanatory variables like PPReg and ACE.

SIR does not get rid of some explanatory variables themselves but may reduce the dimension of a space of explanatory variables. It is based on the model (SIR model)

$$y = f(\beta_1^T x, \beta_2^T x, \cdots, \beta_K^T x, \varepsilon),$$

where x is the vector of p explanatory variables, β_k ($k = 1, 2, \cdots, K$) are unknown vectors, ε is independent of x, and f is an arbitrary unknown function on R^{K+1}. The purpose of SIR is to estimate the vectors β_k when this model holds. If we get the β_k's, we can reduce the dimension of x to K. Hereafter, we shall refer to any linear combination of β_k as effective dimensional reduction (e.d.r.) direction.

Li [5] developed algorithms for the SIR model, SIR1 and SIR2. The author also proposed an algorithm for the SIR model named SIRpp [7]. But, most SIR algorithms, including SIR1, SIR2, and SIRpp, assume that the distribution of explanatory variables is Normal or elliptically symmetric distribution. This restriction is very severe for actual data analysis.

The goal of this paper is to remove the restriction of SIR with *relative projection pursuit*; relative projection pursuit is an extension of ordinary projection pursuit. The relative projection pursuit searches a singular structure in a target dataset based on a degree of difference between the distribution of the projected target dataset and that of the reference dataset designated by the user.

13.2 Algorithms for SIR Model

We describe the brief introduction of SIR algorithms and give notations.

Li [5] proposed an algorithm to find e.d.r. directions and named it SIR1. The goal of SIR1 is not to find the function f, but to get the e.d.r. space, i.e., to find K vectors $\beta_1, \beta_2, \cdots, \beta_K$: e.d.r. directions. When the distribution of X is elliptically symmetric, the centered inverse regression $E[X|y] - E[X]$ is contained in the linear subspace spanned by $\beta_k^T \Sigma_{XX}$ ($k = 1, 2, \cdots, K$), where Σ_{XX} denotes the covariance matrix of X.

Here is the algorithm of SIR1 for the data: (y_i, x_i) ($i = 1, 2, \cdots, n$).

SIR1 algorithm

1. Sphering x: $\tilde{x}_i = \hat{\Sigma}_{xx}^{-\frac{1}{2}}(x_i - \bar{x})(i = 1, 2, \cdots, n)$, where $\hat{\Sigma}_{xx}$ is the sample covariance matrix and $\bar{x}$ is the sample mean of x.

2. Divide range of y into H slices, $I_1, I_2, \cdots, I_H$; let the proportion of the y_i that falls in slice h be $\hat{p}_h$.
3. Within each slice, compute the sample mean of the $\tilde{x}_i$'s, denoted by $\hat{m}_h$ ($h = 1, 2, \cdots, H$), so that $\hat{m}_h = \frac{1}{n\hat{p}_h} \sum_{y_i \in I_h} \tilde{x}_i$.
4. Conduct a (weighted) principal component analysis for the data $\hat{m}_h$ ($h = 1, 2, \cdots, H$) in the following way; form the weighted covariance matrix $\hat{V} = \sum_{h=1}^{H} \hat{p}_h \hat{m}_h \hat{m}_h^T$, then find the eigenvalues and the eigenvectors for $\hat{V}$.
5. Let the K largest eigenvectors of $\hat{V}$ be $\hat{\eta}_k$ ($k = 1, 2, \cdots, K$).
   Output $\hat{\beta}_k = \hat{\Sigma}_{xx}^{-\frac{1}{2}} \hat{\eta}_k$ ($k = 1, 2, \cdots, K$) for estimations of e.d.r. directions.

The main idea of SIR1 is to use $E[X|y]$. $E[X|y]$ is contained in the space spanned by e.d.r. directions, but there is no guarantee that $E[X|y]$ span the space. So, Li [5] also proposed another algorithm, SIR2. SIR2 uses $Cov[X|y]$.

SIR2 algorithm
1. Same as Step 1 of SIR1 algorithm.
2. Same as Step 2 of SIR1 algorithm.
3. Within each slice, compute the sample covariance matrix $\hat{V}_h$:
   $\hat{V}_h = \frac{1}{n\hat{p}_h - 1} \sum_{y_i \in I_h} (\tilde{x}_i - \hat{m}_h)(\tilde{x}_i - \hat{m}_h)^T$.
4. Compute the mean over all slice covariances:
   $\bar{V} = \sum_{h=1}^{H} \hat{p}_h \hat{V}_h$.
5. Compute a variance of slice covariances:
   $\hat{V} = \sum_{h=1}^{H} \hat{p}_h (\hat{V}_h - \bar{V})^2$.
6. Let the K largest eigenvectors of $\hat{V}$ be $\hat{\eta}_k$ ($k = 1, 2, \cdots, K$).
   Output $\hat{\beta}_k = \hat{\Sigma}_{xx}^{-\frac{1}{2}} \hat{\eta}_k$ ($k = 1, 2, \cdots, K$).

Mizuta [7] proposed an algorithm for the SIR model with projection pursuit (SIRpp). SIRpp uses the conditional distribution $X|y$ itself.

SIRpp Algorithm
1. Same as Step 1 of SIR1 algorithm.
2. Same as Step 2 of SIR1 algorithm.
3. Conduct a projection pursuit in K dimensional space for each slice.
   We get H projections: $(\alpha_1^{(h)}, \cdots, \alpha_K^{(h)})$, ($h = 1, 2, \cdots, H$).
4. Let the K largest eigenvectors of $\hat{V}$ be $\hat{\eta}_k$ ($k = 1, 2, \cdots, K$).
   Output $\hat{\beta}_k = \hat{\Sigma}_{xx}^{-\frac{1}{2}} \hat{\eta}_k$ ($k = 1, 2, \cdots, K$) for estimations of e.d.r. directions,
   where $\hat{V} = \sum_{h=1}^{H} w(h) \sum_{k=1}^{K} \alpha_k^{(h)} \alpha_k^{(h)T}$ and $w(h)$ is a weight determined by the size of the slice and the projection pursuit index.

Steps 1 and 2 are the same as those of SIR1 and SIR2. The H projections in Step 3 are regarded as e.d.r. directions on the coordinates of $\tilde{x}$. We get H projections and combine them into $\hat{V}$ in Step 4; this is similar to a singular value decomposition.

13.3 Relative Projection Pursuit

In this section, we would like to propose a new method for projection pursuit to construct a new SIR algorithm.

Projection pursuit is a method to find out "interested" linear projection of the data. This is done by assigning a numerical "interestingness" index to each projection and by maximizing the index. The definition of interestingness is based on how much the projected data deviate from normal distribution. The index is called the projection index. The method of projection pursuit is determined by the projection index. There are several projection indexes. Let $f_\alpha(u)$ denote density function of projected variable u, $\Phi(X)$ denote the distribution function, and $\phi(u)$ denote the density function of standard normal distribution.

Friedman Index

$$R = 2\Phi(X) - 1, \quad J = \int_{-1}^{1} \left(P_R(R) - \frac{1}{2} \right)^2 dR$$

Hall Index

$$J = \int_{-\infty}^{\infty} (f_\alpha(u) - \phi(u))^2 du$$

Moment Index

$$J = \int_{-\infty}^{\infty} f_\alpha(u) \log f_\alpha(u) du - \int_{-\infty}^{\infty} \phi(u) \log \phi(u)$$

We redefine "interestingness" as degree of a difference from the distribution of a reference dataset. The new degree of interestingness is based on the difference between the distribution of the projected target dataset and that of the reference dataset designated by the user. We call this degree relative projection index.

Hiro [3] proposed a relative projection index named *Area based index*:

$$I_A(\alpha) = \int \| F_1(x) - F_2(x) \| dx,$$

where $F_1(x)$ is empirical cumulative distribution of the projected target dataset and $F_2(x)$ is empirical cumulative distribution of the projected whole dataset. It is very easy to extend the index to more than one dimensional projected distribution.

13.4 SIRrpp

We can construct a new SIR algorithm with relative projection pursuit: SIRrpp. The algorithm of SIRrpp is almost the same as SIRpp except for step 3.

SIRrpp Algorithm
1. Same as Step 1 of SIRpp algorithm.
2. Same as Step 2 of SIRpp algorithm.
3. Assign the whole dataset to the reference dataset and assign each slice, which is a subset of whole dataset, to the target dataset. Conduct a relative projection pursuit in K dimensional space for each slice. We get H projections: $(\alpha_1^{(h)}, \cdots, \alpha_K^{(h)})$, $(h = 1, 2, \cdots, H)$.
4. Same as Step 4 of SIRpp algorithm.

Because relative projection pursuit finds projections far from the reference dataset, we do not assume that the distribution of explanatory variables is a specific distribution.

We evaluate the SIRrpp algorithm with a model of multicomponents:

$$y = \sin(x_1) + \cos(x_2) + 0 \cdot x_3 + \cdot x_4 + 0 \cdot x_5 + \sigma \cdot \varepsilon$$

to generate data $n = 1000$, where $\sigma = 0.5$. At first, five variables x_1, x_2, x_3, x_4, x_5 are generated by mixed normal distribution: $0.5N(0,1) + 0.5N(0,1)$. We generate ε with $N(0,1)$ and calculate a response variable y with the above model.

The ideal e.d.r. directions are contained in the space spanned by two vectors $(1,0,0,0,0)$ and $(0,1,0,0,0)$.

These are the results of relative projection pursuit for each slice of the data.

slices	projections
slice 1	(-0.1047 0.7601 -0.2799 -0.4164 -0.3993)
	(-0.9929 -0.0572 0.0039 0.0810 0.0641)
slice 2	(0.9733 0.1480 -0.0518 -0.1505 0.0728)
	(-0.1592 0.9633 0.1641 -0.0843 0.1123)
slice 3	(0.8937 0.3103 -0.0954 0.3004 -0.0736)
	(-0.3520 0.8808 0.2036 0.1567 -0.1846)
slice 4	(0.9876 -0.1091 -0.0081 -0.1057 0.0380)
	(0.1498 0.8677 0.2149 0.4050 -0.1197)
slice 5	(0.9961 0.0197 -0.0371 0.0267 0.0726)
	(-0.0695 0.7650 -0.3725 0.1877 0.4856)

All projections are practically e.d.r. directions: $(\alpha, \beta, 0, 0, 0)$, $\alpha^2 + \beta^2 = 1$. In step 4 of the SIRrpp algorithm, we get eigenvalues of $\hat{V}$: 4.9031, 3.7814, 0.6432, 0.5052, 0.1669. First and second eigenvalues are large and the rest are almost zero. The first and second eigenvectors of $\hat{V}$ are

(0.996470 -0.068780 0.01081 -0.04120 -0.02237)

(-0.068309 -0.992732 0.05703 0.05326 -0.06103).

They are almost perfect results.

13.5 Concluding Remarks

In this paper, we use the area based relative projection index for relative projection pursuit. But, there are some possibilities of other relative projection indexes. We will investigate other indexes for relative projection pursuit.

Relative projection pursuit is useful for other applications, for example, subset selection, cluster analysis, graphical representation of multidimensional data, etc.

References

[1] J. H. Friedman. Exploratory Projection Pursuit. *Journal of the American Statistical Association*, **82**, pages 249–266, 1987.

[2] J. H. Friedman and J. W. Tukey. A Projection Pursuit Algorithm for Exploratory Data Analysis. *IEEE Trans. on Computer*, **c-23**, **9**, 881–890, 1974.

[3] S. Hiro, Y. Komiya, H. Minami and M. Mizuta. Projection Index using Empirical Distribution Function (in Japanese). In *Proceedings of Info. Hokkaido 2002*, pages 128–129, 2002.

[4] K. Koyama, A. Morita, M. Mizuta, and Y. Sato. Projection Pursuit into Three Dimensional Space (in Japanese). *The Japanese Journal of Behaviormetrics*, **25(1)**, pages 1–9, 1998.

[5] Li, Ker-Chau. Sliced Inverse Regression for Dimension Reduction. *Journal of the American Statistical Association*, **86**, pages 316–342, 1991.

[6] M. Mizuta. A New Algorithm for Sliced Inverse Regression with Projection Pursuit. (in Japanese) In *Proceedings of Japan Statistical Society 1998*, pages 158–159, 1998.

[7] M. Mizuta. Sliced Inverse Regression with Projection Pursuit. In *Applied Stochastic Models and Data Analysis. Instituto Nacional de Estatística*, H. Bacelar-Nicolau, F. Costa Nicolau, and J. Janssen (Eds.), pages 51–56, 1999.

[8] M. Mizuta. Projection Pursuit into High Dimensional Space and its Applications. *Bulletin of the International Statistical Institute, 52nd Session*, pages 313–314, 1999.

14

Using Genetic Programming to Improve the Group Method of Data Handling in Time Series Prediction

M. Hiassat, M.F. Abbod, and N. Mort
University of Sheffield, Sheffield, UK

CONTENTS

14.1	Introduction	257
14.2	The Data	258
14.3	Financial Data	259
14.4	Weather Data	259
14.5	Processing of Data	260
14.6	The Group Method of Data Handling (GMDH)	261
14.7	Genetic Programming (GP)	262
14.8	GP-GMDH	263
14.9	Results and Discussion	264
14.10	Conclusion and Further Work	267
	References	268

In this paper we show how the performance of the basic algorithm of the Group Method of Data Handling (GMDH) can be improved using Genetic Programming (GP). The new improved GMDH (GP-GMDH) is then used to predict two currency exchange rates: the US Dollar to the Euro and the US Dollar to the French Franc. It is also used to predict the mean monthly maximum temperatures in Queen Alia International Airport. The performance of the GP-GMDH is compared with that of the conventional GMDH. Two performance measures, the root mean squared error and the mean absolute percentage error, show that the GP-GMDH algorithm appears to perform better than the conventional GMDH algorithm.

14.1 Introduction

Forecasting future trends of many observable phenomena remains of great interest to a wide circle of people. This requirement has maintained a high rate of activity in various research fields dedicated to temporal prediction methodologies.

Two such important application domains are financial markets and environmental systems, to mention but examples. Predicting such systems has been attempted for decades but it remains such a challenging task for a wide array of modelling paradigms.

The foreign exchange market is a large business with a large turnover in which trading takes place round the clock and all over the world. Consequently, financial time series prediction has become a very popular and ever growing business. It can be classified as a real world system characterized by the presence of non-linear relations. Modelling real world systems is a demanding task where many factors must be taken into account. The quantity and quality of the data points, the presence of external circumstances such as political issues and inflation rate make the modelling procedure a very difficult task.

A survey of the different methods available for modelling non-linear systems is given in Billings (1980).

Some researchers tried auto-regressive methods to predict foreign currency exchange rates (Chappell (1995)). Episcopos & Davis (1995) used the GARCH and ARIMA statistical methods to identify the model. These methods have not always produced good results, which has urged scientists to explore other more effective methods.

During the last two decades adaptive modelling techniques, like neural networks and genetic algorithms, have been extensively used in the field of economics. A list of examples using such methods is given in Deboeck (1994) and Chen (1994).

An extension to the genetic algorithm paradigm (Holland (1975)) is the versatile genetic programming method introduced by Koza (1992). Scientists were quick to use this method in many aspects of mathematical modelling.

An alternative non-linear modelling method, which was introduced in the late sixties, is the Group Method of Data Handling (Ivakhnenko (1968)). Since its introduction researchers from all over the world who used the GMDH in modelling were astonished by its prediction accuracy. Many of these applications were in the field of time series prediction. Parks et al. (1975) used the GMDH to find a model for the British economy. Ikeda et al. (1976) used a sequential GMDH algorithm in river flow prediction. Hayashi and Tanaka (1990) used a fuzzy GMDH algorithm to predict the production of computers in Japan. Robinson and Mort (1997b) used an optimised GMDH algorithm for predicting foreign currency exchange rate.

In Section 14.5 we describe how the GMDH and GP can be used in conjunction with each other (GP-GMDH) to improve the prediction accuracy of the standard GMDH algorithm when it is applied to time series in the form of financial and weather data.

14.2 The Data

In this paper both the GP-GMDH and the conventional GMDH algorithms were used to make one step ahead prediction of the exchange rate from US Dollars to French Francs (denoted USD2FFR), US Dollars to Euros (USD2EURO) and for predicting

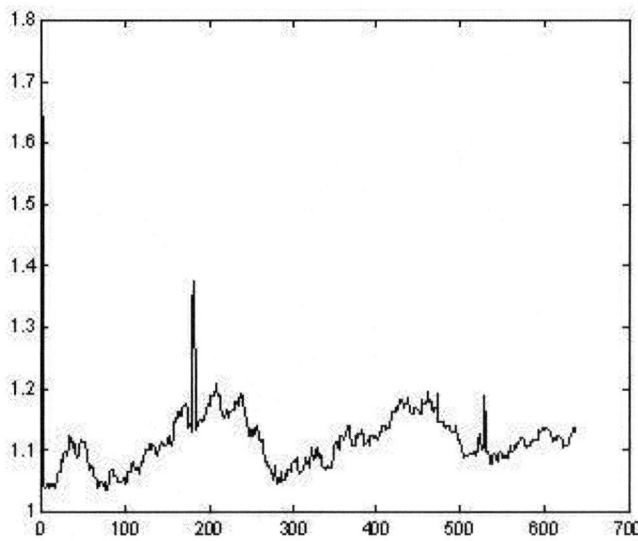

FIGURE 14.1
USD2EURO from April 2, 2000 to December 31, 2001.

the mean monthly maximum temperature in Queen Alia International Airport.

14.3 Financial Data

Values from 2 April, 2000 to 31 December, 2001 for both exchange rates were obtained from the website *www.oanda.com*, a total of 639 points for each exchange rate (Figures 14.1 and 14.2). The first 600 points were used in the training and checking of the GMDH algorithm. The last 39 points were unseen by the algorithm throughout its computation. The performance of the algorithm was evaluated on the last 35 points of the data.

14.4 Weather Data

Predicting weather data is not a straightforward process as there are many variables that affect each other and all need to be considered in the prediction of any one of them.

The mean monthly values of evaporation, humidity, wind speed, precipitation and minimum temperature recorded during the period from January 1995 to December

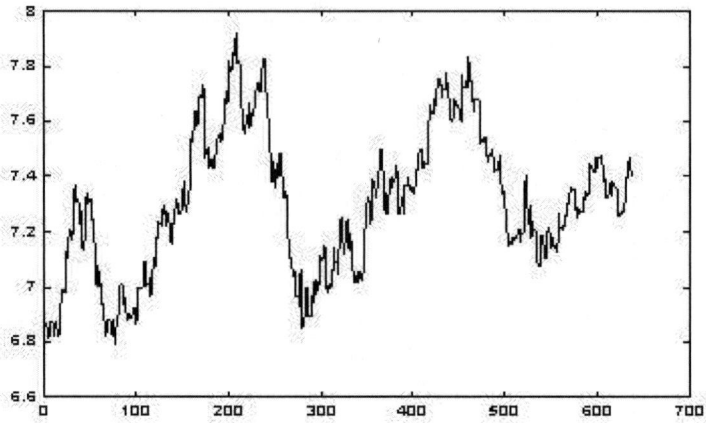

FIGURE 14.2
USD2FFR from April 2, 2000 to December 31, 2001.

1995 in Queen Alia International Airport were used in the building process of the GMDH algorithm which, in turn, was used for predicting the corresponding maximum temperature values. The values for the year 1995 remained unseen by the algorithm except in its assessment process. Figure 14.3 shows the maximum temperature values for the period mentioned above.

14.5 Processing of Data

The GMDH algorithm accepts raw values of any size in its building process and the whole procedure of training, running and evaluating the algorithm could be carried out without pre-processing the data. However, when dealing with weather and financial data it is important to consider the seasonal patterns and the presence of extreme values within the cycle of points that might contribute to noise and, hence, affect the overall accuracy of the computed algorithm. Thus, the five point moving average for both sets of data was computed and used instead of the raw data points. This procedure was then followed by normalising the data using:

$$x_t = \frac{r_t - \bar{r}}{\sigma_t} \qquad (14.1)$$

where $\bar{r}$ is the mean of the data and σ_t is its standard deviation.

The new series will have zero mean and unit variance. This is important as it ensures that the size of the variable does not reflect its importance to the output and, hence, no single variable will dominate the others.

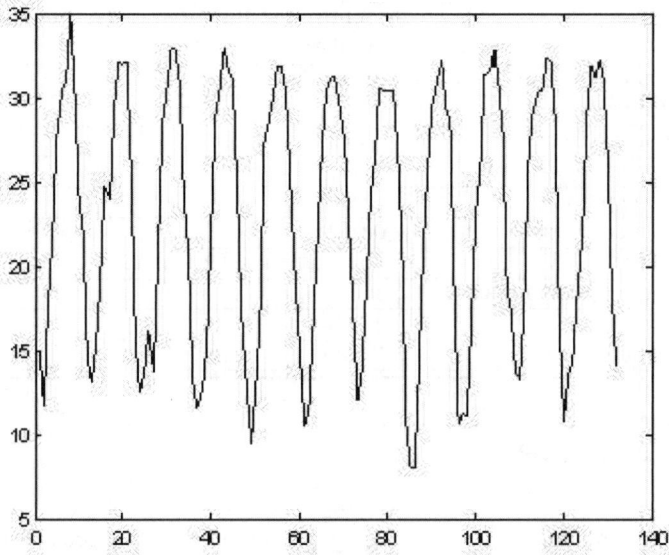

FIGURE 14.3
Mean monthly maximum temperature values.

Having been normalised the data will then be put in a multi-input single-output formation.

The financial data is considered to be autoregressive, i.e., the output value at time 't' can be predicted from k previous values of the series at times $t-1, t-2, \ldots, t-k$. Throughout this paper k will be considered to be 5.

The normalised weather data will also be put in a multi-input single-output formation, the input being evaporation, humidity, wind speed, precipitation and minimum temperature while the output is the maximum temperature.

14.6 The Group Method of Data Handling (GMDH)

It was developed by Ivakhnenko (1968) as a rival to the method of stochastic approximation. The proposed algorithm is based on a multilayer structure using, for each pair of variables, a second order polynomial of the form:

$$y = a_0 + a_1 x_i + a_2 x_j + a_3 x_i x_j + a_4 x_i^2 + a_5 x_j^2 \qquad (14.2)$$

where x_i and x_j are input variables and y is the corresponding output value. The data points are divided into training and checking sets. The coefficients of the polynomial are found by regression on the training set and its output is then evaluated

Parameters	Values
Objective:	Identify the function, given input and output data
Terminal set:	[input data points, integers from −5 to 5]
Function set:	[+, -, ×, %, sin, cos, exp]
Population size:	300
Crossover probability:	0.95
Mutation probability:	0.05
Reproduction probability:	0.05
Selection:	Tournament selection, size 4.
Number of generations:	5
MDP:	4
Initialisation method:	'Grow'

TABLE 14.1
Koza tableau for the GP run.

and tested for suitability using the data points in the checking set. An external criterion, usually the mean squared error (mse), is then used to select the polynomials that are allowed to proceed to the next layer. The output of the selected polynomials becomes the new input values at the next layer. The whole procedure is repeated until the lowest mse is no longer smaller than that of the previous layer.

The model of the data can be computed by tracing back the path of the polynomials that corresponded to the lowest mse in each layer.

14.7 Genetic Programming (GP)

During the last decade Genetic Programming has emerged as an efficient methodology for teaching computers how to program themselves.

Firstly, a set of functions and a set of terminals are defined in such a way that the functions chosen are able to represent the problem at hand. A population of computer programs is generated by randomly selecting members from the function and terminal sets. The output of each of these programs is evaluated and compared to the actual value by using some fitness measure, again, usually the mean squared error. According to their fitness, genetic operators are applied to the individuals creating a second population of computer programs. The procedure is repeated until the required number of generations has been reached. The individual with the best fitness measure is considered to be the model for the data.

The genetic operators employed in the GP run are mainly crossover, mutation and reproduction. They are implemented during the GP run according to pre-set parameters. Koza introduced a lucid form of listing the parameters in a tableau named after him. A list of the parameters used for the GP run in this paper is given in Table 14.1.

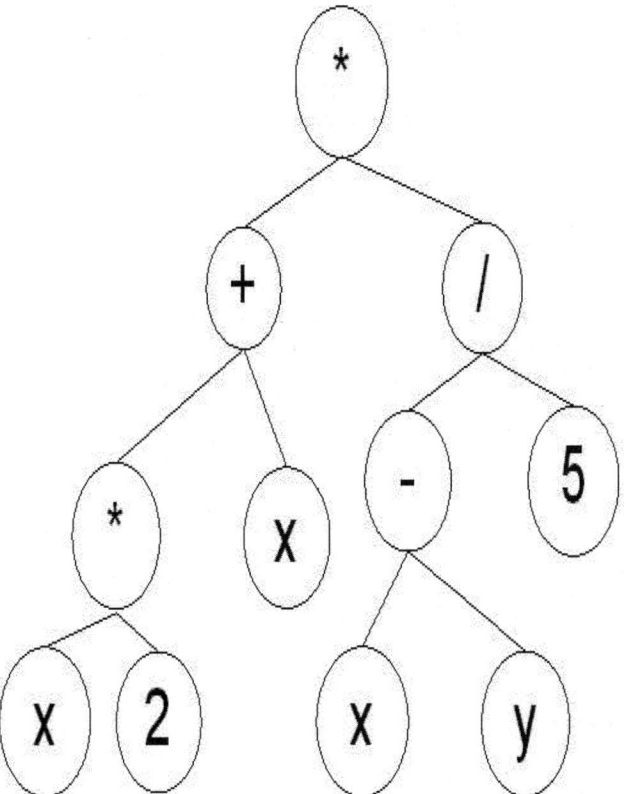

FIGURE 14.4
A parse-tree program.

The most popular form of representing the individual programs is the parse-tree representation, originally introduced by Koza (1992) in his pioneering book. It is a collection of terminal and function nodes interpreted in a depth-first, left-to-right postfix manner. Figure 14.4 shows a program represented in a parse-tree. The parse-tree is decoded to give:

$$(2x+x)[(x-y)/5] = 3x(x-y)/5.$$

14.8 GP-GMDH

The GMDH network, as mentioned earlier, uses a quadratic polynomial as the transfer function in each layer. A question arises: what if the relationship between the input and the output is not best described by a quadratic polynomial? This leads to

	MAPE	RMSE
Conventional GMDH	3.408	0.0484
GP-GMDH	2.3966	0.0360

TABLE 14.2
Results for USD2EURO.

another question: if the conventional quadratic polynomial was replaced by a function that described the input-output relationship more accurately, would this lead to an improvement in the prediction accuracy of the GMDH algorithm?

The GP-GMDH algorithm is similar to the conventional GMDH algorithm except that the transfer function is not necessarily a quadratic polynomial. Instead, GP is applied to the data prior to the GMDH run in order to find the best function that maps the input to the output. This function will later be used to replace the conventional quadratic in the GMDH network. It is important to note that the GP run is not applied to the data points in order to find an exact mapping between the input and the output but to find a general form of the functional mapping between them, i.e., linear, quadratic, cubic, logarithmic, trigonometric, ….etc. A more accurate model of the data will be computed by the GMDH network.

14.9 Results and Discussion

Two performance measures were used in assessing the accuracy of the conventional GMDH and the GP-GMDH: the mean absolute percentage error, denoted MAPE, (Equation 3) and the widely used root mean squared error, RMSE (Equation 4).

$$MAPE = \frac{1}{n} \sum_{i=1}^{n} \frac{(absY_i - Z_i)}{Y_i} \times 100\% \qquad (14.3)$$

$$RMSE = \sqrt{\frac{1}{n} \sum_{i=1}^{n} (Y_i - Z_i)^2} \qquad (14.4)$$

where n is the number of variables, Y is the actual output and Z is the predicted output.

The results for both networks when applied to the entire data are given in Tables 14.2, 14.3 and 14.4.

It is evident from the values of both measures that the GP-GMDH performs better than the conventional GMDH. This improvement is more significant in the weather data.

Values of the percentage improvement in both performance measures for all the data are given in Table 14.5.

	MAPE	RMSE
Conventional GMDH	3.6574	0.3708
GP-GMDH	3.0690	0.3062

TABLE 14.3
Results for USD2FFR.

	MAPE	RMSE
Conventional GMDH	31.06	23.58
GP-GMDH	18.79	14.12

TABLE 14.4
Results for maximum temperature.

	MAPE Percentage improvement	RMSE Percentage improvement
USD2EURO	29.7	25.6
USD2FFR	16.1	17.4
Maximum Temperature	39.5	40.1

TABLE 14.5
Percentage improvement to the performance measures.

Graphs of actual, predicted by the conventional GMDH algorithm and predicted by GP-GMDH algorithm for the USD2EURO, USD2FFR exchange rates and the maximum temperature values are shown in Figures 14.5, 14.6 and 14.7, respectively.

The prediction performance of the GMDH network depends on the number of generations over which the algorithm is allowed to evolve. The results given in this paper were produced after only 5 generations.

Several GMDH runs, using both networks, were carried out, each with a different number of generations. It was found that as the individuals were allowed to evolve over a higher number of generations, the value of the minimum of the selection criterion in each generation was decreased. On the other hand, it was found that the performance measures became progressively worse. This was due to the fact that the algorithms became overspecialised for the data they were trained on to the detriment of their ability to predict the unseen data.

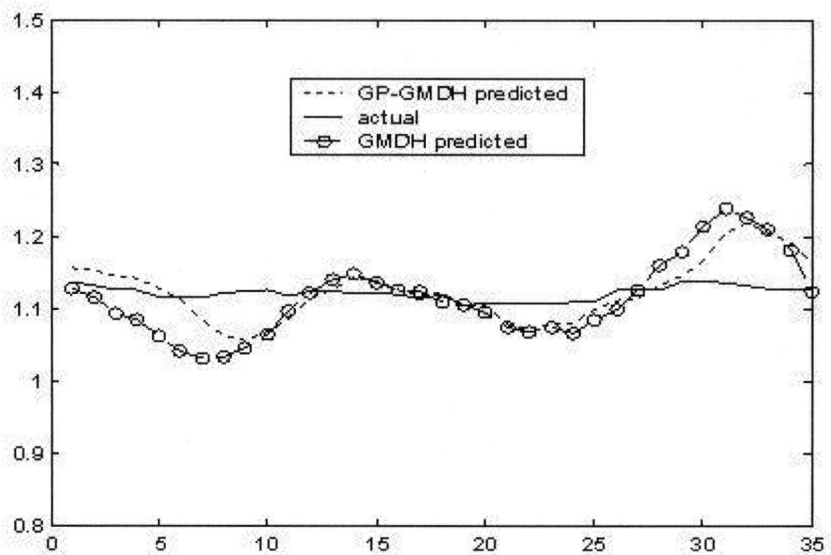

FIGURE 14.5
Graphs of actual and predicted USD2EURO.

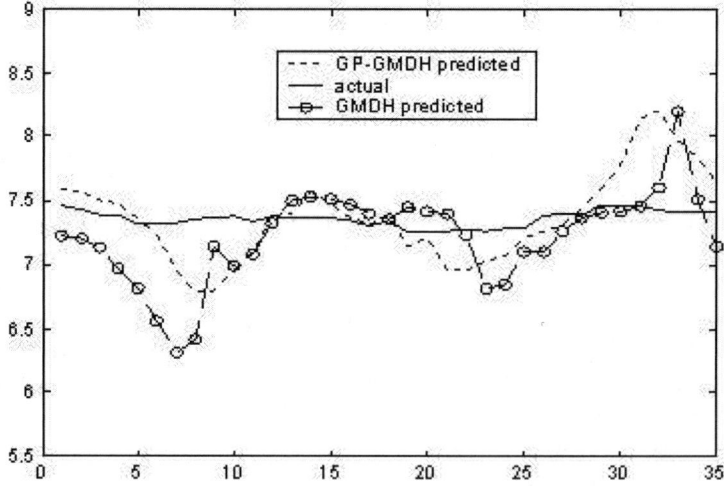

FIGURE 14.6
Graphs of actual and predicted USD2FFR.

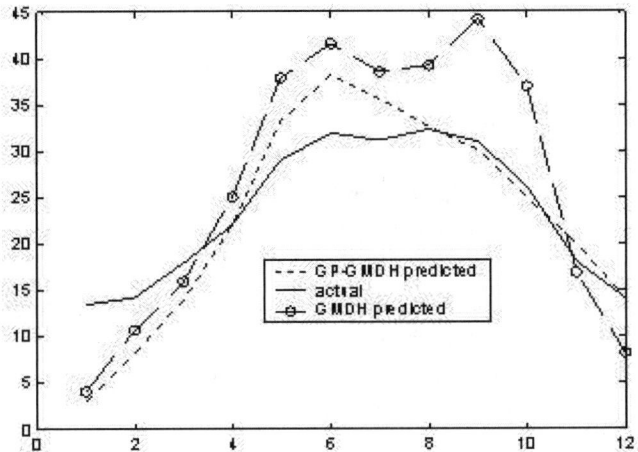

FIGURE 14.7
Graphs of actual and predicted maximum temperature.

14.10 Conclusion and Further Work

It was shown in this paper that the performance of the conventional GMDH algorithm can be improved significantly if some information about the type of the relationship between the input and output was available and used in the GMDH run.

The fitness of the best individual in each generation improved while the individuals were allowed to evolve over more generations. This had the reverse effect on the overall performance of the network for the unseen data points. This is an area that is in need of further investigation in order to find a suitable point for terminating the building of the polynomial process.

When the same procedure carried out in this paper was repeated a few times using a different size of training and checking sets, it was noticed that the performance of both GMDH networks, particularly the conventional one, was greatly affected. This leads to the following hypothesis: there might exist a rule for dividing the sample of data that when applied the accuracy of the GMDH algorithm reaches its optimum. Work needs to be carried out to investigate the validity of this hypothesis.

The work carried out in this paper has provided an insight into the way the GMDH deals with time series prediction. While it was shown that it is possible to improve its prediction performance, the GMDH remains a robust and popular method of mathematical modelling.

References

Billings, S.A. (1980). Identification of non-linear systems – a survey, *IEE Proceedings D. Control Theory and Applications*, Vol. 127, Iss. 6, pp 272-285.

Chappell, D. Padmore, J. Mistry, P. and C. Ellis (1995). A threshold model for the French Franc/Deutschmark exchange rate, *Journal of Forecasting*, Vol. 15, No. 3, pp 155-164.

Chen, C. H. (1994). Neural Networks for Financial market prediction, *IEEE International Conference on Neural Networks*, 7, 1199-1202.

Deboeck, G. (Ed.) (1994). *Trading of the edge: Neural, genetic, and fuzzy systems for chaotic financial markets*. John Wiley and Sons, New York.

Episcopos, A. and Davis, J. (1995). Predicting returns on Canadian Exchange Rates with Artificial Neural Networks and EGARCH-M Models. In *Neural Networks Financial Engineering, Proceedings of the third International Conference on Neural Networks in the Capital Markets*, Refenes, A-P.N., Abu-Mostafa, Y., Moody, J. and Weigend, A. (Eds.), London, World Scientific, Singapore, 135-145.

Hayashi, I. and Tanaka, H. (1990). The fuzzy GMDH algorithm by possibility models and its application. *Fuzzy Sets and Systems 36*. 245-258.

Holland, J. H. (1975). *Adaption in Natural and Artificial Systems*. The University of Michigan Press, Ann Arbor, MI.

Ikeda S., Ochiai, M. and Sawaragi.Y. (1976). Sequential GMDH algorithm and its application to river flow prediction. *IEEE Transaction on Systems, Man and Cybernetics*, July, 1976.

Ivakhnenko, A. G., (1968). The Group Method of Data Handling-A rival of the method of stochastic approximation. *Soviet Automatic Control*, vol 13 c/c of Avtomatika, 1, 3, 43-55.

Koza, J. R. (1992). *Genetic Programming: On the Programming of Computers by Means of Natural Selection*. MIT Press, Cambridge.

Parks, P., Ivakhnenko, A. G., Boichuk, L. M. and Svetalsky, B. K. (1975). A self-organizing model of British economy for control with optimal prediction using the Balance-of-Variables criterion. *Int. J. of Computer and Information Sciences*, vol 4, No. 4.

Robinson, C. and Mort, N. (1997b). Predicting foreign exchange rates using neural and genetic models. *Proceedings of 2nd Asian Control Conference, Seoul, Korea*, July 22-25, vol. 3, pp 115-118.

# 15

Data Mining for Monitoring Plant Devices Using GMDH and Pattern Classification

B.R. Upadhyaya and B. Lu
University of Tennessee, Knoxville

CONTENTS

15.1 Introduction 269
15.2 Description of the Method 273
15.3 Analysis and Results 277
15.4 Concluding Remarks 278
      Acknowledgments 278
      References 278

The application of the group method of data handling technique for modeling dynamic measurements to monitor power plant sensors and field devices is presented. The details of the algorithm, with generalization using rational function approximation, are discussed. The data-driven models are used to generate residuals between the measurements and the predictions of state variables and control functions. This information is then processed for fault detection and isolation using both rule-base analysis and pattern classification techniques. The method is demonstrated by applications to the monitoring of selected devices in a nuclear power plant steam generator system.

15.1 Introduction

For a large-scale industrial system, such as a nuclear power plant, the conditions of optimal performance may be achieved by integrating process control and diagnostics. The latter includes the monitoring of sensors, actuators, controllers, and other critical equipment that are essential for its continued operation. Traditional algorithms generally do not take into consideration inherent feedback among control loops. Because of this process feedback, it is often difficult to isolate faults that may be masked by control actions that try to correct for device faults. Therefore, it is necessary to develop fault detection and isolation (FDI) techniques for application at the system level.

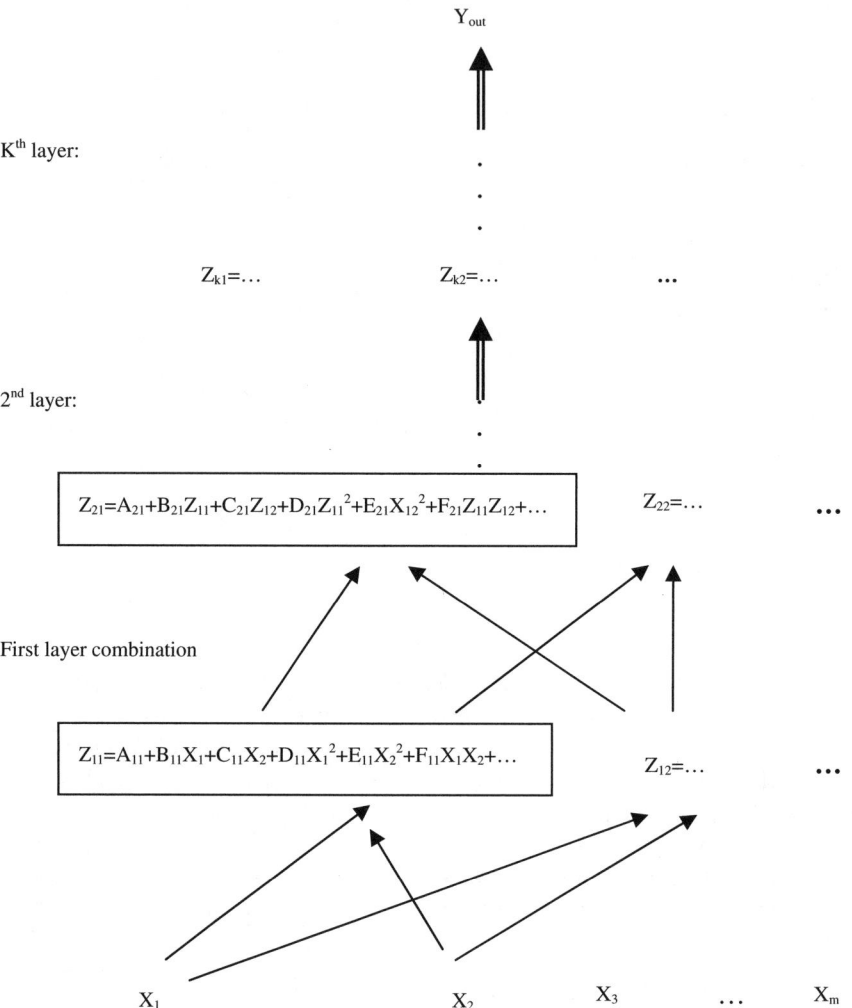

FIGURE 15.1
GMDH model structure.

The approach presented in this paper uses the *Group Method of Data Handling (GMDH)* for characterizing the dynamics of the system. The GMDH model structure is shown in Figure 15.1. Particularly, the GMDH is used to develop nonlinear (with rational functions) predictive models of key system variables and control functions. The models are then used to generate residuals between the measurements and their predictions. The deviation of these residuals from nominal values indicates a possible fault in an instrument channel, a control device, or plant equipment such as a pump. If a fault is indicated, then the properties of the residuals

Statistical Data Mining and Knowledge Discovery 271

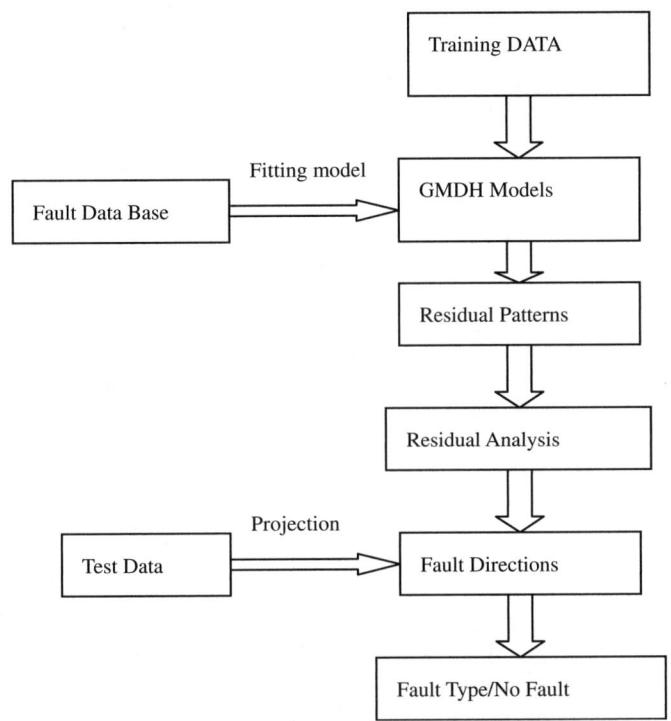

FIGURE 15.2
Structure of the fault detection and isolation (FDI) system.

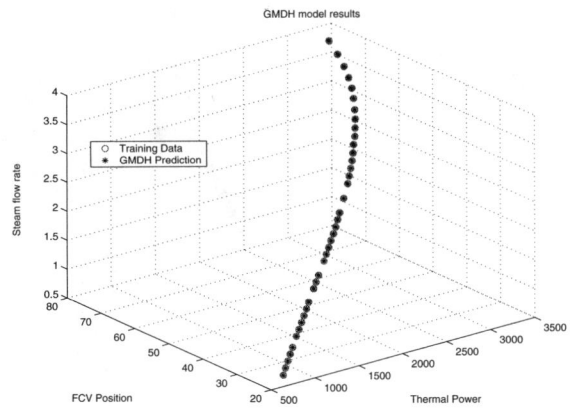

FIGURE 15.3
Steam flow rate model with FCV position and thermal power as model inputs.

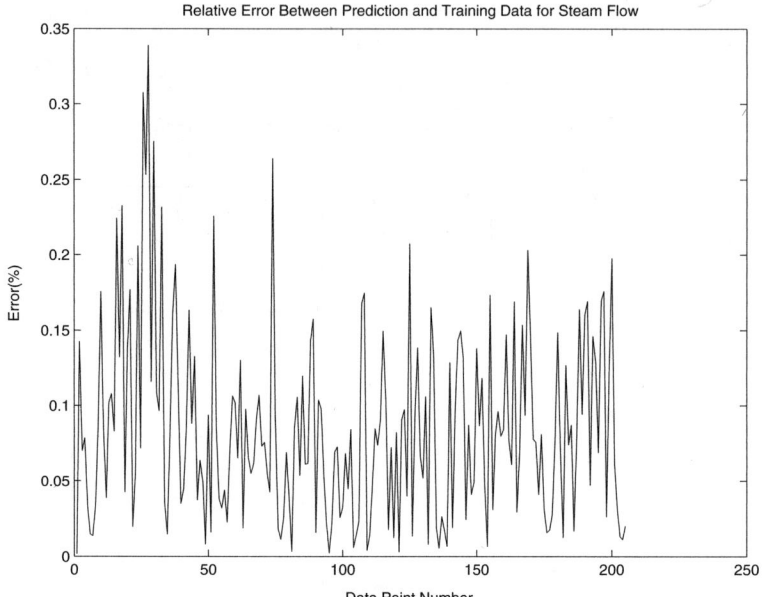

FIGURE 15.4
Error between training data and model prediction for SG steam flow rate.

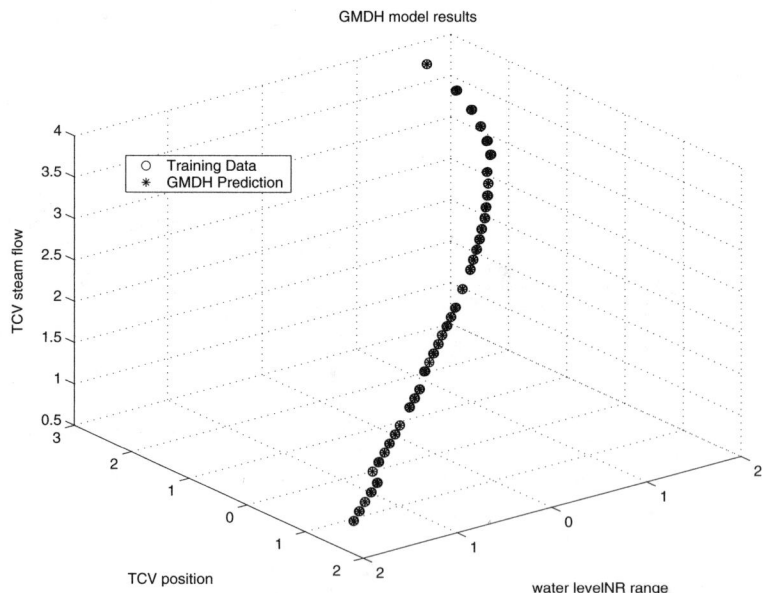

FIGURE 15.5
TCV flow model with TCV position, NR level and three more variables as model inputs.

Statistical Data Mining and Knowledge Discovery

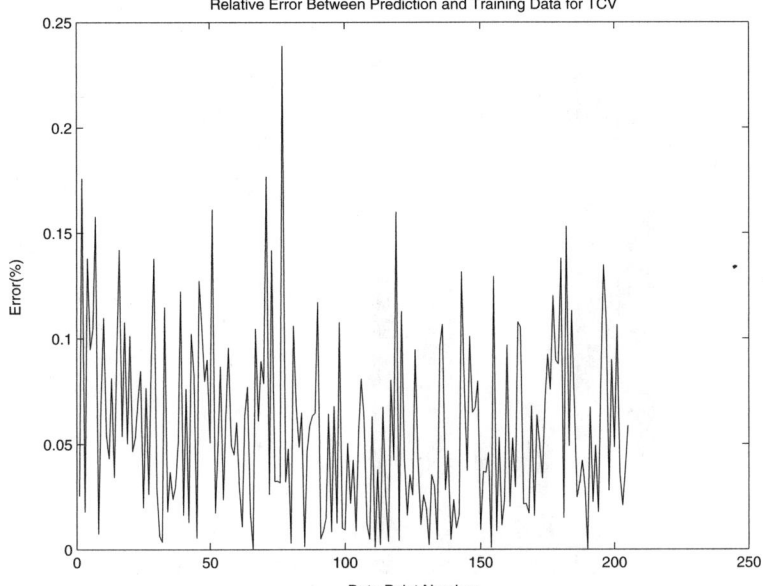

FIGURE 15.6
Error between training data and model prediction for TCV steam flow rate.

are processed to isolate the fault type. A rule-based approach and a principal component analysis (PCA)-based approach are used to perform fault isolation. Both these techniques use the generated residuals. The PCA of the residuals provides a principal direction that dominates a given fault type. In this case the known pattern direction is compared with the test residual direction and their closeness is calculated as a level of confidence in classifying the fault type.

The integrated GMDH and PCA approach has been applied to the steam generator system of a pressurized water reactor to monitor field devices during both steady state and transient operating conditions. The GMDH provides an efficient nonlinear modeling approach and includes rational functions of the measurements at the input level. The complete algorithm has been evaluated for various operating conditions and for the case of several fault scenarios, including a feed pump fault.

15.2 Description of the Method
15.2.1 Group Method of Data Handling (GMDH)

The GMDH is a data-driven modeling method [1] that approximates a given variable y (output) as a function of a set of input variables $\{x_1, x_2, \ldots, x_m\}$ that are closely related to y. The general form is referred to as the Kolmogorov-Gabor polynomial and is given by

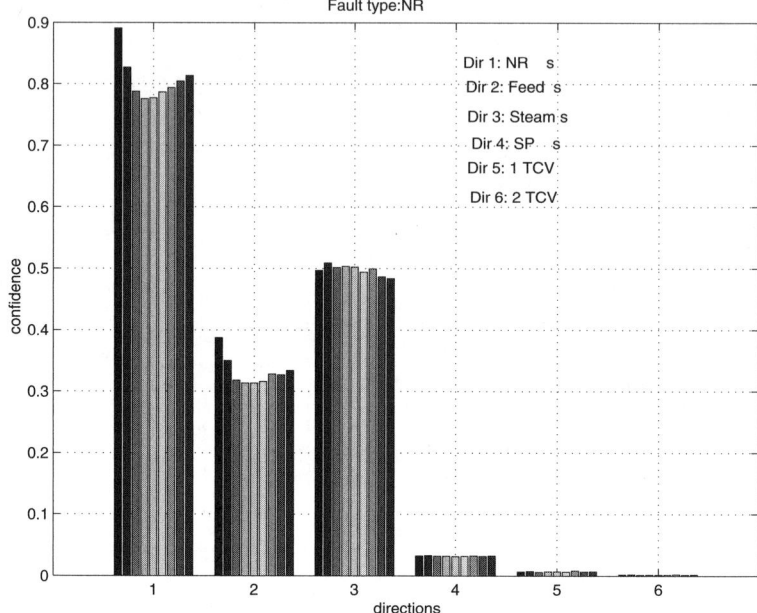

FIGURE 15.7
Static fault direction indicated by PCA residual model, when NR level sensor is under drift fault.

$$y = a_0 + \sum_{i=1}^{m} a_i x_i + \sum_{i=1}^{m}\sum_{j=1}^{m} a_{ij} x_i x_j + \sum_{i=1}^{m}\sum_{j=1}^{m}\sum_{k=1}^{m} a_{ijk} x_i x_j x_k \ldots \quad (15.1)$$

The model is developed in a multi-layer form with each successive layer increasing the order of the lower layer polynomial. As shown in Figure 15.1, the input layer measurements could also include terms that are certain nonlinear functions of the basic measurements, including rational functions. This organization depends on the knowledge of system nonlinearity as indicated by the physics models. The process of approximation continues until the sum-of-squared error (SSE) of overall prediction satisfies a predefined criterion.

$$\text{SSE} = 1/N \sum_{i=1}^{N} (y_i - y_p)^2 \to \min$$

Input combinations of GMDH model is as follows.

$$\left\{ \begin{array}{l} 1, (x_1, x_2), (x_1^2, x_2^2), (x_1 x_2), (\frac{1}{x_1}, \frac{1}{x_2}), (\frac{1}{x_1^2}, \frac{1}{x_2^2}), (\frac{1}{x_1+x_2}, \frac{1}{x_1 x_2}), (\frac{x_1}{x_2}, \frac{x_2}{x_1}), \\ (\frac{x_1}{x_1+x_2}, \frac{x_2}{x_1+x_2}), (\frac{x_1+x_2}{x_1}, \frac{x_1+x_2}{x_2}), \ldots \end{array} \right\}$$

One may consider this algorithm as a statistical learning network. It is reasonable to subdivide a complex relationship into many compact and easily executable pieces, then to apply the advanced regression technique to identify the relational pieces separately. The data set is usually divided into two subsets: the training set and the testing set. The purpose is to do cross validation in order to avoid overfitting in the training phase. Equation (15.2) shows the data structure used in the GMDH algorithm.

$Y = f(X)$

$$\begin{array}{ll} y_1 & x_{11}\ x_{12}\ \ldots\ x_{1m} \\ y_2 & x_{21}\ x_{22}\ \ldots\ x_{2m} \\ \vdots & \vdots \\ y_t & x_{t1}\ x_{t2}\ \ldots\ x_{tm} \\ \vdots & \vdots \\ y_n & x_{n1}\ x_{n2}\ \ldots\ x_{nm} \end{array} \qquad (15.2)$$

The data from 1 to t are used for model fitting, and the data from t+1 to n are used for model validation and to check for over fitting. Figure 15.1 shows the structure usually adopted for the GMDH network, which begins with single input variables and becomes more complicated as the number of layers increases.

The outputs of each layer are sorted in the order of prediction error. Those with values less than a predefined threshold will replace the old predictors in the last generation and pass to the next layer for further combination. The overall sum-squared errors of testing data set are calculated at each generation. An overfitting is found when the test error starts to increase at a certain layer. As a result, the GMDH training process stops as soon as the network begins to simulate the noise included or the number of layers exceeds the preset limit. The multiple regression models help to filter the effect of noise in the prediction of the output y.

The GMDH method described above is a self-organizing modeling method for characterizing the mapping among process variables and control functions. The advantages of this algorithm over other modeling methods include:

The capability of mapping nonlinear relationships between model regressors and model output variables.

The flexible selection of GMDH network structure during training process, instead of the pre-defined structure, as in a neural network, which is also good in extracting nonlinear relations among variables.

Free from the overfitting problem. GMDH method divides the input data into training and checking sets in order to select a good model structure.

Guaranty of convergence.

Several GMDH models have been established for the key devices in a nuclear power plant steam generator system, including narrow range sensor, turbine control valve, and others. The performance of GMDH algorithm is illustrated in the

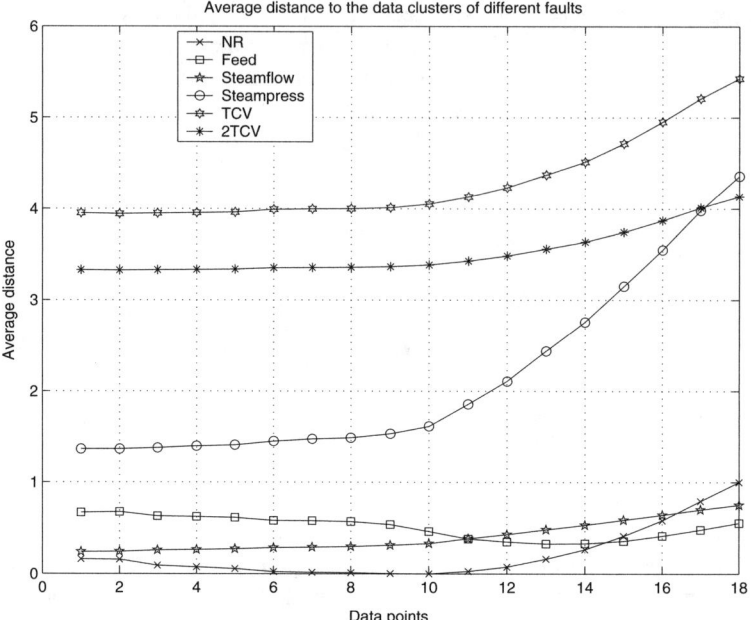

FIGURE 15.8
Fault direction indicated by the nearest neighbor method when the NR sensor is under degradation.

results below. Examples of the development of GMDH models are shown in Figures 15.3–15.6 for the steam generator level and the turbine control valve steam flow rate signals.

15.2.2 Analysis of Residuals for Fault Diagnosis

There are generally two types of residual analysis methods: structural residual analysis (rule-based) and directional residual analysis.

The *Principal Component Analysis (PCA)*, which is a multivariate statistical technique, has been used to characterize the changes in the residual vector directions. The purpose is to reduce a large number of interrelated variables to a relatively small number of variables that account for most of the observed variance information. This is accomplished by linear transformations of the observed variables. The first component accounts for the maximum amount of variance possible, and the rest in decreasing order of contribution. The principal directions are orthogonal with each other. This property is very useful in simplifying the residual patterns and in using them to distinguish among fault types.

The linear nature of PCA makes it less attractive for modeling nonlinear systems. However, since the residuals from the GMDH model have good regularity property, it is feasible to consider PCA in dealing with the residuals from GMDH models. This PCA analysis for residual space is especially useful for transient cases, during which GMDH transient model residuals change with time.

The schematic of data driven FDI using GMDH models is shown in Figure 15.2.

15.3 Analysis and Results

Residual generation is the first step in detecting a device fault. Several GMDH models are developed for the important components related to the steam generator system. Among these are turbine control valve (TCV), narrow range water level sensor, feed control valve (FCV), and feed water flow meter. Figures 15.3–15.6 illustrate the results of model predictions and measurements. It is noted that the training data cover the complete range from near hot zero power to full power levels. Thus the models established can fit a wide range of working conditions, and thus can be used in monitoring related components under various power levels. The selection of predictors is important such that residual classification would be relatively easy, especially for structured residual analysis.

Fault isolation is an important step in FDI procedure in order to implement in future advanced control for nuclear power plants. Different techniques have been studied in order to come up with a reliable approach for isolating fault types that may occur in a steam generator system. Among them, the principal component analysis, applied to the residual space, produced the best results, from the point of view of both accuracy and robustness. This method is based on the assumption that the direction of a specific residual under certain device fault will remain constant during the process. The implementation of PCA has demonstrated its effectiveness in capturing the plant conditions using residual space.

Figure 15.7 illustrates a fault isolation result through the residual space PCA. The PCA is used in this study to find the main residual change direction. The result shows the plots of the residual directions of the measurements for the case when there is a drift or bias fault in the narrow range (NR) SG level sensor. The NR directional signature has the maximum value (about 0.9). The directional signatures for the steam flow and feed flow are not insignificant, primarily because their settings change due to the error in the NR sensor and the controller feedback . Each of the fault direction plots illustrates about 9 steady-state operating conditions.

As compared to this method, Figure 15.8 illustrates another residual analysis result using the nearest neighbor method. The y-axis shows the average distance from the tested condition to the interested fault conditions. The fault type is classified as the one that has the nearest average distance to the test signal.

We should notice that PCA algorithm is pretty data consuming, thus several types of device faults such as FCV degradation are not included in this PCA study, because it is difficult to collect large amount of data for the FCV fault case. This is normal because the fault component has not caused much abnormality in the system. In addition, the feed controller action makes the NR, feed flow and the steam flow sensors hard to isolate during small levels of degradation.

Note fault directions:
1. NR sensor degradation
2. Feed flow sensor degradation
3. Steam flow sensor degradation
4. Steam pressure sensor degradation
5. TCV degradation
6. Steam pressure sensor degradation

15.4 Concluding Remarks

The steam generator system nonlinear properties are characterized by system modeling using GMDH. Furthermore, linear analysis of residual patterns simplifies the work of fault device isolation. The FDI algorithm developed in this study considers both nonlinear properties and simplified fault monitoring through residual analysis. The system anomaly is indicated by large residual values and further modeling of the residual data is useful in isolating the faulty device. The FDI method presented in this paper has been extended to sensor and field device monitoring during plant transients.

Acknowledgments

This research was sponsored by the U.S. Department of Energy, NERI Program, under a grant with The University of Tennessee, Knoxville.

References

Farlow, S.J. (1984). *Self-Organizing Methods in Modeling: GMDH Type Algorithms*, Marcel Dekker, New York.

B.R. Upadhyaya, Lu, B. and Zhao, K. (2001). *Fault Detection and Isolation of Nuclear Plant System Sensors and Field Devices*, Annual Report prepared for the DOE-NERI Project, September.

Ferreira, P.B. and Upadhyaya, B.R. (1999). *On-line Fault Monitoring and Isolation of Field Device Using Group Method of Data Handling*, Proc. MARCON 99, Gatlinburg, Tennessee, Vol. 2, May, pp. 79.01-79.15.

Kaistha, N. and Upadhyaya, B.R. (2001). Fault detection and isolation of field devices in nuclear plant system using principal component analysis, *Nuclear Technology*, Vol. 136, November, pp. 221-230.

Gertler, J., Li, W., Huang, Y. and McAvoy, T.J. (1999). Isolation enhanced principal component analysis, *AIChE Journal*, Vol. 45, p. 323-334.

Mangoubi, R.S. (1998). *Robust Estimation and Failure Detection*, Springer-Verlag, Heidelberg.

16

Statistical Modeling and Data Mining to Identify Consumer Preferences

Francois Boussu[1] and Jean Jacques Denimal[2]

[1]*Ecole Nationale Superieure des Arts et Industries Textiles, Roubaix, and*
[2]*University of Sciences and Technologies of Lille, France*

CONTENTS

16.1 Introduction 282
16.2 Data Mining Method 283
16.3 Application to a Textile Data Set 288
16.4 Conclusion 292
    Acknowledgment 294
    References 294

All along the items design process, the identification of parameters influencing the future sales remains one of the priority of the marketing director. In the apparel industry, textile items collections are mainly processed at meeting periods between the different partners of the firm. Each of them give their own impressions and subjective parameters to forecast the trends to come and the items attributes as well. In most cases, poor statistical tools are used to identify the relations between the items attributes and the historic sales. To fill this gap, we propose in this chapter a data mining technique aiming at explaining the historic sales profiles of items from the knowledge of their attributes. The first step of our approach is based on the PLS regression which allows us to extract the hidden relations (represented by the PLS factors) between the items attributes and their sales profiles. Based on these results, a particular hierarchical clustering of the sales season weeks can then be performed and constitutes the second step of our approach. More precisely, each week is identified by a set of sold items. If this items set remains almost unchanged for two consecutive weeks, then these two weeks are merged. As a consequence, the highest nodes of the hierarchy correspond to the main breakpoints of the sale season. Each of them put on the fore the main changes of purchase behaviors. Moreover, for each of these nodes, graphic plane representations can be obtained displaying weeks, items and items characteristics as well. Therefore, the comparison of the two groups of weeks defining a node and the interpretation of the associated breakpoint can be easily done by the inspection of its corresponding graphic representation.

16.1 Introduction

16.1.1 The Garment Market

In a hard competitive environment, characterizing the garment market, the costs minimization operation is one of the main priorities for an industry to endure season after season. In regards to the purchasing function, from the raw materials to the finished product, a lower price policy is applied to find worldwide corresponding goods (sometimes without the quality requirements) (Batra and Brookstein (2002); Aneja (2002)) [1][2]. The production time is constantly reduced to a minimum. By the same token, the number of items in stock or in progress has to be as low as possible in the POS (points of sales). This logic of permanent costs minimization implies an efficient coordination between the textile actors of the supply chain in order to propose at the right place, at the right time, the fitted items at the right price to the consumers. A methodology of their purchasing acts through the item sales at different POS, proposed by Traci May-Plumlee and Trevor J. Little (2001) [3], makes it possible to identify the items with the highest sale amounts. But no links between sale amounts and item attributes are revealed. However, these links remain essential to understand and then to forecast the sales behaviors evolutions of textile items. Thus, decisions can be made easier with better information on products ("practitioners need to leverage any and all knowledge available to make more informed product decision," Moore et al. (2001) [4]). These main parameters influencing the sales, previously identified, may also be a helpful aid during the building of a new textile items collection, so that the right options may be taken, leading to a future commercial success.

The founder elements, from which a new collection is based, mainly lies on subjective criteria and intuitions. By this way, the financial risk remains high, particularly for new items, which may lead to stop the creation process inside the collection.

This new textile items collection is composed of unchanged items and re-looked items with new descriptive parameters (color, fabric, touch, etc.). Thus, a methodology of sales behaviors analysis linking the historic sales to the items attributes is proposed in this paper. This method is available into a data mining software tool, especially fitted to the strong variations of the textile sales environment and to the short lifetimes of items. An application of this method is proposed using the sales data of a textile firm specializing in sportswear clothes.

16.1.2 Interest of the Proposed Method

Most of the analysis methods of time series lie in a mathematical model based on historic sales. Estimated values are then calculated with a tolerance range (Box and Jenkins (1969)), (Garcia-Cuevas et al. (1981)), (Lewandowski R. (1983)) [5][6][7].

0 ARMA model corresponds to the mathematical model built on the historical sale curve of one item, and often it doesn't take into account the existing interactions between all items sold (Bourbonnais and Usunier (1992)) [8]. Models of ARMAX or ARX type allow us to introduce in the building phase a set of exogenous parameters which enriches the sales explanation (Melard (1990)) [9]. However, all these approaches often remain very complex. In this paper, we propose to build a model explaining the profiles of the items sold from the items characteristics (i.e., color, fabric, ...) using the PLS regression. This model will be used for descriptive purposes when the sales of a past garment collection have to be analyzed and also for forecasting purposes when sales profiles for a new garment collection have to be predicted. The choice of the PLS regression can be justified since it combines theoretical simplicity, efficiency and accuracy in the obtained results.

In this paper, we only present the descriptive part of our methodology. The founder elements of the forecasting part was published in JESA (Boussu and Denimal (2002)) [10].

This descriptive part (Boussu and Denimal (2001)) [11] lies on four successive steps. The first one deals with data preparations necessary to the following steps. The second step aims at extracting relations between sales and items characteristics by using the PLS regression. In the third step, the obtained relations are used for classifying the weeks of the sales season. A partition composed of homogeneous time-periods will be obtained. Finally, the distribution of the items among these time periods is studied in the last and fourth step. Correspondences between each period and their related items will then be obtained. Along these four steps, visualization tools are proposed to help the user in his interpretation work.

16.2 Data Mining Method

16.2.1 From Data to Analyses

Two data tables Y and X as shown in Figure 16.1 are first considered. The former is composed of the sale profiles of items calculated on each week and the latter is a binary table crossing items and their characteristics.

Each cell of the table X crossing the set of items and all the categories of the descriptive parameters (color, fabric, gender,...) contains a value x_{ij} equal to 1 or 0 depending on whether the item i belongs to the category j or not. The table Y crosses the set of items and all the weeks of the sales season. In our case, the value y_{it} represents the value of sale in percentage of the ith item at the tth week. Therefore, the row corresponding to the item i in table Y represents its profile on the whole sales season.

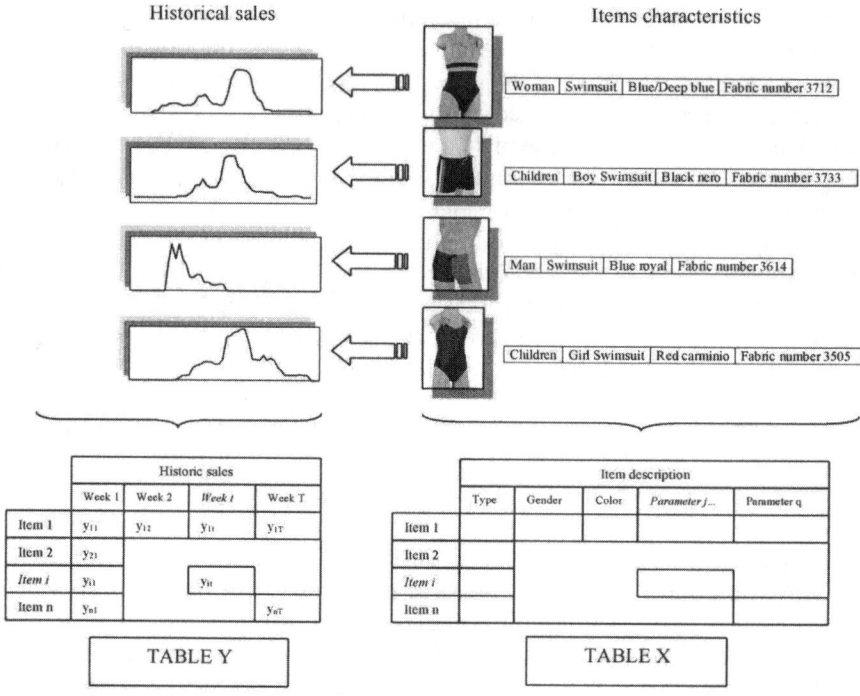

FIGURE 16.1
The data tables.

16.2.2 Proposed Methodology

16.2.2.1 First Step:

The qualitative characteristics (color, fabric, type, gender,...) may be very numerous, defining a large sized table X. We first submit X to Correspondence Analysis (Benzecri (1982)) [12] in order to concentrate the information of X into a smaller sized table, called below reduced X, with little loss of information. This table contains the most significant principal components.

16.2.2.2 Second Step:

A Partial Least Square Regression (PLS Regression, Wold (1966); Esbensen et al. (1984); Martens and Naes (1989); Hoskuldsson (1996)) [13] [14] [15] [16] is then used for the determination of the relations between Y and Reduced X. This last table may be completed by quantitative characteristics, if any, such as price,....

A brief description of this technique is now proposed :

From a theoretical point of view, the PLS regression aims at explaining a set of

q variables $Y = [y^1, y^2, .., y^q]$ from a set of p explanatory variables $X = [x^1, x^2, .., x^p]$. This technique is very useful when p or q become large and sometimes larger than the number of observations and when correlated explanatory variables are observed. The PLS regression can be considered, first as a particular Principal Component Analysis since a set of components is extracted and allows us to obtain graphic plane representations, and second as a modeling procedure since a set of new linear models explaining each response vector y^k is also obtained.

In the first step of the PLS regression, two linear combinations $t^1 = Xw_1$ and $u^1 = Yc_1$, w_1 and c_1 being two vectors respectively composed of p and q coefficients, are searched so that their covariance $cov(t^1, u^1)$ is maximum under the following constraints: $\|w_1\| = \|c_1\| = 1$. Easy calculations show that the vectors w_1 and c_1 are the eigenvectors of the following matrices associated with their respective biggest eigenvalues:

$${}^tX.Y.{}^tY.X.w_1 = \lambda.w_1$$
$${}^tY.X.{}^tX.Y.c_1 = \lambda.c_1$$

A linear combination $t^1 = Xw_1$ is therefore obtained. Simple linear regressions explaining each of the vectors y^k and x^j with respect to t^1 are then carried out. The obtained residual vectors are gathered into two new matrices called X_1 and Y_1.

A second step applies the same process to X_1 and Y_1. Two linear combinations $t^2 = X_1 w_2$ and $u^2 = Y_1.c_2$ are obtained and maximize the covariance $cov(t^2, u^2)$ under similar constraints. This process is resumed as long as the introduction of a new component t^h is judged significant.

This appreciation is based on a cross-validation procedure. More precisely, for each step h, the predicted values $\hat{y}^{th}(l)$ and $\widehat{y_{-i}^{th}}(l)$ are calculated using the model with h components, based on all the observations, then without the observation i. The Residual Sum of squares denoted RSS_{th} and the Predicted Error Sum of Squares denoted $PRESS_{th}$ are first introduced:

$$RSS_{th} = \sum_l \left(y^t(l) - \hat{y}^{th}(l)\right)^2$$

$$PRESS_{th} = \sum_l \left(y^t(l) - \hat{y}_{-i}^{th}(l)\right)^2$$

Then, two criteria are proposed:

$$Q_{th}^2 = 1 - \frac{PRESS_{th}}{RSS_{t(h-1)}}$$

$$Q_h^2 = 1 - \frac{\sum_{t=1}^{q} PRESS_{th}}{\sum_{t=1}^{q} RSS_{t(h-1)}}$$

In SIMCA-P software [17], two rules allow us to decide whether the introduction of a component of order h is significant or not:

Rule 1: $Q_h^2 \geq \left[1 - (0,95)^2\right] = 0,0975$

Rule 2: It can be found at least one index t such that: $Q_{th}^2 \geq 0,0975$. It can be noticed that the rule 1 is more restrictive than the rule 2.

Therefore, using these stopping rules, the PLS regression allows us to extract an orthogonal base composed of PLS factors $t^1, t^2, \ldots, t^r$. New linear models explaining each vector y^k from these PLS factors are then considered.

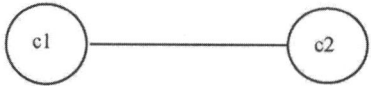

FIGURE 16.2
Representation of a dipole.

In our application, the number S of weeks of the sale season ($S = 52$) represents the number of response variables (Columns of Y). The application of the PLS regression will give us S linear models explaining each response variable with respect to the extracted PLS factors.

16.2.2.3 Third Step:

The aim is to obtain a partition of the sale season. Each obtained group will aggregate consecutive weeks for which the item sales remain unchanged. Between two consecutive groups of weeks, a breakpoint corresponding to major sales behaviors modifications will then be identified. The proposed clustering technique is based on the results of the previous PLS regression and consists in a classification of the response variables (each of them representing a week of the sale season). As regards the classification of the response variables, two approaches are usually applied. The former represents each response variable by its coordinates with respect to the orthogonal base composed of the PLS factors. A usual classification method is then applied, for instance, a hierarchical clustering based on the Ward criterion (Ward (1963)) [18]. The latter, chosen in the following application, considers the orthogonal projections of the response variables into the subspace spanned by the PLS factors. A hierarchical clustering of variables (VARCLUS of SAS (1996)) [19] is then applied to the projected variables. Other techniques of variable clustering are still available and could have been applied and compared (see Rousseeuw and Kaufman (1990); Denimal (2001)) [20][21]. Since this hierarchical clustering gathers, in the same group, positively or negatively correlated variables, each group can be seen as a "dipole" composed of two opposite subgroups of variables (Figure 16.2).

For a dipole $[c_1, c_2]$, one of the groups c_1 and c_2 may be empty. In this case, the dipole can be identified to the remaining non-empty group.

In our application, a dipole represents two subgroups of weeks whose sale behavior differences are explained by opposite item characteristics.

We propose now a brief presentation of the VARCLUS procedure used in the given application. This technique is a descending hierarchical clustering. Therefore, VARCLUS begins with all variables in a single cluster. It then repeats the following steps:

A cluster is chosen for splitting. For each cluster of variables, the Principal Component analysis is carried out on the sub-table associated with this cluster. Depend-

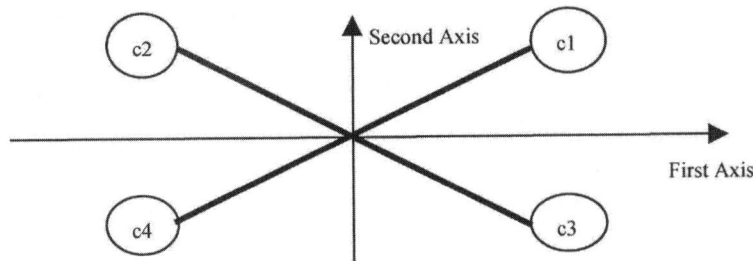

FIGURE 16.3
Graphic representation of a dipole.

ing on the options specified, the selected cluster has either the smallest percentage of variation explained by its cluster component or the largest eigenvalue associated with the second principal component.

The chosen cluster is split into two clusters by finding the first two principal components and assigning each variable to the component with the higher squared correlation ones.

Variables are iteratively assigned to clusters to maximize the variance accounted for the cluster components.

VARCLUS stops when each cluster has only a single eigenvalue greater than one, thus satisfying a popular criterion for determining the sufficiency of a single underlying factor dimension.

Besides, since each cluster is represented by its first component, it is then possible, for each node, to obtain a graphic plane displaying the representative variables of the two groups merging at this node. It is enough to submit to Principal Component Analysis the two-column table composed of these two representative variables. The variables of the two groups merging at the considered node can also be projected in the obtained principal plane as additional elements. Since the items and the categories of the original qualitative variables (color, fabric, ...) can also be represented in the previous representation, a helpful tool of interpretation for each node of the hierarchy is therefore proposed to the user.

In Figure 16.3, a graphic representation is given for a node aggregating the two dipoles $[c_1, c_4]$ and $[c_2, c_3]$

As a stopping rule is also available in the VARCLUS procedure in order to identify the levels where the hierarchy has to be stopped, a set composed of the retained nodes and a partition of the sale season are then determined.

16.2.2.4 Fourth Step:

Based on this partition of the sale season, a classification of items is then carried out by classical techniques (for instance, based on the Ward criterion) applied on the contingency table crossing items and time periods. Graphic representations can be obtained by shading the cells of the previous table with different levels of gray in order to visualize the most important associations between item groups and time periods.

16.2.3 Data Visualization Tools

Different graphic representations for the partition of the sale season into time periods are proposed :
 a) Classical representation of the hierarchy (Figure 16.4).
 b) Circular representation of the hierarchy (Figure 16.5 and Figure 16.6).
 c) Graphic plane representations associated with the nodes (Figure 16.7 and Figure 16.8).
 d) Shaded tables visualizing associations between items and periods (Figure 16.9 and Figure 16.10).

To sum up, the main goal of these graphic representations, displaying the data analysis results, is to give a complete and synthetic view of the sale season to the user.

16.3 Application to a Textile Data Set

16.3.1 Classical and Circular Representations of the Hierarchy

The data-mining method has been applied to a set of data sales extracted from a database of a garment maker of sportswear items. By application of our previously described method, an hierarchical classification can be built on the 52 weeks of the 1994 year. The application of the VARCLUS procedure leads us to a partition composed of 11 different sales periods and to a set of nodes (Figure 16.4). As previously explained, the group of variables obtained at each node can be considered as a dipole. As an example, the dipole corresponding to the highest node opposes the variables 1, 2, 3, 4 (time periods) to the others (see Figure 16.4). For some dipoles, one of the opposed two groups is empty (see the node merging the 10th and 11th time periods). Moreover, to each node of the hierarchy, a plane representing the merged variables is proposed (see §16.2.2.3). For instance, an illustration of this plane is given in Figure 16.4 for the node grouping the 1, 2, 5, 6 time periods.

An other graphic representation of the same hierarchy is now given in Figure 16.5. As well known, a hierarchy can be considered as a succession of partitions. This succession is more clearly displayed in a circular representation. It can be noticed that the smallest circle represents four variable groups coming from the two dipoles (1-2 ; 5-6) and (3-4 ; 7-8-9-10-11). These four big classes roughly represent the four seasons. The seasonal factor is then retrieved by the method. By the same, the largest circle corresponds to the 11 optimal time periods.

If different consecutive sales season years are considered, a spiral representation could be contemplated (see Figure 16.6). In our application, only one year season has been analyzed.

Statistical Data Mining and Knowledge Discovery   289

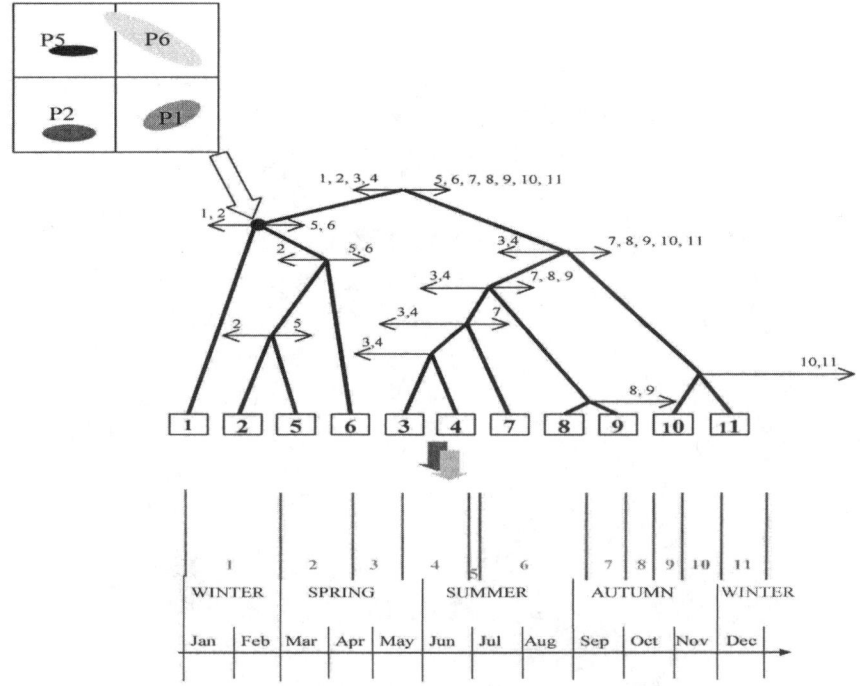

FIGURE 16.4
Classical representation of the hierarchy and the resulted partition.

The identification of these 11 sales periods brings a new knowledge of the sales evolution of all the textile items of the collection. Some periods can be easily explained due to their concordance with the main seasons of the year as winter or summer. The breakdowns between periods can be explained by the calendar events as the 5th period which represents a turning point between the spring's end and the summer's beginning. This cut-point seems to be strict and precisely located. The boundary dividing the 1st period and the 2nd period can be explained by the end of the sales season in February and the beginning of the summer collection in March. By the same, the start of the new school term at the beginning of September also shows the strong change between the 6th and 7th period.

16.3.2 Graphic Plane Representations Associated with Nodes

As previously said, a particular Principal Component Analysis (PCA) is carried out for each node. We propose below the graphic representations given by the two PCA associated with two nodes of the hierarchy including the highest one. To remain as clear as possible, all the points have not been represented, but just the most outstanding ones.

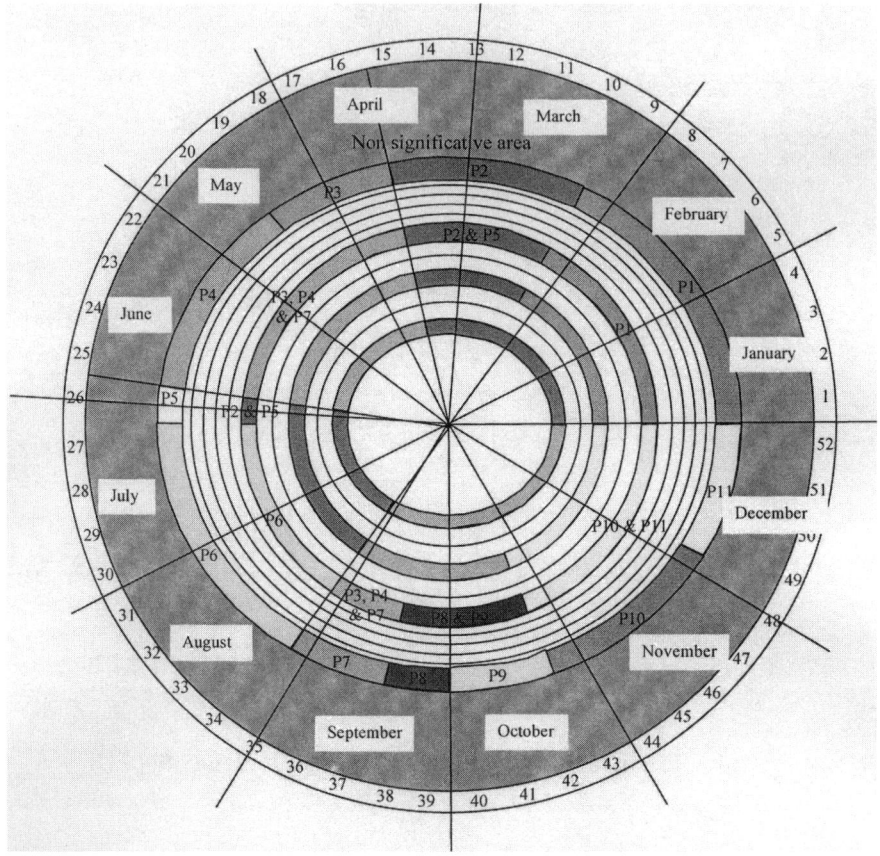

FIGURE 16.5
Circular representation of the hierarchy.

Considering the graphic representation associated to the highest node (Figure 16.7), a new knowledge is then revealed to the practitioner, showing the distribution of the sales periods coupled with the main items attributes. Boy swimsuits items are mainly sold during the July and August period. In opposition, girl tights items are mainly sold during the January and February period. The woman tights and man shorts items are mainly sold during the October, November and December period. On the contrary, man swimsuits items are principally sold from March to middle of April.

In the same way, the other nodes of the hierarchy could be explained through the inspection of their associated graphic representations. We have chosen, for example, to present the node merging the periods 3 and 4 (Figure 16.8). In this case, the corresponding dipole created at this node is composed of the single class 3, 4. Thus, the graphic representation associated with this node will show the similarities and the

Statistical Data Mining and Knowledge Discovery

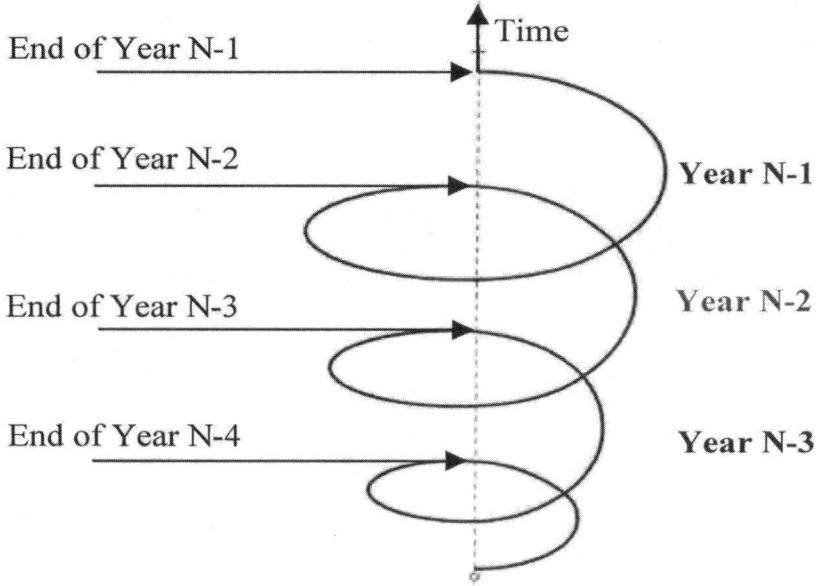

FIGURE 16.6
Spiral representation of successive sales seasons.

dissimilarities observed between these two periods. It can be noticed that the first one gathers the weeks 16 to 19 and the second one the weeks 20 to 25. The transition between these two periods seems to be due to the turning point of Easter day. The man swimsuits are mainly located to the sales period before Easter day, as opposed to girl leotards occurring to the sales weeks after Easter day. This new information brings a new understanding of the sales items evolution during the sales season. Attributes of these items contribute to give an explanation of the sales distribution during the merged weeks from 16 to 25.

16.3.3 Shaded Tables Visualizing Associations Between Items and Periods

A hierarchical classification is carried out from the contingency table crossing items and the previous 11 time periods by using the Ward clustering method. A cut point of the hierarchy is determined by the application of the Mojena and Wishart technique [22] based on the Ward criterion. A partition of 8 item groups (labeled from A to H) is then obtained. In the aggregated table (Figure 16.9), profiles of these 8 item groups along the 11 optimal time periods are displayed. In order to visualize the most important associations, a gray scale is introduced. The more black the case is, the more important association is. As a consequence, permanent and seasonal items

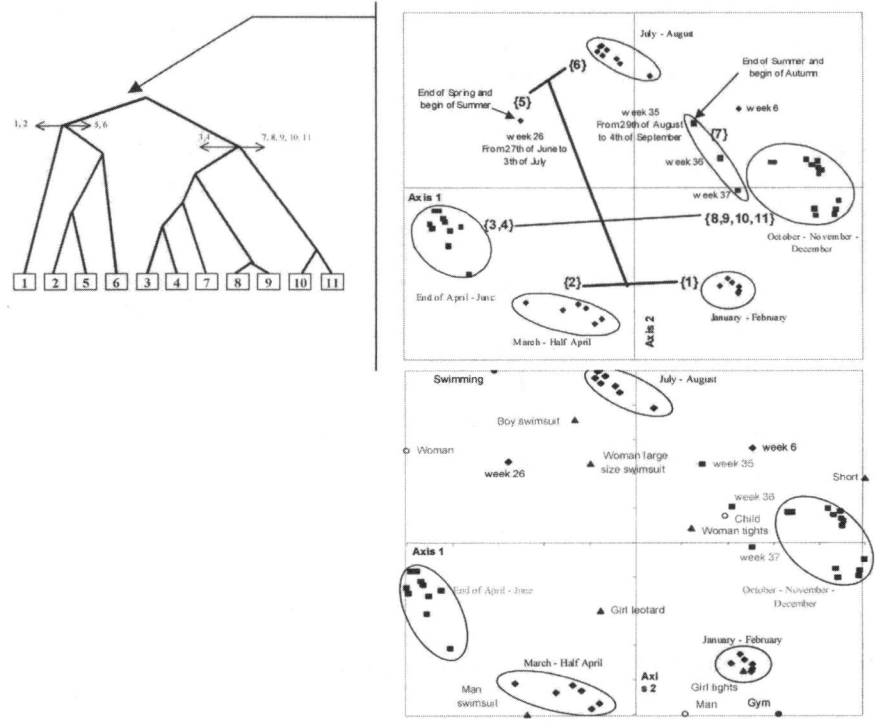

FIGURE 16.7
Hierarchical distribution of sales periods and explanation of the sales season.

have been roughly identified. A second table (Figure 16.10) describes the contents of the different 8 item groups.

16.4 Conclusion

The proposed methodology, well adapted to the constraints of the textile sales environment, first splits the sales season into homogeneous periods and second identifies the items attributes characterizing each of them. Data visualization tools help the user to obtain quickly the information previously hidden in the data. As an example, the graphic plane representation associated with the highest node of the hierarchy allows us to obtain a global view of the whole season. This global view is then completed by the other plane representations. The latter associated with lower nodes may be considered as a close-up of different parts of the sales season. Therefore, a complete understanding of the sales season is then obtained, which will help the chief executive to plan a new textile items collection for the next season taking into account the knowledge acquired from the previous one.

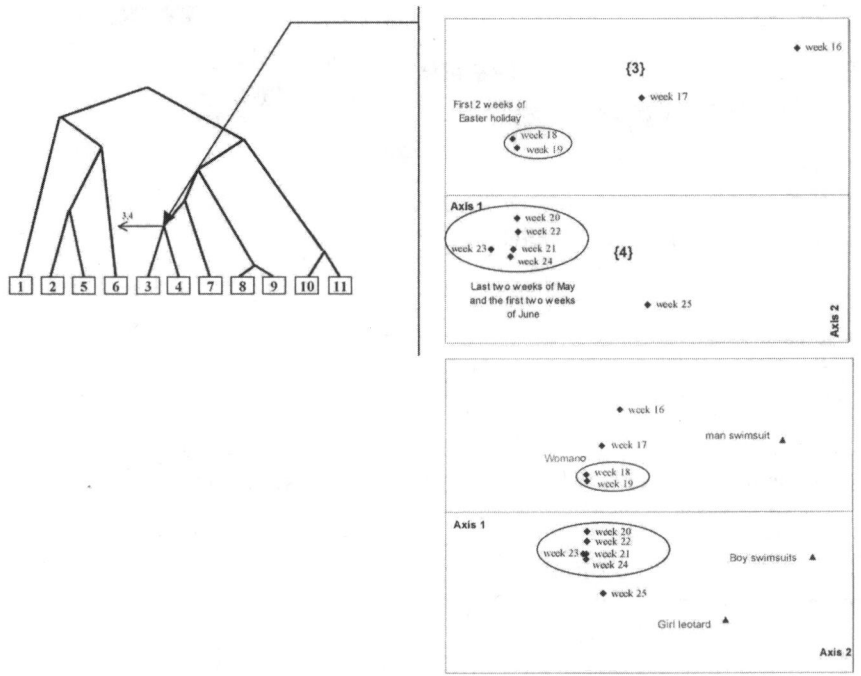

FIGURE 16.8
Explanation of the merging evolution of the 3rd and 4th periods.

Items group		WINTER		SPRING			SUMMER			AUTUMN			
		Jan	Feb	Mar	Apr	May	Jun	Jul	Aug	Sep	Oct	Nov	Dec
		Optimal Periods											
		1	2	3	4	5	6	7	8	9	10	11	
A	Permanent items	13,1		5,16	7,2	3		12,2	6,16	8,8	14,5	11	1,1
B		7,2	11,9	8,27		5			8,88	4,8	5,63	5,44	1
C		0	2,77	10	14,5	2		13,6	8,8	10,7	15,3		2,5
D	Seasonal items	0				5	0	0	0	0	0	0	0
E		0	3,45		52,9	11	8,47	0	0	0	0	0	0
F		1,09	4,15	7,75		4	56,7	4,3	1,5	1,94	1,76	0,2	
G		0	1,18	5,66	13,2	3	52,3	9,78	4,2	4,92	4,73	0,8	
H		0	0	0	0	0	0	0	3	16,4	38,9	42	

FIGURE 16.9
Visualization of the association between the 8 item groups and the 11 optimal time periods.

Type	Swim				Gym					
Gender	Woman	Child	Man		Woman			Child		
Description	Bathing suit	Girl and Boy bathing suit	Bathing suit	Short	Tights	Leotard	Cyclist	Tights	Leotard	Cyclist
A										
B										■
C					■					
D			■							
E	■	■			■					
F	■									
G										
H			■							

FIGURE 16.10
Description of the contents of each item group.

Acknowledgment

The authors want to thank the data-processing and logistic manager and chief executive of the firm for giving us the data sales of the sportswear items.

References

[1] Batra, S.K. and Brookstein, D. (2002). Rethinking the U.S. "textile industry." In *2nd World Textile AUTEX conference*, Bruges, Belgium, July 1-3, 2002.

[2] Aneja, A.P. (2002). Transforming textile. In *2nd World Textile AUTEX conference*, Bruges, Belgium, July 1-3, 2002.

[3] Traci, M.P. and Trevor, J.L. (2001). Consumer purchase data as a strategic product development tool, *Journal of Textile and Apparel, Technology and Management*, Volume 1, Issue 3.

[4] Moore, M., Cassill, N., Herr, D. and Williamson, N. (2001). Marketing fashion color for product line extension in the department store channel, *Journal of Textile and Apparel, Technology and Management*, Volume 1, Issue 2, 2001.

[5] Box,, G.E.P. and Jenkins, G.M. (1969). *Time series analysis — Forecasting and Control*. Prentice Hall, New York.

[6] Garcia-Cuevas, G.J., Kirton, T. and Lowe, P.H. (1981). Demand forecasting for an integrated fashion business, *Clothing Research Journal*, pp. 3-15.

[7] Lewandowski, R. (1983). *La Prévision à Court Terme*, Dunod Editions, France.

[8] Bourbonnais, R. and Usunier, J.C. (1992). *Pratique de la Prévision des Ventes — Conception de Systèmes*, Economica Editions, France.

[9] Melard, G. (1990). *Methodes de Prévision à Court Terme*, Ellipses Editions, Bruxelles.

[10] Boussu, F. and Denimal, J.J. (2002). Estimation des comportements de vente d'articles textiles, *Revue JESA, Journal Européen des Systèmes Automatisés*, 2(36), pp. 223-244.

[11] Boussu, F. and Denimal, J.J. (2001). Hierarchical Classification of Linear Models coming from a PLS Regression. Application to Textile Sale Data Mining. In *Workshop ICDM: Integrating Data Mining and Knowledge Management*, San Jose, California, November 29 to December 2.

[12] Benzecri, J.P. (1982). *L'analyse des données*, Dunod Editions, France.

[13] Wold, H. (1966). Estimation of Principal Components and Related Models by Iterative Least Squares. In *Multivariate Analysis*, Krishnnaiah, P.R.(ed.), Academic Press, New York, pp. 391-420.

[14] Esbensen, K., Schonkopf, S. and Midtgaard, T.(1994). Multivariate Analysis in Practice. In *CAMO, Olav Tryggvasons gt. 24*, N-7011, Norway, Trondheim.

[15] Martens, H. and Naes, T. (1989). *Multivariate Calibration*. John Wiley and Sons, New York.

[16] Hoskuldsson, A. (1996). Prediction methods in science and technology. In *Basic Theory*, Thor Publishing, Denmark.

[17] Umetri, A. B. (1996). Simca-P for windows, graphical software for multivariate process modeling. In Umetri A.B., Box 7960, S-90719 Umea, Sweden.

[18] Ward, J.H. (1963). Hierarchical grouping to optimize an objective function, *Journal of the American Statistical Association*, 58, pp. 236-244.

[19] SAS/STAT (1996). In *User's Guide*, SAS Institute Inc., Cary, NC.

[20] Rousseuw, P.J. and Kaufmann, L. (1990). *Finding groups in data. An introduction to cluster analysis*. John Wiley and Sons, New York.

[21] Denimal, J.J. (2001). Hierarchical Factorial Analysis. In *10th Symposium of Applied Stochastic Models and Data Analysis*, Volume 1, Compiègne, France.

[22] Mojena, R. and Wishart, D. (1980). Stopping rule for Ward's clustering method. In *Compstat 80, Proceedings in Computational Statistics*, Physica Verlag, Wien, pp. 426-432.

17

Testing for Structural Change Over Time of Brand Attribute Perceptions in Market Segments

Sara Dolničar and Friedrich Leisch
University of Wollongong, and Vienna University of Technology, Austria

CONTENTS

17.1 Introduction	297
17.2 The Managerial Problem	298
17.3 Results from Traditional Analysis	299
17.4 The PBMS and DynPBMS Approaches	300
17.5 Summary	306
Acknowledgments	306
References	307

17.1 Introduction

Branding is a major strategic issue in times of increasing competition. Companies that market branded products routinely conduct market research studies investigating the image of their own brand as well as the image of the competitors. Despite acknowledgment of the importance of brand image as well as the routine in analyzing market data on a regular basis, the traditional approaches suffer from misconceptions that can be overcome by simultaneously analyzing three-way data with respect to segmentation, positioning and competition. Dynamic perceptions based market segmentation (dynPBMS), based on the PBMS approach [5, 1], is a tool that achieves this goal, offering a number of advantages:

- Generic product images are revealed in addition to brand-specific images.

- Consumer heterogeneity is automatically accounted for in the process.

- All strategic marketing issues (segmentation, positioning and competition) are treated simultaneously thus avoiding the problems occurring when sequential analyses and managerial decisions have to be taken and consequently the entire strategy cannot be optimized.

17.2 The Managerial Problem

This article is the result of a cooperation with an international company from the chemical industry that provided the data set for the empirical study. Brands are treated anonymously. The management interest in improved data analysis results from the motivation

- to understand the image of the own brands on the marketplace,

- to gain insight in the images of the competing brands,

- to evaluate the amount of competition on the marketplace,

- to be supported in making the integrated strategic decision of which segment to address with which brand image (image position) at a predefined level of competition.

A wide variety of tools has been proposed in the past to tackle the strategic issues of segmentation, positioning and competition (comprehensively outlined in [6] and [4], but most of them treat these issues as independent or sequential. Even in preference maps, including both perceptions and preferences of consumers, the heterogeneity of consumers (the reason for segmentation) is not automatically accounted for. The PBMS approach [5, 1] simultaneously deals with these issues, deriving insights and recommendations from one single analysis based on the same empirical data set. Dynamic PBMS is a simple extension of PBMS, additionally revealing shifts in the attribution of brands over generic perceptual positions over multiple periods of time.

In this article, the traditional approach (as described to us as standard approach within the market research department of the company) of treating the managerial questions is compared to the dynPBMS approach pointing out the consequences for managerial decision support. For this purpose dishwashing brand survey data from the years 2000 and 2001 for an eastern European country are explored. Respondents stated whether each of 25 listed product attributes applies to five dishwashing brands or not. The three-way data include 25 attributes and five brands, one of which was only included in 2000. The sample size is 517 in the year 2000 and 516 in 2001. Only women were questioned. The total row number in the data set consequently equals to 4649. A very large amount of missing data was detected: 1492 pure zero vectors indicating either a missing perception on the brand or a missing evaluation.

Statistical Data Mining and Knowledge Discovery

		A	B	C	D	E	avg
Q1	want to buy	64	26	77	29	12	46
Q2	gentle to hands	67	25	78	28	11	46
Q3	removes grease	70	32	81	33	12	51
Q4	good cleaning power	70	32	81	34	13	51
Q5	dishes shiny	71	34	81	35	13	52
Q6	good smell	69	30	79	33	11	49
Q7	universal use	65	30	71	31	11	46
Q8	economic	64	28	69	33	14	46
Q9	good value for money	63	28	67	31	14	45
Q10	cheap	37	34	20	39	22	31
Q11	a lot of foam	69	37	77	37	14	51
Q12	modern brand	70	21	81	36	12	49
Q13	pleasant smell	68	27	78	33	11	48
Q14	refill avail.	73	19	77	40	9	49
Q15	trustworthy	70	33	82	34	13	51
Q16	nice color	69	28	80	36	13	50
Q17	effective lukewarm	64	27	75	30	12	46
Q18	bottle easy to handle	74	37	81	41	16	55
Q19	easy to rinse off	71	36	78	39	14	53
Q20	thick liquid	69	29	79	35	11	50
Q21	easy to dose	73	38	81	43	15	55
Q22	expensive	40	13	72	14	4	32
Q23	like in ad	42	9	51	15	3	27
Q24	antibacterial	49	13	64	18	6	34
Q25	vinegar	47	9	56	14	3	30

TABLE 17.1
Results from typical traditional marketing survey analysis: Percentage of agreement per question (Q1–Q25) for each of the five brands A–E and overall average.

17.3 Results from Traditional Analysis

17.3.1 Brand Image Analysis

Analysis of variance resulted in brand profiles and the evaluation of brand differences. Each attribute turns out as being significant at the 99.9% level. The percentage of agreement values are given in Table 17.1. Each column represents the brand profile for one brand; the last column provides the overall average value.

The brand profiles arrived at are not very informative. No distinct images can be derived. Mostly, it is purely the level of agreement that contrasts brands. The only two attributes deserving further mentioning are "cheap" and "expensive." Considering these items and the remaining 23 as one single piece of information (which well mirrors the brand profiles arrived at) two kinds of brands seem to exist in the womens' minds: those that are very attractive and offer most advantages of a top dishwashing liquid, but are perceived as rather expensive (A and C) and those that do not offer high quality but are cheap (D, B and E).

Even when additional information is taken into account and included into analysis in the sense of an *a priori* subsample definition, no distinct profiles emerge. Neither income, nor education, city type or age help to reveal any perceptual images of the brands studied. Not even the distinction between users of the brands and non-users provides additional insights into the criteria of differentiation. The only effect of the latter approach is that users show a higher agreement level for "their" brand, shifting the entire values higher.

Comparing the attributes assigned to each brand over two years does not result in clear image changes. Significance of results varies over attributes and brands not following any logic or being interpretable as a result of advertising campaigns.

17.3.2 Competition Analysis

Competition is typically deducted from studying aggregated data, as, e.g., the market share. As choice data were not available, the survey question about frequency of use is explored. The resulting distribution indicates that brands C and A would be believed to be toughest competitors in the market with 44% and 31% market share, respectively. The remaining brands do not even reach the 10% border.

The analysis suggests the following insights: the relevant image attributes on the dishwashing market are "quality" and "price." Brands are perceived differently with regard to these criteria. Brands A and C are competing in the marketplace for the "high-quality" image. No dramatic image changes have occurred, not even image changes that would have been expected as result of advertising action.

17.4 The PBMS and DynPBMS Approaches

17.4.1 General Principles

A general principle of PBMS is that market segments can be defined as *generic* positions in image space (independent of brand, date, respondent, ...). This corresponds to the underlying central question: *"How can a product possibly be seen?"* The consumer population is assumed to be heterogeneous, such that no global models can capture the market structure.

One state-of-the-art approach is to use parametric mixtures to model consumer heterogeneity; see [8] for a comprehensive introduction. However, mixture models make rigid assumptions on the distribution of data and for several popular distributions (e.g., the binomial or multinomial) can only be used if repeated measurements per individual are available. Hence, it makes sense to complement the parametric models by nonparametric approaches using fewer assumptions on the data generating process. As we will show below, results from nonparametric procedures revealing heterogeneity can be used directly and give much more insight into the structure of the data than traditional global models. The approach could also be used as an exploratory step before parametric (mixture) model building.

17.4.2 Complexity Reduction

The idea of perceptions based market segmentation (PBMS) can best be described as a stepwise process. Starting point is a three-way data set with one row in the data set representing the information provided by *one respondent* with respect to *one brand* evaluating a number of *variables* (here questions Q1–Q25). A *generic* perceptual position is now defined as a brand profile with consumer and brand information removed; the three-way data set is reduced to a matrix by collapsing the brand dimension and stacking the consumer × question matrices for each brand on top of each other.

DynPBMS is a natural generalization for multi-way tables, most namely for repeated surveys over time as in our application. We have two three-way data sets (from 2000 and 2001), which are joined to one matrix of generic positions over time by ignoring (in this step of the analysis) both brand and time of each profile. However, the space of generic positions is still rather high-dimensional ($d = 25$ dimensions in our case). Fitting a mixture model that accounts for consumer heterogeneity is both computationally demanding and needs a huge number of respondents in order to avoid the curse of dimensionality (e.g., see [3]).

Following [5] we reduce the d-dimensional brand images $x = (x_1, \ldots, x_d)'$ to univariate variables c with nominal scale, $c \in \{1, \ldots, C\}$, indicating cluster membership. This compression is performed using standard vector quantization techniques like k-means clustering. The compression algorithm should preserve as much information as possible for the subsequent tests on market heterogeneity, hence the choice of clustering algorithm makes a difference [7]. We chose to use the classic k-means clustering algorithm mostly for the following reasons:

- Minimum variance partitions are optimal for several important decision problems, e.g., centered likelihood ratio for discriminant problems [5].

- The algorithm is simple, well understood and familiar to many practitioners.

- The cluster centers are mean values, which in the case of our binary data corresponds to percentage of agreement and is the natural summary for this kind of data.

Figure 17.1 shows the cluster centers from k-means with $k = 7$ centers. The number of clusters was determined by choosing the most stable solution over several repetitions. The bars represent the cluster centers, i.e., the percentage of respondents answering "Yes" to the respective question within the segment. The horizontal lines show the total mean (last column in Table 17.1 for comparison). Cluster #4 almost completely agrees with the global sample mean, whereas Cluster #5 is an answer tendency with "No" to all questions. Clusters #6 and #7 have high agreement

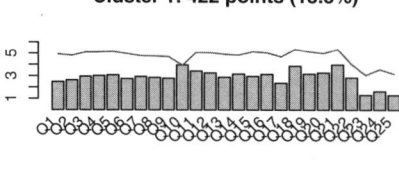
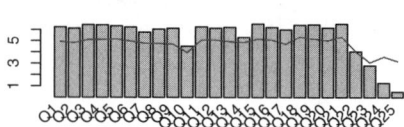
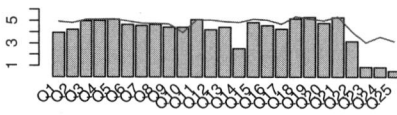
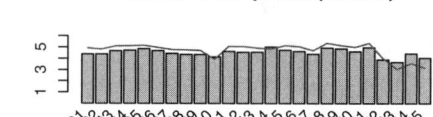
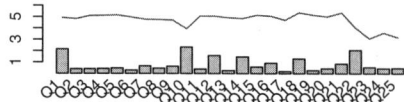
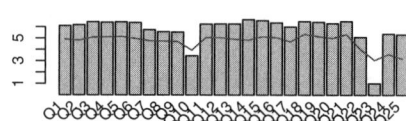
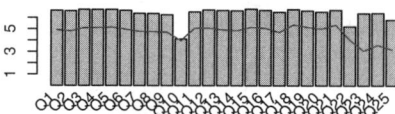

FIGURE 17.1
Cluster profiles (bars) versus overall mean values horizontal lines.

to all questions except Q10 ("cheap"), the difference between the two is whether customers see the product as it is advertised, i.e., if advertising and daily product perception agree (Q23).

Note that the number of clusters is not really important for the subsequent steps of the analysis, because we use the clustering algorithm as vector quantization technique, projecting the d-dimensional space onto a 1-dimensional nominal scale. The only important thing is that the partition is fine enough to capture the consumer heterogeneity. Figure 17.2 shows a 2-dimensional projection of the cluster centers using multi-dimensional scaling [2]. The circles represent the size of the clusters. The thickness of the connecting lines in the neighborhood graph is proportional to the number of data points having the respective other center as 2nd closest. This helps a little bit to understand how close the projection is to the cluster relations in

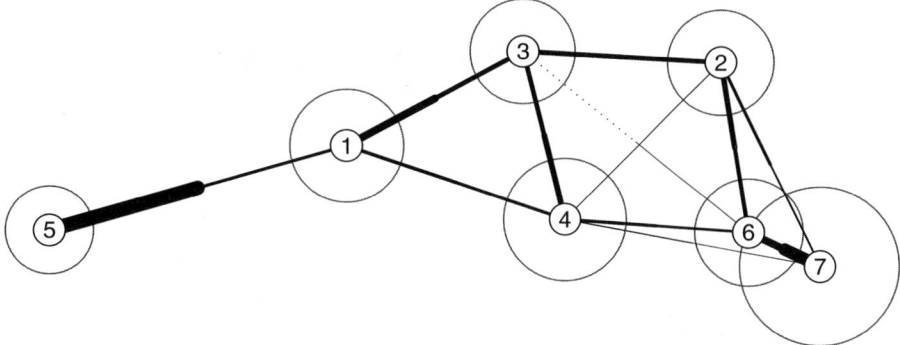

FIGURE 17.2
Neighborhood graph of the clusters.

original space, e.g., in Figure 17.2 it looks as if #6 were in between #4 and #7. The connecting line between #4 and #7 shows that the three clusters form a triangle and that partitions #4 and #7 share a common hyperplane as border.

17.4.3 Tests on Heterogeneity

The result from clustering is a grouping of perceptual patterns that allows insights into generic perceptions of dishwashing liquids as well as (once brand information is revealed) the strength of association of each brand with each particular generic image position. As brands and time information have not been used in the complexity reduction step, we can use standard statistical tests on the independence of categorical variables.

Under the null hypothesis of no differences between the perception of the different brands, all brands should be distributed uniformly over the seven clusters. Table 17.2 shows a contingency table of brands by cluster; Pearson's χ^2 test for independence rejects the null with $p < 2.2e - 16$.

Given heterogeneity, the natural next question is which segments deviate from independence. Let N be the total number of observations, t_{cb} be the entry in row b and column c of the contingency table, and let $t_{c.}$ and $t_{.b}$ denote the row and column totals, respectively. If the number of brands B and number of clusters C are large, then we can assume the residuals

$$r_{cb} = \frac{(t_{cb} - t_{c.}t_{.b}/N)^2}{t_{c.}t_{.b}/N}$$

to be approximately independent χ_1^2 and use the quantiles of the χ^2 distribution together with a correction for multiple testing to search for significant entries in the contingency table.

	A	B	C	D	E
1	59	139	25	160	39
2	116	56	114	69	13
3	50	171	25	96	22
4	146	93	83	157	18
5	35	71	24	78	48
6	133	27	179	38	4
7	311	33	436	56	3

TABLE 17.2
Contingency table of brands (A–E) and clusters (1–7).

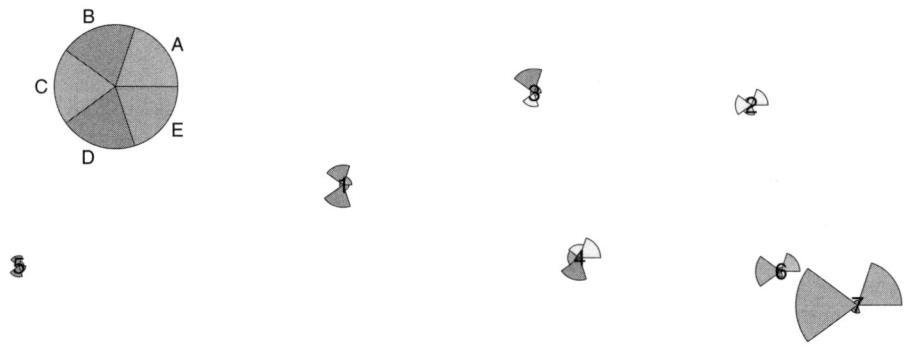

FIGURE 17.3
Distribution of brands over clusters.

If B or C is small, we have to use permutation tests: draw random tables with the same column and row sums as the observed table and use the maximum residual

$$\max_{c,b} r_{cb}$$

as test statistic (this already corrects for multiple testing on all elements of the matrix). Figure 17.3 shows a visualization of the results from permutation tests: Each pie chart corresponds to one cluster (and hence one row of the contingency table); the size of the slices is proportional to the corresponding element t_{cb} of the table. Colored slices correspond to significant residuals (dark shading: $\alpha = 0.01$, light shading: $\alpha = 0.05$); white slices are not significant; e.g., cluster #7 contains significantly more profiles from brands A and C than expected under independence.

In addition to brand and year, we also have information on which brand was used most often by which respondent in the months preceding the respective survey. Figure 17.4 shows the results from cross-tabulating segments, choice and time. TRUE:2000 corresponds to the brand used most often in 2000 by a respondent,

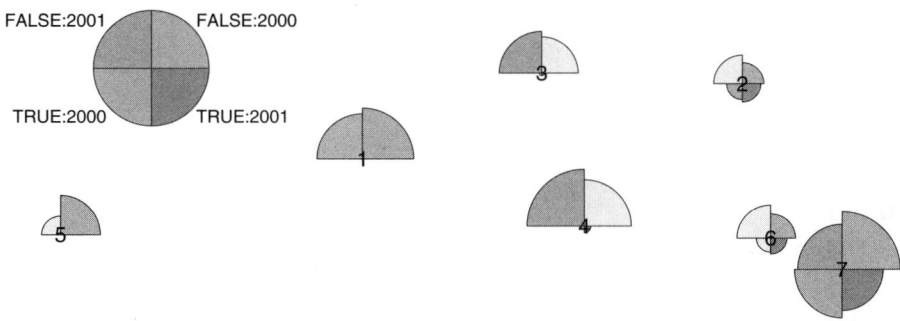

FIGURE 17.4
Distribution of most often used brands per year over clusters.

FALSE:2000 to the remaining 4 brands. It can easily be seen that only clusters #2, #6 and #7 are attractive perceptual position, as almost all choices are contained in these segments. The market is also dynamic: the size of cluster #7 decreases from 2000 to 2001 (both in choices and non-choices), while #2 and #6 are increasing. As the only difference between #6 and #7 is agreement between perception and advertising of the respective brand, this finding has immediate consequences for the marketing strategy. Almost all zero profiles (#5) are from the year 2000, meaning that either respondents in 2001 were more motivated to answer all questions or that the different products had a much more distinct profile, i.e., consumer awareness of the different brands was higher.

17.4.4 Competition Analysis

The concept of competition in dynPBMS is based on disaggregate perceptions. Competition is believed to be encountered, when one individual places two or more brands at the same position, thus denoting perceptual substitutability. Analyzing the competitive relations between the brands based on the 7 cluster grouping of perceptions leads to the coefficients given in Table 17.2. The coefficients indicate the percentage of the respondents that locate pairs of brands at the same position.

There are two groups of brands competing in the marketplace: the high-profile brands A-C, and the low-profile brands B-D-E. However, competition is less pronounced than what would have been expected from the traditional analysis; the majority of consumers (about 60%) perceives the two competing brands A and C differently. Also, the disappearance of brand E did not increase competition between B and D in 2001: the latter two increased competition with brand C (the market leader), while B-D competition remained constant.

This can be explained by the fact that B and D are perceived differently by consumers: B is overrepresented in cluster #3, while D is in cluster #4. Both are not very attractive positions with only few choices. A natural strategy for B is to try to attack position #2, while D could go for #7. Another immediate consequence for B is to

	A	B	C	D	E
B	0.21				
C	0.38	0.12			
D	0.27	0.38	0.14		
E	0.16	0.39	0.08	0.42	

TABLE 17.3
Competition coefficients for 2000.

	A	B	C	D
B	0.19			
C	0.41	0.14		
D	0.25	0.39	0.21	

TABLE 17.4
Competition coefficients for 2001 (brand E was only available in 2000).

rethink their advertising strategy, because consumers do not think that the product is as in the commercials.

17.5 Summary

We have used a case study from an eastern European detergent market to introduce the dynPBMS approach for market segmentation. Brand images are clustered to generic positions in perceptual space, which can subsequently be used to test for differences in how consumers perceive different brands and measure competition between brands. In addition to standard PBMS we also track perceptions over time and test for structural changes in the market. Although the procedure is fully non-parametric and makes only minimal assumptions about the data generating process, all claims are supported by statistical tests that account for random fluctuations.

Acknowledgments

This piece of research was supported by the Austrian Science Foundation (FWF) under grant SFB#010 ('Adaptive Information Systems and Modeling in Economics and Management Science'). We thank our partners from industry for making the data set available for research purposes and granting permission to publish our results.

References

[1] Christian Buchta, Sara Dolnicar, and Thomas Reutterer. (2000). *A nonparametric approach to perceptions-based marketing: Applications.* Interdisciplinary Studies in Economics and Management. Springer-Verlag, Berlin, Germany.

[2] Cox, T. F. and Cox, M. A. A. (1994). *Multidimensional Scaling.* Chapman and Hall, London.

[3] Hastie, T., Tibshirani, R. and Friedman, J. (2001). *The Elements of Statistical Learning (Data Mining, Inference and Prediction).* Springer-Verlag, Heidelberg.

[4] Lilien, G. L. and Rangaswamy, A. (1998). *Marketing Engineering — Computer-Assisted Marketing Analysis and Planning.* Addison-Wesley, Reading, MA.

[5] Mazanec, J. A. and Strasser, H. (2000). *A nonparametric approach to perceptions-based marketing: Foundations.* Interdisciplinary Studies in Economics and Management. Springer-Verlag, Berlin, Germany.

[6] Myers, J. H. (1996). *Segmentation and Positioning for Strategic Marketing Decisions.* American Marketing Association, Chicago.

[7] Rahnenführer, J. (2002). Multivariate permutation tests for the k-sample problem with clustered data. *Computational Statistics*, 17, 165-184.

[8] Wedel, M. and Kamakura, W. A. (1998). *Market Segmentation — Conceptual and Methodological Foundations.* Kluwer Academic Publishers, Boston.

18

Kernel PCA for Feature Extraction with Information Complexity

Zhenqiu Liu and Hamparsum Bozdogan
University of Tennessee, Knoxville, USA

CONTENTS

18.1 Introduction 310
18.2 Kernel Functions 312
18.3 Kernel PCA 314
18.4 EM for Kernel PCA and On-line PCA 318
18.5 Choosing the Number of Components with Information Complexity 319
18.6 Computational Results 320
18.7 Conclusions 321
    Acknowledgments 321
    References 321

In this paper, we deal with modelling or extracting information from an unlabelled data sample. In many real world applications appropriate preprocessing transformations of high dimensional input data can increase overall performance of algorithms. Feature extraction tries to find a compact description of the interesting features of the data. This can be useful for visualization of higher dimensional data in two or three dimensions or for data compression. It can also be applied as a preprocessing step that enables reducing the dimension of the data to be handled by a subsequent model. In this paper, we mainly concentrate on kernel PCA for feature selection in a higher dimensional feature space. We first introduce the usefulness of EM algorithm for standard PCA. We then present the kernel PCA. Kernel PCA is a nonlinear extension of PCA based on the kernel transformation (Scholkopf, Smola, and Muller 1997). It requires the eigenvalue decomposition of a so-called kernel matrix of size $N \times N$. In this contribution we propose an expectation maximization approach for performing kernel principal component analysis. Moreover we will introduce an online algorithm of EM for PCA. We show this to be a computationally efficient method especially when the number of data points is large. The information criteria of Bozdogan together with others are used to decide the number of eigenvalues.

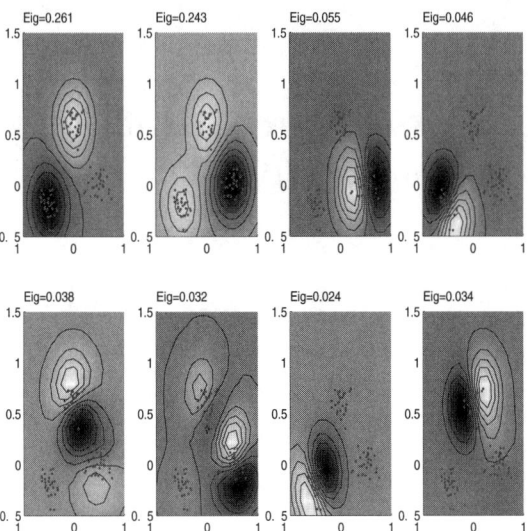

FIGURE 18.1
Nonlinear component contours using the PE kernel.

18.1 Introduction

Let $\mathbf{x}^n$ be an d dimensional data i.e., $\mathbf{x}^n = (x_1^n, \ldots, x_d^n) \in R^d$. Further let

$$D = \{x^1, x^2, \ldots, x^N\}$$

denote the available random sample from the probability distribution of the random vector x. No explicit assumptions on the probability density of the vectors (variables) are made in PCA, as long as the first and second order statistics are known or can be estimated from the sample. It is essential in PCA that the elements are mutually correlated, and there is some redundancy in $\mathbf{x}$, making the PCA possible. If the elements are independent, nothing can be achieved by PCA.

Principal component analysis has several important properties. First, in the optimal (in terms of mean squared error) linear scheme we may compress a set of high dimensional vectors into a set of lower dimensional vectors and then reconstruct. Second, the model parameters can be computed directly from the data, for example by diagonalizing the sample covariance. Third, compression and decomposition are easy operations to perform given the model parameters, since they require only matrix multiplications.

Despite these attractive features, PCA has several shortcomings (Roweis 1998). One is the naive methods for finding the principle component directions have trouble with high dimensional data or large number of data points. Another shortcoming

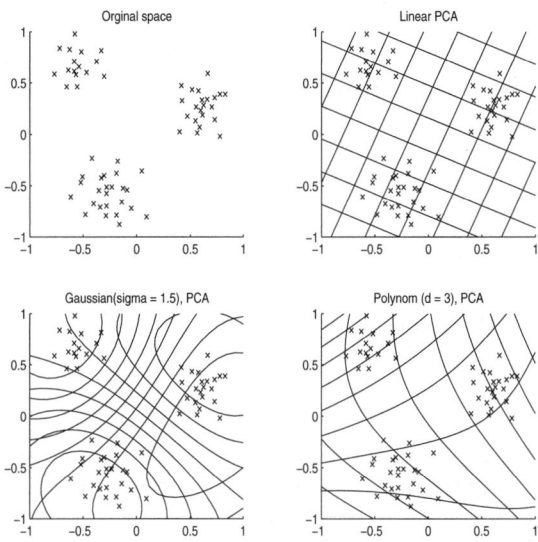

FIGURE 18.2
Nonlinear component contours of different PCAs.

of the standard approach to PCA is that it is not obvious how to deal properly with missing data. Incomplete data points must either be discarded or completed using a variety of ad hoc interpolation methods. Finally, the PCA model itself suffers from a critical flaw which is independent of the techniques used to compute its parameters: it does not define a proper probability model in the space of the input.

In the last couple of years, in the literature there have been many papers published about the PCA. PCA trained using the EM algorithm seems to be an attractive way of doing standard PCA. For feature extraction, see, e.g., Roweis (1998). Of course, a host of other approaches exists for doing PCA. A general technique is to first compute the sample covariance matrix, which is $O(d^2 N)$, followed by any general method which solves a symmetric eigenvalue problem (Golub and Van Loan 1996). The more advanced methods are able to extract a specific number l of principal eigenvectors and are in general $O(ld^2)$. One can avoid computing the sample covariance matrix and its typical problems with a small amount of data in a high-dimensional space, by computing the singular value decomposition of the $N \times d$ matrix containing the training data (Ripley 1996). A disadvantage of these techniques is that, in general, they require storing the entire covariance matrix or the entire data matrix. This has motivated the development of incremental techniques from the fields of neural networks. One class of methods use some form of Hebbian learning on a one layer neural network to find the principal subspace (Diamantaras and Kung 1996).

The EM algorithm for PCA combines several of the advantages of the above methods. It doesn't require computing the covariance matrix and is only $O(ldN) + O(l^2 d)$ when extracting the l principal eigenvectors.

Principal component analysis can be viewed as a limiting case of a particular class of linear Gaussian models, assuming that **x** was produced by a linear transformation of some l dimensional latent variable z plus additive Gaussian noise. Denoting the transformation by a $d \times l$ matrix **C**, and the noise by **v** (with covariance matrix **R**) the generative model can be written as

$$\mathbf{x} = \mathbf{Cz} + \mathbf{v} \qquad \mathbf{z} \sim \mathcal{N}(\mathbf{0}, \mathbf{I}) \qquad \mathbf{v} \sim \mathcal{N}(\mathbf{0}, \mathbf{R}).$$

The latent or cause variables **z** are assumed to be identically distributed according to a unit spherical Gaussian. Since **v** is also independent and normally distributed (and we assume independent **z**), the model simplifies to a single Gaussian model for **x**, which we can write explicitly:

$$\mathbf{x} \sim \mathcal{N}(\mathbf{0}, \mathbf{CC}^\mathbf{T} + \mathbf{R}),$$

where $\mathbf{x} \in R^d$ and $\mathbf{z} \in R^l$, respectively. It is shown in (Roweis and Ghahramani 1998; Tipping and Biship 1999) that as the noise level in the model becomes infinitesimal the PCA model is recovered, i.e., when $R = lim_{\varepsilon \to 0} \varepsilon I$, the posterior density then becomes a delta function

$$P(\mathbf{z}|\mathbf{x}) = \delta(\mathbf{z} - (\mathbf{C}^\mathbf{T}\mathbf{C})^{-1}\mathbf{C}^T\mathbf{x}),$$

and the EM algorithm is a straightforward least square projection, which is given below. We denote the matrix of data observation as $\mathbf{X} \in R^{d \times N}$ and the matrix of latent variables as $\mathbf{Z} \in R^{l \times N}$. Then

$$E-Step: \quad \mathbf{Z} = (\mathbf{C}^\mathbf{T}\mathbf{C})^{-1}\mathbf{C}^\mathbf{T}\mathbf{X}. \tag{18.1}$$

$$M-Step: \quad \mathbf{C}^{\mathbf{new}} = \mathbf{XZ}^\mathbf{T}(\mathbf{ZZ}^\mathbf{T})^{-1}. \tag{18.2}$$

After briefly recalling the main idea of kernel functions and kernel PCA, we show how we can use EM for kernel PCA to solve the eigenvalue problem and make kernel PCA tractable on large data set. The main contribution of this paper is to provide a new version of kernel PCA, and to explore its applications. Online EM algorithm for PCA is also briefly discussed.

Figures 18.1 to 18.7 all relate to the three worked examples shown our computational results in Section 18.6.

18.2 Kernel Functions

In this section, we pursue a different approach of making a model nonlinear, by kernel functions $k : R^d \times R^d \to R$ on pairs of points in data space. If these kernel functions satisfy a certain condition (Mercer's condition), they correspond to nonlinearly mapping the data in a higher dimensional *feature* space F by a map $\Phi : R^d \to F$ and taking the dot product in this space (Vapnik, 1995):

$$K(x,y) = \Phi(x).\Phi(y). \tag{18.3}$$

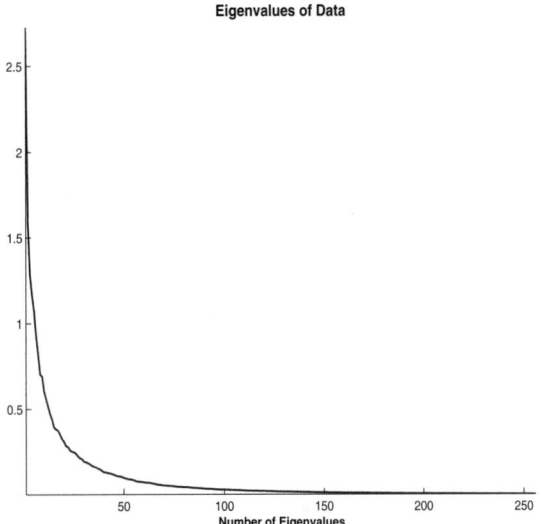

FIGURE 18.3
Eigenvalues.

This means that any linear algorithm in which the data only appear in the form of dot products $x_i.x_j$ can be made nonlinear by replacing the dot product by kernel function $K(x_i, x_j)$ and doing all the other calculations as before. The main idea of the dot product operation is that it enables us to work in the feature space without having to map the data into it. The best known example using this idea is the support vector machine (SVM) in which a linear classification method based on hyperplanes is transformed into a powerful nonlinear method by kernel functions. Some examples of valid (that is, satisfying Mercer's condition) kernels are:

1. Polynomial kernel:
$$K(\mathbf{x}^i, \mathbf{x}^j) = (\mathbf{x}^i.\mathbf{x}^j)^p;$$

2. Radial Basis Function (RBF) kernels:
$$K(\mathbf{x}^i, \mathbf{x}^j) = exp[-\frac{||\mathbf{x}^i - \mathbf{x}^j||^2}{(2\sigma^2)}];$$

3. PE kernels (a generalization of Gaussian kernel):
$$K(\mathbf{x}^i, \mathbf{x}^j) = exp[-(\frac{||\mathbf{x}^i - \mathbf{x}^j||^2}{r^2})^\beta];$$

4. Sigmoid kernels:
$$K(\mathbf{x}^i, \mathbf{x}^j) = tanh[a(\mathbf{x}^i.\mathbf{x}^j)],$$

which all correspond to a dot product in a high dimensional feature space. For the polynomial kernel of degree p, for example, the feature space consists of all products

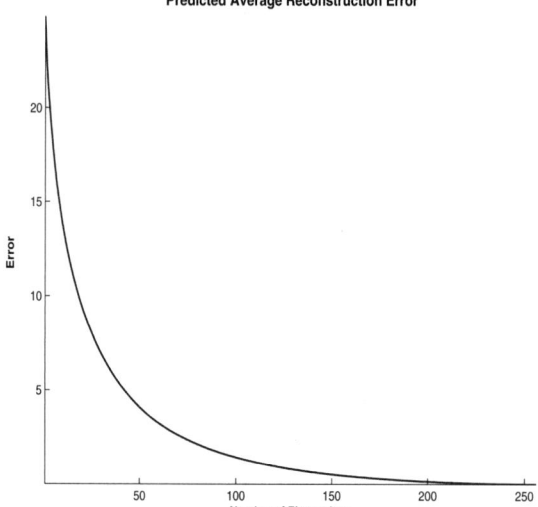

FIGURE 18.4
Predicted reconstruction error.

of entries up to order p, a quantity which grows like d^p. Recently, the kernel trick has also been applied to Fisher discriminant analysis (Mika, Ratsch, Scholkopf, and Muller 1999; Baudat and Anouarf 2000) and PCA (Scholkopf, Smola, and Muller 1997). The latter is created kernel PCA and is based on a formulation of PCA in terms of the dot product matrix instead of the covariance matrix. This makes it possible to extract nonlinear features by solving an eigenvalue problem similar to PCA.

18.3 Kernel PCA

The standard formulation of PCA is an eigendecomposition of the covariance matrix of the data. We will see that PCA can also be carried out on the dot product matrix. This is a well-known fact in the literature (Kirby and Sirovish 1990, Schokopf, Smola, and Muller 1998), but the following proof that we provide is more elegant and shorter than the previous ones.

Let $\{\mathbf{x}^n\}$ be the data set with N examples (observations) of dimension d. We suppose that the data set is centered: $\sum_N \mathbf{x}^n = \mathbf{0}_d$. The $d \times N$ matrix $\mathbf{X} = (\mathbf{x}^1, \mathbf{x}^2, \ldots, \mathbf{x}^N)$ represents the data in a compact form. Standard PCA is based on finding the eigenvalues and orthonormal eigenvectors of the (sample) covariance matrix of size $d \times d$:

$$\mathbf{C} = \frac{1}{N}\mathbf{X}\mathbf{X}^\mathrm{T}.$$

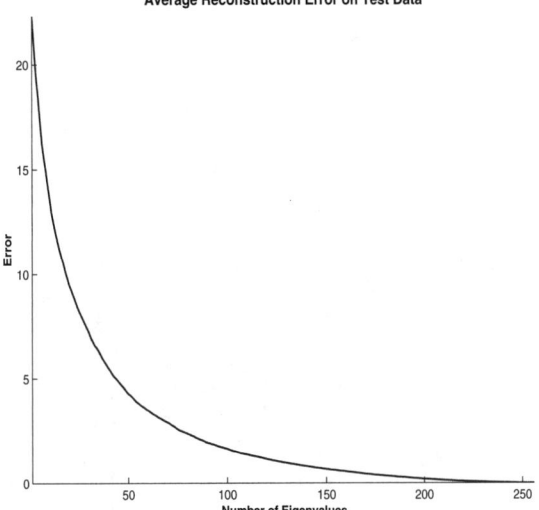

FIGURE 18.5
Average reconstruction error.

The matrix in terms of dot products we are interested in is the dot product matrix of size $N \times N$:

$$\mathbf{K} = \frac{1}{N}\mathbf{X}^T\mathbf{X}.$$

Claim 1:
There is a one to one correspondence between the nonzero eigenvalues related to eigenvectors $\{\mathbf{v}^k\}$ of $\mathbf{C}$, and the nonzero eigenvalues related to eigenvectors $\{\mathbf{u}^k\}$ of $\mathbf{K}$ and they have the same eigenvalues $\lambda_1, \lambda_2, \ldots, \lambda_p$ (of course $p \leq min(d,N)$) and

$$\mathbf{v}^k = \frac{\mathbf{X}\mathbf{u}^k}{\sqrt{\lambda_k}} \tag{18.4}$$

$$\mathbf{u}^k = \frac{\mathbf{X}^T\mathbf{v}^k}{\sqrt{\lambda_k}} \tag{18.5}$$

where the scaling by $\sqrt{\lambda_k}$ normalizes the eigenvectors.

Proof: Let $\mathbf{v}$ be an eigenvector of the covariance matrix $\mathbf{C}$ with eigenvalue λ: $\mathbf{XX}^T\mathbf{v} = \lambda\mathbf{v}$. Then:

$$\mathbf{X}^T\mathbf{X}(\mathbf{X}^T\mathbf{v}) = \mathbf{X}^T(\mathbf{XX}^T\mathbf{v}) = \lambda\mathbf{X}^T\mathbf{v},$$

so λ is also an eigenvalue of the dot matrix $\mathbf{X}^T\mathbf{X}$ with corresponding eigenvector $\mathbf{X}^T\mathbf{v}$ provided $\mathbf{X}^T\mathbf{v} \neq \mathbf{0}_N$ which follows from:

$$\lambda \neq 0 \quad \Rightarrow \quad \lambda\mathbf{v} \neq \mathbf{0}_d \quad \Leftrightarrow \quad \mathbf{XX}^T\mathbf{v} \neq \mathbf{0}_d \quad \Rightarrow \quad \mathbf{X}^T\mathbf{v} \neq \mathbf{0}_N.$$

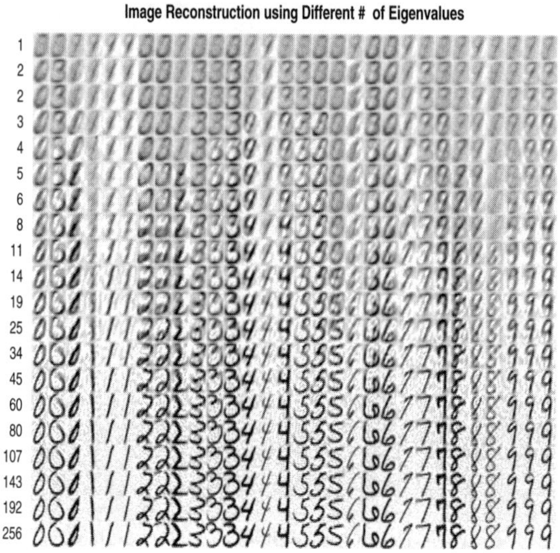

FIGURE 18.6
Reconstructed image.

So we only need to take the nonzero eigenvalue related eigenvectors into account. By symmetry (in $\mathbf{X}$ and $\mathbf{X}^T$), we can also conclude that each nonzero eigenvalue related eigenvector of the dot product matrix $\mathbf{X}^T\mathbf{X}u = \lambda u$ corresponds to an eigenvector $\mathbf{X}u$ of the covariance matrix with eigenvalue λ. The one to one correspondence as stated in the theorem follows after a straightforward normalization of the eigenvectors $\mathbf{u}$ for the dot product matrix (i.e., $||u|| = 1$). One can normalize the eigenvectors $\mathbf{v}$ for the covariance matrix using

$$\mathbf{v}^T\mathbf{v} = \mathbf{u}^T\mathbf{X}^T\mathbf{X}\mathbf{u} = \lambda \mathbf{u}^T\mathbf{u} = \lambda.$$

Given the normalization of $\mathbf{v}$, we can find $\mathbf{u}^T\mathbf{u} = \lambda$. Therefore, the theorem is proved.

A direct consequence of the theorem is that one can perform PCA for feature extraction entirely in terms of the dot products by calculating the product matrix $\mathbf{K}$, and determining its orthonormal eigenvectors u^k and its eigenvalues λ_k, and then projecting a point $\mathbf{x} \in R^d$ onto the principal eigenvectors $\mathbf{v}^k$ in data space as defined by (18.4):

$$\mathbf{x}^T\mathbf{v}^k = \frac{\mathbf{x}^T\mathbf{X}u^k}{\sqrt{\lambda_k}} = \left[\sum_{i=1}^N u_i^k(\mathbf{x}.\mathbf{x_i})\right]/\sqrt{\lambda_k}, \qquad (18.6)$$

in which the data also appear only in a dot product. This means that we can map the data points into a high-dimensional feature space F by $\Phi: R^d \Rightarrow F$ and still perform PCA feature extraction in F without explicitly performing this map using the kernel functions.

When mapping the data into feature space, the dot product matrix becomes the so-called kernel matrix of size $N \times N$:

$$\mathbf{K_{ij}} = \Phi(\mathbf{x}^i).\Phi(\mathbf{x}^j) = \mathbf{K}(\mathbf{x}^i, \mathbf{x}^j), \qquad (18.7)$$

where we use the kernel function (18.3). Let the eigenvectors of $\mathbf{K}$ be $\{\mathbf{u}^k\}$, as before, with the corresponding eigenvalues $\{\lambda_k\}$. The principal eigenvectors of the covariance matrix of the mapped data lie in the span of the Φ-images of the training data:

$$\mathbf{x}^k = \left[\sum_{i=1}^{N} u_i^k \Phi(\mathbf{x}^i)\right] / \sqrt{\lambda_k}. \qquad (18.8)$$

Feature extraction can again be done by projecting a point $\Phi(\mathbf{x})$ onto the principal eigenvectors $\mathbf{v}^k$ in the feature space:

$$\Phi(\mathbf{x}).\mathbf{v}^k = \left[\sum_{i=1}^{N} u_i^k \Phi(\mathbf{x}).\Phi(\mathbf{x}^i)\right] / \sqrt{\lambda_k} = \left[\sum_{i=1}^{N} u_i^k K(\mathbf{x}, \mathbf{x}^i)\right] / \sqrt{\lambda_k}. \qquad (18.9)$$

This leads to the following algorithm, which is formulated entirely in terms of the kernel function.

Algorithm 2:

1. Input:

    - A matrix of training samples: $\mathbf{X} = (\mathbf{x}^1 \mathbf{x}^2 \ldots \mathbf{x}^N)$.
    - A kernel function $K: R^d \times R^d \to R$.

2. The training Process:

    for $i = 1$ to N do

        for $j = 1$ to N do

            $K_{ij} = K(\mathbf{x}^i, \mathbf{x}^j)$

        end

    end

    $\mathbf{E} = ones(N, N)$

    $\mathbf{K} = (\mathbf{E} - \frac{1}{N}\mathbf{E})\mathbf{K}(\mathbf{E} - \frac{1}{N}\mathbf{E})$ (Centering the training data).

    Determine eigenvectors $\{\mathbf{u}^k\}$ and eigenvalues $\{\lambda_k\}$ of $\mathbf{K}/N$ using the EM algorithm or traditional singular value decomposition

    For each k $\mathbf{u}^k$ is an eigenvector corresponding to a nonzero eigenvalue do

        $\mathbf{u}^k = \mathbf{u}^k / \sqrt{\lambda_k}$

    end.

3. Feature extraction of the first l nonlinear principle components of the test data $\mathbf{t}^1, \mathbf{t}^2, \ldots, \mathbf{t}^l$. assume $\lambda_1 \geq \lambda_2 \geq \ldots \lambda_l$

for $i = 1$ to l do
    for $j = 1$ to N do
        $\mathbf{K}^{test}_{ij} = K(\mathbf{t}^i, \mathbf{x}^j)$
    end
end
$F = ones(N,L)/N$
$\mathbf{K}^{test} = \mathbf{K}^{test} - F'\mathbf{K} - \mathbf{K}^{test}\mathbf{E} + F'\mathbf{K}\mathbf{E}$ (Centering the test data)
$\mathbf{U} = (\mathbf{u}^1 \mathbf{u}^2 \ldots \mathbf{u}^l)$
$\mathbf{T} = \mathbf{K}^{test}\mathbf{U}$

where $\mathbf{T}$ is the $N \times l$ matrix of the first l nonlinear component of $\mathbf{t}^1, \ldots, \mathbf{t}^l$.

Kernel PCA corresponds exactly to the usual linear PCA in the high dimensional feature space F and, therefore, has all the properties of PCA in F. Because of the nonlinearity of the map Φ, the features extracted in the input data space are done in a nonlinear fashion.

We need to mention that Kernel PCA has several disadvantages. First, nonlinear PCA involves evaluating the kernel function N times for each principal component of the new pattern while for the standard PCA only the dot product of two d-dimensional vectors is needed. Therefore Kernel PCA is much slower. Second, standard methods for solving eigenvalue problems need to store the entire $N \times N$ kernel matrix which can become infeasible for a large number of samples N.

18.4 EM for Kernel PCA and On-line PCA

The application of the EM algorithm for PCA (see equations (18.1), (18.2)) to kernel PCA is very straightforward. We need to center the kernel matrix $\mathbf{K}$ using the Algorithm 2 first. Then, letting $\mathbf{B} \in R^{N \times l}$ and $\mathbf{Z} \in R^{l \times N}$, the EM for kernel algorithm is given as follows:

$$E - Step: \quad \mathbf{Z} = (\mathbf{B}^T\mathbf{K}\mathbf{B})^{-1}\mathbf{B}^T\mathbf{K}. \qquad (18.10)$$

$$M - Step: \quad \mathbf{B}^{new} = \mathbf{Z}^T(\mathbf{Z}\mathbf{Z}^T)^{-1}. \qquad (18.11)$$

To use this algorithm, we first initialize $\mathbf{B}$ randomly, and then do the iteration until the algorithm converges.

A new online algorithm of the PCA is given below. This algorithm can do the PCA without having to store the entire matrix. Assume the data have zero mean. The algorithm is derived from equations (18.1) and (18.2) in a straightforward manner as follows.

E-step:

$$\mathbf{P} = (\mathbf{C}^T\mathbf{C})^{-1}\mathbf{C}^T$$
$$\mathbf{Q} = \mathbf{0}_{(d \times l)}; \quad \mathbf{R} = \mathbf{0}_{(l \times l)}$$
for $n = 0$ to N **do**
$$\langle \mathbf{z}^n \rangle = \mathbf{P}\mathbf{x}^n$$
$$\mathbf{p} = \mathbf{x}^n \langle \mathbf{z}^n \rangle^T; \mathbf{P} = \mathbf{P} + \mathbf{p}$$
$$\mathbf{q} = \langle \mathbf{z}^n \rangle \langle \mathbf{z}^n \rangle^T; \mathbf{Q} = \mathbf{Q} + \mathbf{q}$$
end

M-step:

$$\mathbf{C} = \mathbf{P}\mathbf{Q}^{-1}$$

The above algorithm can be extended to the kernel PCA with little modifications.

18.5 Choosing the Number of Components with Information Complexity

How many eigenvalues or eigenvectors are needed in the kernel PCA? To answer this question, in this paper, we introduce several information based model selection criteria to choose the number of eigenvalues or eigenvectors needed in the kernel PCA. We first start with the classic Akaike's (1973) information criterion (AIC). This is defined by

$$\mathbf{AIC}(p) = n\log_e(2\pi) + n\log_e(\frac{(y - \mathbf{H}\alpha)^T(y - \mathbf{H}\alpha)}{n}) + n + 2(p+1).$$

Schwarz (1978) Bayesian criterion (SBC)(or BIC) is given by

$$\mathbf{SBC}(p) = \frac{n + (\log_e n - 1)p}{n(n-p)}(y - \mathbf{H}\alpha)^T(y - \mathbf{H}\alpha).$$

Consistent Akaike's information criterion (CAIC) of Bozdogan (1987) is given by

$$CAIC(p) = n\log_e(2\pi) + n\log_e(\frac{(y - \mathbf{H}\alpha)^T(y - \mathbf{H}\alpha)}{n}) + n + (\log_e n + 1)p.$$

Finally, the information measure of complexity (ICOMP) criterion of Bozdogan (1988, 1990, 1994, 2000) is defined by

$$\mathbf{ICOMP}(p) = n\log_e(2\pi) + n\log_e\hat{\sigma}^2 + n + (p+1)\log_e(\frac{tr(\mathbf{H}^T\mathbf{H})^{-1} + \frac{2\hat{\sigma}^2}{p}}{p+1})$$
$$- \log_e|(\mathbf{H}^T\mathbf{H})^{-1}| - \log_e(\frac{2\hat{\sigma}^2}{n}).$$

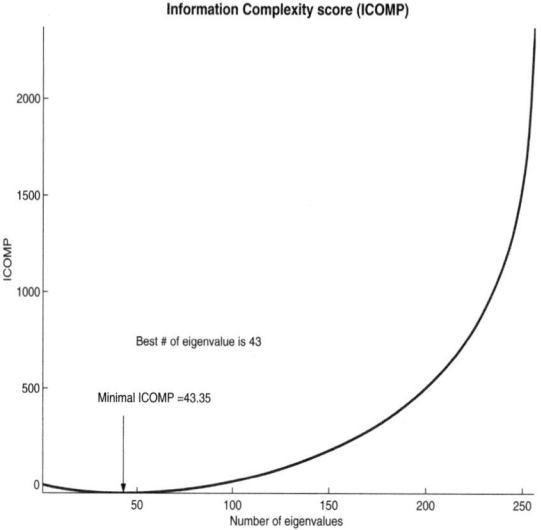

FIGURE 18.7
ICOMP scores.

where

$$\hat{\sigma}^2 = \frac{(y - \mathbf{H}X)^T(y - \mathbf{H}X)}{n - p}.$$

In what follows, in our computational results, we use ICOMP only. Certainly, researchers can choose their other favorite criteria.

18.6 Computational Results

Our first toy example is a data set that consists of three Power Exponential clusters in R^2. This toy problem is similar to an example that appears in the original paper of Scholkopf et al. (1998). However, here we are using the PE kernel instead of the Gaussian kernel to try to capture the nonnormality of the input data set. Our example using the PE kernel is: $exp(-(\frac{||\mathbf{x}-\mathbf{y}||^2}{0.1})^\beta)$, where β is a free parameter. For $\beta = 1.2$, we have the Figure (18.1).

Contour lines in Figure (18.1) indicate levels of constant principle component value. The first two nonlinear principle components separate three clusters. The next five split up each of the clusters.

Our second example is also a similar two dimensional toy problem. This time, we carry out the principle component analysis using different methods and different kernels. The contours of the results are shown in Figure (18.2).

Our third example is a gray image reconstruction problem using the online EM PCA algorithm. The data contains 1900 sample observations that belong to 10 different classes (numbered 0 - 9). Additional 100 samples are used for testing. Figures 18.3 to 18.7 show the tradeoff between the quality of the reconstructions and the number of dimensions.

Figure (18.7) shows that the best ICOMP value is -43.35 and the related number of principle components is 43. From Figure (18.6) we know that the image is clear enough to be distinguished when the number of eigenvalues is 43. Therefore ICOMP works well for this PCA problem.

18.7 Conclusions

Kernel PCA using EM algorithm can be used as the first stage of SVM classification and regression. It is also a useful tool in feature extraction. Our computational results show that kernel PCA using EM algorithm provides an alternative tool to the standard PCA. It can give huge savings in computing time especially when we try to extract small number of eigenvalues from large data sets. Of course, there are some unsolved problems when kernel PCA is applied to data compression. For example, the outcome of the kernel PCA feature extraction lies in feature space. We do not need to have a pre-image in input data space. Each eigenvector lies in the feature space too. There is no technique available for finding approximate pre-images for those values in the feature space. Our future work will address these issues and problems. On the other hand, information measure of complexity (ICOMP) criterion and other regularization procedures may be applied to the kernel PCA nonlinear regression models. We are currently working such problems, and our results will be published elsewhere.

Acknowledgments

This work is based on the results of the Ph.D. thesis of the first author under the supervision of Professor Bozdogan. The first author would like to express his sincere gratitude to Professor Bozdogan. The results of this paper would not have been possible without his guidance, knowledge, encouragement and patience.

References

Aapo, H., Juha, K., and Erkki, O. (2001). *Independent Component Analysis*. John Wiley, New York.

Akaike, H. (1973). Information theory and an extension of the maximum likelihood principle. In B.N. Petrov and F. Csáki (Eds.), *Second international symposium on information theory*, Budapest: Académiai Kiadó, 267-281.

Baudat, G. and Anouar, F. (2000). Generalized discriminant analysis using a kernel approach. *Neural Computation*, 12(10), 2385-2404.

Bozdogan, H. (1987). Model selection and Akaike's Information Criterion (AIC): The general theory and its analytical extensions. *Psychometrika,* 52(3), 345-370.

Bozdogan, H. (1988). ICOMP: a new model-selection criterion. In *Classification and related methods of data analysis*, H. H. Bock (Ed.), Elsevier Science Publishers, Amsterdam, 599-608.

Bozdogan, H. (1990). On the information-based measure of covariance complexity and its application to the evaluation of multivariate linear models. *Communications in Statistics, Theory and Methods*, 19, 221-278.

Bozdogan, H. (1994). Mixture-model cluster analysis using a new informational complexity and model selection criteria. In *Multivariate Statistical Modeling*, H. Bozdogan, (Ed.), Vol. 2, Proceedings of the First US/Japan Conference on the Frontiers of Statistical Modeling: An Informational Approach, Kluwer Academic Publishers, Dordrecht, the Netherlands, 69-113.

Bozdogan, H. (2000). Akaike's information criterion and recent developments in information complexity. *Journal of Mathematical Psychology*, 44, 62-91.

Dempster, A. P., Laird, N. M., and Rubin, D. B. (1977). Maximum Likelihood from incomplete data via the EM algorithm. *J. Roy. Statist. Soc. B*, 39, 1-38.

Diamantaras, K. I. and Kung, S. Y. (1996). *Principal Component Neural Networks (Theory and Applications)*. John Wiley, New York.

Golub, G. H. and Van Loan, C. F. (1997). *Matrix Computation*. The John Hopkins University Press, Baltimore, 3rd edition.

Kirby, M. and Sirovich, L. (1990). Application of the Karhunen-Loeve procedure for characterization of human faces. *IEEE Trans. Pattern Analysis and Machine Intelligence*, 12, 103-108.

Mika, S., Ratsch, G., Weston, J. , Scholkopf, B., and K.R. Muller. (1998). Fisher discriminant analysis with kernels. *Proceedings of IEEE Neural Networks for Signal Processing Workshop*.

Roweis, S. (1998). EM for PCA and SPCA. *Neural Information Processing Systems*, 10, 626-632.

Scholkopf, B., Smola, A., and Muller, K.R. (1997). Kernel principal component analysis. In *ICANN'97*.

Scholkopf, B. Bruges, C., & Muller, K.R. (1998). Nonlinear component analysis as a kernel eigenvalue problem. *Neural Computation,*10, 1299-1319.

Schwarz, G. (1978). Estimating the dimension of a model. *Ann. Statist.*, 6, 461-464.

Vapnik V. (1995). *The Nature of Statistical Learning Theory*. Springer-Verlag, New York.

19

Global Principal Component Analysis for Dimensionality Reduction in Distributed Data Mining

Hairong Qi, Tse-Wei Wang, and J. Douglas Birdwell
University of Tennessee, Knoxville, USA

CONTENTS

19.1 Introduction 324
19.2 Principal Component Analysis 326
19.3 Global PCA for Distributed Homogeneous Databases 327
19.4 Global PCA for Distributed Heterogeneous Databases 330
19.5 Experiments and Results 331
19.6 Conclusion 336
      References 337

Previous data mining activities have mostly focused on mining a centralized database. One big problem with a centralized database is its limited scalability. Because of the distributed nature of many businesses and the exponentially increasing amount of data generated from numerous sources, a distributed database becomes an attractive alternative. The challenge in distributed data mining is how to learn as much knowledge from distributed databases as we do from the centralized database without costing too much communication bandwidth. Both unsupervised classification (clustering) and supervised classification are common practices in data mining applications, where dimensionality reduction is a necessary step. Principal component analysis is a popular technique used in dimensionality reduction. This paper develops a distributed principal component analysis algorithm which derives the global principal components from distributed databases based on the integration of local covariance matrices. We prove that for homogeneous databases, the algorithm can derive the global principal components that are exactly the same as those calculated based on a centralized database. We also provide quantitative measurement of the error introduced in the recompiled global principal components when the databases are heterogeneous.

19.1 Introduction

Data mining is a technology that deals with the discovery of hidden knowledge, unexpected patterns and new rules from large databases. In an information society where "we are drowning in information but starved for knowledge [8]," data mining provides an effective means to analyze the uncontrolled and unorganized data and turns them into meaningful knowledge.

The development of different data mining technologies has been spurred since the early 90s. Grossman [4] classified data mining systems into three generations: The first generation develops single or collection of data mining algorithms to mine vector-valued data. The second generation supports mining of larger datasets and datasets in higher dimensions. It also includes developing data mining schema and data mining languages to integrate mining into database management systems. The third generation provides distributed data mining in a transparent fashion. Current commercially available data mining systems mainly belong to the first generation.

With the advances in computer networking and information technology, new challenges are brought to the data mining community, which we summarize as follows: 1) Large dataset with increased complexity (high dimension); 2) New data types including object-valued attributes, unstructured data (textual data, image, etc.) and semi-structured data (html-tagged data); 3) Geographically distributed data location with heterogeneous data schema; 4) Dynamic environment with data items updated in real time; and 5) Progressive data mining which returns quick, partial or approximate results that can be fine-tuned later in support of more active interactions between user and data mining systems.

The focus of the previous data mining research has been on a centralized database. One big problem with a centralized database is its limited scalability. On the other hand, many databases nowadays tend to be maintained distributively not only because many businesses have a distributed nature, but that growth can be sustained more gracefully in a distributed system. The paper discusses the problem of distributed data mining (DDM) from geographically distributed data locations, with databases being either homogeneous or heterogeneous.

Data mining in distributed systems can be carried out in two different fashions: data from distributed locations are transferred to a central processing center where distributed databases will be combined into a data warehouse before any further processing is to be done. During this process, large amounts of data are moved through the network. A second framework is to carry out local data mining first. Global knowledge can be derived by integrating partial knowledge obtained from local databases. It is expected that by integrating the knowledge instead of data, network bandwidth can be saved and computational load can be more evenly distributed. Since the partial knowledge only reflects properties of the local database, how to integrate this partial knowledge into the global knowledge in order to represent characteristics of the overall data collection remains a problem. Guo et al. addressed in [5] that in distributed classification problems, the classification error of a global model should, at worst, be the same as the average classification error of local models, at best, lower than the error of the non-distributed learned model of the same domain.

Popularly used data mining techniques include association rule discovery [11], clustering (unsupervised classification) and supervised classification. With the growth of distributed databases, distributed approaches to implement all the three techniques have been developed since early 90s.

Chan and Stolfo proposed a distributed meta-learning algorithm based on the JAM system [2], which is one of the earliest distributed data mining systems developed. JAM [10] stands for Java Agents for Meta-learning. It is a multi-agent framework that carries out meta-learning for fraud detection in banking systems and intrusion detection for network security. In the distributed meta-learning system, classifiers are first derived from different training datasets using different classification algorithms. These "base classifiers" will then be collected or combined by another learning processing, the meta-learning process, to generate a "meta-classifier" that integrates the separately learned classifier. Guo and Sutiwaraphun proposed a similar approach named distributed classification with knowledge probing (DCKP) [5]. The difference between DCKP and meta-learning lies in the second learning phase and the forms of the final results. In DCKP, the second learning phase is performed on a probing set whose class values are the combinations of predictions from base classifiers. The result is one descriptive model at the base level rather than the meta level. The performance reported from the empirical studies of both approaches vary from dataset to dataset. Most of the time, the distributed approach performs worse than the non-distributed approach. Recently, there has been significant progress in DDM and there are approaches dealing with massive datasets that do better than the non-distributed learned model [9].

Kargupta et al. [7] proposed collective data mining (CDM) to learn a function which approximates the actual relationship between data attributes by inductive learning. The key idea of CDM is to represent this function as a weighted summation of an orthonormal basis. Each local dataset, generates its own weights corresponding to the same basis. Cross terms in the function can be solved when local weights are collected at a central site. He also studied distributed clustering using collective principal component analysis (PCA) [6]. Collective PCA has the same objective as global PCA. However, in collective PCA, local principal components, as well as sampled data items from local dataset, need to be sent to a central site in order to derive the global principal components that can be applied to all datasets. In global PCA, no data items from the local database are needed in the derivation of the global principal components.

Except for the CDM approach proposed by Kargupta, most of the current DDM methods deal with only homogeneous databases.

Almost all DDM algorithms need to transfer some data items from local databases in order to derive the global model. The objective of global PCA is to derive the exact or high-precision global model, from homogeneous or heterogeneous databases respectively, without the transfer of any local data items.

19.2 Principal Component Analysis

Principal component analysis (PCA) is a popular technique for dimensionality reduction which, in turn, is a necessary step in classification [3]. It constructs a representation of the data with a set of orthogonal basis vectors that are the eigenvectors of the covariance matrix generated from the data, which can also be derived from singular value decomposition. By projecting the data onto the dominant eigenvectors, the dimension of the original dataset can be reduced with little loss of information.

In PCA-relevant literature, PCA is often presented using the eigenvalue/eigenvector approach of the covariance matrices. But in efficient computation related to PCA, it is the singular value decomposition (SVD) of the data matrix that is used. The relationship between the eigen-decomposition of the covariance matrix and the SVD of the data matrix itself is presented below to make the connection. In this paper, eigen-decomposition of the covariance matrix and SVD of the data matrix are used interchangeably.

Let X be the data repository with m records of dimension d ($m \times d$). Assume the dataset is mean-centered by making $E[X] = 0$. A modern PCA method is based on finding the singular values and orthonormal singular vectors of the X matrix as shown in Eq. 19.1,

$$X = U\Sigma V^T \tag{19.1}$$

where U and V are the left and the right singular vectors of X, and Σ is a diagonal matrix with positive singular values, $\sigma_1, \sigma_2, \cdots, \sigma_d$ ($d = \text{rank}(X)$, assuming $d < m$), along the diagonal, arranged in descending order.

Using covariance matrix to calculate the eigenvectors, let $C = E[X^T X]$ represent the covariance matrix of X. Then the right singular vectors contained in V of Eq. 19.1 are the same as those normalized eigenvectors of the covariance matrix C (Eq. 19.2). In addition, if the nonzero eigenvalues of C are arranged in a descending order, then the kth singular value of X is equal to the square root of the kth eigenvalue of C. That is, $\lambda_k = \sigma_k^2$.

$$C = V\Sigma^2 V^T \tag{19.2}$$

The paper presents an algorithm to calculate the global principal components from distributed databases by only transferring the eigenvectors and eigenvalues (or the singular vectors and the singular values) of the local covariance matrix instead of the original data set. We assume the dimension of the data (d) is much less than the number of data samples (m). We prove that in homogeneous databases, the global principal components derived are exactly the same as those derived from a centralized data warehouse. We also quantitatively measure the error introduced to the integrated global principal components when the databases are heterogeneous.

19.3 Global PCA for Distributed Homogeneous Databases

We first derive the global PCA algorithm assuming the distributed databases are homogeneous and the dimension of the dataset is much less than the number of data samples ($d \ll m$).

Let $X_{m \times d}$ and $Y_{p \times d}$ be two distributed databases of the same dimension (d). X is a matrix of m rows and d columns, and Y of p rows and d columns. The number of columns is in fact the dimension of the data samples in the database, and the number of rows is the number of data samples. Assume that $m, p \gg d$. We present Lemma 19.1 and provide the proof.

LEMMA 19.1
If matrices $X_{m \times d}$ and $Y_{p \times d}$ are mean-centered, that is, $E[X] = E[Y] = 0$, then

$$\text{eig}[(m-1)cov(X) + (p-1)cov(Y)] = \text{eig}[(m+p-1)cov(\begin{bmatrix} X \\ Y \end{bmatrix})] \qquad (19.3)$$

where $\text{eig}[A]$ denotes the eigenvectors and the eigenvalues of matrix A.

Proof: Since $E[X] = 0$ and $E[Y] = 0$, we have

$$E\begin{bmatrix} X \\ Y \end{bmatrix} = 0$$

According to the definition of the covariance matrix,

$$cov(X) = \frac{1}{m-1} \sum_{k=1}^{m} (X_k - E[X])^T (X_k - E[X])$$

$$= \frac{1}{m-1} X^T X$$

and similarly,

$$cov(Y) = \frac{1}{p-1} Y^T Y$$

Therefore, we have the left hand side of Eq. 19.3

$$(m-1)cov(X) + (p-1)cov(Y) = X^T X + Y^T Y$$

The right hand side of Eq. 19.3 can also be derived in a similar way:

$$cov(\begin{bmatrix} X \\ Y \end{bmatrix}) = \frac{1}{m+p-1} \begin{bmatrix} X \\ Y \end{bmatrix}^T \begin{bmatrix} X \\ Y \end{bmatrix}$$

$$= \frac{1}{m+p-1} \begin{bmatrix} X^T & Y^T \end{bmatrix} \begin{bmatrix} X \\ Y \end{bmatrix}$$

$$= \frac{1}{m+p-1} (X^T X + Y^T Y)$$

Therefore, the right hand side of Eq. 19.3 is also equal to

$$(m+p-1)\frac{1}{m+p-1}(X^TX+Y^TY) = X^TX+Y^TY$$

We can extend Lemma 19.1 to the case of multiple distributed databases. Let X_i represent the local database of d dimension and i the index of distributed databases where $i = 1 \cdots r$. The global principal components can be derived by Eq. 19.4,

$$eig[((\Sigma_{i=1}^r m_i) - 1)\begin{bmatrix} X_1 \\ \vdots \\ X_r \end{bmatrix}] = \\ eig[(m_1 - 1)cov(X_1) + \ldots + (m_r - 1)cov(X_r)] \quad (19.4)$$

where $m_i (i = 1, \cdots, r)$ is the number of samples in the distributed database i. Eq. 19.4 says that the principal components of the combined matrix (the global principal components) can be derived from the distributed databases through the covariance matrices assuming the distributed databases are homogeneous. We have shown in Eq. 19.1 and Eq. 19.2 that the covariance matrix can be calculated if the singular values and singular vectors are known.

Based on the above analysis, we design the global principal components derivation algorithm for distributed homogeneous databases. Let X_i denote the local dataset. X_i has m_i samples and is of d dimension. $i = 1 \cdots r$ is the index of different dataset locations. The algorithm is carried out in two steps:

Step 1: At each local site, calculate the singular values and the singular vectors of the local database X_i using SVD method, as shown in Eq. 19.5.

$$X_i = U_i \Sigma_i V_i^T \quad (19.5)$$

where according to Eq. 19.2, the columns of V_i are the eigenvectors of the covariance matrix of X_i, and the singular values ($\sigma_i = (\sigma_{i1}, \sigma_{i2}, \cdots, \sigma_{id})$) along the diagonal of Σ_i are the square root of the eigenvalues of the covariance matrix of X_i.

Step 2: Transfer the singular values (Σ_i), the singular vectors (V_i), and the number of data samples m_i from the local site (i) to another site ($j = i+1$). That is, transfer the covariance matrix and the number of data samples from the local site to another site. Let the knowledge transfer process be carried out serially. Reconstruct the covariance matrix based on data from site i and site j as shown in Eq. 19.6.

Statistical Data Mining and Knowledge Discovery

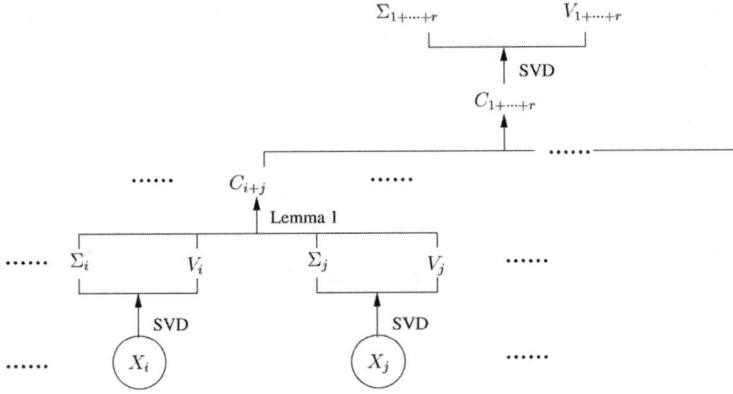

FIGURE 19.1
Illustration of global PCA for distributed homogeneous databases.

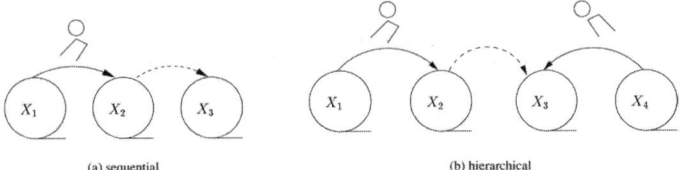

FIGURE 19.2
Two scenarios can be used to integrate local singular vectors and singular values.

$$C_{i+j} = \tfrac{1}{m_i+m_j-1}((m_i-1)C_i + (m_j-1)C_j)$$
$$= \tfrac{1}{m_i+m_j-1}((m_i-1)V_i\Sigma_i^2 V_i^T + (m_j-1)V_j\Sigma_j^2 V_j^T) \quad (19.6)$$

where C_i, C_j are the covariance matrices of X_i, X_j respectively, and C_{i+j} is the covariance matrix of

$$\begin{bmatrix} X_i \\ X_j \end{bmatrix}$$

Step 2 will continue until $C_{1+2+\cdots+r}$ is generated. We can then use SVD method to derive the global principal components of the distributed datasets. This process is also illustrated in Fig. 19.1.

During this learning process, only the singular vectors, the singular values, and the number of samples in each dataset are transferred. Yet, this process generates exactly the same global principal components as if calculated from a central database. The data transferred in the proposed approach is at the order of $O(rd^2)$ compared to the transfer of the original local database which is at the order of $O(rmd)$, where $m \gg d$.

Step 2 can also be carried out hierarchically. Figure 19.2 shows two different integration scenarios.

The proposed approach is described in detail in Algorithm 19.1.

Algorithm 19.1: Global PCA in distributed homogeneous databases.

Data: local dataset X_i of size $m_i \times d$, the number of distributed datasets, $r, i = 1, \cdots, r$.
Result: Global principal components V_G.
% *The following session can be done in parallel at local sites*;
Mean-center X_i such that $E[X_i] = O$ (a $1 \times d$ zero vector);
SVD: $X_i = U_i \Sigma_i V_i^T$ where the non-zero singular values along the diagonal of Σ_i form the vector σ_i;
% *The following session can be done serially or hierarchically*;
$i = 1$;
while $i < r$ **do**
    transfer V_i and σ_i to where $X_{j=i+1}$ is located;
    Reconstruct the covariance matrix C_{i+j} using Eq. 19.6;
    increase i by 1
end
$C_G = C_{1+\cdots+r}$;
$C_G = V_G \Sigma_G^2 V_G^T$;
V_G is the global principal components.

19.4 Global PCA for Distributed Heterogeneous Databases

The global PCA algorithm presented in Sec. 19.3 can also be used if the databases are heterogeneous, except that the global principal components are not accurate any more if we only transfer the singular values and singular vectors as shown in Eq. 19.8. Assume again that X and Y are two databases at two different locations. Assume the structure of X and Y are not the same. The dataset X is of d_X dimension, and Y of d_Y dimension. X and Y are related through a public key. For example, different departments of a hospital might use different databases to record patient's information. Patient's personal data can be organized in one table and patient's diagnostic history might be stored in another table. However, patient's ID is unique which is used as a public key to link these two tables. Without loss of generality, assume X and Y have the same number of samples. That is, X is an $m \times d_X$ matrix, and Y an $m \times d_Y$ matrix. The combined covariance matrix of $[X\ Y]$ can then be calculated as Eq. 19.8.

$$\text{cov}([X\ Y]) = \frac{1}{m-1} [X\ Y]^T [X\ Y]$$

$$= \frac{1}{m-1} \begin{bmatrix} X^T \\ Y^T \end{bmatrix} [X\ Y] \quad (19.7)$$

$$= \frac{1}{m-1} \begin{bmatrix} X^T X & X^T Y \\ Y^T X & Y^T Y \end{bmatrix}$$

$$= \frac{1}{m-1} \begin{bmatrix} m*cov(X) & X^T Y \\ Y^T X & m*cov(Y) \end{bmatrix} \quad (19.8)$$

If we assume data are transferred from where X locates to where Y locates, then the error introduced in the global principal components (Eq. 19.8) actually comes from the estimation of X since Y is the local dataset. Therefore, the key problem in deriving the global principal components from distributed heterogeneous databases is how to estimate local dataset when the computation is away from that local site.

According to SVD algorithm, X can be decomposed as Eq. 19.9,

$$X = u_1 \sigma_1 v_1^T + u_2 \sigma_2 v_2^T + \cdots + u_j \sigma_j v_j^T + \cdots + u_d \sigma_d v_d^T \quad (19.9)$$

where u_j is the jth column vector of the left singular matrix of X, v_j the jth column vector of the right singular matrix of X, and σ_j the jth singular value of X. The singular values are arranged in descending order, i.e., $\sigma_1 > \sigma_2 > \cdots > \sigma_j \cdots > \sigma_d$. Usually, the first component in Eq. 19.9 ($u_1 \sigma_1 v_1^T$) contains most of the information of X and thus would be a good estimation of X. In other words, besides transferring the singular vectors and singular values, we also transfer u_1, the first column vector of the left singular matrix of X. The loss of information by estimating X using only the first component in Eq. 19.9 can be formulated using Eq. 19.10,

$$\varepsilon = \frac{\sum_{j=2}^{d} \sigma_j}{\sum_{j=1}^{d} \sigma_j} \quad (19.10)$$

Therefore, the amount of data transferred among heterogeneous databases is at the order of $O(rd^2 + m)$. The more u_j's transferred, the more accurate the estimation to X, the more data need to be transferred as well.

Applying the above analysis to Eq. 19.8, we have

$$cov([X\ Y]) = \frac{1}{m-1} \begin{bmatrix} m*cov(X) & \tilde{X}^T Y \\ Y^T \tilde{X} & m*cov(Y) \end{bmatrix}$$

where $\tilde{X} = \sum_{i=1}^{t} u_{xi} \sigma_{xi} v_{xi}^T$ approximates X. t is the number of u_j's transferred. The loss of information is then calculated by

$$\varepsilon = \frac{\sum_{j=t+1}^{d} \sigma_j}{\sum_{j=1}^{d} \sigma_j}$$

19.5 Experiments and Results

Experiments are done on three data sets (Abalone, Pageblocks, and Mfeat) from the UCI Machine Learning Repository [1]. We use Abalone and Pageblocks

Data Set	Nr. of Attributes	Nr. of Classes	Nr. of Samples
Abalone	8	29	4177
Pageblocks	10	5	5473
Mfeat	646	10	2000

TABLE 19.1
Details of data sets used in the simulation.

to simulate the homogeneous distributed environment, and Mfeat, the heterogeneous distributed environment. The details of all data sets are shown in Table 19.1. We adopted two metrics to evaluate the performance of global PCA: the *classification accuracy* and the *Euclidean distance* between the major components derived based on the global PCA and a local PCA respectively. For the purpose of simplification, we choose the minimum distance classifier, where a sample is assigned to a class if its distance to the class mean is the minimum. In each subset, 30% of the data are used as the training set, and the other 70% for the test set.

Here, we outline the PCA and classification processes designed in our experiments given the distributed data sets (including both the training and test sets). Assume X_i is a subset at location i, X_i^{Tr} the training set, X_i^{Te} the test set, where $X_i = \begin{bmatrix} X_i^{Tr} & X_i^{Te} \end{bmatrix}^T$.

- Step 1: Apply PCA on X_i^{Tr} to derive the principal components and use those components which keep most of the information as P_i. A parameter indicating the information loss (ε) is used to control how many components need to be used. In all the experiments, an information loss ratio of 10% is used.

- Step 2: Project both X_i^{Tr} and X_i^{Te} onto P_i to reduce the dimension of the original data set, and get PX_i^{Tr} and PX_i^{Te} respectively.

- Step 3: Use PX_i^{Tr} and PX_i^{Te} as the local model for local classification. The local classification accuracy is averaged and compared to the classification accuracy derived from the global PCA.

- Step 4: Calculate the distance between the major component in P_i and that in the global principal component for performance evaluation.

19.5.1 Global PCA for Distributed Homogeneous Databases

Abalone is a data set used to predict the age of abalone from physical measurements. It contains 4177 samples from 29 classes. We randomly divide the whole data set into 50 homogeneous subsets of the same size. All the subsets have the same number of attributes (or features). Pageblocks is a data set used to classify all the blocks of the page layout of a document that has been detected by a segmentation process. It has 5473 samples from 5 classes. We also randomly divide this data set into 50 homogeneous subsets.

Figures 19.3 and 19.4 show the performance comparisons with respect to the classification accuracy and Euclidean distance on the Abalone data set. We observe

Statistical Data Mining and Knowledge Discovery

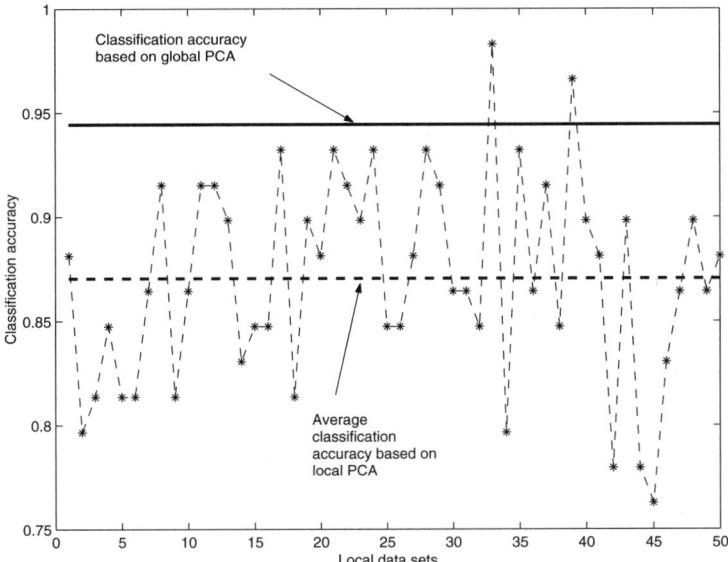

FIGURE 19.3
Classification accuracy comparison. Note: the upper solid straight line indicates the classification accuracy based on the global principal components. The lower dash straight line is the averaged local classification accuracy based on local principal components at each of the 50 subsets (`Abalone`).

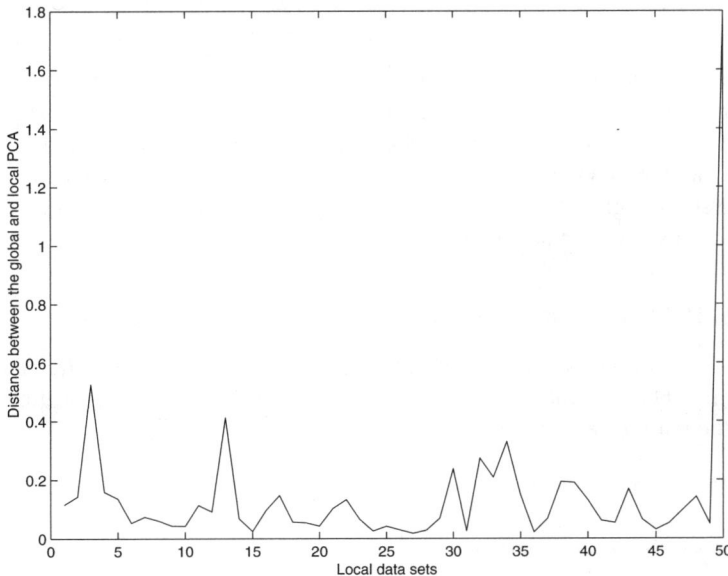

FIGURE 19.4
Euclidean distance between the major components derived from the global PCA and the local PCA (`Abalone`).

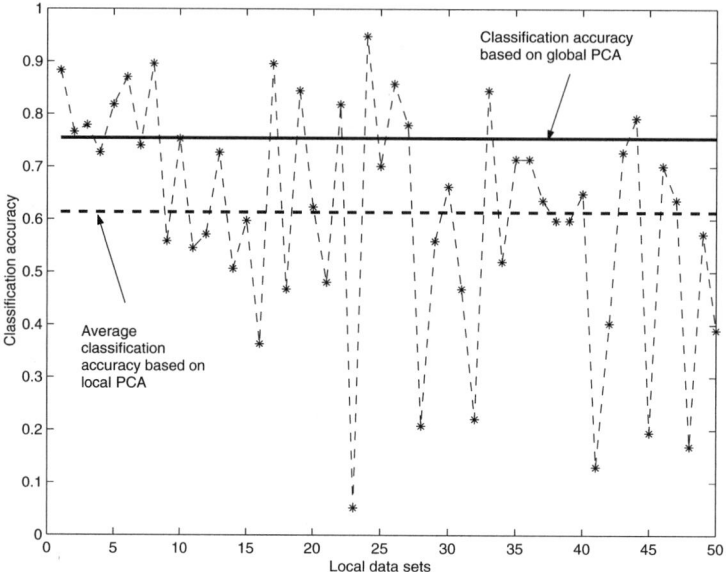

FIGURE 19.5
Classification accuracy comparison. Note: the upper solid straight line indicates the classification accuracy based on the global principal components. The lower dash straight line is the averaged local classification accuracy based on local principal components at each of the 50 subsets (`Pageblocks`).

(Figure 19.3) that even though some of the local classification accuracy is higher than the accuracy using the global PCA, the average local accuracy (0.8705) is 7.8% lower than the global classification accuracy (0.9444). Similar patterns can be observed from Figures 19.5 and 19.6 which are results generated from the `Pageblocks` data set. For this data set, the global classification accuracy (0.7545) is 23% higher than the averaged local classification accuracy (0.6135).

19.5.2 Global PCA for Distributed Heterogeneous Databases

`Mfeat` is a data set that consists of features of handwritten numerals (0–9) extracted from a collection of Dutch utility maps. Six different feature selection algorithms are applied and the features are saved in six data files.

1. `mfeat-fac`: 216 profile correlations

2. `mfeat-fou`: 76 Fourier coefficients of the character

3. `mfeat-kar`: 64 Karhunen-Love coefficients

4. `mfeat-mor`: 6 morphological features

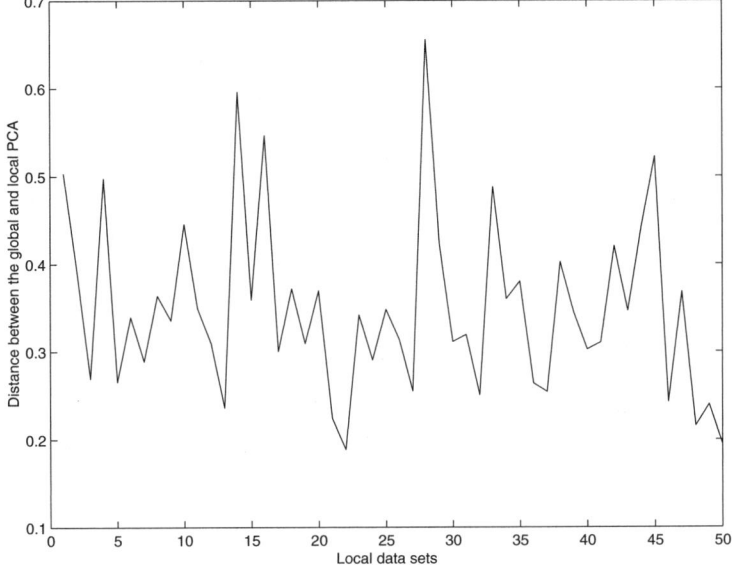

FIGURE 19.6
Euclidean distance between the major components derived from the global PCA and the local PCA (Pageblocks).

5. mfeat-pix: 240 pixel averages in 2×3 windows

6. mfeat-zer: 47 Zernike moments

Each data file has 2000 samples, and corresponding samples in different feature sets (files) correspond to the same original character. We use these six feature files to simulate a distributed heterogeneous environment.

Figure 19.7 shows a comparison between the global and local classifications. Notice that the global classification accuracy is calculated with the assumption that no information is lost, that is, all the u_j's are transferred and the local data set is accurately regenerated. However, in real applications, this is very inefficient since it consumes a tremendous amount of computer bandwidth and computing resources. Figure 19.8 shows the trade-off between the classification accuracy and the amount of u_j's being transferred between local data sets. We use

$$\varepsilon = \frac{\sum_{j=t+1}^{d} \sigma_j}{\sum_{j=1}^{d} \sigma_j}$$

to calculate the information loss and t is the number of u_j's transferred. We observe that when only one u_j is transferred, the information loss is about 40%, but the classification accuracy is, interestingly, a little bit higher than that calculated with

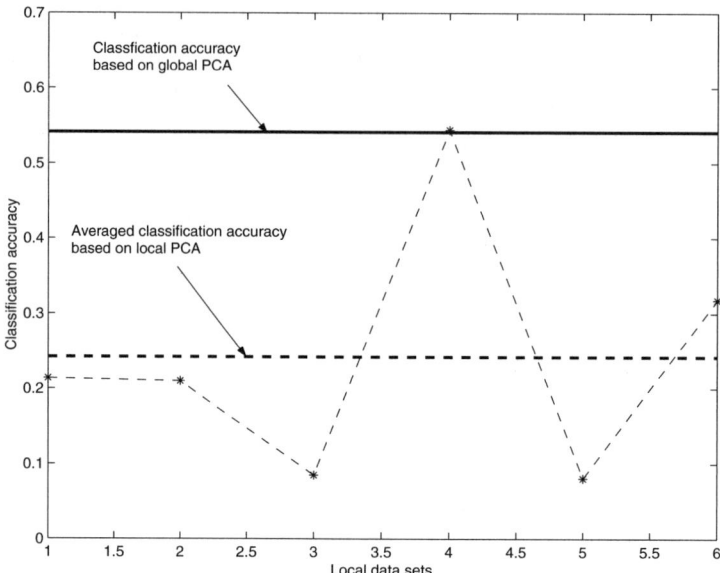

FIGURE 19.7
Classification accuracy comparison. Note: the upper solid straight line indicates the classification accuracy based on the global principal components (calculated based on all features). The lower dash straight line is the averaged local classification accuracy based on local principal components at each of the 6 subsets (`Mfeat`).

all u_j transferred. As the number of transferred u_j's increases to 10 and 20, the information loss drops to about 15% and 10% respectively, but the classification accuracy does not change. Actually, it converges to the accuracy derived when all u_j's are transferred. Figure 19.8 shows a good example on the effectiveness of the first component ($u_1 \sigma_1 v_1^T$) in approximating the original data set (Eq. 19.9).

19.6 Conclusion

This paper discusses the problem of distributed data mining. It develops an algorithm to derive the global principal components from distributed databases by mainly transferring the singular vectors and singular values of the local dataset. When the database is homogeneous, the derived global principal components are exactly the same as those calculated from a centralized database. When the databases are heterogeneous, the global principal components cannot be accurate using the same algorithm. We quantitatively analyze the error introduced with respect to different amounts of local data transferred.

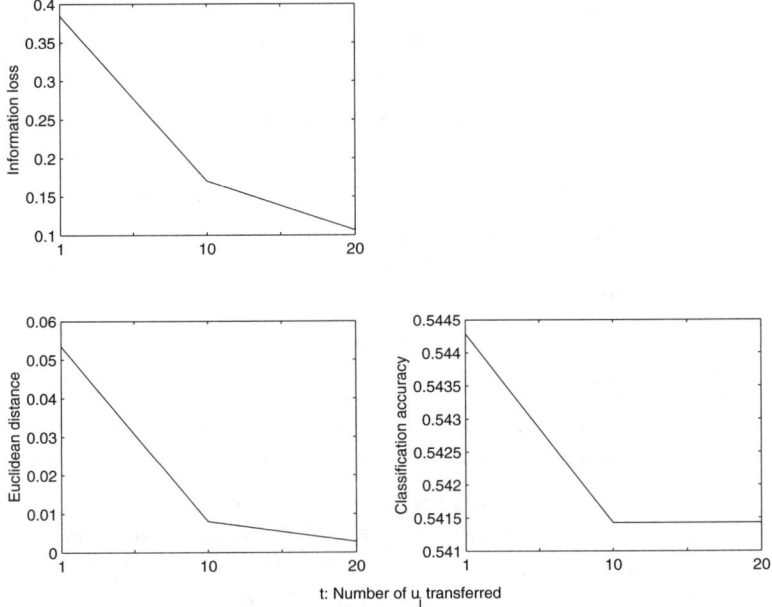

FIGURE 19.8
Effect of the number of left singular vectors (u_j) transferred. Top-left: information loss (ε) vs. t. Bottom-left: Euclidean distance between the major component derived from the global PCA with t amount of u_j transferred and the major component derived from the global PCA with all u_j's transferred. Bottom-right: Classification accuracy vs. t.

References

[1] Blake, C. L. and Merz, C. J. (1998). UCI repository of machine learning databases. http://www.ics.uci.edu/mlearn/MLRepository.html. University of California, Irvine, Department of Information and Computer Sciences.

[2] Chan, P. and Stolfo, S. (1993). Toward parallel and distributed learning by meta-learning. In *Working Notes AAAI Work Knowledge Discovery in Databases*, AAAI Press, pp. 227-240.

[3] Duda, R. O., Hart, P. E. and Stork, D. G. (2001) *Pattern Classification*. John Wiley and Sons, New York, 2nd edition.

[4] Grossman, R. L. (1997). Data mining: challenges and opportunities for data mining during the next decade. http://www.lac.uic.edu, May.

[5] Guo, Y. and Sutiwaraphun, J. (2001). *Advances in Distributed Data Mining*, chapter 1: Distributed Classification with Knowledge Probing, AAAI Press, pp. 1-25.

[6] Kargupta, H., Huang, W., Sivakumar, K. and Johnson, E. (2000). Distributed clustering using collective principal component analysis. *Under review in Knowledge and Information Systems*.

[7] Kargupta, H., Park, B., Hershberger, D. and Johnson, E.(2002). *Advances in Distributed Data Mining*, chapter Collective data mining: a new perspective toward distributed data mining. AAAI Press. Submitted for publication.

[8] Naisbitt, J. and Aburdene, P. (1990). *Megatrends 2000: Ten New Directions for the 1990's*. Morrow, New York.

[9] Provost, F. J. and Kolluri, V.(1999). A survey of methods for scaling up inductive algorithms. *Data Mining and Knowledge Discovery*, 3(2), pp. 131-169.

[10] Stolfo, S. et al. (1997). JAM: Java agents for meta-learning over distributed databases. In *Proceedings Third International Conference on Knowledge Discovery and Data Mining*, D. Heckerman, H. Mannila, D. Pregibon, and R. Uthurusamy (Eds.), AAAI Press, Menlo Park, CA, pp. 74-81.

[11] Zaki, M. J. (1999). Parallel and distributed association mining: A survey. *IEEE Concurrency*, October-December, pp. 14-25.

20

A New Metric for Categorical Data

S. H. Al-Harbi, G. P. McKeown and V. J. Rayward-Smith
University of East Anglia, Norwich, UK

CONTENTS

20.1 Introduction 339
20.2 Dissimilarity Measure 340
20.3 D_{CV} Metric 343
20.4 Synthetic Examples 345
20.5 Exploiting the D_{CV} Metric 348
20.6 Conclusions and Future Work 349
      References 350

A measure of the closeness between two objects in high dimensions is essential to most clustering algorithms. In a metric space, the closeness between two objects is modelled by a distance function that satisfies the triangle inequality. Most earlier work on metrics focussed on continuous fields. However, many of the fields in data mining consist of categorical data which describe the symbolic values of objects. In this chapter, we introduce a new metric for categorical data that is derived from the Mahalanobis metric.

20.1 Introduction

Cluster analysis, which is the process of classifying objects into subsets of similar objects, is an important task of data mining. Many data mining applications require clustering of high-dimensional data sets into homogeneous partitions from which interesting groups may be discovered. Applications exist in diverse areas, e.g.,

Disease: Finding a virus similar to a given one from a large virus dataset or finding groups of viruses with certain common characteristics [11].

Social services: Clustering to identify groups with particular requirements (e.g., the elderly) would economize on resources, and improve the allocation [10].

City Planning: Identifying groups of houses and buildings according to type, use, architecture, value and location [2].

Marketing: Help market analysts identify distinct groups in their customer base, and then use this knowledge to develop marketing strategies [1].

Many of the fields in data mining consist of categorical data which describe the symbolic values of objects. The most important types of categorical data can be classified as follows.

- Ordinal data: induces an ordering of objects. As well as distinguishing between $x = y$ and $x \neq y$, the ranking of the objects can be used to obtain an inequality, $x > y$ or $x < y$. Examples of ordinal scale data include number of children, level of education and ranks.

- Nominal data: an object has one of two or more values but no ordering can be given to these values. Examples of nominal scale data include the names of viruses and cities. Binary data is a special case where the number of values is two. Examples of binary data include gender (female and male) and smoking status (smoker and non-smoker).

Since ordinal data can be ordered, it can be transformed into integer values. These values are not necessarily sequential. For instance the values of 'level of education' need not be the same distance apart, e.g., 'First degree', 'Master' and 'PhD' could be transformed into 1, 3 and 7. However, it is not feasible to order nominal data. Therefore, there is a need for metrics that can adequately deal with nominal data.

In this chapter we introduce a new metric that uses the inverse of a relationship matrix, and is based on *Cramer's V* statistic [14]. In addition, a weight can be given to each field to give it greater or lesser importance.

20.2 Dissimilarity Measure

The problem of clustering data points is defined as follows: Given a set of points in high-dimensional space, how does one partition points into clusters so that the points within each cluster are "similar" to one another, and the points in different clusters are "dissimilar"? Thus, clustering is the task of grouping together similar objects in a data set.

Similarity is fundamental to the definition of a cluster and a measure of the similarity between two objects drawn from the same feature space is essential to most clustering algorithms. In a metric space, the dissimilarity between two objects is modelled with a distance function that satisfies the triangle inequality. It gives a numerical value to the notion of closeness between two objects in a high-dimensional space.

DEFINITION 20.1 *Let M be a non-empty space and for each $x, y \in M$ let $\delta(x, y)$ be a real number satisfying*

- $\delta(x,y) = 0$ if and only if $x = y$;
- $\delta(x,y) = \delta(y,x)$ for each $x, y \in M$;
- $\delta(y,z) \leq \delta(y,x) + \delta(x,z)$ for each x, y and $z \in M$.

Then δ is called a metric or distance on M; and M, together with δ, is called a metric space (M, δ). The objects of the set M are also called the points of the metric space (M, δ).

More details of metric spaces can be found, for example, in [4]. Most of the existing metrics are appropriate for continuous fields. For example, the following are defined over R^2 and are generalised in the obvious way to R^n:

1. Manhattan metric: $\delta((x_1,y_1),(x_2,y_2)) = |x_1 - x_2| + |y_1 - y_2|$.

2. Euclidean metric: $\delta((x_1,y_1),(x_2,y_2)) = \sqrt{(x_1 - x_2)^2 + (y_1 - y_2)^2}$.

3. Chebychev metric: $\delta((x_1,y_1),(x_2,y_2)) = max\{|x_1 - x_2|, |y_1 - y_2|\}$.

Even when the above metrics are used, care has to be taken. The data sets might need to be scaled in order to avoid one or more features overpowering other features. For example, let $x = (2, 100)$, $y = (7, 500)$ and $z = (1, 600)$ be three point in R^2. Then the Euclidean distance between x and the other two points is as follows.

- $\delta(x,y) = \sqrt{(-5)^2 + (-400)^2} = 200.062$.
- $\delta(x,z) = \sqrt{(1)^2 + (-500)^2} = 223.609$.

Accordingly, x is closer to y. However, if the second feature had been scaled by dividing through by 10, then the Euclidean distance is as follows.

- $\delta(x,y) = \sqrt{(-5)^2 + (-4)^2} = 6.403$.
- $\delta(x,z) = \sqrt{(1)^2 + (-5)^2} = 5.099$.

Now, x is closer to z; obviously the Euclidean distance was almost entirely dominated by the second feature.

20.2.1 Mahalanobis Distance

A further distance measure, proposed originally by Mahalanobis [13], and now known as the Mahalanobis distance, D_M has been used in clustering techniques [6]. This measure is given by:

$$D_M(x,y) = \sqrt{(x-y)V^{-1}(x-y)^T}. \tag{20.1}$$

where V is the covariance matrix of the distribution of objects. The covariance of two fields measures their tendency to vary together, where the variance is the average of the squared deviation of a field from its mean. All of the covariances v_{ij} can be collected together into a covariance matrix $V = [v_{ij}]$. The covariance matrix has the following important properties.

(1) If field i and field j tend to increase together, then $v_{ij} > 0$.

(2) If field i tends to decrease when field j increases, then $v_{ij} < 0$.

(3) If field i and field j are independent, then $v_{ij} = 0$.

The Mahalanobis metric has the advantage over other metrics because it caters for the correlation between variables. As an example, in the extreme case, one field might be an exact copy of another field. Both fields contribute to the distance. For instance, let $x = (1,1)$, $y = (3,4)$ and $z = (5,2)$ be three points in R^2. If a traditional metric such as the Euclidean metric is used then

- $\delta(x,y) = \sqrt{13}$,
- $\delta(x,z) = \sqrt{17}$.

So x is closer to y than to z. However, if a new field is created and is given exactly the same values as the second field, such that $x = (1,1,1)$, $y = (3,4,4)$ and $z = (5,2,2)$, then

- $\delta(x,y) = \sqrt{22}$,
- $\delta(x,z) = \sqrt{18}$

and x is closer to z than to y, which is the reverse of the previous case.

The use of the Mahalanobis metric solves such problems (e.g., correlation) as it automatically accounts for the scaling of the coordinate axes. On the other hand, the Mahalanobis metric does have some limitations.

(1) The Mahalanobis metric cannot measure the distance between categorical fields since the covariance matrix is appropriate only for continuous fields.

(2) The Mahalanobis metric scales all the fields so that they have equal size or magnitude, which is not always practical in data mining applications.

As a result of this, this chapter proposes a solution to these problems by presenting a new metric, D_{CV}, which uses *Cramer's V* statistic [14]. D_{CV} is based on the Hamming metric which deals with nominal data. Moreover, D_{CV} is derived from the Mahalanobis metric. Unlike the Mahalanobis metric, the D_{CV} metric uses the relationship matrix of nominal fields. Further, D_{CV} can take into account a user-defined weight for each field.

20.3 D_{CV} Metric

If the fields are categorical, special metrics are required, since distance between their values cannot be defined in an obvious manner. The Hamming distance is the most popular measurement that is used to compute the distance between nominal data. If p and q are nominal values, the Hamming distance is defined as follows:

$$\delta_H(p,q) = \begin{cases} 0 & \text{if } p = q, \\ 1 & \text{otherwise.} \end{cases} \quad (20.2)$$

If p, q are n-tuples of categorical values, then we define the Hamming distance between them to be:

$$\delta_H(p_1, q_1) + \ldots + \delta_H(p_n, q_n), \quad (20.3)$$

where n is the number of categorical values. However, the Hamming distance has some limitations due to its lack of ability to handle any relationships between fields.

Let x and y be two objects described by nominal data, where $x = (x_1, \ldots, x_n)$ and $y = (y_1, \ldots, y_n)$. Then, we can introduce a new dissimilarity metric between x and y, thus

$$D_{CV}(x,y) = \sqrt{\delta_H(x,y)\, C^{-1}\, \delta_H(x,y)^T}, \quad (20.4)$$

where C is the relationship between fields and $\delta_H(x,y)$ is defined to be the vector of the Hamming metric of corresponding nominal values. The relationship between two fields measures their correlation. All of the relationship $c(s,t)$ can be collected together into a relationship matrix $C = [c_{st}]$, which is defined as follows.

$D = D_1 \times \ldots \times D_n$ is the domain of the database. A general record $r \in D$ is of the form $r = (r_1, \ldots, r_n)$ where $r_i \in D_i$ determines the value of attribute A_i. Let $D_s = \{u_1, \ldots, u_I\}$, $D_t = \{v_1, \ldots, v_J\}$. Then a contingency table for D_s and D_t is

$$\text{contingency-table}(D_s, D_t) = [N_{ij}], \quad (20.5)$$

where $N_{ij} = |\{r : r \in D, r_i = u_i \text{ and } r_j = v_j\}|$. Define $K_i = \sum_{j=1}^{J} N_{ij}$, $L_j = \sum_{i=1}^{I} N_{ij}$, $M = \sum_{i=1}^{I} K_i = \sum_{j=1}^{J} L_j$; then the chi-square value for D_s, D_t is computed by

$$\chi_{st}^2 = \sum_{i,j} \frac{(M N_{ij} - K_i L_j)^2}{M K_i L_j}. \quad (20.6)$$

We then define the *Cramer's V* statistic [14] by

$$c_{st} = \sqrt{\frac{\chi_{st}^2}{N \min(I-1, J-1)}}. \quad (20.7)$$

Equation (20.7) measures how D_s and D_t are related, giving a value between 0 and 1. A value of zero indicates no correlation (i.e., independent fields), and a value of one indicates a strong correlation. Figure 20.1 shows an example of a contingency table between gender and smoking status.

	Male	Female	
Smoking	75	450	525
Non-smoking	340	65	405
	415	515	930

FIGURE 20.1
An example of a contingency table.

For this example,*

$$\chi_{gs}^2 = \frac{((930\times75)-(415\times525))^2}{930\times415\times525} + \frac{((930\times340)-(415\times405))^2}{930\times415\times405}$$

$$+ \frac{((930\times450)-(515\times525))^2}{930\times515\times525} + \frac{((930\times65)-(515\times405))^2}{930\times515\times405}$$

$$= 446.2097.$$

Then, the relationship between gender and smoking-status is computed by *Cramer's V* statistic as follows.

$$c_{gs} = \sqrt{\frac{446.2097}{930\min(2-1,2-1)}} = 0.692.$$

From the above figure, there appears to be quite a significant relationship between gender and smoking-status.

20.3.1 Weights of Fields

To weight a field means to give it greater or lesser importance compared to other fields when measuring the distances between fields. If no weights are given to fields, then the methods of clustering are applied to a data set in the hope that previously unnoticed and potentially useful groups will emerge. However, this approach would seem appropriate only if no information at all is available about the relevance of the different fields. An alternative approach gives positive weights to selected fields, where a zero weight is given to any field not selected.

---

*For notational convenience we chose g to stand for gender and s for smoking status.

Different approaches of measuring weights have been proposed in the literature. The first approach measures the weights based on the intuitive judgements of what is important [6]. In other words, the investigator gives weights to fields based on his understanding of the data. An alternative approach is to choose the weights to be the inverses of the variances. With this variance weighting, the distance between the objects does not change irrespective of any change in the units of measurement. Thus, a low weight is given to a field that has high value of variance [16, 7].

In the D_{CV} metric, the nominal field takes a weight

$$w_r = \frac{\max_{1 \leq i \leq I} \{N_i\}}{N}, \qquad (20.8)$$

where N_i is the frequency of each value in the nominal field and N is the total number of records. Moreover, in the D_{CV} metric, weights will be associated with the diagonal of S^{-1}, such that

$$C^{-1} = \begin{bmatrix} w_1 c_{11}^{-1} & \cdots & c_{1n}^{-1} \\ \vdots & \ddots & \vdots \\ c_{n1}^{-1} & \cdots & w_n c_{nn}^{-1} \end{bmatrix}, \qquad (20.9)$$

where c_{kl}^{-1} is the element of the invertible matrix of *Cramer's V* statistic between fields.

20.4 Synthetic Examples

To get a better feel for how the D_{CV} performs, we consider two synthetic examples using limited data in order to simplify the analysis of the output. We assume that there is a strong relationship between the fields in the first example, unlike the second example, in which there is none. Further, objects are given binary values so that both the D_{CV} and D_M metrics can be applied.

Example 1: Figure 20.2 shows the objects of the first data set in $M = \{0,1\}^2$, i.e., each object represents a value in two dimensions. Some values are repeated to establish a relationship between fields. When *Cramer's V* is computed, a value of 0.675 results, indicating that there is a strong relationship between the two fields. The distances between x^1 and other objects are computed by using the Mahalanobis and the D_{CV} metrics respectively. Figures 20.3 and 20.4 show these distances.

Observe that in both tables all objects can be ordered relative to x^1 in the same way. Also the objects from each table can fall into two clusters. The first, which contains $x^1, \ldots, x^{11}$, shares the patterns $(0,0)$ and $(1,1)$ as shown in Figure 20.2. The

Object	Field 1	Field 2
x^1	0	0
x^2	1	1
x^3	1	1
x^4	1	1
x^5	1	1
x^6	0	0
x^7	0	0
x^8	1	1
x^9	1	1
x^{10}	1	1
x^{11}	0	0
x^{12}	1	0
x^{13}	0	1

FIGURE 20.2
The objects of the first data set.

Object	x^1
x^1	0
x^2	2.16
x^3	2.16
x^4	2.16
x^5	2.16
x^6	0
x^7	0
x^8	2.16
x^9	2.16
x^{10}	2.16
x^{11}	0
x^{12}	2.68
x^{13}	2.68

FIGURE 20.3
The distances of data set 1 by using the D_M metric.

second cluster contains x^{12} and x^{13} which shares the patterns of $(0,1)$ and $(1,0)$. Or we can have three clusters: with patterns $(0,0)$, $(1,1)$ and $(0,1) \vee (1,0)$.

Example 2: Figure 20.5 shows the objects of the second data set in $M = \{0,1\}^3$. When *Cramer's V* is computed for each pair of fields, a value of 0 results, indicating that there is no relationship between the three fields. The distances between x^1 and other objects are computed by using the Mahalanobis and the D_{CV} metrics respectively. Figures 20.6 and 20.7 show these distances.

Object	x^1
x^1	0
x^2	1.09
x^3	1.09
x^4	1.09
x^5	1.09
x^6	0
x^7	0
x^8	1.09
x^9	1.09
x^{10}	1.09
x^{11}	0
x^{12}	1.35
x^{13}	1.35

FIGURE 20.4
The distances of data set 1 by using the D_{CV} metric.

Object	Field 1	Field 2	Field 3
x^1	0	1	1
x^2	0	1	1
x^3	0	1	0
x^4	1	0	1
x^5	1	0	0
x^6	1	0	1
x^7	1	1	1
x^8	1	1	1

FIGURE 20.5
The objects of the second data set.

Object	x^1	x^2	x^3	x^4	x^5	x^6	x^7	x^8
x^1	0	0	2.29	2.16	3.15	2.16	2.53	2.53

FIGURE 20.6
The distances of data set 2 by using the D_M metric.

Object	x^1	x^2	x^3	x^4	x^5	x^6	x^7	x^8
x^1	0	0	$\sqrt{1}$	$\sqrt{2}$	$\sqrt{3}$	$\sqrt{2}$	$\sqrt{1}$	$\sqrt{1}$

FIGURE 20.7
The distances of data set 2 by using the D_{CV} metric.

Observe that there is a slight difference when the objects are ordered relative to x^1 in each table. In Figure 20.6, $x^4 = (1,0,1)$ and is closer to $x^1 = (0,1,1)$ than to $x^7 = (1,1,1)$ and vice versa in Figure 20.7. However, there is no correlation between the fields, and x^4 and x^1 have different values occurring in two of their respective fields. The D_{CV} metric reflects the dissimilarity of these values and, in this respect, can be said to perform better than D_M.

We may also observe that the D_{CV} and Hamming metrics work identically when there is no relationship between the fields. In this case any two objects will be closer to each other if they share similar values. Additionally, we can see that each value in Figure 20.7 is exactly the square root of the corresponding Hamming distance (as expected).

20.5 Exploiting the D_{CV} Metric

The D_{CV} metric can be applied in many disciplines such as unsupervised clustering, case-based reasoning and supervised clustering, and these will be explored in the following sections.

20.5.1 k-Means Algorithm

Cluster analysis has been classified according to the different methods used. Partitioning methods (also known as optimization clustering) have been widely used in the data mining environment, because of their scalability and efficiency.

The well-known k-means algorithm [12] is the most popular partitioning algorithm. It uses an iterative, hill climbing technique. Starting with an initial k partition, objects are moved from one partition to another in an effort to improve the result of clustering.

The biggest advantage of the k-means algorithm in data mining applications is its efficiency in clustering large data sets. The k-means algorithm usually uses the simple Euclidean distance which is only suitable for hyperspherical clusters, and its use is limited to numeric data. However, the most distinct characteristic of data mining is that it deals with categorical data. Huang [8] presented an algorithm, called k-modes, to extend the k-means paradigm to categorical objects. k-modes uses the Hamming metric. However, the Hamming metric does not take into account any correlations between the fields, but in this case k-modes may be adapted to use the D_{CV} metric.

20.5.2 Case-Based Reasoning

Case-Based Reasoning (CBR) is a computational paradigm in which an artificial problem solver finds solutions to new problems by adapting solutions that were used

Statistical Data Mining and Knowledge Discovery

to solve old problems [3]. A case-based reasoner has a case library and each case describes a problem and a solution to that problem. The reasoner solves new problems by adapting relevant cases from this library.

To solve a problem, a case-based reasoning method can retrieve a case (or cases), which is similar to the current one from its library. The retrieved case is used to suggest a solution which is then reused and tested for success. If necessary, the solution is then revised. Finally the current problem and its solution are retained as a new case. Thus the retrieval stage, which is based on measuring the similarity (or distance) of a given case to other cases in the library, is crucial to the success of case-based reasoning methods. However, the descriptions of the cases in the library often involve many categorical fields, and some of these categorical fields also have strong correlations. When this so, the retrieval engine will need some assistance in selecting the most suitable case, and here the D_{CV} metric can be usefully employed.

20.5.3 Supervised Clustering

Clustering, in general, is defined as grouping similar objects together by optimizing some quality measurement for each cluster such as within-group distances. Since clustering generally works in an unsupervised fashion, it is not necessarily guaranteed to group the same type (class) of objects together. In this case, supervision needs to be introduced to partition the objects that have the same label into one cluster. This is done by assigning an appropriate weight to the metric for each field.

The D_{CV} metric can be used in the supervised clustering of categorical data. Weights can be introduced so that records with identical labels tend to lie in similar clusters.

20.6 Conclusions and Future Work

Clustering has typically been a problem related to continuous fields. However, in data mining, often the data values are categorical and cannot be assigned meaningful continuous substitutes. This chapter has been a study of this problem and a new metric for nominal data has been proposed. The new metric takes into account the relationships between fields, and more important fields take more weight. The weight is derived from the frequency of values within the nominal field. The D_{CV} metric can be applied to many disciplines such as cluster analysis and case-based reasoning.

Data mining is distinct from other traditional applications of cluster analysis in that data sometimes contain both numeric and categorical values. To solve this issue, the continuous data can be discretised [5] and then we can use the D_{CV} metric. The determination of suitable metrics to be used on mixed data allowing for correlation is an open research topic.

This work has presented a new and exciting approach to the problems inherent in the effective analysis of data. Categorical data, in particular, deserves more attention in the future, and this chapter is an important contribution to that endeavor. The results of these investigations are promising and prospects of more successful analyses are good.

References

[1] Berry, M. and Linoff, G. (1997). *Data Mining Techniques: For Marketing, Sales, and Customer Support*. John Wiley and Sons, New York.

[2] Berson, A., Thearling, K. and Smith, S. (1999). *Building Data Mining Applications for CRM*. McGraw-Hill Professional Publishing, New York.

[3] Bradley, K., Rafter, R. and Smyth, B. (2000). *Case-Based User Profiling for Content Personalisation. Adaptive Hypermedia and Adaptive Web-Based Systems*. Springer-Verlag, Heidelberg.

[4] Copson, E. T. (1968). *Metric Spaces*. Cambridge University Press, London.

[5] Debuse, J.C.W. and Rayward-Smith, V. J. (1968). Discretisation of continuous commercial database features for a simulated annealing data mining algorithm, *Journal of Applied Intelligence*, 285-295.

[6] Everitt, B. (1974). *Cluster Analysis*. Social Science Research Council.

[7] Hartigan, J. (1975). *Clustering Algorithms*. John Wiley and Sons, New York.

[8] Huang, Z. (1997). A Fast Clustering Algorithm to Cluster Very Large Categorical Data Sets in Data Mining. SIGMOD Workshop on Research Issues on Data Mining and Knowledge Discovery, Tucson, Arizona.

[9] Huang, Z. (1997). Clustering Large Data Sets with Mixed Numeric and Categorical Values. Proceedings of the First Pacific-Asia Conference on Knowledge Discovery and Data Mining, 21-34.

[10] Jolliffe, I. T., Jones, B. and Morgan, B. (1982). Utilising cluster: a case study involving the elderly, *J. Roy. Statist. Soc.* Volume 145, 224-236.

[11] Jourdan, L., Dhaenes, C. and Talbi, E. G. (2001). An Optimization Approach to Mine Genetic Data. METMBS'01/Session Biological Data Mining and Knowledge Discovery, 40-46.

[12] MacQueen, J. (1967). Some methods for classification and analysis of multivariate observations. *Proceeding of the 5th Berkeley Symposium*, 281-297.

[13] Mahalanobis, P. C. (1936). On generalized distance in statistics. *Proceedings of the National Inst. Sci.*, India, Volume 12, 49-55.

[14] Nagpaul, P. S. (1999). *Guide to Advanced Data Analysis using IDAMS Software*. National Institute of Science Technology and Development Studies, New Delhi, India.

[15] Kim, B. S. and Park S. B. (1986). A Fast k Nearest Neighbor Finding Algorithm Based on the Ordered Partition. In *IEEE Transactions on Pattern Analysis and Machine Intelligence, PAMI-8*, No. 6, 61-766.

[16] Sokal, R. R. and Sneath, P. H. A. (1963). *Principles of Numerical Taxonomy*. Freeman, San Francisco, CA.

21

Ordinal Logistic Modeling Using ICOMP as a Goodness-of-Fit Criterion

J. Michael Lanning and Hamparsum Bozdogan
University of Tennessee, Knoxville, USA

CONTENTS

21.1 Introduction	353
21.2 Model Selection Criteria	356
21.3 Ordinal Logistic Regression	359
21.4 Example Problem: Diabetes Severity	367
21.5 Conclusions	369
Acknowledgments	369
References	370

21.1 Introduction

Ordinal logistic regression is a relatively new method now widely used for analyzing ordinal data. There has been very little work on model selection in ordinal logistic regression. In this paper we are interested in applying an informational complexity criterion for best subset selection in ordinal logistic regression models and for goodness-of-fit in proportional odds and nested cumulative link models.

The information criteria used in this paper are based on the *Kullback-Leibler* (*KL*) (1951) information (or distance). These include Akaike's (1973) Information Criteria (*AIC*), which measures loss of information as a lack of fit (maximized log likelihood function) plus a lack of model parsimony (two times the number of estimated parameters), and an information measure of complexity (*ICOMP*) criterion that extends the *AIC* with a penalty due to increased complexity of the system. For more on *ICOMP*, see Bozdogan (2003) in this volume.

The ordinal logistic model selection using the information criteria provides a simple, effective, and objective method for the selection of a best approximating model of the data set while allowing a direct ordering of the models for comparison.

A simulation and a data set in which the severity of diabetes is ranked on an ordinal scale of one to three is analyzed to give an example and to test the model selection criteria.

Subsets	AIC	ICOMP		CAICF	DEV	Misclass
		COVB	IFIM			
1234	23.90	-139.12	-121.48	76.82	**11.9**	**2**
123	33.78	77.63	88.29	78.83	23.78	5
124	35.96	-28.98	-19.27	90.69	25.96	5
134	25.49	-122.83	-109.68	74.54	15.49	3
234	**23.27**	**-146.71**	**-128.81**	**69.23**	13.27	3
12	159.85	209.61	215.68	210	151.85	30
13	31.86	68.17	78.84	69.88	23.86	5
14	42.33	54.7	63.41	88.81	34.3	6
23	39.53	1.18	11.6	82.8	31.53	7
24	35.51	-26.77	-17.64	82.65	27.51	7
34	28.58	-107.01	-95.62	72.93	20.58	6
1	197.08	262.26	268	236.96	191.08	46
2	305.83	322.19	326.18	346.37	299.83	95
3	39.49	34.92	44.95	74.4	33.49	7
4	40.49	50.12	58.15	78.73	34.49	6

TABLE 21.1
Values of the model selection criteria for Diabetes Data.

Model	Parameter	Value	Std. Err
1234	Constant 1	6.3467	433.2365
	Constant 2	42.6379	25.7069
	Beta 1	-2.4652	2.3943
	Beta 2	-6.6809	4.4795
	Beta 3	9.4294	4.7371
	Beta 4	18.2862	9.7423
234	Constant 1	13.3185	455.9319
	Constant 2	50.5269	23.9944
	Beta 2	-8.3761	4.7611
	Beta 3	7.8746	3.8406
	Beta 4	21.4296	10.7072

TABLE 21.2
Diabetes model parameters.

One could use a simple device for regression-like analysis of ordinal data by attaching a score to each category.

$$Rating : Bad \Leftrightarrow Good$$
$$Score : 1 \Leftrightarrow 4$$

While this is often a good first step in exploratory analysis of the data, there are several drawbacks.

- No invariance to merging of adjacent categories

- Predicted scores are often out of range (i.e., negative)

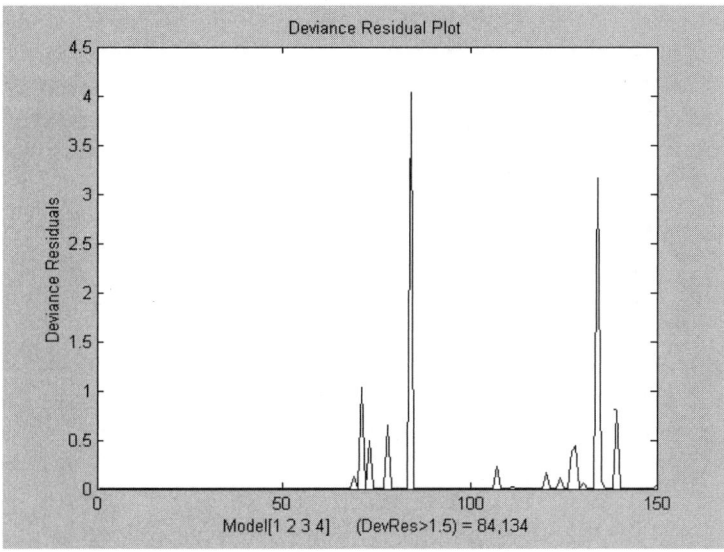

FIGURE 21.1
Deviance plot for model including X_1, X_2, X_3, and X_4.

- Scores are 'arbitrary' (differences are not equal at different points on the scale)
- Nonnormal distribution of errors.

Often used for a dichotomous response is logistic regression :

$$logit(\pi) = \left(\frac{\pi}{1-\pi}\right). \tag{21.1}$$

Modified to take into account more than two levels, there is the multinomial or base line logit model where the coefficients are log-odds comparing category $Y = k$ to a baseline category, $Y = 0$.

$$g_j(x) = \ln\left[\frac{\pi_j(x)}{\pi_0(x)}\right] = \beta_{j0} + x'\beta_j. \tag{21.2}$$

The problem is that the multinomial model does not take in account the ordinal nature of the outcome.

The most popular ordinal logistic model is the proportional odds model which compares the probability of an equal or smaller response, $Y \leq i$, to the probability of a larger response, $Y > i$ (the cumulative logits). Ordinal logistic regression is a relatively new method now widely used for analyzing ordinal data in finance, market research, medicine, and other areas, where the response variable in the model takes ordinal values such as:

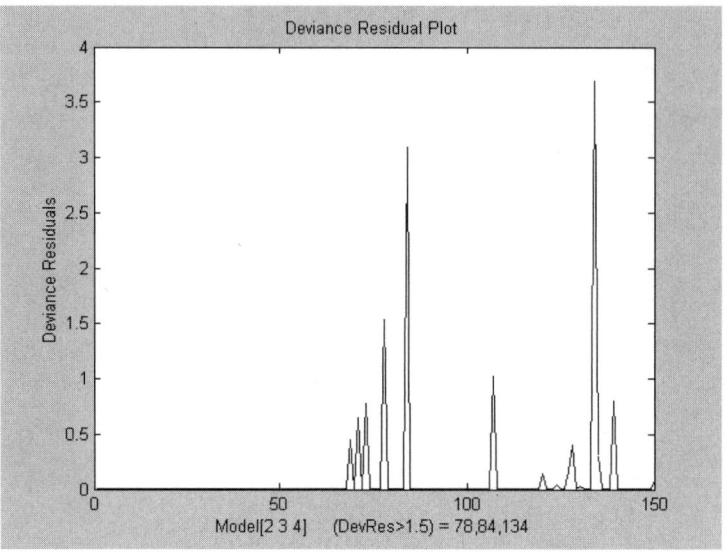

FIGURE 21.2
Deviance plot for model including X_2, X_3, and X_4.

- Credit Card Risk Analysis
- Classification of Disease (none, some, severe)
- Job Performance (inadequate, satisfactory, peak performer)

21.2 Model Selection Criteria

There has been very little work on model checking in ordinal logistic regression. In this paper we apply an Informational Measure of Complexity (ICOMP) criterion of Bozdogan (1988, 1990a, 1994, 2000, 2003) for best subset selection and goodness-of-fit in the proportional odds model.

The information criteria used in this paper are based on the *Kullback-Leibler* (*KL*) (1951) information (or distance). These include Akaike's (1973) Information Criteria (*AIC*) which measures loss of information as a lack of fit (maximized likelihood function) plus a lack of model parsimony (two times the number of estimated parameters). The Informational Measure of Complexity (*ICOMP*) criteria extend the *AIC* criteria with a penalty due to increased complexity of the system.

The specific criteria used in this paper are

- Akaike's (1973) information criterion (*AIC*):

$$AIC = -2\log L(\widehat{\theta}) + 2(\# \, model \, parameters), \quad (21.3)$$

where $-2\log L(\widehat{\theta})$ is obtained from:

$$LR = 2\sum_{i=1}^{n} y_{i,observed} \ln\left[\frac{y_{i,observed}}{y_{i,expected}}\right]. \quad (21.4)$$

- Bozdogan's (1990) information complexity (*ICOMP*) criterion based on finite sampling distribution of the parameter estimates is given by:

$$ICOMP(\widehat{Cov}(\widehat{\beta})) = n\ln(2\pi) + n\ln(\widehat{\sigma}^2) + n + 2C_1(\widehat{Cov}(\widehat{\beta})) \quad (21.5)$$

where $C_1(\circ)$ is a maximal information theoretic measure of complexity of a covariance matrix $\widehat{Cov}(\widehat{\beta})$ defined by

$$C_1(\widehat{Cov}(\widehat{\beta})) = \frac{q}{2}\log\left[\frac{tr(\widehat{Cov}(\widehat{\beta}))}{q}\right] - \frac{1}{2}\log|\widehat{Cov}(\widehat{\beta})|, \quad (21.6)$$

where

$$\widehat{Cov}(\widehat{\beta}) = \widehat{\sigma}^2(X'WX)^{-1}, \quad (21.7)$$

and where:

$$W_{(n\times n)} = diag[n_1\widehat{p}_1(1-\widehat{p}_1),\ldots,n_n\widehat{p}_n(1-\widehat{p}_n)], \quad (21.8)$$

$$\widehat{\sigma}^2 = \frac{1}{n}\sum_{i=1}^{n}\frac{(y_i - n_i\widehat{p}_i)^2}{n_i\widehat{p}_i(1-\widehat{p}_i)}. \quad (21.9)$$

- Information complexity (*ICOMP*) criterion of the estimated inverse Fisher information matrix (*IFIM*), *ICOMP(IFIM)* is:

$$ICOMP(IFIM) = -2\log L(\widehat{\theta}) + C_1(\widehat{F}^{-1}(\widehat{\theta})), \quad (21.10)$$

where the complexity of the accuracy of the parameter estimates of the model as measured by *IFIM* is given by

$$C_1(\widehat{F}^{-1}(\widehat{\theta})) = \frac{s}{2}\log\left[\frac{tr(\widehat{F}^{-1}(\widehat{\theta}))}{s}\right] - \frac{1}{2}\log|\widehat{F}^{-1}(\widehat{\theta})|, \quad (21.11)$$

and where the estimated *IFIM* for the model is:

$$\widehat{F}^{-1}(\widehat{\theta}) = \begin{bmatrix} \widehat{\sigma}^2(X'WX)^{-1} & 0 \\ 0' & \frac{2\widehat{\sigma}^4}{n} \end{bmatrix}. \quad (21.12)$$

- Bozdogan's (1987) consistent *AIC* with Fisher information matrix (*CAICF*) is:

Subsets	AIC	ICOMP COVB	ICOMP IFIM	CAICF	DEV	Misclass
1234	10	16.21	55.3	84.4	0	0
123	8	12.81	51.78	78.4	0	0
124	8	8.82	47.49	76.76	0	0
134	8	13.07	51.86	76.35	0	0
234	8	8.81	47.83	76.8	0	0
12	6	9.51	48.41	65.79	0	0
13	6	11.67	51.92	69.81	0	0
14	6	8	47.25	67.6	0	0
23	6	8.4	46.97	68.93	0	0
24	6	5.23	43.66	67.98	0	0
34	6	5.56	45.8	69.21	0	0
1	75.84	79.43	85.76	102.75	71.84	16
2	127.83	129.86	134.49	153.32	123.83	27
3	**4**	3.89	43.39	60.95	0	0
4	**4**	**2.88**	**42.13**	**58.69**	0	0

TABLE 21.3
Values of the model selection criteria for nested diabetes data, Y = {1,2}.

Model	Parameter	Value	Std. Err
3	Constant 1	-64.3	3.59
	Beta 3	-26.1	1.39
4	Constant 1	-58.3	2.97
	Beta 4	-74.1	3.58

TABLE 21.4
Nested diabetes model parameters, Y={1,2}.

$$CAICF = n\log(2\pi) + n\log(\widehat{\sigma}^2) + n + k[\log(n) + 2] + \log|\widehat{F}| \quad (21.13)$$

where $|\widehat{F}|$ denotes the determinant of the *estimated FIM* which is the inverse of *IFIM*, and where $-2\log L(\widehat{\theta})$ is obtained from the log likelihood ratio (*LR*) Chi-square:

$$LR = 2\sum_{i=1}^{n} y_{i,observed} \ln\left[\frac{y_{i,observed}}{y_{i,expected}}\right]. \quad (21.14)$$

21.2.1 Computational Software

The *MATLAB* programs were developed and used to analyze ordinal logistic regression data based on the existing programs of Bozdogan's (1990b) from his lecture notes and using the *LOGIST* module of Smyth's (1999) StatBox 4.1.

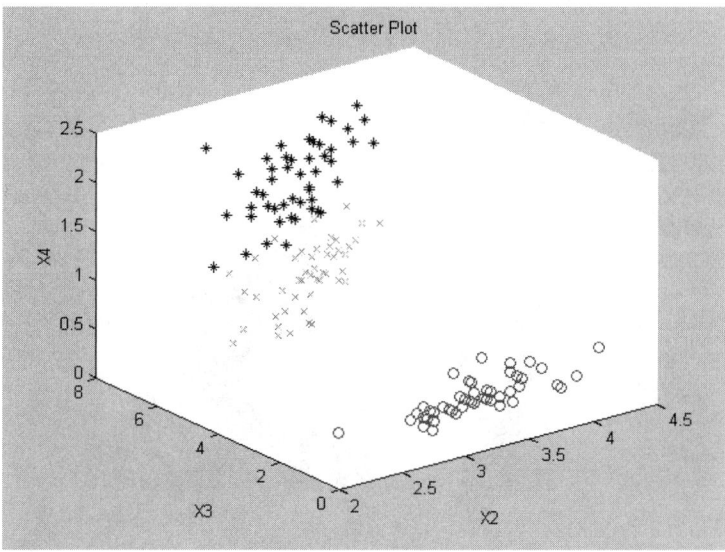

FIGURE 21.3
Scatter plot of variables X_2, X_3, and X_4.

21.3 Ordinal Logistic Regression

A natural way to a baseline view of ordinal data is to postulate the existence of an underlying latent (unobserved) variable, Z, associated with each response (Fox, 1997). The range of Z is dissected by $m-1$ boundaries into m regions where α_k are category boundary cutoffs within the model, and the response Y is given by

$$Y_i = \begin{Bmatrix} 1 & z_i \leq \alpha_1 & \pi_1 \\ 2 & \alpha_1 < z_i \leq \alpha_2 & \pi_2 \\ \vdots & \vdots & \vdots \\ m-1 & \alpha_{m-2} < z_i \leq \alpha_{m-1} & \pi_{m-1} \\ m & \alpha_{m-1} < & \pi_m \end{Bmatrix} \quad (21.15)$$

The general aim is to relate $\pi_1,...,\pi_m$ to explanatory variables $X_1, X_2,...,X_p$ and to take account of the ordering among the categories by using different functions of $\pi_1,...,\pi_m$ which exploit the ordering.

Consider two values, X_1, X_2 of vectors of explanatory variables and define the cumulative probability as

$$\gamma_j = \pi_1 + ... + \pi_j \quad \text{where} \quad j = 1,...,m-1, \quad (21.16)$$
$$\gamma_m = 1.$$

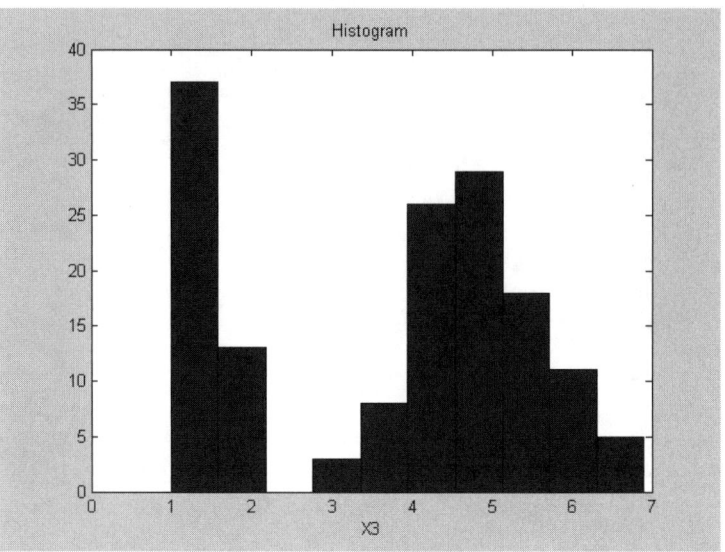

FIGURE 21.4
Histogram for variable X_3.

If $\gamma_j(X_1) < \gamma_j(X_2)$ for all $j = 1,...,m-1$, then there is a clear sense in which the response can be said to be systematically higher at X_1 than at X_2 and the two distributions are said to be stochastically ordered (Firth, 2001).

Common models in which stochastic ordering holds can be modeled as sets of nested dichotomous variables: the cumulative link models, and the continuation-ratio logits models.

21.3.1 Cumulative Link Models

The underlying latent (unobserved) variable, Z, associated with each response can be assumed to be drawn from a continuous response centered on a mean value that varies from individual. This mean value is then modeled as a linear function of the respondent's covariate vector (Johnson, 1999).

Suppose

$$Y = X'B + \varepsilon \qquad (21.17)$$

where ε is a normally distributed error with unit variance. Y is not observed but a coarsely categorized version. Then

$$\gamma_j = P(Y < \alpha_j) = \Phi[\alpha_j - X'B], \qquad (21.18)$$
$$\Phi^{-1}(\gamma_j) = \alpha_j - X'B.$$

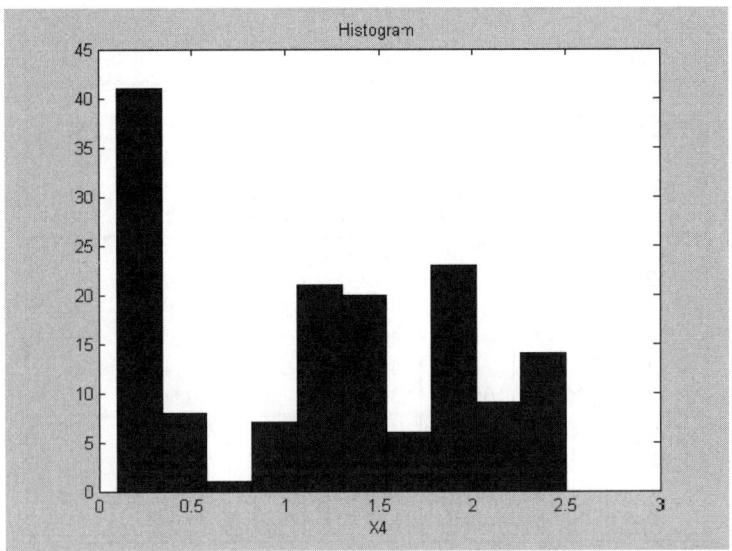

FIGURE 21.5
Histogram for variable X_4.

This is the cumulative 'probit' model.
Cumulative link models can be defined as a generalized linear model:

$$\eta_i = g(\mu_i) = \alpha_j - X''B \tag{21.19}$$

where $g(\mu_i)$ is a link function that transforms the expectation of the dependent variable $\mu_i \equiv E(Y_i)$ to the linear predictor η_i (Myers, 2002).

21.3.2 Cumulative Logit (Proportional Odds) Model

The cumulative 'logit' model

$$\text{logit}(\gamma_j) = \alpha_j - X'B \tag{21.20}$$

corresponds to the regressions errors, ε, having a logistic distribution instead of normal.

The proportional odds models compare the probability of an equal or smaller response, $Y \leq j$, to the probability of a larger response, $Y > j$ (the cumulative logits)

$$p_j(x) = \ln\left[\frac{P(Y \leq j \mid x)}{P(Y > j \mid x)}\right] = \ln\left[\frac{\sum_{i=0}^{j} \pi_i}{\sum_{i=j+1}^{K} \pi_i}\right] \tag{21.21}$$

$$= \ln\left[\frac{\gamma_j}{1 - \gamma_j}\right] = \alpha_j - x'\beta.$$

Subsets	AIC	ICOMP		CAICF	DEV	Misclass
		COVB	IFIM			
1234	21.9	27.2	38.04	65.92	11.9	2
123	31.77	36.62	45.68	71	23.77	5
124	33.9	35.75	43.78	73.38	25.9	5
134	23.49	27.82	37.87	62.49	15.49	3
234	**21.27**	**26.52**	**37.35**	**59.63**	**13.27**	**3**
12	121.9	125.07	129.74	155.02	115.9	29
13	29.85	34.74	43.89	63.87	23.85	5
14	39.29	41.85	49.44	72.99	33.29	6
23	37.54	41.39	49.82	70.44	31.51	7
24	33.4	33.4	40.92	66.31	27.4	7
34	26.56	30.04	39.42	59.67	20.56	6
1	121.35	124.53	129.17	148.29	117.35	27
2	192.14	193.15	195.93	217.82	188.14	51
3	37.43	41.74	50.51	64.77	33.43	7
4	37.42	38.26	45.55	64.26	33.42	6

TABLE 21.5
Values of the model selection criteria for nested diabetes data, Y = {2,3}.

Model	Parameter	Value	Std. Err
234	Constant 1	-50.5265	23.9946
	Beta 1	8.376	4.7611
	Beta 2	-7.8745	3.8406
	Beta 3	-21.4296	10.7072

TABLE 21.6
Diabetes nested model with parameters, Y = {2,3}.

The negative sign of the linear predictor is a convention ensuring that high values of $x'\beta$ lead to increased probability for higher categories.

An extension of logistic regression, *cumulative logit model* is also known as the *proportional odds model*, the most popular ordinal logistic model. It is called a proportional odds model since it assumes that each logit follows a linear model with a separate intercept parameter but other regression parameters are constant (proportional) across all cumulative logits for different levels.

In a nested dichotomous variable, this would be solved as a set of simultaneous models as shown below:

$$[1,2,...,m] -- \Longrightarrow [1 \mid 2,...,m] \quad (21.22)$$
$$\Longrightarrow [1,2 \mid ...,m]$$
$$\Longrightarrow [1,2,... \mid m].$$

21.3.3 Proportional Hazard Model

Another common regression model for ordinal data is the proportional hazards model, given by the log-log link

$$g(\gamma_j) = \log[-\log(1-\gamma_j)] = \alpha_j - X'B \quad (21.23)$$

If $1 - \gamma_j$ is interpreted as the possibility of survival beyond time category j, this model may be considered as a discrete version of the proportional hazards (PH) model, (Johnson, 1999)

The error term, ε, of this model is that of the extreme value distribution.

21.3.4 Continuation-Ratio Model

The 'backward' continuation-ratio model compares each response, $Y = i$, to all lower responses, $Y < i$

$$p_j(x) = \ln\left[\frac{P(Y=j\mid x)}{P(Y<j\mid x)}\right] \quad (21.24)$$

$$= \ln\left[\frac{\pi_j}{\gamma_{j-1}}\right] = \alpha_j - x'\beta.$$

In a nested dichotomous variable, this would be solved as a set of simultaneous models as shown in the following figure:

$$[1,2,...,m] --\Longrightarrow [1\mid 2]$$
$$--\Longrightarrow [1,2\mid ...]$$
$$--\Longrightarrow [1,2,...\mid m].$$

Continuation-ratios are popular because of their appealing interpretation. Although 'forward' continuation-ratio models are more common,

$$p_j(x) = \ln\left[\frac{P(Y=j\mid x)}{P(Y \geq j\mid x)}\right]. \quad (21.25)$$

In ordinal response modeling, the interest is in the odds of a higher state measured with lower states in steps. For example, what are the odds of continuing to college based on the completion of high school; and in the next step, what is the completion of post secondary education based on the completion of college (Fox, 1997).

21.3.5 Category Boundary Cutoffs (Correlated Data)

In ordinal response data, there is often a lack of independence in the covariates since they are often multiple measurements made on the n observations within each response category m. These cluster-specific categories (and covariates) are modeled with category boundary cutoffs, α_k.

Model Eqn 1	Model Eqn 2	AIC	DEV	Misclass
1234	1234	31.898	**11.899**	2
123	123	39.772	23.772	5
124	124	41.902	25.902	5
134	134	31.492	15.492	3
234	**234**	**29.266**	**13.266**	3
12	12	124.803	112.803	29
13	13	35.850	23.850	5
14	14	45.287	33.287	6
23	23	43.512	31.512	7
24	24	39.400	27.400	7
34	34	32.564	20.564	6
1	1	190.023	182.023	38
2	2	260.493	252.493	68
3	3	41.432	33.432	7
4	4	41.421	33.421	6
3	**1234**	**25.899**	**11.899**	**2**
3	**234**	**25.266**	**13.266**	**3**
4	**1234**	**25.899**	**11.899**	**2**
4	**234**	**25.266**	**13.266**	**3**

TABLE 21.7
Summary of values of the model selection criteria.

Subsets	AIC	ICOMP		CAICF
		COVB	IFIM	
1234	12	11	11	1
123	37	22	20	23
124	0	2	2	0
134	0	3	3	0
234	0	0	1	0
12	0	1	0	0
13	0	1	1	0
14	0	1	1	1
23	0	1	1	0
24	0	3	3	0
34	0	0	0	0
1	0	0	0	0
2	0	1	3	0
3	0	0	0	0
4	1	4	4	25

TABLE 21.8
Simulation model: $N = 100$.

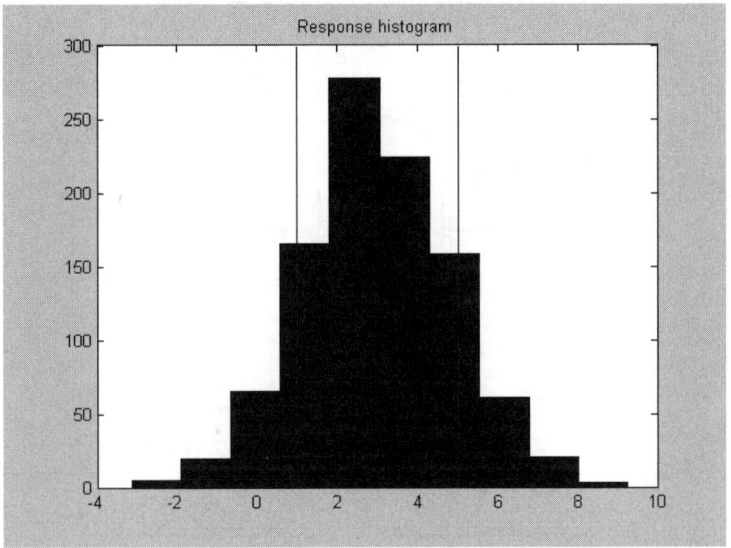

FIGURE 21.6
Histogram of simulation data.

The effect of the α_k is to increase the correlation among responses within a cluster relative category to the correlation between categories. [The basic idea is that the underlying logistic probabilities for observations have a common value of α that provide a 'baseline' interpretation between clusters.] Thus the within-cluster correlation increases with increasing σ_α^2 and vice versa, (Hosmer, 2000).

The numerical methods of log-linear models are sensitive to the number of clusters and cluster size and one must be careful when fitting cluster-specific models.

For example,

- If the intracluster correlation is very small, then the software may fail to converge to a solution.

- If the intracluster correlation is too high, then the coefficients estimates may become unstable.

Examples of each will be seen in the case study.

21.3.6 Model Selection

Selection of the appropriate model depends on the structure of the data and on the analyst interest. Below are listed some considerations (Firth, 2001).

- All three models describe forms of stochastic ordering.

Subsets	AIC	ICOMP		CAICF
		COVB	IFIM	
1234	8	14	14	0
123	42	23	23	43
124	0	2	2	0
134	0	1	1	0
234	0	4	3	0
12	0	0	0	0
13	0	0	0	0
14	0	1	1	0
23	0	1	1	0
24	0	2	3	0
34	0	1	1	0
1	0	0	0	0
2	0	0	0	0
3	0	0	0	0
4	0	1	1	7

TABLE 21.9
Simulation model: $N = 200$.

- The proportional odds (PO) and hazards (PH) models are natural in situations where the ordinal response is thought to represent division of an underlying continuous scale.

- The PH and PO models are invariant under a reversal of categories (the signs of the regression coefficients change).

- The PH and PO models are also invariant under collapsing of the categories (the regression coefficients do not change).

- The continuation-ratio is not invariant, and the forward and backward models are not equivalent and yield different results. Care must be used in choosing the continuation model.

Another major consideration is the availability of software to fit the models. The proportional odd models are now becoming standard in statistical software. Add-in programs for ordinal regressions are also becoming increasingly available.

All these considerations are important, but the main consideration is the fit of the data. Using binary regression, these models can be developed as defined in the nested dichotomous variables given in the above sections. Using this method allows each intersection to be optimized on fit to the data in regards to variable selection since, if the assumption of the PO model is false, it may lead to invalid results and interpretation.

21.4 Example Problem: Diabetes Severity

Consider the diabetes data set from Andrews and Herzberg (1985). This data set includes $n = 150$ responses where the dependent variable is an ordinal response on the severity of the patient's disease, $Y = $ *Patient diabetes severity (1,2,3)*, and the four predictor variables are continuous: X_1, X_2, X_3, and X_4.

$AIC, ICOMP(\widehat{Cov}(\widehat{\beta})), ICOMP(IFIM)$, and $CAICF$ are implemented as the model selection criteria to choose the best subset logistic regression model and see if they produce the same or different subsets.

21.4.1 Proportional Odds Model

Fitting the Proportional Odds Model, the information criteria results can be found in Table 21.1 with the corresponding deviance and number of misclassified responses.

While the minimum number of misclassifications is with the full set of predictor variables, all the selection criteria choose variables two, three, and four as the best prediction set; but if we look at the deviance values between the two models, we see that the added variable does not add any statistical significance to the model. Also, the standard errors of model parameters, Table 21.2, show a stronger fit for the reduced model.

21.4.2 Residual (Outlier) Analysis

Associated with each of the multinomial observations are $m = 3$ categories. In ordinal data if you know of the probability p_{ij} for $m - 1$ of the categories, the probability of the last is known. Therefore, there are potentially $m - 1$ residuals for each of the n observations. Because of the increase in dimensionality, it is not clear how classical (Pearson, deviance, etc.) residuals should be displayed (Johnson, 1999).

While the *Deviance* (Log-likelihood Ratio (*LR*) Chi-Square) is being used for model selection for the *AIC* and *CAIC*, the deviance contributions from individual observations should be examined. Observations that contribute disproportionately to the overall deviance should be regarded with suspicion.

The deviance plots for each of the top two models are given in Figure 21.1 and 21.2. Note that the values with the high deviance are also the missclassified observations for each of the models.

Removal of the misclassified values led to failure of the modeling code for the first reason given in the discussion of boundary cutoffs. The values are located in the second and third clusters and may be providing the leverage that define the clusters. Remember, the clusters are determined by the modeler, not the modeling technique. The software may be failing to converge to a solution because the intracluster correlation is very small or because there are only two clusters in the data.

Figure 21.2 is the scatter plot for the best fitting model: ($Y = 1$, circle; $Y = 2$, cross; $Y = 3$, star).

21.4.3 Nested Dichotomous Models

The main assumption of the proportional odds model is that while each logit follows a linear model with a separate intercept parameter the other regression parameters are constant (proportional) across all cumulative logits for different levels.

This may or may not be true.

While this assumption is made with an expert understanding of the process under study, often it is made with no understanding of the modeling implications and simply because it is the method available.

One way to check this assumption is through the use of simultaneous nested dichotomous models as described in the preceding sections. While the model is not as clean as the proportional odds models, it can be optimized on subset selection and allow for a more complete understanding of the data for each dichotomous step.

21.4.4 Nested Cumulative Link Dichotomous Models

For the Proportional Odds Dichotomous Model, each 'intersection' will be checked for the best subset selection, and then the final probabilities will be computed and the overall model checked for the best subset selection.

Checking for the best subset between categories one and two, we see that **model [4]** for all the criteria is chosen. *AIC* also chooses **model [3]** as a possible choice.

The parameters and histogram for each of the models is given below. What is not readily apparent is that this model would give an unstable result for the coefficients in some modeling programs, even though the overall fit will be very significant with no misclassifications.

Referring to the previous scatter plot and the histogram in Figure 21.3 and 21.4, it can be seen that the intracluster correlation is high to the correlation between category one and category two. There is a 'wide' area for the placement for the line, and the intercept, α, has a large variance and will be determined highly insignificant and unstable. While this is not true for the modeling program used in this report, this is the result when using JMP.

Checking for the best subset between categories two and three, we see that the same model is chosen as the proportional odds model, including coefficients and misclassifications.

The *AIC* values for the overall model fit are as follows. The best proportional model is still [234], but the coefficient values will be different between equations. The best model overall is [3 or 4] and [234 or 1234].

21.4.5 Nested Continuation-Ratio Link Dichotomous Models

The continuation ratio nested model gives identical results (the model equations will have a different interpretation) and therefore will not be presented.

21.4.5.1 Simulation:

A ordinal response data set was simulated to test the fit criteria.
The independent variables are defined as:

$$X_1 \sim N(6,1)$$
$$X_2 \sim N(0,1)$$
$$X_3 \sim N(-4,1)$$
$$X_4 \sim X_1 + X_2 + X_3 + 0.5 * N(0,1) + 1$$

The response variable is defined as

$$y = X_1 + X_2 + X_3 + 0.5 \times N(0,1).$$

As shown in Figure 21.6, the response was divided into three categories.

The data was simulated for $N = 100$ and 200 observations for 50 replications in order to see how many times each criteria would hit the correct model of [123]. The lower number of observations was set by the modeling program's ability to converge to a solution.

The best selection criteria as N increased is *CAICF*, since it was able to distinguish between the true variables X_1, X_2, X_3 and a closely related fourth variable X_4.

21.5 Conclusions

The ordinal logistic model selection using information criteria provided a simple, effective, and objective method for the selection of a best approximating model of the diabetes data set while allowing a direct ordering of the models for comparison. The criteria proved simpler and more effective than traditional variable selection methods with manual and computational stepwise procedures, and allow the user to pursue other cumulative link models other than the proportional odds models.

While more work is needed in the development of informational complexity criterion in application to ordinal logistic regression, it is a viable option for best model subset selection and goodness-of-fit.

Acknowledgments

The first author extends his appreciation and thanks to Dr. Bozdogan in guiding and supervising him on this interesting research problem.

References

Akaike, H. (1973). Information theory and an extension of the maximum likelihood principle. In B.N. Petrov and F. Csáki (Eds.), *Second international symposium on information theory*, Académiai Kiadó, Budapest, 267-281.

Andrews, D.F. and Herzberg, A.M. (1985). *Data*, Springer-Verlag, New York.

Bozdogan, H. (1987). Model selection and Akaike's Information Criterion (AIC): The general theory and its analytical extensions. *Psychometrika,* 52(3), 345-370.

Bozdogan, H. (1988). ICOMP: a new model-selection criterion. *Classification and related methods of data analysis*, H. H. Bock (Ed.), Elsevier Science Publishers, Amsterdam, 599-608.

Bozdogan, H. (1990a). On the information-based measure of covariance complexity and its application to the evaluation of multivariate linear models.*Communications in Statistics, Theory and Methods*, 19, 221-278.

Bozdogan, H. (1990b). *Lecture Notes in Stat 677: Statistical Modeling and Model Evaluation: A New Information-Theoretic Approach*, Department of Statistics, the University of Tennessee.

Bozdogan, H. (1994). Mixture-model cluster analysis using a new informational complexity and model selection criteria. In *Multivariate Statistical Modeling*, H. Bozdogan (Ed.), Vol. 2, Proceedings of the First US/Japan Conference on the Frontiers of Statistical Modeling: An Informational Approach, Kluwer Academic Publishers, Dordrecht, the Netherlands, 69-113.

Bozdogan, H. (2000). Akaike's information criterion and recent developments in information complexity. *Journal of Mathematical Psychology*, 44, 62-91.

Bozdogan, H. (2003). Intelligent statistical data mining with information complexity and genetic algorithms. In *Statistical Data Mining and Knowledge Discovery*, H. Bozdogan (Ed.), Chapman & Hall/CRC, Boca Raton, FL.

Firth, D. (2001). *Lecture Notes in Advanced Social Statistics*. Department of Statistics, the University of Oxford.

Fox J. (1997). *Applied Regression Analysis, Linear Models, and Related Methods.* Sage Publications, Newbury Park, CA.

Hosmer, David W. (2000). *Applied Logistic Regression*, 2nd ed. John Wiley and Sons, New York.

Hosmer, D.W. and Lemeshow, S. (2000). *Applied Logistic Regression.* John Wiley and Sons, New York.

Johnson, V.E. and Albert, J.H. (1999). *Ordinal Data Modeling*. Springer-Verlag, New York.

Kullback, S. and Leibler, R. (1951). On information and sufficiency. *Ann. Math. Statist.*, 22, 79-86.

Myers, R.H., Montgomery, D.C., and Vining, G.G. (2002). *Generalized Linear Models*. John Wiley and Sons, New York.

Smyth, G. K. (1999). StatBox 4.1: A statistics toolbox for Matlab. University of Queensland, Brisbane (www.maths.uq.edu.au/~gks/matlab/statbox.html).

22

Comparing Latent Class Factor Analysis with the Traditional Approach in Data Mining

Jay Magidson and Jeroen K. Vermunt
Statistical Innovations Inc., USA, and Tilburg University, The Netherlands

CONTENTS

22.1 Introduction	373
22.2 The Basic LC Factor Model	375
22.3 Examples	376
22.4 Conclusion	381
References	383

A major goal of data mining is to extract a small number of meaningful "factors" from a larger number of variables available on a database. While traditional factor analysis (FA) offers such a data reduction capability, it is severely limited in practice because it requires all variables to be continuous, and it uses the assumption of multivariate normality to justify a linear model. In this paper, we propose a general maximum likelihood alternative to FA that does not have the above limitations. It may be used to analyze combinations of dichotomous, nominal, ordinal, and count variables and uses appropriate distributions for each scale type. The approach utilizes a framework based on latent class (LC) modeling that hypothesizes categorical as opposed to continuous factors, each of which has a small number of discrete levels. One surprising result is that exploratory LC factor models are identified while traditional exploratory FA models are not identified without imposing a rotation.

22.1 Introduction

A major goal of data mining is to extract a relatively small number of meaningful "factors" from a larger number of variables available on a database. While traditional factor analysis (FA) offers such a data reduction capability, it is severely limited in practice for 4 reasons:

1. It requires all variables to be continuous.

2. It uses the assumption of multivariate normality to justify a linear model.

3. It assumes that the underlying latent variables (factors) are measured on an interval or ratio scale.

4. Results are generally not unique – in order to interpret the solution users must select from among possible "rotations," each of which provides a somewhat different result.

Although justified only for continuous variables, FA is frequently used in practice with variables of other scale types including dichotomous, nominal, ordinal, and count variables. In such cases, the linearity assumption will generally be violated, as the true model will typically be nonlinear. In particular, when the observed variables are dichotomous, FA users have sometimes observed the occurrence of non-informative extraneous factors on which variables having a common skewness (i.e., similar marginal distributions) tend to have large factor loadings. It is possible that such factors serve as proxies for various nonlinearities in the model.

Even when the first 2 assumptions hold true, in the case that one or more *latent* variables is dichotomous, statistical inferences used in maximum likelihood FA are not valid as such tests assume that the factors are multivariate normal.

A promising alternative to FA, proposed by Magidson and Vermunt (2001) utilizes a framework based on latent class (LC) modeling. This latent class approach to factor analysis (LCFA) hypothesizes dichotomous or ordered categorical (ordinal) as opposed to continuous factors, and is especially suited for categorical variables. While this methodology resolves each of the 4 FA problems stated above, it has its own limitations. In particular, when used in the exploratory setting, the following limitations have been noted:

1. LCFA has primarily been applied in confirmatory applications involving a relatively small number of variables. Recent advances in computing power and the availability of new efficient algorithms suggest that LCFA may be applicable in larger exploratory settings, but this has not yet been tested.

2. The LCFA analogs to the "loadings" used in FA are given by log-linear parameters, which are not so easy to interpret.

In this paper, we use real data to compare LCFA with FA in situations where the assumptions from FA are violated. For simplicity, we have limited our current study to examples where the manifest variables are all dichotomous. To facilitate this comparison, we linearize the latent class model, transforming the log-linear effects to linearized parameters comparable to traditional loadings used in FA. Two data sets are used for this comparison. The first utilizes data analyzed previously by LCFA (Magidson and Vermunt, 2003) which yields results that are clearly nonlinear. The second involves 19 dichotomous indicators from the Myers-Briggs Type Indicator, designed to measure 2 latent dimensions of personality, hypothesized by Karl Jung to be dichotomous.

The LCFA model is described in section 22.2 along with a brief history of LC models. Section 22.3 presents results from 2 data examples, where the Latent GOLD computer program was used to estimate the LC models. The results are summarized in section 22.4.

22.2 The Basic LC Factor Model

The LC Factor model was originally proposed for use with nominal manifest and dichotomous latent variables in various confirmatory applications (Goodman, 1974). This model was extended for use with ordinal *latent* variables and for *manifest* variables of differing scale types – dichotomous, ordinal, continuous, and count variables – by Vermunt and Magidson (2000). A *basic* LC factor model consisting of K mutually independent dichotomous factors was proposed by Magidson and Vermunt (2001) for general exploratory applications. For the expository purposes of this paper, we limit to applications of this exploratory model. For other applications involving more complex LCFA models see Magidson and Vermunt (2003).

Let θ_k denote a value of one of the K dichotomous latent variables. Without loss of generality we assume that θ_k can take on two values, 0 and 1. Let y_j denote a value on one of the J observed variables. The most common parameterization of the basic LC factor model is in terms of unconditional and conditional probabilities. For example, for 4 nominal variables, a basic 2-factor LC model can be expressed in terms of the joint probability $P(\theta_1, \theta_2, y_1, y_2, y_3, y_4)$:

$$P(\theta_1, \theta_2, y_1, y_2, y_3, y_4) = P(\theta_1, \theta_2) P(y_1|\theta_1, \theta_2) P(y_2|\theta_1, \theta_2)$$
$$P(y_3|\theta_1, \theta_2) P(y_4|\theta_1, \theta_2), \qquad (22.1)$$

where the conditional probability parameters are restricted by logit models. More precisely, the conditional probability for manifest variable j is assumed to be equal to

$$P(y_j|\theta_1, \theta_2) = \frac{\exp(\beta_{j0y_j} + \beta_{j1y_j}\theta_1 + \beta_{j2y_j}\theta_2)}{\sum_{y_j} \exp(\beta_{j0y_j} + \beta_{j1y_j}\theta_1 + \beta_{j2y_j}\theta_2)}. \qquad (22.2)$$

For the basic factor LC model, the latent variables are assumed to be independent of one another. Thus, we have the following additional constraint:

$$P(\theta_1, \theta_2) = P(\theta_1) P(\theta_2). \qquad (22.3)$$

The constraints of the type in equation (22.2) restrict the conditional response probabilities in a manner similar to traditional FA by excluding the higher-order interaction terms involving θ_1 and θ_2. The β parameters can be viewed as category-specific "loadings" on the factor concerned, expressed as log-linear parameters. Note that one identifying constraint has to be imposed on each set of β parameters.

If variable j were instead ordinal or dichotomous, equation (22.2) becomes

$$P(y_j|\theta_1, \theta_2) = \frac{\exp(\beta_{j0y_j} + \beta_{j1} y_j \theta_1 + \beta_{j2} y_j \theta_2)}{\sum_{y_j} \exp(\beta_{j0y_j} + \beta_{j1} y_j \theta_1 + \beta_{j2} y_j \theta_2)}. \qquad (22.4)$$

in which case a single loading for variable j on each of the 2 factors is given by β_{j1} and β_{j2}, respectively.

More generally, let θ denote a vector of K latent variables and $\mathbf{y}$ a vector of J observed variables. Then the model becomes:

$$f(\theta, \mathbf{y}) = f(\theta) f(\mathbf{y}|\theta) = f(\theta) \prod_{j=1}^{J} f(y_j|\theta) \qquad (22.5)$$

where $f(\theta, \mathbf{y})$ denotes the joint probability density of the latent and manifest variables, $f(\theta)$ the unconditional latent probabilities, and $f(y_j|\theta)$ the conditional density for variable j given a person's latent scores. The primary model assumption in equation (22.5) is that the J observed variables are independent of each other given the latent variables. That is, as in traditional FA, the latent variables explain all of the associations among the observed variables.

The conditional means of each manifest variable are restricted by regression type constraints; that is, by a regression model from the generalized linear modelingfamily. The following distributions and transformations are used:

Scale type	Distribution $f(y_j|\theta)$	Transformation $g(.)$
dichotomous	binomial	logit
nominal	multinomial	logit
ordinal	multinomial	restricted logit
count	Poisson	log
continuous	normal	identity

In equations (22.2) and (22.4), we gave the form of the regression models for dichotomous, nominal, and ordinal variables.

Parameters can be estimated by maximum likelihood using EM or Newton-Raphson algorithms, or combinations of the two. Maximum likelihood estimation of the LCFA model is implemented in the Latent GOLD program (Vermunt and Magidson, 2000).

22.3 Examples

In this section we compare results obtained from the latent class factor model with the traditional linear factor model.

22.3.1 Rater Agreement

For our first example we factor analyze ratings made by 7 pathologists, each of whom classified 118 slides as to the presence or absence of carcinoma in the uterine cervix (Landis and Koch, 1977). Agresti (2002), using traditional LC models to analyze these data, found that a 2-class solution does not provide an adequate fit to these data. Using the LCFA framework, Magidson and Vermunt (2003) confirmed that a

		Factor θ_1 = 1 (True -)		Factor θ_2 = 0 (True +)	
		Factor θ_1		Factor θ_2	
		1	0	1	0
Rater		0.35	0.18	0.31	0.16
F					
	-	1.00	0.99	**0.80**	0.11
	+	0.00	0.01	0.20	0.89
D					
	-	1.00	0.98	**0.61**	0.11
	+	0.00	0.02	0.39	0.89
C					
	-	1.00	1.00	0.22	0.14
	+	0.00	0.00	0.78	0.86
A					
	-	0.94	0.59	0.01	0.00
	+	0.06	**0.41**	0.99	1.00
G					
	-	0.99	0.46	0.01	0.00
	+	0.01	**0.54**	0.99	1.00
E					
	-	0.94	0.28	0.03	0.00
	+	0.06	**0.72**	0.97	1.00
B					
	-	0.87	0.01	0.03	0.00
	+	0.13	**0.99**	0.97	1.00

TABLE 22.1
Estimates of the unconditional and conditional probabilities obtained from the 2-factor LC Model.

single dichotomous factor (equivalent to a 2-class LC model) did not fit the data but that a basic 2-factor LCFA model provides a good fit.

Table 22.1 presents the results of the 2-factor model in terms of the conditional probabilities. These results suggest that factor 1 distinguishes between slides that are "true positive" or "true negative" for cancer. Factor 2 is a nuisance factor, which suggests that some pathologists bias their ratings in the direction of a "false +" error while others exhibit a bias towards "false -" error. Overall, these results demonstrate the richness of the LCFA model to extract meaningful information from these data. Valuable information includes an indication of which slides are positive for carcinoma, as well as estimates of "false +" and "false -" error for each rater.

The left-most columns of Table 22.2 list the estimates of the log-linear parameters for these data. Although the probability estimates in Table 22.1 are derived from

	Log-linear		Communalities based on		Linearized model		
Rater	θ_1	θ_2	Linear terms only		Total	θ_1	θ_2
F	7.2	3.4	0.45	0.60	0.53	0.38	0.40
D	6.0	2.6	0.47	0.54	0.62	0.26	0.26
C	7.2	0.5	0.68	0.68	0.82	0.04	0.04
A	7.7	2.4	0.72	0.75	0.82	0.18	-0.16
G	10.1	5.2	0.76	0.82	0.82	0.27	-0.25
E	6.4	3.8	0.65	0.75	0.72	0.35	-0.31
B	5.3	6.3	0.59	0.76	0.60	0.47	-0.42

TABLE 22.2
Log-linear and linearized parameter estimates for the 2-factor LC Model.

these quantities (recall equation 22.2), the log-linear estimates are not as easy to interpret as the probabilities.*

Traditional factor analysis fails to capture the differential biases among the raters. Using the traditional rule of choosing the number of factors to be equal to the number of eigenvalues greater than 1 yields only a single factor. (The largest eigenvalue is 4.57, followed by 0.89 for the second largest.) For purposes of comparison with the LCFA solution, we fit a 2-factor model using maximum likelihood for estimation.

Table 22.3 shows the results obtained from both varimax and quartimax rotations. The substantial differences between these loadings is not a reliable method for extracting meaningful information from these data.

The right-most columns of Table 22.2 present results from a linearization of the LCFA model using the following equation to obtain "linearized loadings" for each variable j:

$$E(y_j|\theta_1, \theta_2) = \rho_{j0} + \rho_{j1}\theta_1 + \rho_{j2}\theta_2 + \rho_{j12}\theta_1\theta_2. \qquad (22.6)$$

These 22.3 loadings have clear meanings in terms of the magnitude of validity and bias for each rater. They have been used to sort the raters according to the magnitude and direction of bias. The log-linear loadings do not provide such clear information.

The loading on θ_1 corresponds to a measure of validity of the ratings. Raters C, A, and G who have the highest loadings on the first linearized factor show the highest level of agreement among all raters (Magidson and Vermunt, 2003). The loading on θ_2 relates to the magnitude of bias and the loading on $\theta_1\theta_2$ indicates the direction of the bias. For example, from Table 22.1 we saw that raters F and B show the most

---

*For example, the log-linear effect of A on θ_2, a measure of the validity of the ratings of pathologist A, is a single quantity, exp(7.74)=2,298. This means that among those slides at level 1 of θ_2, the odds of rater A classifying a "true +" slide as "+" is 2,298 times as high as classifying a "true -" slide as "+". Similarly, among those slides at level 0 of θ_2, this expected odds ratio is also 2,298. The linear measure of effect is easier to interpret, but is not the same for both types of slides. For slides at level 1 of θ_2, the probability of classifying a "true +" slide as "+" is .94 higher (.99-.06=.93), while for slides at level 0 of θ_2, it is .59 higher (1.00 - .41=.59), a markedly different quantity.

		Varimax Rotation		Quartimax Rotation	
		Factor		Factor	
Rater	Comm-unalities	θ_1	θ_2	θ_1	θ_2
F	0.49	0.23	0.66	0.55	0.43
D	0.60	0.29	0.72	0.63	0.45
C	0.62	0.55	0.56	0.77	0.18
A	0.73	0.71	0.48	0.85	0.03
G	0.86	0.83	0.42	0.92	-0.09
E	0.78	0.82	0.31	0.86	-0.18
B	0.69	0.80	0.24	0.80	-0.22

TABLE 22.3
Results obtained from a 2-factor solution from traditional factor analysis.

bias, F in the direction of "false -" ratings and B in the direction of "false +". The magnitude of the loadings on the nonlinear term is highest for these 2 raters, one occurring as "+," the other as "-."

Table 22.2 also lists the communalities for each rater, and decomposes these into linear and nonlinear portions (the "total" column includes the sum of the linear and nonlinear portions). The linear portion is the part accounted for by $\rho_{j1}\theta_1 + \rho_{j2}\theta_2$, and the nonlinear part concerns the factor interaction $\rho_{j12}\theta_1\theta_2$. Note the substantial amount of nonlinear variation that is picked up by the LCFA model. For comparison, the right-most column of Table 22.4 provides the communalities obtained from the FA model.

22.3.2 MBTI Personality Items

Our second example consists of 19 dichotomous items from the Myers-Briggs Type Indicator (MBTI) – 7 indicators of the Sensing-iNtuition dimension, and 12 indicators of the Thinking-Feeling personality dimension. These items are designed to measure 2 hypothetical personality dimensions, which were posited by Carl Jung to be latent dichotomies.

The log-likelihood values obtained from fitting 0, 1, 2, 3 LC factor models are summarized in Table 22.4. Strict adherence to the BIC, AIC, CAIC or similar criterion suggests that more than 2 latent factors are required to fit these data due to violations of the local independence assumption. This is due to similar wording[†] used in several of the S-N items and similar wording used in some of the T-F items.

[†]For example, in a 3-factor solution, all loadings on the third factor are small except those for S-N items S09 and S73. Both of these items ask the respondent to express a preference between "practical" and a second alternative (for item S09, "ingenious;" for item S73, "innovative").

Model	Log-likelihood (LL)	% of LL Explained	Time in seconds ‡
0-Factor	72804	0.00	1
1-Factor	55472	0.24	5
2-Factor	46498	0.36	11
3-Factor	43328	0.40	27

TABLE 22.4
Results of estimating LC factor models.

In such cases, additional association between these items exists which is not explainable by the general S-N (T-F) factor. For our current purpose, we ignore these local dependencies and present results of the 2-factor model.

The right-most column of Table 22.2 shows that estimation time is not a problem. Estimation of the 3-factor model using the Latent GOLD computer program took only 27 seconds on a 2000 Megahertz computer.

In contrast to our first example, the decomposition of communalities in the right-most columns of Table 22.5 shows that a linear model can approximate the LCFA model here quite well. Only for a couple of items is the total communality not explained to 2 decimal places by the linear terms only. The left-most columns of Table 22.5 compares the log-linear and linearized "loadings" for each variable. The fact that the latter numbers are bounded between -1 and +1 offers easier interpretation.

The traditional FA model also does better here than the first example. The first four eigenvalues turn out to be 4.4, 2.8, 1.1 and 0.9. For comparability to the LC solution, Table 22.6 presents the loadings for the 2-factor solution under Varimax and Quartimax rotations. Unlike the first example where the corresponding loadings showed considerable differences, these two sets of loadings are quite similar. The results are also similar to the linearized loadings obtained from the LCFA solution.

The right-most column of Table 22.6 shows that the communalities obtained from FA are quite similar to those obtained from LCFA. Generally speaking, these communalities are somewhat higher than those for LCFA, especially for items S27, S44, and S67 (highlighted in bold).

Figure 22.1 displays the 2-factor bi-plot for these data (see Magidson and Vermunt, 2001). The plot shows how clearly differentiated the S-N items are from the T-F items on the 2-factors. The 7 S-N items are displayed along the vertical dimension of the plot, which is associated with factor 2, while the T-F items are displayed along the horizontal dimension, which is associated with factor 1. This display turns out to be very similar to the traditional FA loadings plot for these data. The advantage of this type of display becomes especially evident when nominal variables are included among the items.

	Log-linear		Linearized		Communalities based on	
Item	θ_1	θ_2	θ_1	θ_2	Linear terms only	Total
S02	0.03	**-1.51**	-0.01	**-0.61**	0.37	0.37
S09	0.01	**-1.16**	0.00	**-0.50**	0.25	0.25
S27	-0.03	**1.46**	0.01	**0.55**	0.30	0.30
S34	0.07	**-1.08**	-0.03	**-0.45**	0.21	0.21
S44	0.11	**1.13**	-0.04	**0.47**	0.22	0.22
S67	0.06	**1.54**	-0.02	**0.53**	0.28	0.28
S73	0.01	**-1.05**	0.00	**-0.46**	0.21	0.21
T06	**-1.01**	0.53	**0.43**	0.19	0.22	0.22
T29	**-1.03**	0.59	**0.44**	0.20	0.23	0.23
T31	**1.23**	-0.47	**-0.52**	-0.15	0.29	0.29
T35	**1.42**	-0.29	**-0.55**	-0.09	0.31	0.32
T49	**-1.05**	0.65	**0.44**	0.22	0.24	0.25
T51	**-1.32**	0.30	**0.53**	0.09	0.29	0.29
T53	**-1.40**	0.77	**0.56**	0.22	0.36	0.36
T58	**1.46**	-0.12	**-0.62**	-0.03	0.38	0.38
T66	**1.23**	-0.27	**-0.54**	-0.09	0.30	0.30
T70	**-1.07**	0.61	**0.43**	0.19	0.22	0.23
T75	**1.01**	-0.39	**-0.45**	-0.14	0.22	0.22
T87	**1.17**	-0.45	**-0.50**	-0.15	0.28	0.28

TABLE 22.5
Log-linear and linearized parameter estimates and communalities for the 2-factor LC Model as applied to 19 MBTI items.

22.4 Conclusion

In this study, we compared LCFA with FA in 2 cases where the assumptions from FA were violated. In one case, the resulting linear factor model obtained from FA provided results that were quite similar to those obtained from LCFA even though the factors were taken to be dichotomous in the LCFA model. In this case, decomposition of the LCFA solution into linear and nonlinear portions suggested that the systematic portion of the results was primarily linear, and the linearized LCFA solution was quite similar to the FA solution. However, the LCFA model was able to identify pairs and small groups of items that have similar wording because of some violations of the assumption of local independence.

In the second case, LCFA results suggested that the model contained a sizeable nonlinear component, and in this case the FA result was unable to capture differential

| Item | Quartimax Rotated Factor Matrix | | Varimax Rotated Factor Matrix | | Comm- |
| | Factor | | Factor | | unalities |
	1	2	1	2	
S02	0.08	**-0.63**	0.06	**-0.63**	0.40
S09	0.07	**-0.50**	0.06	**-0.50**	0.26
S27	-0.06	**0.62**	-0.05	**0.62**	**0.38**
S34	0.07	**-0.46**	0.06	**-0.46**	0.22
S44	-0.02	**0.55**	0.00	**0.55**	**0.30**
S67	-0.02	**0.64**	-0.01	**0.64**	**0.41**
S73	0.06	**-0.46**	0.05	**-0.46**	0.21
T06	**-0.49**	0.09	**-0.49**	0.10	0.25
T29	**-0.49**	0.10	**-0.49**	0.11	0.25
T31	**0.56**	-0.04	**0.56**	-0.05	0.32
T35	**0.58**	0.05	**0.58**	0.04	0.34
T49	**-0.50**	0.13	**-0.50**	0.15	0.27
T51	**-0.57**	-0.03	**-0.57**	-0.02	0.33
T53	**-0.61**	0.09	**-0.61**	0.10	0.38
T58	**0.64**	0.11	**0.64**	0.10	0.42
T66	**0.58**	0.05	**0.58**	0.03	0.33
T70	**-0.49**	0.10	**-0.49**	0.11	0.25
T75	**0.50**	-0.03	**0.50**	-0.04	0.25
T87	**0.55**	-0.04	**0.55**	-0.05	0.30

TABLE 22.6
Results from traditional factor analysis of the 19 MBTI items.

biases between the raters. Even when a second factor was included in the model, no meaningful interpretation of this second factor was possible, and the loadings from 2 different rotations yielded very different solutions.

Overall, the results suggest improved interpretations from the LCFA approach, especially in cases where the nonlinear terms represent a significant source of variation. This is due to the increased sensitivity of the LCFA approach to all kinds of associations among the variables, not being limited as the FA model to the explanation of simple correlations.

The linearized LCFA parameters produced improved interpretation, but in the nonlinear example, a third (nonlinear) component model was needed in order to extract all of the meaning from the results. This current investigation was limited to 2 dichotomous factors. With 3 or more dichotomous factors, in addition to each 2-way interaction, additional loadings associated with components for each higher-order interaction would also be necessary. Moreover, for factors containing 3 or more levels, additional terms are required. Further research is needed to explore these issues in practice.

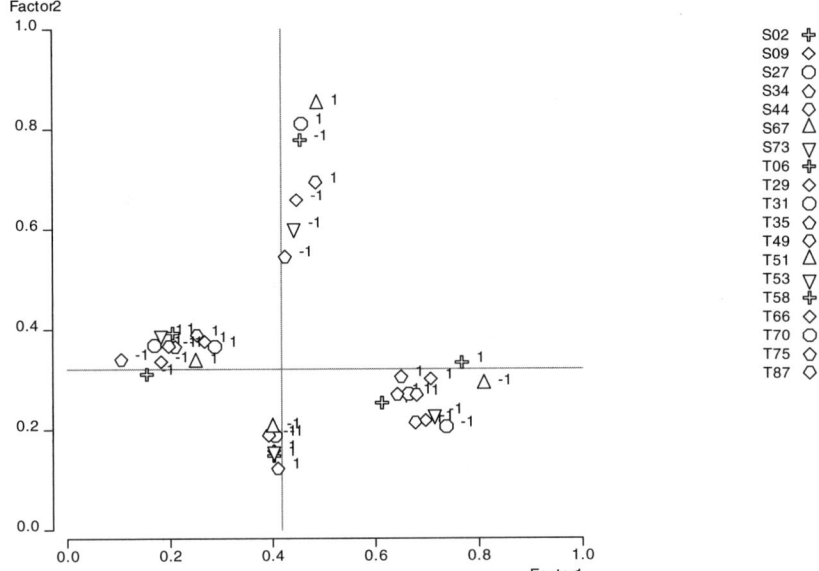

FIGURE 22.1
2-factor bi-plot.

References

Agresti, A. (2002). *Categorical Data Analysis*. Second Edition. New York: Wiley.

Goodman, L.A. (1974). Exploratory latent structure analysis using both identifiable and unidentifiable models, *Biometrika*, 61, 215-231.

Landis, J.R. and Koch, G.G. (1977). The measurement of observer agreement for categorical data, *Biometrics*, 33, 159-174.

Magidson, J. and Vermunt, J.K. (2001). Latent class factor and cluster models, bi-plots and related graphical displays, *Sociological Methodology*, 31, 223-264.

Magidson, J. and Vermunt, J.K. (2003). Latent class models, chapter in D. Kaplan (editor), *Handbook of Quantitative Methods in Social Science Research*, Sage Publications, Newbury Park, CA.

Vermunt, J.K. and Magidson, J. (2000). *Latent GOLD 2.0 User's Guide*. Belmont, MA: Statistical Innovations Inc.

23

On Cluster Effects in Mining Complex Econometric Data

M. I. Bhatti
Sultan Qaboos University, Muscat, OMAN

CONTENTS

23.1 Introduction 386
23.2 The Model 387
23.3 An Algorithm for Full Maximum Likelihood Estimation 389
23.4 Application of the Model 392
23.5 Fixed Coefficient Regression Models 394
23.6 Concluding Remarks 395
    Appendix: A1 Sampling Design 396
    Appendix: A2 The Measurements of the Variables 397
    References 397

In the last few years there has been a significant growth of research in mining complex databases, which have been generated from pattern, longitudal, time series, panel and/or sample surveys and their application in econometrics and other social sciences. Indeed, in the last few years, the tremendous growth in the use of sample surveys methods in data mining in the presence of cluster and/or block effects has dichotomized the subject of econometrics due to the nature and problems in the economics data and continuing innovation in computing technology.

    Often the data arising from these areas are naturally in clusters or blocks. When regression models are applied to data obtained from such clusters, regions, blocks, subblocks or multiblocks (i.e., from multistage-cluster sample design), the regression errors can be expected to be correlated within ultimate clusters or subclusters. As one would expect, ignoring such correlation can result in inefficient estimators, and in seriously misleading confidence intervals and hypothesis tests. This paper develops a regression model and efficient estimation procedure for the cluster effects associated with multi-factor economic data. An application of a clustered regression model to Bangladesh agricultural data demonstrates its usefulness in the area of data mining and knowledge discovery.

23.1 Introduction

In a world that is increasingly becoming competitive, data- and computing-rich, best practices demand greater use of statistics in decision-making, business, computing applications, data mining, economics and government. Two important tools of data mining (DM) are complex surveys and model building. Cost considerations often mean that survey data are gathered in clusters or sub-clusters of observations that may be influenced or affected by common factors. The best examples concern geographical grouping of regional block as clusters. In DM and knowledge discovery, one may view clustering and regression as a function of DM, machine learning, statistics and pattern recognition as algorithms of DM, business, marketing, finance, digital libraries, data warehousing, WWW, etc., as the best known applications of DM. Recently, Bhatti and Thalib (2000) and Thalib and Bhatti (1999) noted that how a small fraction of a cent over many transections at different tellers and branches of a financial institution could make a big difference in terms of a bank's overall return. They also noted how a negligible (non-significance) correlation among various claims variables contributed a significant amount of monetary benefits to the insurance company.

Data miners, economists and statisticians (who need to gather data before making important decisions or giving much needed advice) are increasingly using regression analysis based on survey data. It is common practice for survey data to be collected in clusters and the standard linear regression model to be fitted to such data. To analyse such a body of data the classical linear regression model that assumes fixed regression coefficients and spherical disturbances may not always be appropriate, as has been pointed out by Brook and King (1994), Holt, Smith and Winter (1980), Scott and Holt (1982), King and Evans (1986), Bhatti (1991), Wu and Bhatti (1994) and Bhatti (2000, 2001), among others. Since there are situations in which economic structures change or socio-economic and demographic background factors differ, it is possible that the response parameters may vary over clusters, groups or regions. To illustrate, equal amounts of labour and capital in a particular production process may yield different levels of output over different clusters in view of technical progress, labour efficiency and managerial ability that may vary from cluster to cluster. Similarly, identical applications of fertilizer to different blocks or clusters may yield different outputs because of variation in average temperature, land fertility, rainfall and agricultural land practice.

The main aim of this paper is to investigate and develop an efficient estimation procedure for the linear regression model with stochastic and fixed coefficients, based on clustered survey data. The focus of our investigation is to estimate cluster effects, ρ, cluster-wise heteroscedasticity, and variances of the random coefficients. The structure of the rest of this paper is as follows. In the subsequent sections, the stochastic coefficient regression model with cluster effects is introduced. In Section 23.3, an algorithm for the efficient maximum likelihood estimator (EMLE) is presented, using Baltagi's (1996) approach for an error component model. Section 23.4 presents

Statistical Data Mining and Knowledge Discovery

an application of the EMLE method to the estimation of unknown parameters, using Bangladesh data. Section 23.5 considers fixed coefficient models and compares estimation results to the stochastic model. The final section contains some concluding remarks and suggestions for further research in relation to cluster effects and DM in this field.

23.2 The Model

Following Bhatti (2000, 2001), we assume that n observations are available from a two-stage sample with **c** clusters. Let $m(i)$ be the number of observations from the ith cluster so that $n = \sum_{i=1}^{c} cm(i)$. For ease of notation, we will use a^i to denote ith quantity 'a' associated with the ith cluster while $(a)^i$ will denote quantity 'a' raised to the power i. An exception will be σ^2, which has its usual meaning. Let us consider the regression model[1]

$$y_j^i = \sum_{k=1}^{p} \beta_k x_{jk}^i + u_j^i \qquad (23.1)$$

for observations $j = 1, 2, ..., m(i)$ from clusters $i = 1, 2, ..., c$, with dependent variables y_j^i and p independent variables x_{jk}^i, which are assumed nonstochastic, the first of which is a constant. Baltagi (1996) follows a similar version but in panel data framework. Here in model (23.1), we assume that the regression errors u_j^i are independent between clusters but equicorrelated within clusters. Hence for (23.1), $E(u_j^i) = 0$ for all i and j;

$$E\left(u_j^i u_t^s\right) = \sigma^2 \delta_{is} \left\{\rho + (1-\rho)\delta_{jt}\right\}, \qquad (23.2)$$

where $0 \leq \rho \leq 1, \delta_{ii} = 1, \delta_{ij} = 0$, for $i \neq j$. They also assumed that the regression coefficients, β_k; $k = 1, 2, ..., p$ are constant.

In certain applications based on data with a clustering structure, the assumption of response parameter, β_k, being constant may not be appropriate. For example, Hoque (1991) in a similar study with a different data set used the Langrange multiplier test (i.e., Rao's (1973) efficient score test, and Wu and Bhatti (1994) point optimal (PO) test) for testing the null hypothesis of fixed regression coefficients against an alternative that they are stochastic. He rejected the null in favour of the alternative hypothesis. Therefore, in this paper it may be reasonable to assume that the parameters, β_k and σ^2, in (23.1) and (23.2) are changing from cluster to cluster. Thus we consider the intercluster random coefficients model[2], which regards the coefficients as having constant means and constant variance-covariance's over different clusters and additionally it allows cluster-wise heteroscedasticity in the disturbance terms, u_j^i. Thus, model (23.1) with intercluster random coefficients can be expressed as,

$$y_j^i = \sum_{k=1}^{p} \beta_k^i x_{jk}^i + u_j^i \qquad (23.3)$$

for $j = 1, 2, ..., m(i)$, and $i = 1, 2, ..., c$. Further, the intercluster random coefficients, β_k^i can be decomposed into a deterministic component (mean) and a random component (deviation from mean). Thus, for the i'th cluster, the regression coefficients can be written as[3]

$$\beta_k^i = \beta_k + \varepsilon_j^i; \ k = 2, ..., p \tag{23.4}$$

$$\left.\begin{array}{l} E\left(\varepsilon_k^i\right) = 0, \text{for all } i \text{ and } k, \\ Var\left(\varepsilon_k^i\right) = \sigma_k^2, \ k = 2, ..., p, \\ Cov\left(\varepsilon_k^i, \varepsilon_l^j\right) = 0, \text{for all } i, j, k \text{ and } l \\ \text{such that either } i \neq j \text{ or } k \neq l, \\ Cov\left(\varepsilon_k^i, u_l^j\right) = 0, \text{for all } i, j, k \text{ and } l \end{array}\right\} \tag{23.5}$$

Also, x_{jk}^i is always independent of ε_j^i and u_j^i. Then

$$\left.\begin{array}{l} E\left(\beta_k^i\right) = \beta_k, \text{for all } i \text{ and } k, \\ Var\left(\beta_k^i\right) = \sigma_k^2, \text{for all } i \text{ and } k. \end{array}\right\} \tag{23.6}$$

Under (23.4), (23.5) and (23.6), i.e., for the i'th cluster the variance term σ^2 in (23.2) is $(\sigma^i)^2$ — the regression model (23.3) may be written as[4]

$$y_j^i = \sum_{k=1}^{p} \beta_k x_{jk}^i + V_j^i; \ j = 1, 2, ..., m(i), \text{ and } i = 1, 2, ..., c \tag{23.7}$$

where

$$V_j^i = \sum_{k=2}^{p} \varepsilon_j^i x_{jk}^i + u_j^i. \tag{23.8}$$

Note that (23.5) and (23.6) imply that the mean, variance and covariances of V_j^i are as follows:

$$E(V_j^i) = E\left(\sum_{k=2}^{p} \varepsilon_j^i x_{jk}^i + u_j^i\right)$$

$$= E\left(\sum_{k=2}^{p} \varepsilon_j^i x_{jk}^i\right) + E\left(u_j^i\right)$$

and

$$\begin{aligned} E\left(V_j^i V_t^s\right) &= E\left[\left(\sum_{k=2}^{p} \varepsilon_k^i x_{jk}^i\right)\left(\sum_{k=2}^{p} \varepsilon_k^s x_{tk}^s\right)\right] + E\left[u_j^i u_t^s\right] \\ &= \delta_{is}\left(\sum_{k=2}^{p} \sigma_k^2 x_{jk}^i x_{tk}^i\right) + (\sigma^i)^2 \delta_{is}\left\{\rho + (1-\rho)\delta_{jt}\right\} \\ &= (\delta^1)^2 \delta_{is}\left\{\left(\sum_{k=2}^{p} \frac{\sigma_k^2}{(\sigma^1)^2}\right) x_{jk}^i x_{tk}^i + \frac{(\sigma^i)^2}{(\sigma^1)^2}\left\{\rho + (1-\rho)\delta_{jt}\right\}\right\} \\ &= (\delta^1)^2 \delta_{is}\left\{\left(\sum_{k=2}^{p} \lambda_k x_{jk}^i x_{tk}^i\right) + \mu^i\left\{\rho + (1-\rho)\delta_{jt}\right\}\right\} \end{aligned} \tag{23.9}$$

where[5]

$$\lambda_k = \frac{\sigma^2}{(\sigma^1)^2}, \text{ for } k = 2,...,p, \text{ and } \mu^i = \frac{(\sigma^i)^2}{(\sigma^1)^2}, i = 1,2,...,c.$$

For ease of notation, the term $(\sigma^1)^2$, the disturbance variance for the first cluster, in the remainder of the paper will be denoted by σ^2. Therefore, the model (23.7) can be more compactly written in matrix form as

$$y = X\beta + v. \tag{23.10}$$

Now, let $Var(V^i) = \sigma^2 \Omega^i$ for the i'th cluster then, (23.9) implies that

$$\Omega^i = D^i + F^i,$$

where D^i is the matrix whose (j,t)'th element is obtained by

$$\sum_{k=2}^{p} \lambda_k x^i_{jk} x^i_{tk}, \tag{23.11}$$

and F^i is of the form

$$F^i = \mu^i \left[(1-\rho) I_{m(i)} + \rho E_{m(i)} \right] \tag{23.12}$$

where $I_{m(i)}$ is the $m(i) \times m(i)$ identity matrix and $E_{m(i)}$ is an $m(i) \times m(i)$ matrix whose elements are all equal to one. It follows from (23.11) and (23.12) that $v \sim N(0, \sigma^2 \Omega)$ where $\Omega = \oplus_{i=1}^{c} \Omega^i$ is block diagonal. For any X matrix in (23.10), the distribution of y is determined by $\beta, \sigma^2, \rho, \lambda = (\lambda_2, ..., \lambda_k)'$ and $\mu = (\mu^1, ..., \mu^c)'$.

In the next section we will develop an algorithm in the spirit of Ansley (1979) and King (1986) for finding the true maximum likelihood estimates of the unknown, under the constraints that λ's and μ's be strictly positive. This solves the problem of negative estimates of variances of the coefficients. However, this boundary condition of having only nonnegative variances means that standard methods of estimating the standard errors of the estimates cannot be used. An obvious solution is to use the bootstrap method to estimate them. An overview of the theory and application of bootstrapping is provided by Efron (1979, 1982), Efron and Tibshirani (1986) while Raj (1989) and Brooks and King (1994) discuss its application to random coefficient models.

23.3 An Algorithm for Full Maximum Likelihood Estimation

As we know from the previous section, $v \sim N(0, \sigma^2 \Omega)$, where Ω is a block diagonal matrix. It is important to note that the matrix Ω has the Cholesky decomposition

$\Omega = LL\prime$, such that

$$L = \begin{pmatrix} T^1 & 0 & . & . & 0 \\ 0 & T^2 & . & . & . \\ . & . & T^3 & 0 & . \\ . & . & 0 & . & . \\ 0 & . & . & . & T^c \end{pmatrix};$$

where T^i is an $m(i) \times m(i)$ lower triangular matrix of the i'th cluster, i.e.,

$$\Omega^i = T^i T^{i\prime}.$$

If w^i_{jk}; denotes the (j,k)'th element of Ω^i then nonzero elements of T^i can be found by the following recursive scheme:

$$t^i_{11} = (\omega^i_{11})^{\frac{1}{2}}; \tag{23.13}$$

$$t^i_{j1} = \omega^i_{j1}/t^i_{11}; \text{where } j = 1,\ldots,m(i). \tag{23.14}$$

The off-diagonal elements of T^i can be obtained by the formula,

$$t^i_{jk} = \frac{1}{t^i_{kk}} \left(\omega^i_{j1} - \sum_{p-1}^{k-1} t^i_{kp} t^i_{jp} \right), \text{ for } k < j,\ldots \tag{23.15}$$

whereas the diagonal elements can be obtained by the formula

$$t^i_{jj} = \left(\omega^i_{jj} - \sum_{k=1}^{j-1} (t^i_{jk})^2 \right). \tag{23.16}$$

Now, the model (23.10) can be transformed as

$$L^{-1}y = L^{-1}X\beta + L^{-1}v$$

and may conveniently be written as

$$\tilde{y} = \tilde{X}\beta + \tilde{V} \tag{23.17}$$

such that $\tilde{V} \sim N(0, \sigma^2 I_n)$. The transformed vector $\tilde{y}$ can be obtained by the recursive relationship

$$\tilde{y}^i_1 = y^i_1/t^i_{11} \tag{23.18}$$

and so on; the j'th value of the i'th cluster of y is

$$\tilde{y}^i_j = \frac{1}{t^i_{jj}} \left(y^i_j - \sum_{k=1}^{j-1} t^i_{jk} \tilde{y}^i_k \right). \tag{23.19}$$

Similarly, the matrix X may be transformed recursively as follows:

$$\tilde{X}^i_{1k} = \tilde{X}^i_{1k}/t^i_{11} \text{ where } k = 1,\ldots,p, \tag{23.20}$$

and so on; the (j,k)'th element of i'th cluster of transformed matrix $\widetilde{X}$ can be obtained by:

$$\widetilde{X}^i_{jk} = \frac{1}{t^i_{jj}} \left(\widetilde{X}^i_{jk} - \sum_{k=1}^{j-1} t^i_{jk} \widetilde{X}^i_{1k} \right). \tag{23.21}$$

The log likelihood of the original model (23.10) and the transformed model (23.17) is:

$$\begin{aligned}\ell\left(\beta,\sigma^2,\rho,\lambda,\mu\right) &= const - \tfrac{n}{2}\log\sigma^2 - \tfrac{1}{2}\log|\Omega| \\ &\quad - \tfrac{1}{2\sigma^2}(y-X\beta)'\Omega^{-1}(y-X\beta) \\ &= const - \tfrac{n}{2}\log\sigma^2 - \log|L| \\ &\quad - \tfrac{1}{2\sigma^2}\left(\widetilde{y}-\widetilde{X}\beta\right)'\left(\widetilde{y}-\widetilde{X}\beta\right), \end{aligned} \tag{23.22}$$

where the determinant of the i'th cluster of L can easily be calculated by

$$\hat{e}_i = \hat{\eta}_i \left(|L|\right)^{1/n} \tag{23.23}$$

Setting $\partial \ell / \partial \beta$ and $\partial \ell / \partial \sigma^2$ to zero and solving, we obtain

$$\hat{\beta} = (\widetilde{X}'\widetilde{X})^{-1}\widetilde{X}'\widetilde{y} \tag{23.24}$$

$$\hat{\sigma}^2 = \hat{\eta}'\hat{\eta}/n \tag{23.25}$$

respectively, where

$$\hat{\eta} = (\hat{y} - \widetilde{X}\hat{\beta}) \tag{23.26}$$

is the OLS residual vector from (23.17). Substituting (23.24) and (23.25) into (23.22) yields the concentrated log likelihood

$$\begin{aligned}\tilde{\ell} &= c - \tfrac{n}{2}\log\hat{\eta}'\hat{\eta} - \log|L| \\ &= c - \tfrac{n}{2}\left[\log\left\{\hat{\eta}(|L|)^{\frac{1}{n}}\right\}'\left\{\hat{\eta}(|L|)^{\frac{1}{n}}\right\}\right] \\ &= c - \tfrac{n}{2}[\log\hat{e}'\hat{e}] \\ &= c - \tfrac{n}{2}\log\sum_{j=1}^n (\hat{e}_j)^2\end{aligned}$$

where c is a constant and

$$\hat{e}_i = \hat{\eta}_i \left(|L|\right)^{\frac{1}{n}}. \tag{23.27}$$

Therefore, the estimation problem reduces to minimizing the sum of squares of

$$\hat{S} = \sum_{j=1}^n \hat{e}_j^2$$

with respect to ρ, λ_k; $(k=2,...,p)$ and μ^i; $(i=2,...,c)$, given that $\mu^1 = 1$. This may be obtained by using a standard nonlinear least squares algorithm to minimize $\hat{S}$, where for any given ρ, λ_k and μ^i; $\hat{e}_i$ ($i=1,2,...,n$) are obtained as follows:

(i) Transform y and X to $\tilde{y}$ and $\tilde{X}$, respectively, using (23.10), (23.13)-(23.16), (23.17), (23.18)-(23.21) and at the same time progressively calculate $|L|$ via (23.23).

(ii) Compute $\widehat{\beta}$ and $\widehat{\eta}$ using (23.24) and (23.26) and the use of (23.27) to calculate $\widehat{e}_i$.

When the values of $\widehat{\rho}$, $\widehat{\lambda}$, and $\widehat{\mu}$ that minimize $\widehat{S}$ have been found, the MLE of β is $\widehat{\beta}$ from step (ii) of the final iteration, while σ^2 can be evaluated by using the final value $\widehat{\eta}$ in (23.25). This procedure converges to a solution of the first-order conditions for maximizing (23.22) that may or may not correspond to the global maximum (see Oberhofer and Kmenta (1974)).

23.4 Application of the Model

In this section we use the Cobb-Douglas production function to estimate unknown stochastic parameters by using the random coefficients model discussed in the previous sections. The model is applied to Bangledesh agricutural data for the year 1996-97, collected from 600 farms of the seven selected districts of Khulna and Rajshahi divisions. Due to computational ease and brevity, we will consider two independent random samples of size 20 farms from each district (clusters) of both divisions. The detailed sampling design and measurement of variables are given in appendix A.

The model (23.7), in the form of unrestricted Cobb-Douglas production functions (linear in the logarithms), under (23.4), (23.5) and (23.6), can generally be written as

$$y_j^i = \sum_{k=1}^{p} \beta_k x_{jk}^i + V_j^i, \ldots \quad (23.28)$$

where y_j^i is the log of output for the j'th farm in the i'th cluster and x_{jk}^i is the log of a $(1 \times p)$ vector of functions of values of inputs associated with the j'th farm on the i'th cluster, such that the first element of the x_{jk}^i is assumed to be one. Thus, we can write model (23.28) as:

$$\log(y_j^i) = \beta_1 + \beta_2 \log(X_{j2}^i) + \beta_3 \log(X_{j3}^i) + \beta_4 \log(X_{j4}^i) + V_j^i, \quad (23.29)$$

where

y_j^i: Total value of output per acre for j'th farm in the i'th cluster, in thousands Taka,

X_{j2}^i: Labour input per acre in mandays of j'th farm in the i'th cluster,

X_{j3}^i: BC (biological-chemical) input per acre in thousands Taka, of j'th farm in i'th cluster,

X_{j4}^i: Size of j'th farm in i'th cluster (district) in acres,

and the random variable y_j^i has the distributional properties as in (23.9), (23.10) and (23.11).

Using the likelihood and the concentrated likelihood functions (23.22) and (23.27), respectively, on the Cobb-Douglas production function (23.28), generally, and (23.29), particularly, we can obtain the estimates of the unknown parameters by the Levenberg-Marguardt algorithm. Thus, the estimated model (23.29) based on the first set of 140 randomly selected farms is

$$\log(y_j^i) = -0.272 + 0.675\log(X_{j2}^i) + 0.0351\log(X_{j3}^i) + 0.0347\log(X_{j4}^i). \quad (23.30)$$

Similarly, the estimated model (23.29) based on the second set of 140 selected farms is

$$\log(y_j^i) = -0.269 + 0.674\log(X_{j2}^i) + 0.033\log(X_{j3}^i) + 0.04\log(X_{j4}^i). \quad (23.31)$$

The estimated values of the parameters $\mu^i = \frac{(\sigma^i)^2}{\sigma^2}$ for $i = 2,...,7$ clusters from both the samples are given in Table 23.1 below.

The estimated results in Table 23.1 demonstrate that there exist a high districtwise heteroscedasticity in all the seven districts of Khulna and Rashahi divisions. It is due to different geographical locations, cultural and economic factors; the farmers' motivations are quite different in the two divisions. The Khulna division is the second largest industrial division of the country. Therefore, one can expect extrafarm job openings here which makes the opportunity cost of labour much higher compared to that of the Rashahi division.

The main reason for poor economic results in all districts of Rajshahi division is due to its geographical location and the wholly dependent agrobased industry, which is always affected by climate and weather conditions, e.g., cyclones, floods and droughts. During the monsoon, it has an excess of water, which affects the Rajshahi division causing considerable damage to its cultivated lands. This restricts farmers to grow particular crops that can resist floodwater. Moreover, during the dry season, this division faces a shortage of water (see Hossain (1990)). This creates an irrigation problem and, hence, watering the plants involves huge capital investment in the form of water dams and/or deep tubewells. Therefore, farm activities in the Rajshahi are different from that of Khulna and, hence, are the result of high cluster-wise heteroscedasticity. The estimates of the parameters λ_k's, which are the ratio of the variances of random coefficients to the variance of the error term of the first cluster, i.e., $\lambda_k = \sigma_k^2/\sigma^2$ for $k = 2,...,4$, are given in Table 23.2 (see equation (23.9) for the re-parameterization of the λ's and μ's in our model).

Parameters	$\hat{\sigma}$	$\hat{\rho}$	μ^2	μ^3	μ^4	μ^5	μ^6	μ^7
Sample 1 from Model (23.30)	0.051	0.0017	0.381	0.223	0.024	0.049	0.078	0.082
Sample 2 from Model (23.31)	0.0472	0.0065	0.363	0.22	0.028	0.043	0.083	0.082

TABLE 23.1
Estimated values of the parameters based on models (23.30) and (23.31).

k	β_k Sample 1	β_k Sample 2	λ_k Sample 1	λ_k Sample 2	σ_k Sample 1	σ_k Sample 2
2	0.683	0.681	0.2194	0.2076	0.0191	0.017
3	0.042	0.042	0.0622	0.0155	0.0112	0.0101
4	0.043	0.048	0.5217	0.4710	0.0233	0.0311

TABLE 23.2
Some estimates of random coefficient model.

The estimates given in model (23.30), (23.31) and in Tables 23.1 and 23.2 provide a local maximum for the criterion function but they do not necessarily correspond to the global maximum required.

Furthermore, the high elasticity of labour as compared to other variables in models (23.30) and (23.31) is due to the following reasons. Firstly, Bangladesh is a labour intensive country and hence labour is very cheap as compared to land and/or BC inputs, etc. Secondly, the shape and small size of the farms prevents the owners from utilizing new technology in order to reap a high level of output. In such environments labour contributions could of course be more important than capital (i.e., land and BC inputs). However, one should not forget that there must be some limit for the number of labourers working for a given size of the farm. On the other hand, the estimated coefficients of BC inputs and that of farm size are 0.043 and 0.042 in model (23.30) and 0.042 and 0.048 in model (23.31), respectively. These results support the empirical work reported by Hoque (1991), Wu and Bhatti (1994), Parikh (2000), Parikh and Radhakrishna (2002) and Ali (2002), among others.

23.5 Fixed Coefficient Regression Models

The model (23.1), under (23.2), is similar to that of the random effects model or one-way error component model used by econometricians and other social scientists in the analysis of panel and/or time-series data. A simple (re)formulation appropriate in this case is

$$y_{it} = \sum_{k=1}^{p} \beta_k x_{itk} + u_{it}, (i = 1, 2, ..., N, t = 1, 2, ..., T)$$

where

$$u_{it} = \mu_i + v_{it}, \qquad (23.32)$$

in which $i = 1, 2, ..., N$, where N stands for the number of individuals (e.g., households) in the sample and $t = 1, 2, ..., T$, where T stands for the length of the observed time series. Each of the μ_i's, $(i = 1, ..., N)$, are called an individual effect and v_{it} is the usual (white noise) error term. In this reformulation (at this stage) it is assumed that every cluster has the same number of observations (T).

k	β_k			StanError, σ_k			T
	(23.30)	(23.31)	(23.32)	(23.30)	(23.31)	(23.32)	(23.32)
2	0.683	0.681	0.564	0.021	0.020	0.112	5.0748
3	0.042	0.042	−0.044	0.011	0.005	0.069	−1.0289
4	0.043	0.048	0.0867	0.032	0.030	0.053	1.04778

TABLE 23.3
Some estimates of random and fixed coefficient models.

The pioneers Balestra and Nerlove (1966), Wallace and Hussain (1969) and Maddala (1971) have drafted the basic outline of the model (23.32) which is a special case of (23.3) under equations (23.4) to (23.8). Here we assume that

1. The random variables μ_i and υ_{it} are mutually independent.
2. $E(u_{it}) = 0$. This implies that $E(\mu_i) = 0$ and $E(\upsilon_{it}) = 0$
3. $Var(\mu_i) = \begin{cases} \sigma_\mu^2, \text{for } i = i' \\ 0, \text{otherwise} \end{cases}$
4. $Var(\upsilon_{it}) = \begin{cases} \sigma_\upsilon^2, \text{for } i = i', t = t' \\ 0, \text{otherwise.} \end{cases}$

In comparing (23.1) with (23.32), it is noted that $u_{it} = \mu_i + \upsilon_{it}$, $\sigma^2 = \sigma_\mu^2 + \sigma_\upsilon^2$, and $\rho = \sigma_\mu^2/\sigma^2$.

The only difference between (23.1) and (23.32) is that in model (23.32) the i'th cluster consists of the time-series of the i'th individual and the number of observations in a 'cluster' is T, the length of the time series. In the econometrics literature, this model is also called the oneway error component model (refer to Bhatti (2001) for useful references therein). This model is frequently being used to model panel data in the econometrics literature. Bhatti (1995) discussed this model in detail and it has been called as the twostage linear regression (2SLR) model whereas Wu and Bhatti's (1994) model is said to be three-stage (3SLR) models. For a recent review on these models, one can refer to Bhatti (2001). Empirical comparison of estimates of fixed (23.32) and random coefficient models (23.30) and (23.31) is given in Table 23.3.

Surprisingly, fixed coefficient model (23.32) reconfirms our results of the stochastic fitted models (23.30) and (23.31) for the high elasticity of labour contribution. However, negative relationship between farm size outputs may explain the stochastic patterned in the data structure and labour redundancy theory with increase in technology and the quality of BC, for example, a typical case of underdeveloped countries like Bangladesh.

23.6 Concluding Remarks

In this paper we have developed and illustrated efficient estimation procedures for the linear regression model with stochastic coefficients, clusterwise heteroscedasticity and intracluster correlation, based on two-stage clustered survey data. Following Hoque (1991), we applied a two-stage clustered sampling procedure, restricted by computational convenience, to Bangladesh data from the selected districts of Khulna and Rajshahi divisions. Hoque (1991) used a random coefficient approach, but his estimates are different from ours because he ignored the heteroscedasticity between clusters and equicorrelation within clusters. We find strong evidence of clusterwise heteroscedasticity in our Bangladesh data. If this is ignored, we suspect that the estimates might be inefficient. We recommended the use of bootstrapping procedures for the estimation of standard errors of random coefficients. Summarising these results, we can conclude that, given sufficient detail of survey design such as in our case of the Bangladesh data, one can obtain efficient and optimal estimates of unknown parameters. To gain these efficient estimates, we have used a full maximum likelihood estimator procedure by implementing the simple algorithm outlined above.

Further theoretical and applied research on regression models, using survey data, is possible. For example, an extension of this study to three-stage models using a random coefficients model approach when regression coefficients vary at district and divisional levels is in progress. Another area of interest could be of testing heteroscedasticity and random coefficients for two- and three-stage models.

Appendix: A1 Sampling Design

The survey is based on two-stage cluster sampling. The first-stage sampling units are districts of Khulna and Rajshahi division. From each district 20 farms are randomly selected. The districtwise farm distribution of each division is given below:

Division/District	Number of farms
Khulna	
Jessore	78
Khulna	92
Kushtia	79
Satkhira	80
Subtotal	329
Raishahi	
Natore	87
Nawabgunj	85
Rajshahi	99
Subtotal	271
Total	**600**

Appendix: A2 The Measurements of the Variables

The measurements of the variables used in this experiment are as follows:

(a) **Gross output:** This is the money value of all the crops grown during the year 1986-87. It has been evaluated at the relevant cropwise market prices (in thousand of Taka).

(b) **BiologicalChemical (BC) input:** This includes both high yielding variety (HYV) and local variety of seeds, the chemical fertilizers, pesticides and insecticides. BC input per acre is measured in money terms, i.e., in thousands of Taka.

(c) **Human labour:** The data on human labour are given in adult mandays. This includes family as well as hired labour. In order to compute the wagebill, family labour is assigned an imputed value that is equal to the average of the wages of casual hired labour and permanently hired labour.

(d) **Size of the farm (land):** This is measured in terms of acres. We take care of the differences in land quality across clusters partly by applying the random coefficient method in estimating the production functions.

References

Ali, M. (2002). Historical ex-post and ex-ante forecasts for three kinds of pulse in Bagladesh: Masu, Gram and Khesuri, *Unpublished PhD dissertation* Jahangir Nagar University, Bangladesh.

Ansley, C.F. (1979). An algorithm for the exact likelihood of a mixed autoregressive-moving average process, *Biometrika* 66, 59-65.

Balestra, P. and Nerlove, M. (1966). Pooling cross section and time series data in estimation of a Dynamic Model: The demand for natural gas, *Econometrica* 34, 585-612.

Baltagi, B. (1996). *Econometrics analysis of panel data*. John Wiley and Sons, New York.

Bhatti, M. I. (2000). On optimal testing for the equality of equicorrelation: An example of loss in power, *Statistical Papers,* 41, 345-352.

Bhatti, M. I. (2001). Environmetric analysis in complex surveys, *Complexity,* 6, *41-55.*

Bhatti, M. I. (1995). *Testing regression models based on sample survey data*, Avebury, England.

Bhatti, M.I. (1991). Optimal testing for cluster effects in regression models, *The Third Pacific Area Statistical Conference PrePrints,* pp. 401-404, The Pacific Statistical Institute, Tokyo, Japan.

Bhatti, M.I. and King, M.L. (1990). A Betaoptimal test for equicorrelation coefficients, *Australian Journal of Statistics,* 32, 87-97.

Brook and King (1994). Hypothesis testing of varying coefficient regression models: Procedures and applications, *Pakistan Journal of Statistics,* 10, 301-357.

Efron, B. (1979). Bootstrap methods: another look at the jackknife, *Annals of Statistics,* 7: 126.

Efron, B. (1982). *The Jackknife, the Bootstrap, and other resampling plans,* Society for Industrial and Applied Mathematics, Philadelphia.

Effron, B. and R. Tibshirani (1986). Bootstrap methods for standard errors, confidence intervals and other measures of statistical accuracy, *Statistical Science,* 1, 54-77.

Holt, D., Smith, T.M.F. and Winter, P.D. (1980). Regression analysis of data from complex surveys, *Journal of Royal Statistical Society,* A, 143, 474-487.

Hoque, A. (1991). An application and test for a random coefficient model in Bangladesh agriculture, *Journal of Applied Econometrics,* Vol. 6, 77-90.

Hossain, M. (1990). Natural calamities, instability in production and food policy in Bangladesh, *The Bangladesh Development Studies,* Vol. XVIII, No. 4, 33-54.

Hsiao, C. (1986). *Analysis of Panel Data.* Cambridge University Press, London.

Judge, G.G., Griffiths, W.E., Hill, R.C., Lutkepoht, H., and Lee, T.C. (1985). *The Theory and Practice of Econometrics.* John Wiley and Sons, New York.

King, M.L. and Evans, M.A. (1986). Testing for block effects in regression models based on survey data, *Journal of the American Statistical Association,* Vol. 81, No. 395, 677-679.

King, M.L. (1986). Efficient estimation and testing of regressions with a serially correlated error component, *Journal of Quantitative Economics,* Vol. 2, 231-247.

Maddala, G. S. (1977). *Econometrics.* McGraw-Hill, New York.

Oberhofer, W. and Kmenta, J. (1974). A general procedure for obtaining maximum likelihood estimates in generalized regression models, *Econometrica,* 42, 579-590.

Parikh, K. S. (2000). India development report 2000, Oxford University Press, New Delhi.

Parikh, K. S., and Radhakrishna, R. (2002). India development report 2002, Oxford University Press, New Delhi.

Raj, B. (1989). The peril of underestimation of standard errors in a randomcoefficients model and the bootstrap, unpublished manuscript. Invited paper presented in the Department of Econometrics, Monash University, 1989.

Rao, C. R. (1973). *Linear Statistical Inference and Its Applications.* John Wiley and Sons, New York.

Scott and Holt, D. (1982). The effect of twostage sampling on ordinary least squares methods, *Journal of the American Statistical Association,* 77, 848-854.

Swamy, P.A.V.B (1970). Efficient inference in random coefficient regression models, *Econometrica,* Vol. 38, 311-323.

SenGupta, A. (1987). On tests for equicorrelation coefficient of a standard symmetric multivariate normal distribution, *Australian Journal of Statistics,* 29, 49-59.

Wallace, T. D. and Hussain, A. (1969). The use of error components model in combining cross section with time series data, *Econometrica,* 37, 55-72.

Wu, P. and Bhatti, M. I. (1994). Testing for block effects and misspecification in regression models based on survey data, *Journal of Statistical Computation and Simulation,* 50, 75-90.

Notes:

[1] If we assume $n = \sum_{i=1}^{c} m(i)$ and $\sigma^2 = 1$, then the model (23.1) becomes a standard symmetric multivariate model (see Bhatti and King, 1990 and Bhatti, 2000).

[2] Alternatively, known as stationary random coefficient models, e.g., see Hsiao (1986) and Baltagi (1996), which ignore equicorrelation within clusters.

[3] Note that there is an identification problem if the intercept term is also assumed to follow (23.4).

[4] If we asume $\varepsilon_k^i = 0$ then the inter-cluster random coefficient model reduces to a model with fixed coefficients and heteroscedastic variances. If we further assume $\varepsilon_k^i = 0$, and $(\sigma^i)^2$, then it will become a special case of Bhatti (2000) model.

[5] Swamy's (1970) model ignores equicorrelation within clusters and considers heteroscedasticity, i.e., $(\sigma_k^i)^2$; $k = 1, ..., p$, whereas, in our model, the variance terms of the diagonal elements of i'th cluster are $(\sigma^i)^2$, i.e., constant within clusters.

24

Neural Network-Based Data Mining Techniques for Steel Making

Ravindra K. Sarma, Amar Gupta, and Sanjeev Vadhavkar
Massachusetts Institute of Technology, USA

CONTENTS

- 24.1 Introduction 402
- 24.2 Productivity from Information Technology (PROFIT) Initiative 403
- 24.3 Description of Predictive Model 406
- 24.4 NNRUN – ANN Training Suite 407
- 24.5 Results and Analysis 409
- 24.6 Conclusions 411
    - Acknowledgments 412
    - References 412

The blast furnace is the heart of any steel mill, where raw materials, such as coke and sinter, are combined to produce pig iron, the precursor of steel. The hot metal temperature (HMT) is an important indicator of the state of the blast furnace, as well as the quality of pig iron produced. Traditionally, due to the highly complex and non-linear relationships between the various chemical inputs and HMT, models based on conventional statistical forecasting techniques have provided very poor results. To mitigate this problem, the paper highlights a neural network based approach to modeling a blast furnace to generate accurate HMT predictions. Issues such as data processing and augmentation, as well as optimal neural network architectures, are discussed. This paper presents in detail a neural network-training suite, NNRUN, which automates the search for the optimal neural network configuration given user-defined boundaries. The paper presents some of the research findings including data pre-processing, modeling and prediction results based on HMT data received from the industrial blast furnace of a leading steel manufacturer in Asia. Feed-forward neural networks with a single hidden layer have been found to be very accurate predictors of HMT. A prototype system based on the neural network based methodology is currently being implemented at the blast furnace. The relevant research for this paper was conducted by members of the **Productivity from Information Technology Initiative at MIT,** where research is being conducted into the use of neural networks for a wide variety of application domains, ranging from optimization of inventory operations to automated reading of handwritten bank checks.

24.1 Introduction

With advances in database technologies, companies have started storing large amounts of historical data. Over the past decade, there has been an increasing interest in using artificial neural networks (ANNs) to mine these large databases to capture useful patterns and relationships. ANN based data mining has been applied in a multitude of domains, including finance [1], inventory reduction [2] [3] [4], electronic commerce [5] and medicine [6].

ANNs have also been used in industrial applications for tasks such as modeling and predicting complex industrial processes. For the most part, ANNs have been used for their ability to capture arbitrary non-linear and highly complex relationships between the inputs and outputs of processes. In addition, neural networks are becoming increasingly attractive in data mining of large corporate databases because they require no prior domain knowledge and because they are computationally efficient [7].

The focus of this paper is to analyze and interpret the use of ANNs in the context of a steel mill's blast furnace operations. The blast furnace is where inputs such as coke, iron ore and sinter are combined in a complex chemical process, yielding liquid pig iron, the pre-cursor of steel. The hot metal temperature (HMT) is an important indicator of the internal state of a blast furnace as well as of the quality of the pig iron being produced [8]. Hence, steel-makers and blast furnace operators would like to predict these quality parameters based on current and past conditions of the furnace, as well as on the levels of the various input chemicals used. This would provide them with information regarding the quality of the steel produced, and would allow them to take corrective action if future HMT predictions indicate sub-optimal operating conditions.

Unfortunately, researchers have not been able to find a precise function mapping these input variables to HMT. The production of pig iron involves complicated heat and mass transfers and introduces complex relationships between the various chemicals used. Most of the time, these relationships are non-linear and therefore cannot be accurately estimated by standard statistical techniques or mass-transfer equations [9]. Therefore, many have turned to ANNs as a means of modeling these complex inter-variable relationships. Attempts have been made by researchers to use ANNs to predict the silicon content of pig iron produced from a blast furnace [10]. Due to the success of this previous work, and the fact that silicon content is directly related to HMT, it seems natural to use neural networks in order to predict HMT.

Hence, the purpose of this paper is to examine the ability of feed-forward neural networks to predict the HMT of pig iron based on 12 input parameters that reflect the current and past conditions of the blast furnace. The prediction horizons for the networks presented here range from 1 to 8 hours. Along the way, various data challenges and solutions are presented, as well as a neural-network training suite that automatically finds the best-performing neural multi-layer perceptron (MLP) network. The paper then explains how prediction depends on the number of hidden nodes and layers used. The relationship between prediction accuracy and prediction horizon is also discussed. Finally, the paper presents conclusions and areas of further work.

24.2 Productivity from Information Technology (PROFIT) Initiative

Research performed by faculty and students from multiple departments and schools at MIT under the aegis of the PROFIT Initiative, based at MIT's Sloan School of Management, focuses on the use of information technology in both the private and public sectors to enhance productivity in many areas ranging from finance to transportation, and from manufacturing to telecommunications. Research at MIT shows that the likelihood of success in utilizing information technology to increase productivity is a function of several technical and non-technical factors. To attain success, there are three prerequisites – a careful determination of strategic applications, an intelligent selection of technologies and an ability to incorporate appropriate changes in the organizational structure. The absence of even one of these factors will lead to failure.

PROFIT is currently characterized by four primary focal areas of research. These are as follows:

- Knowledge Acquisition, which deals with the issue of eliciting information and knowledge from sources that are not computer-based. These can range from information on paper based documents to information maintained solely in the human mind;

- Knowledge Discovery, which deals with the issue of mining of huge amounts of historical and current information in numerical, textual, and other formats;

- Knowledge Management, which focuses on integration of disparate pieces of information in order to meet a particular need; and

- Knowledge Dissemination, which deals with extracting knowledge that is tailored to the needs to each user.

Unlike current approaches that tend to focus on one aspect only, researchers of PROFIT emphasize an integrated approach that attaches appropriate weightage to each of the four facets. In Figure 24.1, a small subset of our sponsor organizations is shown, along with their respective areas of interest. The work described in this paper transcends multiple areas of research and is aligned most closely to the Knowledge Discovery area.

Sponsors and Test Sites: Varied Emphasis

```
KNOWLEDGE                                              KNOWLEDGE
ACQUISITION                                            DISSEMINATION

        Integris  Ministry of Education, Brazil
                  Polaroid Corporation
                  Ministry of Science & Technology, Brazil

                            MITRE Corporation
                                                US Air Force
                       Federal Aviation Administration
        "Medicorp"           Defense Logistics Agency
        "Steelcorp"
        "Bankcorp"           DARPA
                                                World Bank

KNOWLEDGE                                              KNOWLEDGE
DISCOVERY                                              MANAGEMENT
```

FIGURE 24.1
Different organizations emphasize different facets: few adopt multifaceted approach.

Within the broad area of "Knowledge Discovery and Data Mining," very diverse applications are being addressed. This diversity is reflected in the following two examples:

(i) Use of Recurrent Neural Networks for Strategic Data Mining of Sales Information

With hundreds of chain stores and with revenues of several billion dollars per annum, *Medicorp* is a large retail distribution company that dispenses pharmaceutical drugs to customers in a number of states in the United States. Just as any other retailer in its position, *Medicorp* carries a large standing inventory of products ready to deliver on customer demand. Unsatisfied customers frequently turn to competing stores, and *Medicorp* loses potential profits in such cases. The problem is how much quantity of each drug should be kept in the inventory at each store and warehouse. *Medicorp* incurs significant financial costs if it carries excess quantities of drugs relative to the customer demand; especially because pharmaceutical drugs have limited shelf-lives. Historically, *Medicorp* has maintained an inventory of approximately a billion dollars on a continuing basis and has used traditional regression models to determine inventory levels for each of the items.

The approach involved a regression study of historical data to compute a seasonally-adjusted estimate of the forecasted demand for the next three week period. This estimated demand is the inventory level that *Medicorp* keeps, or strives to keep, on a continuing basis. For this purpose, neural network based data mining and knowledge discovery techniques were used to optimize inventory levels. Strategic data mining techniques were used to achieve strategic corporate goals for customer satisfaction while simultaneously cutting down the current inventory. Neural networks were used to predict future sales because of their power to generalize trends and their ability to store relevant information about past sales.

Prototype based on these networks was successful in reducing the total level of inventory by 50% in *Medicorp*, while maintaining the same level of probability that a particular customer's demand will be satisfied. Additional information is available in [20].

(ii) System for Processing Handwritten Bank Checks Automatically

In the US and many other countries, bank checks are preprinted with the account number and the check number in MICR ink and format; as such, these two numeric fields can be easily read and processed using automated techniques. However, the amount field on a filled-in check is usually read by human eyes, and involves significant time and cost, especially when one considers that about 68 billion checks are processed per annum in the US alone. The system described in this paper uses the scanned image of a bank check to "read" the check.

There are four main stages in the system focus on: the detection of courtesy amount block within the image; the segmentation of string into characters; the recognition of isolated characters; and the postprocessing process that ensures correct recognition. Image pre-processing involves: conversion from gray scale into black and white pixels; organizing the information in connected components; and location of strings in a page with unspecified format. The output of the preprocessor serves as the input to the segmentation module. The latter takes advantage of the results of the recognition module, via a feedback mechanism. The neural network architecture employs a set of four neural networks of different types that are run in parallel to minimize the likelihood of erroneous readings. This architecture offers a superior accuracy and performance, as compared to structures comprised of single nets only. Finally, the post processing module takes advantage of contextual information in monetary amounts. This module has been developed as a generalized syntactic checker based on deterministic finite automata techniques. The post processing module also provides the string of the amount in a standard format, hence providing the information needed for processing financial transactions on an international basis.

This approach has been applied to read American and Brazilian bank checks, with appropriate differences in the two sets of implementations. The algorithms and techniques used to read bank checks can also be applied to other environments that can require reading of handwritten documents or other documents of poor quality. Additional information is available in [21].

24.3 Description of Predictive Model

The standard multi-layer perceptron (MLP) model has become the architecture of choice due to its success in previous work, both in our own research group at MIT and at other places. The feed-forward network had provided accurate prediction results both in the blast furnace domain and with other chemical processes [11]. Time-delay neural networks (TDNNs) were also examined, primarily because there exist time lags between the instant when an input is changed and when the effect of the change is manifested in the output HMT value. TDNNs are capable of capturing these lags during training, and storing this knowledge implicitly in the connections of the network. On the other hand, if one is to use an MLP model with back-propagation learning, the time lag between a particular input and HMT must be decided ahead of time and the variables in the training examples must be adjusted accordingly before learning begins. This corresponds to explicit memory, which is presented to the network by the inputs.

Initial prediction results as well as past experience by the research group [2] revealed that the MLP network was more accurate in predicting HMT. In addition, time-delay networks take a much longer time to learn. As will be described later, NNRUN, the automated tool used to find the best neural network, tries a multitude of hidden layer configurations. The use of TDNNs, in this case, would force NNRUN to take a much longer time to converge to its final solution.

The model constructed consists of 15 input variables, each lagged in time from the output HMT by an appropriate amount. 12 of the input variables used are chemical inputs into the blast furnace as well as byproducts of the steel-making process. These include coal injection, heat flux, ore/coke ratio, oxygen enrichment, steam flow, wind flow, carbon dioxide and hydrogen. Three additional binary variables are used that indicate the specific sensor from which the HMT is measured. In addition to these 15 inputs, an extra input, the last measured HMT value, is also used as an input. According to past work and neural network theory [12], it has been shown that a neural network with one hidden layer is capable of modeling any arbitrary function between a set of inputs and outputs. As the mapping function needs to become increasingly complex, the number of hidden nodes in the layer must also increase. However, others in the literature have noted that in practice, two-hidden layer networks have been able to capture certain relationships with greater accuracy [13]. Therefore, this paper examines both one-hidden layer and two-hidden layer networks and compares the results.

24.4 NNRUN – ANN Training Suite

NNRUN provides a menu-driven interface to perform customized data cleansing and manipulation, as well as a means to automate the search for the optimal neural network, given a set of training and testing data.

24.4.1 Data Manipulation

Raw furnace data must be transformed into a more useful form before they can be presented as learning examples to the neural network. These techniques try to overcome the problems of missing data, scaling of data and lack of data. The initial data set consisted of approximately 30,100 data points, measured at 1-minute intervals. After consulting the domain experts at the blast furnace, it was suggested that we use hourly data to perform training. This type of hourly averaging can suppress some of the measurement noise that is present in the 1-minute data. However, averaging every contiguous group of 12 data points would leave only 30100/60 ≈ 501 data points to be split between testing and training phases. Therefore, the moving window averaging concept was adopted to perform hourly averaging. Every contiguous set of 10 data points was first averaged to create a dataset of 3010 data points at 10-minute intervals. The first m 10-minute interval data points were averaged into one hourly data point. Next, this window was shifted down by one 10-minute data point, and the next m data points were averaged. If the initial 10-minute data set had N number of rows, using a window of size m resulted in an averaged data set of size N- m + 1. Therefore, each new data point contained ten minutes of new information. This is why the 10-minute data, as opposed to 1-minute data, were used for purposes of the moving window averaging; each data points carried 10 minutes, rather than 1 minute, of new information. At the same time, potential measurement errors at the 10-minute level were suppressed by averaging the "new" 10-minute point with (m-1) other 10-minute data points. Since the goal was to obtain hourly data, m=6 and the number of data points in the new dataset was 3100 – (6 – 1) = 3095, a significant improvement over the 501 data point sets mentioned earlier.

Neural networks, along with many other statistical learning algorithms, are sensitive to the scale and variance of the input variables. For this reason, normalizing of variables is often performed [14]. This normalization renders values for each variable that are between 0 and 1. The normalization formula used was:

$$X_{ij} - \min\{X_i\}/(\max\{X_i\} - \min\{X_i\}) \tag{24.1}$$

where X_{ij} is jth value of the ith input, the value that is to be normalized. Max$\{X_i\}$ and Min$\{X_i\}$ are the maximum and minimum values of the ith input variable respectively. This gave all of the variables the same range of values, along with relatively similar means and variances. These methods allow the neural network to capture more easily the relationship between a change in inputs and the change in the output, avoiding distortion caused by wide differences in scale and variation.

24.4.2 Automated Search For Best Network

In order to find the best performing neural network for a given set of data, it is necessary to find the optimal MLP hidden-node configuration, defined to be the network whose predictions on the validation sample exhibit the lowest mean square error (MSE). NNRUN provides the user a choice, through menus, to select the number of hidden layers that the network should have, as well as a minimum and maximum number of nodes for each hidden-layer that should be considered. Therefore, if one wants to find the best two-hidden layer network, and assuming a case where the number of hidden nodes in the range [1,10] for the first layer and nodes in the range [1,5] in the second layer, the total number of network configurations trained will be 10 * 5 = 50.

Typically, the initial dataset is divided into a training set, which comprises 80% of the data, and the testing or validation set, which makes up the other 20%. In the event the number of data points in the testing set is small, if performance of various neural nets is compared using only one particular partition of data, the best performing network will necessarily be the scenario that best describes the particular data subset, and not necessarily the one that best describes the overall mapping. To alleviate this problem, NNRUN allows the user to set the number of random runs. This parameter allows the user to train the neural networks on a large number (up to the number of data points) of different testing/training partitions of the original data set. This results in the selection of the ANN hidden layer/node configuration with the best mean performance over different partitions. This also ensures that the "best" configuration reflects the general properties of the mapping and not a particular choice of data partition. If the number of runs chosen is m, then one can choose the best node configuration such that: $(MSE_1 + MSE_2 + \ldots + MSE_m) / m$ is minimized, where MSE_n is the mean square error over the nth randomized testing data set.

In addition, the user can also specify whether the different partitions are selected randomly or sequentially from the main data set. Once the best network configuration is identified, it is retrained on the default training set in order to produce the "best mean" network. Based on the results of running NNRUN with different numbers of runs, it was confirmed that the ANN exhibiting the lowest error on the default data partition rarely provides the best mean-performance ANN. Further, it was observed that, for the best mean network, the mean square error (MSE) indicators of performance are significantly higher for the default partition as compared to the MSE for randomized train/test selections. It is possible that this discrepancy is the result of fundamental changes in the properties of the mapping in the time period covering the train/test partition.

The number of random runs typically used was 3. The reason for choosing this value is to set an upper bound on search time. If one takes the above example of restricting the first and second hidden-layer node configurations to [1, 10] and [1, 5] respectively, and one sets the number of random runs to 3, the total number of training/testing sessions that the system would have to endure is 10 * 5 * 3 + 1 = 151.

24.5 Results and Analysis

Although neural network theory has mathematically proven that a one hidden layer network (3-layer net) can approximate any input-output mapping [12], some researchers have suggested that feed-forward networks with 2 hidden layers (4-layer net) can offer increased prediction accuracy in specific cases [13]. Therefore, this paper examines the ability of both one and two hidden layer networks and compares their performance.

Both three-layer and four-layer networks were trained in order to predict HMT 1, 2, 3, 4, 5, 6, 7 and 8 hours into the future. NNRUN, described in Section 24.3, was used to find the optimal networks for each prediction horizon. For three-layer networks, the size of the hidden layer was varied from 1 to 30 nodes. For four-layer networks, each of the two hidden layers ranged from 1 to 12 nodes. These boundaries were established in order to avoid excessive computation time. Allowing for three random runs and running on Sun Ultra 5 workstations, three-layer simulations would take 30 hours to complete and four-layer simulations would take 40 hours to finish.

There are three main measures that were used to evaluate network performance and have been cited in many papers [2]. These are: the Pearson correlation coefficient, the average error (AE) and the Normalized Mean Square Error (NMSE). The Pearson coefficient is useful because it measures how well the model predicts *trends* in the output variable. A coefficient of 1 indicates that the model is predicting trends with the highest possible accuracy, while a value of −1 means the model is not predicting trends at all. The average error is just the average difference (in degrees C) between the actual HMT and that predicted by the network.

NMSE compares the accuracy of the model's predictions versus predicting the mean [14]. An NMSE value less than 1 indicates that the model performs better than the mean, while a value greater than 1 means that the model performs worse than the mean. The performance of all trained models was evaluated on the last 20% of the entire dataset, which was the default validation data set.

After training both three-layer and four-layer networks on the same data, it was determined that the networks with two-hidden layers did not provide improved accuracy over the single-hidden layer models.

Although 2-hidden layer and 1-hidden layer networks perform at relatively the same level of accuracy for shorter prediction horizons, the 1-hidden layer networks do show greater accuracy once the prediction horizon is larger than 4 hours. What this could mean is that for predictions closer in the future, a relatively less complex four-layer model is required to predict HMT accurately. However, once the prediction horizons increase past 4 hours, the complexity of the two-hidden layer network may lie outside the search space of possible node configurations set when training using NNRUN. In general, for one and two hidden layer networks, the number of hidden nodes tends to increase as the prediction horizon increases. The reason is that as the model tries to predict further into the future, it cannot rely as heavily

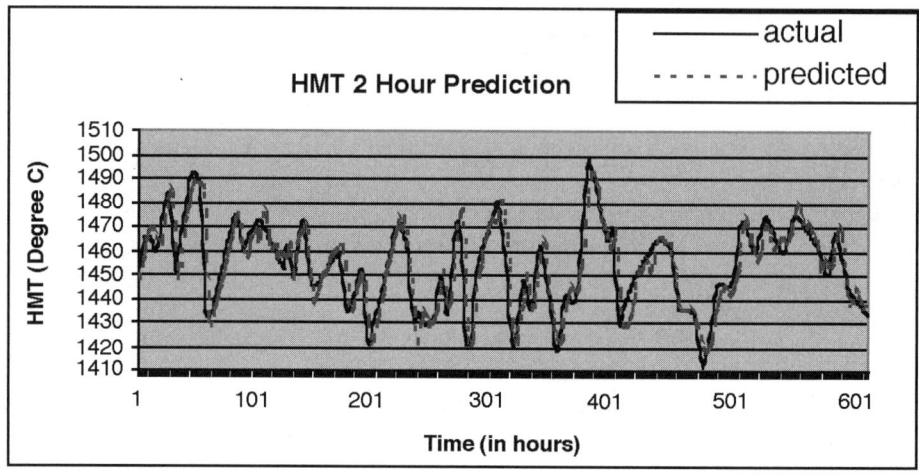

FIGURE 24.2
2-hour HMT results. Configuration: 1 hidden layer with 12 nodes. NMSE: .0986; Correlation: 0.984.

on the last known HMT value (which is used as an input) when predicting future HMT.

In general, the Pearson coefficient values for the best overall performing networks range from 0.986 for 1-hour prediction to 0.837 for 8-hour prediction. NMSE ranges from 0.0284 for the 1-hour network to 0.306 for the 8-hour network. Average error ranges from 2.92 to 6.95 degrees Celsius. Thus, although the prediction accuracy deteriorates with increasing prediction horizon, it is clear that overall prediction capability is very favorable. The fact that the Pearson coefficient does not fall below 0.837 indicates that each network has significant ability to predict the trends of HMT. Figures 24.2-24.4 illustrate the performance of networks used to predict HMT 2 hours, 4 hours and 8 hours into the future.

While the 2 hour and 4 hour predictions are much smoother and more accurate, the 8 hour predictions appear to be more jagged and not as close to the actual values. Even in the 8-hour case, the trends of the HMT are predicted very well. For the blast furnace operator, knowing the trends of future HMT is as important as knowing the actual future HMT value when deciding upon what actions to take.

It is important to note that the complexity of the neural network configuration that performs best over all random partitions, or runs, is generally higher than the node configuration that performs best only on the default dataset. For example, for 4-hour prediction, the best mean configuration contains 15 hidden nodes, while the best default configuration contains only 7 hidden nodes. One reason for this finding could be that the best mean network configuration requires increased generalization to perform well over test data sampled from many different regions of the overall dataset.

Statistical Data Mining and Knowledge Discovery 411

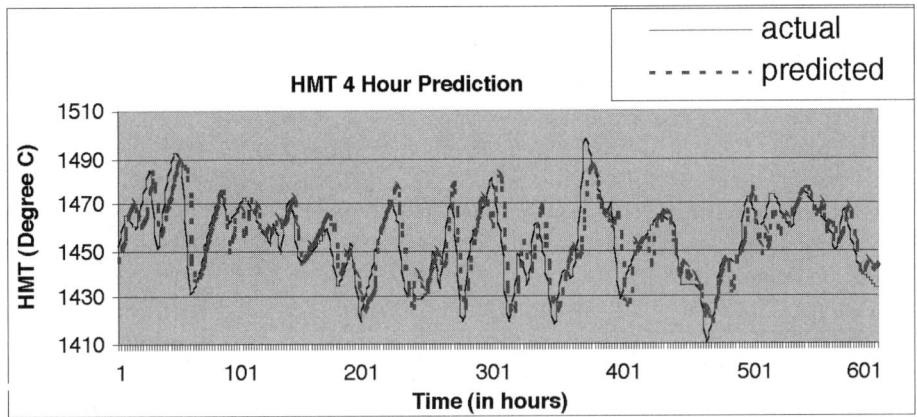

FIGURE 24.3
4-hour HMT results. Configuration: 1 hidden layer with 15 nodes. NMSE: .241; Correlation: 0.878.

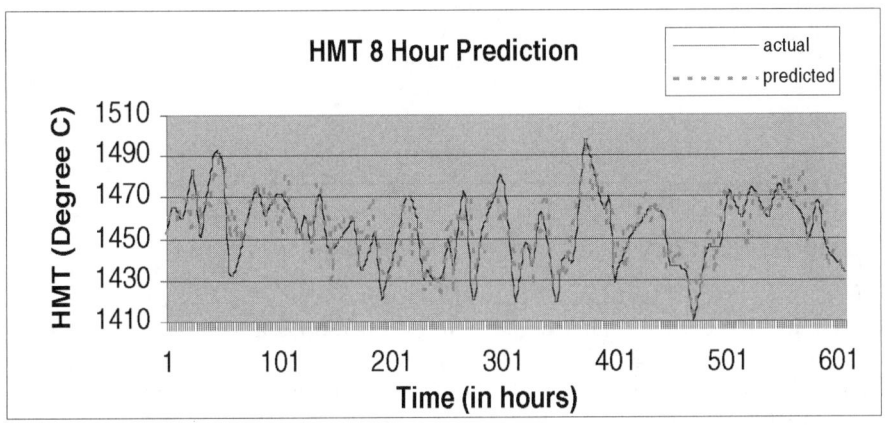

FIGURE 24.4
8-hour HMT results. Configuration: 1 hidden layer with 15 nodes. NMSE: .301; Correlation: 0.839.

24.6 Conclusions

The rapid growth of databases with sensor data has overwhelmed the traditional, interactive approaches to data analysis in blast furnaces and created a need for a new generation of tools for intelligent and automated discovery in large databases. Knowledge discovery in databases presents many interesting challenges within the context of providing computer tools for exploring large data archives. The forecasting of hot metal temperatures (HMT) in blast furnaces is a nascent application for ANN based strategic data mining and was explored in this paper.

The paper presented results from one of the several research projects currently underway in the Sloan School of Management in the broad area of strategic data mining [2] [3] [4] [15]. Earlier efforts from this research group concentrated on the use of multi layer perceptron (MLP) and time-delay neural networks (TDNN) for inventory control for a large pharmaceutical distribution company. The prototype from the latter research endeavor was successful in reducing the total level of inventory by 50%, while maintaining the same level of customer satisfaction.

This paper presented the design and implementation highlights of a multi layer perceptron ANN model used to predict HMT data. The predicted results provided a good indicator of the trends and had strong (high amplitude) predictions. Various modeling techniques used by the research group were described in this paper. In particular, data cleansing techniques used for live blast furnace data were discussed in the paper. During the course of this research effort, the research team developed NNRUN –a menu-driven interface to perform customized data cleansing and manipulation, as well as to automate the search for the optimal neural network, given a set of training and testing data. Though using the proposed architecture will not mitigate all the problems caused by the lack of data of good quality, this architecture is geared towards prediction tasks based on available data.

Acknowledgments

The authors would like to thank Ashish Mishra for help in preparing this paper. In addition, the authors thank other members of the Data Mining research group at the Sloan School of Management for their help in testing various ANN models. Proactive support from *Steelcorp,* throughout the entire research endeavor, is greatly appreciated.

References

[1] Prokhorov, D., Saadm, E., and Wunsch, D. (1998). Comparative Study of Stock Trend Prediction Using Time Delay, Recurrent and Probabilistic Neural Networks. In *IEEE Transactions on Neural Networks*, Vol. 9, No.6, Nov.

[2] Bansal, K., Gupta, A., and Vadhavkar, S. (1998). Neural Networks Based Forecasting Techniques for Inventory Control Applications, *Data Mining and Knowledge Discovery*, Vol. 2.

[3] Bansal, K., Vadhavkar, S., and Gupta, A. (1998). Neural Networks Based Data Mining Applications for Medical Inventory Problems, *International Journal of Agile Manufacturing*, Volume 1, Issue 2, pp. 187-200, Urvashi Press, India.

[4] Reyes, C., Ganguly, A., Lemus, G., and Gupta, A. (1998). A hybrid model based on dynamic programming, neural networks, and surrogate value for inventory optimization applications, *Journal of the Operational Research Society*, Vol. 49, pp. 1-10.

[5] Gupta, A., Vadhavkar, S., and Au, S. (1999). Data Mining for Electronic Commerce, *Electronic Commerce Advisor*, Volume 4, Number 2, September/October, pp. 24-30.

[6] Penny, W. and Frost, D. (1996). Neural Networks in Clinical Medicine, *Medical Decision Making: an International Journal of the Society for Medical Decision Making*. Vol.16, No. 4.

[7] Rumelhart, D.E., Hinton, G.E., and Williams, R.J. (1986). Learning representation by back-propagating error, *Nature*, 323, 533-536.

[8] Biswas, A.K. (1984). *Principles of Blast Furnace Ironmaking*, SBA Publications.

[9] *Ullmann's Encyclopedia of Industrial Chemistry*, 5th complete revised edition. VCH 1985. Vol. A 14, 517-540.

[10] Bulsari, A., Saxen, H., and Saxen B. (1992). Time-series prediction of silicon in pig iron using neural networks, *International Conference on Engineering Applications of Neural Networks (EANN '92)*.

[11] Bhat, N. and McAvoy, T.J. (1990). Use of Neural Nets For Dynamic Modeling and Control of Chemical Process Systems, *Computers in Chemical Engineering*, Vol. 14, No. 4/5, pp. 573-583.

[12] Smith, M. (1993). *Neural Networks for Statistical Modeling*. pp. 111-133. Van Nostrand Reinhold, New York.

[13] Banks, B. (1999). Neural Network Based Modeling and Data Mining of Blast Furnace Operations. MIT M.Eng Thesis, Sept.

[14] Weigend, A.S. and Gershenfeld, N.A. (1993). Results of the time series prediction competition at the Santa Fe Institute, *IEEE International Conference on Neural Networks*, pp. 1786-1793. IEEE Press, Piscataway, NJ.

[15] Agrawal, A., Gupta, A., Hussein, K., and Wang, P. (1996). Detection of courtesy amount block on bank checks, *Journal of Electronic Imaging*, Vol. 5(2), April.

[16] Osamu, L., Ushijima, Y. and Toshiro, S. (1992). Application of AI techniques to blast furnace operations, *Iron and Steel Engineer*, October.

[17] Knoblock, C., (ed.)(1996). Neural networks in real-world applications, *IEEE Expert*. August, pp. 4-10.

[18] Bhattacharjee, D., Dash S.K., and Das, A.K. (1999) Application of Artificial

Intelligence in Tata Steel, *Tata Search 1999*.

[19] Hertz, J., Krogh, A., and Palmer, R.G. (1991). *Introduction to the Theory of Neural Computation*. Addision-Wesley, Reading, MA.

[20] Shanmugasundaram, J., Nagendra Prasad, M.V., Vadhavkar, S., and Gupta, A. *Use of Recurrent Neural Networks for Strategic Data Mining of Sales*, http://ssrn.com/abstract_id=300679.

[21] Palacios, R. and Gupta, A. *A System for Processing Handwritten Bank Checks Automatically*, http://papers.ssrn.com/abstract=302874.

25

Solving Data Clustering Problem as a String Search Problem

V. Olman, D. Xu, and Y. Xu
Oak Ridge National Laboratory, Oak Ridge, TN, USA

CONTENTS

25.1	Introduction	415
25.2	Mathematical Framework	417
25.3	Stability of MST Structure Under Noise	421
25.4	Statistical Assessment of Identified Clusters	422
25.5	Applications	423
25.6	Discussion	428
	Acknowledgments	429
	References	429

The various high-throughput efforts such as the Human Genome Project have opened the flood gate of biological data, including enormous amount of sequences, structure, expression, and interaction data. The rates of data generation far exceeds our current capability of analysis and interpretation. New ideas and approaches are urgently needed to establish greatly improved capabilities for biological data analysis. Data clustering is fundamental to mining a large quantity of biological data. In this paper, we present a new approach to address this challenge based on a rigorous relationship between data clusters and a sequential representation derived from the Prim algorithm for constructing a minimum spanning tree of a data set. This approach converts a clustering problem to a problem of partitioning a one-dimensional profile (a sequential representation), which facilitates easy identification of "dense" clusters from a noisy background. We have applied the method to a number of data mining problems for high-throughput biological data, including cluster identification in gene expression profiles and regulatory binding site identification. The results have shown that our method can identify underlying patterns from large-scale biological data effectively and efficiently.

25.1 Introduction

The Human Genome Project has started a new revolution in biological science, which is fundamentally changing how biological research is done. As a result, we are now witnessing an unprecedented flood of biological data being generated by high-throughput production facilities at rates that far exceed our current ability to understand these data. The high-throughput biological data include, for example, (a) gene and protein sequences generated by world-wide sequencing efforts [1, 2], (b) gene and protein expression data from microarray facilities [3, 4] and mass spectrometry facilities [5, 6], (c) protein structure data generated by structural genomics centers [7], and (d) protein-protein interaction data from two-hybrid systems [8, 9]. Hidden in these and other large data sets is the information that reflects the existence, activity, and functionality of biological machineries at different levels in living organisms. A common feature of these data sets is that they are generally unstructured. Strong capabilities of deciphering the information hidden in these data are essential for successfully transforming the experimentally-based biological science to a new information-based science [10]. Development of such capabilities represents a highly challenging problem.

Data clustering has been a popular technique for grouping unstructured data sharing of common or similar features. It facilitates recognition of patterns shared by some subsets of the data, and identification of significant hidden signals. Data clustering is often used as the first step in mining a large quantity of data. The basic idea of clustering can be stated as follows. For a given set of data points (e.g., multi-dimensional vectors), group the data into clusters so that (a) data of the same cluster have similar features, and (b) data of different clusters have dissimilar features. Similarity between data points is typically defined by a *distance* measure; and the clustering quality is measured by a specified *objective function*. Thus a clustering problem can be formally defined as an optimization problem, which partitions the data set to optimize a specified objective function. For biological data analysis, the optimization problem is typically a combinatorial optimization problem. Clustering has been used or could be potentially used to solve or provide partial solutions to many high-throughput biological data analysis problems, including gene expression data clustering [3, 4, 11], sequence-, structure-, or function-based protein classification [12, 13, 14], and protein domain identification based on structure [15, 16] or sequence information [17, 18].

K-means [19], neural networks [20], and self-organizing maps [21] are among the most popular clustering techniques for biological data analyses. They have been widely used in gene expression data analysis [3, 4, 11], protein classification [14], and predictions of genes' splice sites and translation starts [22, 23]. While these approaches have clearly demonstrated their usefulness in real applications, a few basic problems should not be overlooked: (1) Virtually none of these methods can guarantee to find the global optimum in an efficient and rigorous manner for any non-trivial clustering objective functions, making it difficult to rigorously assess the effectiveness of these methods. (2) Many of these approaches use simple geometric shapes, e.g., piece-wise hyperplanes, to separate clusters, making it very difficult for them to deal with clustering problems with complex cluster boundaries, e.g., clusters that cannot be contained in non-overlapping convex sets (or even worse, with holes inside, which may contain other clusters). (3) There is no general and effective mechanism, within these clustering techniques, to carry out statistical analysis and to determine the number of clusters in a data set. (4) None of these classical clustering techniques are adequate for addressing the *cluster identification problem*, i.e., identification of data clusters with outstanding common or similar features from such a problem, as we have found, can be used to formulate many biological data analysis problems, where data points of well-defined clusters may not appear in a vacuum but rather in a more general (noisy) background. Simply partitioning a data set into clusters often will not lead to effective identification of these well-defined clusters.

To address these difficulties encountered by traditional clustering methods, we have recently developed a new framework for multi-dimensional data clustering, based on a graph-theoretic concept, called *minimum spanning trees* (MSTs) [24, 25]. A minimum spanning tree is generally considered as a *skeleton* of a graph. For many purposes, a minimum spanning tree can capture the key essential information of a graph. The foundation of our MST-based clustering framework is that a multi-dimensional data set can be represented as a minimum spanning tree, without losing any essential information for the purpose of clustering. Hence, under our general definition of a *cluster*, a clustering problem on a multi-dimensional data set can be rigorously solved as a tree partitioning problem, which leads to efficient and rigorous clustering algorithms.

MSTs have long been used for data classification in the field of image processing and pattern recognition [26, 27]. We have also seen some limited applications in biological data analysis [28]. One popular form of these MST applications is called the *single-linkage cluster analysis* [29]. Our study on these methods has led us to believe that all these applications have used the MSTs in some heuristic ways, e.g., cutting long edges to separate clusters, without fully exploring their power and understanding their rich properties related to clustering.

In this paper, we report two new results based on our previous rigorous results about MSTs *versus* clustering and a number of highly attractive properties of the MSTs [24, 25]. The first new result is that we have further converted a tree-partition problem to a problem of partitioning a one-dimensional profile for clustering. The second new result is a capacity to solve the cluster identification problem, which has not been addressed in our recent publications [24, 25]. We use two applications, i.e., cluster identification for gene expression profiles and regulatory binding site identification, to demonstrate the effectiveness of our approach.

25.2 Mathematical Framework

In this section, we will introduce our clustering technique and its mathematical foundation. Based on a rigorous relationship between a minimum spanning tree representation of a data set and clusters in the data set, we can represent a data set as a one-dimensional sequence such that each data cluster will be represented as a substring of sequence. Considering the page limit, we provide here only sketches of the proofs for all the theorems. Their full proofs will be shown elsewhere (Olman et al., in preparation).

25.2.1 Definition of Cluster

To put our discussion on data clustering on a solid mathematical ground, we need a formal definition of a cluster. Our intuition about clusters is that *intra-cluster distances among neighbors should be significantly smaller than any inter-cluster distances*. This intuition can be formalized as follows, which we call the *separability condition* of a cluster [25]:

Definition 1: Let D be a data set and $dist(u,v)$ denote the distance between any pair of data u,v in D. The **necessary condition** for any $C \subseteq D$ to be a cluster is that for any non-empty partition $C = C_1 \cup C_2$, the closest data point $d \in D - C_1$ to C_1 (measured by $dist$) must be from C_2, or in a formal way,

$$\arg\min dist(d \in D - C_1, C_1) \in C_2,$$

where the distance between a point to a data set means the distance between the point and its closest data point in the set. □

Here we provide only the necessary condition of a cluster since we believe that the sufficient condition of a cluster ought to be problem-dependent. This definition captures the essence of our intuition about a cluster.

A **cluster identification problem** is defined as to identify all data clusters (satisfying **Definition 1**) from a noisy data set.

25.2.2 MST-Representation of High-Dimensional Data

Let $D = \{d_i\}_{i=1}^N$ be a set of k-dimensional data with each $d_i = \{d_i^1, ..., d_i^k\}$. We define a weighted undirected graph $G(D) = (V,E)$ as follows. The vertex set $V = \{d_i | d_i \in D\}$ and the edge set $E = \{(a,b) | \text{ for } a,b \in D \text{ and } a \neq b\}$. Each edge $(a,b) \in E$ has a distance (or weight), $dist(a,b)$, between vertices a and b, which could be the Euclidean distance or other distance measures. Note that the *distance* does not have to be a *metric*. A *spanning tree* T of a (connected) weighted graph $G(D)$ is a connected subgraph of $G(D)$ such that (i) T contains every vertex of $G(D)$, and (ii) T does not contain any cycle. A *minimum spanning tree* is a spanning tree with the minimum total distance. In this paper, any connected component of a MST is called a *subtree* of the MST.

A minimum spanning tree of an undirected graph can be found by the classical Prim's algorithm [30]. The basic idea of the algorithm can be outlined as follows: *the initial solution is a singleton set containing an arbitrary vertex; the current partial solution is repeatedly expanded by adding the vertex (not in the current solution) that has the shortest edge to a vertex in the current solution, along with the edge, until all vertices are in the current solution*. A simple implementation of Prim's algorithm runs in $O(\|E\|\log(\|V\|))$ time [31], where $\|\cdot\|$ represents the number of elements in a set.

25.2.3 Relationship between MSTs and Clusters

We have observed, from a number of application problems, that data points of the same cluster tend to form a subtree of the MST representing the data set. If this is generally true, a clustering problem could be formulated and solved as a problem of partitioning a tree to optimize some objective function. Potentially, this could significantly reduce the computational complexity of a clustering problem. Based on the formal definition of cluster (Definition 1), we previously proved the following theorem [25]:

THEOREM 25.1
For any given data set D and a distance measure dist(), let T be a MST representing D with its edge-distances defined by dist(). If $C \subseteq D$ is a cluster satisfying the above definition, then all C's data points form a connected component of T. □

The implication of Theorem 1 is that to do clustering, all we need to do is to find a right objective function and to partition the MST into subtrees which optimizes this objective function. The following theorem establishes an interesting relationship between Prim's algorithm and data clusters. Let $V(k, a)$ represent the set of the first k vertices selected by Prim's algorithm with a being the first vertex selected.

THEOREM 25.2
A subset $C \subset D$ satisfies the necessary condition of a cluster if for any $a \in D$ there exists a $k \geq 1$ such that $V(k+||C||-1, a) - V(k-1, a) = C$.

To prove this theorem, we first define an operation G defined for any subset $A \subset D$:

$$G(A) = A \cup \{s | s \in D - A \text{ with the minimum distance to } A)\}. \tag{25.1}$$

We have the following result:

Lemma 1. If subset $C \subset D$ satisfies the necessary condition of a cluster, then for any $B \subseteq C$

$$G^{||C||-||B||}(B) = C, \tag{25.2}$$

i.e., applying the G-operation $(||G|| - ||B||)$ times to the set starting from B will cover the whole subset C.

Proof: Let us assume that is not true, and let $B \subseteq C$ that does not satisfy (25.2). So there exists $d \in G^{||C||-||B||}(B) \cap (D - C)$. We assume without loss of generality, $d \in G(B)$ (if not we can always expand B). Hence there exists $b \in B$ such that

$$dist(b, d) < \min\ dist(a \in B, C - B). \tag{25.3}$$

Since C satisfies the necessary condition of a cluster and $b \in C$, we have $G^{||C||-1}(\{b\}) = C$. However, this contradicts the upper bound of the inequality (25.3) since the inequality implies that d will be added to $G^{||C||-1}(\{b\})$ before any other elements of $C - B$ can be added. However we know $d \notin G^{||C||-1}(\{b\})$. This contradiction implies the correctness of the Lemma 1. □

A simple proof-by-contradiction can prove the correctness of Theorem 25.2, through an application of Lemma 1. We omit further details.

Theorem 25.2 states that after including any element from a subset satisfying the necessary condition of a cluster, Prim algorithm would pick all the elements in the cluster before moving to an element outside the cluster. Such a property gives us a one-dimensional representation for a cluster:

Definition 2. For a weighted graph $G(D)$ representing a data set D, $R_{D,a}$ is called D's *sequential representation* if $a \in D$ is the first vertex of $G(D)$ selected by an application of Prim's algorithm when constructing a minimum spanning of D, and

$$R_{D,a}(k) = (k^{th} \text{ selected vertex}, \text{distance of } k^{th} \text{ selected edge}), k = 1, \ldots, \|D\| - 1, \tag{25.4}$$

and

$$R_{D,a}(0) = (\emptyset, \infty); \quad R_{D,a}(\|D\|) = (\text{last vertex selected}, \infty). \tag{25.5}$$

For the two fields, we denote them as $R_{D,a}.V$ and $R_{D,a}.E$, respectively. □

Definition 3. A substring $R_{D,a}[i,j]$, from i^{th} to j^{th} positions of $R_{D,a}$, is called a *valley* if

$$\max_{i < k \leq j} R_{D,a}(k).E < \min\{R_{D,a}(i).E, R_{D,a}(j+1,a).E\}. \tag{25.6}$$

Based on **Definition 3**, we have the following results.

THEOREM 25.3
Any valley of $R_{D,a}$ corresponds to a subtree of D's MST, i.e., vertices from the valley form a connected component of the MST.

Proof: Let's assume that this is not true. So there is a valley $R_{D,a}[i,j]$ which contains a vertex k that connects with vertex i in the MST through vertices outside of $R_{D,a}[i,j]$. Let k be the first such vertex selected by Prim's algorithm after i is selected. Hence $R_{D,a}(k).E < R_{D,a}(i).E$, by the definition of a valley. But this contradicts to the selection order of Prim's algorithm. Hence we have proved the theorem. □

This theorem implies that a cluster identification problem can be solved as finding certain substrings (valleys) from a linear sequence (a sequential representation of the data set). The following theorem states that there is a one-to-one correspondence between *valleys* in a sequential representation and data clusters in a data set.

THEOREM 25.4
*For any data set D and any sequential representation, $R_{D,a}$, of D, $C \subseteq D$ forms a cluster (satisfying **Definition 1**) if and only if its vertices form a valley in $R_{D,a}$.* □

The proof of Theorem 25.4 can be done by direct applications of Theorems 25.2 and 25.3, which we omit. Theorem 25.4 states that all data clusters from a noisy data set can be found by identifying all valleys in the sequential representation of the data set, which can be done easily in linear time after a minimum spanning tree has been constructed for the data set. This sequential representation scheme can also be used to deal with the classical clustering problem, i.e., to partition a data set into non-overlapping "clusters."

THEOREM 25.5
Any data set with N elements can be partitioned into K subsets, $K < N$, such that each subset satisfies **Definition 1**. □

25.3 Stability of MST Structure Under Noise

The foundation of our MST-based clustering framework is the relationship between data clusters and subtrees of a MST representing the data set. As long as the property that a data cluster is represented by connected subtree in the MST, our framework will be applicable and maintain its rigorousness in finding all the data clusters. The question is how stable this relationship is for real biological data, particularly in the presence of noise. While research is under way to rigorously study this issue, we will present an example to show that this relationship is quite stable under heavy noise.

We have conducted the following test on a 2D gray-level image. In this simple test, we use a 2-dimensional grey-scale (ranging from 0 to 255) image with four letters "ORNL" appearing in a uniform background (Figure 25.1 (i)). We have constructed a graph representation of this image as follows. Each pixel is represented as a vertex of the graph, and each pair of adjacent pixels has an edge connecting them. An edge's distance is defined as the absolute value of the gray-level difference between its two end pixels. We then construct the MST of this graph. A 5-way partitioning of the MST, by cutting 4 longest edges, extracts accurately the four letters from the background. Now we add noise to the data set, by changing 70% of the pixels to random gray levels between 0 and 255. Figure 25.1 (ii) shows the resulting image, where the letters are hardly recognizable. Then we build a MST of this noisy data set using the same distance definition, and construct the sequential representation of the MST. Using the knowledge that there are four significant data clusters (representing the four letters), we extracted the four largest data clusters through identifying the four largest non-overlapping valleys. We then label the corresponding pixels of these valleys (along with the four neighbors of each such pixel) as "black" and the rest of the pixels as "white." Figure 25.1 (iii) shows the resulting image. Apparently, we lost very little accuracy for each of the five components. What this example demonstrates is that most of the data points in the original data clusters (the four letters and the background) still stay together as connected components in the new MST, even in the presence of heavy noise. This explains why our clustering framework stays effective for real applications (see next section) even when some of the data "clusters" may not rigorously follow **Definition 1**.

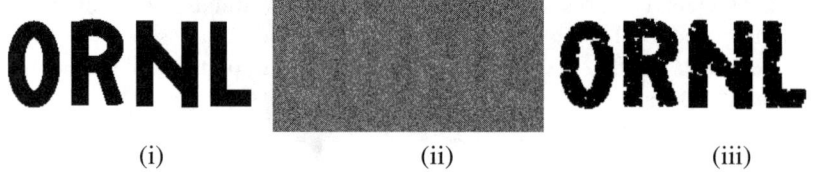

FIGURE 25.1
Noise and image segmentation. (i) A 2-D gray-level image with **256×512 pixels**.
(ii) Image of (i) with **70%** of pixels changed to random numbers $\in [0,255]$. (iii)
Segmented image of the noisy image (ii).

25.4 Statistical Assessment of Identified Clusters

An identified data cluster, by our algorithm, could be a "real" cluster with outstanding features that is different from its surrounding regions, or an "accidental" cluster that is formed by chance and generally does not exhibit significantly different features when compared to its background. In this section, we outline an approach to assess the statistical significance of each identified data cluster. The essence of our approach is to measure the average edge distance within a cluster (represented as a valley) and the minimum distance among the edges connecting this cluster with outside, and assess the statistical significance of the ratio between these two values.

Let us consider our probabilistic model in a one-dimensional case. Let $x_1, x_2, ..., x_n$ be a series of independent equally distributed observations (data points) from $[0,1]$. Without changing notation we will assume $x_i < x_{i+1}$, $i = 0, 1, 2, ..., n$, where $x_0 = 0, x_{n+1} = 1$. The MST of this data is trivial: for $root = 0$ the sequential representation is $x_{i+1} - x_i, i = 0, 1, 2, ..., n$. Let $B = \min\{x_1, 1 - x_n\}$, $A_n = \sum_{i=1}^{n-1}(x_{i+1} - x_i)/(n-1)$, where A_n is average edge length of the sequential representation of the edges of the cluster. We assume $x_1, x_2, ..., x_n$ is identified as a cluster, and x_0 and x_n connect to other data points in the background. According to Theorem 25.4, this series should satisfy the *Condition*

$$\{B > x_{i+1} - x_i, i = 2, 3, ..., n-1\}, \quad (25.7)$$

i.e., the condition that the boundary edges are longer than edges within a cluster. Then we carry out satistical analysis to check what is the likelihood that this *Condition* is satisfied by chance. If the likelihood is low, then the cluster is very significant, and *vice versa*. Our statistical significance analysis is based on value B/A_n under the hypothesis that all observations $x_i, i = 1, 2, ..., n$ are from a Uniform distribution at $[0,1]$ and satisfy the *Condition*. In other words we analytically calculate the function

$$h(t,n) = \text{probability}(B/A_n > t | Condition). \quad (25.8)$$

If our observed data significantly deviate from the hypothesis then $h(z,n)$ calculated from real observations, where z is observed value of the ratio B/A_n, should be

Statistical Data Mining and Knowledge Discovery

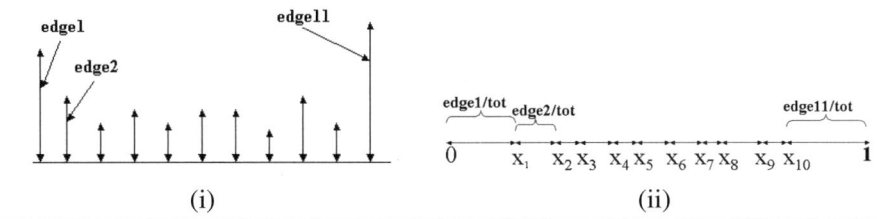

FIGURE 25.2
Statistical assessment of an identified cluster. (i) The sequential representation of the cluster with 11 edges, where the edge 1 and the edge 11 represent connections to the data outside the cluster (background). (ii) Normalized edges of (i) on a one-dimensional plot in [0,1], where $x_i - x_{i-1}, i = 1, 2, ..., 11$ represents the edge i normalized by the sum of all edges (*tot*).

very small. It would mean that our uniformity hypothesis should be rejected and the cluster should be considered as real with statistical significance $h(z,n)$. Calculations of $h(z,n)$ are based on the fact that under the uniformity hypothesis the vector $(x_1, x_2 - x_1, ..., x_n - x_{n-1})$ has the Dirichlet distribution [32]. We omit further details of this calculations.

This model can be applied to an identified valley (data cluster) as follows. Let $(e_2, ..., e_{n-1})$ be a valley and e_1 and e_n are the edges immediately outside of the valley. Let $x_i = \sum_{j \leq i} e_j$, for $i \in [1, n]$ and $x_0 = 0$. Now the above discussions can be applied directly to the edge distances with a normalization. Figure 25.2 shows the relationship between the edge distances within a valley and the x_i variables of the above discussion.

25.5 Applications

In this section, we present applications of our clustering method to three problems: a simulated data set for clustering, regulatory binding site identification problem, and cluster identification in microarray gene expression data.

25.5.1 Partitioning of Simulated Data

We use the following simulated data set to compare our clustering algorithm to the K-means clustering approach. The data set, as shown in Figure 25.3(i), is made of data points in 2-dimensional space, generated randomly. Visually it consists of two distinct clusters. We first applied our approach to build a MST of the data set and a sequential representation of the MST. Figure 25.3(i) shows the sequential represen-

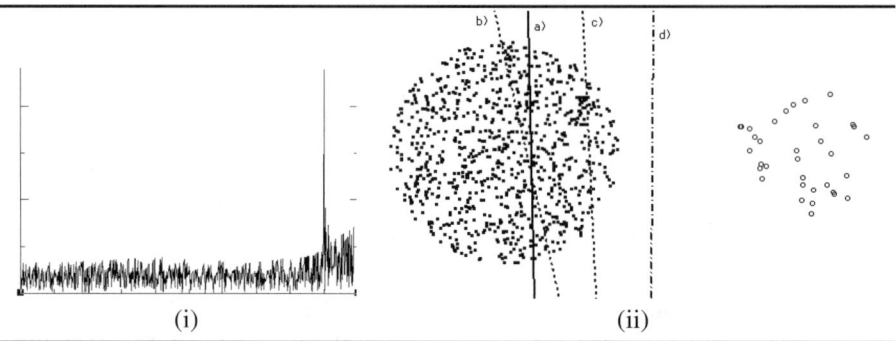

FIGURE 25.3
A simulated data set, in two dimensional space, consisting of two natural clusters. (i) Sequential representation of the data set. (ii) The four lines, (a), (b), (c), and (d), represent four clustering results by a K-means algorithm, using different seeds as starting points.

tation. Clearly it consists of two large and deep valleys, separated by a tall wall. The two valleys correspond perfectly with the two data clusters. This is clearly a simple clustering problem. However this simple problem could present difficulties to other clustering approaches. Now we show clustering results by a K-means approach. When using different seeds (randomly selected) as starting points, the K-means algorithm may give different clustering results. Figure 25.3(ii) shows four such clustering results, represented by four separating lines (a), (b), (c), and (d). Though the correct solution (d) is among the calculated solutions, it does not represent the "optimal" solution for the typical objective function in a K-means algorithm, i.e., the total distance between all the data points and the centers of the clusters they belong to. It may be possible to find a particular objective function whose minimum corresponds to the correct clustering of this specific example. However finding the right objective function for each individual application could be an awkward and unnatural process.

25.5.2 Regulatory Binding Site Identification

We have applied our clustering method to the regulatory binding site identification problem. A gene's mRNA expression level is regulated by proteins, which bind to specific sites in the gene's promoter region, called *binding sites* [33]. Binding sites for the same protein are generally conserved on the sequence level, across all genes regulated by this protein. Identification of genes with the same binding sites can provide hints about which genes may work in the same biological processes. Operationally, the problem of identifying regulatory binding sites can be defined as follows. Given a list of genomic sequences covering genes' promoter regions, identify short (e.g., 5 - 30) "conserved" sequence fragments, which are over-represented [33]. There are a number of existing software programs, e.g., CONSENSUS [34],

MEME [35], for this problem. However, it is clear that the problem is far from being solved.

Unlike any existing methods, we have formulated the binding-site identification problem as a cluster identification problem. Consider a set of N sequences (from the upstream regions of genes). We assume that the binding sites we are searching for have the following characteristics: (1) the data densities of clusters formed by these binding sites are higher than that of the overall background; (2) the position-specific information content [36] of the gapless multiple-sequence alignment among the k-mers of these clusters is relatively higher; and (3) k-mers of each such cluster cover at least M of the N sequences, with $M \leq N$. We carried out the following four steps for the binding-site identification. The first step is the search for the most frequent short (5 letters) substring S. The reasoning behind it is that any set of binding sites has continuous substring with high position-specific informational content. The second step is to form the block of maximal length L from words containing this substring S, and reassess the length of new block (L') by cutting the extended L-mers in the cluster from both sides till the first positions with informational content more than 0.1. We define the distance $dist(w_1, w_2)$ between two words (w_1 and w_2) of length L' using the position-specific information content as a weight:

$$dist(w_1, w_2) = \sum_{i=1}^{L'} IC[i](2 - f[i][w_1[i]] - f[i][w_2[i]] + |f[i][w_1[i]] - f[i][w_2[i]]|),$$
(25.9)

where $f[i][nt], i = 1, 2 \ldots L'$; $nt = a, c, g, t$ is the frequency profile of the block. The third step is to build the sequential representation in the space of L'-mers with the distance $dist(w_1, w_2)$. The last step is to search for valley in the sequential representation and to check statistical significance of a cluster as described in section 25.4.

25.5.2.1 A Case Study on CRP Binding Sites

The CRP binding site represents a challenging case for identification of regulatory binding sites [33], and has been one of the standard test cases for binding-site identification programs. The test set consists of 18 sequences with 23 experimentally verified CRP binding sites, with site being a 22mers. The best results by any existing software can identify 17 or 18 of these 23 sites [37], with an unspecified number of false positives. We have applied our cluster identification framework to the CRP data set, with the result

$$L = 28 \; ; \; L' = 22 \; ; \; S = tgtga \, .$$
(25.10)

Figure 25.4 (i,ii) shows the sequential representation of all the 22mers from the 18 CRP sequences. As we can see, most of the true CRP sites (represented as triangles) appear in the deep valley in this sequential representation.

In addition to running our clustering algorithm on the CPR data set, we have run the program also on an enlarged CRP data with 18 randomly generated DNA sequences to test the robustness of our approach (see Figure 25.4 (ii,iv)). Table 25.1 summarizes the detailed prediction results along with their statistical significance assessments. As we can see, when the program selects a data cluster with 26 elements

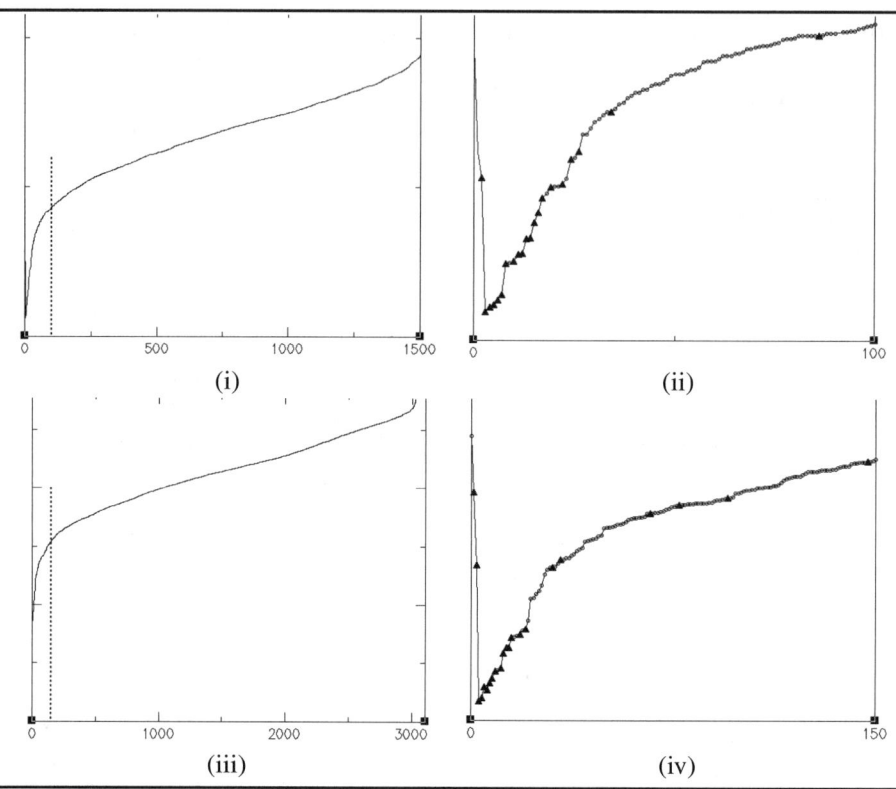

FIGURE 25.4
The sequential representation of all the 22-mers from the CRP data set (i,ii) and the CRP data with additional 18 randomly generated DNA sequences (iii, iv). (i,iii) are for the whole data set and (ii,iv) are for the part from 0 to the marked dashed lines in (i,iii), i.e., enlarged. Each triangle represents a known CRP binding site and each circle represents a non-CRP binding site.

([1, 26]), 20 of them are true CRP sites with a high statistical significance. Similarly when the program selects a smaller cluster with 24 elements ([1, 24]), we get 19 true CRP binding sites (one fewer CRP site) but with lower false positive and a higher statistical significance. Also we can see, when applied to the enlarged data set with noise, the performance of the program drops only slightly.

25.5.3 Cluster Identification in Gene Expression Profiles

We have also applied our clustering framework to the microarray gene expression data. As probably the most explosively expanding tool for genome analysis, microchips of gene expression have made it possible to simultaneously monitor the expression levels of tens of thousands of genes under different experimental condi-

Statistical Data Mining and Knowledge Discovery

TABLE 25.1
The statistical significance of identified CRP clusters.

1	23	6.58E-1	18
1	24	7.41E-5	19
1	26	2.59E-5	20
1	27	4.08E-4	21
2	17	3.39E-2	15
2	20	4.95E-4	16
2	21	3.67E-5	17
2	23	8.46E-4	17
2	25	1.85E-3	18
2	27	7.02E-3	18

The first and second columns are boundary positions of the selected valleys. The fourth column is the statistical significance of the cluster, and the last column is the number of true binding sites in the selected cluster. The first five rows are selection results on the original CRP data set, and the last five rows show the results on the original CRP data set plus 18 random sequences added as noise.

tions [3, 4, 11]. This provides a powerful tool for studying how genes collectively react to changes in their environments, providing hints about the structures of the involved gene networks. One of the basic problems in interpreting the observed expression data is to identify correlated expression patterns of genes representing the basic challenge in this clustering problem. There are a number of existing computational methods/software for analyzing gene expression data, based on clustering techniques like K-means [19], hierarchical clustering [4], or self-organizing maps [21]. One of the main problems with all these clustering techniques is that they are generally inadequate in identifying "dense" data clusters from the noisy background as they are designed to partition a data set into "clusters" no matter if any "clusters" exist or how many exist.

The cluster identification problem for gene expression profiles can be defined as follows. Let $d_i = (e_1^i, ..., e_t^i)$ represent the expression levels of N genes over a time series (or different experimental conditions) 1 through t of gene i. The goal is to find a set of K clusters in D, i.e., $\{D_1,...,D_K\}$, such that (1) the gene expression patterns within any cluster D_j, $j = 1, 2, ..., K$, are similar; (2) the gene expression patterns between any two different clusters D_j and D_k, $j \neq k$, are distinct; (3) the gene expression profiles in the genes not included in $\{D_1,...,D_K\}$ do not form any significant cluster and any of these genes do not resemble the pattern in any cluster D_j, $j = 1, 2, ..., K$.

We have applied our clustering program to a number of data sets of microarray gene expression data. The example we show here is a set of 145 differentially ex-

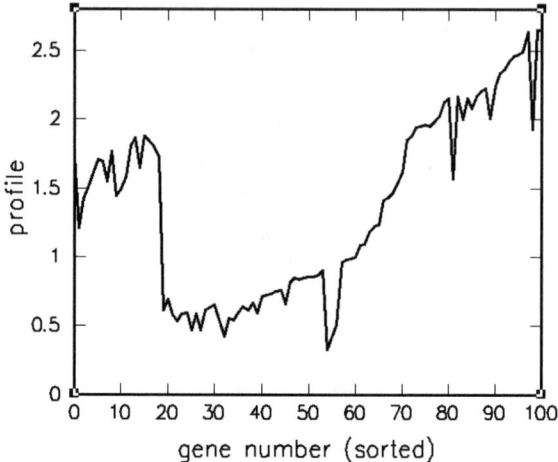

FIGURE 25.5
The ordered representation plot for gene expression data related to yeast amino acid transport, where the valley in the middle of the plot indicates a "dense" cluster.

pressed genes from yeast under the experimental condition to identify genes possibly involved in the amino acid transport pathway. Figure 25.5 shows part of the sequential representation of the data set. We can see clearly that there is a "dense" cluster in the middle of the figure. Five genes are in this dense cluster: PHO5, BAP2, BAP3, AGP1, and TAT1. Based on our previous knowledge and experimental results, we know that these five genes are part of the amino acid transport pathway in yeast. This information, which cannot be obtained from other methods, is very important to understand the pathway.

25.6 Discussion

By representing a multi-dimensional data set as a sequential representation, we can rigorously reduce a multi-dimensional data clustering problem to a substring search problem. The simplicity of a one-dimensional problem made it possible to develop efficient and rigorous clustering algorithms. When compared to the existing clustering techniques as mentioned above, our MST-based clustering framework has the following strengths, as demonstrated in this paper:

- The dimensionality of the data set to be clustered becomes irrelevant since we will be working on a one-dimensional sequence rather than high dimensional data.

- The complexity of cluster boundaries generally becomes irrelevant since we can transform the shapes of clusters while keeping its representing MST structure intact. This is in contrast with most of the existing clustering algorithms, which attempt to use simple geometric shapes, e.g., hyperplanes, to separate clusters, and hence are dependent on the complexity of the cluster boundaries. In fact, our method focuses on the separability (instead of the geometric shapes) of clusters and and is more reliable to detect separable clusters than methods like K-means as demonstrated in the paper.

- The relationship between clusters and valleys of the sequential representation, as the cornerstone of our approach, allows us to identify a cluster whose pattern is substantially different from the background. This is particularly useful for pattern recognition in biological data. Traditional clustering methods generally do not have such a capacity.

- The computational efficiency of our algorithm, facilitated by the simplicity of a one-dimensional sequential representation, allows us to effectively provide many other useful features relevant to clustering, in particular, the statistical assessment of clustering results.

While we presented only preliminary application results in two application areas, e.g., gene expression data analysis and regulatory binding-site identification, we found that many other biological data analysis problems, as mentioned in the Introduction, could potentially be solved or partially solved using this approach. We expect our method can be very useful for analyzing the high-throughput biological data in general.

Acknowledgments

The authors thank Dr. Gary Stormo for providing us the CRP binding site data. The work was supported by ORNL LDRD funding and by the Office of Biological and Environmental Research, U.S. Department of Energy, under Contract DE-AC05-00OR22725, managed by UT-Battelle, LLC.

References

[1] E. S. Lander et al. (2001). Initial sequencing and analysis of the human genome. *Nature*, 409, 860–921.

[2] J. C. Venter et al.(2001). The sequence of the human genome. *Science*, 291, 1304–1351.

[3] M. B. Eisen, P. T. Spellman, P. O. Brown, and D. Botstein.(1998). Cluster analysis and display of genome-wide expression patterns. *Proc. Natl. Acad. Sci. USA*, 95,14863–14868.

[4] X. Wen, S. Fuhrman, G. S. Michaelsand D. B. Carr, S. Smith, J. L. Barker, and R. Somogyi.(1998). Large-scale temporal gene expression mapping of central nervous system development. *Proc. Natl. Acad. Sci. USA*, 95,334–339.

[5] M. M. Young, N. Tang, J. C. Hempel, C. M. Oshiro, E. W. Taylor, I. D. Kuntz, B. W. Gibson, and G. Dollinger.(2000). High throughput protein fold identification by using experimental constraints derived from intramolecular crosslinks and mass spectrometry. *Proc. Natl. Acad. Sci. USA*, 97,5802–5806.

[6] M. Mann, R. C. Hendrickson, and A. Pandey.(2001). Analysis of proteins and proteomes by mass spectrometry. *Annu. Rev. Biochem.*, 70, 437–473.

[7] National Institute of General Medical Sciences. Pilot projects for the protein structure initiative (structural genomics).(1999). *http://www.nih.gov/grants/guide/rfa-files/RFA-GM-99-009.html*, June:RFA GM–99–009.

[8] S. Fields and O. K. Song.(1989). A novel genetic system to detect protein-protein interactions. *Nature*, 340, 245–246.

[9] P. Uetz, L. Giot, G. Cagney, T. A. Mansfield, R. S. Judson, J. R. Knight, D. Lockshon, V. Narayan, M. Srinivasan, P. Pochart, A. Qureshi-Emili, Y. Li, B. Godwin, D. Conover, T. Kalbfleisch, G. Vijayadamodar, M. Yang, M. Johnston, S. Fields, and J. M. Rothberg.(2000). A comprehensive analysis of protein-protein interactions in saccharomyces cerevisiae. *Nature*, 403, 623–627.

[10] U.S. Department of Energy. Genomes to Life program. *http://DOEGenomesToLife.org/*, April, 2001.

[11] G. Sherlock.(2000). Analysis of large-scale gene expression data. *Curr. Opin. Immunol.*, 12, 201–205.

[12] A. Bateman, E. Birney, R. Durbin, S. R. Eddy, F. D. Finn, and E. L. L. Sonnhammer.(1999). Pfam 3.1: 1313 multiple alignments match the majority of proteins. *Nucleic Acids Research*, 27, 260–262.

[13] A. G. Murzin, S. E. Brenner, T. Hubbard, and C. Chothia.(1995). Scop: a structural classification of proteins database for the investigation of sequences and structures. *J. Mol. Biol.*, 247, 536–540.

[14] A. Bairoch.(1993). The ENZYME data bank. *Nucleic Acids Research*, 21, 3155–3156.

[15] L. Holm and C. Sander.(1994). Parser for protein fodling units. *Proteins: Struct. Funct. Genet.*, 19, 256–268.

[16] Ying Xu, Dong Xu, and Harold N. Gabow.(2000). Protein domain decomposition using a graph-theoretic approach. *Bioinformatics*, 16,1091–1104.

[17] F. Corpet, J. Gouzy, and D. Kahn.(1999). Recent improvements of the ProDom database of protein domain families. *Nucleic Acids Research*, 27, 263–267.

[18] X. Guan and L. Du.(1998). Domain identification by clustering sequence alignments. *Bioinformatics*, 14, 783–788.

[19] Ralf Herwig, Albert J. Poustka, Christine Mller, Christof Bull, Hans Lehrach, and John O'Brien.(1999). Large-scale clustering of cdna-fingerprinting data. *Genome Res.*, 9,1093–1105.

[20] J. Herrero, A. Valencia, and J. Dopazo.(2001). A hierarchical unsupervised growing neural network for clustering gene expression patterns. *Bioinformatics*, 17,126–136.

[21] P. Tamayo, D. Slonim, J. Mesirov, Q. Zhu, S. Kitareewan, E. Dmitrovsky, E. S. Lander, and T. R. Golub.(1999). Interpreting patterns of gene expression with self-organizing maps: methods and application to hematopoietic differentiation. *Proc. Natl. Acad. Sci. USA*, 96,2907–2912.

[22] Ying Xu, Richard J. Mural, J. R. Einstein, Manesh Shah, and E. C. Uberbacher.(1996). GRAIL: A multi-agent neural network system for gene identification. *Proc. IEEE*, 84,1544–1552.

[23] D. Kulp, D. Haussler, M. G. Reese, and F. H. Eeckman.(1996). A generalized hidden Markov model for the recognition of human genes in DNA. *Proc. Int. Conf. Intell. Syst. Mol. Biol.*, 4,134–142.

[24] Y. Xu, V. Olman, and D. Xu.(2001). Minimum spanning trees for gene expression data clustering. In S. Miyano, R. Shamir, and T. Takagi, (Eds.), *Proc. 12th Int. Conf. on Genome Informatics (GIW)*, 24–33. Universal Academy Press, Tokyo.

[25] Ying Xu, Victor Olman, and Dong Xu.(2002). Clustering gene expression data using a graph-theoretic approach: An application of minimum spanning trees. *Bioinformatics*, 18, 536–545.

[26] R. O. Duda and P. E. Hart.(1973). *Pattern Classification and Scene Analysis*. Wiley-Interscience, New York.

[27] R. C. Gonzalez and P. Wintz.(1987). *Digital Image Processing (second edition)*. Addison-Wesley, Reading, MA.

[28] D. J. States, N. L. Harris, and L. Hunter.(1993). Computationally efficient cluster representation in molecular sequence megaclassification. *ISMB*, 1,387–394.

[29] J. C. Gower and G. J. S. Ross.(1969). Minimum spanning trees and single linkage analysis. *Applied Statistics*, 18,54–64.

[30] R. C. Prim.(1957). Shortest connection networks and some generalizations. *Bell System Technical Journal*, 36,1389–1401.

[31] T. H. Cormen, C. E. Leiserson, and R. L. Rivet.(1989). *Introduction to Algorithms*. MIT Press, Cambridge.

[32] S. S. Wilks.(1962). *Mathematical Statistics*. John Wiley and Sons, New York.

[33] G. D. Stormo and G. W. Hartzell 3rd.(1989). Identifying protein-binding sites from unaligned DNA fragments. *Proc. Natl. Acad. Sci. USA*, 86,1183–1187.

[34] G. Z. Hertz and G. D. Stormo.(1999). Identifying DNA and protein patterns with statistically significant alignments of multiple sequences. *Bioinformatics*, 15, 563–577.

[35] T. L. Bailey and M. Gribskov. Methods and statistics for combining motif match scores. *J. Comput. Biol.*, 5:211–221, 1998.

[36] T. D. Schneider, G. D. Stormo, L. Gold, and A. Ehrenfeucht.(1998). Information content of binding sites on nucleotide sequences. *J. Mol. Biol.*, 188, 415–431.

[37] C. E. Lawrence and A. A. Reilly.(1990). An expectation maximization (em) algorithm for the identification and characterization of common sites in unaligned biopolymer sequences. *Proteins: Struct. Funct. Genet.*, 7, 41–51.

26

Behavior-Based Recommender Systems as Value-Added Services for Scientific Libraries

Andreas Geyer-Schulz,[1] Michael Hahsler,[2] Andreas Neumann,[1] and Anke Thede[1]
[1] Universität Karlsruhe (TH), Germany, [2] WU-Wien, Austria

CONTENTS

26.1 Introduction 433
26.2 Recommender Services for Legacy Library Systems 435
26.3 Ehrenberg's Repeat-Buying Theory for Libraries 439
26.4 A Recommender System for the Library of the Universität Karlsruhe (TH) 448
26.5 Conclusion 451
    Acknowledgment 451
    References 451

Amazon.com paved the way for several large-scale, behavior-based recommendation services as an important value-added expert advice service for online book shops. In this contribution we discuss the effects (and possible reductions of transaction costs) for such services and investigate how such a value-added service can be implemented in the context of scientific libraries. For this purpose we present a new, recently developed recommender system based on a stochastic purchase incidence model, present the underlying stochastic model from repeat-buying theory and analyze whether the underlying assumptions on consumer behavior hold for users of scientific libraries, too. We analyzed the logfiles with approximately 85 million HTTP-transactions of the web-based online public access catalog (OPAC) of the library of the Universität Karlsruhe (TH) since January 2001 and performed some diagnostic checks. The recommender service is fully operational within the library system of the Universität Karlsruhe (TH) since 2002/06/22.

26.1 Introduction

Recommender systems are regarded as strategically important information systems for e-commerce. Amazon.com, one of the most profitable internet companies, aggressively and successfully uses recommender services for building and maintaining customer relationships. Recommender services are attractive for both companies and their customers because of their capability to reduce transaction costs:

For companies they

- reduce the cost of customer service and support by shifting customers to web-based self-service platforms,

- improve cross- and up-selling revenues,

- support product managers by automatically generating additional product information,

- support marketing research by continuous consumer panel analysis.

For customers they

- reduce search cost and lead to a better overview of available products,

- support the discovery of related products and product groups,

- reveal market leaders and standard products.

The potential of recommender systems to reduce transaction costs in a educational and research environment has been analyzed in detail in [19]. Several innovative and experimental digital libraries, namely ResearchIndex [29] whose tools are described in [5] and the digital libraries of the ACM [1] and the IEEE [23], exploit these advantages, although with different types of services. Several digital library and web search engine projects implemented services and interfaces to support the user's process of search and information extraction. An example is the Stanford Digital Library Project [21] within the scope of which the system Fab [2] [3] was developed. Fab is a combination of a content-based and a collaborative recommender system that filters web pages according to content analysis and creates usage profiles for user groups with similar interests as well. Popescul et al. [32] have experimented with estimating collaborative filter models by latent variable models represented as Bayesian networks in the context of ResearchIndex. On the ResearchIndex dataset a Bayesian network with the structure of the classical diagnostic model has been evaluated by Pennock et al. [31]. Another example is PADDLE [22], a system dealing with the information overload caused by the mass of documents in digital libraries by introducing customization and personalization features. Inquirus 2 is a prototype of a personalized web search engine which uses automatic query modification and a personalized result scoring function [20]. Furthermore the UC Berkeley Digital Library Project [41] offers users to build personalized collections of their documents of interest. Recommendation services for digital libraries and their evaluation methods are discussed by Bollen and Rocha [6]. However, traditional scientific libraries seem to be late to realize the potential of recommender services for scientists and students alike. Our main objective is to reorganize scientific libraries with the help of recommender systems to customer oriented service portals with a reputation of above average service quality. For students, university teachers, and researchers an essential advantage of recommender systems is the reduction of search and evaluation cost for information products and the reduction of information overload by customization and personalization features. A recent study of the usage of electronic scientific information in academic education in Germany indicates a severe need for such systems [26]. In addition, recommender systems trigger customer oriented procurement processes in libraries which will improve the service quality of libraries.

This article is structured into three parts:

1. In Section 26.2 we discuss how recommender systems can be integrated with a legacy library system. We describe a loosely coupled distributed system which minimizes the required changes in the legacy system. It builds on the software pattern of active agents presented in [15]. The system uses a variant of a generic architecture for recommender systems shown in [18].

2. In Section 26.3 we transfer a stochastic model from repeat-buying theory for recommender systems in libraries. We adapt the model for anonymous groups of users of the same information product and use this model to identify statistically significant purchase co-occurrences.

3. In Section 26.4 we present a case study of this system at the library of the Universität Karlsruhe (TH).

26.2 Recommender Services for Legacy Library Systems

We describe recommender services and their integration with legacy library systems in the language of software patterns, an approach made popular by Gamma et al. [13]. In the following we repeatedly refer to the software pattern of agents described in Russell and Norvig [36] which has served as the basic building block for the pattern of a virtual library with active agents [15] [16] for defining a generic reference architecture for recommender services [18]. Russell and Norvig's agent pattern describes the interaction between an agent and its environment. The environment is perceived by the sensors of the agent, sensor data is aggregated and inferences are drawn by the reasoning component of the agent and, finally, the agent influences its environment by acting on its inferences. In the library setting, we simplify our agent by separation of labor which leads to three specialized agent types, namely user observation agents, aggregation agents, and recommendation agents which together provide one or more recommender services. These agents are distributed and loosely coupled; their cooperation is asynchronous. The collaboration of the components of the recommender services implemented at the library of the Universität Karlsruhe (TH) is shown in Figure 26.1. The organization is a compromise between consistency and performance requirements.

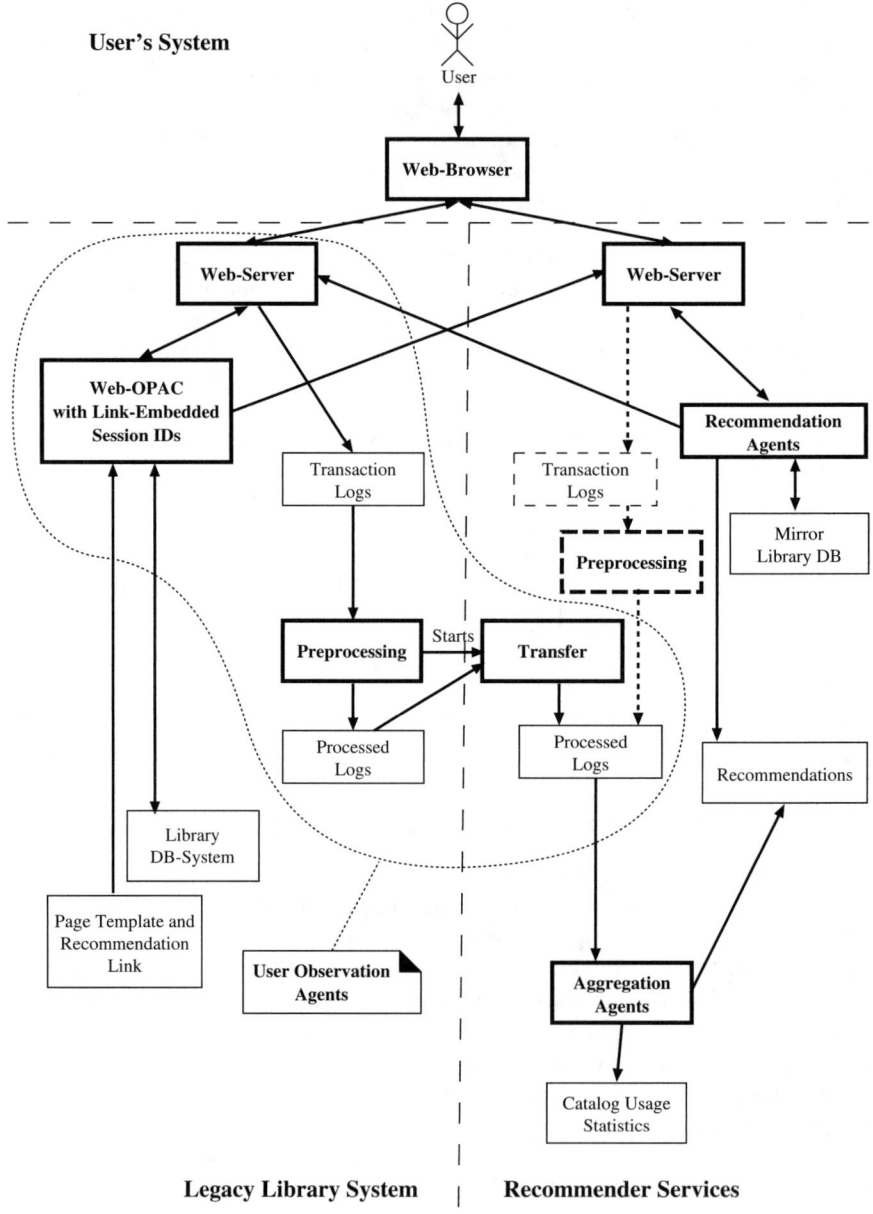

FIGURE 26.1
The architecture of the legacy library system with loosely coupled recommender services of the Universität Karlsruhe (TH).

Statistical Data Mining and Knowledge Discovery 437

For behavior based recommendation services we need at least market baskets or purchase histories. Market baskets correspond to anonymous but session level data, purchase histories to user session data. In the current implementation only anonymous, session level data are collected. This implies that the behavior of a single user is not observed and that the privacy of users is respected.

User observation agents record the relevant transactions of a user. Several server-side recording mechanisms and their suitability for session identification have been discussed in the literature:

HTTP-logs. As Cooley [9] has shown heuristics for session identification for pure HTTP-logs range from 40 % to 60 % correctly identified sessions due to the combined effects of ISP proxy-servers and rotating IP addresses.

HTTP-logs with link embedded session IDs. Link embedded session IDs considerably improve the accuracy of session identification. However, three problem areas remain: First, robot identification [39], second, public terminals which are accessed by several users sequentially, and third, the complete implementation of link embedding in the OPAC.

HTTP-logs with cookies. An advantage of the cookie mechanism compared to link embedded session IDs is that sessions can be identified without changes in legacy applications and that cookies are not included in bookmarks and thus do not lead to session restarts after potentially long periods of time [18]. The disadvantage of cookies is that a certain percentage of users will refuse to accept cookies.

Instrumented and specialized transaction logging with cookies. This approach makes preprocessing of log-files obsolete at the price of instrumenting the application. See [18].

The web-OPAC of the library of the Universität Karlsruhe (TH) already maintained session state with link embedded session IDs in order to host the library systems of a network of 23 libraries in the south-west of Germany. The library's development system principles include the renouncement of cookies and require minimal change to the existing system. Because of these requirements link embedded session IDs are the session recording mechanism of choice in the current implementation. The web server of the university library collects HTTP-logs with link embedded session IDs which are periodically posted via HTTP to the recommendation server after local preprocessing. Preprocessing on the library server includes extraction of HTTP GET requests with session IDs. Preprocessing on the recommendation server implements session splitting after a break of 15 minutes to take care of public access terminals in the library building and session restarts from bookmarks. In Figure 26.1 the components of the current user observation agent are combined to a subsystem in a dotted bubble.

However, a considerable simplification is possible. Whenever a user requests the detailed view of a document (book, journal, multimedia file etc.) with the meta data of the document the page-building procedure of the web-OPAC tests whether recommendations exist for this document by calling a CGI-script on the web server of the recommender service (the arrow from the web-OPAC to the web server on the right-hand side in Figure 26.1). The primary motivation for this existence test is that a link to recommendations for a document is only shown to the user if recommendations exist. The consequences of the existence test for recommendations are twofold. On the one hand, the recommender service and its network connection to the library system must immediately accommodate the traffic resulting from all users of an instrumented web-OPAC. If either limits in network bandwidth or local processing power lead to high response times in this test, the test can be omitted by unconditionally presenting a link to a recommendation page - even if it is empty. On the other hand, the information necessary to compute market baskets is mirrored in the transaction logs of the recommender service so that the periodic posting of session data from the legacy library system to the recommender service is redundant. The drawback is that only session data of libraries offering the recommender service would be collected in this way. This would reduce the amount of data collected and it would have negative consequences for the analysis of stochastic models and on the number of recommendations generated. Preprocessing on the recommendation server remains functionally identical and is still necessary.

After preprocessing the aggregation agent computes market baskets, estimates a logarithmic series distribution (LSD) for the stochastic consumer behavior model presented in Section 26.3, and identifies and extracts outliers as recommendations. In addition, basic diagnostic statistics are provided for recommender management. The aggregation agent performs incremental updates periodically. Because of the extreme sparseness of observations relative to the total amount of documents of the library (15 million), the memory of the recommender is kept. We expect that the recommender service will profit of several years of memory. However, the effects of memory length on the quality of the recommender as well as the repeat buying behavior of library users must be investigated.

The recommendation agent resides on the recommendation server and consists of two CGI-scripts. The first implements the existence test for recommendations for a document. The script is invoked by a dynamic image link and returns an image containing the recommendation link or otherwise a transparent image if no recommendations are available for this document. The link invokes the second script which generates recommendation pages with the corporate identity of the university library and its associated libraries. A crash of the recommendation server is handled in the following way: Because the HTTP-protocol is stateless, embedded requests to dynamic images are separate requests of the user's browser to the recommendation server. If an image is not retrievable the detailed inspection page of a document is nevertheless loaded and shown, albeit with broken image symbols and alternate tag displayed.

Performance considerations for the generation of recommendation pages again determine the actual design. Figure 26.1 shows the Mirror Library DB component connected by a double arrow to recommendation agents which in turn perform a query with the identification of an information object on the web-OPAC of the legacy library system in order to obtain the meta data of this information object in the university library's traditional MAB format (Maschinelles Austauschformat für Bibliotheken - German machine exchange format for libraries [10]). This query is depicted by the directed arrow from recommendation agents to the web server on the legacy library system. Functionally, the mirror library database system's sole purpose is to reduce the load caused by the generation of recommendation pages as much as possible. Whenever the recommendation agent builds a recommendation page, it first tries to retrieve the information from the mirror library database. If this fails, a query is directed to the web-OPAC and the resulting meta data in MAB format is converted, first stored into the mirror library database, and second inserted into the recommendation page.

Therefore, as shown in Figure 26.1 the interface between the legacy library system and the recommendation service consists of a single dynamic image link in the template of the detailed document view, two CGI-scripts for the existence test and for the generation of the recommendation page, the meta data request for document details, and the periodic transfer of web server transaction logs.

26.3 Ehrenberg's Repeat-Buying Theory for Libraries

When discussing repeat-buying theory in the context of a library for the first time, the idea was met with considerable skepticism, because of the at first sight seemingly obvious arguments that the users of a library almost never borrow a book twice or more often and that they rarely pay for the books. As we will show in this section, repeat-buying theory is nevertheless the method of choice for libraries, too, since these objections do not hold. Our argumentation will be structured in two parts. First, we rehearse repeat-buying theory in a classical consumer panel setting. Then, we will argue that the regularities of the observable stochastic purchasing (or weaker borrowing or inspection) processes in a library can be sufficiently described by repeat-buying theory.

In purchasing a non-durable consumer product a consumer basically makes two decisions: the decision to purchase a product of a certain product class (purchase incidence) and the decision to choose a certain brand (brand choice). Ehrenberg's main conceptual insight is that repeat-buying behavior can be adequately modeled by formalizing the purchase incidence process of a single brand. As a result Ehrenberg's repeat-buying theory is of a considerable simplicity and elegance: *Of the thousand and one variables which might affect buyer behavior, it is found that nine hundred and ninety-nine usually do not matter. Many aspects of buyer behavior can be predicted simply from the penetration and the average purchase frequency of an item, and even these two variables are interrelated* (A. S. C. Ehrenberg (1988) [11]).

Historically, repeat-buying theory was developed for the analysis of consumer panels. A consumer panel consists of a sample of consumers who report their purchases completely and faithfully to a marketing research company as, e.g., A. C. Nielsen. Such a full report contains the sequence of all purchases of a consumer over an extensive period of time for all outlets and is called the purchase history of a consumer. The list of products purchased at a single trip to the store is called a market basket. In a consumer panel the identity of each consumer is known and an individual purchase history can be constructed from the union of all market baskets of a single consumer. Crucial for the success of consumer panel analysis was the choice of purchase occasions as unit of analysis. A purchase occasion is a binary variable coded as one if a consumer has purchased at least one item of a product in a trip to a store and zero otherwise. The number of items purchased as well as package sizes are ignored. One of the earliest uses of purchase occasions can be attributed to L. J. Rothman [38].

Analysis is carried out in distinct time-periods (such as 1-week, 4-week, quarterly periods) conforming with other standard marketing reporting practices. A particular simplification resulting from this time-period orientation is that most repeat-buying results for any given item can be expressed in terms of penetration and purchase frequency. The penetration is the proportion of consumers who buy an item at all within a given period. The purchase frequency w is the average number of times these consumers buy at least one item in the period. The mean purchase frequency w is itself the most basic measure of repeat-buying in Ehrenberg's theory [11] and in this contribution.

The lower level of Figure 26.2 illustrates the basic idea of Ehrenberg's purchase incidence models: a consumer in a panel purchases a specific consumer product following a stationary Poisson process. This process is independent of the other purchase processes of the consumer. The rationale is that in each household certain consumer products are stored and only restocked as soon as the household runs out of the item (e.g., coffee, soap, toothpaste, ...). Chatfield et al. [8] proved that aggregating these purchase processes over a population of consumers under the (quite general) assumption that the parameters μ of the Poisson distributions of the purchase processes of the individual consumers (the long run average purchase rates) follow a truncated Γ-distribution results in a logarithmic series distribution (LSD).

The LSD is a one parameter (q) distribution which gives according to Ehrenberg [11] the probability that a specific product is purchased a total of 1, 2, 3, ..., r times without knowing the number of non-buyers. Its frequency distribution $P(r$ purchases), its mean w (the mean purchase frequency), and its variance σ^2 are shown in Formulas 26.1, 26.2, and 26.3, respectively. Note that $\sigma^2 > w$ is a characteristic of the LSD distribution. For further details on the LSD distribution, see Johnson and Kotz [24].

$$P(r \text{ purchases}) = \frac{-q^r}{r\ln(1-q)}, \quad r \geq 1 \qquad (26.1)$$

$$w = \frac{-q}{(1-q)\ln(1-q)} \qquad (26.2)$$

Statistical Data Mining and Knowledge Discovery

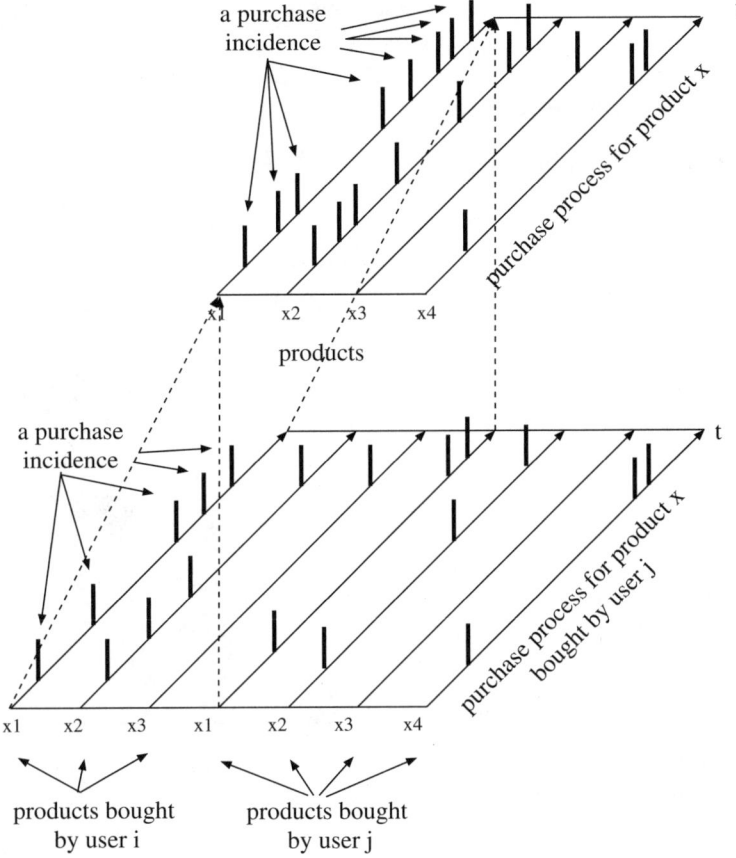

FIGURE 26.2
Purchase incidences as independent stochastic processes.

$$\sigma^2 = \frac{w}{(1-q)} - w^2 = \frac{-q\left(1 + \frac{q}{\ln(1-q)}\right)}{(1-q)^2 \ln(1-q)} \qquad (26.3)$$

Next, we summarize the assumptions on consumer purchase behavior which lead to a LSD:

1. The share of never-buyers in the population is unknown. In the classic consumer panel setting, this assumption is usually unnecessary. However, in Internet environments and for library networks, this assumption definitely holds and is necessary. The implication of this is that this restricts our analysis to the LSD-model which in consumer panel analysis serves only as an approximation for the negative binomial distribution (NBD) model [11].

2. The purchases of a consumer in successive periods is Poisson distributed with an average μ which can be observed in the long run if a purchase is

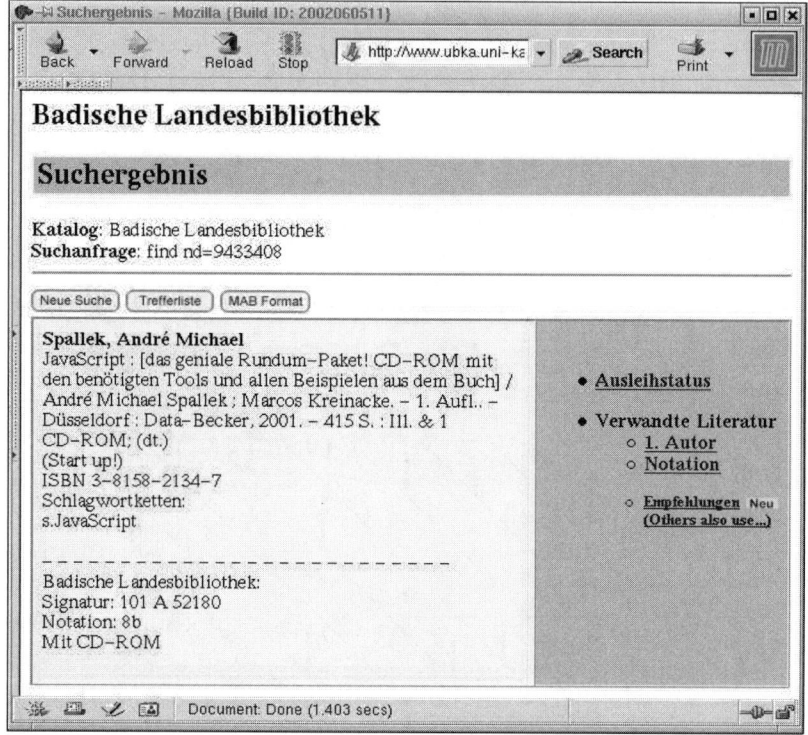

FIGURE 26.3
Detailed view of documents.

independent of previous purchases (as is often observed) and a purchase occurs in an irregular manner that seems random (see Wagner and Taudes [40]).

3. The distribution of μ in the population follows a truncated Γ-distribution so that the frequency of any particular value of μ is given by $(ce^{-\mu/a}/\mu)d\mu$, for $\delta \leq \mu \leq \infty$, where δ is a very small number, a a parameter of the distribution, and c a constant so that $\int_\delta^\infty (ce^{-\mu/a}/\mu)d\mu = 1$.

Ehrenberg's argument [11, p. 259] for a Γ-distribution of the μ in the population of consumer purchase processes is the following: If for different products $x_1, x_2, x_3, x_4, \ldots$ the average purchase rate of x_1 is independent of the purchase rates of the other products, and $\frac{x_1}{(x_1+x_2+x_3+x_4+\ldots)}$ is independent of a consumer's total purchase rate of buying all the products then it can be shown that the distribution of μ must be a Γ-distribution. In several consumer panel studies these independence conditions have been shown to hold at least approximately (for example see [35],[7],[33],[37]).

4. The market is stationary or in equilibrium. This is violated, e.g., when new brands in a consumer product market are launched. For libraries, new acquisi-

tion of books is an example for the violation of this assumption. Still, as long as new acquisitions constitute only a tiny fraction when compared to the full collection, we assume that this condition still tends to hold for most documents most of the time.

That these assumptions lead indeed to an LSD distribution can be seen from Chatfield's proof whose most important steps we repeat here for the sake of completeness:

1. The probability p_r of r purchases of a consumer is $\frac{e^{-\mu}\mu^r}{r!}$ (Poisson).

2. By integration over all consumers in the truncated Γ-distribution:

$$p_r = c \int_\delta^\infty \frac{e^{-\mu}\mu^r}{r!} \frac{e^{-\frac{\mu}{a}}}{\mu} d\mu = \frac{c}{r!(1+\frac{1}{a})^r} \int_\delta^\infty e^{-(1+\frac{1}{a})\mu}((1+\frac{1}{a})\mu)^{r-1} d(1+\frac{1}{a})\mu$$

For $r \geq 1$ and setting $t = (1+1/a)\mu$ and $q = \frac{a}{1+a}$ we get approximately (because δ is very small):

$$p_r = \frac{c}{r!(1+\frac{1}{a})^r} \int_\delta^\infty e^{-t} t^{r-1} dt \approx \frac{c}{r!(1+\frac{1}{a})^r}\Gamma(r) = c\frac{q^r}{r} = q p_{r-1}(r-1)/r$$

3. For $r \geq 1$, $\sum p_r = 1$ holds. Therefore, by analyzing the recursion we get $p_1 = \frac{-q}{\ln(1-q)}$ and $p_r = \frac{-q^r}{r\ln(1-q)}$. (Compare with Formula 26.1.)

In the library environment we now identify a purchase incidence with the closer inspection of a detailed document view recorded by the web server of the OPAC. The reason for this is that, work lies in the search cost which the user incurs when inspecting document details. For information products this has been shown to hold in [17]. In this context a market basket corresponds to all detailed document views in a single user session. For the library setting we consider the upper level of Figure 26.2. The basic idea is that we treat anonymous market baskets as a consumer panel with unobserved consumer identity. This implies that the purchase process of a document which we can observe is an aggregation of all purchase processes of all users of the library which inspect a certain detailed document view. In Figure 26.2 this aggregation process is illustrated for document x_1 by the dotted arrows from the lower to the upper level. In consumer panel analysis such aggregations have not been of interest yet. However, e.g., for planning the capacity of local nodes of a telephone system similar aggregate processes (of incoming calls) are traditionally modelled as Poisson-processes for the analysis as queueing systems.

Although penetration is easily measured within personalized systems here penetration is of less concern because in the library setting the proportion of library users in the population is unknown due to the anonymity of market baskets.

For giving recommendations, we consider document pairs. That is for some fixed document x in the set X of documents of the library the purchase frequency of pairs of (x,i) with $i \in X \setminus x$. The probability $p_r(x \wedge i)$ that users make r inspections of detailed document views x and i during the same sessions which follow independent Poisson processes with means μ_x and μ_i is [25]: $p_r(x \wedge i) = \frac{e^{-\mu_x}\mu_x^r}{r!} \frac{e^{-\mu_i}\mu_i^r}{r!}$. For our recommender services for document x we need the conditional probability that document i has been inspected under the condition that document x has been inspected in the same session. Because of the independence assumption it is easy to see [17] that the conditional probability $p_r(i \mid x)$ is again Poisson distributed by

$$p_r(i \mid x) = \frac{p_r(x \wedge i)}{p_r(x)} = \frac{\frac{e^{-\mu_x}\mu_x^r}{r!} \frac{e^{-\mu_i}\mu_i^r}{r!}}{\frac{e^{-\mu_x}\mu_x^r}{r!}} = \frac{e^{-\mu_i}\mu_i^r}{r!} = p_r(i).$$

With the help of self-selection [28] we can identify purchase processes for each library user segment – a set of anonymous users with common interests that inspected a document pair in the same session. The occurence of repeat-purchases in a library setting on the aggregate level is best explained by the way research is done at a university. Today research is organized as a communication-intensive team-effort including university teachers and students. Repeat purchases on the aggregate level are now triggered by several informal word-of-mouth processes like, e.g., the tutoring of students in a seminar, the recommendations given in various feedback and review processes etc. A second effect which triggers repeat-purchases is the complementary nature of the net of science, e.g., several independent application-oriented research groups in marketing research, telecommunications, statistics, and operations research apply Poisson-processes in their field of study. For each of these segments we can identify the purchase histories as follows [17]: For each document x the purchase history for this segment contains all sessions in which x has been inspected. For each pair of documents (x,i) the purchase history for this segment contains all sessions in which (x,i) has been inspected. The stochastic process for the segment (x,i) – n library users that have inspected document x and another document i – is represented by the sum of n independent random Bernoulli variables, which equal 1 with probability p_i, and 0 with probability $1 - p_i$. The distribution of the sum of these variables tends to a Poisson distribution. For a proof see Feller [12, p. 292]. Assuming that the parameters μ of the segments' Poisson distributions follow a truncated Γ-distribution, Chatfield's proof can be repeated and we thus establish that the probability of r inspections of document pairs (x,i) follow a LSD.

However, we expect that non-random occurrences of such pairs occur more often than predicted by the logarithmic series distribution because of the way research and teaching is organized at a research university and that we can identify non-random occurrences of such pairs and use them as recommendations. For this purpose the logarithmic series distribution for the whole market (over all consumers) from market baskets is estimated from anonymous web-sessions. We compute the mean purchase frequency w and solve Equation 26.2 for q, the parameter of the LSD. By comparing the observed repeat-buying frequencies with the theoretically expected frequencies we identify outliers as recommendations.

Statistical Data Mining and Knowledge Discovery 445

TABLE 26.1
Algorithm for computing recommendations. See also [17].

1. Compute for all documents x in the market baskets the frequency distributions $f(x_{obs})$ for repeat-purchases of the co-occurrences of x with other documents in a session, that is of the pair (x, i) with $i \in X \setminus x$. Several co-occurrences of a pair (x, i) in a single session are counted only once.
   (Frequency distribution.)

2. Discard all frequency distributions with less than l observations.
   (Current setting: $l = 10$.)

3. For each frequency distribution:

   (a) Compute the **robust** mean purchase frequency w by trimming the sample by removing x percent of the high repeat-buy pairs.
   (Current setting: $x = 20\%$.)

   (b) Estimate the parameter q for the LSD-model from
   $w = \frac{-q}{(1-q)(\ln(1-q))}$ with a bisection method.
   (Alternative: Newton method.)

   (c) Apply a χ^2-goodness-of-fit test with a suitable α between the observed and the expected LSD distribution $f(x_{exp})$ with a suitable partitioning.
   (Current settings: 0.01 and 0.05.)

   (d) Determine the outliers in the tail. Compute for each r of repeat-buys the ratio s_r of the observed frequency to the expected frequency according to the LSD-model: $s_r = \frac{f_r(x_{obs})}{f_r(x_{exp})}$.
   If $s_r \leq t$ with t a suitable threshold, then all documents in class r are recommended.
   (Current setting: $t = 0.5$.)

The LSD-model limits the kind of market analysis that can be conducted. For example, analysis of the behavior of different types of library users (e.g., light and heavy users) is possible only with a full NBD-model (see Ehrenberg [11]).

A recommendation for a document x simply is an outlier of the LSD-model – that is a document y that has been used more often in the same session as could have been expected from independent random choice acts. A recommendation reveals a complementarity between documents.

The main purpose of the LSD-model in this setting is to separate non-random co-occurrences of information products (outliers) from random co-occurrences (as expected from the LSD-model). We use the LSD-model as a benchmark for discovering regularities.

In Table 26.1 we present the algorithm we currently use for computing document

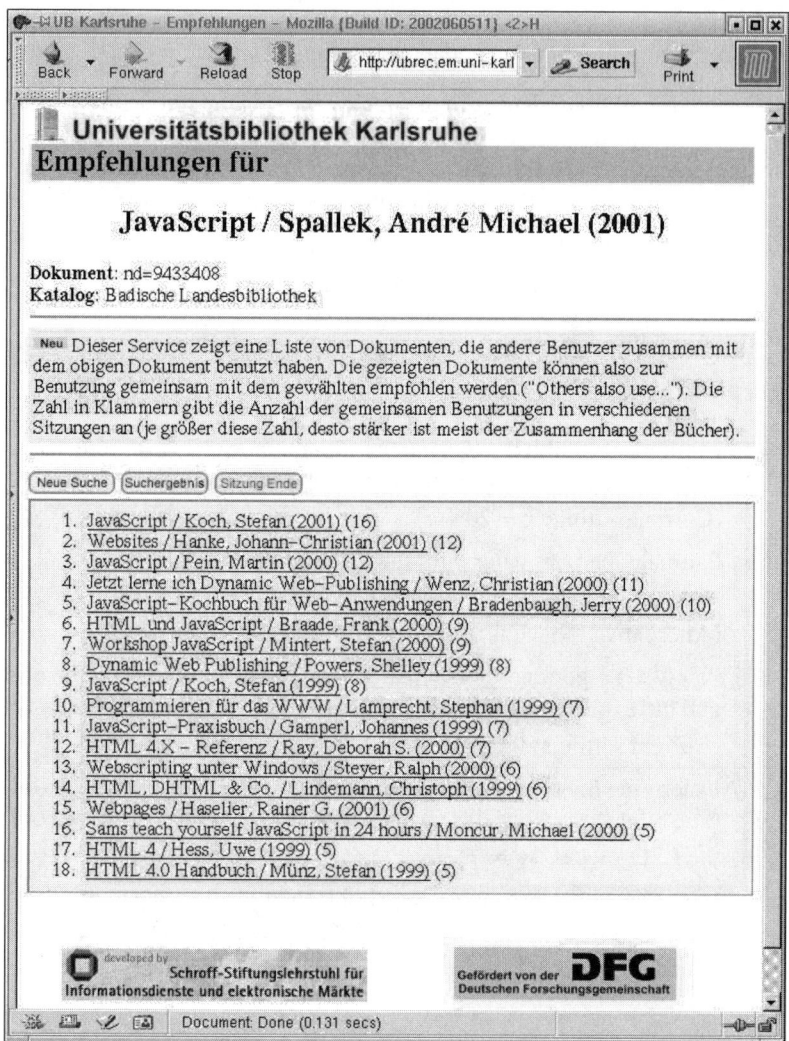

FIGURE 26.4
Recommendation list.

recommendations for the university library's recommender service. As necessary in repeat-buying theory, step 1 of the algorithm counts repeated usage of two information products in a single session only once. A rationale for this correction is that repeated inspection of detailed meta data for documents in a single session reflects the user's decision process leading to a lending decision. Step 2 of the algorithm discards all frequency distributions with a small number of observations. The reason is that no valid LSD-model can be estimated and that we did not yet investigate the rationale for and the combinatorics of very small sample discrete distributions (e. g., binomial distributions). Of course, the implication is that for these cases no recommendations are given. For each remaining frequency distribution, step 3 computes the mean purchase frequency, the LSD parameter, and the outliers as recommendations.

High repeat-buy outliers may have a considerable impact on the mean purchase frequency and thus on the parameter of the distribution. The statistical standard procedure for outliers is trimming the sample (step 3a). By computing a robust mean the chances of finding a significant LSD-model are considerably improved. Detailed statistics for this are provided in our case study on the library of the Universität Karlsruhe (TH) in Tables 26.2 and 26.3 in Section 26.4.

In step 3d outliers are identified as belonging to classes with r repeat-buys if the ratio of the expected random co-occurences according to the LSD-model to the observed co-occurences is below a certain threshold. The threshold can be interpreted as the maximum accceptable percentage of random co-occurences recommended. Several other options for determining the outliers in the tail of the distribution are possible:

1. Outliers at r are above $\sum_r^\infty f_r(x_{exp})$.

2. Set β as the acceptable type two error for recommendations that is recommending a document although it is only a random co-occurrence. Accept all documents in classes $r\ldots\infty$ with $\sum_r^\infty f_r(x_{exp}) < \beta$. From the boundary class $r+1$ draw j documents at random (anyway you like) as long as $\beta - \sum_r^\infty f_r(x_{exp}) > j \cdot \frac{f_{r+1}(x_{exp})}{n \cdot f_{r+1}(x_{obs})}$.

These options lead to variants of the recommender service which exhibit different first and second type errors. However, at the moment, a more in-depth analysis of these effects remain to be done on the library data.

As Table 26.2 in Section 26.4 shows, recommendations are identified with this model – even if the LSD-model estimated can not be tested for significance (column II of Table 26.3) or if the LSD-model is not significant (column V Table 26.3). The reason for this is that we use the LSD-model as an approximation of an underlying stationary stochastic purchase process which we remove in order to present the non-random outliers as recommendations. Especially for documents observed over a longer period of time, combinations with documents recently bought by the library obviously violate assumptions underlying the LSD-model, because pairs with a recently bought document had a smaller chance to be inspected together in a session than pairs of older documents. Nevertheless, for relatively short time periods and periods of small library growth, we hold the LSD-model to be a robust first approximation and thus a useful filter of randomness. For the cases in column V of Table 26.3, for example, we plan to study models from the recently discovered class of scale-free network models as suggested by Barabási [4].

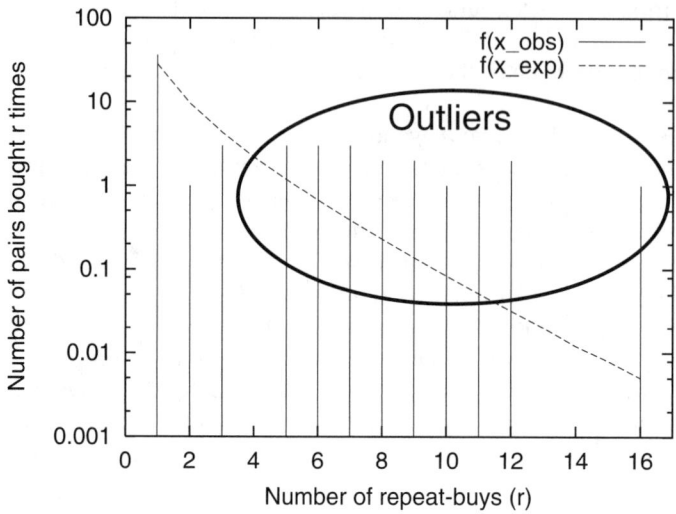

FIGURE 26.5
Logarithmic plot of the frequency distribution of JavaScript by Spallek.

26.4 A Recommender System for the Library of the Universität Karlsruhe (TH)

In this chapter we present the integration of a recommender service based on Ehrenberg's repeat-buying theory into the legacy library system of the Universität Karlsruhe (TH) and analyze some sample data from the observation period of 2001/01/01 to 2002/05/30.

Figure 26.3 shows the detailed inspection page of documents including author (Spallek, André Michael), title (JavaScript), publisher, keywords, etc. In the darker bar on the right hand side the link to recommendations (Empfehlungen (Others also use ...)) appears only if recommendations can be given (as is the case here). Figure 26.4, for example, displays the recommendation page for JavaScript by Spallek. The recommendations are ranked by the number of co-purchases with JavaScript, which can be seen in brackets.

As Figure 26.5 shows, the framework described in the previous chapter holds for the JavaScript example. The observed frequency distribution $f(x\text{ obs})$ corresponds to the ranking by decreasing number of repeated co-purchases in Figure 26.4. Recommendations are the outliers, i.e., products that have been bought together more often than expected by the stochastic model. More specifically, an LSD-model with a robust mean of 1.851 and a parameter $q = 0.676$ passes a χ^2-goodness-of-fit test at $\alpha = 0.01$ ($\chi^2 = 9.851$, which is below 10.828, the critical value at $\alpha = 0.01$) (see Table 26.2).

Statistical Data Mining and Knowledge Discovery 449

```
# Web-site: 9433408BLB_OPAC
# Total number of observations: 58
# Max repeat-buys: 16
# Sample mean=3.37931034482759 and var=13.6147443519619
# Case: E var>mean
# Estimate for q=0.875726879692078

# Robust estimation: Trimmed begin 0: 0 / end 0.2: 11
#                    (11 observations)
# Robust estimation: Number of observations: 47
# Robust mean=1.85106382978723 and var=2.93526482571299
# Robust estimate for q=0.675936790466309

# Plot: Observed repeat-buys and robust estimated LSD
# r repeat-buys   nf(x_obs)   nf(x_exp)   f(x_exp)/f(x_obs)   show
       1             36         28.194          0.783            0
       2              1          9.529          9.529            0
       3              3          4.294          1.431            0
       4              0          2.177            -              0
       5              3          1.177          0.392            1
       6              3          0.663          0.221            1
      ...            ...         ...            ...             ...
      16              1          0.005          0.005            1
# Recommendations found with threshold=0.5: 18

# Robust estimate performs better with chi-square value: 9.851 #
Chi-square test threshold with alpha=0.05 and 1 d.f.:3.841 #
Chi-square test threshold with alpha=0.01 and 1 d.f.:10.828 #
Sample comes from LSD with alpha=0.01 # Col: IV
```

TABLE 26.2
Statistics for JavaScript by Spallek

The library of the Universität Karlsruhe (TH) is hosting the OPACs of 23 libraries in the south-west of Germany as an internet service provider and recommendations are generated within all of them. While recommendations are generated for the whole network of hosted libraries, currently recommendations are given only in the web-OPAC of the library of the Universität Karlsruhe (TH) and in those libraries which use the same page template as this library (the most important of these is the Badische Landesbibliothek (State Library of Baden - a part of Baden-Württemberg which is a state of the Federal Republic of Germany)). As some of our examples show the user, upon inspection of the recommendations, might see that these recommendations cross catalog boundaries and thereby increase the awareness of users for documents in other libraries whose OPACs are hosted by the catalog recommendations provide a new quality of user-service which is currently unavailable in all other traditional library systems. For students and researchers of the Universität Karlsruhe (TH) cross catalog recommendations to the Badische Landesbibliothek are expected to have a high impact and utility because of the short (walking) distance from the university campus to the Badische Landesbibliothek.

The statistical results for the sample data of the 23 libraries hosted by the library of the Universität Karlsruhe (TH) are summarized in Table 26.3. From the 15 million

	I q undef.	II no χ^2 (< 3 classes)	III Sign. $\alpha = 0.05$	IV Sign. $\alpha = 0.01$	V Not sign.	Σ
A Obs. < 10	1,302,529 (0)	55,675 (9,522)	0 (0)	0 (0)	0 (0)	1,358,204 9,522
B $\bar{x} = 1$	212,152 (0)	0 (0)	0 (0)	0 (0)	0 (0)	212,152 (0)
C $\bar{x} > \sigma^2$ $r \leq 3$	1,150 (0)	134,268 (32,216)	656 (529)	4,491 (2,393)	6,059 (3,205)	146,624 (38,343)
D $\bar{x} > \sigma^2$ $r > 3$	0 (0)	31,225 (31,158)	3,802 (3,802)	6,838 (6,803)	13,034 (12,126)	54,899 (53,889)
E $\sigma^2 > \bar{x}$	0 (0)	1,0442 (10,442)	5,528 (5,528)	3,135 (3,135)	5,508 (5,508)	24,613 (24,613)
Σ	1,515,831 (0)	231,610 (83,338)	9,986 (9,859)	14,464 (12,331)	24,601 (20,839)	1,796,492 (126,367)

(n) indicates n lists with recommendations

TABLE 26.3
Detailed results for observation period 2001/01/01 to 2002/05/30.

documents contained in the combined library catalog 1,796,492 have been inspected by users together in a session with at least one other document. For 126,367 of these products, lists of recommendations with a total of 966,504 entries (not shown in the table) have been generated.

The current implementation features incremental updates of market baskets with a complexity of $O(n^2)$ in time and space with n the number of items updated. Only for updated market baskets the LSD-models are re-estimated. Since the upper bound is reduced by a reduction of the update period this improves the scalability of the algorithm. Simple association rule algorithms compute market baskets essentially in the same way. However, the advantage of this algorithm is that the only parameter for the LSD estimation, the mean, can be computed for updated market baskets only and does not depend on global values like support and confidence.

The recommendation server is currently located on a standard PC with a 1,2 GHz AMD Athlon processor and 1,5 GB main memory, running Mandrake Linux (Kernel Version 2.4.17). The recommender software is implemented in Perl (5.6), with MySQL as the underlying database system. Real time monitoring is necessary for operating such a system reliably. For this purpose network traffic and several machine parameters are monitored constantly and are graphically processed for inspection with the mrtg package (see [30]).

Due to the recency of the introduction of the system no systematic evaluation of the acceptance of recommendations by end users and experts has been carried out yet. A systematic traffic analysis including recommender usage is in preparation.

26.5 Conclusion

In this contribution we have reported on the development of a recommender system and its integration into the legacy library system of the Universität Karlsruhe (TH) which is the first of its kind and which works for a collection of documents one order of magnitude larger than amazon.com. For library systems, we have shown for the first time that Ehrenberg's repeat-buying theory is valid, too, and that this theory provides an excellent, scalable foundation for the identification of non-random outliers as recommendations. Our implementation requires only a minimal interface with the web-OPAC of the legacy library system provided that session state is kept in the OPAC. In addition, the update complexity is limited by an incremental update to $O(n^2)$ in time and space with n the number of items updated. The recommender service is distributed; failure of the recommender service does not disrupt the operation of the web-OPAC of the legacy library system. The unexpected discovery of cross-library recommendations throughout the libraries hosted at the Universität Karlsruhe (TH) provides for an improved service level of the system which has not been available in the previous system. In principle, we expect cross-library recommendations to have the effect of increasing the awareness of students and researchers to all the libraries hosted - and thus of improved access not only to the 0.8 million documents of the university library, but to all 15 million documents of the library network.

Acknowledgment

We gratefully acknowledge the funding of the project "Scientific Libraries in Information Markets" ("Wissenschaftliche Bibliotheken in Informationsmrkten") by the Deutsche Forschungsgemeinschaft (DFG) within the scope of the research initiative "Distributed Processing and Delivery of Digital Documents" (DFG-SPP 1041 "V^3D^2: Verteilte Vermittlung und Verarbeitung Digitaler Dokumente").

References

[1] ACM. ACM digital library, 2002. http://www.acm.org/dl/.

[2] Balabanovic, M. (1997). An adaptive web page recommendation service. In Proceedings of the 1st International Conference on Autonomous Agents, February, Marina del Rey, CA.

[3] Balabanovic, M. and Shoham, Y. (1997). Fab: Content-based, collaborative recommendation. *Communications of the ACM*, 40(3), 66-72, March.

[4] Barabasi, A.-L. (2002). *Linked - The New Science of Networks*. Perseus Publish-

ing, Cambridge.

[5] Bollacker, K., Lawrence, S., and Giles, C. L. (2000). Discovering relevant scientific literature on the web. *IEEE Intelligent Systems*, 15(2), 42-47, March/April.

[6] Bollen, J. and Rocha, L. M. (2000). An adaptive systems approach to the implementation and evaluation of digital library recommendation systems. In *Proceedings of the 4th European Conference on Digital Libraries*, J. Borbinha and T. Baker, (Eds.), Vol. 1923 of LNCS, pp. 356-359. Springer, Heidelberg.

[7] Charlton, P. and Ehrenberg, A. S. C. (1976). Customers of the LEP, *Applied Statistics*, 25, 26-30.

[8] Chatfield, C., Ehrenberg, A. S. C., and Goodhardt, G. J. (1966). Progress on a simplified model of stationary purchasing behavior, *Journal of the Royal Statistical Society A*, 129, 317-367.

[9] Cooley, R. W. (2000). Web Usage Mining: Discovery and Application of Interesting Patterns and Web Data. PhD thesis, Faculty of the Graduate School, University of Minnesota. Advisor: Jaideep Srivastava.

[10] Die Deutsche Bibliothek, editor. (1999). *MAB2 - Maschinelles Austauschformat für Bibliotheken*. Die Deutsche Bibliothek, Frankfurt, 2 edition.

[11] Ehrenberg, A. S. C. (1988). *Repeat-Buying: Facts, Theory and Applications*. Charles Griffin and Company Ltd, London, 2 edition.

[12] Feller, W. (1971). *An Introduction to Probability Theory and Its Application*, Volume 2. John Wiley, New York, 2 edition.

[13] Gamma, E., Helm, R., Johnson, R., and Vlissides, J. (1995). *Design Patterns: Elements of Reusable ObjectOriented Software. AddisonWesley Professional Computing Series*. AddisonWesley Publishing Company, Reading, MA.

[14] Gaul, W. and Ritter, G., editors. (2002). Classification, Automation, and New Media, volume 20 of *Studies in Classification, Data Analysis, and Knowledge Organization*, Heidelberg. Gesellschaft für Klassifikation e.V. (German Classification Society) http://www.gfkl.de, Springer-Verlag. Proceedings of the 24th Annual Conference of the Gesellschaft für Klassifikation e.V., pp. 535, University of Passau, March 15-17, 2000.

[15] Geyer-Schulz, A. and Hahsler, M. (2001). Pinboards and virtual libraries - analysis patterns for collaboration. Technical Report 1, Institut für Informationsverarbeitung und -wirtschaft, Wirtschaftsuniversitat Wien, Augasse 2-6, A-1090Wien.

[16] Geyer-Schulz, A. and Hahsler, M. Software reuse with analysis patterns. In Ramsower [34], pages 1156-1165. Dallas Texas.
http://aisel.isworld.org/article.asp?Subject$_I$D = 11 &Publication$_I$D = 30.

[17] Geyer-Schulz, A., Hahsler, M., and Jahn, M. A customer purchase incidence model applied to recommender services. In Kohavi et al. [27],25-47.

[18] Geyer-Schulz, A., Hahsler, M., and Jahn, M. (2000). Recommendations for virtual universities from observed user behavior. In Gaul and Ritter [14], pages 273-280. Proceedings of the 24th Annual Conference of the Gesellschaft für Klassifikation e.V.,535 University of Passau, March 15-17.

[19] Geyer-Schulz, A., Hahsler, M., and Jahn, M. (2001). Educational and Scientific Recommender Systems: Designing the Information Channels of the Virtual University. *International Journal of Engineering Education*, 17(2), 153-163.

[20] Glover, E., Lawrence, S., Gordon, M. D., Birmingham, W., and Giles C. L. (1999). Recommending web documents based on user preferences. In SIGIR 99 Workshop on Recommender Systems, Berkeley, CA, August.

[21] The Stanford Digital Libraries Group. The Stanford digital library project. *Communications of the ACM*, 38(4):, 59-60, April 1995.

[22] Hicks, D., Tochtermann, K., and Kussmaul, A. (2000). Augmenting digital catalogue functionality with support for customization. In Proceedings of 3rd International Conference on Asian Digital Libraries.

[23] IEEE. IEEE digital library, 2002. http://www.ieee.org/products/ onlinepubs/.

[24] Johnson, N. L., Kemp, A. W., and Kotz, S. (1993). *Univariate Discrete Distributions*. Wiley Series in Probability and Mathematical Statistics. John Wiley, 2nd edition.

[25] Johnson, N. L., Kotz, S., and Balakrishnan, N. (1997). *Discrete Multivariate Distributions*. John Wiley, New York, 1 edition.

[26] Klatt, R., Gavriilidis, K., Kleinsimlinghaus, K., and Feldmann, M. (2001). Nutzung und Potenziale der innovativen Mediennutzung im Lernalltag der Hochschulen. BMBF-Studie, http://www.stefi.de/.

[27] R. Kohavi, B. M., Masand, M., Spilioupolou, and Srivastava, J. editors. (2002). *WEBKDD 2001 - Mining Web Log Data Across All Customer Touch Points*, Volume 2356 of LNAI, Springer-Verlag, Berlin.

[28] Milgrom, P. and Roberts, J. (1992). *Economics, Organization and Management*. Prentice-Hall, Upper Saddle River, NJ.

[29] NEC Research Institute. Researchindex, 2002. http://citeseer.nj. nec.com/.

[30] Oetiker, T. and Rand, D. Multi Router Traffic Grapher. http://people.ee.ethz.ch/ oetiker/webtools/mrtg/.

[31] Pennock, D., Horvitz, E., Lawrence, S., and Giles, C. L. (2000). Collaborative filtering by personality diagnosis: A hybrid memory- and model-based approach. In Proceedings of the 16th Conference on Uncertainty in Artificial Intelligence, UAI, pp. 473-480, Stanford, CA.

[32] Popescul, A., Ungar, L., Pennock, D., and Lawrence, S. (2001). Probabilistic models for unified collaborative and content-based recommendation in sparse-data environments. In 17th Conference on Uncertainty in Artificial Intelligence, pp. 437-

444, Seattle, Washington, August 25.

[33] Powell, N. and Westwood, J. (1978). Buyer-behaviour in management education, *Applied Statistics*, 27, 69-72.

[34] Ramsower, R. editor. (2002). *Procs. 8th AMCIS* (Americas Conference on Information Systems 2002), USA, August. AIS. Dallas Texas.
http://aisel.isworld.org/article.asp?Subject$_I$D = 11 &Publication$_I$D = 30.

[35] Aske Research. The structure of the tooth-paste market. Technical report, Aske Research Ltd., London, 1975.

[36] Russell, S. and Norvig, P. (1995). *Artificial Intelligence: A Modern Approach - The Intelligent Agent Book*. Prentice-Hall, Upper Saddle River, NJ. Introduction and survey of AI.

[37] Sichel, H. S. (1982). Repeat-buying and a Poisson-generalised inverse Gaussian distributions, *Applied Statistics*, 31, 193-204.

[38] S.R.S. The S.R.S. motorists panel. Technical report, Sales Research Service, London, 1965.

[39] Tan, P.-N. and Kumar, V. (2002). Discovery of web robot sessions based on their navigational patterns. *Data Mining and Knowledge Discovery*, 6, 9-35.

[40] Wagner, U. and Taudes, A. (1987). Stochastic models of consumer behaviour. *European Journal of Operational Research*, 29(1), 1-23.

[41] Wilensky, R., Forsyth, D., Fateman, R., Hearst, M. Hellerstein, J., Landay, J., Larson, R., Malik, J., Stark, P., Twiss, R., Tygar, D., Van House, N., Varian, H., Baird, H., Hurley, B., Kopec, G., Hirata, K., Li, W.-S., and Amir, A. (1999). Reinventing scholarly information dissemination and use. Technical report, University of California, Berkeley, CA. http://elib.cs.berkeley.edu/pl/about.html.

27

GTP (General Text Parser) Software for Text Mining

Justin T. Giles, Ling Wo, and Michael W. Berry
University of Tennessee, Knoxville, USA

CONTENTS

27.1 Introduction	455
27.2 Model Facilitated by GTP	456
27.3 GTP Usage and Files Generated	457
27.4 Overview of GTP Options	458
27.5 Query Processing with GTPQUERY	464
27.6 Example	464
27.7 Versions of GTP and GTPQUERY	469
27.8 Code Evolution	470
27.9 Future Work	470
Acknowledgment	470
References	471

Because of the seemingly transparent nature of search engine design and use, there is a tendency to forget the decisions and tradeoffs constantly made throughout the design process, which ultimately affect the performance of any information retrieval (IR) system. One of the major decisions is selecting and implementing any underlying computational model within a single (but integrated) software environment. We present the latest release, an object-oriented (C++ and Java) software environment called GTP (or General Text Parser) which can be used by both novice and experts in information modeling to (i) parse text (single files or directories), (ii) construct sparse matrix data structures (with choices of different term weighting strategies), (iii) perform selected matrix decompositions for the representation of terms, documents, and queries in a reduced-rank vector space, and (iv) convert user-supplied natural language queries into appropriate query vectors for cosine-based matching against term and/or document vectors in that vector space.

27.1 Introduction

With the enormous growth in digital text-based information, the efficiency and accuracy of search engines is a growing concern. In order to improve performance, novices and experts in information modeling need ways to study and evaluate various information retrieval (IR) models. Limitations exist in large part due to the absence of publicly available software capable of facilitating such modeling. To address this void in modeling software, we present an object oriented software environment called General Text Parser (GTP). GTP is public domain software, which is freely available for anyone to download.*

GTP provides users with the ability to parse ASCII text as well as other forms of text (PostScript, PDF, etc.) via user-generated filters. For the more advanced user, GTP is equipped to construct sparse matrix data structures (based on different term weighting choices) and then perform matrix decompositions for the representation of terms, documents, and queries in a reduced-rank vector space. The underlying IR model facilitated by GTP is latent semantic indexing (or LSI) [3, 5], although with little effort by the user, the LSI-specific modules may be removed and replaced by an alternative model. Finally, GTP is capable of converting user-supplied natural language queries, through the GTPQUERY module, into appropriate query vectors for cosine-based matching against term and/or document vectors in the reduced-rank vector space generated.

This paper does not discuss in great detail the theoretical development of vector-space modeling and LSI (see [3, 4]). Section 27.2 provides a brief overview of LSI in order to facilitate understanding of the processes of GTP. The general flow of GTP is discussed in Section 27.3 with a follow-up section covering the details of the several command-line arguments of GTP. A new addition to the GTP package is GTPQUERY (Section 27.5), which is used for query processing. An example run of GTP and GTPQUERY is illustrated in Section 27.6, and Section 27.7 presents the various versions of GTP including the most recent Java release. Section 27.8 briefly discusses the code evolution from Fortran to Java. Finally, Section 27.9 presents future improvements to be made to GTP and GTPQUERY.

27.2 Model Facilitated by GTP

GTP is a software package that provides text parsing of small to large document collections and matrix decomposition for use in information retrieval applications. GTP has the ability to parse any document (using tag filters) and produce a list of keys (or words that have been extracted by the parser). Beyond being a simple text parser, GTP uses a vector-space approach to text modeling [6]. In using the vector-space approach, the documents and queries are represented as vectors of the terms parsed, basically creating a term-by-document matrix. The elements of this matrix are frequencies (or weighted frequencies) of terms (rows) with respect to their corresponding documents (columns).

---

*http://www.cs.utk.edu/~lsi

The specific vector-space model exploited by GTP is latent semantic indexing (LSI). LSI expands on the general vector-space approach by exploiting a low-rank approximation of the term-by-document matrix [3, 6, 7]. LSI analyzes the global patterns of terms and word usage, thus allowing documents with dissimilar terms to have closely related vectors. To achieve this, LSI performs singular value decomposition (SVD) on the term-by-document matrix [3], whose nonzero elements may be weighted term frequencies. Term weighting is often used when performing the SVD. Using term weights, instead of raw frequencies, may increase or decrease the importance of terms (Section 27.4). Thus allowing the meaning of a document to rise to the surface instead of having the raw frequencies determine content.

27.3 GTP Usage and Files Generated

GTP is executed by the command *gtp* followed by a sequence of command line arguments. The basic command looks like the following

gtp filename –c common_words_file –t temp_dir

where *filename* is a file or directory of documents to be parsed, *common_words_file* is the file containing the common words to be ignored, and *temp_dir* is a directory where temporary working files are stored. When this command sequence is used, GTP traverses the directory structure(s) and inserts the files found into a red-black tree. GTP then maneuvers through the red-black tree and parses each document into keys. The only items generated by GTP at this point are the *keys* database, *RUN_SUMMARY /LAST_RUN* (Figure 27.1), and uncompressed *rawmatrix* (Figure 27.2) files (see Figure 27.3 for the general flow of GTP processing and Table 27.1 for a list of frequently generated files).

With the use of more options, GTP may produce several other files in varying formats. The *output* file, created by specifying the $-O$ option, is a binary file that contains all the vector (term and document) and singular value information produced by the SVD. The layout of the output file is as follows: header information consisting of the number of terms parsed, number of documents encountered, and the number of factors used; term vectors for all terms parsed; document vectors for all documents parsed; singular values computed. A Perl script called *readOutput* is provided with the software package, which displays the data in the output file in ASCII format.

The keys (*keys.pag* and *keys.dir* in C++; *keys* in Java) file is a database (dbm) of all the terms that were parsed in the GTP run. Stored with the terms is the term id that is a numeric value starting at 1 and incremented by 1 for each new term that is parsed. So, the first term parsed has an id of 1. The next new term encountered has an id of 2, and so on. The final information stored with the term and its id is the global weight of the term. The global weight is calculated based on options specified by the user, and takes into account all occurrences of the term in all the documents

File name	Type	Description (Section)
RUN_SUMMARY	ASCII	Summary of options used (27.3)
LAST_RUN	ASCII	Summary of options used on most recent GTP run (27.3, 27.5)
keys.dir/keys.pag - C++ keys - Java	DBM	Database of keys generated (27.3, 27.5)
Output	Binary	Vector information generated by SVD (27.3, 27.5, 27.6)
rawmatrix/rawmatrix.Z	ASCII/ Compressed	Raw term-by-document matrix (27.3)
matrix.hb/matrix.hb.Z	ASCII/ Compressed	Contains the Harwell-Boeing compressed matrix. (27.3)
TITLES	ASCII	List of document titles. (Table 27.2)
lao2	ASCII	Summary of SVD calculation.
larv2	Binary	File of SVD vectors. Use the readVect script for viewing.
lalv2	Binary	File of SVD vectors. Use the readVect script for viewing.
nonz	ASCII	Total terms in the document collection, including those not parsed.

TABLE 27.1
List of common files that GTP generates. A brief description of each file is given along with a pointer (reference) to the section describing the file.

being parsed, not just a single document. Under Solaris and Linux, the database that is used is Berkeley 4.3 BSD. Under Java, the World Wide Web Consortium (W3C) Jigsaw database package is used.

The *rawmatrix* or *rawmatrix.Z* file contains the term-by-document matrix in raw format (Figure 27.2). This file has the format of document number followed by term id/weight pairs for each term in the document. For large document collections, this file could be large; for this reason GTP compresses the *rawmatrix* by default. *matrix.hb* is a file that holds the sparse term-by-document matrix in Harwell-Boeing compressed format. The Harwell-Boeing format is also known as compressed column storage (CCS). CCS stores all nonzero elements (or frequencies) of a sparse term-by-document matrix by traversing each column. Stored with the frequencies are row and column pointers [3]. By default the *matrix.hb* file is compressed.

27.4 Overview of GTP Options

As GTP has grown into the sizable program (over 13,000 lines of code), it has increased in the number of command line arguments to an almost unbearable point. Even expert users have a difficult time keeping all the options straight. A wordy dialogue about each option would be as unbearable as the number of options available.

```
#
# Variables set when keys database created (i.e., constants):
#
extra_chars =
numbers = false
df = 1
gf = 1
local = tf
global = (null)
stop_file = ../../etc/common_words
nterms = 161
ndocs = 7
ncommon = 1000
minlen = 2
maxlen = 25
maxline = 10000
normal_doc = no normalization
delimiter = end of file only
log_file = none
temp_dir = /a/berry/bay/homes/giles/linuxgtp_orig/src3.1/run/tmp
keephb = true
keepkeys = false
decomposition= false
filter(s) =
../../filters/blfilter
../../filters/filter
#
# Variables that can be changed when SVD is run
#
run_name = Test Run 1 of gtp
file_dir = /a/berry/bay/homes/giles/linuxgtp_orig/src3.1/sample
nfact = 0
##
##Keys database created Sat Jul 13 16:19:12 EDT 2002
```

FIGURE 27.1

Example of the *RUN_SUMMARY* and *LAST_RUN* files. These files log all options the user requested at runtime. The *LAST_RUN* file only contains options relevant to the last run of GTP.

```
7 161
doc 1:
123 1.0000 80 3.0000 10 1.0000 30 1.0000 150 1.0000 144 1.0000 83 2.0000 89
1.0000 24 1.0000 53 1.0000 62 1.0000 9 1.0000 25 1.0000 60 2.0000 64 2.0000
51 1.0000 142 1.0000 110 1.0000 34 1.0000 140 1.0000 54 1.0000 159 1.0000
147 2.0000 66 1.0000 118 1.0000 155 1.0000 161 1.0000 129 1.0000 49 1.0000
153 1.0000 47 1.0000
doc2:
```

FIGURE 27.2

Example of the *rawmatrix* file, in which each record is composed of the document number followed by term id/weight pairs of terms that exist in that document.

With that in mind, a table has been created to explain each option and its dependencies on other options in the command line (Table 27.2).

A few of the options deserve more explanation than what the table provides. The -*d* and -*g* options can be a bit confusing to the new user. Both of these options determine the threshold of the local and global raw frequencies of terms. If the -*d* option is set at 2, this means that before a term is included in the keys database, it must occur more than twice in the document. Consequently, if the value is set at 0, then there is no minimum requirement for the frequency of a term in any particular document. The -*g* option acts in a similar fashion, but reflects the minimum threshold for the global frequency of a term. If the -*g* option is set at 2 then a term must occur more than twice in an entire document collection before it is included in the keys database. As with the -*d* option, if the value is set at 0, then there is no minimum frequency requirement. For small document collections, it is strongly advised to set both the local (-*d*) and global (-*g*) thresholds to 0 in order to capture all useful terms.

Another option that can be confusing to a new user is the -*w* option, which involves different term weighting schemes. Term weighting is especially important for vector space IR models (such as LSI). The importance of terms may increase or decrease depending on the type of weighting that is used. In determining which local weighting to use, the vocabulary and word usage patterns of the document need to be considered [3]. If the collection spans general topics (news feeds, magazine articles, etc.), using raw term frequency (tf) would suffice. If the collection were small in nature with few terms in the vocabulary, then binary frequencies would be the best to use.

In determining the global weight, the likelihood that the collection will change needs to be considered. If a collection is static, the inverse document frequency (idf) is a good choice [3]. In general, the document collection will work well with some weighting schemes and poorly with others. Any knowledge of the term distribution associated with a document collection before running GTP could be extremely helpful in determining which weighting scheme to use.

Arg	Additional Args.	Description	Dependencies
-help		Summarize options.	
-q		Suppress progress summary.	
-h		Create the Harwell-Boeing compressed matrix. Default is to not create it.	Required if using -z option.
-u		Keep the Harwell-Boeing compressed matrix in an uncompressed file (on output) if the matrix is created.	-h
-N		Include numbers as keys.	
-D		Do not create Unix compatible dbm key files (keys.dir/keys.pag in C++; keys in Java). Default is to generate them.	Do not use if you are to perform queries.
-K		Keep the keys file created in the temporary directory specified by the "-t temp_dir" argument.	
-T		Consider the first line of each document (up to 200 characters) to be the title of the document. Before this line is parsed, it will be written to the file *TITLES* in the current directory. Each title line in this file will exist on its own line.	
-s		Normalize the document length. This ensures a unit length for columns in the term-by-document matrix.	
-m	Int	Set a new minimum key length of *int* for the parser.	
	Ex: -m 5	The default minimum length is 2.	
-M	Int	Set a new maximum key length of *int* for the parser.	

TABLE 27.2

List of command-line options for GTP. Column 1 shows the argument. Column 2 shows additional options for the specified argument as well as examples. Column 3 gives a brief description of each argument. Column 4 shows which other arguments the current one depends on.

Arg	Additional Args.	Description	Dependencies
	Ex: -M 35	The default maximum length is 20.	
-L	Int	Specify a new maximum line length of *int*. If any	
	Ex: -L 1000	record being parsed exceeds *int* characters in length before a carriage return/line feed character, the user is informed of this and the portion of the record that caused the overrun is printed to the screen. The default maximum is 10,000.	
-S	Int	Set the maximum number of common words to use to	
	Ex: -S 2000	*int*. The default value is 1,000.	
-d	Int	Change the threshold for document frequency of any	
	Ex1: -d 0 Ex2: -d 2	term to *int*. Default is 1.	
-g	Int	Change the threshold for global frequency of any	
	Ex1: -g 0 Ex2: -g 4	term to *int*. Default is 1.	
-e	"Extra_characters"	Specify a string of characters, each of which	
	Ex: "()$%"	will be considered a valid character, in addition to all default characters, when tokenizing keys.	
-f	Filter1 [opts] [filter2 [opts] ... filterN [opts]]	Specify filters to pass each file through before the parser looks at it. If a filter	At least one filter must be specified if -f is used.
	Ex1: -f zcat html_filter Ex2: -f zcat "grep computer"	has options, it needs to be surrounded by quotes.	
-o	Filename	Specify that the key, id# global frequency,	
	Ex: -o keystable	document frequency, and weight of all keys are to be written to "filename".	

TABLE 27.2 continued...

Statistical Data Mining and Knowledge Discovery

Arg	Additional Args.	Description	Dependencies
-B	New_delimiter Ex: -B /newdoc/	Specify that a new document delimiter is needed. New_delimiter must be alone on a line in the file and must match exactly for GTP to recognize it. It can be up to 198 characters. Default is a blank line.	Cannot be used if -x is being used.
-x		Indicate that there is to be no delimiter other than the end of file.	Cannot be used if -B is being used.
-w	Local global Ex: -w log entropy or Ex: -w entropy log	Specify a custom weighting scheme. Local and global refer to local and global weighting formulas. Local can be tf (term frequency), log, or binary. Global can be normal, idf, idf2, or entropy. Default local is tr and global is not calculated.	
-R	Run_name Ex: -R "Medical Docs"	Specify a name for the current run of GTP.	
-z	sdd rank inner_loop_criteria tolerance	Performs semi-discrete decomposition. [3]	Cannot use if using -z svd1 ...; -h
-z	svd1 desc lanmax maxprs	Performance singular value decomposition. [3, 5, 6]	Cannot use if using -z sdd ...; -h
-O		Specify that the *output* file is to be in one binary file for SVD. This is needed if you are going to use GTPQUERY.	-z sdv1 ...
-Z		Specify if parse procedure should be skipped so that an available matrix can be decomposed via SVD or SDD.	-h -z svd1 ... or -z sdd ...

TABLE 27.2
continued...

27.5 Query Processing with GTPQUERY

GTPQUERY relies completely on files produced by a standard GTP run. Those files are *output*, *keys* (or *keys.pag* and *keys.dir* in C++; *keys* in Java), and LAST_RUN (Section 27.3). Query processing will fail if these files are not in the working directory.

Query processing is performed by finding a cosine similarity measure between a query vector and document vectors. Query vectors are generated by summing the term vectors of terms in the query (the term vectors are generated in GTP) then scaling each term vector dimension by the inverse of a corresponding singular value [3, 5]. In this way, the query vector can be considered a *pseudo*-document. In other words, the query vector mimics a document vector and may be projected into the term-document space [7]. At this point, if the user opted to scale the query vector it is done using the singular values produced by GTP. The scaling is done to emphasize the more dominant LSI factors (or dimensions). Cosine similarity is then calculated between the query vector and document vectors and the process is repeated if there are more queries. Options for GTPQUERY are provided to assist in query parsing and how the results are presented (Table 27.3).

The files that GTPQUERY produces are strictly results files. Each file has a prefix of *q_result.#*, where # is a number starting with 1. The number represents the corresponding number id of the query that was performed. The file contains a list of document ids and cosine similarity measures organized by most relevant to least relevant (Figure 27.4).

27.6 Example

To illustrate the process of running GTP and GTPQUERY, a small example is provided.

1. The document collection to be parsed is one file with each document separated by a blank line.

Numerical Libraries and The Grid

The Semantic Conference Organizer Software

GTP: Software for Text Mining

Arg	Add. Args.	Description
-help		Summarize options.
-S		Scale the query vector by the singular values before calculating cosine similarity.
-n	Int	Set the number of factors to use. Default is the value of *nfact* found in
	Ex: -n 15	LAST_RUN file generated by GTP.
-u	Float	Set the upper threshold value for query results returned. If the upper threshold
	Ex: -u 0.75	is set to 0.75, then all query results returned will be equal to or less than 0.75 (default is 1).
-l	Float	Set the lower threshold value for query results returned. If the upper threshold
	Ex: -l 0.25	is set to 0.25, then all query results returned will be greater than or equal to 0.25 (default is -1).
-k	Int	Set the number of results returned to *int* (default is all).
	Ex: -k 20	
-f	Filter1 [opts] [filter2 [opts] ... filterN [opts]]	Specify filters to pass each file through before the parser looks at it. If a filter has options, it needs
	Ex1: -f zcat html_filter Ex2: -f zcat "grep computer"	to be surrounded by quotes.
-B	New_delimiter	Specify that a new query delimiter is needed. *New_delimiter* must be
	Ex: -B /newquery/	alone on a line in the file and must match exactly for the query processing to recognize it. It can be up to 198 characters, and the default delimiter is a single blank line. Cannot be used in conjunction with the -x option.
-x		Indicate that there is to be no delimiter other than the end of file. This cannot be used in conjunction with the -B option.

TABLE 27.3
List of command-line options for GTPQUERY. Column 1 shows the arguments. Column 2 includes any additional arguments to be added to the root argument. Column 3 displays a brief description of each argument. There are no dependencies for each argument.

2. The GTP command is invoked using the command below. GTP provides the user with messages regarding what it is currently processing.

   gtp ../sample -c ./common_words -t ./tmp -h -z svd1 sample -d 0 -g 0 -O -w log entropy

   Creating keys — Mon Jun 24 16:45:51 EDT 2002
   Calculating term weights — Mon Jun 24 16:45:51 EDT 2002
   Creating raw matrix — Mon Jun 24 16:45:51 EDT 2002
   Creating Harwell-Boeing matrix — Mon Jun 24 16:45:51 EDT 2002
   matrix size: 3 x 10 nelem: 11
   Decompose Harwell-Boeing matrix — Mon Jun 24 16:45:51 EDT 2002
   Using svd method – las2 Mon Jun 24 16:45:51 EDT 2002
   time for gtp is 0.000000
   time for decomposition is 0.000000
   Total time is 0.000000
   Writing summary to RUN_SUMMARY — Mon Jun 24 16:45:51 EDT 2002

3. Once GTP has terminated, the *keys* and binary *output* files will have been created. Those generated by this example may be seen below: **Keys file:**

Key	ID	Global Weight
Conference	1	1.000000
Grid	2	1.000000
Gtp	3	1.000000
Libraries	4	1.000000
Mining	5	1.000000
Numerical	6	1.000000
Organizer	7	1.000000
Semantic	8	1.000000
Software	9	0.369070
Text	10	1.000000

Output file (ASCII equivalent created using *readOutput* on binary file produced):

Header
terms = 10
docs = 3
factors = 3
commentSize = 20
updatedTerms = 0 * not activated *
updatedDocs = 0 * not activated *
comment = Creating output file

Output file continued ...
Term Vectors

Term 0	(conference)
0	0.3908561766
1	-0.3573666215
2	-0.1973721683

Term 9	(text)
0	0.3908561766
1	0.3573666215
2	0.1973721683

Document Vectors

Document 0 (Numerical Libraries and the Grid)
0	0.0000000000
1	-0.4834610820
2	0.8753658533

...

Document 2 (GTP: Software for Text Mining)
0	0.7071067691
1	0.6189771295
2	0.3418586254

Singular Values	
0	1.2537220716
1	1.2003111839
2	1.2003111839

4. A query may now be performed using the above *keys* and *output* files. The queries used for this example are two queries in a single file, *queryfile*, delimited by a single blank line.

> Numerical Software
> Text Mining Software

5. The command used for the query processing exploits scaling by the singular values as the only optional command line argument.

> *gtpquery queryfile -c ./common_words -S*
>
> Query 1 done.
> Query 2 done.

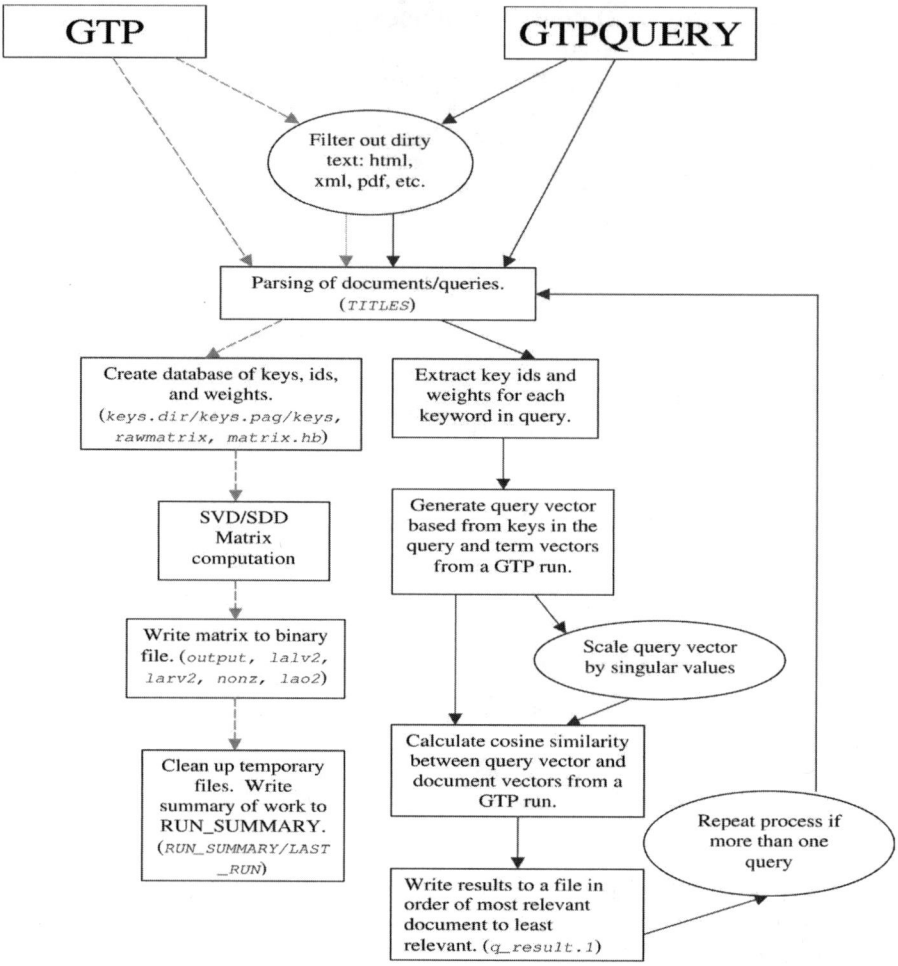

FIGURE 27.3
Flowchart of GTP and GTPQUERY. Files produced are listed in parentheses.

Doc ID	Cos. Similarity
50	0.975631
2	0.756432
14	0.500123
...	...

FIGURE 27.4
Query results file example.

6. Once the query processing is done, a file for each query processed will have been generated. In this case, the files would be named *q_result.1* and *q_result.2*. Each file is shown below (only numerical values would be written; items in parentheses are not included in the results files).

q_result.1 (Numerical Software)		q_result.2 (Text Mining Software)	
1 0.755929	(Numerical Libraries and the Grid)	3 1	(GTP: Software for Text Mining)
3 0.654654	(GTP: Software for Text Mining)	1 5.04984e-17	(Numerical Libraries and the Grid)
2 5.27521e-09	(The Semantic Conference Organizer Software)	2 -1.40715e-16	(The Semantic Conference Organizer Software)

This example illustrates using GTP as a means to parse documents and generate factors using SVD. After running GTP, the example performed a query using files generated by GTP. As stated before, GTP may be used in many other ways besides parsing and performing decomposition. One may strictly use GTP as a means to parse documents and generate a database of keys and frequencies. Titles of documents (first line of the document) may also be extracted.

27.7 Versions of GTP and GTPQUERY

There are several different versions of GTP that are supported. For Solaris and Linux based machines there is a C++ version. Also provided for Solaris is a parallel version based on MPI (Message Passing Interface) [9], which performs only the SVD computations in parallel. A Java version has recently been released and has been successfully executed on Solaris, Linux, and MacOS X platforms. The Java version has not been tested on Windows as of yet. There has, however, been a successful port of the Solaris C++ version to work with Borland Builder on the Windows platform. The Windows version is not supported at this time. All versions include the query-processing module except the parallel and Windows version.

There are no differences between the Solaris and Linux C++ versions. There are, however, a few differences between the C++ and Java versions. The most obvious is that Java is slower. Since Java uses a virtual machine, calculations are performed at a much slower rate. This is most noticeable when running GTP on a large document collection. As an example, GTP was run using the option to perform the SVD. The document collection used was about 48MB in size, consisting of almost 5,000 documents and over 42,000 unique terms parsed. Time for completion using the C++ version was about 560 seconds. Time for completion using the Java version was about 1.5 hours. Possible solutions to fix this slowdown are discussed later (Section 27.9). Secondly, the Java version is not capable of accepting user-generated filters for the parsing process. The Java version does, however, provide an internal HTML filter. The user can create his/her own filters in Java and incorporate them into GTP.

27.8 Code Evolution

The original design of the GTP parser was based on C code and shell scripts originally distributed by Telcordia Technologies, Inc. (formerly Bellcore). The SVD code was originally written in Fortran [2], converted to C [4], finally converted to C++ for GTP. Hence, the GTP code to date is basically C code wrapped in C++. Since GTP does not use genuine C++ code, true object-oriented techniques (OO) and features were not incorporated. The Java version, which was converted from the C++ version, solves some of the OO mistakes due to the numerous built-in Java classes and the ease of use of these classes.

27.9 Future Work

What does the future hold for GTP? Currently in development is a graphical user interface (GUI) front-end that is written in Java. This GUI will be compatible with all versions of GTP (C++ and Java). The GUI has been a long awaited addition to GTP and will solve many of the issues surrounding the multitude of command-line options that users are plagued with currently. The GUI is currently slated to control GTP runs (parsing and matrix decomposition) as well as controlling queries and displaying results using the current query module [8].

Also being developed is the ability to remotely store files generated by a GTP run as well as the ability to perform a query using the remotely stored files. This is being done using IBP and Exnode technologies [1]. By using the remote storage locations, or IBP depots, a user will have the ability to run GTP on large document collections and not need to worry about local hard drive space restraints. These IBP depots have the ability to allow users to store gigabytes of information for a limited time.

Acknowledgment

This research was supported in part by National Science Foundation under grant no. NSF- EIA-99-75015.

References

[1] Beck, M., Moore, T., and Plank, J. (2002). An End-to-End Approach to Globally Scalable Network Storage. In *Proceedings of the ACM SIGCOMM 2002 Conference*, Pittsburgh, PA, August 19-23.

[2] Berry, M.W. (1990). Multiprocessor Sparse SVD Algorithms and Applications. PhD Thesis, University of Illinois at Urbana-Champaign, Urbana, IL, October.

[3] Berry, M. and Browne, M. (1999). *Understanding Search Engines: Mathematical Modeling and Text Retrieval*. SIAM, Philadelphia, PA.

[4] Berry, M.W., Do, T., O'Brien, G., Krishna, V., and Varadhan, S. (1993). SVDPACKC (Version 1.0) User's Guide. Technical Report No. CS-93-194, Department of Computer Science, University of Tennessee.

[5] Berry, M.W., Drmač, Z., and Jessup, E.R. (1999). Matrices, Vector Spaces, and Information Retrieval. *SIAM Review* 41(2),335-362.

[6] Hughey, M.K. (2000). Improved Query Matching Using kd-Trees: A Latent Semantic Indexing Enhancement. *Information Retrieval* (2), 287-302, *Information Retrieval* (2), 287-302, 2000.

[7] Letsche, T.A. (1997). Large-Scale Information Retrieval with Latent Semantic Indexing. *Information Sciences*, (100), 105-137.

[8] Lynn, P.A. (2002). Evolving the General Text Parser (GTP) Utility into a Usable Application via Interface Design. MS Thesis, Department of Computer Science, University of Tennessee, Knoxville, December.

[9] Snir, M., Otto, S., Huss-Lederman, S., Walker, D., and Dongarra, J. (1995). *MPI: The Complete Reference*. MIT Press, Cambridge, MA.

28

Implication Intensity: From the Basic Statistical Definition to the Entropic Version

Julien Blanchard, Pascale Kuntz, Fabrice Guillet, and Regis Gras
Ecole Polytechnique de l'Universite de Nantes, France

CONTENTS

28.1 Introduction 473
28.2 First Definitions 475
28.3 Entropic Version 476
28.4 Experimental Results 478
28.5 Conclusion 483
     References 484

Filtering relevant and intelligible information via quantitative measures of quality remains one of the most sensitive phases of a rule mining process. In order to explicitly take the dataset sizes into account contrary to the classical confidence, and also to highlight the "natural" non-symmetrical feature of the implication notion, Gras has defined the implication intensity which measures the statistical surprisingness of the discovered rules. However, like numerous measures of the literature, this latter does not take into account the contrapositive $\bar{b} \Rightarrow \bar{a}$ which could yet allow to reinforce the assertion of the implication between a and b. Here, we introduce a new measure based on the Shannon entropy to quantify the imbalances between examples and counter-examples for both the rule and its contrapositive. Numerical comparisons of this measure with the confidence and Loevinger's index are given on both synthetic databases and real data of various types from human resource management and from lift breakdowns. We compare the statistical distributions of the number of rules retained by these indexes and underline the interest, in a decision process, of rules having a different behavior depending on the chosen measure.

28.1 Introduction

Association rules of the form $a \Rightarrow b$ have become the major concept in data mining to represent quasi-implicative relationships between itemset patterns. From the seminal works of Agrawal *et al.* [1], numerous algorithms have been proposed to efficiently mine such rules in large databases. All of them attempt to extract a restricted set of relevant rules easy to interpret for decision-making, but comparative experiments show that results may vary with the choice of rule quality measures. In the rich literature devoted to this problem, measures of interestingness are often classified in two categories: the subjective (user-driven) ones and the objective (data-driven) ones. Subjective measures aim at taking into account unexpectedness and actionability relatively to a prior knowledge (see [19], [16] for review), while objective measures give priority to statistical criteria such as coverage, strength, significance ... (e.g., [3], [13], [20]).

Among the latter, the most commonly used criterion is the combination of the support -or frequency- $f(a \wedge b)$, which indicates whether the variables involved in the itemsets a and b occur reasonably often together in the dataset, with the confidence -or conditional probability- $c(a \Rightarrow b)$ which is the fraction of objects that satisfy b among the objects that satisfy a. However, it is now well known that confidence presents two major faults: it does not vary when the size of $f(b)$ or of the transaction set T varies and it is insensitive to the dilatation of $f(a)$, $f(b)$ and of the cardinality of T (e.g., [7] for details). Other measures, coming from the statistical literature, calculate a link -or an absence of link- between itemsets but, like χ^2, they often do not clearly specify the direction of the relationship. Brin proposes in [5] to look for some correlated itemsets (positive or negative dependence validated by the χ^2 value). His interestingness measure relies on one cell in the contingency table without taking advantage of the imbalances which can be found between two different cells and which indicate an existing rule.

In order to explicitly take the dataset size into account, and also to highlight the "natural" non-symmetrical feature of the implication, Gras [9] has defined the *implication intensity* $\varphi(a \Rightarrow b)$ which aims at quantifiying the "surprise" of an expert faced with the improbable small number of counter-examples in comparison with the data number. Similarly, like Freitas [8], we here consider that subjective aspects may be partly measured by objective terms and we focus on the importance to discover "small disjuncts" in the dataset. With that aim in view, the implication intensity is based on a probabilistic model which allows to precisely measure the statistical significance of the discovered rules. The general limits of significance of testing methods in data mining have been underlined by different authors [12]. Nevertheless, the implication intensity has been experimentally shown to be robust to small variations [6]. Besides, numerical experiments on both synthetic and real-world data have justified its combination with more classical measures ([11], [14]).

However, the experiments have also highlighted two limits of the original measure for large datasets. First, it tends to be not discriminant enough when the size of T dramatically increases; its values are close to 1 even though the inclusion $A \subset B$, where A (resp. B) is the subset of transactions which contains a (resp. b), is far from being perfect. Secondly, like numerous measures proposed in the literature, it does not take into account the contrapositive $\overline{b} \Rightarrow \overline{a}$ which could allow to reinforce the affirmation of the good quality of the implicative relationship between a and b.

To overcome these difficulties, we propose to modulate the value of the surprise quantified by the implication intensity by taking into account both the imbalance between $card(A \cap B)$ and $card(A \cap \overline{B})$ associated with $a \Rightarrow b$ and the imbalance between $card(A \cap \overline{B})$ and $card(\overline{A} \cap \overline{B})$ associated with the contrapositive $\overline{b} \Rightarrow \overline{a}$ [10]. We here introduce this recent measure, called the *entropic implication intensity*, based on the Shannon entropy to non-linearly quantify these differences.

The next section briefly recalls the main definitions and properties of the basic implication intensity. In Section 28.3, we explain how to weigh it later by a function of the conditional Shannon entropy. Numerical comparisons of this new measure with the confidence and Loevinger's index are given in Section 28.4 on both synthetic databases and real data of various types from human resource management and from lift breakdowns. We compare the statistical distributions of the number of rules retained by these indexes and underline the interest, in a decision process, of rules having a different behavior depending on the chosen measure.

28.2 First Definitions

Let us now consider a finite set T of n transactions described by a set I of p items. Each transaction t can be considered as an itemset so that $t \subseteq I$. A transaction t is said to contain an itemset a if $a \subseteq t$ and we denote by $A = \{t \in T; a \subseteq t\}$ the transaction set in T which contains a and by $\overline{A}$ its complementary set in T.

An association rule is an implication of the form $a \Rightarrow b$, where a and b are disjoined itemsets ($a \subset I$, $b \subset I$, and $a \cap b = \emptyset$). In practice, it is quite common to observe a few transactions which contain a and not b without having the general trend to have b when a is present contested. Therefore, with regards to the cardinal n of T but also to the cardinals n_A of A and n_B of B, the number $n_{A \cap \overline{B}} = card(A \cap \overline{B})$ of counter-examples must be taken into account to statistically accept to retain or not the rule $a \Rightarrow b$. Following the likelihood linkage analysis of Lerman [15], the implication intensity expresses the unlikelihood of counter-examples $n_{A \cap \overline{B}}$ in T.

More precisely, we compare the observed number of counter-examples to a probabilistic model. Let us assume that we randomly draw two subsets X and Y in T which respectively contain n_A and n_B transactions. The complementary sets $\overline{Y}$ of Y and $\overline{B}$ of B in T have the same cardinality $n_{\overline{B}}$. In this case, $N_{X \cap \overline{Y}} = card(X \cap \overline{Y})$ is a random variable and $n_{A \cap \overline{B}}$ an observed value. The association rule $a \Rightarrow b$ is *admissible* for a given threshold $1 - \sigma$ if σ is greater than the probability that the number of counter-examples in the observations is greater than the number of expected counter-examples in a random drawing, i.e., if $\Pr(N_{X \cap \overline{Y}} \leq n_{A \cap \overline{B}}) \leq \sigma$.

The distribution of the random variable $N_{X \cap \overline{Y}}$ depends on the drawing mode [9]. In order to explicitly take the asymmetry of the relationships between itemsets into account, we here restrict ourselves to the Poisson distribution with $\lambda = n_A n_{\overline{B}}/n$. For cases where the approximation is justified (e.g., $\lambda > 3$), the standardized random variable $\tilde{N}_{X \cap \overline{Y}} = (card(X \cap \overline{Y}) - \lambda)/\sqrt{\lambda}$ is approximatively $N(0,1)$-distributed. The observed value of $\tilde{N}_{X \cap \overline{Y}}$ is $\tilde{n}_{A \cap \overline{B}} = (n_{A \cap \overline{B}} - \lambda)/\sqrt{\lambda}$.

Definition 1. The implication intensity of the association rule $a \Rightarrow b$ is defined by $\varphi(a \Rightarrow b) = 1 - \Pr(\widetilde{N}_{X \cap \overline{Y}} \leq \widetilde{n}_{A \cap \overline{B}})$ if $n_B \neq n$; otherwise $\varphi(a \Rightarrow b) = 0$.
The rule is retained for a given threshold $1 - \sigma$ if $\varphi(a \Rightarrow b) \geq 1 - \sigma$.

28.3 Entropic Version

The previous definition essentially measures the significance of the rule $a \Rightarrow b$. However, taking the contrapositive $\overline{b} \Rightarrow \overline{a}$ into account could reinforce the assertion of the implication between a and b. Moreover, it could improve the quality of discrimination of φ when the transaction set T increases: if A and B are small compared to T, their complementary sets are large and vice versa.

For these reasons, we here introduce a weighted version of the implication intensity $\phi(a \Rightarrow b) = (\varphi(a \Rightarrow b) \cdot \tau(a,b))^{1/2}$ where $\tau(a,b)$ measures the imbalance between $n_{A \cap B}$ and $n_{A \cap \overline{B}}$ -associated with $a \Rightarrow b$- and the imbalance between $n_{A \cap \overline{B}}$ and $n_{\overline{A} \cap \overline{B}}$ -associated with its contrapositive. Intuitively, the rule-induced surprise measured by ϕ must be softened (resp. confirmed) when the number of counter-examples $n_{A \cap \overline{B}}$ is high (resp. small) for the rule and its contrapositive considering the observed numbers n_a and $n_{\overline{b}}$. Here, we follow an axiomatic approach of the measurement of imbalances.

A well known index for taking the imbalances into account non-linearily is the Shannon conditional entropy [18]. The conditional entropy $H_{b/a}$ of cases (a and b) and (a and $\overline{b}$) given a is defined by

$$H_{b/a} = -\frac{n_{a \cap b}}{n_a} \log_2 \frac{n_{a \cap b}}{n_a} - \frac{n_{a \cap \overline{b}}}{n_a} \log_2 \frac{n_{a \cap \overline{b}}}{n_a}$$

and, similarly, the conditional entropy $H_{\overline{a}/\overline{b}}$ of cases ($\overline{a}$ and $\overline{b}$) and (a and $\overline{b}$) given $\overline{b}$ is defined by

$$H_{\overline{a}/\overline{b}} = -\frac{n_{a \cap \overline{b}}}{n_{\overline{b}}} \log_2 \frac{n_{a \cap \overline{b}}}{n_{\overline{b}}} - \frac{n_{\overline{a} \cap \overline{b}}}{n_{\overline{b}}} \log_2 \frac{n_{\overline{a} \cap \overline{b}}}{n_{\overline{b}}}$$

We can here consider that these entropies measure the average uncertainty of the random experiments in which we check whether b (resp. $\overline{a}$) is realized when a (resp. $\overline{b}$) is observed. The complements of 1 for these uncertainties $I_{b/a} = 1 - H_{b/a}$ and $I_{\overline{a}/\overline{b}} = 1 - H_{\overline{a}/\overline{b}}$ can be interpreted as the average information collected by the realization of these experiments; the higher this information, the stronger the guarantee of the quality of the implication and its contrapositive.

Intuitively, the expected behavior of the new measure ϕ is determined by three stages:

1. a slow reaction to the first counter-examples (robustness to noise),

2. an acceleration of the reject in the neighborhood of the balance,

3. an increasing rejection beyond the balance -which was not guaranteed by the basic implication intensity φ.

More precisely, in order to have the expected significance, our model must satisfy the following constraints:

1. Integrating both the information relative to $a \Rightarrow b$ and that relative to $\bar{b} \Rightarrow \bar{a}$ respectively measured by $I_{b/a}$ and $I_{\bar{a}/\bar{b}}$. A product $I_{b/a} \cdot I_{\bar{a}/\bar{b}}$ is well adapted to simultaneously highlight the quality of these two values.

2. Raising the conditional entropies to the power of a fixed number $\alpha > 1$ in the information definitions to reinforce the contrast between the different stages detailed below: $\left((1-H^{\alpha}_{b/a}) \cdot (1-H^{\alpha}_{\bar{a}/\bar{b}})\right)^{1/\beta}$ with $\beta = 2\alpha$ to remain of the same dimension as φ.

3. The need to consider that the implications have lost their inclusive meaning when the number of counter-examples is greater than half of the observations of a and $\bar{b}$ (which seems quite natural). Beyond these values we consider that each of the terms $(1-H^{\alpha}_{b/a})$ and $(1-H^{\alpha}_{b/a})$ is equal to 0. Let $f_a = n_a/n$ (resp. $f_{\bar{b}} = n_{\bar{b}}/n$) the frequency of a (resp. $\bar{b}$) on the transaction set and $f_{a\cap\bar{b}} = n_{a\cap\bar{b}}/n$ be the frequency of counter-examples. The proposed adjustment of the information can easily be defined by

$$\widehat{I^{\alpha}}_{b/a} = 1 - H^{\alpha}_{b/a} = 1 + \left(\left(1 - \frac{f_{a\cap\bar{b}}}{f_a}\right)\log\left(1 - \frac{f_{a\cap\bar{b}}}{f_a}\right) + \frac{f_{a\cap\bar{b}}}{f_a}\log\left(\frac{f_{a\cap\bar{b}}}{f_a}\right)\right)^{\alpha} \text{ if } f_{a\cap\bar{b}} \in \left[0, \frac{f_a}{2}\right[\text{ ; otherwise } \widehat{I^{\alpha}}_{b/a} = 0$$

and

$$\widehat{I^{\alpha}}_{\bar{a}/\bar{b}} = 1 - H^{\alpha}_{\bar{a}/\bar{b}} = 1 + \left(\left(1 - \frac{f_{a\cap\bar{b}}}{f_{\bar{b}}}\right)\log\left(1 - \frac{f_{a\cap\bar{b}}}{f_{\bar{b}}}\right) + \frac{f_{a\cap\bar{b}}}{f_{\bar{b}}}\log\left(\frac{f_{a\cap\bar{b}}}{f_{\bar{b}}}\right)\right)^{\alpha} \text{ if } f_{a\cap\bar{b}} \in \left[0, \frac{f_{\bar{b}}}{2}\right[\text{ ; otherwise } \widehat{I^{\alpha}}_{\bar{a}/\bar{b}} = 0$$

Definition 2. The imbalances are measured by $\tau(a,b)$ -called the *inclusion index*- defined by

$$\tau(a,b) = \left(\widehat{I^{\alpha}}_{b/a} \cdot \widehat{I^{\alpha}}_{\bar{a}/\bar{b}}\right)^{1/2\alpha}$$

and the weighted version of the implication intensity -called the *entropic implication intensity* (EII)- is given by

$$\phi(a \Rightarrow b) = (\varphi(a \Rightarrow b) \cdot \tau(a,b))^{1/2}$$

For simplicity sake, we chose $\alpha = 2$ for numerical applications. Figure 28.1 shows the difference between the ϕ distributions for $\alpha = 1$ and $\alpha = 2$; the expected reaction

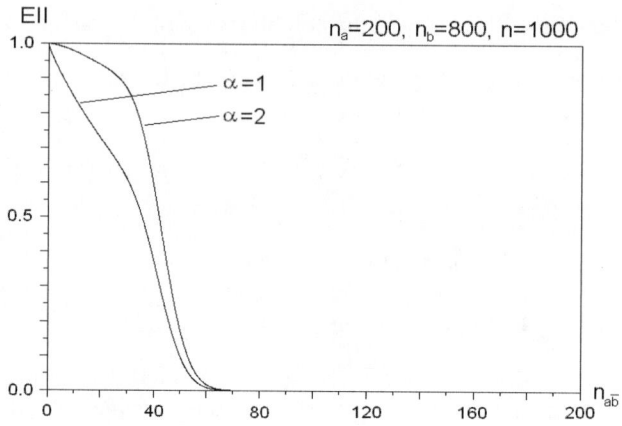

FIGURE 28.1
EII with $\alpha=1$ and $\alpha=2$.

faced with the counter-example increase is clearly highlighted with $\alpha = 2$. More generally, α may be interpreted as the selectivity of EII index that may be tuned depending on the nature of data : the lower α, the more EII decreases with counter-examples and the more discriminant the rule ranking is (e.g., in the MUSHROOMS experiment of Figure 28.7.(a), the results show a large and inextricable set of 100%-confidence rules that could be reduced and better ranked by using $\alpha =1$).

28.4 Experimental Results

We here compare how confidence and EII evaluate the interest of rules on three synthetic databases of different sizes and three real ones. Association rules were mined with a low support threshold (between 0.1% and 10% depending on the data) to avoid premature elimination of potentially interesting rules ("small disjuncts"). For each case, we compare rule distributions for confidence and EII. Due to recent promising results [4], we have added Loevinger's index [17] to our comparisons.

28.4.1 Experiments with Synthetic Data

We have generated synthetic databases using the well known procedure proposed by Agrawal and Srikant [2]. Let us recall that these data simulate the transactions of customers in retail businesses. Results are here presented for the databases T5.I2.D100k, T10.I4.D100k, and the dense database T10.I4.D5k (see Figure 28.2), which are representative of a larger set of experiments.

Roughly speaking, Figure 28.3 shows that the EII seems to prune fewer rules

	Items	Transactions	Average length of transactions	Discovered association rules (for this support threshold)
T10.I4.D5k	12	5 000	10	97 688 (10%)
T5.I2.D100k	1 000	100 000	5	10 426 (0.1%)
T10.I4.D100k	1 000	100 000	10	478 894 (0.1%)

FIGURE 28.2
Synthetic data characteristics.

than the confidence for high thresholds. Therfore, we cannot deduce general behaviors for the two indexes because they obviously depend on the data characteristics. Nethertheless, from a more precise study of the individual behavior of each rule, we discriminated three basic situations:

1. most of the rules with a good confidence (e.g., > 90%) have a good EII (e.g., > 0.9), and vice versa,

2. some rules can be conserved by the EII while they are rejected by the confidence even with quite a low threshold (e.g., around 0.7),

3. some rules can be conserved by the confidence while they are rejected by the EII (sometimes with a score of 0).

The detailed repartitions of rules for the three cases are given in Figure 28.4. To illustrate cases 2 and 3, Figure 28.5 shows samples of rules from T10.I4.D5k and T10.I4.D100k whose quality measure depends on the chosen index.

The rules of case 3 are of poor interest. Even if they are little contradicted, they are not statistically surprising and/or their contrapositives have a weak inclusion quality. Our studies show that Loevinger's index, by assigning them low scores, is also well adapted to reject these rules.

On the other hand, rules of case 2 are potentially very interesting. They perfectly meet the initial objectives of data mining ("to find the nuggets"): these rules are *a priori* unexpected by domain experts because they do not correspond to strong inclusions, but in spite of their relatively high number of counter-examples they are statistically surprising and their contrapositives have a strong inclusion quality. In practice, these rules should be kept for a subsequent semantic analysis by domain experts.

28.4.2 Experiments with Real Data

We used three real databases, presented in Figure 28.6. The UCI database MUSHROOMS (www.ics.uci.edu/~mlearn/MLRepository.html), classical in machine learning, is now used for association rule discovery.* The database LBD is a set of lift

---

*For our experiments we used a maximal size of 4 items for the itemsets and we deleted the attributes with only one value in the data.

(a) T10.I4.D5k

(b) T5.I2.D100k

(c) T10.I4.D100k

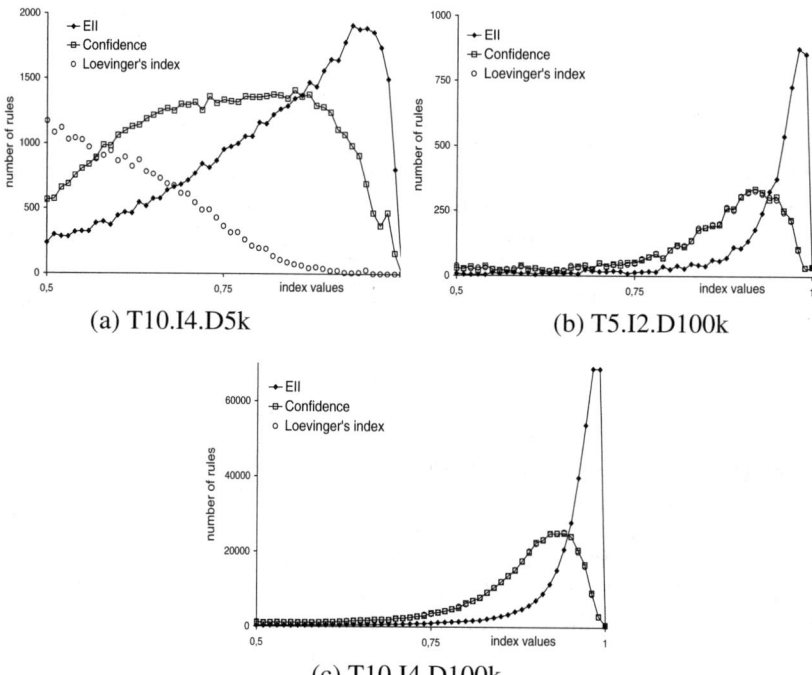

FIGURE 28.3
Rule distribution for synthetic data.

	T10.I4.D5k	T5.I2.D100k	T10.I4.D100k
Rules of case 1	20 099 (21%)	4 262 (41%)	314 581 (66%)
Rules of case 2	4 341 (4%)	310 (3%)	17 731 (4%)
Rules of case 3	551 (1%)	0	0

case 1: EII > 0.8 and Confidence > 80%, case 2: EII > 0.8 and Confidence < 75%, case 3: EII < 0.75 and Confidence > 80%

FIGURE 28.4
Rule distribution among the three cases for synthetic data.

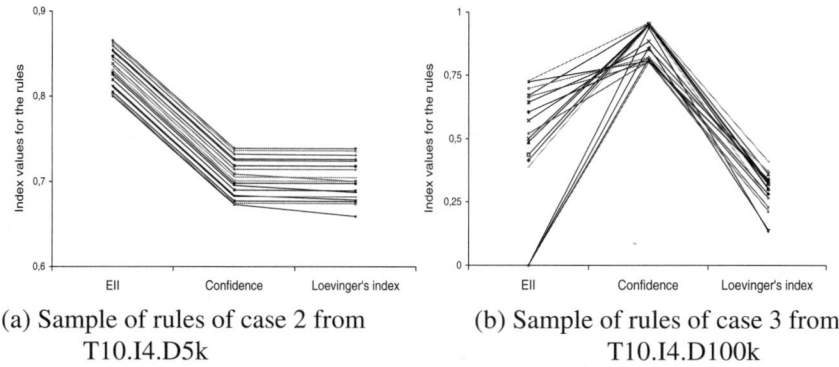

(a) Sample of rules of case 2 from T10.I4.D5k

(b) Sample of rules of case 3 from T10.I4.D100k

FIGURE 28.5
Examples of rules of cases 2 and 3.

	Items	Transactions	Average length of transactions	Discovered association rules (for this support threshold)
MUSHROOMS	118	8 416	22	123 228 (12 %)
LBD	92	2 883	8,5	43 930 (1%)
EVAL	30	2 299	10	28 938 (4%)

FIGURE 28.6
Real data characteristics.

breakdowns provided by the breakdown service of a lift manufacturer. EVAL is a database of profiles of workers' performances which was used by the firm Performanse SA to calibrate a decision support system in human resource management [6].

We can see on Figure 28.7 that rule distributions may be quite different depending on the databases. On LBD and EVAL the EII filters less than the confidence for high thresholds, while on MUSHROOMS the confidence is less filtering.

Figure 28.8 shows that the three studies present some rules of the above mentioned case 2. For example, the rule mined over LBD $(C12 \& C35 \& M24) \Rightarrow (C30)$, where the items are types of breakdowns for a lift (lock, brakes, safety stop, fuses...), has a low confidence of 70% with a good EII of 0.83. This rule is one of the rules which have been judged very interesting by domain experts.

Moreover, a few rules coming from MUSHROOMS belong to case 3, like the rule $(CLASS = EDIBLE \& GILL\_SPACING = CLOSE) \Rightarrow (RINGS\_NUMBER = ONE)$ which has a very good confidence of 92% while its EII is around 0.4. The rule $(GILL\_SIZE = BROAD) \Rightarrow (GILL\_ATTACHMENT = FREE)$ with a confidence set to 96% is totally rejected by the EII with a score of 0. Also, Loevinger's index allows to exclude the rules of case 3 in MUSHROOMS.

Let us notice that the EII computation time increases linearly with the number of discovered rules (see Figure 28.9).

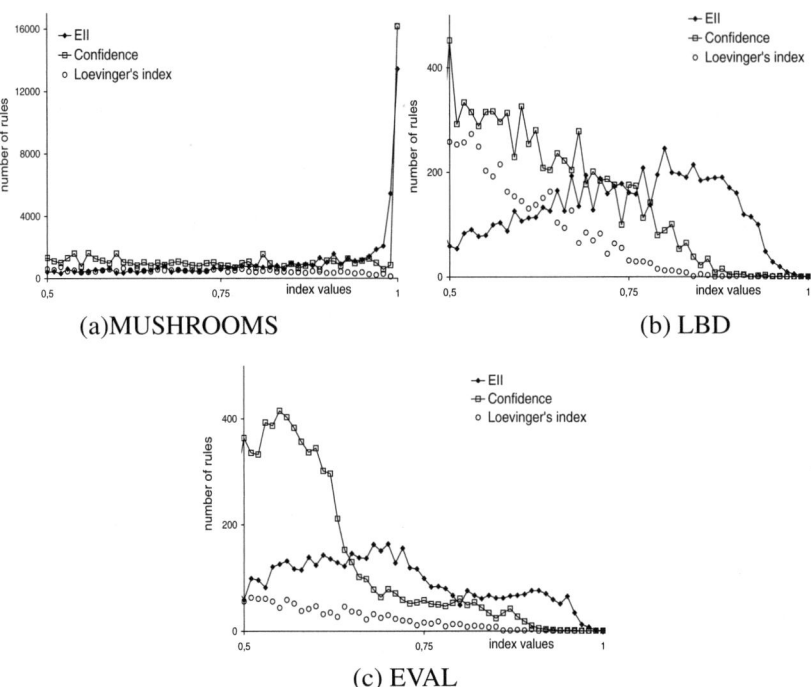

FIGURE 28.7
Rule distribution for real data.

	MUSHROOMS	LBD	EVAL
Rules of case 1	32 689 (27%)	411 (1%)	402 (1%)
Rules of case 2	3 130 (2,6%)	1 440 (3%)	428 (1%)
Rules of case 3	1 851 (2%)	0	0

(same thresholds as table 28.4)

FIGURE 28.8
Rule distribution among the three cases for real data.

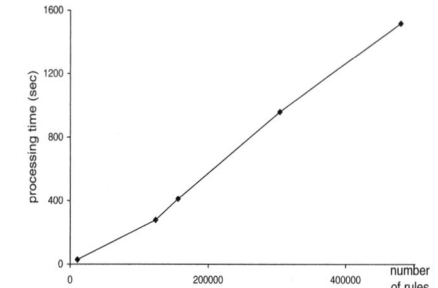

Our experiments were performed on a 500MHz bi-Pentium3 PC with 1GB of memory, under a Linux 2.4.17 operating system.

FIGURE 28.9
EII computation time.

28.5 Conclusion

In this paper we have developed an extension of the implication intensity which takes into account the quality of the rule contrapositive. By including the rule statistical significance and the inclusion strength of the rule, our model allows to discover a subjective aspect -the rule surprisingness- with an objective measure. Moreover, it evolves non-linearly with the counter-example number and makes the discovery of "small disjuncts" easier. The entropic implication intensity has been recently integrated in the software CHIC devoted to the statistical implicative analysis in order to process large datasets. We are currently studying its application to the discovery of prediction rules in sequences.

The experimental comparisons of EII with the confidence have highlighted two interesting features when these measures do not select the same rules: in various databases, we find both a subset of non-surprising rules with a good confidence but a low EII, and a promising subset of potentially interesting rules that are rejected by the confidence but conserved by the EII. We have shown the relevance of some of these rules on real-life data for decision-making. These results confirm the limits of a single measure for modeling the different aspects of the interestingness of a rule (e.g., [3]). Most works are based on the search of a consensus between results found by different measures. However, when we are looking for "nuggets" such as for instance behavioral niches, the permutations in partial orders defined by a set of measures also give precious information. Moreover, in a multicriteria analysis perspective, the determination of Pareto's optima is undoubtedly interesting. Although, on a theoretical point of view, this characterization is here very difficult as the measures used have a very different nature, we believe that the continuation of the feature typology we have started could allow to improve the numerical experiments necessary to a better understanding of this problem.

References

[1] Agrawal, R., Imielinsky, T., and Swami, A. (1993). Mining association rules between sets of items in large databases. In *Proc. of the ACM SIGMOD'93*, pp. 207–216.

[2] Agrawal, R. and Srikant, R. (1994). Fast algorithms for mining association rules. In *Proc. of the 20th Int'l Conf. on Very Large Databases (VLDB '94)*, pp. 487–499.

[3] Bayardo, R. J. and Agrawal, R. (1999). Mining the most interesting rules. In *Proc. of the 5th Int. Conf. on Knowledge Discovery and Data Mining*, pp. 145–154.

[4] Bernard, J.M. (2002). Implicative analysis for multivariate binary data using an imprecise Dirichlet model. *J. of Statistical Planning and Inference*, to appear.

[5] Brin, S., Motwani, R., and Silverstein, C. (1997). Beyond market baskets: Generalizing association rules to correlations. In *Proc. of ACM SIGMOD Conf. on Management of Data SIGMOD'97*, pp. 265–276.

[6] Fleury, L. (1996). *Knowledge discovery in a human resource management database (in French)*. PhD thesis, University of Nantes, France.

[7] Fleury, L., Briand, H., Philippe, J., and Djeraba, C.(1995). Rule evaluation for knowledge discovery in databases. In *Proc. of the 6th Conf. on Database and Expert System Appl.*, pp. 405–414.

[8] Freitas, A. (1999). On rule interestingness measures. *Knowledge-Based Systems Journal*, 12(5), 309–315.

[9] Gras, R. (1996). *The statistical implication - A new method for data exploration (in French)*. La Pensee Sauvage, editor.

[10] Gras, R., Kuntz, P. and Briand, H. (2001). Les fondements de l'analyse statistique implicative et quelques prolongements pour la fouille de donnes. *Mathmatiques et Sciences Humaines*, 39(154–155),9–29.

[11] Guillaume, S., Guillet, F., and Philippe, J. (1998). Improving the discovery of association rules with intensity of implication. In *Proc. of the 2nd Eur. Conf. of Principles of Data Mining and Knowledge Discovery*, pp. 318–327. L.N.A.I. 1510.

[12] Hand, D., Mannila, H., and Smyth, P. (2001). *Principles of data mining*. The MIT Press, Cambridge, MA.

[13] Hilderman, R. and Hamilton, H. (1999). Knowledge discovery and interestingness measures: a survey. Technical Report 99-04, University of Regina.

[14] Kuntz, P., Guillet, F., Lehn, R., and Briand, H. (2000). A user-driven process for mining association' rules. In *Proc. of the 4th Eur. Conf. of Principles of Data Mining and Knowledge Discovery*, pp. 160–168. L.N.A.I. 1910.

[15] Lerman, I.C. (1993). Likelihood linkage analysis classification method. *Biochimie*, 75, 379–397.

[16] Liu, B., Hsu, W., Mun, L., and Lee, H. (1999). Finding interesting patterns using user expectations. *Knowledge and Data Engineering*, 11(6), 817–832.

[17] Loevinger, J. (1947). A systematic approach to the construction and evaluation of tests of abilities. *Psychological Monographs*, 61(4).

[18] Shannon, C.E. and Weaver, W. (1949). *The mathematical theory of communication*. Univ. of Illinois.

[19] Silberschatz, A. and Tuzhilin, A. (1995). On subjective measures of interestingness in knowledge discovery. In *Proc. of the First Int. Conf. on Knowledge Discovery and Data Mining*, pp. 275–281.

[20] Tan, P. and Kumar, V. (2000). Interestingness measures for association patterns: a perspective. Technical Report TR00-036, University of Minnesota.

29

Use of a Secondary Splitting Criterion in Classifying Forest Construction

Chang-Yung Yu and Heping Zhang[1]
Yale University, New Haven, USA

CONTENTS

29.1 Introduction	487
29.2 A Secondary Node-Splitting Criterion	488
29.3 The Formation of a Deterministic Forest	488
29.4 Comparison Data	489
29.5 Discussion	491
Acknowledgments	494
References	494

[1]To whom reprint requests should be addressed. E-mail: heping.zhang@yale.edu

29.1 Introduction

Microarray technology has unveiled a great opportunity for tumor and cancer classifications [7, 5, 10, 12, 17]. The classic approach does not discriminate among tumors with similar histopathologic features, which may vary in clinical course and in response to treatment [7]. Microarray data monitor gene expression profiles from thousands of genes simultaneously. Appropriate use of such rich information can lead to improvement in the classification and diagnosis of cancer over the classic morphologic approaches.

This microarray technology has also created new data-mining challenges in the sense that we usually have a lot of number of predictors and yet a small number of samples. In this article, we are concerned with an issue arising from classifying multi-class tumor cells using microarray data. Specifically, when the frequencies of the cell types are imbalanced, the standard splitting criterion tends to overlook the classes with least frequencies. To address this problem and to improve the classification accuracy, we introduce a secondary splitting criterion in the construction of deterministic forests. Using two published data sets and based on cross-validation, we demonstrate the improvement in prediction of the deterministic forest as a result of such a secondary splitting criterion.

It is known in the field of machine learning that the use of forest improves the classification accuracy over a single tree. Breidman[4] and Zhang[19] confirmed this observation in the context of microarray data analysis and introduced a procedure for constructing a deterministic forest that retains high prediction precision and is easily reproducible. Thus, the focus of this paper is to apply our proposed secondary node-splitting criterion to the determinist forest and evaluate the benefit of this proposal.

29.2 A Secondary Node-Splitting Criterion

Before describing the construction of a forest, we need to describe how a single tree can be grown [3, 14, 15, 16, 18]. Suppose we have data from n units of observations (e.g., samples). Each unit contains a vector of feature measurements (e.g., gene expression levels) and a class label (e.g., normal or cancer). A classification tree is formed by recursively partitioning a given set of observations into smaller and smaller groups (called nodes) using the feature information such that the distribution of the class membership within any node becomes more and more homogeneous. Figure 29.1 is a classification automatically generated by RTREE (can be downloaded from http://peace.med.yale.edu program using the leukemia data set described below. In Figure 29.1, the entire sample (the circle on the top, also called the root node) of 72 cells is split into two sub-groups, which are called daughter nodes. The choices of the selected predictor and its corresponding cut-off value are designed to purify the distribution of the response; namely, separating different tissues from each other. One popular node impurity measure is the entropy$\sum_i p_i \log(p_i)$where p_i is the probability of a sample within the node to be of label i. The goodness of split is measured by a weighted sum of the within-node impurities. When analyzing microarray data, we have noted that such an impurity measure tends to overlook the contribution from classes with relatively small p_i. To resolve this difficulty, we propose to pool the more frequent classes together to re-calculate the impurity as the secondary criterion. When splitting a node, if there exists more than one covariate with best impurity measure, we use the secondary criterion to refine the order of the node splits.

29.3 The Formation of a Deterministic Forest

To improve both the classification precision and interpretation, Zhang[19] proposed a deterministic process by collecting competitive trees to form a forest. Specifically, for any given data set, we consider top 20 splits of the root node and top 3 splits of the

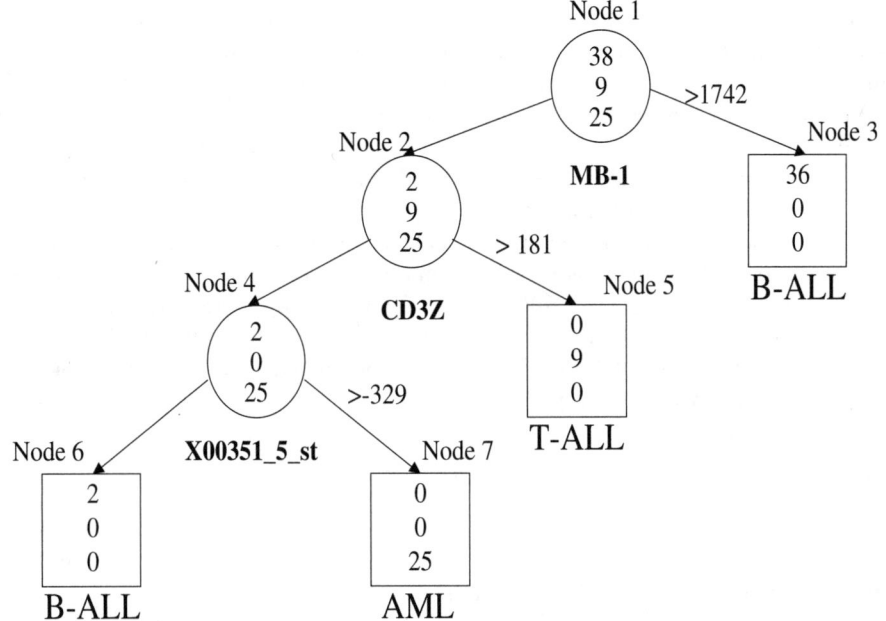

FIGURE 29.1
A tree structure produced automatically by RTREE program for the leukemia data set. The circles represent internal nodes that are split further. The boxes are terminal nodes without a split. Inside each node are the counts of B-ALL (top), T-ALL (middle), and AML (bottom) cells. Under each internal node is the gene whose expression is used to split the node with the splitting value on its right. Under each terminal node is the class label that dominates the classes of the cells in that node.

two daughter nodes of the root node. A second criterion as described above is applied in case that one goodness of split criterion cannot decide the ranking of the splits. The collection process is terminated once we reach 100 trees. This size of 100 trees is heuristic, as it is so in the formation of a random forest. Nonetheless, our experience suggests that it is a reasonably large and manageable size, and seems to achieve the two aims set forth. Figure 29.1 shows a tree structure produced automatically by RTREE program for the leukemia data set.

29.4 Comparison Data

We selected two commonly used data sets in microarray data analysis to demonstrate the benefit of using the secondary splitting criterion for the classification based on deterministic forests.

The first data set is on leukemia[7] that was downloaded from the website http://www-genome.wi.mit.edu/cancer. It includes 25 mRNA samples with acute myeloid leukemia (AML), 38 samples with B-cell acute lymphoblastic leukemia (B-ALL), and 9 samples with T-cell acute lymphoblastic leukemia (T-ALL). Expression profiles were assessed for 7,129 genes for each sample. The question is whether the microarray data are useful in classifying the three types of leukemia. The number of T-ALL cells is notably less than the other two.

Our second example is the lymphoma data set by Alizadeh[1]. Data are available on the three most prevalent adult lymphoma malignancies: 29 B-cell chronic lymphocytic leukemia (B-CLL), 9 follicular lymphoma (FL), and 46 diffuse large B-cell lymphoma (DLBCL). We analyzed the data from 3,198 genes that have relatively more information from all 84 samples. This lymphoma data set can be downloaded from http://llmpp.nih.gov/lymphoma.

29.4.1 Comparison through Cross-Validation

To obtain an unbiased estimate of the misclassification rate and to base our comparison on it, we report the error rates based on the cross-validation. We used both leave-one-out and 5-fold cross-validation.

For the leave-one-out procedure, we save one sample as a test sample and use the rest of the samples as the learning sample to construct the forest. With n original samples, the procedure takes n runs and each sample serves once as the test sample. With so few original samples in most of current microarray experiments, this jackknifing procedure retains the maximum number of samples in the learning sample, which is expected to increase the stability of the constructed forest.

On the other hand, with only one test sample, the error-rate estimate may be highly variable. To address this concern, we also conduct 5-fold cross validation by saving one-fifth of the samples as the test samples. The 5-fold cross validation were repeated 10 times for a better estimate of prediction error rate. As displayed in Figure 29.2, the secondary criterion reduces the error rates in the deterministic forests for both the leukemia data set and lymphoma data set.

29.4.2 Understanding the Deterministic Forest

As discussed in Zhang[19], reducing the misclassification rate is one objective, and our second objective is to understand the genes that participate in the forest formation. To the second end, Zhang[19] proposed to assess the number of different genes appearing in the deterministic forests, and the frequencies of the genes used. This reveals the importance of the genes in classifying tumor tissues in the respective data sets. For the leukemia data set, 35 different genes appeared in the forest of 100 trees. For the lymphoma data set, 40 different genes appeared in the forest of 100 trees. Figures 29.3 and 29.5 present the frequencies of the genes that are used relatively frequently among the two data sets, respectively. A high frequency is indicative of the importance of a gene in the respective classification. Figures 29.4 and 29.6 display a tree based on the "most important" genes in respective data sets.

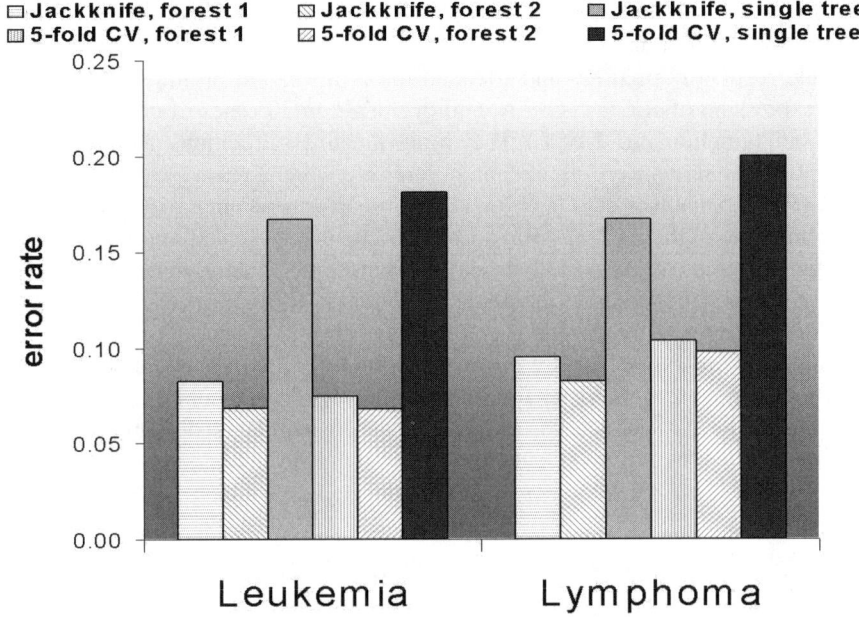

FIGURE 29.2
Error rates of deterministic forests: with (forest 2) and without (forest 1) the secondary node splitting criterion and using the jackknife and 5-fold cross-validation.

29.5 Discussion

To understand the scientific meaning of our results, we conducted a MEDLINE search afterwards and discovered that most of the genes that we found important have also been examined in the related contents. It is important to remind us that those important genes were determined among several thousands of genes according the frequency appeared in the forest. Thus, the chance of selecting a gene with scientific relevance is very small.

In relation to Figure 29.3, Hashimoto et al. [8] examined twenty-three cases of precursor T cell lymphoid malignancies with respect to CD79a (MB-1) expression. Their results suggest that CD79a is expressed weakly and transiently in immature T-lineage cells. Yu and Chang[13] also observed that human MB-1 was expressed by B cell lines. Herblot et al.[9] studied the E2A (TCF3) activity in B-cell development. Their observations provide evidence for a gradient of E2A activity that increases from the pre-pro-B to the pre-B stage and suggest a model in which low levels of E2A (as in pro-B cells) are sufficient to control cell growth, while high levels (in pre-B cells) are required for cell differentiation.

For the genes in Figure 29.5, Bai et al.[2] investigated the expression of the cyclin-dependent kinase inhibitor (CDKI) p27 protein in relation to the expression of the cell cycle regulators p53, Rb and p16 and the proliferation profile as determined by the expression of Ki67, cyclin A, and cyclin B1 in 80 cases of de novo diffuse large B-cell lymphomas (DLBCL). They found that three alterations in the combined p27/p53/Rb/p16 status were significantly correlated with increased expression of cyclin B1 (P =.005). Nilson et al.[11] found that the AF-4 gene on human chromosome 4q21, a member of the AF-4, LAF-4 and FMR-2 gene family, was involved in reciprocal translocations to the ALL-1 gene on chromosome 11q23, which were associated with acute lymphoblastic leukemias. Delmer et al.[6] reported overexpression of cyclin D2 (CCND2) in chronic B-cell malignancies.

In summary, we exploit the use of classification trees in tumor and cell classifications through gene expressions. To improve the classification and prediction accuracy, we introduced a secondary node-splitting for constructing a deterministic forest and demonstrated the improvement through two published and commonly used data sets.

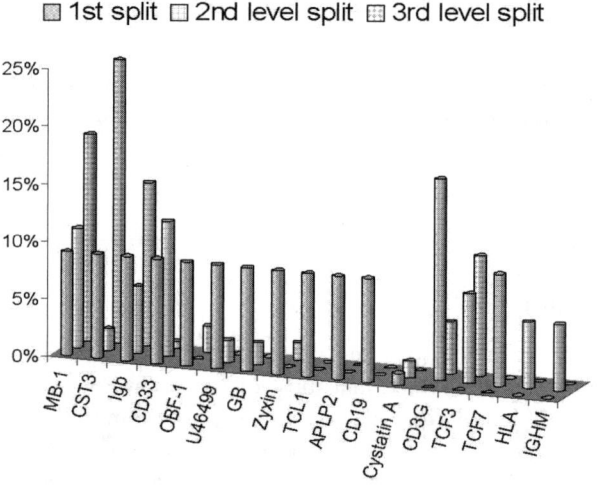

FIGURE 29.3
Frequencies of genes used in classifying leukemia data set. The 1st split, 2nd level split, and 3rd level split refers to the split of the root node, the split of the daughter nodes of the root node, and the split of the grand daughter nodes of the root node, respectively. Genes used with low frequencies are not shown.

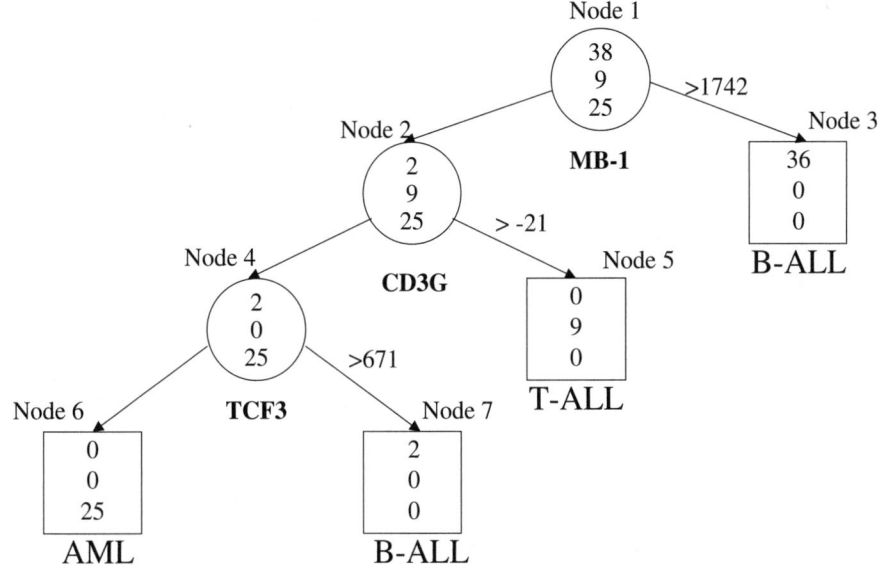

FIGURE 29.4
A tree structure based on the "most important" genes for the leukemia data set.

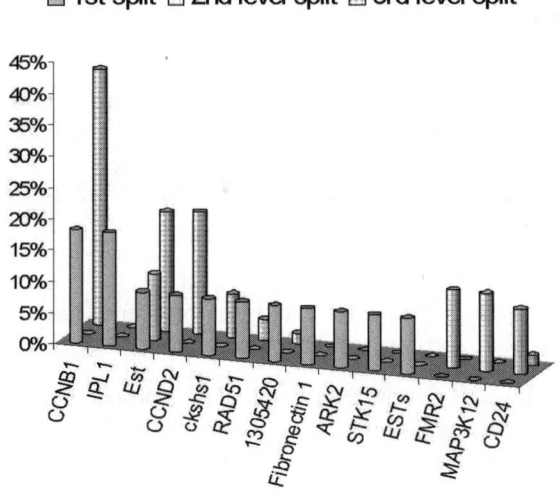

FIGURE 29.5
Frequencies of genes used in classifying lymphoma data set.

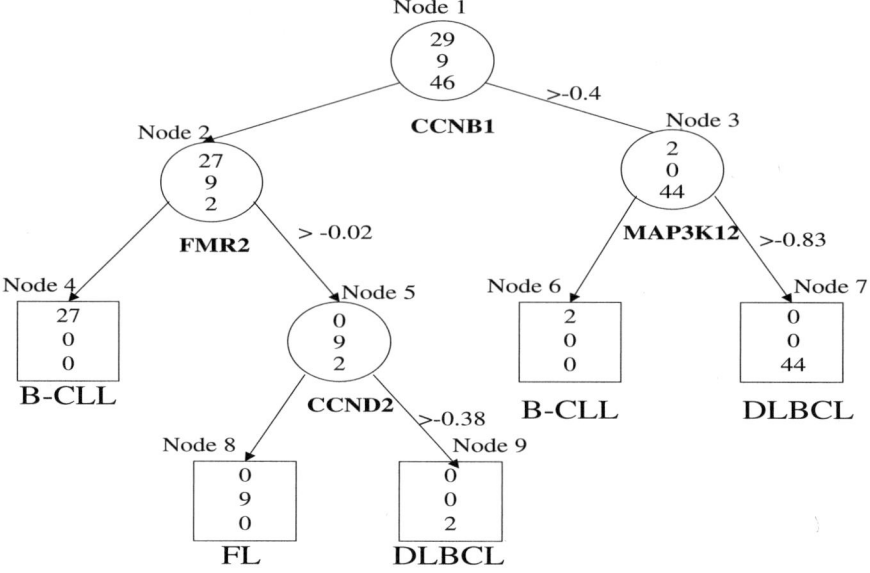

FIGURE 29.6
A tree structure based on the "most important" genes for the lymphoma data set.

Acknowledgments

This research was supported in part by NIH grants DA12468 and AA12044.

References

[1] Alizadeh, A. et al. (2000). Distinct types of diffuse large B-cell lymphoma identified by gene expression profiling. In *Nature*, 403, 503-511.

[2] Bai, M. et al. (2001). Low expression of p27 protein combined with altered p53 and Rb/p16 expression status is associated with increased expression of cyclin A and cyclin B1 in diffuse large B-cell lymphomas. In *Mod. Pathol.*, 14, 1105-1113.

[3] Breiman, L., Friedman, J., Stone, C., and Olshen, R. (1984). *Classification and Regression Trees*. Wadsworth, CA.

[4] Breiman, L. (2001). Random Forest. In *Machine Learning*, 45, 5–32.

[5] Brown, M. P. S. et al. (2000). Knowledge-based analysis of microarray gene expression data by using support vector machines. In *Proc. Natl. Acad. Sci. USA*, 97, 262–267.

[6] Delmer, A. et al. (1995). Overexpression of cyclin D2 in chronic B-cell malignancies. In *Blood*, 85, 2870–2876.

[7] Golub, T. R. et al. (1999). Molecular classification of cancer: Class discovery and class prediction by gene expression monitoring. In *Science*, 286, 531-537.

[8] Hashimoto, M., Yamashita, Y., and Mori, N. (2002). Immunohistochemical detection of CD79a expression in precursor T cell lymphoblastic lymphoma/leukaemias. In *J. Pathol.*, 197, 341–347.

[9] Herblot, S., Aplan P.D., and Hoang, T. (2002). Gradient of E2A activity in B-cell development. In *Mol. Cell. Biol.*, 22, 886–900.

[10] Moler, E. J., Chow, M. L., and Mian, I. S. (2000). Analysis of molecular profile data using generative and discriminative methods. In *Physiol. Genomics*, 4, 109–126.

[11] Nilson, I. et al. (1997). Exon/intron structure of the human AF-4 gene, a member of the AF-4/LAF-4/FMR-2 gene family coding for a nuclear protein with structural alterations in acute leukaemia. In *Br. J. Haematol.*, 98, 157–169.

[12] Xiong, M. M., Jin, L., Li, W., and Boerwinkle, E. (2000). Computational methods for gene expression-based tumor classification. In *Biotechniques*, 29, 1264–1270.

[13] Yu, L. M. and Chang T.W. (1992). Human mb-1 gene: complete cDNA sequence and its expression in B cells bearing membrane Ig of various isotypes. In *J. Immunol.*, 148, 633–637.

[14] Zhang, H. P. and Bracken, M. B. (1995). Tree-based risk factor analysis of preterm delivery and small-for-gestational-age birth. In *Amer. J. Epidemiol.*, 141, 70-78.

[15] Zhang, H. P., Holford, T., and Bracken, M. B. (1996). A tree-based method of analysis for prospective studies. In *Stat. Med.*, 15, 37-50.

[16] Zhang, H. P. and Singer, B. (1999). *Recursive Partitioning in the Health Sciences* Springer, New York.

[17] Zhang, H. P., Yu, C. Y, Singer, B., and Xiong, M. (2001). Recursive partitioning for tumor classification with gene expression microarray data. In *Proc. Natl. Acad. Sci. USA*, 98:, 6730–6735.

[18] Zhang, H. P. and Yu, C.Y. (2002a). Tree-based analysis of microarray data for classifying breast cancer. In *Front Biosci.*, 7, 63-67.

[19] Zhang, H. P. and Yu, C.Y. (2002). Cell and Tumor Classifications Using Gene Expression Data: Forests Versus Trees. Technical Report, Department of Epidemiology and Public Health, Yale University School of Medicine.

30

A Method Integrating Self-Organizing Maps to Predict the Probability of Barrier Removal

Zhicheng Zhang and Frédéric Vanderhaegen
University of Valenciennes, Le Mont Houy, France

CONTENTS

30.1 Introduction	498
30.2 A Method Integrating Self-Organizing Maps Algorithm	498
30.3 Experimental Results	503
30.4 Discussions	507
30.5 Conclusions	509
Acknowledgments	509
References	510

Barrier Removal (BR) is a particular violation in the field of human reliability analysis. The analysis of BR may be undertaken in terms of benefit, cost and possible deficit. Moreover, during the BR analysis, the data of all three indicators for each barrier class are usually provided in terms of some performance criteria, e.g., productivity, quality, safety and workload. This paper addresses the problem of how to balance the multi-variable BR data on different performance criteria and capture the complex nonlinear relationships that exist between these sub-criteria. The application of artificial intelligent techniques, which can analyze the multi-dimensional BR indicator data with the sophisticated visualization technique, is vital for the sustainable study of BR.

In this paper, the Self-Organizing Maps (SOM) algorithm is used in the analysis and modeling of BR study. The unsupervised SOM (USSOM), the supervised SOM (SSOM) and the Hierarchical SOM (HSOM) algorithms are used comparatively to support the anticipation of BR for a changed barrier and redesign the human machine system specifying new barriers. Based on the SOM maps obtained from the training, predictions can be made prospectively for a changed barrier, even if some barrier indicator data for the barrier are incomplete. The application of proposed method in the BR study for a series of experiments on a railway simulator illustrates its feasibility. It is concluded that the proposed method provides an effective analyzing and diagnosing tool to understand the interrelationships contained in the multi-dimensional BR data, and then to support the designer to reconfigure a barrier. It has considerable potential not only in the study of experimental situation, but also in the real-world practice.

30.1 Introduction

Human Reliability Analysis (HRA) is a primary analytical tool for risk management, in particular for predicting and preventing negative impacts of human error on complex systems' safety [1]. Designers of complex systems have to specify barriers to protect the corresponding human-machine system from the negative consequences of errors or failures [2]. Sometimes, users of such specified machines voluntarily do not respect the prescriptions of designers. Such a human behavioral deviation is a violation [3-5]. In the field of HRA, a safety related violation named as Barrier Removal (BR) has been recently taken into account [6-9]. It's a particular violation which is made without any intention to subjectively damage the human-machine system. When a barrier is to be removed, the users are facing a risk from which they were protected, but obtain an immediate benefit by compromising between performance criteria.

The analysis of BR can be undertaken in terms of benefit, cost and possible deficit [5,6]. In a survey, it has been concluded that the perceived risk and perceived benefit cannot be independently evaluated [10], as well as the possible deficit. There is often a compromise between them. Moreover, during the BR analysis, for each barrier class, the data of all three indicators (benefit, cost, possible deficit) are provided in terms of some sub-criteria, e.g., productivity, quality, safety and workload. In order to balance three BR indicators on different performance criteria and then to anticipate removal result so as to redesign the barrier, an artificial neural network method, which can analyze the multi-dimensional BR indicator data with the sophisticated visualization technique, is developed in the following section. And the third section applies it to a railway simulator experimentation. Some issues are discussed in Section 30.4, and conclusions are drawn in the final section.

30.2 A Method Integrating Self-Organizing Maps Algorithm

30.2.1 Problematic in BR Data Analysis

According to Hollnagel [14], a barrier is defined as an obstacle, an obstruction or a hindrance that may either:

- prevent an action from being carried out or a situation to occur,
- prevent or lessen the severity of negative consequences.

Four classes of barriers are distinguished as material, functional, symbolic and immaterial barriers. Based on the identification of two barrier groups according to the physical presence or absence of four classes of barriers [6], a model of the removal of a given barrier that integrates three distinct attributes has been developed by considering both the positive and the negative consequences of such a human behavior [13].

The consequences of BR consist of direct consequences:

- The immediate **cost** of removal: in order to remove a barrier the human operator has to modify sometimes the material structure, and/or the operational mode of use. That usually leads to an increase in workload and may also have negative consequences on productivity or quality. These negative consequences are immediate and acceptable by the users.

- The expected **benefit**: a barrier removal is goal driven. Removing a barrier is immediately beneficial and the benefits outweigh the costs, i.e., they are sufficiently high to accept to support the costs.

Secondly, a barrier that is removed introduces a potentially dangerous situation, i.e., there may be some potential consequences. So, the removal of a barrier has also a **possible deficit** considered by users as a latent and unacceptable negative consequence.

The relationships between three BR indicators at a given time t can be shown as in Figure 30.1. In Figure 30.1, there are some extreme cases from the theoretical point of view, e.g., the partial zone of "benefit" in which there is not any overlapped part with "cost" and "possible deficit" means that the benefit of BR is 100%, and relative cost and possible deficit are nonexistent or insignificant. If this zone is located at the area overlapped with "cost" and non-overlapped with "possible deficit," that means that there is compromise between "benefit" and "cost," the possible deficit of the BR is nonexistent or insignificant.

Usually, the decision on the removal of a barrier is made among three indicators; a compromise between these attributes determines the decision of either removing or respecting a barrier.

Moreover, during the BR analysis, for each barrier, the levels of all three indicators may be provided in terms of, e.g., four performance criteria: productivity, quality, safety and workload. An example of the data variables is given in Table 30.1.

Based on this kind of multi-dimensional data, it isn't very easy to capture the complex nonlinear relationships that exist between these sub-criteria, nor to know the similarity of all barriers; Secondly, when the (re)design of a new barrier needs to be implemented, it's better to predict, first of all, its prospective removal probability, then retrospectively, to integrate the user's viewpoint during the early phase of the (re)design. To this end, a Hierarchical SOM algorithm-based method is proposed in the following text. This is a framework which is intended for assessing the different type of BR data.

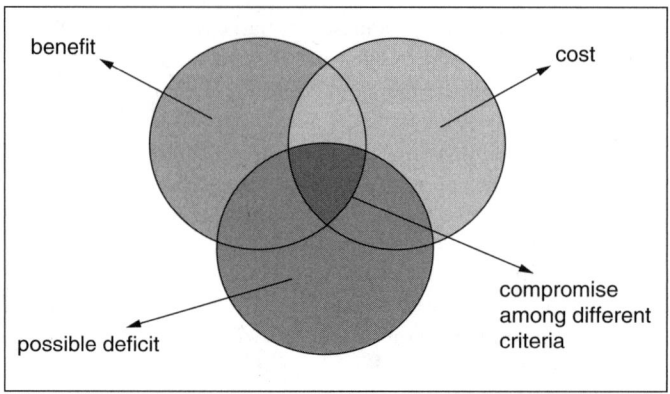

FIGURE 30.1
Three BR attributes and their compromises.

1. Productivity-based criteria	{benefit-productivity, cost-productivity, possible deficit-productivity}
2. Quality-based criteria	{benefit-quality, cost-quality, possible deficit-quality}
3. Safety-based criteria	{benefit-safety, cost-safety, possible deficit-safety}
4. Workload-based criteria	{benefit-workload, cost-workload, possible deficit-workload}

TABLE 30.1
An example of the data variables for BR analysis with 12 variables.

30.2.2 A Hierarchical SOM (HSOM) Algorithm-Based Method

Currently, there have been various neural networks that are being studied. Based on their characteristics, the neural network architectures may be classified into three categories (Figure 30.2) [12]. In Figure 30.2, feedforward networks transform sets of input signals into sets of output signals. The desired input-output transformation is usually determined by external, supervised adjustment of the system parameters. In feedback networks (recurrent), the input information defines the initial activity state of a feedback system. After state transitions, the asymptotic final state is identified as the outcome of the computation. In competitive, unsupervised or self-organizing category neurons, the neighboring neurons in the network compete in their activities and develop iteratively specific detectors for different input signal patterns.

Basically, competitive neural networks are designed to solve the type of problems where the output we require is unknown (unsupervised learning). The output required in such a situation is clusters or categories into which the input falls depending on its similarity with other input. If we use the unsupervised learning algorithm and place the neurons in some sort of order such as a line or a grid, we may wish to

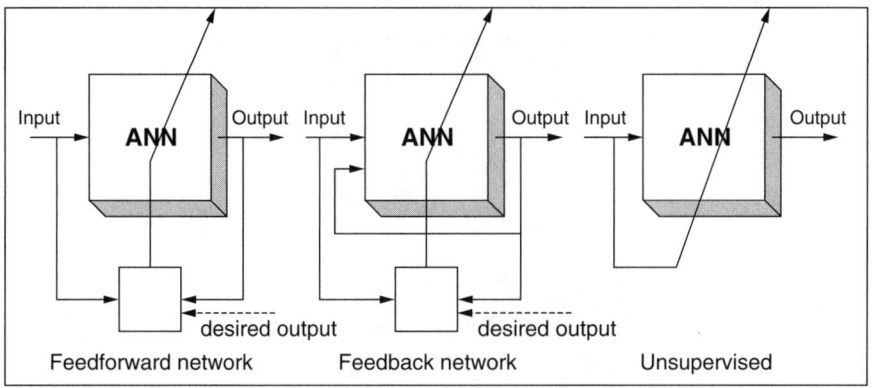

FIGURE 30.2
Neural network models' dotted line illustrates the training scheme.

use information regarding the locations of the nearby winning output units to determine the similarity of input vectors in n-dimensional space. For instance, if ξ_x and ξ_y are two input vectors, K_1 and K_2 are the locations of the corresponding winning output then K_1 and K_2 should get closer as ξ_x and ξ_y get closer. Neural networks such as this are called feature maps. The principle idea behind feature maps is to create a neural network with topology preserving characteristics. Feature maps are trained on input vectors using rules that aim to iteratively arrange the neurons in the maps so as to approximate the topology-preserving properties. Thus the paradigm is often referred to as Self-Organizing Maps (SOM).

The SOM algorithm is based on the unsupervised learning principle [15, 16]. It has been applied extensively within entire fields of industry ranging from engineering sciences to medicine, from biology to economics [11, 17]. The SOM can be used at the same time to both deduce the amount of data by clustering, and for projecting the data nonlinearity onto a lower-dimensional display. Figure 30.3 shows a 12-dimensional input vector projected into 2-dimensional space.

The SOM consist of two layers: the input layer and competitive layer (output layer) which is usually a two-dimensional grid. Both of these layers are fully interconnected. The input layer has as many neurons as it has indicator data (e.g., safety-based criteria: benefit-safety, cost-safety, possible deficit-safety). Let m be the number of neurons in the input layer, and let n the number of neurons in the output layer which are arranged in a rectangular or hexagonal patterns (see Figure 30.3 and Figure 30.4). Each neuron in the input layer is connected to each neuron in the output layer. Thus, each neuron in the output layer has m connections to the input layer. Each one of these connections has a synaptic weight associated with it. Let W_j be the weight vector associated with the connection between m input neurons $i = 1,\ldots,m$ and one output $j = 1,\ldots,n$. The neurons of the maps are connected to adjacent neurons by a neighborhood relation. Each neuron k is represented by an m-

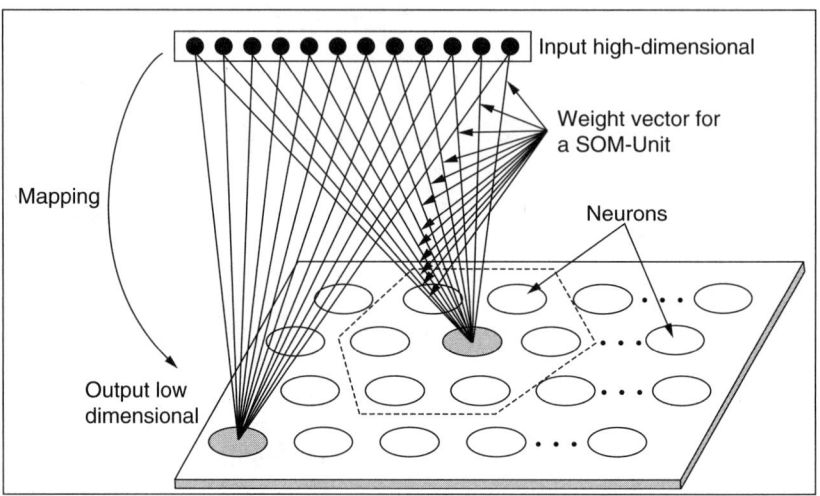

FIGURE 30.3
Graphical illustration of a SOM architecture.

dimensional prototype vector $W_k = [W_{k1}, \ldots, W_{km}]$, where $k = j = 1, \ldots, n$. On each training step, a data sample ξ is selected and the nearest unit, best matching unit (BMU),* is found from the map. The prototype vectors of the BMU and its neighbors on the grid are moved towards the sample vector. A high-dimensional vector is mapped into a lower-dimensional space.

During the BR experiments, it was observed that there were some BR indicator data whose corresponding removal results have been registered whereas some BR data had not had this type of registration. In order to deal with not only the data set with the removal recording but also the data set without the removal recording, a Hierarchical SOM (HSOM) framework is proposed as Figure 30.5; its algorithm procedure is shown in the Table 30.4. For the data set with the removal recording, supervised SOM (SSOM) algorithm is used (see Table 30.3), and for those data without the removal recording, unsupervised SOM (USSOM) algorithm (see Table 30.2) may therefore be integrated with the relative observations to identify the corresponding output neuron groups.

Supervised learning here means that the classification of each ξ_s in the training set is known; the corresponding ξ_s (refer to the Table 30.3) value must be used during the training [15]. In the process of recognition of a redesigned barrier indicator data ξ, only its ξ_s part is compared with the corresponding part of weight vectors.

Based on the corresponding HSOM maps obtained from the training, predictions can be made prospectively for a redesigned/reconfigured barrier, even if some bar-

---

*BMU: the output layer neuron whose weight vector is closest to the input vector ξ is called Best-Matching Unit (BMU).

Statistical Data Mining and Knowledge Discovery

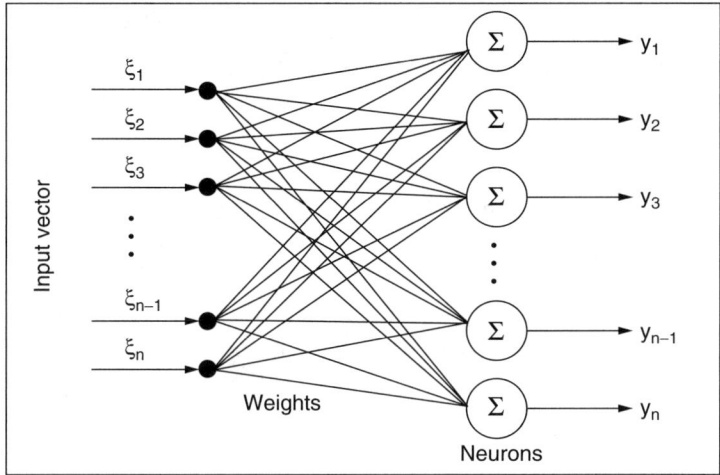

FIGURE 30.4
The basic SOM structure.

rier indicator data for the barrier are incomplete/missing. It may therefore be, as a decision making support, used to analyze both the qualitative and quantitative BR indicator data.

30.3 Experimental Results

To study the feasibility of BR analysis, some railway experiments have been implemented on an experimental platform. The platform simulates train movements from some depots to other ones by crossing several exchange stations on which human operators convert products placed on the stopped train. In the process of the train traffic flow controlled by a human controller, several risks have been identified. In order to limit relative risks and to control the traffic flow, several barriers have been proposed. They are composed by the immaterial barriers and the material barriers [5]. Immaterial barriers such as procedures that constrain the human controllers' behavior are exemplified by respect for timing knowing that it is better to be in advance.

Besides the immaterial barriers, there are material barriers such as signals with which human controllers have to interact:

- Signals to prevent traffic problems related to the inputs and the outputs of trains from depots.
- Signals to prevent traffic problems at the shunting device.
- Signals to control inputs and outputs at the transformation areas.

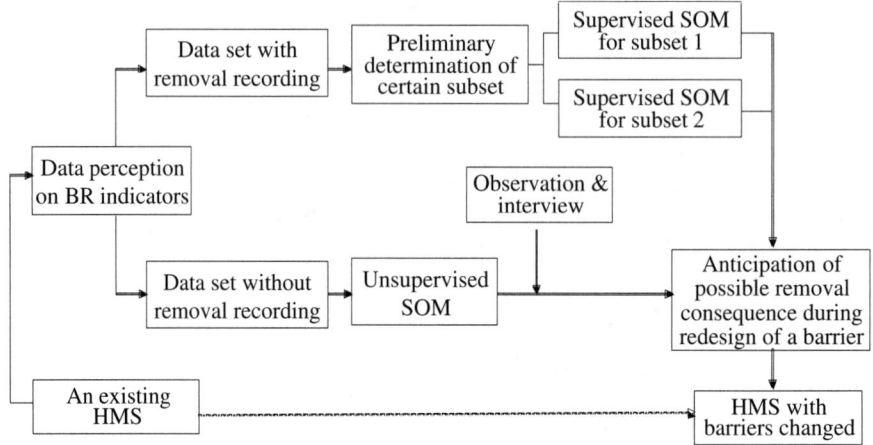

FIGURE 30.5
A hierarchical SOM (HSOM) flowchart.

- Signals to inform the treatment of the content of a train is in course.

During the experiments in which the proposed HSOM was applied, human controllers could select the signals that they wanted to remove or maintain; that means (s)he may remove several barriers which were being judged as removable. After the experiment, they answer a questionnaire on the evaluation of the interest of the removal of family of barriers in terms of benefit, cost, possible deficit. They should take into account four performance criteria:

- The quality related to the advancement of the planning.
- The production related to the percentage of product treated at the stations.
- The traffic safety in terms of:
    - Collision,
    - Derailment,
    - Synchronization of movement announcement message at transformation stations.
- The human workload related to the occupational rate.

The study of collected data (totally 1600 sample units have been used for the multiperformance mode) according to different criteria has been implemented. SOM Toolbox [15] has been used for some basic function computations. All the computer code including the prediction process have been finalized in MATLAB 5.3 and 6.0.

For a same barrier and its three BR indicators, there are different values from the different performance criteria of the human-machine system. BC indicators can be compared between different barriers and different controllers. The SSOM algorithm

USSOM 1:	Determine the topology of the map and the number of the neurons, e.g., if the number of data samples is given as p, the number of the neurons can be determined with a heuristic formula of $5\sqrt{p}$; 2D grid is suitable for the BR data analysis [9] and the hexagonal grid can usually represent the forms of the barrier classes better than the rectangular one [15].
USSOM 2:	Initialize the weight vectors with small random values. The initial $W_j(j=1,\ldots,n)$ are given small random values, or other initialization methods can be adopted which allows the computation/training of the SOM faster (e.g., W_j are initialized linearly) [16].
USSOM 3:	Choose the next training sample vector in the training data set.
USSOM 4:	Choose the BMU neurons W_c, which is closest to the input vector $\xi(t)$ according to $$\|\xi - W_c\| = \min \|\xi - W_j\| (j=1,\ldots,n)$$ where $\|\cdot\|$ is the distance measure. The BMU, denoted as c, is the unit whose weight vector has the greatest similarity with the input sample. The similarity is usually defined by means of a distance measure, typically Euclidian distance.
USSOM 5:	Update Wc(t) and other neurons belonging to its topological neighborhood towards the sample $\xi(t)$ according to: $$W_j(t+1) = \begin{cases} W_j(t) + \eta\phi[\xi(t) - W_j(t)] & \forall i \in N_c(t), \\ W_j(t) & \forall i \notin N_c(t), \end{cases}$$ where η is learning rate, ϕ is the neighborhood function, $0 \le \eta\phi \le 1$. The learning rate η is decreased during time and forces the weight vector to converge in the training process.
USSOM 6:	Stop, if some optimal number of iteration steps is done, or else continue from step 3.

TABLE 30.2
The USSOM algorithm.

has been used in the analysis of experimental data in terms of mono-performance mode (3 input dimensions) and multi-performance mode (21 input dimensions) [9]. Seven mono-performance modes are (an example of its input vector can be found in Table 30.6):

1. The quality related to the advancement of the planning;

2. The production related to the percentage of product treated at the stations;

3. The face-to-face collision;

4. The overtaking collision;

5. The derailment;

6. The synchronization of movement announcement message at transformation stations;

7. The workload related to the occupational rate.

SSOM 1:	Determine the topology of the map and the number of the neurons.
SSOM 2:	Initialize the weight vectors with small random values.
SSOM 3:	Present the input feature vector in the training data set. Input vectors are formed of two parts ξ_s and ξ_u, where ξ_s is the BR indicator data vector whose structure is same as the one of the USSOM algorithm, and ξ_u is the label vector in which the removal result is taken into account.
SSOM 4:	Similar steps like USSOM4, USSOM5, USSOM6.

TABLE 30.3
The SSOM algorithm.

HSOM 1:	Collection of acquired BR indicator data. Skip to HSOM 4 if encountered data set include the removal recording.
HSOM 2:	Apply USSOM (Table 30.2).
HSOM 3:	Identify corresponding barrier classes with relative observations.
HSOM 4:	Preliminary determination of certain parallel subset, e.g., experimental BR data may be grouped into several subset in terms of controllers' nationalities (two subset in the section 3). The SSOM (Table 30.3) can be used in the training of each subset.
HSOM 5:	Identification of indicator data for a redesigned barrier.
HSOM 6:	Provide a predictive removal probability for the redesigned barrier.

TABLE 30.4
The HSOM algorithm.

In the multi-performance mode, seven above mentioned performance criteria are taken into account entirely and comprehensively; there are 21 variables (21 dimensional input data for the part $g\xi_s$) for each barrier in the input layer.

In the USSOM training, there is only one label that indicates the identification and the observation result of corresponding barrier, e.g., (Where "*Cro1B1*" means controller No.1 and the first barrier for him, the observation result is "removed"), Table 30.5.

In the SSOM training, there is another separate label (see Table 30.6) that contains the recorded removal information besides barrier identification. The difference between the SSOM and the USSOM is that ξ_u in SSOM algorithm encompasses not only the identification label, but also the removal label (first label of each barrier indicator data, e.g., "Yes")

To illustrate the feasibility of the proposed method, the previous 15 controllers were selected as the training set. Once the training is completed, the following 4 controllers were considered as the prediction set. Both the SSOM and the USSOM algorithms were used in the prediction of the removal results for the 4 controllers in terms of (mono-)multi-performance mode. Table 30.7 shows the comparison of the prediction accuracies. Here the prediction accuracy is defined as:

Statistical Data Mining and Knowledge Discovery 507

ξ_s Part			ξ_u Part
benefit-safety	cost-safety	possible deficit-safety	Identification
0.8	0.2	0.2	Cro1B1
......			......
0.2	0.2	1.0	Non7B4
......			......

TABLE 30.5
The composition of input vector for USSOM.

ξ_s Part			ξ_u Part	
benefit-safety	cost-safety	possible deficit-safety	Removal	Identification
0.8	0.2	0.2	Yes	Cro1B1
......			......	
0.2	0.2	1.0	No	Non7B4
......			......	

TABLE 30.6
The composition of input vector for SSOM.

$$Accuracy = \frac{\sum N(s)}{\sum_{i=1}^{m} N(\xi i)}$$

where $N(s)$ is number of scenarios which have same predictive removal status as ones from the observations, $N(\xi_i)$, $i = 1,\ldots,m$ means the total number of scenarios whose removal results have been anticipated.

In Table 30.7, for the same BR experimental data, USSOM and SSOM have been used respectively to provide the prediction for the following 4 controllers, and the prediction accuracies have been calculated with the above formula. It can be seen from the table that the SSOM algorithm may give a little bit better prediction rates for the same data set (column "USSOM" and "SSOM"). And it can be seen also that the HSOM gives the best prediction results (column "HSOM"). Although USSOM provides the lowest prediction rate, it has its own inherent advantage, as it doesn't need the removal recoding for the training. Additionally, in multi-performance mode, it is noted that, with the HSOM, the BR data can be analyzed in terms of any combination of the performance criteria if necessary.

30.4 Discussions

Three algorithms, USSOM, SSOM and HSOM, have been used respectively to predict the barrier removal status in this paper; their prediction accuracies are compared.

Performance mode	Criteria	Prediction accuracies		
		USSOM	SSOM	HSOM
Mono-performance mode	Quality	31%	75%	69%
	Productivity	25%	50%	57%
	Face-to-face collision	31%	44%	60%
	Overtaking collision	38%	56%	66%
	Derailment	31%	44%	57%
	Synchronization	56%	56%	54%
	Workload	56%	63%	51%
	Sub-means	38%	55%	59%
Multi-performance mode	Synthetic /comprehensive	50%	56%	82%

TABLE 30.7
The comparison of the prediction accuracies between USSOM, SSOM and HSOM.

It can be seen from Table 30.7 that the prediction accuracies of the multi-performance mode are higher than the ones of the mono-performance mode. More BR indicators (21 variables) in the multi-performance mode are taken into account during the training, whereas BR indicators (3 variables) in each mono-performance mode are put into the training. It indicates that the BR behaviour description of human controllers from the multi-viewpoint is better than the one from the mono-viewpoint.

However, during the identification of the final removal result, a barrier has been judged "removed" so long as one barrier in the same class is removed. In the same class, several barriers have similar features and functions, e.g., there are totally 6 signals for input/output movements at the depots. Some controllers removed a few signals, and the others removed all 6 signals; both of the cases have been identified "removed" at this stage.

It has been found out that there is a difference between the barriers which belong to same barrier class in the questionnaire sheets, e.g., it was observed that the signals for output movements at the depots are always removed; in contrast, the ones for input movement were sometimes respected. So the prediction accuracy may be higher if the barrier class could be further detailed in the questionnaire in the future.

The prediction accuracy of HSOM is the mean value of two SSOM subset prediction rates. The two subset are grouped by the controllers' nationalities in the paper. The data can be equally grouped by other ways.

Notice that, during the data analysis of BR experiments, for each barrier, besides the four performance criteria: productivity, quality, safety and workload, there is also another criterion which may affect controllers' behaviors, e.g., individual advantage criteria such as motivation, free time, etc. The study incorporating these criteria may lead to the identification of new BR indicator.

Additionally, the perception error of risk should be considerably pointed out. During the experiment, the human controller estimates by him/herself the qualitative levels of each indicator in terms of four performance criteria. Moreover, it was the first time for all testers to participate in the experiments; the perception error of risk is therefore unavoidable. It may be partly corrected by comparing the corresponding objective performance data measured during the experiments.

There were more than 20 controllers who have participated in the experiments. The predictive error may arise in cases where less data are available. The more numerous the BR data are, the more realistic and objective the anticipation of BR probability will be.

30.5 Conclusions

The Self-Organizing Map (SOM) is an effective neural network for analysis and visualization of high-dimensional data. It maps nonlinear statistical relationships between high-dimensional input data into simple geometric relationships on a usual two-dimensional grid. The mapping preserves the most important topological and metric relationships of the original data elements and, thus, inherently clusters the data. Based on the SOM maps obtained from the training set, predictions can be made for the unknown/redesigned barriers. Prospective analysis can be equally implemented to foresee the predictive removal probability for the barrier. This can be used to support the evaluation of existing barriers and the (re)design process.

At this stage of the experiments, the BR analysis only focuses on the subjective indicator data anyway the BR analysis based on the objective performance data could be implemented. Moreover, the HSOM proposed in this paper has been applied to the analysis of data from the railway experiments. By comparing between USSOM, SSOM and HSOM algorithms for the same BR data set, the proposed HSOM is found out to have the highest prediction rate. Depending on the experience feedback in some real industry fields, the further validation of HSOM should be performed.

It is argued that because of the complex nonlinear relationships between the BR variables, classical linear statistical methods are unreliable and not so easy to visualize the results. As artificial neural network approaches, using the HSOM algorithm to model the encountered problems in BR analysis is an efficient way to study multi-dimensional BR data. In the future, the comparative BR study with other potentially suitable approaches could be planned and implemented. The final refined method will be applied in an European 5th Framework Programme, Urban Guided Transport Management System (*UGTMS*).

Acknowledgments

The railway experimental simulator platform was developed by LAMIH at the University of Valenciennes (France), in collaboration with Delft University of Technology (Netherlands). Authors would like to thank P. Polet , P. Wieringa, and students from the Technical University of Delft and from the University of Valenciennes for their contribution to this project.

References

Kirwan, B. (1997). The development of a nuclear chemical plant human reliability management approach: HRMS and JHEDI, *Reliability Engineering and System Safety*, 56, pp. 107-133.

Kecklund L. J., Edland A., Wedin P., and Svenson, O. (1996). Safety barrier function analysis in a process industry: a nuclear power application. *International Journal of Industrial Ergonomics*, 17, pp. 275-284.

Reason, J. (1990). *Human error*, Cambridge University Press, New York.

Isaac, A., Shorrock, S. T., and Kirwan, B. (2002). Human error in European air traffic management: the HERA project, *Reliability Engineering and System Safety*, 75, pp. 257-272.

Vanderhaegen, F., Polet, P., Zhang, Z., and Wieringa P. A. (2002). Barrier removal study in railway simulation, *PSAM 6*, Puerto Rico, USA, June.

Polet P., Vanderhaegen F., and Wieringa P.A. (2001). Theory of safety-related violations of system barriers, *Cognition, Technology and Work*, accepted in 2002, to be published.

Zhang Z., Polet P., and Vanderhaegen V. (2002). Toward a decision making support of Barrier Removal, 21st European Annual Conference on Human Decision Making and Control, Glasgow, Scotland, July.

Polet, P., Vanderhaegen, F., and Amalberti, R.(2001). Modeling border-line tolerated conditions of use (*BTCUs*) and associated risks. *Safety Science*, accepted in 2001, to be published.

Zhang Z., Polet P., Vanderhaegen V., and Millot P. (2002). Towards a method to analyze the problematic level of Barrier Crossing, *lm13/Esrel2002*, Lyon, France, pp. 71-80.

Mccormick, N. J. (1981). *Reliability and Risk Analysis, Methods and Nuclear Power Applications*, Academic Press, Inc., New York.

Simula, O., Vesanto, J., Alhoniemi, E., and Hollmen, J. (1999). *Analysis and Modeling of Complex Systems Using the Self-Organizing Map*, Springer-Verlag, Heidelberg, pp. 3-22.

Kohonen, T. (1990). The self-organizing map, *Proceedings of the IEEE*, Vol. 78(9), pp. 1464-1480.

Polet, P., Vanderhaegen, F., Millot, P., and Wieringa, P. (2001). Barriers and risk analysis, 8th *IFAC/IFIP/IFORS/IEA Symposium on Analysis*, Design and Evaluation of Man-Machine Systems, Kassel, Germany.

Hollnagel, E. (1999). Accident and barriers, 7th *European Conference on Cognitive*

Science Approaches to Process Control, Villeneuve d'Ascq, France, pp. 175-180.

Kohonen, T. (2001). *Self-Organizing Maps*. Third edition, Springer-Verlag, Heidelberg.

Kohonen, T. (1998). Self-organizing map, *Neurocomputing*, 21(1), pp. 1-6.

Kaski, S., Kangas, J., and Kohonen, T. (1998). Bibliography of self-organizing map (SOM) papers: 1981-1997, *Neural Computing Surveys*, Vol. 1.

European Commission, GROWTH Work programme 2001-2002, Work programme for RTD actions in support of "*Competitive and sustainable growth*" 1998-2002 Edition, December 2000.

31

Cluster Analysis of Imputed Financial Data Using an Augmentation-Based Algorithm

H. Bensmail and R. P. DeGennaro
University of Tennessee, Knoxville, TN, USA

CONTENTS

31.1 Introduction 513
31.2 Data and Preliminary Tests 514
31.3 Clustering and Bayesian Data Augmentation 518
31.4 Bayesian Model Selection for Choosing the Number of   Clusters 523
31.5 Analysis of Financial Data 523
31.6 Discussion 525
    Acknowledgments 526
    References 526

This paper introduces and applies a new statistical modelling technique to carry out cluster analysis on imputed financial companies data that offer a direct investment plan. We show how this new method correctly classifies the companies without Dividend Reinvestment Plans (DRIPS), and determines misclassified companies.

31.1 Introduction

In this paper, we introduce and apply a novel statistical modelling technique based on the on-going work of Bensmail and Bozdogan (2003a,b) to cluster analyze imputed financial data (DeGennaro 2003). We have two main purposes to achieve: one, to forecast (supervised clustering), and two, to find homogeneous groups within the data (unsupervised clustering). We stress that this is a flexible modelling approach in the following sense: we handle large and complex data structures with missing observations with mixed structure, that is, data types with both quantitative and qualitative measurements present. We achieve this by mapping the data to a new structure which is free of distributional assumptions in choosing homogeneous groups of observations (Bensmail and Bozdogan 2002).

    Classification methods have a long history of productive uses in business and finance. Perhaps the most common are discrete choice models. Among these, the multinomial logit approach has been used at least as far back as Holman and Marley (in Luce and Suppes, 1965). McFadden (1978) introduced the Generalized Extreme Value model in his study of residential location. Koppelman and Wen (1997) and Vovsha (1997) have recently developed newer variations. The nested logit model of Ben-Akiva (1973) is designed to handle correlations among alternatives. Other variations of multinomial logic have been developed or used by Koppelman and Wen (1997) and Bierlaire, Lotan, and Toint (1997). More recently, Calhoun and Deng (2000) use multinomial logit models to study loan terminations.

Another form of discrete choice model is cluster analysis. Shaffer (1991) is one example. He studies federal deposit insurance funding and considers its influence on taxpayers. Dalhstedt, Salmi, Luoma, and Laakkonen (1994) use cluster analysis to demonstrate that comparing financial ratios across firms is problematic. They argue that care is necessary even when the firms belong to the same official International Standard Industrial Classification category. von Altrock (1995) explains how fuzzy logic, a variation of cluster analysis, can be useful in practical business applications.

Though not discrete choice models, methods that produce a continuous variable can be used as classification methods. For example, credit scoring uses information to produce a continuous variable called the credit score. Lending institutions overlay this continuous score with a grid, producing discrete categories. For example, applicants with a score below a certain point might be rejected automatically. Applicants above a specified higher point may be accepted automatically. Scores falling between these trigger points might be given further investigation. See Mester (1997) for an example. Altman (2000) follows a somewhat similar approach to update the popular method of zeta analysis.

Related to the problem of classifying data is the issue of determining the number of categories. Some methods can determine the number of classes without providing evidence on which observations fall within each class. For example, Baillie and Bollerslev (1989) use cointegration methods to study the number of common stochastic trends in a system of exchange rates. In this case, it makes little economic sense to attempt to classify exchange rates along some dimension. Instead, Baillie and Bollerslev calculate the number of common stochastic trends to gain insight regarding the extent of market efficiency and potentially profitable trading opportunities.

31.2 Data and Preliminary Tests

We apply this new approach to a sample of companies that offer direct investment plans and a corresponding, size-matched set of companies without such plans. Dividend Reinvestment Plans and a more general class of investments, Direct Investment Plans, allow investors to avoid investment channels typically used in the past, such as securities brokers. A Dividend Reinvestment Plan is a mechanism that permits shareholders to reinvest their dividends in additional shares automatically. No broker is involved, unless he is the agent of the plan administrator. If the firm does not restrict its plan to current shareholders, then the plan is also what is called a Direct Investment Plan, also known as a Super DRIP. Transactions costs are typically much lower than when using traditional brokerage accounts.

DRIPS are not a different class of security, such as swaps or options. They are simply a new way of selling the traditional equity security. The privileges and obligations of equity ownership are unchanged. For example, DRIP investors receive the usual mailings and they retain all voting rights. Tax implications are unaffected, and stock splits are handled exactly as if the investor were using a traditional brokerage account. Readers seeking more detailed information about such plans should see DeGennaro (2003).

Data are from the firms listed in The Guide to Dividend Reinvestment Plans (1999) and the Compustat data base. These data are a subset of those used in the forthcoming work of DeGennaro (2003), and include 36 financial variables. Because DRIP firms tend to be much larger in terms of total assets than companies without such plans (DeGennaro, 2001), we match the 906 DRIP companies with available data to a sample of firms without such plans, for a total of 1812 companies. We use total assets in 1999 as our matching variable. Some companies have missing values for certain variables, but this is not a serious problem given the new proposed method; indeed one of the strengths of this approach is that it handles such characteristics. From the perspective of the financial economist, these data provide information that may let us determine the likelihood that companies without plans will adopt one. Given the results of Dubofsky and Bierman (1988), the ability to predict such an adoption before the marginal investor can do so represents a potentially profitable trading opportunity. In addition, companies that administer direct investment plans that seek new customers can produce a list of firms most likely to be interested in purchasing their services. The reverse is also possible: we can improve our predictions of which companies are likely to abandon their plans, and plan administrators can improve their predictions about which customers are at greatest risk to become former customers. Predicting changes in plan terms may also be possible.

Table 31.1 presents sample statistics. Only three variables (Total Assets, Net Income, and After Tax Return on Total Assets) have no missing values. Five variables are only available for financial institutions, so about six of every seven observations is missing for these. Still, we have upwards of 1650 observations for most variables. Note that the two S&P rating codes are categorical.

Because of certain screens to eliminate extreme observations (DeGennaro, 2003), almost all observations on all variables lie within a reasonable range. Exceptions occur for certain ratios with denominators near zero. For example, Compustat defines the Payout Ratio as essentially the dollar amount of dividends paid to common shareholders divided by earnings. Because earnings can be near zero, ratios can be large in absolute value. Even these cases, though, are relatively rare.

Table 31.2 contains the number of observations for the subsets of firms with and without DRIPs, and where meaningful, the means for each group. It also reports t-ratios testing the equality of the means. The first question of interest is the efficacy

TABLE 31.1
Sample statistics

Variable	N	Mean	Std Dev	Minimum	Maximum
Total Assets MM$	1,812	14,140.70	45,776.10	6.38	575,167
Property, Plant and Equipment MM$	1,682	2,534.27	6,332.99	0	94,043
Property, Plant, and Equipment (Capital Expenditures) MM$	1,463	510.6	1,762.14	-5.7	30,549
Research and Development Expense MM$	698	262.93	799.06	0	7,100
Net Sales MM$	1,809	5,289.74	13,163.40	0	173,215
Payout Ratio	1,755	36.1	166.41	-3,626.04	3,192.31
Dividend Yield	1,682	2.81	10.15	0	394.45
Common Shares Outstanding MM	1,765	194.88	460.09	0	6,133.40
Common Shares Traded	1,680	165.82	514.06	0	8,129.70
Treasury Stock - Number of Common Shares MM	1,775	9.79	47.32	0	994.8
Common Shareholders M	1,387	36.92	156.99	0	4,206.32
Employees M	1,620	21.33	54.26	0	1,140
Sale of Common and Preferred Stock MM$	1,469	105.11	468.08	-1.44	10,694.70
Purchase of Common and Preferred Stock MM$	1,417	123.02	431.38	-0.12	6,645
Pretax Income MM$	1,810	547.68	1,503.17	-3,889	15,942
Net Income (Loss) MM$	1,812	358.58	1,016.22	-2,501.60	10,717
S&P Senior Debt Rating Code	1,038	10.21	3.47	2	27
S&P Commercial Paper Rating - Historical Code	500	102.33	0.91	101	107
Risk-Adjusted Capital Ratio (Tier 1)	255	10.4	3.95	5.6	34.7
Risk-Adjusted Capital Ratio (Total)	259	13.75	5.14	6.9	57.06
Non-performing Assets MM$	261	93.96	313.5	0	3,075
Provision for Loan/Asset Losses MM$	267	77.58	288.02	-175	2,837
Net Interest Margin (Ratio)	262	4.03	1.06	0.85	12.24
Interest Expense Per Share	1,417	4.74	100.12	0	3,628.12
Net Profit Margin	1,807	4.75	47.96	-1,324.84	726.95
PreTax Interest Coverage	1,470	22.48	474.47	-7,122.29	14,481.70
PreTax Profit Margin	1,807	8.87	56.58	-1,324.84	1,187.23
PreTax Return On Assets	1,810	4.8	11.4	-117.33	157.33
Operating Income Before Depreciation to Total Assets	1,682	10.25	10.02	-97.89	80.2
After Tax Interest Coverage	1,470	16.35	466.84	-8,144.57	14,480.50
After Tax Return On Common Equity	1,801	9.8	270.12	-6,812.12	8,563.59
After Tax Return On Total Assets	1,812	2.78	9.73	-117.33	157.33
Debt Ratio	1,810	0.69	0.23	0	2.74
Market To Book	1,669	2.96	8.82	-238.17	121.53
P/E at Fiscal Year End	1,682	18.39	101.13	-1,693.80	1,437.50
Earnings Per Share	1,727	1.68	9.11	-51.66	276.02

TABLE 31.2
Means and t-tests, 906 companies with DRIP plans compared to 906 companies without.

Variable	Number of Observations		Mean		t-statistic
	No plan	DRIP plan	No plan	DRIP plan	
Total Assets MM$	906	906	14,412	13,870	0.25
Property, Plant and Equipment MM$	851	831	2,428	2,644	-0.7
Property, Plant, and Equipment (Capital Expenditures) MM$	751	712	535.05	484.81	0.54
Research and Development Expense MM$	317	381	265.96	260.4	0.09
Net Sales MM$	904	905	4,737	5,842	-1.79
PayoutRatio	875	880	19.34	52.77	-4.23**
Dividend Yield	777	905	1.46	3.96	-5.07**
Common Shares Outstanding MM	862	903	181.43	207.73	-1.2
Common Shares Traded	774	906	191.9	143.56	1.92
Treasury Stock - Number of Common Shares MM	884	891	5.16	14.39	-4.12**
Common Shareholders M	675	712	23.46	49.65	-3.17**
Employees M	800	820	18.49	24.1	-2.08*
Sale of Common and Preferred Stock MM$	757	712	155.93	51.07	4.32**
Purchase of Common and Preferred Stock MM$	706	711	75.49	170.21	-4.16**
Pretax Income MM$	905	905	473.8	621.55	-2.09*
Net Income (Loss) MM$	906	906	313.83	403.33	-1.88
S&P Senior Debt Rating Code	491	547	N/A	N/A	N/A
S&P Commercial Paper Rating - Historical Code	163	336	N/A	N/A	N/A
Risk-Adjusted Capital Ratio (Tier 1)	107	148	10.44	10.37	0.13
Risk-Adjusted Capital Ratio (Total)	110	149	14.22	13.41	1.24
Non-performing Assets MM$	109	152	125.77	71.15	1.39
Provision for Loan/Asset Losses MM$	115	152	107.12	55.23	1.46
Net Interest Margin (Ratio)	111	151	3.91	4.11	-1.47
Interest Expense Per Share	678	739	8.4	1.38	1.32
Net Profit Margin	902	905	1.3	8.2	-3.06**
PreTax Interest Coverage	735	735	30.04	14.91	0.61
PreTax Profit Margin	902	905	5.45	12.28	-2.57*
PreTax Return On Assets	905	905	3.3	6.31	-5.66**
Operating Income Before Depreciation to Total Assets	857	825	9.16	11.38	-4.56**
After Tax Interest Coverage	735	735	22.87	9.84	0.53
After Tax Return On Common Equity	896	905	14.79	4.85	0.78
After Tax Return On Total Assets	906	906	1.53	4.04	-5.53**
Debt Ratio	905	905	0.69	0.69	0.44
Market To Book	766	903	3.07	2.87	0.46
P/E at Fiscal Year End	777	905	20.8	16.31	0.91
Earnings Per Share	822	905	1.64	1.73	-0.21

of the size-matching procedure. Because the number of DRIP firms is a fairly large proportion of the total firms in the size range, there is simply no good match for all companies. In such cases, we match with the closest available company, even though this sometimes means that an individual firm is perhaps 10% larger or smaller than its matched company. This procedure works well under the circumstances, though. Companies without DRIPs are a little bigger than those with plans, but the difference is less than 4% and is insignificant by any conventional standard.

Table 31.2 shows that several variables do differ significantly. For example, DRIP companies have higher payout ratios and dividend yields (the table is constructed so that a negative t-ratio means companies with plans have the larger value). They generally have higher margins before taxes, and generally, higher earnings. They purchase more shares on the open market (probably to meet the needs of the plan), but sell fewer shares (probably because they tend to grow less rapidly than companies without plans). None of the t-ratios reject the equality of means for variables unique to financial institutions, possibly due to the smaller samples. Economic reasons for these results and further tests are in DeGennaro (2003). For our purposes, the point is that these differences hold promise for partitioning the data in the last section.

We also conduct our tests on a subset of these data. This smaller data set uses only 16 of the 36 variables in Table 31.1 and Table 31.2. Gathering data is costly and researchers would prefer to collect a smaller data set if the information loss is minimal. Thus, we use this smaller data set to check the ability of the cluster analysis method in partitioning the data correctly. (The variables in the subset of the data are printed in the tables using italics.)

31.3 Clustering and Bayesian Data Augmentation

In this section without going into technical details, we briefly discuss Bayesian data augmentation based on the ongoing work of Bensmail and Bozdogan (2003 a,b) which we will apply to clustering and data mining the imputed financial data as described above.

Cluster analysis has been developed mainly through the invention of empirical, and lately Bayesian study of ad hoc methods, in isolation from more formal statistical procedures. In the literature, it has been found that basing cluster analysis on a probability model can be useful both for understanding when existing methods are likely to be successful and for suggesting new methods. For this, see, e.g., Hartigan (1975), Kaufman and Rousseeuw (1990), Bozdogan (1994), Gelman et al. (1995), Gordon (1999), and Bensmail and Bozdogan (2002).

One assumes that the population of interest consists of K different subpopulations $G_1, \ldots, G_K$ and that the density of a p-dimensional observation $\mathbf{x}$ from the kth subpopulation is $f_k(\mathbf{y}, \theta_k)$ for some unknown vector of parameters θ_k ($k = 1, \ldots, K$). Given observations $\mathbf{y} = (\mathbf{y}_1, \ldots, \mathbf{y}_n)$, we let $v = (v_1, \ldots, v_n)^t$ denote the unknown identifying labels, where $v_i = k$ if $\mathbf{y}_i$ comes from the kth subpopulation. Clustering data using a mixture distribution framework was successful lately and many authors proposed different approaches. Good sources of references are the paper by Hosmer (1973a, 1973b). In most cases, the data to be classified are viewed as coming from a mixture of probability distributions (Tan and Chang 1972; Bozdogan 1994; McLachlan and Basford 1988), each representing a different cluster, so the likelihood is expressed as

$$p(\theta_1, \ldots, \theta_K; \pi_1, \ldots, \pi_K | \mathbf{x}) = \prod_{i=1}^{n} \sum_{k=1}^{K} \pi_k f_k(\mathbf{y}_i | \theta_k), \tag{31.1}$$

where π_k is the probability that an observation belongs to the kth component ($\pi_k \geq 0; \sum_{k=1}^{K} \pi_k = 1$).

Clustering data with missing values has always been difficult. In many cases, sample means were used to replace the missing values and then any clustering methods were applied to the complete data for the analysis. Recently, the EM algorithm (Dempster, Laird, and Rubin (1977)) has been used to overcome the limitations of the average and the maximum likelihood estimators. Within the Bayesian framework, similar to the usual EM algorithm, a data-augmentation (DA) algorithm (Tanner and Wong, 1987) has been proposed.

When $\mathbf{y}$ represents an observation from the sample, we use $\mathbf{y}_{obs}$ for the observed complete part of the data and $\mathbf{y}_{miss}$ the missing one. Here we want to estimate the parameter θ given in (1) based on $\mathbf{y} = (\mathbf{y}_{miss}, \mathbf{y}_{obs})$. The data (observed and missing) should be clustered in K clusters; the cluster $G_1, \ldots, G_K$ are unknown. Each observation y_i belonging to a cluster G_k is supposed to be a random variable drawn from a normal distribution $N_p(\mu_k, \Sigma_k)$ where μ_k and Σ_k are the mean and covariance matrix of the cluster G_k such that

$$(y_i | \mu_k, \Sigma_k) \sim N_p(\mu_k, \Sigma_k). \tag{31.2}$$

The distribution function of a sample $(y_1, \ldots, y_{n_k})$ representing a subpopulation G_k is given by

$$p(y_1, \ldots, y_{n_k} | \mu_k, \Sigma_k) \propto |\Sigma_k|^{-n_k/2} \exp\left(-\frac{1}{2} \sum_{i=1}^{n_k} (y_i - \mu_k)^t \Sigma_k^{-1} (y_i - \mu_k)\right) \tag{31.3}$$

$$= |\Sigma_k|^{-n_k/2} \exp\left(-\frac{1}{2} tr W_k \Sigma_k^{-1}\right),$$

where $n_k = \sum_{i \in G_k} I\{v_i = k\}$, $W_k = \sum_{i; v_i = k} (y_i - \bar{y}_k)(y_i - \bar{y}_k)^t$, $\bar{y}_k = \frac{1}{n_k} \sum_{i; v_i = k} y_i$.

In the Bayesian clustering approach, one needs to estimate the posterior distribution of the parameter θ involved given its prior distribution. When y_{miss} denote a subvector of y containing the missing components, the posterior distribution of the parameter θ given the observed data y_{obs} is

$$f(\theta | y_{obs}) = \int f(\theta | y_{miss}, y_{obs}) f(y_{miss} | y_{obs}) dy_{miss} \tag{31.4}$$

which is a mixture of the posterior distribution of θ given the data (observed and missing) where the mixing proportion is given by the marginal conditional distribution of y_{miss}. This is typically very difficult to use, as it often cannot even be expressed in a closed form (without integral).

A very useful method for getting around these difficulties and exploring $f(\theta|y_{obs})$ is the data augmentation (DA) algorithm. The term data augmentation refers to methods for constructing iterative algorithms via the introduction of unobserved data or latent variables. For deterministic algorithms, the method was popularized in the general statistical community by the seminal paper of Dempster, Laird, and Rubin (1977) on the EM algorithm for maximizing a likelihood function or more generally a posterior density. For stochastic algorithms, the method was popularized in the statistical literature by Tanner and Wong (1987), data augmentation algorithm for posterior sampling, and in the physics literature by Swendsen and Wang (1987), algorithm for sampling from Ising and Potts models (Cipra, 1987) (and its generalizations) in the physics literature, the method of data augmentation is referred to as the method of auxiliary variables. Data augmentation schemes were used by Tanner and Wong to make simulation feasible and simple, while auxiliary variables were adopted by Swendsen and Wang (1987) to improve the speed of iterative simulation. In general, however, constructing data augmentation schemes that result in both simple and fast algorithms is a matter of art in that successful strategies vary greatly with the observed-data models being considered (Tierney, 1994).

In the following, we will describe the DA algorithm for imputing the missing data. For more details, see Bensmail and Bozdogan (2003a,b).

The algorithm iterates as follows:

To go from an iteration (t) to an iteration $(t+1)$ we do the following:

1. **I**-step: *imputation* : generate

$$y_{miss}^{(t+1)} \sim f(y_{miss}|y_{obs}, \theta^{(t)}). \tag{31.5}$$

2. **P**-step: *posterior estimation* : generate

$$\theta^{(t+1)} \sim f(\theta|y_{obs}, y_{miss}^{(t)}). \tag{31.6}$$

31.3.1 Imputation

To calculate equation (31.5) we use the following Lemma from Anderson (1984):

If y is a random variable having a multivariate normal distribution, then the conditional distribution of any subvector of y given the remaining elements is once again multivariate normal. If we partition y into subvectors $y = (y_1, y_2)$, then $p(y_1|y_2)$ is (multivariate) normal such that

$$y_1|y_2 \sim N\left(\mu_1 + \Sigma_{12}\Sigma_2^{-1}(y_2 - \mu_2), \Sigma_1 - \Sigma_{12}\Sigma_2^{-1}\Sigma_{21}\right), \tag{31.7}$$

where
$$y_1 \sim N(\mu_1, \Sigma_1), \text{ and } y_2 \sim N(\mu_2, \Sigma_2), \tag{31.8}$$
and
$$\Sigma_{12} = \Sigma_{21} = Cov(y_1, y_2). \tag{31.9}$$

Case of one missing value and many are observed:

Suppose that an observation $y = (y_1, y_2, ..., y_p)$ has one missing value. Let's consider $z_1 = y_1$ the missing value and $z_2 = (y_2, ..., y_p)$ the remaining observed values. Then the only information needed are parts of the vector mean $\mu = (\mu_1, ..., \mu_p)$ and the covariance matrix Σ. Given the mean μ and given the covariance matrix

$$\Sigma = \begin{pmatrix} \sigma_{11} & \sigma_{12} & \cdots & \sigma_{1p} \\ \sigma_{21} & \sigma_{22} & \cdots & \sigma_{2p} \\ \vdots & \vdots & \ddots & \vdots \\ \sigma_{p1} & \cdots & \cdots & \sigma_{pp} \end{pmatrix}$$

the only input we need are the first row of the covariance matrix except the first variance term, which means the vector $\sigma_{1k(-1)} = (\sigma_{12}, \sigma_{13}, ... \sigma_{1p})$ and the covariance matrix minus the first row and the first column. This gives us the matrix

$$\Sigma_{-(1,1)} = \begin{pmatrix} \sigma_{22} & \cdots & \sigma_{2p} \\ \vdots & \ddots & \vdots \\ \sigma_{p2} & \cdots & \sigma_{pp} \end{pmatrix}. \tag{31.10}$$

Now we can use these new blocks to estimate the missing value $z_1 = y_1$ by generating the data from a normal distribution

$$z_1 | z_2 \sim N \begin{pmatrix} \mu_1 + \sigma_{1k(-1)} \Sigma_{-(1,1)} (y_2 - \mu_2, ..., y_p - \mu_p)^t, \\ \sigma_{11} - \sigma_{1k(-1)} \Sigma_{-(1,1)} \sigma^t_{1k(-1)}. \end{pmatrix} \tag{31.11}$$

General case:

For the general case, we have multivariate data $y = (y_1, y_2, ..., y_p)$ where two y_j and y_h or more are missing and the others are observed. Using the same schema as before, the only information needed are parts of the vector mean μ and the covariance matrix Σ. Using Anderson's Lemma (1984), $(y_j, y_h) | (y_2, ..., y_p, \mu, \Sigma)$ is normally distributed with mean vector $\tilde{\mu}$ and covariance matrix $\tilde{\Sigma}$ as described in Bensmail and Bozdogan (2003b). Here we will not describe the details of the calculating $\tilde{\mu}$ and $\tilde{\Sigma}$; see the previous work for more details.

31.3.2 Posterior Estimation

To estimate the parameter μ and Σ, we need to specify priors on those parameters. Here we use conjugate priors for the parameters π which is a *Dirichlet* distribution $Dirichlet(\alpha_1, ..., \alpha_K)$.

Since the log-likelihood is a quadratic form in μ_k, the conjugate prior distribution of μ_k is given by:

$$\mu_k|\Sigma_k \sim N_p(\xi_k, \Sigma_k/\tau_k), \tag{31.12}$$

and a conjugate prior of Σ_k is given by

$$\Sigma_k \sim W_p^{-1}(m_k, \Psi_k). \tag{31.13}$$

The posterior distribution of μ_k and Σ_k given the missing and observed data is then given by:

$$\mu_k|y_{miss}, y_{obs}, \Sigma_k \propto N_p((\xi_k + n_k\bar{y}_k)/(n_k + \tau_k), \Sigma_k/(n_k + \tau_k)), \tag{31.14}$$

and

$$\Sigma_k|y_{miss}, y_{obs}, v \sim W_p^{-1}\left(n_k + m_k, \Psi_k + W_k + \frac{n_k\tau_k}{n_k + \tau_k}(\bar{y}_k - \xi_k)(\bar{y}_k - \xi_k)^t\right). \tag{31.15}$$

31.3.3 Algorithm

We estimate the parameters by simulating from the joint posterior distribution of y_{miss}, π, θ, and v using the Gibbs sampler (Smith and Roberts 1993, Bensmail et al. 1997, Bensmail and Bozdogan 2003b). In our case this consists of the following steps:

1. Simulate the classification variables v_i according to their posterior probabilities $(t_{ik}, k = 1, ..., K)$ conditional on π, y_{miss}, and θ, namely

$$t_{ik} = \frac{\pi_k f(y|\mu_k, \Sigma_k)}{\sum_{h=1}^{K} \pi_h f(y|\mu_h, \Sigma_h)}; i = 1, ..., n. \tag{31.16}$$

2. Simulate the missing values y_{miss} given y_{obs} from

$$y_{miss} \sim f(y_{miss}|y_{obs}, \mu_k, \Sigma_k). \tag{31.17}$$

3. Simulate the vector π of mixing proportions according to its posterior distribution conditional on the v_i's. It consists of simulating π from its conditional posterior distribution, namely $\pi \sim Dirichlet\ (\alpha_1 + \Sigma I\{v_i = 1\}, ..., \alpha_K + \Sigma I\{v_i = K\})$.

4. Simulate the parameters μ_k and Σ_k according to their posterior distribution

$$\Sigma_k^{(t+1)}|y_{obs}, y_{miss}^{(t)} \sim W^{-1}\left(n_k + m_k, \Psi_k + W_k + \frac{n_k\tau_k}{n_k + \tau_k}(\bar{y}_k - \xi_k)(\bar{y}_k - \xi_k)^t\right) \tag{31.18}$$

$$\mu^{(t+1)}|y_{obs}, y_{miss}, \Sigma^{(t+1)} \sim N((\xi_k + n_k\bar{y}_k)/(n_k + \tau_k), \Sigma_k/(n_k + \tau_k)), \tag{31.19}$$

where $\bar{y}_k$ and W_k are the sample mean and covariance matrix of the data, and W^{-1} denotes the inverse Wishart distribution.

31.4 Bayesian Model Selection for Choosing the Number of Clusters

The most important component of any cluster analysis algorithm is finding the number of clusters. Different criteria for model selection and how to choose the number of clusters have been investigated in the literature by many authors. For this, see, for example, Bozdogan (1994) where Akaike's (1973) information criterion (AIC) and its variants along with a new information measure of complexity (ICOMP) criterion of Bozdogan (1988, 1990, 1994, 2002) have been developed and utilized. Further, Celeux and Soromenho (1996) developed and used normalized entropy criterion (NEC) to assess the number of components in a given data set. The new work of Bensmail and Bozdogan (2003a,b) develops ICOMP in choosing the number of components in both multivariate kernel mixture-model and Bayesian kernel mixture-model cluster analysis of mixed and imputed data.

For comparative purposes, in this paper, we use Schwarz's (1978) Bayesian criterion (SBC), although regularity conditions for this may not hold for mixture models. However, there is considerable theoretical and practical support for its use.

SBC, which is an approximation of the Bayes factor, is defined by:

$$SBC(M_k) = -2\log L(\tilde{\theta}_k, M_k) + m(k)\log(n_k), \tag{31.20}$$

where $L(\tilde{\theta}, M_k)$ is the likelihood of the posterior mode $\tilde{\theta}$ for the model M_k (here the number of components is k), and $m(k)$ is the number of parameter to estimate and n_k is the sample size of the subpopulation G_k.

31.5 Analysis of Financial Data

We apply this new approach to a sample of companies that offer direct investment plans and a corresponding, size-matched set of companies without such plans. Dividend Reinvestment Plans and a more general class of investments, Direct Investment Plans, allow investors to avoid investment channels typically used in the past, such as securities brokers. A Dividend Reinvestment Plan is a mechanism that permits shareholders to reinvest their dividends in additional shares automatically. No broker is involved, unless he is the agent of the plan administrator. If the firm does not restrict its plan to current shareholders, then the plan is also what is called a Direct Investment Plan, also known as a Super DRIP. Transactions costs are typically much lower than when using traditional brokerage accounts.

DRIPS are not a different class of security, such as swaps or options. They are simply a new way of selling the traditional equity security. The privileges and obligations of equity ownership are unchanged. For example, DRIP investors receive the usual mailings and they retain all voting rights. Tax implications are unaffected, and stock splits are handled exactly as if the investor were using a traditional brokerage account. Readers seeking more detailed information about such plans should see DeGennaro (2003).

Using the Data augmentation and the Gibbs sampler, we run the algorithm for 1000 iterations. The SBC resulting in Table 31.3 shows that the two clusters were proposed by SBC which is consistent with the information we have originally from the data. With two clusters, the confusion matrix is given by Table 31.4 which gives us an error rate of misclassification equal to 0.034 (3.4%).

k	SBC
1	7818.19
2	7680.90
3	8798.92
4	8448.44

TABLE 31.3
SBC values for different number of components.

k	No Plan	Plan	Total
No Plan	851	55	906
Plan	5	901	906
Total	856(cluster1)	956(cluster2)	n = 1812

TABLE 31.4
Confusion matrix.

In the following, we summarize the estimated parameters using the first four estimates of the vector mean (it will be space consuming to report the whole mean vector and the whole covariance matrix posterior mode). The first four estimates of the posterior mean for the cluster 1 (chosen by SBC) is

$$\hat{\mu}_1 = (12044.36, 4205.21, 187.64, 204.47)$$

and their related posterior covariance matrix estimator is

$$\hat{\Sigma}_1 = \begin{pmatrix} 1774899.9384 & -238289.5187 & 608.8653 & -2883.1619 \\ -238289.5187 & 116291.2842 & 1625.8510 & -646.0837 \\ 608.8653 & 1625.8510 & 142.7815 & -167.2418 \\ -2883.1619 & -646.0837 & -167.2418 & 394.3522 \end{pmatrix}$$

The four terms of the posterior estimated mean for the second cluster is

$$\hat{\mu}_1 = (13909.44, 5839.01, 206.34, 142.99)$$

and their related posterior covariance matrix estimator is

$$\hat{\Sigma}_2 = \begin{pmatrix} 2152933.044 & -416870.6140 & 2459.4332 & 1029.5514 \\ -416870.614 & 238102.3010 & 3120.4234 & 300.1279 \\ 2459.433 & 3120.4234 & 246.0917 & 103.6611 \\ 1029.551 & 300.1279 & 103.6611 & 126.7641 \end{pmatrix}$$

31.6 Discussion

What economic or managerial implications can we draw from this study? Table 31.4 is the key. The first row shows that this new method correctly classifies 851 of the companies without DRIPS, meaning that 55 companies have been misclassified. According to the model, they should have DRIPS, but in reality, they do not. One interpretation is that the model is simply wrong about 6% of the time when it is used to identify companies with DRIPS. However, another interpretation is that these companies are likely candidates to adopt a plan. A plan administrator for DRIPS could do far worse than contacting the representatives of these 55 companies to gauge their interest in introducing a DRIP. This is because these companies' financial data show that some aspect of their operations corresponds to firms that typically operate a DRIP. These firms are probably the most likely candidates to start a plan. The second row shows that the procedure does even better for firms that have no DRIP: only *five* companies classified as having no DRIP actually have them, while 901 are correctly classified as having a DRIP. Applying the same reasoning as for the first row, the managerial interpretation is that the plan administrator is most likely to lose these *five* companies as customers – the data indicate that some aspect of their financial statements corresponds with firms that do not operate a DRIP. Other financial applications of this method are easy to find. First, it has obvious value to regulators. Consider the problem of mortgage lending discrimination. Regulators have long been charged with monitoring fairness. Essentially, the problem reduces to determining whether members of one race are equally likely to be denied a mortgage compared to similarly situated member of other races. This problem is extremely difficult for any of several reasons (readers should see Black, Boehm, and DeGennaro 2001 and Black, Boehm, and DeGennaro 2003 for details). Part of the problem is missing data. For example, loan officers often fail to collect all of the usual data for loan applications that are almost sure to be denied, because continuing to collect it is likely to be a waste of time. In addition, institutions sometimes gather information that other lenders ignore. This also produces missing values. Because this paper's approach handles missing data well, we conjecture that regulators could identify rejected applicants that, at least according to the method, could easily have been approved. Given that regulatory resources are scarce, it makes sense to concentrate on the cases that are most likely to be problems. Managers in the private sector, of course, see the matter from the other side. They might use the method to insure compliance with regulations rather than to identify lapses. In addition, this could identify potential profit opportunities. After all, the model identifies a pool of mortgage applications that were denied, yet which had financial characteristics very similar to other applications that were approved. By studying this pool of rejections, management could possibly refine its approval process so that profitable loans are less likely to be missed.

Acknowledgments

We express our gratitude to Professor Bozdogan for editing, commenting, and simplifying the presentation of this paper.

References

Akaike, H. (1973). Information theory and an extension of the maximum likelihood principle. In B.N. Petrov and F. Cski (Eds.), *Second International Symposium on Information Theory*, Acadmiai Kiad, Budapest, 267-281.

Altman, Edward I. (2000). Predicting Financial Distress of Companies: Revisiting the Z-Score and Zeta Models. Working paper, July 2000.

Anderson, T. W. (1984). *An Introduction to Multivariate Statistical Analysis*, 2nd Edition. John Wiley, New York.

Baillie, R. and Bollerslev, T. (1989). Common Stochastic Trends in a System of Exchange Rates. *Journal of Finance*, 44, 167-181.

Ben-Akiva, M.E. (1973) Structure of passenger travel demand models. Ph.D. thesis, Department of Civil Engineering, MIT, Cambridge, Ma.

Bensmail, H. and Bozdogan, H. (2002). Regularized kernel discriminant analysis with optimally scaled data. In *Measurement and Multivariate Analysis*, S. Nishisato, Y. Baba, H. Bozdogan, and K. Kanefuji, (Eds.), Springer, Tokyo, Japan, 133-144.

Bensmail, H. and Bozdogan, H. (2003a). Multivariate kernel mixture-model cluster analysis for mixed data. Working paper.

Bensmail, H. and Bozdogan, H. (2003b). Bayesian kernel mixture-model cluster analysis of mixed and imputed data using information complexity. Working paper.

Bensmail, H., Raftery, A., Celeux, G. and Robert, C. (1997). Inferences for model-based cluster analysis. *Computing and Statistics*, 7, 1-10.

Bierlaire, M., Lotan, T. and Toint, Ph. L. (1997). On the overspecification of multinomial and nested logit models due to alternative specific constants. *Transportation Science*. Forthcoming.

Black, H. A., Boehm, T. P., and DeGennaro, R. P. (2003). Is there discrimination in overage pricing? *Journal of Banking and Finance*. Forthcoming.

Black, H. A., Boehm, T. P., and DeGennaro, R. P. (2001). Overages, mortgage pricing and race. *International Journal of Finance*, 13, 2057-2073.

Bozdogan, H. (1987). Model selection and Akaike's Information Criterion (AIC): The general theory and its analytical extensions. *Psychometrika,* 52(3), 345-370.

Bozdogan, H. (1988). ICOMP: a new model-selection criterion. In *Classification and Related Methods of Data Analysis*, H. H. Bock (Ed.), Elsevier Science Publishers, Amsterdam, 599-608.

Bozdogan, H. (1990). On the information-based measure of covariance complexity and its application to the evaluation of multivariate linear models. *Communications in Statistics, Theory and Methods*, 19, 221-278.

Bozdogan, H. (1994). Mixture-model cluster analysis using a new informational complexity and model selection criteria. In *Multivariate Statistical Modeling*, H. Bozdogan, (Ed.), Vol. 2, Proceedings of the First US/Japan Conference on the Frontiers of Statistical Modeling: An Informational Approach, Kluwer Academic Publishers, Dordrecht, the Netherlands, 69-113.

Bozdogan, H. (2000). Akaike's information criterion and recent developments in information complexity. *Journal of Mathematical Psychology*, 44, 62-91.

Calhoun, C. A. and Yongheng, D. (2000). A dynamic analysis of fixed and adjustable-rate mortgage terminations. *The Journal of Real Estate Finance and Economics*, 24, # 1 & 2.

Cipra, B. A. (1987). An introduction to the ising model. *Amer. Math. Monthly*, 94, 937-959.

Dalhstedt, R., Timo, S., Martti, L., and Laakkonen, A. (1994). On the usefulness of standard industrial classifications in comparative financial statement analysis. *European Journal of Operational Research*, 79, No. 2, 230-238.

DeGennaro, R. P. (2003). Direct investments: A primer. Federal Reserve Bank of Atlanta Economic Review. Forthcoming.

Dempster, A.P., Laird, N.M. and Rubin, D.B. (1977). Maximum likelihood from incomplete data via the EM algorithm (with discussion). *J. R. Statist. Soc. B.*, 39, 1-38.

Dubofsky, D. and Bierman, L. (1988). The effect of discount dividend reinvestment plan announcements on equity value. *Akron Business and Economic Review*, 19, 58-68.

Gelman, A., Carlin, J. B., Stern, H. S., and Rubin, D. B. (1995). *Bayesian Data Analysis*. Chapman and Hall, London.

Guide to Dividend Reinvestment Plans (1999). *Temper of the Times Communications, Inc.*

Hartigan, J. A. (1975). *Clustering Algorithms*. John Wiley, New York.

Hosmer, D.W. (1973a). On maximum likelihood estimator of the parameters of a mixture of two normal distributions when the sample size is small. *Commun. Statist.*, 1, 217-227.

Hosmer, D.W. (1973b). A comparison of iterative maximum likelihood estimates of the parameters of a mixture of two normal distributions under three different types of sample. *Biometrics*, 29, 761-770.

Kaufman, L. and Rousseeuw, P. J. (1990). *Finding Groups in Data*, John Wiley, New York.

Koppelman, F. S. and Chieh-Hua Wen. (1997). The paired combinatorial logit model: properties, estimation and application. *Transportation Research Board*, 76th Annual Meeting, Washington, DC, January 1997.

Luce, R. D. and P. Suppes. (1965). Preference, utility and subjective probability. In *Handbook of Mathematical Psychology*, R. D. Luce, R. R. Bush, and E. Galanter, (Eds.), John Wiley, New York.

McFadden, D.(1978). Modelling the choice of residential location. In *Spatial Interaction Theory and Residential Location*, A. Karlquist et al., (Eds.), North-Holland, Amsterdam, 75-96.

McLachlan, G.J. and Basford, K.E. (1988). *Mixture Models Inference and Applications to Clustering*. Marcel Dekker, Inc., New York.

Mester, Loretta J. (1997). What's the point of credit scoring? Federal Reserve Bank of Philadelphia Business Review, September/October, 3-16.

Schwarz, G. (1978). Estimating the dimension of a model. *Annals of Statsitics*, 6, 461-464.

Shaffer, S. (1991). Aggregate deposit insurance funding and taxpayer bailouts. *Journal of Banking and Finance*, September.

Smith A.F. and Roberts G.O. (1993). Bayesian computation via the Gibbs sampler and related Markov chain Monte Carlo methods. *J. Royal Stat. Soc. B*, 55, 3–23.

Swendsen, R. H. and Wang, J. H. (1987). Nonuniversal critical dynamics in Monte Carlo simulations. *Physical Review Letters*, 58, 86-88.

Tan, W.Y. and Chang, W.C. (1972). Some comparisons of the method of moments and the method of maximum likelihood in estimating parameters of a mixture to two normal densities. *J. Amer. Statist. Assoc.*, 67, 702-708.

Tanner, M. A. and Wong, W. H. (1997). The calculation of posterior distributions by data augmentation. *Journal of the American Statistical Society*, 82(398), 528-550.

Tanner, M.A. and Wei, G.C.G. (1990). A Monte Carlo implementation of the EM-Algorithm and the poor man's data Augmentation algorithms. *Journal of the American Statistical Association*, 85, 699–704.

Tierney, L (1994). Markov chains for exploring posterior distributions (with discussion). *Ann. Statist.*, 22, 1701-1758.

von Altrock, C. (1995). *Fuzzy Logic and Neuro Fuzzy Applications Explained*. Inform Software Corp., Germany, Prentice Hall.

Vovsha, P. (1997). Cross-nested logit model: an application to mode choice in the Tel-Aviv metropolitan area. *Transportation Research Board*, 76th Annual Meeting, Washington, DC, January 1997.

32
Data Mining in Federal Agencies

David L. Banks and Robert T. Olszewski
U.S. Food and Drug Administration, Rockville, MD, and University of Pittsburgh, Pittsburgh, PA, USA

CONTENTS

32.1 Data Quality 529
32.2 Indexing Data 534
32.3 Screening for Structure with Locally Low Dimension 537
32.4 Estimating Exposure 545
      References 546

Federal agencies in the United States collect enormous quantities of data. Recently, they have begun to attempt to apply data mining to extract additional insights from their collections.

This paper examines four areas that particularly affect data mining in the U.S. government: data quality, mathematical ways to find representative cases, methods to screen out datasets for which data mining efforts are unlikely to be successful, and estimation of risk in databases of spontaneous reports. These are non-trivial problems, but progress on any of these fronts could significantly improve the quality of data analysis for the benefit of the public.

32.1 Data Quality

The U.S. government runs on low-quality data, and it generally runs pretty well. But every manager feels keenly the need to make better decisions, and one of the limitations to smart planning by means of data mining is poor data. This section describes issues with data quality at the U.S. Department of Transportation. The fact that the agency experiences problems with data quality does not in any way distinguish it from other agencies; in fact, the forthrightness with which the Bureau of Transportation Statistics has addressed those problems is unusual.

The U.S. Department of Transportation maintains approximately 160 databases, of all kinds and sizes. About 60 of them are key to the official business of the agency; the others generally represent internal personnel systems, document libraries, or databases that are of very specialized interest. Some of the most important databases are:

- FARS, the Fatality Analysis Reporting System, which captures police reports and related information on all fatal automobile accidents in the U.S.;

- HPMS, the Highway Performance Monitoring System, which is used to estimate the number of miles travelled on public roads, broken out by geography and type of road;

- DIMS, the Defect Information Management System, which contains data on automobile defect reports; and

- NPTS, the Nationwide Personal Travel Survey, which summarizes data from a nationwide household survey of the transportation choices and needs of American families.

These databases include many different kinds of data, collected in many different ways. Some of the data come from partner agencies, within or outside the Department of Transportation. It may be collected from commercial sources, public surveys, mandatory reporting systems, citizen-generated reports, or from secondary analyses of primary data.

The Bureau of Transportation Statistics is responsible for advising the Department of Transportation on data quality issues that affect DOT databases. To that end, the Office of Data Quality has begun a systematic examination of the key databases, looking for quality shortfalls that diminish the success of the database in achieving its purposes. The Office of Data Quality is also involved with the establishment of TranStat, an intermodal transportation database that serves as a warehouse and allows one-stop access for many of the major DOT databases. This warehousing project enforces a special urgency in addressing data quality issues, since it offers a unique opportunity for quality review of databases that are being incorporated into TranStat.

32.1.1 First Steps

In 2000, Congress asked the Bureau of Transportation Statistics to perform in-depth audits of data quality for four randomly chosen DOT databases. Those audits found that one database was quality-capable, two databases had serious problems that diminished their utility, and one database was fundamentally unable to support its purpose. This finding was a trigger for the formation of the Office of Data Quality. Also, the four audits brought home the fact that a full-scale quality check is both expensive and time-consuming. Consequently, BTS explored ways in which data quality auditing efforts should be managed and resourced.

One proposal for helping to focus quality efforts more efficiently was the development of a database report card. The design of the report card went through several iterations, but the motivation was to acquire an instrument that could quickly and in-

Statistical Data Mining and Knowledge Discovery

expensively determine what kinds of data quality problems were likely to be present. This would enable managers to prioritize attention to the most problematic databases.

Many different kinds of report cards are possible, and the one used should be tailored to the particular circumstances of the database and the agency. But the fairly generic version that was tried at the Department of Transportation evaluated data quality in terms of the following eight criteria:

1. *Sampling Methods.* The key concern in this criterion is whether issues of survey coverage, non-response bias, household bias, frame bias, respondent bias, and so forth have been properly addressed. Ideally, the database documentation would include some discussion of total survey error. Obviously, not all of the DOT databases contain survey data, but there are analogous problems of representation and generalization that arise very broadly.

    In terms of this criterion, raters assign a numerical score to the database: a "2" implies that good attention has been paid to sampling issues, a "1" implies that improvement is possible but that there do not seem to be flaws that affect routine use of the database, and a "0" implies that the utility of the database has been compromised.

2. *Verification Process.* Any significant database should have a process in place to review and verify the entries. Ideally, this process would take a random sample of the records (perhaps 1% of the total) and independently check their accuracy. In practice, such verification can be time-consuming and expensive. Partial credit is given to systems that have some kind of verification protocol in place, provided it is used regularly. A database receives a numerical grade (2, 1, or 0) depending on whether a stringent and sufficient protocol is routinely used.

3. *Documentation.* Without documentation, there is hardly any point in having a database. This is especially true when service databases are available over the Internet, or intended for use by many diverse customers.

    The report card assesses the adequacy of such metadata impressionistically. Good documentation should discuss the limitations of the data and its provenance, as well as the data definitions. Reviewers look at the available documentation, and decide whether it is adequate (2), mostly adequate (1), or generally unsatisfactory (0).

4. *Review Committee.* No matter how clever the data capture process, nor how established the database, there should always be a periodic review of the data management system. The review committee should have a broad brief for action and its membership should extend beyond the program staff to include user and supplier representation. Full marks require an active committee that has made some change to the process within the last two years; if there is no active committee, the rater assigns a 0.

5. *Relevance.* There is always a degree of inertia in data collection processes, which works against the need to have relevant, useful data in the collection. As

databases age, they come to serve different purposes than were originally intended. And the problem that drove the initial use may also change. Therefore this portion of the assessment lists the main uses of the database, and checks that each item captured is needed by a clearly defined customer to support a decision or satisfy a regulatory requirement. The grades reflect the degree to which the data have direct applications.

6. *Accessibility.* In government, there are many legacy database management systems that use old-fashioned software and run on old-fashioned platforms. To assess the accessibility of a database, one of the members of the Office of Data Quality is assigned to use the database for a reasonable period of time. The final grade depends on how frustrated that person is at the end of the effort.

7. *Cross-DOT Coordination.* There are many data collection programs in DOT, but their efforts are not always efficiently aligned. For example, a person has 365 days to linger before death in a train wreck, but only 30 days to die in an automobile accident. Similarly, survey questions about automobile travel can be usefully combined with collection efforts aimed at air travel. The extent to which this type of coordination occurs in a database determines the grade it receives on this quality dimension.

8. *Burden.* There is a great temptation to overload surveys and other data collection instruments. It requires discipline to ensure that only directly useful information is acquired. Overloaded data collection instruments tend to be expensive and to produce unreliable data.

This portion of the report card concerns the total respondent burden imposed by the collection program. If that burden is too large, then the quality of the reported data tends to decay. Therefore every instrument should be piloted, and the comments of test respondents about the points they find tiresome should guide instrument revision. A good grade on this criterion requires clear evidence that the database administrators have addressed the need to minimize burden.

For each of the eight components of the report card, raters give a grade from 0 to 2. A 0 indicates substantial failure on that factor, whereas a 2 indicates good performance (at least compared to the norm within the agency). The scale is crude; for example, it does not capture the relative costs of achieving improvement on the different criteria, nor does it necessarily reflect the impact of each criterion on the overall utility of the database. But this kind of scale enables a composite assessment of problems, and pinpoints areas in which gains can most readily be made.

Experiments indicate that the report card can be scored relatively quickly, usually within a few days, which compares favorably with the time needed for a database audit. However, the scoring cannot be done by the program manager in charge of the database; experience indicates that the program personnel are boundlessly optimistic about the quality of their data, compared to independent raters.

32.1.2 Using Poor Quality Data

Regrettably, government statisticians must learn to co-exist with poor quality data. Surveys, administrative forms, and other data collection techniques are expensive to administer carefully and difficult to verify. Fortunately, most policy decisions are not tremendously sensitive to the quality of the data. If a few errors on the Census form or a few lies on the Nationwide Personal Travel Survey diary were to invalidate the utility of those projects, then the wheels of federal statistics would grind to a halt.

Given that we must live with inadequate data quality, what steps can statisticians take to reduce the influence of bad data? One obvious strategy is to use robust estimators; in particular, we urge the use of S-estimators, which can perform well even when just more than half of the data are correct. See Rousseeuw and Yohai [18] for a discussion of S-estimators, and Sakata and White [19] for a discussion of breakdown points.

S-estimation works very well for many univariate parameters, giving robust estimates of central tendency, dispersion, and association. It performs less well for multivariate parameters, such as estimation of a covariance matrix—in such applications the breakdown point depends on the dimension, and thus the method cannot accommodate a very large percentage of poor-quality data.

The biggest obstacle to using S-estimators in federal statistics is that there is no robust procedure for estimating a proportion from survey data. And estimates of proportions are ubiquitous outputs from federal statistics programs. Such estimates probably play a larger role in framing national policy than estimates of location, dispersion, or association.

Other potential obstacles to the use of S-estimators (and other robust procedures) are that:

1. They are less efficient than classical procedures. But this should be set against the fact that government databases used for data mining tend to be very large, and the fact that the assumptions needed to claim efficiency for the classical procedures are generally unrealistic in practice.

2. Sometimes it is necessary to explain the estimate to a politician. But if agencies only undertook work that led to results that could be explained to elected officials, then perhaps even less would get done.

3. SAS does not easily support high-end robust procedures. But one should look to the future; the incoming generation of new federal statisticians is far more comfortable with software and computational complexity than is the imminently retiring crop of senior statisticians.

On the whole, the obstacles to the use of robust procedures do not seem strong enough to prevent their eventual adoption for routine use in federal programs. We believe that accelerating this inevitability will do much to circumvent the quality barriers that presently exist for many data mining efforts.

32.1.3 Estimating the Probability of Bad Data

As a research topic, we note that not all data are equally likely to have poor quality. Most survey researchers agree that the accuracy of a particular item depends upon the complexity of the question, the sensitivity or delicacy of the information, the burden of the survey, the demographics of the respondent, and many other factors. Similarly, for non-survey data, such as police reports on traffic fatalities, some items are far more reliable than others.

As statisticians, it is possible for us to build a logistic regression model that predicts the probability that a data item is correct as a function of explanatory variables. The appropriate explanatory variables may change from situation to situation, but such issues as complexity, sensitivity, burden, and so forth are all likely to be useful regressors. Ultimately, this kind of approach could help in targeting quality improvement efforts. It enables auditors to stratify their validation tests to items that are most likely to be problematic, and it could highlight the design factors and item issues that contribute to bad data.

Similarly, it would be helpful for survey statisticians to have logistic regression models that estimate the probability that a particular subject will respond, or respond truthfully. And it would be useful to build nonparametric regression models, perhaps using MARS [9] or CART [4], that enable prediction of the total cost of a survey.

Each of these efforts involves using data mining tools to improve the quality of data that will subsequently be mined for other purposes. This kind of self-reflexivity is common in machine learning applications (e.g., boosting [10] to improve the performance of classification rules) and offers a paradigm for improving the performance of our federal data systems. By collecting and analyzing data about how we collect and analyze data, we can better discover what works, when it works, and how much it costs.

32.2 Indexing Data

Data mining is an iterative process. As structure is discovered, the results suggest new questions and guide new inquiries. Once a federal agency has data of adequate quality, or has developed procedures that are resistant to realistic levels of poor quality, then it becomes worthwhile to plan the first phase of the data mining effort.

There are many approaches to the first phase, and the best choice depends strongly upon the context in which the agency operates, its mission, and the kind of data that are available. This section describes one strategy that may be useful across many situations.

32.2.1 A First-Pass Method

Suppose you are a statistician for the Internal Revenue Service or the U.S. Census Bureau. You have a large, complex database of tax forms or census returns. You would like to obtain a first-pass characterization of the data, in a way that can be easily communicated and which suggests new questions.

To do this, one can try to find the m cases (tax forms, returns) that are most spread out among the data. These cases maximize their mutual distances, and give a representative view of the kinds of variation that occur in the database. Some of the m cases will be quite normal, but many will be exceptional, and there is insight from both. For example, in the context of tax forms, one would like to use an algorithm which ensures that one of the m cases is a middle-class two-parent family with two children, that one of the m cases is someone on welfare, that one of the cases is a retiree, and so forth. But one also wants to see the man who claims 57 children, and the woman who holds 14 jobs, and the child with $40 million dollars in earned income.

If the database is not thoroughly accurate, many of the exceptional cases will turn out to be data errors. From this perspective, looking at cases with maximum mutual distance can help flag mistakes and detect outliers. But it is probably more useful to iterate, removing wrong observations and rerunning the algorithm until the exceptional cases are true observations. There *are* men in the U.S. who correctly claim 57 children as dependents, and women with 14 jobs, and rich children; and these are exactly the cases that are interesting to a data miner who wants to gain insight.

Similarly, the unexceptional cases are also interesting. The two-parent families, the retirees, and the person on welfare all capture basic economic lifestyles that a data miner needs to understand. To the extent that these cases characterize large segments of society, they can serve as a guide to policy formulation. And the exceptional cases show the boundaries in which policy must successfully operate. For policy considerations, our sense is that m should be between 20 and 50; beyond that, it becomes difficult for managers to see the procedural implications.

The overall strategy of finding mutually distant cases has several antecedants. Cutler and Breiman [5] proposed the method of archetypes, in which each observation is represented by a mixture of a finite number of archetypes. Flury [8] developed a method of principal points that looks for cases that may be viewed as cluster centers; this is closely related to the ideas in k-means clustering [17]. And electrical engineers have long-studied the problem of quantization [11], in which one attempts to summarize a dataset by a small number of pseudo-observations.

But the proposed method is different from each of these. In contrast to the archetypal and quantization approaches, the m cases found through this algorithm are actual records in the dataset; this enables policy-makers to be more concrete in their thinking, and prevents logically inconsistent multivariate records (except insofar as such records arise in practice). And in contrast to the method of principal points, this method does not depend upon where the data are concentrated—it looks only at the inter-case distances, and not at the empirical probability mass function. Obviously, in some situations it may be useful to consider using these alternative methods, but the proposed technique still seems generally valuable when one is just starting the data mining activity.

32.2.2 Estimating Distance Functions

The first major problem in implementing the methodology outlined in this section concerns the definition of distance. A naive Euclidean metric would put equal weight upon a differences in zip code and differences in the number of wives. But ideally, the distance metric should reflect the scientific or policy interest in the data, and may change from application to application.

One method for estimating an appropriate metric is to use expert judgment in the following way. Have a scientist or policy maker examine a small random fraction of the data, and give an expert opinion about the distance or dissimilarity between each pair of cases. These expert opinions will not, in general, constitute a true metric, but multidimensional scaling [3] can be used to estimate intercase distances that conform as closely as possible to the opinions but still respect the mathematical properties of a metric.

These estimated distances do not determine a metric that can be imposed upon the entire dataset; they represent only the distances between the random fraction of cases examined by the expert. It is necessary to impute a metric over the entire space from the distances between these cases. But this estimation might be done through a nonparametric regression analysis that uses covariate information (i.e., all the values supplied in the tax form, the census return, or other documentation) to find a function that predicts the distance. This would tend to select the items that contributed (consciously or unconsciously) to the expert's judgement, and downweight or drop items that the expert thought were irrelevant to the inquiry.

It may be that the estimated distance function obtained from a nonparametric regression analysis will be sufficient for practical purposes. But we note that a mathematician would and should object that the nonparametric function is not, in general, itself a metric function. We know of no kind of functional analysis that offers an analogue to multidimensional scaling such that it could determine the metric function which agrees most closely with a given regression function. This is a deep problem, but fortunately it is one that is probably not essential to solve.

32.2.3 Computation

The second major problem that arises in implementing this methodology is computational. To determine a set of m cases with maximal mutual distance, one might have to calculate all distances between each pair of cases, and then do a complex search among those to find the most-separated set. This is worse than an $\mathcal{O}(n^2)$ operation, where n is the number of observations, and would be infeasible for datasets of the size that commonly arise in federal statistics programs.

But there are shortcuts. First, one may be able to work with a large random subset of the data and still obtain useful results. Second, one could find a minimum spanning tree for the data, and then use that to improve the efficiency of search for maximally separated cases. Third, one could "coarsen" the data by a crude partition, and then work only with elements in different regions of the partition. None of these suggestions is particularly attractive, but smart computer scientists are likely to be able to find adequate approximate solutions.

Clearly, the entire problem of indexing is very much of an open area for research. We believe that this kind of approach would be useful, not just to federal agencies but to other researchers engaged in first-stage data mining.

32.3 Screening for Structure with Locally Low Dimension

Federal agencies have many large datasets, and numerous important problems. But not all problems are tractable. It is useful to have some procedure for screening out those situations in which data mining is a viable strategy from those in which it will fail, thereby avoiding the investment of high-level technical time in fruitless analysis. This section proposes such a screening procedure.

Classical statistical methods were designed to work for low-dimensional data. But data mining (and related methods, from simple regression to MARS, CART, and more exotic machine learning techniques) quickly becomes unreliable in high dimensions; this phenomenon is called the "curse of dimensionality" (COD). There are three nearly equivalent formulations of the COD, each offering a different perspective on the problem:

1. The number of possible structural relationships increases faster than exponentially with dimension. To see this, consider just the subclass of polynomial regression models of degree 2 or less with explanatory variables of dimension p. A simple combinatorial argument shows that there are $2^{1+p+p(p+1)/2} - 1$ models among which the data must discriminate, and thus one needs large quantities of data.

2. When the dimensionality is large, almost all datasets are sparse. To exemplify this, suppose one has n points uniformly distributed in the unit cube in $\mathbb{R}^p$. Then the proportion of data one expects within a subcube with side length $d < 1$ is d^p, which goes to zero as p increases. Therefore the local information about the structure quickly becomes small for any fixed sample size n.

3. In high dimensions, almost all datasets show multicollinearity (and its nonparametric generalization, concurvity); this makes prediction unstable in certain regions. Multicollinearity occurs when the values of the explanatory variables lie on or near a proper subspace of $\mathbb{R}^p$, and concurvity occurs when they lie close to a smooth submanifold in $\mathbb{R}^p$. If p is large, then the number of possible subspaces and submanifolds is very large, making it almost certain that such concentration is present simply by chance [20].

These illustrations have been couched in the context of regression, but the ideas extend to other situations. Detailed discussion of this topic and its consequences may be found in Hastie and Tibshirani [13].

Historically, methods of multivariate statistical analysis sidestepped the COD by imposing strong model assumptions that restricted the potential complexity of the fitted models, thereby allowing sample information to have non-local influence. But now there is growing demand for data mining techniques that make weaker model assumptions and use larger datasets. This has led to the rapid development of a number of new methods; in the regression domain, prominent methods are MARS, PPR, LOESS, ACE, AVAS, GAM, CART, neural nets, and wavelets. The structure discovery domain is a bit less developed, but there are now techniques for factor analysis, principal components analysis, and cluster analysis that employ projection pursuit, recursive partitioning, and other ideas that have been central to the success of the regression techniques.

However, none of these methods is capable of handling true high-dimensional data. The ones that are sometimes successful must assume some kind of locally low-dimensional structure; if they happen to assume a structure that does an adequate job of describing the situation, then they work very well, but if not, then they fail. Hastie and Tibshirani [13] discuss how the new-wave methods are designed to work well when particular kinds of structure are present. In contrast, methods that don't assume such local structure (e.g., simple local averaging) are usually unsuccessful because they confront the full force of the COD.

To be a bit more specific, note that MARS, PPR, neural nets, and wavelets look hard to select a small set of variables that are influential in a particular region (MARS and wavelets) or a particular direction (PPR and neural nets). MARS and wavelets do not assume that the same variables are active everywhere, which is a great advantage, but it is doubtful whether they are particularly successful in handling regions where the local functional dependence involves more than about four variables. Similarly, PPR and neural nets are most effective when the regression surface in a given direction is dominated by the behavior of a small number of explanatory variables. In an alternate path to a comparable end, GAM, ACE, and AVAS all assume a simple additive structure that precludes the interactions that make high-dimensions so difficult; this assumption posits a different kind of local simplicity that enables an evasion of the COD. Banks, Olszewski, and Maxion [1] describe a comparison of the performances of new-wave methodologies that highlights these issues.

Our perspective is that some problems are intrinsically too hard for statisticians to solve with the data available. It therefore becomes valuable to find a screening tool to determine when a dataset has simple structure that makes it potentially amenable to a modern computer-intensive analysis, as opposed to when a dataset is so complex that no method has realistic hopes of discovering useful information. To this end, we propose a strategy for screening datasets that applies to problems of either regression or structure discovery, and show the results of a designed experiment that implements our strategy for the structure discovery form of the problem.

As a final point, we note that recent work has shown that in a narrow, technical sense, neural nets [2] and PPR [24] evade the COD. For a rich class of functions, the mean squared error in their regression fits increases linearly in the dimension of the data. However, these results are asymptotic, and do not appear to translate into any useful comparative dominance, as demonstrated either by practice or simulation studies. In fact, Banks, Olszewski, and Maxion [1] found that neural net methods were notably poor in their comparative performance across a range of situations.

32.3.1 Screening Strategy

The simplest and first case to consider is that of structure discovery, which is more akin to principal components analysis than to regression. Here the data consist of vectors $\mathbf{X}_1, \ldots, \mathbf{X}_n$ in $\mathbb{R}^p$, and one wants to discover whether there is some hidden regularity.

We call this the "crumpled napkin problem" because of the following illustration. Suppose during dinner with Persi Diaconis (a mathematician who is also a magician), he draws a large number of dots on his napkin, crumples it loosely, and causes the napkin to become invisible, so that only the dots may be seen. From cursory inspection, it appears that the dots are a featureless blob in space; but if one looks very closely, and if there are enough dots, one could in principle discover that the points lie on the hidden two-dimensional manifold that is the surface of the napkin. The clue that enables that insight is the fact that in sufficiently small subregions of the volume containing the dots, the dots tend to lie on nearly flat two-dimensional surfaces. Thus the local dimensionality is in fact two except near the folds in the napkin, despite the apparent three-dimensionality.

Following this heuristic, our analytical strategy is to place the center of a small hypersphere in $\mathbb{R}^p$ at random in the smallest right hyperparallelepiped containing the data. The radius of the sphere is then adjusted so that the sphere contains a fixed number of points. (In our work, that fixed number is $2p + 1$, but this should probably be adjusted upward; the danger with larger values is that the sphere is so large that it typically includes "folds" of the napkin, distorting the results, and pointing up the delicate balance between sample size requirements and the amount of folding that can be accommodated.) At each placement, we record the points that lie inside the sphere, and perform a principal components analysis on them. The number of eigenvalues that contribute appreciably to the trace of the covariance matrix indicates the approximate local dimensionality of the data. (In our work, we estimate the local dimensionality as the number of eigenvalues needed to sum to 80% of the trace, but this is a choice of convenience rather than principle.) Finally, we average the local estimates of dimension; if the result is much smaller than p, we have good reason to hope that there is simple structure hidden in the data, and thus that the dataset might repay further study. But if the result is not much smaller than p, this suggests that no currently available analysis can succeed, and time would be better spent on other projects.

The previous strategy is still a bit too simple. Suppose that one's data fill out the locus between two p-dimensional spheres of different radii, each centered at **0**. Then a randomly-placed fixed-radius sphere will typically find either no points within its ambit (when it lies in empty region of the smaller sphere), or it will estimate a local dimensionality of p, when it is located inside the outer sphere but outside the inner sphere. Thus the proposed strategy does not notice structure caused by regions of data sparsity. To repair this deficiency, we make a second analysis that is a slight variation on the strategy described previously. As before, we place random hyperspheres in the data cloud, but these have fixed radius (as is described in the following subsection). We then count the number of observations within the sphere at each random position; if the number falls below a threshold (we use $2p$), then the region is declared sparse. At the end of each run, we record the proportion of positions that were sparse.

When both analyses are complete, we examine both the proportion of sparse sites and the average local dimensionality. If the former number is large or the latter number is small, this implies the presence of interesting structure.

There has been previous research that bears on this problem. Shepard and Carroll [21] made an early attempt at "uncrumpling the napkin" using two approaches; one involves a proximity measure (which is a bit like minimum spanning tree methods in cluster analysis) and the other involves examination of local smoothness. The latter strategy is more closely related to our perspective, but their technique is parametric in spirit and entails the explicit determination of the napkin's folds. They call this second approach "parametric mapping" and seek a numerical solution that identifies the smoothest function that expresses the observed data (with noise) as a function of values in a space of lower dimension q, where q is determined by the user. From their examples, it seems most useful when the apparent p is very small (about $p = 4$) and the dimensionality of q is even smaller. By construction, their solution does not allow different values of q for different regions of $\mathbb{R}^p$, whereas our method explicitly recognizes the potential for such variation.

More recently, Kruskal [15] developed a multidimensional scaling approach to the parametric mapping problem. This method is based upon the Gateaux derivative and poses a number of difficult numerical subproblems, for which Kruskal provides solution strategies. Also, Hastie and Stuetzle [12] have developed a method of principal curves that offers (in two dimensions) an attractive approach to the parametric mapping problem. However, the goal of uncrumpling seems too ambitious, at least at the first stage. Our interest is the humbler task of simply determining whether an estimate of local dimensionality might warrant a more athletic analysis of the kind these other authors consider.

32.3.2 The Designed Experiment

This experiment calibrates the screening strategy described previously for the situation in which data on a q-dimensional manifold is presented in $\mathbb{R}^p$, for $p \geq q$. The particular structure of the manifold that we consider is the q-dimensional boundary of the unit p-dimensional hypercube. For example, uniform data on the 1-boundary of a 3-dimensional cube would have points that lie (apart from noise) on the 12 edges of the cube; in contrast, uniform data on the 2-boundary of the cube would have points that lay (apart from noise) on the 6 faces of the cube. And clearly, when $q = p = 3$, there is no structure present that anyone would be interested to discover. We wish to examine how well average local dimensionality and sparsity do in finding the cases for which $q < p$.

Before describing the simulation experiment in more detail, we note that the choice of the q-dimensional boundary of a p-dimensional cube as the example manifold is driven by several considerations:

1. For a fixed p and all values of q ($q \leq p$), the covariance matrix of the entire dataset is (up to noise) of the form $\sigma^2 \mathbf{I}$; thus a typical naive analysis based on correlations would fail to find the hidden structure.

2. If one uses X-gobi or some other data projection and rotation scheme [23], then from nearly every angle, the data appear uninteresting (i.e., spherically symmetric noise). This is an instantiation of a theorem by Diaconis and Freedman [6], which says that in high dimensions, nearly every projection of a dataset appears normally distributed.

3. The simulation task is easy. As shown by an induction argument given in Sommerville [22], a p-dimensional cube has $2^{p-q} \binom{p}{q}$ different q-dimensional boundaries, each of which is itself a q-dimensional cube. Thus one simulates uniformly in the unit cube in $\mathbb{R}^q$, then pads the vectors with $p - q$ additional components, at each of the $\binom{p}{q}$ possible choices for insertions, with zeroes and/or ones. That is, to produce a particular q-dimensional face, one selects the $p - q$ components at which insertions will be made, and then assigns one of the 2^{p-q} possible patterns of zeroes and ones.

This geometric structure makes generalization to higher dimensions straightforward. Of course, a different kind of manifold might lead to different simulation results. But to preclude nonidentifiabililty, one needs to ensure that the underlying manifold cannot assume arbitrarily large numbers of folds or creases, as that situation cannot be distinguished from a truly p-dimensional manifold.

The experiment consists of 20 replications at each combination of the following factor levels:

1. Dimension. We take all values of (p, q) such that $7 \geq p \geq q \geq 1$. (A preliminary experiment took even larger values of p, but that proved time-intensive as data sparsity became a problem.)

2. Noise. All sample observations (uniform on the q-surface) are corrupted by independent p-variate Gaussian noise with mean $\mathbf{0}$ and covariance matrix $\sigma^2 \mathbf{I}$ where σ^2 takes two levels: 0.02 and 0.1. (This amount of noise is relatively small, but since the effect of noise becomes confounded with the amount of crumpling, as reflected in the number of joinings of q-dimensional faces, we chose to focus on the simplest version of the problem.)

3. Sample Size. We consider two levels; the general formula is $n = 2^q k$, where $k = 10, 15$. (This allows the sample sizes at each level of this factor to vary

according to the dimension, reflecting the unequal informational demands imposed by the COD.)

This design is not intended as a stringent test of the strategy, but rather establishes the general sensitivity of our implementational code to choices of sphere size and the threshold values for the eigenvalue sum.

For completeness, we note that the algorithm used in the simulation experiment differs slightly from the heuristic sketched in the previous section. In order to avoid the technical difficulties that result from trying to place hyperspheres at random in an arbitrary dataset volume, we make it a practice to first "sphere" the data. This is done by subtracting off the sample mean and premultiplying the result by the square root of the inverse of the sample covariance matrix S; i.e., the transformed data vector Y_i is found as

$$Y_i = S^{-1/2}(X_i - \bar{X}).$$

The result is that the sphered dataset has mean 0 and covariance matrix I. This affine transformation does not affect the local dimensionality of the problem.

The first results of the experiment are shown in Table 32.1. The entries show the average of the average local dimensionality over the 20 replications of the treatment combinations, and the corresponding standard errors. The factor levels determine the small sample size, low-noise regime (or $k = 10$, $\sigma^2 = .02$).

q							
7							5.03
							.003
6						4.25	4.23
						.004	.010
5					3.49	3.55	3.69
					.003	.010	.012
4				2.75	2.90	3.05	3.18
				.006	.009	.015	.012
3			2.04	2.24	2.37	2.50	2.58
			.010	.010	.009	.011	.009
2		1.43	1.58	1.71	1.80	1.83	1.87
		.014	.007	.007	.012	.012	.012
1	.80	.88	.92	.96	.95	.95	.98
	.000	.005	.010	.013	.006	.009	.007
$p=1$	2	3	4	5	6	7	

TABLE 32.1

The value of p indicates the apparent dimension, while q is the true dimension of the data. In each double row, the top number is the estimate of q, while the bottom number is the standard error of that estimate.

From Table 32.1, it is clear that the estimates of q are extremely stable across different values of p. The estimates tend to increase slightly with p, but appear to reach a bounding asymptote, as one would expect. Also, note that the estimates are all somewhat lower than the true value of q. This is also to be expected, since

Statistical Data Mining and Knowledge Discovery 543

within each hypersphere, the principal components analysis declares only as many dimensions as are needed to explain 80% of the total variation in the enclosed data.

For other levels of the design factors, a similar stability is found. Interested readers may obtain many such tables by contacting the authors.

The second portion of the simulation experiment concerns sparsity, and the results are shown in Table 32.2. This table displays the average sparsity proportion over the 20 replications of the design. The factor levels shown in the table correspond to large sample size and the high-noise situation (or $k = 15$ and $\sigma^2 = 0.1$). The full set of tables is available from the authors.

q							
7							41.0
6						39.1	52.2
5					34.4	45.3	53.2
4				32.3	36.2	46.1	55.9
3			29.1	27.0	34.7	48.6	57.9
2		28.4	26.5	32.0	41.6	46.6	55.2
1	28.5	40.1	45.8	51.0	51.3	51.0	52.5
	p=1	2	3	4	5	6	7

TABLE 32.2
The value of p indicates the apparent dimension, while q is the true dimension of the data. The number in a row indicates the proportion of spheres that did not contain at least $2p$ observations.

The results in Table 32.2 show that as p increases, the proportion of hyperspheres that are sparse increases. This is a natural consequence of the second formulation of the COD; to a degree, it also follows from the geometry of the particular crumpled surface that we explore. In general, p-cubes built from q-dimensional boundaries are hollow when $q < p$, and thus by construction the data should contain a volume that is sparse. This points up the delicate interplay between sample size, noise, and the amount of crumpledness in the underlying structure.

In the simulations used to produce Table 32.2, our program took the fixed radius to be

$$r = \left(\frac{3p \left(\frac{\sqrt{p}}{2} \right)^p}{2^p k \binom{p}{q}} \right)^{\frac{1}{p}},$$

which aims at ensuring that the expected number of points inside the hypersphere is $3p/n$, with an inflation factor to scale for the COD (this assumes uniformity in the p-dimensional unit sphere, which seems a sensible approximate description of the null distribution after sphering the data). But other choices are worth consideration; in particular, we now recommend that one try to ensure that (under uniformity) the probability of a random hypersphere being sparse be fixed across comparisons at some common value v for all values of p and n. To achieve this, one would use the relationship between the binomial sum and the beta function by setting

$$\begin{aligned} v &= P[\text{less than } 2p+1 \text{ values}] \\ &= \sum_{j=0}^{2p} (r^p)^j (1-r^p)^{n-j} \\ &= \frac{n!}{(2p)!(n-2p-1)!} \int_{r^p}^{1} x^{2p}(1-x)^{n-2p-1} dx \end{aligned}$$

where r^p is the probability of inclusion in the sampling hypersphere as derived from the formula for the volume of a p-dimensional sphere. Solving this incomplete beta function for r is computationally intensive, but standardizes comparisons across the rows and columns in Table 32.2 and the related tables not shown in this paper.

32.3.3 Regression

We want to extend the structure discovery approach to regression analysis. The way to do this is to replace the principal components analysis at each random placement of the small hypersphere with a principal components stepwise regression. The number of components that are selected for inclusion in the model represents the local dimensionality of the functional relationship between the explanatory variables and the response. When this number is low, there is hope that MARS, ACE, GAM, PPR, or one of the other new wave methods might be tuned to discover the kind of relationship that exists.

Of course, this implementation requires a bit more judgment. One must determine the levels of significance in the repeated tests used for variable selection in stepwise regression, and one should also set a minimum value for the coefficient of determination, below which one does not feel that the strength of the local relationship is sufficiently strong to warrant further study. In this spirit, one can also calculate the local average coefficient of determination which, if small, might persuade one that an analysis is bootless, despite a low average local dimensionality. This would occur, for example, if the explanatory variables had locally low-dimensional structure, but were independent or nearly independent of the response variables.

Of course, even if our technique finds that there is a locally low-dimensional structure relating the response to the explanatory variables, there is no guarantee that any of the new-wave regression methods will be successful in sorting this out. Our sense is that in many cases one will need to use the results of the method we employ to segment the space into disjoint regions within which a particular regression method is useful. This segmentation might be carried out with respect to either the explanatory variables, the response variable, or both. Related discussion occurs in Li [16].

32.4 Estimating Exposure

As a closing note, a common data mining problem in federal agencies revolves around estimates of exposure from spontaneous reports. For example:

- The Consumer Products Safety Commission must identify products that may cause fires based on reports from homeowners or fire departments.

- The U.S. Food and Drug Administration must identify vaccines or drugs that cause rare adverse reactions, based on reports from patients or medical examiners.

- The National Highway Transportation Safety Administration must identify makes of automobiles that are prone to accidents, based on complaints by owners and police reports.

- Consular officers must identify regions that abuse human rights, based on reports of deaths or disappearances by media, church groups, or family members.

In each of these cases one wants to estimate risk. This requires a numerator (the number of bad outcomes) divided by a denominator (the exposure). But the available data from spontaneous reports only provide direct information on the numerator.

To be specific, suppose one wants to estimate the fatality rate from automobiles for last year, in order to decide whether safety is improving. Ideally, that would be done by dividing the total number of fatal accidents by the total number of miles driven on U.S. roads. The Fatality Analysis Reporting System provides excellent data on the numerator, but the Highway Performance Monitoring System gives only an imprecise estimate of the denominator. Since the delta method shows that the variance of a ratio is

$$\text{var}(X/Y) = (\mathbb{E}[X]/\mathbb{E}[Y])^2 \left[\frac{\text{var}[X]}{\mathbb{E}[X]^2} + \frac{\text{var}[Y]}{\mathbb{E}[Y]^2} - \frac{2\text{Cov}[X,Y]}{\mathbb{E}[X]\mathbb{E}[Y]} \right]$$

then the uncertainty in the denominator can easily be more important than the uncertainty in the numerator. Thus accuracy in estimating fatality rates would be most improved by focusing resources upon estimating the number of miles that people drive.

32.4.1 Categorical Data

The Adverse Event Reporting System (AERS) may be thought of as a table whose rows are drugs and whose columns are adverse events (e.g., stroke, stomachache, gastrointestinal bleeding, etc.). In each cell there is a count of the number of people who took a given drug and reported a specific adverse event. For obvious reasons, the U.S. Food and Drug Administration would like to be able to identify the most common side-effects associated with particular drugs.

But AERS data are not, on the face of it, sufficient to the task. A few strokes or stomachaches are to be expected in any large patient population. There is only a safety issue when those events are disproportionately associated with a given drug. But it is very difficult to determine how many people use particular drugs; physicians believe that much prescribed medication sits on a shelf and is never used. And if the drug causes headaches or stomachaches, people are even less likely to use it, creating a bias in reporting rates.

Nonetheless, there are some strategies that offer help in the AERS situation. Du-Mouchel [7] has proposed a Bayesian data mining technique that enables one row of the AERS matrix to stand as a proxy for exposure in the others. Conceptually, the ratio of adverse events between two drugs (rows) should be the same across all columns (events), unless the drug in one row is a causitive factor in the specific kind of event. In that case, the ratio will be different in that column. There are many more details in this strategy; since one has Poisson event counts under the null model of no causation, then it is useful to use the geometric mean of the empirical Bayes posterior distribution of the relative risk. This is essentially a shrinkage argument, to deflate the false signals that arise by chance in a large table with many cells that have low numbers.

This is still only a partially satisfactory solution. It does not take proper account of the underreporting bias [14], and it does not use all of the medical and prescription rate information that is available. Nonetheless, in the AERS application, it is being used with some success.

In federal agencies, there are many datasets that contain spontaneous event reports, and these are often important for public health and safety. It would be a great step forward to further develop this kind of methodolgy, enabling better estimates of risk to guide policy formulation.

References

[1] Banks, D.L., Olszewski, R.T., and Maxion, R. (2003). Comparing methods for multivariate nonparametric regression. To appear in *Communications in Statistics: Simulation and Computation*.

[2] Barron, A.R. (1994). Approximation and estimation bounds for artificial neural networks. *Machine Learning*, **14**, 115–133.

[3] Borg, I. and Groenen, P.J.F. (1997). *Modern Multidimensional Scaling*. Springer-Verlag, New York.

[4] Breiman, L., Friedman, J., Olshen, R.A., and Stone, C. (1984). *Classification and Regression Trees*, Wadsworth, Belmont, CA.

[5] Cutler, A. and Breiman, L. (1994). Archetypal analysis. *Technometrics*, **36**, 338–347.

[6] Diaconis, P. and Freedman, D. (1984). Asymptotics of graphical projection pursuit. *Annals of Statistics*, **12**, 793–815.

[7] DuMouchel, W. (1999). Bayesian data mining in large frequency tables, with an application to the FDA spontaneous reporting system. *The American Statistician*, **53**, 177–202.

[8] Flury, B. (1990). Principal points. *Biometrika*, **77**, 33–41.

[9] Friedman, J.H. (1991). Multivariate additive regression splines. *Annals of Statistics*, **19**, 1–66.

[10] Freund, Y. and Schapire, R.E. (1996). Experiments with a new boosting algorithm. In *Machine Learning: Proceedings of the Thirteenth International Conference*, 148–156. Morgan Kaufmann, San Mateo, CA.

[11] Gersho, A. and Gray, R.M. (1992). *Vector Quantization and Signal Compression*. Kluwer Academic Publishers, Norwell, MA.

[12] Hastie, T. and Stuetzle, W. (1989). Principal curves. *Journal of the American Statistical Association*, **84**, 502–516.

[13] Hastie, T.J. and Tibshirani, R.J. (1990). *Generalized Additive Models*, Chapman and Hall, New York.

[14] van der Heijden, P.G.M., van Puijenbroek, E.P., van Buuren, S., and van der Hofstede, J.W. (2002). On the assessment of adverse drug reactions from spontaneous reporting systems: the influence of under-reporting on odds ratios. *Statistics in Medicine*, **21**, 2027–2044.

[15] Kruskal, J. B. (1975). Locally linear and locally isometric mapping. In *Theory, Methods, and Applications of Multidimensional Scaling and Related Techniques*. National Science Foundation, Washington, DC, pp. 27–33.

[16] Li, K.-C. (1991). Sliced inverse regression for dimension reduction (with discussion). *Journal of the American Statistical Association*, **86**, 316–327.

[17] MacQueen, J.B. (1967). Some methods for classification and analysis of multivariate observation. In *Proceedings of the 5th Berkeley Symposium on Mathematical Statistics and Probability*, ed. by L. LeCam and J. Neyman. University of California Press, Berkeley, pp. 281–297.

[18] Rousseeuw, P. and Yohai, V. (1984). Robust regression by means of S-estimators. In *Robust and Nonlinear Time Series Analysis*, Lecture Notes in Statistics No. 26, ed. by J. Franke, W. Härdle, and D. Martin. Springer-Verlag, Berlin, pp. 256–272.

[19] Sakata, S. and White, H. (1998). Breakdown points. In *Encyclopedia of Statistical Sciences, Update Volume 3*, ed. by S. Kotz, C. B. Read, and D. Banks. John Wiley and Sons, New York, pp. 84–89.

[20] Scott, D. and Wand, M.P. (1991). Feasibility of multivariate density estimates. *Biometrika*, **78**, 197–205.

[21] Shepard, R.N. and Carroll, J.D. (1966). Parametric representation of nonlinear data structures. In *Multivariate Analysis: Proceedings of an International Symposium Held in Dayton, Ohio, June 14-19, 1965*, ed. by P. R. Krishnaiah, Academic Press, New York, pp. 561–592.

[22] Sommerville, D.M.Y. (1958). *An Introduction to the Geometry of N Dimensions*. Dover, New York.

[23] Swayne, D.F., Cook, D., and Buja, A. (1991). XGobi: Interactive dynamic graphics in the X window system with a link to S. *Proceedings of the American Statistical Association Section on Statistical Graphics*, 1–8. ASA, Alexandria, VA.

[24] Zhao, C. and Atkeson, P. (1992). *Advances in Neural Information Processing Systems*, **4**, 936–943.

33

STING: Evaluation of Scientific & Technological Innovation and Progress in Europe Through Patents

S. Sirmakessis,[1] K. Markellos,[2] P. Markellou,[3] G. Mayritsakis[4], K. Perdikouri,[5] A. Tsakalidis,[6] and Georgia Panagopoulou[7]

[1-6]*Computer Technology Institute, and* [7]*National Statistical Services of Greece, IT Division, Greece*

CONTENTS

33.1	Introduction	549
33.2	Methodology for the Analysis of Patents	550
33.3	System Description	559
33.4	Technology Indicators	563
33.5	Conclusion	568
	References	569

33.1 Introduction

Nowadays, the increase of the volume of data stored into different computer systems is so huge that only one extremely reduced portion of these data (typically between 5 to 10%) can be effectively analyzed. The use of techniques of automatic analysis allows us to valorize in a more efficient way the potential wealth of information that the textual databases represent.

The old technology must be considered today as the main equipment for the description of the scientific and technological evolution. The existing systems of interrogating databases allow users to understand completely a query and provide them with references concerning the subject they are interested in which the references used in our study will be the patent references.

In general, the analysis and comparison of the scientific and technological activity between countries and/or enterprises, with the help of brevets, is made through a priori classifications and different types of indicators. Describing them in this way allows scientists to free the tendencies and the essential points in the peak fields and to place them according to the industrial activity worldwide. On the other hand, it does not allow a multi-dimensional comparison, neither of the countries and activity fields, nor of the concurrence within the same activity field.

In this paper, we give an answer to the problem of the lack of the brevets' multidimensional analysis. All this study is based on the principles and methods of textual analysis. This type of approach allowed us to manage in an elegant way data that are difficult to use, such as the patents. The aim is to show effectively how the use of methods, like the hierarchic classification, makes possible to answer questions, applied by industry, concerning the interactions existing between the different fields of activity and the poles of innovation that are being created in these fields. We also describe in a detailed way the different step-by-step treatments applied to patents database, in order to get all necessary information required to find the position of the European industry in the international environment.

This type of analysis and decision-making assist tool will enormously facilitate the experts' web, and at the same time decrease the risks of making mistakes or eventually forgetting something that could be issued when not estimating in their entirety the links and relations between patents.

A classificatory approach is therefore the most suitable, in order to respond to problems like those posed by the technological alert. With this approach two patents belong to the same class, not only because they cover the same sectors, but also because they are seldom shared with other patents.

We should also mention the appearance of some interesting and not too easy to reveal phenomena on the databases, such as the existence of a priori patents with no direct relation, combining equivalent technologies. Textual analysis seems to be, because of that, perfectly appropriate for the bibliometric analysis. It does not neglect any information, even if its weak presence gives to it an *a priori* minor character.

Of course, many problems (algorithmic or conceptual) that we have met remain internally complicated and still require the discovery of satisfactory theoretical solutions. However, the work already done in the different disciplines has gained today a sufficient critical volume, in order to permit the realization of the performed techniques and effectively introduce the application of results. In this paper we present the way in which we use the international patent classification hierarchy, in order to produce meaningful results, as well as the methodology applied to clustering. The results of the study are also presented.

33.2 Methodology for the Analysis of Patents

The proposed methodology provides a multidimensional analysis of patent data. This enables multidimensional comparisons between the countries and/or the sectors, while it also allows identification of competition within the same sector. Interactions that exist between various domains of technological activity and the poles of innovation that exist inside these domains are captured. The proposed technique of

Statistical Data Mining and Knowledge Discovery 551

automatic analysis allows exploiting the information stored in patent databases, in a more effective way. The innovative character of the methodology proposed in this project consists in the fact that it does not only use the first digits of the IPC code of a patent, but also any other information that is stored in the classification record of a patent. This approach enables comparisons between countries, companies and specific sectors, as well as the extraction of other useful conclusions. Furthermore, through this approach we have the ability to analyze scientific and technological innovation and progress in Europe at three different levels.

- Firstly, analysis can be performed at the *level of a sector*. This means that a specific sector can be isolated in order to be analyzed and consequently identify technological evolution, which is not very evident. More specifically, for the analysis we use the IPC codes and/or the text describing a patent in order to create homogeneous classes from which technological trends can be identified and derive useful information. Variables that are not involved in the main part of the analysis, such as the companies submitting the patents, the inventors, the countries in which the patent is submitted, etc. would enrich the result of the classification as complementary analysis variables.

- The same analysis could be performed at the *level of all sectors*. This would enable us to obtain information about scientific and technological activity per selected sector with relation to the set of companies submitting patents in this specific sector, for a specific year or for several years.

- Furthermore, analysis at the *level of a country* is available. Through this analysis, homogeneous groups of countries are formed, which show the progress of the scientific and technological analysis in the different countries of Europe. Indicators regarding the competitive level of each country are extracted, as well as listings of the countries that are active in a specific technological domain, etc.

The kind of information described above is produced by data analysis methods and more specifically by classification techniques. The production of homogeneous clusters is based on methods, a brief presentation of which will be provided next in this document.

The basic steps of the analysis are presented below:

- Textual analysis of the IPC codes and the texts describing the patents.

- Multiple Factor analyses based on boostrap techniques for controlling the stability of the method.

- Creation of homogeneous classes of patents based on their codes and texts that describe the patents, using the methods of correspondence and cluster analysis. The objective of this stage is to look for families of patents characterized by their similarities in terms of shared technologies.

33.2.1 Textual Analysis Techniques

As already mentioned, textual analysis techniques form the basis of the developed methodology for the analysis of patents. Textual analysis of the codes and titles or abstracts describing a patent is applied. Some basic concepts of textual analysis are presented, in order to have a complete view of the undertaken statistical methodology for the exploitation of patent data.

In every statistical problem the following procedure is followed: firstly, we identify the nature of the problem and formulate it according to specific statistical or probabilistic models. The type of data may lead to various types of analysis. A pre-processing of the data may be necessary before involving them in any kind of analysis. Also, the pre-processing phase may include the testing of hypotheses or models. Finally, for the interpretation of the results many activities may be necessary, such as a critical evaluation of the hypotheses and models, etc. However, the need for analyzing texts is increasing in many fields of scientific research. Statistical methods rely on measurements and counts based on objects that are to be compared. In the case that textual units are under consideration, these should be analyzed through the use of discrete, qualitative variables, such as the counts, rather than with variables of continuous nature. Generally, the statistical analysis of texts is quite complicated since every text possesses a sequential or syntagmatic dimension; therefore its formulation is too complex. In addition the relationships between words of a text should be taken into account and could be brought into light through counts. Counting elements and adding them together means that they are treated as identical occurrences. Before performing any kind of analysis, textual data should be decomposed in simpler lexical units. Several methods of lexicometric processing exist that help identify specific units of the text upon which counts are carried out. In order to choose units from the text the procedures of segmentation, identification, lemmatization, disambiguation can be applied. Segmentation consists in subdividing the text into minimum units, i.e., units that are not to be subdivided further. Then follows the phase of identification, i.e., the grouping of identical units. Once the segmentation unit is defined then textual statistics methods are applied. Furthermore, the elements resulting from segmentation can be lemmatized. In this case identification rules should be established so that words arising from the different inflections of a lemma are grouped together. The main steps of a lemmatization are the following:

- Verb forms are out into the infinitive.

- Nouns are put into the singular.

- Elisions are removed.

Automatic lemmatization requires a disambiguation, including a morpho-syntactic analysis and some times a pragmatic analysis. In some cases, in order to have a systematic determination of the lemma to which a form in a text belongs, a prior disambiguation is required. This need for disambiguation arises in many cases such as: when a given unit corresponds to inflectional forms of different lemmas, or when units of the same etymological source exist. In other cases ambiguities concerning the syntactic function of a word have to be removed, requiring a grammatical analysis of the sentence containing it. So, this procedure assists the automatic identification of the morpho-syntactic categories (noun, verb, adjective, etc.) of the words in the documents. In this way, we can filter non-significant words on the basis of their morpho-syntactic category.

In addition, there are cases where the meaning of words is closely related to the way they appear together. In these cases, the identification of repetitive segments may be another solution for identifying lexical units that could be used in the statistical analysis. Textual data analysis, when used for extracting information from documents, relies on a cluster analysis based on the chi-square distance between the lexical profiles. For each of the resulting clusters characteristic words, i.e., words with a frequency in the cluster significantly higher than the one expected according to a predefined probabilistic model, are extracted. Each of the clusters is then represented by a characteristic document, which is the document in the cluster that contains the most characteristic words.

After the pre-processing of the data and in order to proceed with the analysis, several types of methods can be applied for obtaining useful results. Firstly, it should be mentioned that computer-based processing of textual data is greatly simplified by applying a technique called numeric coding. This technique consists in giving a numeric code to each word involved in the analysis. This code is associated with each occurrence of the word. Then a quantitative analysis of the vocabulary is performed. In fact, a table of frequencies of each word is obtained, on which the next steps of the analysis of data will be based. In addition, indexes and concordances of the data can be produced in order to provide a different perspective from the one obtained when having a sequential reading of the corpus. Consequently, an alphabetic index can be obtained, where words that participate in the analysis are arranged in alphabetical order. There is also the ability to obtain lexical tables, as well as to take into account repeated segments. It is important to have the ability to identify segments since the meaning of words is closely related to the way they appear in compound words or in phrases and expressions that can either inflect or completely change their meanings. So, in several cases it is useful to count larger units consisting of several words. These elements can be analyzed in the same way as words. In addition in such analysis there is always the problem of misleading segments, which are identical because of the existence of punctuation marks. In order to face this situation the status of strong separator or sentence separator is assigned to some of the punctuation marks (such as period, exclamation point, question mark). Also, weak punctuation marks are defined (such as comma, semicolon, colon, hyphen, quotation marks and parentheses). These delimiters are called sequence delimiters. Apart from them exist the word delimiters, which are treated as characters called blanks or spaces.

33.2.2 Correspondence and Cluster Analysis Techniques

The main idea behind this approach is to represent the patents in a high dimensional vector space, in which each of the available codes represents a dimension. Repre-

Role & use of statistical techniques (factor & cluster analysis)	
Input :	Frequency tables with words in rows and codes in columns (or the inverse).
Statistical processing of the frequency table:	✓ Multiple Factor Analyses based on boostrap techniques ✓ Correspondence Analysis (hidden) ✓ Cluster Analysis
How cluster analysis works:	Create groups of words and codes according to the chi-square distance or a predefined similarity criterion
Output of cluster analysis:	✓ Creation of families of patents characterised by their similarities in terms of shared technologies ✓ Relationships between groups of patents
Additional information:	Use of supplementary variables i.e. inventors, assignees, priority year, priority country etc.
Capture of any kind of information based on the results of cluster analysis:	Combination of information derived from groups of patents and supplementary variables for the production of graphs, reports and tables for an informative represenation of desired information

FIGURE 33.1

Process of cluster analysis: input data, processing of data, aim of the analysis, outputs.

senting the patents in such a space allows the visualization of their relative position and groupings, which are indicative of various implicit relationships and can serve as a basis for the analysis of technological innovation. However, because of the intrinsic complexity of any interpretation within highly dimensional vector spaces specific data analysis tools need to be used such as factorial and clustering techniques for textual data.

The main method on which the derivation of good results depends is cluster analysis. However, in some cases, a factor analysis may precede the cluster analysis. In fact the use of factor analysis has a dual goal. Firstly, multiple factor analysis will be performed and through the use of bootstrap techniques the stability of the method will be presented to the user. Thus multiple ellipsoid graphs will be demonstrated enabling the user to draw conclusions about the stability of the method. Secondly, it is under consideration to use correspondence analysis that will not be presented to the user with the aim to ensure the robustness of the cluster analysis. A schematic representation of the idea incorporated in the role and use of the proposed statistical methodology based on factor and cluster analysis is given in Figure 33.1.

33.2.2.1 Factor Analysis (Correspondence Analysis)

Factor analysis (in this case correspondence analysis) allows to approximate (with minimal distortion) the high dimensional representations in the more manageable 2D or 3D spaces that can be directly visualized. So, the role of factor analysis is to find lower-dimensional subspaces, which more accurately approximate the original distributions of points. However, the reduction of dimensionality cannot be obtained without a certain loss of information. Factor analysis is applied to the contingency tables and permits studying the relationships that exist between nominal variables. More specifically the columns of this contingency table represent the modalities of the nominal variable while the rows represent the other variable. In the case of textual data a special contingency table is used where rows represent words or lemmas of words, etc. while the columns are groupings of texts. In a typical correspondence analysis, a cross-tabulation table of frequencies is first standardized, so that the relative frequencies across all cells sum to 1.0. One way to state the goal of a typical analysis is to represent the entries in the table of relative frequencies in terms of the distances between individual rows and/or columns in a low-dimensional space. More analytically, in order to analyze a contingency table we use the repartitions in percentage in the interior of each line or column, i.e., the line-profile or column-profile, which makes comparable the modalities of a variable. The proximities between points are interpreted in terms of similarities. In fact, a geometrical representation of similarities between different modalities of the same variable is performed.

The first step in the analysis is to compute the relative frequencies for the frequency table, so that the sum of all table entries is equal to 1.0. Then this table shows how one unit of mass is distributed across the cells. In the terminology of correspondence analysis, the row and column totals of the matrix of relative frequencies are called the row mass and column mass, respectively. If the rows and columns in a table are completely independent of each other, the entries in the table (distribution of mass) can be reproduced from the row and column totals alone, or row and column profiles. According to the formula for computing the chi-square statistic, the expected frequencies in a table, where the column and rows are independent of each other, are equal to the respective column total times the row total, divided by the grand total. Any deviations from the expected values (expected under the hypothesis of complete independence of the row and column variables) will contribute to the overall chi-square. Thus, another way of looking at correspondence analysis is to consider it as a method for decomposing the overall chi-square statistic (or Inertia=Chi-square/Total N) by identifying a small number of dimensions in which the deviations from the expected values can be represented.

33.2.2.2 Cluster Analysis

The basic objective in cluster analysis is to discover natural groupings of the items. Grouping is done on the basis of similarities or distances. In our case the aim is to look for families of patents characterized by their similarities in terms of shared technologies, i.e., eliminate classes of patents, which are similar in the codes, and words that they have in common. Several similarities measures can be adopted. Usually distances are used for clustering items and correlations to cluster variables. At the first step, when each object represents its own cluster, the distances between those objects are defined by the chosen distance measure. However, once several objects have been linked together, there is the need for defining a linkage rule in order to determine when two clusters are sufficiently similar to be linked together. Several linkage rules exist which are briefly described below. The single linkage method is according to which two clusters could be linked together when any two objects in the two clusters are closer together than the respective linkage distance. That is, we use the "nearest neighbors" across clusters to determine the distances between clusters. This rule produces "stringy" types of clusters, that is, clusters "chained together" by only single objects that happen to be close together. Other linkage rules are the complete linkage (furthest neighbor) method and the **Ward's method**. In the complete linkage method distances between clusters are determined by the greatest distance between any two objects in the different clusters (i.e., by the "furthest neighbors"). The **Ward's method** is distinct from all other methods because it uses an analysis of variance approach to evaluate the distances between clusters. In short, this method attempts to minimize the Sum of Squares (SS) of any two (hypothetical) clusters that can be formed at each step.

Apart from the measures of similarity used for identifying relationships between objects, the grouping into clusters can also be performed through different approaches. Therefore, different clustering algorithms have been created, among which are these of the hierarchical clustering, the k-means algorithm or a mixture of these algorithms.

Hierarchical clustering techniques proceed by either a set of successive mergers or a series of successive divisions. Agglomerative hierarchical methods start with the individual objects. Thus there are initially as many clusters as objects. The most similar objects are first grouped and these initial groups are merged according to their similarities; as the similarity decreases all subgroups are fused into a single cluster. On the contrary, divisive hierarchical methods start from an initial single group of objects, which is subdivided into two subgroups so that the objects in each subgroup are completely different between each other. These subgroups are then further subdivided into dissimilar subgroups and the process ends up when there are as many subgroups as objects, i.e., until each object forms a group. The results of both methods can be displayed in a dendrogram.

Non-hierarchical clustering techniques (such as k-means method) are designed to group items rather than variables into a specific number of clusters, which can either be specified in advance or determined as a part of the clustering procedure. Non-hierarchical methods start either from an initial partition of items into groups or an initial set of seed points that will form the nuclei of clusters.

33.2.2.3 Cluster Analysis of Words and Texts

In the case of textual data, clustering techniques are used for representing proximities between the elements of a lexical table through groupings or clusters.

When methods of hierarchical clustering are used, then we obtain a hierarchy of groups partially nested in one another, starting with a set of elements that are characterized by variables. On the other hand, when direct clustering methods are applied, then simple segments or partitions of the population are produced without the intermediate step of hierarchical cluster analysis.

So, cluster analysis is applied to the column and row matrices of lexical tables. Either the entire set of columns (usually words and sometimes text parts) or the entire set of rows (most often the different text parts) is clustered. Hierarchical agglomeration as already described in the previous section is based on the agglomeration of elements that are close to each other according to the measure of distance used. In the general case, the distances among the elements subjected to cluster analysis are measured using the chi-square distance between the columns of the table. Each of the groupings created at each step, by following this method, constitutes a node. The set of terminal elements corresponding to a node creates a cluster. The representation as a dendrogram of a hierarchical cluster analysis shows that the groups created in the course of a cluster analysis constitute an indexed hierarchy of clusters that are partially nested in one another.

33.2.2.4 Use of Supplementary Variables

Supplementary variables can also be involved in the analysis in order to provide a complete description of the clusters and let us identify information about technological trends, competitors, inventors as well as technological evolution over time and information about priority countries. Below it is shown how additional information can be exploited in order to get a complete view of technological trends and innovation. As already mentioned in previous sections apart from the main variables used in the analysis, i.e., the codes and the abstracts or titles that describe a patent, additional information can be obtained when considering supplementary variables such as inventors, assignees, countries that apply the patent and priority year.

If we take into account the structure of clusters relating to the codes that describe them, then we can derive any other kind of information. Thus, for each cluster considering which codes belong to it and consequently the technological trends it represents, we can have a global view about which companies are especially interested in specific technological sectors, which are the most prominent inventors, the technological activity of different countries and in which sectors, as well as technological evolution over years.

In the following sections we attempt to describe how additional information taking into account supplementary variables can be exploited in order to get results that allow detecting different "situations" related to the technological development and innovation. For reasons of simplicity we present the way supplementary variables can be used for exploiting patent data information in two sections. The first one refers to the societies that deposit patents and what kind of information can be derived from it. The second one refers to the use of two other supplementary variables that describe a patent, those of inventors and priority year. Of course, these are not the only supplementary variables that describe a patent. Therefore, in the two sections mentioned above we describe how these variables can be used in combination with the other supplementary variables. The main aim is to present how the developed statistical methodology offers the ability to exploit all information related to patents and combine different variables in order to get the desirable results, but also an idea of what kind of analysis can be available through the use of this methodology. Furthermore, we should mention that the methodology allows exploiting information in each cluster separately as well as combined information for more than one cluster. As a consequence it is possible for each cluster to exploit information not only from the main variables we used but also from supplementary variables. Below we present how information can be exploited from supplementary variables.

33.2.3 Pre-Processing Steps

33.2.3.1 Transformation of Data

It is important to present the data in the form of a table where each field describing a patent (i.e., assignees, inventors, etc.) will form a column while each patent will form a row. This is a more flexible format of the data that will facilitate their use in the subsequent steps of the procedure but also in the selection of different fields. Furthermore, this will enable us to preserve the relationship that exists between patents and the different fields. It is of great importance to keep up the relationships between different fields since this will enable us to associate supplementary information such as inventors, assignees, etc. to the results obtained from the main part of analysis and especially those of cluster analysis. In order to do this it is therefore necessary to have data sorted according to the number of patent. Therefore we should assign the number of each patent to all fields related to it and then sort according to field. Then for all patents according to their order of appearance in the original data we have a list with all the fields. Thus it is easy to create the table with patents in rows and fields in columns.

33.2.3.2 Selection of Fields Involved in the Analysis

It has already been mentioned that the analysis will mainly be based on the use of codes and either titles or abstracts. However, although there is the ability to download selected fields from the patent database in the case that data are in other forms, we have to choose the fields that will mainly participate in the analysis. These are the main and IC codes as well as titles or abstracts.

33.2.3.3 Transformation of Selected Field in Appropriate Format for Being Used in the Analysis

For continuing the procedures of the analysis it is necessary to appropriately form the data that will participate in the analysis. We should take into account that both the file with titles or abstracts as well as the file with the codes should be transformed. In the case of titles or abstracts the corresponding file should have the format described below. Titles or abstracts should be distinguished among them. Therefore separators should be defined and used. The separators among patents are lines that only contain the symbols "—-" in columns 1 to 4.

Furthermore, the file with the codes that will be involved in the analysis will be treated as the case of numerical data that has to be associated with the file of textual data. The numerical variable is considered nominal with a number of modalities.

Statistical Data Mining and Knowledge Discovery

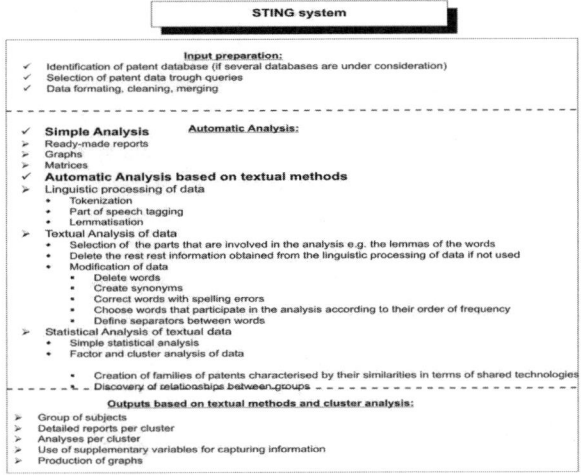

FIGURE 33.2
Basic idea of the way STING works.

Therefore, a file with the labels is created first and a file with the numerical data next. The last file consists of two columns, the first contains the identifiers of patents while in the second column the numerical data are represented.

Additionally, it should be mentioned that in the procedure described above it is possible to use not only the main codes but also IC codes. In this case, special consideration should be given to the way that the relationships between different codes are defined, as well as to which texts (titles or abstracts) these are related. In the development phase, this kind of problem should also be taken into account. Indices denoting which texts the codes are related to should therefore be used.

A breakdown of the developed statistical methodology is presented graphically in Figure 33.2.

33.3 System Description

One of the main objectives of STING project is the design and implementation of a system for the efficient analysis of existing information "hidden" in patent data, in order to produce indicators for the technological innovation in the pan-European level [8],[9], [11],[16], [17],[18]. The system is based on the proposed statistical methodology described in the previous section and focuses on the maximization of end-user's productivity and satisfaction by offering him not only the correct guidance (wizards and help options) but also useful tools and functionalities (filters, charts, reports, etc.). This means on the one hand that the system enables the user to extract only necessary information and exploits it in an effective way for drawing useful conclusions. On the other hand, the system is capable of conforming to continuously changing user needs. Specifically, the target user-groups of the STING system are Science and Research Institutes, Educational Centers (Universities), Statistical Offices, industries, companies, or individuals, etc.

The system consists of three main modules, which integrate a full-operational patent data analysis environment. The functional architecture of STING system is presented in Figure 33.3. It shows the modules-tools of the system and the interactions between them. Each module corresponds to a basic system task, has a pre-specified input and output data format and executes a set of well-defined operations. The main system modules are:

- Database manager module.
- Statistical analysis module.
- Results presentation module.

All the above tools interact and allow easy navigation to the user from the data import level to the analysis and presentation level. It is highlighted by the modular basis of the system, which enables the flexibility of the system to subsequent changes in the used statistical methodologies (addition of new methods, etc.). Furthermore, the structure of the system allows the use of different patent databases.

The different flows are also depicted in the figure, defining the different stages of the analysis and the connections between them. It is also common sense that the natural sequence followed by the flows should be respected for the correct operation and for the robustness of the results. In the following sub-sections the modules of the system as well as the user interface are analytically described.

33.3.1 Database Manager Module

The database manager module is mainly responsible for the patent data import, cleaning and preparation for further processing and analysis.

On a first level the module reads a text file from the MIMOSA search engine and imports it into the STING database (appropriate format). The database fields correspond to the fields describing a patent as presented in the ESPACE ACCESS database of patents. There is no restriction in the database from which will be taken the patent data. According to the user requirement analysis ESPACE ACCESS and ESPACE Bulletin are among the databases most frequently used. Therefore, we used these databases for explaining the statistical methodology through application to real data.

The flexibility of the system to different input databases is achieved through the adoption of specific input formats. Although data from different databases may be used depending on the problem and the information one wants to extract, they are each time standardized to a uniform representation in the system database.

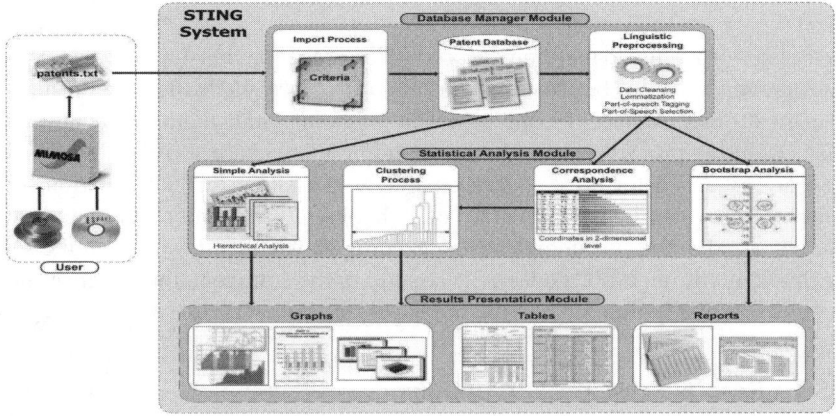

FIGURE 33.3
STING functional architecture.

Before the data import the data are cleaned and filtered. The parser is used for reading the textual data and consequently linguistic preprocessing [2], [7] is applied on them (this includes data cleansing, lemmatization, part-of-speech tagging and part-of-speech selection). The use of a dictionary and of a grammar is necessary for the linguistic processing.

On a final level, the module encodes the textual information describing the patents in a lexical table, which associates the frequencies of the selected words/lemmas with the corresponding patents.

33.3.2 Statistical Analysis Module

The statistical analysis module is mainly responsible for the statistical analysis of data and the production of the technological and scientific indicators. In particular, it applies textual analysis methods on the pre-formatted data, in order to extract valuable information and create the first groups of patents.

There are four different analysis methodologies integrated into the system: simple analysis, correspondence analysis [3], [14], cluster analysis [1], [15], bootstrap analysis. Normally, this module starts after the linguistic processing of data and the creation of a lexical table, which associates the frequencies of the selected words/lemmas with the corresponding patents.

In the case of simple analysis the user can proceed directly to the production of indicators based on the selected database. Otherwise, the user can choose to proceed with a factor analysis on the lexical table and consequently perform the cluster analysis. At the end of cluster analysis the user can explore the homogeneous classes of patents and run the simple analysis in each cluster separately. The aim of the procedure is to identify groups of patents that share common vocabulary and groups of patents that share common technologies in order to derive conclusions about technological trends and innovation.

It is also worthwhile to mention the production of the relationship map that demonstrates the relationships between the clusters or in other words the relationships between the different areas of technology. The technology indicators [6] are also based on the clustering procedure and constitute an important characteristic of the system. These are produced for each cluster separately and allow for identification of the technology on-going in different areas of technology. Furthermore, these indicators are categorized in four different levels depending on whether they refer to the sector of technology (through IPC codes), the country or the continent, the assignees or the inventors and finally time (due to the priority year or other).

33.3.3 Results Presentation Module

The results presentation module is mainly responsible for the data export and the graphical representation of the analysis results.

It is common sense that the visualization of the results is a significant factor for their understanding [10], [19]. This module allows visualization of the desired information in a useful way and is very important for the user in order to fully comprehend their meaning.

Therefore, different options from graphs and tables to ready-made reports are available. The interactivity is an important feature of the system giving to the user the opportunity to intervene in the outputs and adapt these to his real needs. Changes in the colors, types of lines, types of graphs (2-dimensional, 3-dimensional, etc.), fonts, are supported so that one elaborates the results.

Finally, the positioning of the graphs in the space is supported by the system, giving to the user the opportunity to have the optical view he considers appropriate for the visualization of the results.

33.3.4 User Interface

Effective user interfaces generate positive feelings of success, competence, mastery and clarity in the users. However, designing user interfaces is a complex and highly creative process that blends intuition, experience and careful consideration of numerous technical issues. STING system's main aim was the development of a *flexible* and *user-friendly* environment that enables the effective analysis of information stored in patent databases. Especially, novice users have the opportunity to easily navigate the system through an effective graphical user interface and explore every field in patent data analysis.

Hence, the basic user interface specifications that the final system offers include: language/vocabulary, form of dialogue, data entry, windows, use of color, response times, help messages, error messages, system feedback, human-computer interface configuration, documentation, general qualification requirements, [4], [5], [12], [13].

Figure 33.4 provides a first view of the user interface of STING. The system is designed to convey information to users efficiently. For this reason different menus are available, as well as different windows and controls that visualize the functionalities

Statistical Data Mining and Knowledge Discovery 563

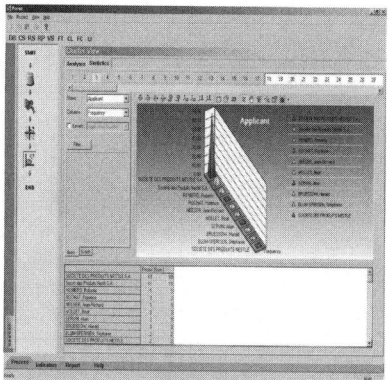

FIGURE 33.4
STING linguistic process.

of the software. Specifically, the main window is separated into sub-windows, each of which describes a different functionality. The basic parts of STING's workspace are the following:

- Main menu.
- STING's Toolbars.
- Tool Window.
- Tool Selector.

The system functionalities and interfaces were tested by groups of users during the validation phase. However, extensive testing and iterative refinement were performed early on to validate the design.

33.4 Technology Indicators

It has already been mentioned that STING will produce indicators either in an overall basis or within clusters. Here particular emphasis is given to the indicators within clusters since they are the result of a specific statistical methodology based on cluster analysis. In addition, these indicators can be categorized according to the patent field to which they are related. More specifically, these are categorized as follows:

- Indicators in the level of areas of technology.
- Indicators in the level of continents/countries/designated states.

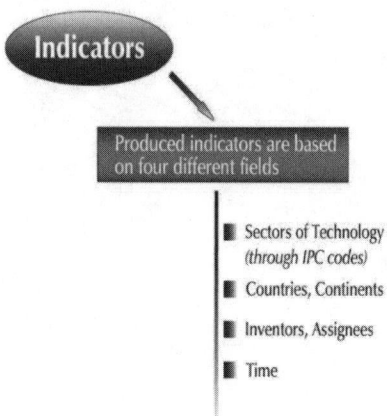

FIGURE 33.5
Categorization of indicators.

- Indicators in the level of assignees/inventors.

- Indicators over time.

A schematic representation of the categorization of indicators is also given in Figure 33.5.

The simplest type of patent indicator is obtained when counting the number of patents satisfying some criteria. These criteria are imposed to other fields such as inventors, assignees, priority countries, priority years or set of criteria imposed to a combination of these fields. In addition counting the number of patents in each cluster either by imposing some criteria or not is an index of great importance since it lets us identify technological tendencies.

33.4.1 Indicators Based on the Technological Sector

The use of cluster analysis allows identification of areas of technology that share common technologies. Each created cluster expresses a specific area of technology. Therefore, there is the ability for each area of technology to define several indicators.

A first indicator is the one that gives the number of patents that correspond to each area of technology. This allows identification of the maturity of a specific area of technology as well as to innovate areas of technology. According to the information one is interested in, one can obtain either the top areas of technology or the less active technologies based on the number of patents.

A more sophisticated indicator about the maturity of each area of technology can be defined as follows. Categorize clusters in "very homogeneous" (this is the case that the major code exists in a percentage greater then 70%), in " relatively homogeneous" (this is the case that the major code exists in a percentage between 55 and 70%) and finally in "nonhomogeneous" (this is the case that a major code does not exist; its percentage is between 35 and 55%) and thus draw conclusions about the homogeneity of clusters as well as about technological activity.

Another indicator may be the dominant codes of each cluster. Then we have at once the major technologies that characterize each area of technology. Percentages or additional information such as how many times they appear in other clusters may also be demonstrated.

33.4.2 Indicators in Level of Continents/Countries/Designated States

The most frequently published indicators are counts of patents taken in a given country, broken down by country of the patentee (the inventor or the applicant) or by priority country (first country where the invention is filed before protection is extended to other countries). However when counting patents applied in a given country by patentees from various countries raises the issue of comparability, i.e., to what extent do countries' shares reflect their technological output. In fact residents in any country have a higher propensity to patent inventions at home than do foreigners. This means that protection for smaller inventions is searched on the local market only. In the sequence we present some indicators that take into account the fields of country, inventor or assignee. These are very simple and are based on the calculation of some simple statistics such as percentages.

33.4.2.1 Level of Continents

For each area of technology, each cluster identifies the patenting activity per continent based on the number of patents or the corresponding percentages. In addition another indicator is that this gives the top areas of technology of each continent or the less active areas of technology for each continent.

33.4.2.2 Level of Countries

A first indicator is that this gives the active countries in each area of technology. Furthermore another indicator is that this specifies the hot areas of technology for specific countries.

33.4.2.3 Level of Designated States

The top designated states (as well as these countries in which the fewest inventions are protected) are a very important element since they give a first view about the strength of the market. Thus a country that is between the top designated states probably indicates the existence of a powerful market. Therefore the ability to identify "strong" markets (i.e., competitive markets) enhances the capabilities of the patent analyst to make good decisions.

Furthermore the countries that are not considered so important, and therefore present a low place in the selected designated states, can be identified.

- The evolution of each country as a designated state over years or for specific years should be presented.
- The selected designated states for USA patents/over years.
- The selected designated states for European patents/over years.
- The selected designated states for Japanese patents/over years.
- The selected designated states for specific European countries patents/over years.
- The average number of designated states per invention.
- Ratio of the selected designated states for USA patents over the totality of patents.
- Ratio of the selected designated states for European patents over the totality of patents.
- Ratio of the selected designated states for Japanese patents over the totality of patents.
- Ratio of the selected designated states for specific European countries patents over the totality of patents.
- For the dominant designated states:
    - Top areas of technology.
    - Top industries.
    - Top inventors.

33.4.3 Indicators for Inventors/Assignees

33.4.3.1 Inventors

In the sequence are presented some statistics based on the notion of inventors.

- Top inventors/less active inventors (also at the level of clusters).
- Average number of inventions per inventor.
- A comparative view of the patenting activity of inventors over years based on the average number of inventions or on patents counts.
- Resident and non-resident inventors.

- Inventors per country, per continent, etc.

The subject of counting the patents relating to the inventors may be faced from different perspectives. According to the patent manual, in the case that the inventors are of different nationalities we should share the patent among the various countries concerned. In measuring a country's patent output this results in fractional counting.

33.4.3.2 Assignees

The field of assignees can be used for a different kind of analysis in order to catch points of interest. Firstly the top assignees as well as the less active are of importance in order to identify the leaders in specific areas of technology, for specific years, etc. Then we should have in mind that these that apply a patent vary from individuals to companies, public or private, universities, etc. Therefore the analyst should be able to define all these categories that will form the basis for different analyses.

Additionally, the distinction between assignees of the same nationality as these of the applicant or of the inventor may be of interest.

- Top assignees/Less active assignees.

- Distinction in companies, institutes, universities, etc.

- Distinction in individuals and societies.

- Distinction in public societies and private societies.

- Distinction in small and big companies.

- Patenting activity of assignees for specific years/over years.

- Average number of assignees per invention.

- Average number of assignees with same nationality of applicant/inventor.

- Average number of assignees with foreigner applicant/inventors.

When patenting by type of assignee is investigated, fractional counts can be used to assign patents to the different groups considered, such as firms, universities, government laboratories, individual inventors and so on.

33.4.4 Indicators over Time

Taking into account the indicators mentioned above, we could derive statistical measures based on the number or percentages of patents for each technology area, as well as for the designated states or inventors. The evolution over time is another feature that helps trace the on-going technology and monitor the novelty of an invention. The field of Priority Year can be used for different kinds of analysis. Firstly one can depict the evolution of patenting activity over time independently of the country of filing. Additionally the evolution over time taking into account the country of filing can be demonstrated. More detailed information can be obtained by combining the field of priority year with this of the inventors. More specifically the inventions can be distinguished in the following categories:

National applications: all applications filed in a national patent office.

Resident applications: all applications filed in a national patent office by inventors residing in a country.

Non-resident applications: all applications filed in a national patent office by persons residing abroad.

33.5 Conclusion

The described system refers to a significant scientific subject, the measurement and assessment of technological innovation through indicators. Specifically, it specializes in the analysis of patents exploiting the totality of information related to them. The fact that we take into account all the information describing a patent, i.e., the codes as well as the titles or abstracts, allows more reliable and complete results. This is the feature that differentiates it from other existing approaches for the exploitation of patent data. Another innovative point is the ability to exploit information stored in various patent databases. Patent data can be reached using filters and downloaded in the appropriate format in order to be involved in the procedures of various supported analysis.

System's statistical methodologies are based on the use of textual and advanced statistical methods such as correspondence and cluster analysis. These statistical procedures permit the effective exploitation of patents enabling the user to capture the desired knowledge in an easy and informative way. Moreover, the automation of the patent data analysis does not require statistical knowledge from non-expert users. The use of the most appropriate statistical tests for ensuring the accuracy and reliability of the method is under consideration. The modular approach ensures system's flexibility and openness to future changes and modifications, e.g., addition of new statistical methods or techniques. Moreover, the system handles dynamically all the available information, regarding patents and indicators. Special consideration was given to user friendliness, interactivity and interoperability.

The produced results can be presented through different ways, which enhance the usability of our system in the domain of patent analysis. The information can be depicted graphically through different kind of graphs such as pie charts, bar charts, etc. In addition, several reports can be derived in order to present information summarizing important features. Another characteristic of the system is the production of ellipsoid graphs as a result of a correspondence analysis. This allows identifying information in an easy way and provides conclusions on a comparative basis.

Finally, it should be also mentioned that efficiency is a very important factor of the system. In order to achieve greater efficiency, in the design of the system a modern and innovative philosophy was followed. More specifically, the following parameters guided the development of the modules:

- Use of open system architecture, to allow the easy adaptation of the system on many different statistical databases;
- Interoperability;
- Development of an integrated processing environment;
- Implementation of a standardized interface.

Taking into consideration the produced indicators and the knowledge extracted from Patent Databases we could propose some improvements in the organization and management of Patent Databases, as a future work.

References

[1] Alderferer, M.S. and Blashfield, R.K. (1986). *Cluster Analysis*. Sage Publications, Inc., Beverly Hills, CA.

[2] Beaugrande, R. and Dressler, W. (1981). *Introduction to Text Linguistics*, Longman, London.

[3] Benzecri, J.P. (1992). *Correspondence Analysis Handbook*, Marcel Dekker, New York.

[4] Brooks, R. (1997). User Interface Design Activities. In Helander et al. 1997, 1461-1473.

[5] Carroll J.M. (Ed.) (1997). Human-Computer Interaction. Part VII of *The Computer Science and Engineering Handbook*, Allen B. Tucker Jr. (Ed.), CRC Press, Inc., Boca Raton.

[6] Chappelier, J., Peristera, V., Rajman, M., and Seydoux, F. (2002) Evaluation of Statistical and Technological Innovation Using Statistical Analysis of Patents, JADT.

[7] Ciravegna, F., Lavelli, A., and Pianesi, F. (1996). Linguistic Processing of Texts Using Geppetto, Technical Report 9602-06, IRST, Povo TN, Italy.

[8] Comanor, W.S. and Scherer, F.M. (1969) Patent Statistics as a Measure of Technical Change. *Journal of Political Economy*, 392-398.

[9] Edelstein, H. (1999). *Introduction to Data Mining and Knowledge Discovery*. Two Crows Corporation.

[10] Fayyad, U., Grinstein, G., and Wierse, A. (2001). *Information Visualization in Data Mining and Knowledge Discovery*. Morgan Kaufmann Publishers.

[11] Fayyad, U., Piatetsky-Shapiro, G., and Smyth, P. (1996). The KDD Process for Extracting Useful Knowledge from Volumes of Data, *Communications of the ACM*, November, Vol. 39, No. 11, 27-34.

[12] Galitz, W. O. (1989; 1993). User-interface Screen Design. QED Information Sciences, Wellesley, MA.

[13] Helander M., Landauer T. K., and Prabhu, P. V. (Eds.) (1997). *Handbook of Human-Computer Interaction*. North-Holland (Second, completely revised edition), Amsterdam.

[14] Hill, M.O. (1974). Correspondence Analysis: a Neglected Multivariate Method. *Journal of Applied Statistics*, Vol. 23, No. 3, 340-354.

[15] Lewis, S. (1991). Cluster Analysis as a Technique to Guide Interface Design, *International Journal of Man-Machine Studies*, 35, 251-265.

[16] Narin, F. (1995). Patents as Indicators for the Evaluation of Industrial Research Output. *Scientometrics*, 34, 3, pp. 489-496.

[17] OECD. (1994). *The Measurement of Scientific and Technological Activities Using Patent Data as Science and Technology Indicators. Patent Manual.*

[18] Schmoch, U., Bierhals, R., and Rangnow, R. (1998). *Impact of International Patent Applications on Patent Indicators. JOINT NESTI/TIP/GSS WORKSHOP*, Room Document No. 1.

[19] Thearling, K., Becker, B., DeCoste, D., Mawby, B., Pilote, M., and Sommerfield D. (2001). Visualizing Data Mining Models. Published in *Information Visualization in Data Mining and Knowledge Discovery*, Usama Fayyad, Georges Grinstein, and Andreas Wierse (Eds.), Morgan Kaufman.

34

The Semantic Conference Organizer

Kevin Heinrich, Michael W. Berry, Jack J. Dongarra, and Sathish Vadhiyar
University of Tennessee, Knoxville, USA

CONTENTS

34.1	Background	571
34.2	Latent Semantic Indexing	572
34.3	Software Issues	573
34.4	Creating a Conference	575
34.5	Future Extensions	579
	Acknowledgment	580
	References	581

The organization of a technical meeting, workshop, or conference involving submitted abstracts or full-text documents can be quite an onerous task. To gain a sense of what topic each submission addresses may require more than just a quick glimpse at the title or abstract. The use of automated indexing and text mining can revolutionize the manner and speed of information assessment and organization. In this work, we demonstrate the use of Latent Semantic Indexing (LSI) for probing and labeling conference abstracts using an intuitive Web interface and client-server internal software design using grid-based middleware such as NetSolve. Automated text parsing and keyword extraction is facilitated using the General Text Parser software (C++) developed in the UTK Department of Computer Science.

34.1 Background

Creating a conference manually can be a burdensome task. After all papers have been submitted, the human organizer must then group the papers into sessions. The session topics can be decided either before or after the organizer has a feel for the material covered in the papers. If the session topics have been pre-conceived, then the organizer must select papers that fit the topic. The other option is to peruse the subject material covered in the papers and discern where natural clusters form and create sessions accordingly. In either case, once a paper has been assigned to a particular session, it cannot belong to another session. This exclusivity causes papers to be grouped together in sub-optimal arrangements so that each topic has a constrained number of papers assigned to it.

Since the average conference has around one hundred papers submitted to it, the organizer must shuffle these papers between topics trying to find a workable fit for the papers and the sessions to which they are assigned. Of course, one person trying to fit fifty to one hundred papers into about twenty sessions will lose context very quickly. Switching rapidly between sessions will cause confusion, and renaming sessions or assigning different topics may cause the entire conference to get reworked. Many times the human organizer will only work with document surrogates such as an abstract or simply the paper title, so often papers will be misclassified due to summarization errors. Also note that a significant amount of time must be spent reading and re-reading abstracts to remember what each paper's subject is. Manually creating a conference takes anywhere from a day to a week or longer. With such a combinatorial problem confronting the person who manually organizes the conference, the need for some sort of automated assistance is justified in hopes of reducing the hours spent in creating a conference.

34.2 Latent Semantic Indexing

In order for the Semantic Conference Organizer to be useful, it must replace the most time-consuming of tasks undertaken when creating a conference—reading. There are several techniques and algorithms used in the field of information retrieval that enable relevant documents to be retrieved to meet a specific need without requiring the user to read each document. The model used by the Semantic Conference Organizer is latent semantic indexing or LSI [1].

Once the document collection is received, it must be parsed into barewords called *tokens*. All punctuation and capitalization is ignored. In addition, articles and other common, non-distinguishing words are discarded. In effect, each document is viewed as a bag of words upon which operations can be performed. Once the bag of words has been formed, a term-by-document matrix is created where the entries of the matrix are the weighted frequencies associated with the corresponding term in the appropriate document.

The weight of a term within a document is a nonnegative value used to describe the correlation between that term and the corresponding document. A weight of zero indicates no correlation. In general, each weight is the product of a local and global component. A simplistic method of obtaining weights is to assign the local component as the frequency of the word within the document and the global component as the log of the proportion of total documents to the number of documents in which the term appears. Such a method is known as a tf-idf (term frequency, inverse-document frequency) weighting scheme [2]. The aim of any scheme is to measure similarity within a document while at the same time measuring the dissimilarity of a document from the other documents within the collection.

The Semantic Conference Organizer uses a log-entropy weighting scheme [3]. The local component l_{ij} and the global component g_i can be computed as

$$l_{ij} = \log_2(1+f_{ij}), \ g_i = 1 + \left(\frac{\sum_j (p_{ij} \log_2(p_{ij}))}{\log_2 n} \right), \ p_{ij} = \frac{f_{ij}}{\sum_j f_{ij}},$$

where f_{ij} is the frequency of the ith term in the jth document, p_{ij} is the probability of the ith term occuring in the jth document, and n is the number of documents in the collection [4]. The weighted frequency for each token is then computed by multiplying its local component by its global component. That is, the term-by-document matrix is defined as

$$M = (m_{ij}), \text{ where } m_{ij} = l_{ij} \times g_{ij}.$$

The aim of using the log-entropy weighting scheme is to downweight high-frequency words while giving distinguishing words higher weight.

Once the $m \times n$ term-by-document matrix, M, has been created, a truncated singular value decomposition of that matrix is performed to create three factor matrices

$$M = K \Sigma D^T,$$

where K is the $m \times r$ matrix of eigenvectors of MM^T, D^T is the $r \times n$ matrix of eigenvectors of $M^T M$, and Σ is the $r \times r$ diagonal matrix containing the r nonnegative singular values of M [5]. The size of these factor matrices is determined by r, the rank of the matrix M. By using only the first s columns of the three component submatrices, we can compute M_s, a rank-s approximation to M. In this case, s is considerably smaller than the rank r. Document-to-document similarity is then computed as

$$M_s^T M_s = (D_s \Sigma_s)(D_s \Sigma_s)^T,$$

and can be derived from the original formula for the rank-s approximation to M [6]. Queries can be treated as *pseudo*-documents and can be computed as

$$q = q_0^T K_s \Sigma_s^{-1},$$

where q_0 is a query vector of the associated term weights [7].

The end result of LSI is a reduced space in which to compare two documents at a broader level. The goal is to map similar word usage patterns into the same geometric space [8]. In effect, documents are compared in a more general sense, so concepts are compared against each other more so than vocabulary.

34.3 Software Issues

The Semantic Conference Organizer is designed to assist a human organizer in creating a conference—it is not a tool for automating conference creation. As such,

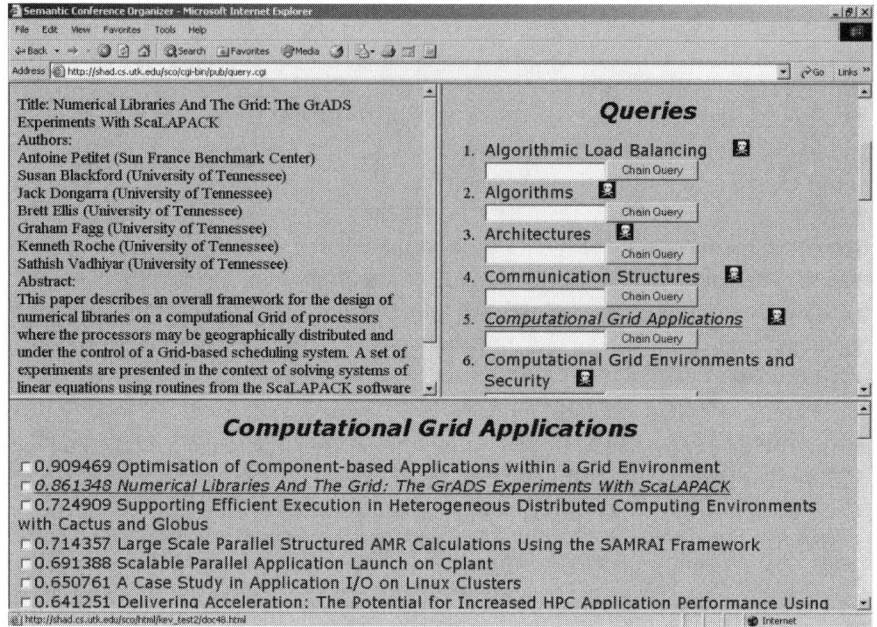

FIGURE 34.1
Sample layout of the Semantic Conference Organizer.

great care was taken to present information to the user without overloading the user with too much information at one time. The three basic actions that an organizer performs to create a conference are reading papers, creating sessions, and grouping papers together to form sessions. Therefore, after a document collection is submitted, the screen is split into three frames in which each of the three aforementioned actions can take place. The right frame is responsible for creating, deleting, and modifying session names, the bottom frame shows how papers semantically fit within a given session and give the user the ability to group papers into a session, and the left frame allows the user to browse a particular document. Figure 34.1 illustrates how splitting the window into three frames enables the user to maintain both a local and a global view of the document collection. Furthermore, it also allows only the requested information to be transmitted across the network at one time, which greatly reduces load time. As discovered in the first attempt at creating the organizer, the delays incurred through CGI can be quite significant if one is attempting to maintain a global perspective on the document collection by transferring the entire document collection with each page load.

Once a document collection is submitted, the text is parsed and keywords are extracted using the General Text Parser (GTP) [9]. Singleton words* are allowed to

---

*A singleton word is one that only occurs once across the entire document collection. Singleton words are discarded in many information retrieval algorithms since a singleton usually does not distinguish a

Statistical Data Mining and Knowledge Discovery   575

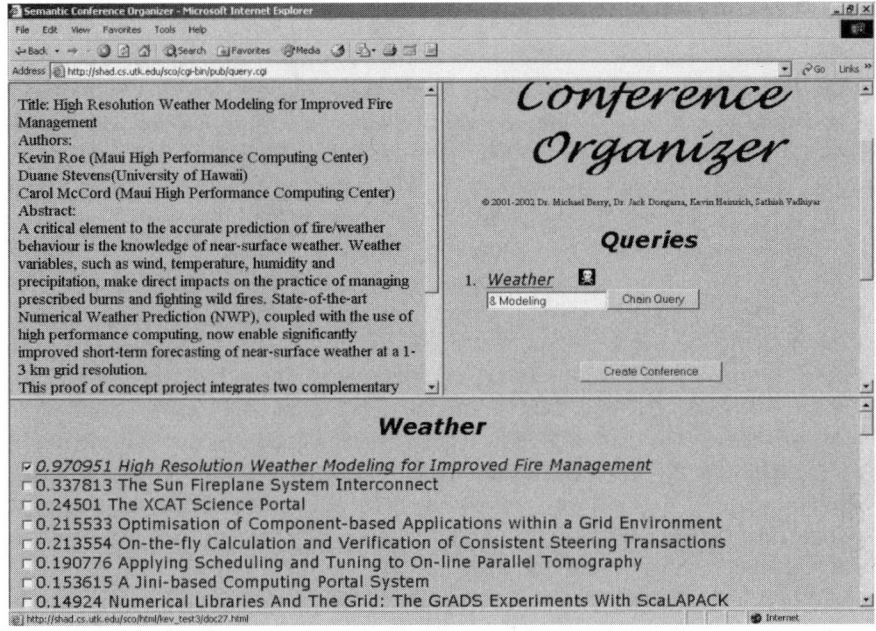

FIGURE 34.2
Return list generated for the query *weather*.

be keywords since abstracts themselves are small. Allowing singleton words also allows the user to query for a specific person and get the intuitive results. LSI is applied to the document collection after keyword extraction. A log-entropy weighting scheme (see Section 34.2) is used to ensure that distinguishing words within an abstract carry more weight.

Queries to the document collection are processed using the query module of GTP. Subsequent queries are only routed through the query module since there is no need to re-parse the document collection if the server has access to it. All other functions of the organizer are accomplished through scripts and simple text files.

34.4 Creating a Conference

34.4.1 A Simple Example

A working version of the Semantic Conference Organizer can be found at http://shad.cs.utk.edu/cop. A simple query of *weather* on the documents from the Supercomput-

---

document from a collection in a meaningful way.

ing 2001 Conference[†] will produce the output shown in Figure 34.2. Once the document collection has been submitted, three frames should appear. The right frame has the list queries. A new query can be added by placing them in the textbox at the bottom of the frame. Clicking on a skull next to a session will delete the entire session, while clicking on a skull next to the most recent query will only delete that query. The ability to delete intermediate queries is not provided. Clicking on a query will show the ranked list of documents for that query in the bottom frame. Clicking on a specific document title will show the entire document in the left frame. The checkboxes next to the document titles are used to lock documents to a query, i.e., assign a paper to a specific session. Once a document has been locked to a specific session it cannot be locked to another unless the original lock is released. Locked documents will appear in white font if the document is locked to another session or black if the document is locked further up the query chain in the same session.

If a given topic does not produce the expected results, the user may wish to modify the topic slightly. To accomplish this, we have added the ability to *chain queries*. Chaining queries is a quick way to compare the results of two different queries. In the context of the organizer, a chained query is a query viewed over time. That is, documents that have appeared in the top twenty over the last several queries will be marked to inform the user that that particular document has done a fairly good job of matching all the previous query terms. In the case of the organizer, all documents are initially colored blue. After a query has been chained, the results new to the top twenty will be colored red. After multiple chains, the documents will have a number in parentheses next to the title indicating the number of consecutive queries that the document has appeared above the threshold.

Chaining is particularly useful to see the effects a single word has on the return list. Typing an ampersand (&) at the beginning of the chained query will append the new query to the previous one. The power of chaining can be seen in Figures 34.2-34.4. Chaining has allowed the user to append *modeling* to the initial query *weather*. Not seeing desired papers appearing in the top of the return list, the user has switched the query to weather-related words. In Figure 34.3, the user has misspelled the word *temperature*. By chaining, one can quickly notice the impact that the correct spelling of *temperature* in Figure 34.4 has in the return list (i.e., the sixth document returned).

Another useful function of chaining occurs when trying to find a session title. After all documents have been locked, one can chain queries until all documents are found high in the return list. If found high in the return list, then the session title has some semantic tie to the documents returned and hopefully will be a helpful start to finding a session title germane to the topic. Note that in Figures 34.5 and 34.6, the user has locked two more papers to the *weather* session. As seen in Figure 34.7, the user initially tries *Global modeling* as a session title to unsatisfactory success. Changing the chained query to simply *modeling*, one notes that all three documents appear in the top three of the return list. Ideally, the three papers will be separate in a similar or (hopefully) more distinguishing way when trying to create a session title.

[†]http://www.sc2001.org/techpaper.shtml

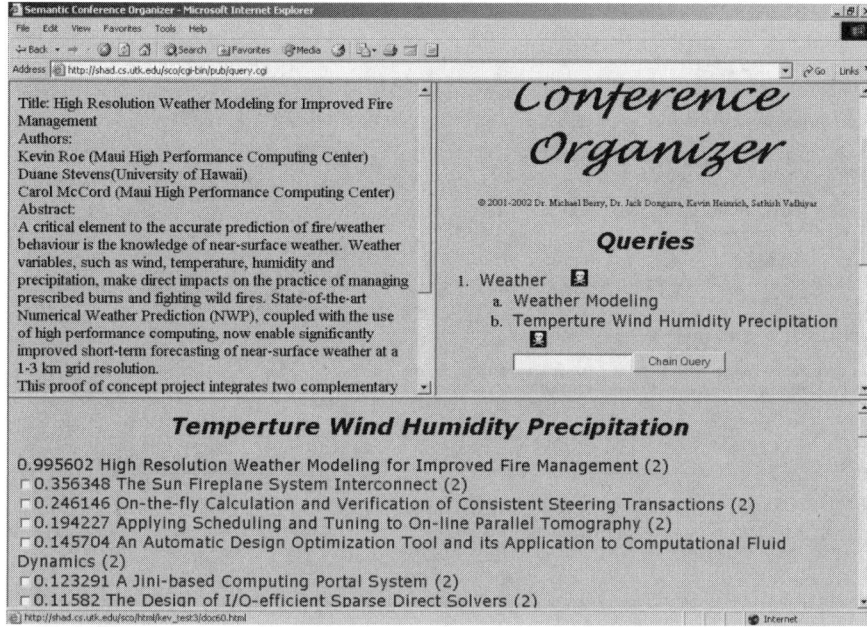

FIGURE 34.3
Note the misspelling of *temperature*.

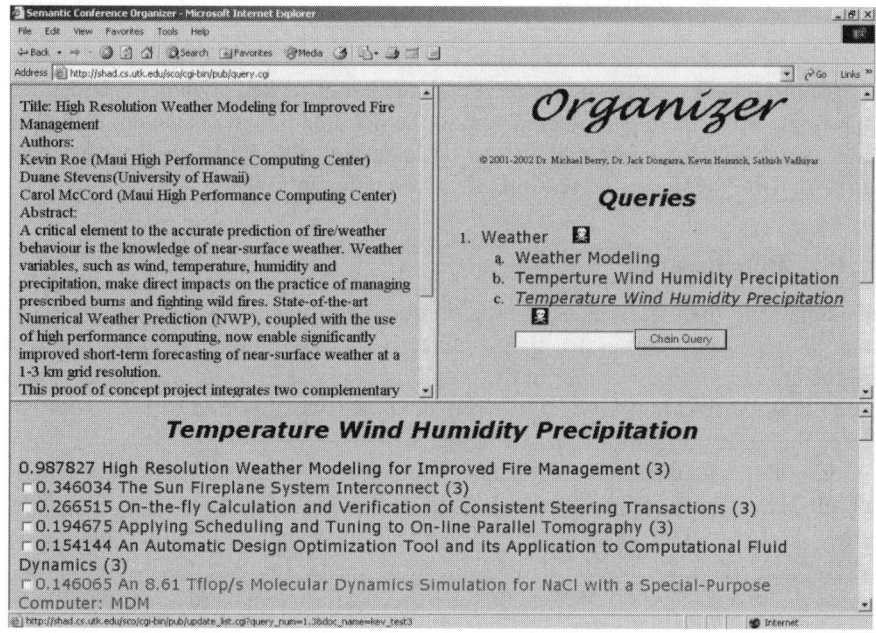

FIGURE 34.4
Notice the sixth document is new to the top 20.

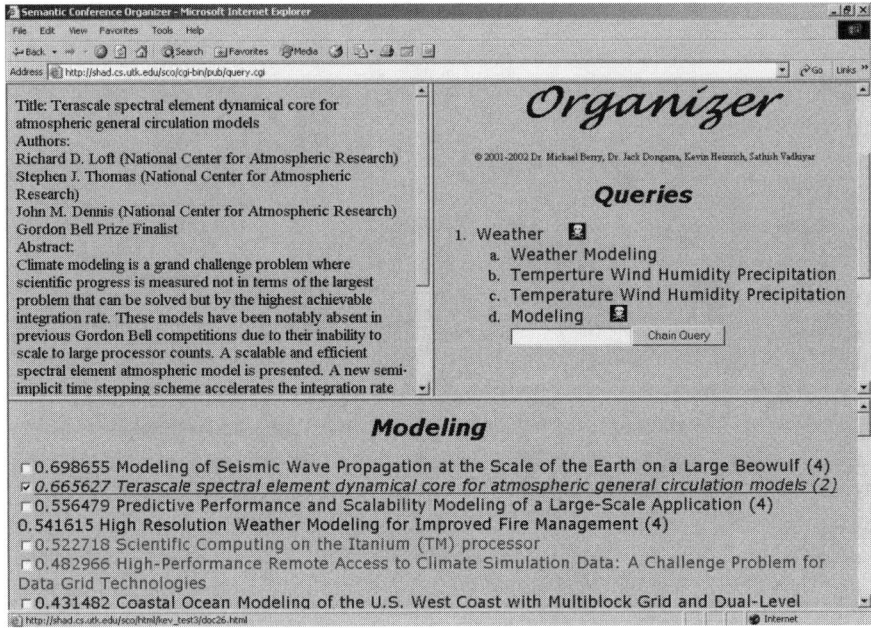

FIGURE 34.5
The second document is locked to the session *weather*.

To create the final conference, simply click on the "Create Conference" button. The list produced is the list of sessions with the list of locked documents under each appropriate session. In parentheses next to the document name is the chained query under which the document was locked. The session title is the most recent chain query followed by the initial session title given in parentheses.

34.4.2 Benchmarks

Benchmarking the effectiveness of the conference organizer is a difficult task because all session groupings are highly subjective. Of the three documents that were assigned to the session *weather* in the previous example,[‡] one appeared in a session titled *Groundbreaking Applications* while the other two appeared in *Sea, Wind, And Fire* in the Supercomputing 2001 Conference.

Continuing with the same document collection, two test conferences were created. In both cases, query chaining was not used. In the biased approach, the Supercomputing 2001 conference was re-created by using the same session titles and locking the corresponding documents if they appeared in the top twenty. Using such an approach, 34 out of the 60 documents were successfully locked to a session. To sim-

---

[‡]Please note that a person who did not specialize in computer weather applications created the example session.

Statistical Data Mining and Knowledge Discovery 579

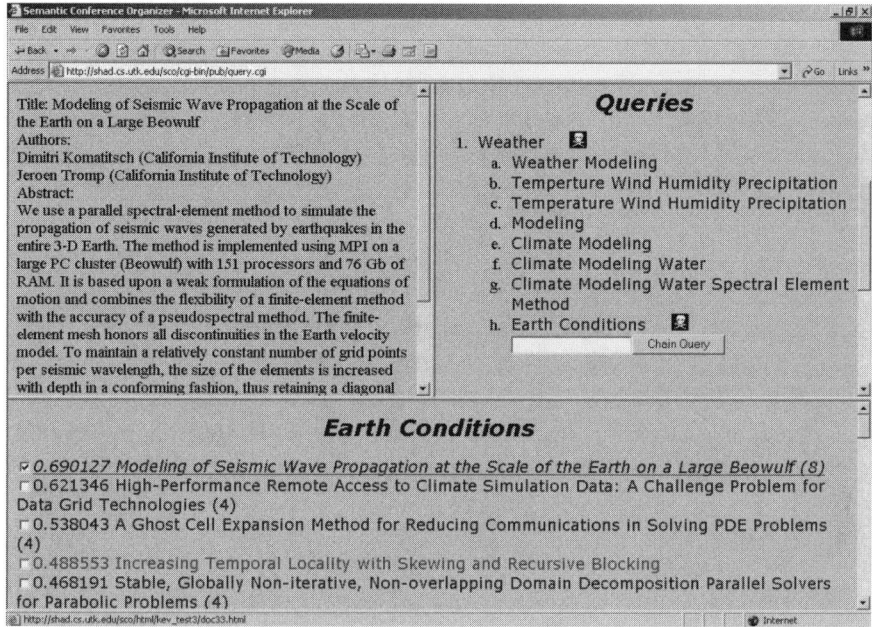

FIGURE 34.6
The third and final document is locked to the session.

ulate an unbiased approach, a simple algorithm was used. First, the same session titles used in the unbiased approach were listed in alphabetical order. Next, any documents in the first session that had a score of .9 or higher were locked. This process was iterated for all twenty sessions. After that, the process was repeated for scores higher than .8 and continued decreasing the threshold by .1 until no document could be locked to a session with less than three documents already locked to it. Using the unbiased approach, 49 out of the 60 documents were locked to sessions. Between the two approaches, only 7 papers were assigned to the same session. Such a disparity in results reemphasizes that a human organizer is essential to oversee conference creation.

34.5 Future Extensions

Currently, all processing and storage of the document collection is done on the webserver itself. Since the Conference Organizer only deals with document surrogates, i.e., abstracts, performing the SVD is not computationally intensive. The natural extension of this is to allow remote processing as well as remote storage on a grid which will enable the possibility of increasing the size of the document collection

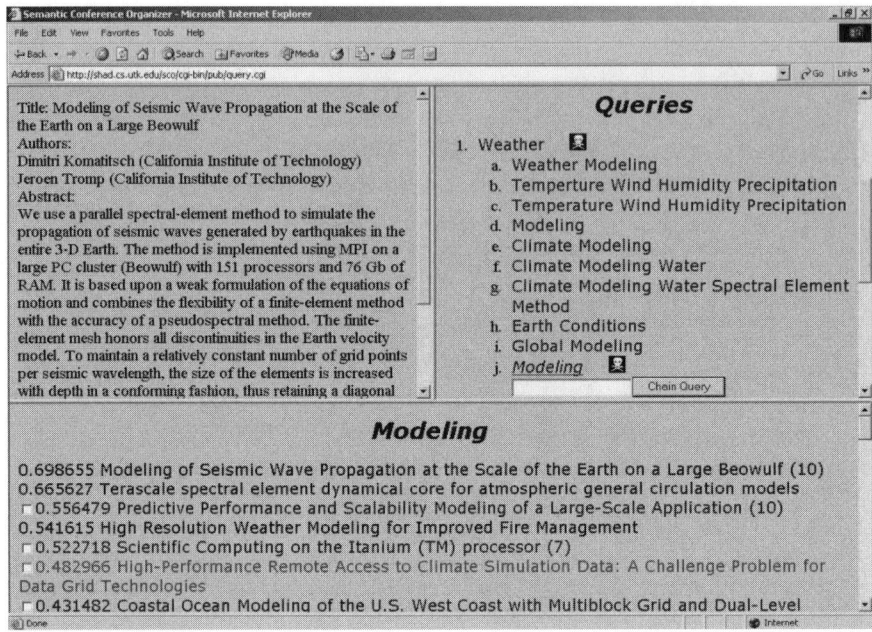

FIGURE 34.7
The three locked documents are ranked in the top four.

to include full documents. Grid-based middleware such as NetSolve[§] can be used to factor the larger term-document matrix used by LSI. Thus, the server will not be as burdened performing computationally intensive tasks and response time will inevitably improve. Given the temporary nature of the information used by this tool, distributed storage software such as the Internet Backplane Protocol[¶] is an ideal way to store the matrix and document collections themselves.

Other small adjustments are also possible for the sake of convenience. The ability to index full documents while only viewing the abstracts is one of these small future conveniences. Alternate methods to transfer the document collection such as IBP or some other method would also be nice extensions. Giving the user more flexibility with the weighting scheme and factors used by LSI is another possible future addition.

Acknowledgment

Research supported in part by the Los Alamos National Laboratory under Contract No. 03891-001-99 49.

[§]http://icl.cs.utk.edu/netsolve/
[¶]http://loci.cs.utk.edu/ibp/

References

[1] S. Deerwester, S. Dumais, G. Furnas, T. Landauer, and R. Harshman. Indexing by Latent Semantic Analysis. *Journal of the American Society for Information Science* 41:391-407, 1990.

[2] R. Baeza-Yates and B. Ribeiro-Neto. *Modern Information Retrieval*. Addison-Wesley, Boston, MA, 1999.

[3] M. Berry and M. Browne. *Understanding Search Engines: Mathematical Modeling and Text Retrieval*. SIAM, Philadelphia, PA, 1999.

[4] M. Berry, Z. Drmač, and E. Jessup. Matrices, Vector Spaces, and Information Retrieval. *SIAM Review* 41:335-362, 1999.

[5] G. Golub and C. V. Loan. *Matrix Computations*. Johns Hopkins, Baltimore, Third ed., 1996.

[6] M.W. Berry. Large Scale Singular Value Computations. *International Journal of Supercomputer Applications* 6:13-49, 1992.

[7] M. Berry and J. Dongarra. Atlanta Organizers Put Mathematics to Work for the Math Sciences Community. *SIAM News* 32:6, 1999.

[8] M. Berry, S. Dumais, and G. O'Brien. Using Linear Algebra for Intelligent Information Retrieval. *SIAM Review* 37:573-595, 1995.

[9] J.T. Giles, L. Wo, and M.W. Berry. GTP (General Text Parser): Software for Text Mining. In *Proceedings of the C. Warren Neel Conference on The New Frontiers of Statistical Data Mining and Knowledge Discovery*, Knoxville, TN, June 22-25, 2002.

Index

accuracy, 138, 141, 151, 152
ACE, 252
Activities of daily living (ADL), 119
adaptive mixtures, 81
AIC, 17, 199, 319, 367, 370, 379
algorithms
    CPS, 153
    PolyScore, 153
All-Volunteer Force (AVF), 234
AMDE, 81
archetypes, 535
Area based index, 254
Army Recruiting Command, 235
artificial neural networks, 402
association rule, 475
asymptotic covariance, 28
attrition, 235
audit, 530
AutoClass, 176
automated scoring, 141, 152
    algorithms, 152
autoregressive, 261
autoregressive model, 63

band signatures, 80
Barrier Removal, 497
Bayes factor, 525
Bayes' Theorem, 58
Bayesian, 141
    analysis, 154
Bayesian criterion (SBC), 525
Bayesian data augmentation, 520
Bayesian estimation, 119
Bayesian method of moments (BMOM), 77
Bayesian methods, 76
Bernoulli, 142

bi-plot, 380
bias, 138, 141, 155, 238
BIC, 379
binary classifier, 197
blast furnace, 401
bootstrap techniques, 554
bounds, 93
boxplots, 80
BR analysis, 503
brand image, 297
brand profiles, 299
C++, 455
CAIC, 199, 319, 367, 379
CAICF, 17, 357
CART, 82, 534
case-based reasoning, 348
categorical data, 340
category boundary, 359
causality
    definition, 59
chemical warfare, 79
classification, 79, 138, 141, 146, 147, 152
    model, 138
    results, 151
classification accuracy, 155, 159
classification and regression trees, 79
classifier, 146
client-server, 571
Cluster analysis, 520
cluster analysis, 339, 554
cluster identification, 415
clustering, 149, 151, 415
co-occurrence cube, 4
collinearity, 219
communality, 380
complexity, 239

complexity criterion, 353
complexity of a covariance matrix, 22
compressed column storage (CCS), 458
confidence intervals, 219
confidentiality, 93
confirmatory science, 2
confusion matrix, 88
connecting the dots, 11
contingency table, 93
contingency tables, 4
continuation-ratio model, 363
contrapositive, 474
controller feedback, 278
convex function, 204
correspondence analysis, 554
cosine similarity, 464
covariance matrix, 326
Cramer's V statistic, 344
cross-validation, 142, 146, 151, 490
 k-fold, 152
crossover, 38
curse of dimensionality, 537

DA algorithm, 522
DAGS, 7
data, 143
 box plots, 59
 missing, 143
 quality, 155
Data augmentation, 522
data cube, 10
data dredging, 2
data mining, 59, 240, 339
data mining (DM), 386
data mining activities, 236
data mining priors, 1
data quality, 237
data snooping, 2
Data visualization, 292
decision tree, 155, 159
decision-maker, 236
decomposable frontier, 100
decomposable graphical model, 100
decomposable log-linear model, 93
deduction, 59

density estimation, 79
deviance, 243
diabetes data, 367
dichotomous latent variables, 375
dichotomous response, 243
dimension-reduction, 251
directional residual analysis, 277
disability data, 93
disaggregation, 71
disclosure limitation, 93
disclosure score, 112
discriminant analysis, 141
dissimilarity, 340, 536
dissimilarity coefficient, 174
distance function, 536
distance measure, 418
distributed data mining, 336
distributed databases, 336
distributed homogeneous databases, 328
distributed PCA, 323
dot product, 315

E step, 179
EM algorithm, 179, 206, 311
entropic implication intensity, 475
error component model, 386
error sum of squares, 242
errors
 measurment, 153
estimation, 71
evaluation, 154
Exnode, 470
exploratory data analysis, 79
exploratory science, 2
ExplorN, 82

factor analysis, 378, 554
false alarm, 91
false negative, 138
false positive, 138
FASTCLUS, 174
Fatality Analysis Reporting System, 545
FCV, 278
FDI, 278

INDEX 585

feasibility intervals, 97
feature, 147, 154
    evaluation, 146
    extraction, 146, 147
    selection, 141, 150
        stepwise, 151
feature selection, 309
feature set, 83
feature space, 309
features
    extraction, 141
filter
    butterworth, 146, 148
fitness function, 37
flat files, 4
follow the dots, 2
forecasting, 73
Friedman Index, 254
FSIMILARITY, 174
functional disability, 119

Galileo, 2
garment market, 282
Gaussian, 81
Gaussian kernel function, 194
Gaussian process, 194
gene expression data, 423
General Text Parser (GTP), 456, 574
generalized linear model, 361, 376
Genetic algorithms, 36
Genetic Programming (GP), 257
GMDH, 270
GMDH network, 276
GoM model, 117
goodness-of-fit, 353
GP-GMDH, 257
Grade of Membership model, 93
graphical model, 97
graphical presentation, 67
greedy algorithm, 106
greedy frontier, 106
Group Method of Data Handling (GMDH), 257

Hall Index, 254

Harwell-Boeing, 458
Hidden Markov Models, 154
hidden Markov models, 9
hierarchical classification, 288
Hierarchical SOM, 497
high dimensional, 6
Highway Performance Monitoring System, 545
histograms, 79
Home security, 1
hot metal temperature, 401
Human Reliability Analysis, 498
hybrid training, 210

ICOMP, 17, 199, 319
ICOMP criterion, 525
ICOMP(IFIM), 29
ill-posed problems, 230
implication intensity, 473
imputation, 155, 159, 162, 163
imputed financial data, 515
independence graph, 97
indexing, 537
inferential sensing, 218
information criteria, 199, 353, 367
information measures of complexity, 15
information processing, 58
Instrumental activities of daily living (IADL), 119
intelligent data mining, 15
iris data, 182

jackknife, 80
jackknifing, 490
Java, 457

K-means algorithm, 424
k-means clustering, 535
kernel density estimation, 81, 223
kernel estimation, 81
kernel functions, 312
kernel mixture-model, 525
kernel PCA, 309
kernel regression, 223

kernel trick, 314
KISS, 60
knowledge discovery, 15, 386, 403
Kullback-Leibler information, 353

L-curve, 226
latent class, 119
latent class model, 374
Latent Gold, 176
Latent GOLD program, 376
Latent Semantic Indexing (LSI), 571
latent semantic indexing (LSI), 457
latent variable, 374
LC model, 374
learning models, 66
leukemia data, 488
Levenberg-Marguardt algorithm, 393
library, 433
linear programming, 97
linear regression model, 31, 386
local independence, 177, 379
log-entropy weighting, 575
log-linear model, 93
logistic regression, 141, 149, 150, 193, 355, 534
    classifier, 138
    models, 142
    modles, 150
LSD-models, 450
lymphoma data, 490

M step, 181
machine learning, 488
Mahalanobis distance, 341
manifest variable, 374
marginal totals, 93
market basket, 450
market segmentation, 297
Markov Chain Monte Carlo (MCMC), 127
MARS, 534
Marshallian macroeconomic model, 74
Matlab, 148
maximum likelihood, 142
MDL, 17

measuring business cycles, 67
metric, 341
microarray data, 487
microarray technology, 487
middleware, 580
military manpower analysis, 233
minimum spanning tree, 431, 537
missing at random, 182
missing value algorithm, 155, 159
missing values, 521
mixed data, 188
mixing coefficients, 81
mixture distribution, 521
mixture model, 210
model
    AR, 147
model complexity, 17
model selection criteria, 319
model-based density estimation, 81
model-based exploratory analysis, 81
modeling, 146, 154
Moment Index, 254
moving average, 146
Mplus, 176
MSE, 243
MSET, 222
multi-layer perceptron, 402
multidimensional scaling, 540
Multimix, 177
multivariate normal, 373
multivariate normal density, 21
mutation, 39
mutual information, 21

National Long Term Care Survey (NLTCS), 119
Nave Bayes, 8
nearest neighbor classifier, 82
nearestneighbor, 278
nested cumulative link models, 353
nested dichotomous model, 368
NetSolve, 571
neural nets, 538
neural networks, 141, 224
Newton-Raphson, 376

INDEX

nonlinear, 374
nonparametric regression, 239, 534
NR sensor, 277
nuisance factor, 377

object-oriented, 455
Office of Data Quality, 530
OPAC, 449
optimal release, 93
ordinal logistic regression, 353, 355
outliers, 65

paper signatures, 80
parallel coordinates, 90
patent data, 550
patents, 550
pattern recognition, 386
PCA, 149, 151, 274, 309
PE kernels, 212, 313
PE mixture, 210
penalized likelihood, 27
pixels, 80
PLS factors, 281
PLS regression, 283
polygraph, 137, 138
    computerizedscoring, 141
    data, 138
    deception, 140
    examination, 138
    instrument, 139
    numerical scoring, 141
    questions, 139
polygrph
    chart, 139
polytope, 97
posterior distribution, 521
PPReg, 252
prediction, 57, 147, 241
predictive density, 65
principal curves, 540
principal points, 535
production function, 392
Projection Pursuit, 251
projective geometry, 81
proportional odds, 353

proportional odds model, 355
prostate cancer data, 182
pseudo-document, 464
purchase incidence model, 440

quadratic classifier, 90
quality measure, 474
quantization, 535
query chaining, 578

radial basis function, 193
random effects model, 394
RBF classification, 194
reagent paper, 80
recommender system, 433
reducible log-linear model, 98
reduction, 59
regression models, 16
regression sum of squares, 242
regression tree, 208
regularization, 217
regularization parameter, 218
relational databases, 4
released frontier, 99
repeat-buying, 435
residual patterns, 277
results, 138, 152
ridge regression, 220
ROC, 151
root mean squared error, 257
rotation, 378
RTREE, 489

S-estimators, 533
SALAD, 79
sample, 149
SBC, 199, 319
scatter plots, 79
scientific method, 2
scientific methodology, 58
scoring algorithms, 138
Self-Organizing Maps, 497
self-organizing modeling, 276
semiparametric density estimation, 79
SEMTSA approach, 58

sensor validation, 222
shifted hats, 82
Sigmoid kernels, 313
signal, 139
    average, 146
    processing, 146
simplicity, 60
Simpson's paradox, 238
singleton words, 574
Singular value decomposition, 7
singular value decomposition, 326
singular value decomposition (SVD), 457
SIR model, 253
SIR with Projection Pursuit, 251
SIRpp, 252
SIRrpp, 254
Snob, 176
sparse matrix, 456
spatial information, 89
spectral filters, 80
Splus, 151
steel-making, 406
STING project, 559
stochastic coefficient regression model, 386
structural econometric models, 61
structural residual analysis, 277
structured query language, 1
subset selection, 17, 199, 353
substring search, 428
Super DRIP, 525
supervised SOM, 497
Support vector machines, 223
surprisingness, 483
surrogate split, 155, 158, 163
SVM classification, 321

TCV, 278
term weighting, 457
term-by-document matrix, 458, 572
test, 150, 151
text parsing, 571
textile sales, 282
textual analysis, 550, 551

tf-idf, 572
Threat matrix, 11
time series, 147
    analysis, 154
time series analysis, 61
time varying parameter models, 70
training, 150, 151
training data, 80
training set, 80
transaction costs, 433
triangulated graph, 97
turning points, 64

unsupervised SOM, 497
unusual facts, 60
utility of data releases, 94

validity, 138
variable selection, 241
variables, 138
vector space, 456
visualization, 79

Wald statistic, 243
wavelengths, 80

X-gobi, 541

Stafford Library
Columbia College
1001 Rogers Street
Columbia, Missouri 65216